The Evolution of Language

Language, more than anything else, is what makes us human. It appears that no communication system of equivalent power exists elsewhere in the animal kingdom. Any normal human child will learn a language based on rather sparse data in the surrounding world, while even the brightest chimpanzee, exposed to the same environment, will not. Why not? How, and why, did language evolve in our species and not in others? Since Darwin's theory of evolution, questions about the origin of language have generated a rapidly growing scientific literature, stretched across a number of disciplines, much of it directed at specialist audiences. The diversity of perspectives – from linguistics, anthropology, speech science, genetics, neuroscience, and evolutionary biology – can be bewildering. Covering diverse and fascinating topics, from Kaspar Hauser to Clever Hans, Tecumseh Fitch provides a clear and comprehensible guide to this vast literature, bringing together its most important insights to explore one of the biggest unsolved puzzles of human history.

W. TECUMSEH FITCH is Professor of Cognitive Biology at the University of Vienna. He studies the evolution of cognition and communication in animals and man, focusing on the evolution of speech, music, and language. He is interested in all aspects of vocal communication in terrestrial vertebrates, particularly vertebrate vocal production in relation to the evolution of speech and music in our own species.

The Evolution of Language

W. TECUMSEH FITCH

CAMBRIDGE
UNIVERSITY PRESS

University Printing House, Cambridge CB2 8BS, United Kingdom

Cambridge University Press is part of the University of Cambridge.

It furthers the University's mission by disseminating knowledge in the pursuit of education, learning and research at the highest international levels of excellence.

www.cambridge.org
Information on this title: www.cambridge.org/9780521677363

© W. Tecumseh Fitch 2010

First published 2010
5th printing 2013

A catalogue record for this publication is available from the British Library

ISBN 978-0-521-85993-6 Hardback
ISBN 978-0-521-67736-3 Paperback

Dedicated to my father

Contents

Figures

Acknowledgments

I began writing this book during a guest Leibniz professorship in Leipzig, Germany, in the winter of 2005–2006. I thank Matthias Middell and the Center for Advanced Studies, Leipzig, for this invitation, Angela Friederici for suggesting the idea, and the University of St. Andrews for leave to accept this professorship. During my stay in Leipzig, Svante Pääbo hosted me as a guest researcher at the Max Planck Institute for Evolutionary Anthropology; Josep Call, Wolfgang Enard, and Angela Friederici supported and enriched my stay there. As Leibniz professor I offered a seminar course on the evolution of language, and I am very grateful to the students in that course for their feedback.

I have been very fortunate to have had a series of excellent teachers and colleagues. My undergraduate teachers in evolutionary biology at Brown, particularly Mark Bertness, Margaret Kidwell, Douglas Morse, Douglas Shapiro, and Jonathan Waage taught me to think rigorously about evolution, while Andrew Schloss in the Music Department introduced me to acoustics and reawakened my interest in mathematics. In graduate school at Brown's Department of Cognitive and Linguistic Sciences, Nelson Francis, Henry Kucera, and Mark Johnson introduced me to quantitative linguistics, and James Anderson introduced me to theoretical neuroscience. During my post-doctoral years at MIT and Harvard, my post-doctoral advisor Marc Hauser showed me how to interact and communicate constructively with scientists from many disciplines, and has been constructively critical ever since. The Research Laboratory of Electronics at MIT, and especially Joseph Perkell, Stefanie Shattuck-Hufnagel, and Kenneth Stevens, provided a supportive but challenging environment for deepening my understanding of speech and its animal homologs. As a faculty member at Harvard, conversations with Noam Chomsky, Daniel Dennett, Terrence Deacon, William D. Hamilton, Nelson Kiang, Marc Hauser, Richard Lewontin, Michael Studdert-Kennedy, and Donald Griffin helped me to see the forest while attending to the trees. As a faculty member at St. Andrews, Gillian Brown, Richard Byrne, Juan-Carlos Gomez, David Perrett, Andrew Whiten, and Klaus Zuberbühler have been fantastic colleagues, both challenging and encouraging.

One teacher deserves special mention: without the intellectual influence of my PhD supervisor, Philip Lieberman, I would probably still be studying fish behavior. Although I know he disagrees with many of my conclusions, I have stood upon his intellectual shoulders in many ways, and I hope he can at least enjoy my views.

Many of the colleagues whose ideas are discussed here have read and critiqued portions of the book. In alphabetical order, I thank Michael Arbib, Derek Bickerton, Rudie Botha, Andrew Carstairs-McCarthy, Noam Chomsky, Simon Conway-Morris, Michael Corballis, Terrence Deacon, Robin Dunbar, Robert Foley, Marc Hauser, Simon Kirby, Peter MacNeilage, William McGrew, Aniruddh Patel, David Reby, Dietrich Stout, Maggie Tallerman, Alison Wray, and Klaus Zuberbühler for their constructive criticisms on one or more chapters. My editor Andrew Winnard has been enthusiastic and critical, in just the right balance, throughout the long process of writing this book, and sharp-eyed Adrian Stenton caught and corrected many infelicities and typos. Robert Ladd, Philip Lieberman, Daniel Mietchen, and Robert Seyfarth read and criticized many chapters, and Gesche Westphal carefully read a draft of the entire manuscript. All of these colleagues offered many suggestions and corrections that have greatly improved the organization and clarity of the final product, for which I am deeply grateful. Of course, none of them necessarily agree with the interpretations here, and all errors and oversights remain my own.

This book is dedicated to my father, William T. S. Fitch, whose unwavering intellectual, material, and emotional support made my somewhat circuitous career trajectory possible.

Introduction

SOME Hindus had brought an elephant for exhibition and placed it in a dark house. Crowds of people were going into that dark place to see the beast. Finding that ocular inspection was impossible, each visitor felt it with his palm in the darkness. The palm of one fell on the trunk. 'This creature is like a water-spout,' he said. The hand of another lighted on the elephant's ear. To him the beast was evidently like a fan. Another rubbed against its leg. 'I found the elephant's shape is like a pillar,' he said. Another laid his hand on its back. 'Certainly this elephant was like a throne,' he said.

The sensual eye is just like the palm of the hand. The palm has not the means of covering the whole of the beast.
— From Rumi's Tales from the Masnavi (translated from Persian by
A. J. Arberry)

Language, more than anything else, is what makes us human: the unique power of language to represent and share unbounded thoughts is critical to all human societies, and has played a central role in the rise of our species in the last million years from a minor and peripheral member of the sub-Saharan African ecological community to the dominant species on the planet today. Despite intensive searching, it appears that no communication system of equivalent power exists elsewhere in the animal kingdom. The evolution of human language is thus one of the most significant and interesting evolutionary events that has occurred in the last 5–10 million years, and indeed during the entire history of life on Earth. Given its central role in human behavior, and in human culture, it is unsurprising that the origin of language has been a topic of myth and speculation since before the beginning of history. More recently, since the dawn of modern Darwinian evolutionary theory, questions about the evolution of language have generated a rapidly growing scientific literature. Since the 1960s, an increasing number of scholars with backgrounds in linguistics, anthropology, speech science, genetics, neuroscience, and evolutionary biology have devoted themselves to understanding various aspects of language evolution. The result is a vast scientific literature, stretched across a number of disciplines, much of it directed at specialist audiences. The purpose of this book is to survey the major issues debated in this literature, from a non-specialist and balanced viewpoint.

The single most significant problem plaguing this field, in my opinion, is aptly symbolized by the parable of the elephant (told above, in one of many forms, by the Sufi poet Rumi). Language is hugely complex, and is so central to humanity that it infiltrates all aspects of human cognition, behavior, and culture. Practitioners of many different disciplines can fairly claim insight into its workings. After twenty years of studying and discussing language evolution, I conclude that many different scholars have reached valid insights about human language, some of them quite far-reaching, but that no one scholar or discipline has yet achieved an adequately comprehensive overview of this complex system. All of us are still exploring the elephant of language in the darkness, all of us with only partial understanding, and each discipline will have its place in the richer description and understanding that all are seeking.

The diversity of perspectives can be bewildering. Where linguist Noam Chomsky sees a highly abstract core of syntax as central to the biology of language, psychologist Michael Tomasello finds it in the human capacity for shared intentions, and speech scientist Philip Lieberman sees it in the motor control of speech. In semantics, psychologist Ellen Markman argues that a suite of detailed constraints on "possible meanings" are critical for language acquisition, while computer scientist Luc Steels envisions meaning as emerging from a broad social, perceptual and motor basis. While neuroscientist Terrence Deacon seeks the neural basis for symbolic thought in the over-developed prefrontal cortex of humans, his colleague Michael Arbib finds it elsewhere, in the mirror neurons that we share with monkeys. While most scholars agree that human language evolution involved some sort of intermediate stage, a "protolanguage," linguist Derek Bickerton argues that this system involved individual words, much like those of a two-year-old child, while anthropologist Gordon Hewes argued that it was gesturally conveyed by the face and hands, and Charles Darwin argued that protolanguage was expressed in the form of song-like phrases. Linguist Allison Wray argues that the link between sounds and meanings was initially holistic, while her colleague Maggie Tallerman sees it as inevitably discrete and compositional. Turning to the selective pressures that made language adaptive, linguists Ray Jackendoff and Steven Pinker cite ordinary natural selection, evolutionary psychologist Geoffrey Miller argues for sexual selection, and I argue that kin selection played a crucial role. Scholars appear evenly split concerning whether language evolved initially for its role in communication with others, or whether its role in structuring thought provided the initial selective advantage. Where some scholars see evolutionary leaps as playing a crucial role, stressing the discontinuities between language and communication in other animals, others stress gradual change and evolutionary continuity between humans and other species. All of these, and many other, issues have been vociferously debated for decades, often with little sign of resolution.

A core argument in this book is that each of the scholars has grasped some truth about language, but that none of these truths are complete in themselves. Language, I will argue, requires the convergence and integration of multiple mechanisms, each of them necessary but no one alone sufficient. From such a multi-component perspective, arguments about which single component is *the* core, central feature of "Language" are divisive and unproductive. Just as the parable urges us to reconcile apparently contradictory perspectives, I believe that an adequate understanding of language evolution requires us to reconcile many of the contrary opinions alluded to above.

In one common variant of the elephant parable, a king calls a group of blind scholars to explore the elephant, and they fall to fighting over their various interpretations. I prefer Rumi's version, for, in the case of language, there is no clear-sighted king who can survey the entire elephant: all of us have only partial insights. Unfortunately, the bellicose conclusion of this second version of the parable often applies to work in language evolution, since rhetorical battles and disciplinary turf-wars have been depressingly pervasive. I have all too frequently seen intelligent, respected scholars accuse each other of "knowing nothing about" language, evolution, the brain, or other relevant topics. Researchers whose perspective champions one or another approach often accuse their colleagues of missing the point, or of failing to understand what "Language" really is.

Because I do not think that anyone, including myself, has an adequate, comprehensive overview of language evolution, this book will not present "the answers" or resolve all debates. Rather, it will provide an overview of many different perspectives on language, and the many types of data relevant to the debates, accepting each as a necessary component of some future synthesis. The data that can help resolve the perennial issues of debate in language evolution come from so many different disciplines (spanning from physics and molecular biology to linguistics, anthropology, and sociology) that no single human could hope to master them all. Thus researchers must cooperate with others to achieve a broader and more satisfactory picture. Answers to the difficult questions about language evolution, which include some of the deepest and most significant questions concerning humanity, require interdisciplinary teamwork of a sort that remains regrettably rare in this field. My central goal in writing this book has been to increase the potential for such collaboration by providing access to the insights from many relevant fields to any interested reader.

The nature of this book

This book provides an introduction to the interdisciplinary study of language evolution, stressing the importance of both modern biology (including neo-Darwinian evolutionary theory, developmental and molecular genetics, and neuroscience) and the modern language sciences (including theoretical linguistics, psycholinguistics, and comparative linguistics). Although biology and linguistics have traditionally traveled quite separate paths, there is growing evidence that a rapprochement and synthesis is in the making (sometimes subsumed under the term "biolinguistics"). This potential for synthesis makes the topic of language evolution both exciting, and ripe for productive interdisciplinary collaboration.

The book fills a currently empty niche. Despite an ever-increasing number of accessible books on language evolution, none attempts a comprehensive overview of the sort given here. Instead, most provide long and detailed arguments favoring one particular hypothesis or point of view. I think the field needs, and is ready for, a dispassionate survey of the available hypotheses, and an even-handed evaluation of their strengths and weaknesses in the light of currently available data. This book is problem-oriented, advocating the hypothesis-testing stance of the mature sciences. I will focus on hypotheses and data that have appeared in peer-reviewed publications in the last two decades, but I have also sought the roots of contemporary ideas and do not ignore older contributions. Although I obviously have my own perspective on these problems and my own judgments about the plausibility of various hypotheses, my goal is to enable interested readers to draw their own conclusions by providing an unbiased overview of the relevant questions, approaches, and data. In order to aid this balance, I have shared draft versions of each chapter with many relevant experts, who have in most cases kindly offered corrections or extensions of my initial attempts (see the Acknowledgments for details).

A pluralistic, multi-component perspective

The central assumption of my approach is that language must be viewed as a composite system, made up of many partially separable components.

Many of these components are widely shared with other animals (such as the capacity for hearing, memory, basic cognition, and vocalization), but a few differentiate humans from our nearest primate cousins (such as vocal learning or complex syntax). Crucially, each of these necessary components of language may conceivably have its own evolutionary history, and rely upon quite separate neural and genetic mechanisms. Although language is a system characterized by seamless interaction between these multiple components, "Language" is not a monolithic whole, and from a biological perspective may be better seen as a "bag of tricks" pieced together via a process of evolutionary tinkering. To the extent that this multi-component perspective is correct, any attempt to single out just one aspect of language as "core" or "central" is a mistake.

A second central aspect of my approach follows from this: I rely on data from a broad array of animal species to inform and test theories of language evolution. Some of the subcomponents of human language are shared with unexpected species. For instance the human capacity for complex vocal learning, allowing children to learn the words of their community's language, is shared with many birds, whales and seals, but not with chimpanzees or indeed any other primate. Investigating such traits demands a very broad comparative approach, encompassing a wide range of species, each chosen with a particular subcomponent of language in mind. The reader will thus find not only detailed discussion of chimpanzees and other primates here, but also whales, birds, honeybees, seals and deer. An exclusive focus on primates alone is misguided, and risks overlooking many species with important lessons to teach us about human language.

Nonetheless, I fully accept the uniqueness of human language: despite relying on a broad suite of biological mechanisms shared with other species, language in its full human form remains unique to our species. Human language gives us the ability to express anything we can think, and to communicate these thoughts via a set of mutually comprehensible signals. Although all animals communicate, this boundless expressivity sets our species off from all others. The fact that humans, alone on our planet, have this particular capacity is no more surprising to evolutionary biologists than other unusual features like the elephant's trunk, bat echolocation, or "radar" in electric fish. All of these "unique" traits, however, share components with other organisms, and language is no different. Based on current understanding of animal communication and cognition, *some* aspect(s) of language must be unique to our species. It remains possible that *every* subcomponent of language is shared with one species or another, and our species is simply the only one lucky enough to integrate them all. More likely, most components are shared, but a few core aspects of the human language capacity remain unique to our species. These are empirical questions, and resolving them requires a close look at the similarities and differences between human language and animal communication and cognition.

The final principle guiding my writing has been optimism about our ability to empirically resolve many current debates. This optimism runs directly counter to the common idea that there are no data relevant to language evolution. It is true that language does not fossilize, and we have no time machines. But this does not entail that the study of language is unscientific, and more than our lack of videotapes of the Big Bang renders cosmology unscientific, or any other historically grounded science from geology to paleontology. We need to rely upon indirect evidence in all of these fields, and available data already put serious constraints upon attempts at modeling language evolution. More importantly, powerful new tools today provide an ever-increasing fund of data that will allow us to actually test hypotheses about the biology and evolution of language. To mention only two, modern non-invasive brain imaging allows us to test models about cognitive "modules" and their relationships. We shall see that such data are directly relevant to Darwin's "musical protolanguage" hypothesis. Similarly, molecular genetic techniques, applied to modern humans, allow us to estimate the times at which genes involved in speech swept through populations of our extinct ancestors. Eventually, as more about the genetic basis for language is learned, this approach may allow us to determine the order in which different components of language evolved in our species. The existence of such new tools opens up the exciting prospect, in the coming decades, of scientifically resolving debates that have dragged on for centuries or even millennia.

Despite reviewing a substantial amount of factual knowledge, this book is as focused on open questions as it is on answers. My goal is to provide the reader with the theoretical tools and factual database to help answer such questions, and offer an invitation to join in the broad, collaborative, interdisciplinary exchange that I firmly believe is necessary for progress. I hope that the reader emerges conversant with several different perspectives or hypotheses about language evolution, and a desire to test them by gathering new data. Such data could be as accessible as observing one's own child acquire language, or searching the Internet for unusual sentence structures; or it might involve multi-million dollar grant proposals in molecular biology or neuroscience. The point is that many questions that can, in principle, be answered have not yet even been asked. I will count myself successful if this book spurs many such new questions, and at least a few answers, in the future.

Plan of the book

The first half of the book is introductory, offering tutorial reviews of evolutionary theory, linguistics, animal cognition, animal communication, and human evolutionary history. By providing an introduction to the main issues and hypotheses, along with concise tutorials on necessary background material, and reviewing the relevant data, I aim to provide a synthetic, comparative overview of the data and disciplines that enter into this rapidly growing field. Specialist terms are used only when necessary (e.g. formant, homology, recursion, transcription factor, epigenesis) and are both explained where first used, and assembled in a glossary. Although I obviously cannot do justice to these many academic disciplines in a single book, the goal of the introductory chapters is to equip readers to explore further, and ultimately to evaluate current models of language evolution themselves. These chapters provide the antidote to any belief that there are no data relevant to language evolution, and although the connections may at first seem quite indirect, all of these data will be put to use later in the book.

The book starts with a survey of evolutionary theory, summarizing the basic principles used in contemporary biology to judge the validity and plausibility of evolutionary hypotheses. Language evolution poses some unique problems, and may even turn out to require additions to contemporary evolutionary theory, but we should not prejudge this issue. Rather, we should employ standard evolutionary logic, well-tested in many different organisms and traits, and only deviate from such logic if the facts require it. Although some theorists seem to believe that language evolution, almost by definition, breaks the normal rules of evolution, I will conclude that this intuition is misguided, and that contemporary evolutionary theory already possesses the conceptual resources to handle, and indeed strongly constrain, theories of language evolution. Furthermore, once these constraints are taken seriously, many aspects of contemporary evolutionary scenarios ("evolutionarios") of language evolution are seen to be inadequate.

Turning next to language itself, I attempt to tease out the separate subcomponents of the language faculty that needed to evolve since our divergence from chimpanzees. I will enumerate a suite of different mechanisms involved in language: summarized under the "three S's" of signal, structure, and semantics. I situate each of these in the traditional subdisciplines of linguistics (phonetics, phonology, syntax, semantics, and pragmatics), but in each case the system in question requires further subdivision to reach the grain of actual biological mechanisms. Chapter 3 doubles as an introduction to linguistics, and a classification of the mechanisms involved in modern human language. Given this preliminary breakdown of mechanisms, we turn in the remaining introductory chapters to studies of animal cognition and communication, investigating which of these many mechanisms are shared with other species, and which appeared to evolve separately in the human lineage. We will pay careful attention to chimpanzees and other primates, but we will also examine more distant relatives (such as birds or seals) because parallel (or "convergent") evolution of human-like traits has much to teach us about the evolution of such traits. This is particularly the case for phonology and syntax, where the study of other species suggests some possible revisions to the traditional view of the phonological and syntactic subsystems. I conclude that each traditional subdivision includes multiple mechanisms, many of them shared with other species. But in each case, at least one subcomponent appears to have evolved in humans since our divergence from the chimpanzee lineage.

In the next section, I provide a whirlwind tour of human evolution, starting from the beginning of life and the first cells. This introduction to our long ancestry shows that most of human biology, including many aspects of behavior and cognition, has very deep roots, long predating our split with chimpanzees about 6 million years ago. I will discuss our last common ancestor with chimpanzees, in detail, and then review the fossil evidence concerning our hominid ancestors. These introductory chapters provide the factual background and key data enabling the reader to evaluate, in a balanced, well-informed manner, current debates.

The second half of the book systematically introduces and evaluates current theories about language evolution, reviewing the many current hypotheses about the stages through which humans passed in our route from our last common ancestor (LCA) with chimpanzees, which lacked language, to modern *Homo sapiens*, which has it. Although this aspect of biolinguistics is sometimes seen as hopelessly speculative, I will argue that the comparative and linguistic data reviewed in the earlier sections allow us to evaluate, and sometimes reject, hypotheses. Constructing viable hypotheses for language evolution that cover this full timespan, and deal adequately with all core components of language without unjustified assumptions, is far from trivial. Furthermore, by considering the hypotheses of different scholars side-by-side, we can see how various combinations of current proposals might work together synergistically to provide greater explanatory coverage. Most fundamentally, this approach in many cases allows *predictions* to be made that can be tested with the ever-increasing flow of data on brain development, animal communication, evolutionary theory, neurolinguistics, and comparative genomics.

I start with a detailed description and analysis of the biology and evolution of speech. Although speech is but one of the suite of components making up language as a whole, the physical tangibility of the speech signal has led to an extensive body of research and clear scientific progress in the last decades. I will discuss the reconfigured anatomy of the human vocal tract ("the descent of the larynx") in detail, because this feature has played a central role in many discussions of language evolution. However, I will conclude that peripheral vocal anatomy is not a controlling factor in the biology of language, and that vocal tract configuration has been over-emphasized in discussions of language evolution. This negative verdict leads to a positive conclusion: that the human speech capacity is grounded in *neural* changes. The trajectory of this line of research, starting with early work of Philip Lieberman and colleagues in the late 1960s, offers an excellent illustration of the power of the comparative method to test hypotheses and resolve debates about language evolution. The speech chapters will demonstrate the value of the comparative, multi-component approach adopted throughout this book.

Next, I address the evolution of other components of language, including syntax and semantics, using the core notion of a "protolanguage" to structure the analysis. All modern theories of language evolution posit one or more intermediate systems, "**protolanguages**," that represent evolutionary precursors to language in its full, modern sense. Most contemporary scholars agree on the explanatory necessity for protolanguage: language did not spring into being all at once, like Athena from Zeus's brow, but developed in stages, each one of them serving some function of its own. However, there is strenuous disagreement about the sequence in which the components appeared, and the nature of the protolanguages they served. Proponents of **lexical protolanguage** suggest that language started with isolated, meaningful spoken words: speech and semantics came first, and syntax last. In contrast, proponents of **gestural protolanguage** suggest that language started in the manual modality, and that syntax and semantics preceded speech. Finally, proponents of **musical protolanguage** argue that speech initially arose as complex learned vocalizations, more like song than speech, and that semantics was added to this system later.

Since protolanguages constitute hypotheses about what a system could have been like, before it was linguistic, the very notion of a protolanguage requires that we abandon preconceptions about one "core" or central aspect of language. An open-minded attitude towards different hypotheses about protolanguage thus goes hand in hand with the multi-component approach. I will stress the testable empirical consequences of each hypothesis, particularly those that would allow us to distinguish between them. Although sometimes denounced as mere fairytales, such evolutionary scenarios are valuable in the study of the biology and evolution of language precisely to the extent that they drive us to gather new data – data that might not otherwise be seen as interesting or worthy of collection. Although we may never know for certain whether *Homo erectus* sang, or if Neanderthals communicated in sign language, posing these questions explicitly can lead to a better empirical understanding of the relations between speech and sign, syntax and semantics, or language and music in modern humans, an understanding of independent scientific value. Furthermore, as the genetic bases for these different systems become better understood, there is a real possibility that some of these debates can be answered more definitively by "fossils" left in the human genome which allow us to discover the sequence of the selective events that drove different evolutionary components to fixation (Enard *et al.*, 2002; Carroll, 2006). Because this exciting possibility remains speculative at present, I think phylogenetic hypotheses must always be viewed circumspectly and seen as generators of questions, and possible answers ("intuition pumps") rather than as ends in themselves. Like all scientific hypotheses, they are proposals to be interrogated, knocked down, and rebuilt, not beliefs to be defended. I will conclude that no one of these models, alone, can fully account for language evolution, and that a successful theory will need to selectively integrate insights from each. This last part of the book provides far more questions than answers, but I will conclude with a summary and prospectus that strikes a cautiously optimistic note about the future of this aspect of biolinguistics. But let us now dive into the theory and data that can help constrain our hypotheses.

The lay of the land: an overview of disciplines and data relevant to language evolution

1 | Language from a biological perspective

On an autumn day in 1947, much like any other, Cathy and Keith Hayes returned to their suburban American ranch house with their newborn infant girl, Viki (Hayes, 1951). After a few difficult days, Viki began feeding well and growing rapidly. She was a very quiet baby, sweet and affectionate, and loved to be held and tickled. She learned to walk early, entering a rambunctious phase and breaking numerous household objects, but eventually her loving parents' gentle discipline bore fruit and she developed into a playful, obedient little girl. By the age of three, Viki could feed and bathe herself, eat with a spoon and drink through a straw, and help with cleaning. She was fond of looking at herself in the mirror, and loved assembling jigsaw puzzles. She enjoyed playing on the backyard swing, climbing trees, and playing peekaboo with the neighborhood children. She was in many ways a normal young girl, with one major exception: Viki did not speak. Not a word. She was able to grunt, scream, and laugh, so her problem was not with vocalization in general; instead it seemed to stem from a neural difficulty specific to spoken language. After consultation with experts, Cathy Hayes instituted a speech training regime, manipulating her young pupil's lips manually and rewarding her with treats whenever she approximated a word. Unfortunately, even these dedicated efforts were mostly in vain: Viki's "vocabulary" reached a plateau of three words (*mama*, *papa*, and *cup*), and even these attempts were breathy and inarticulate: poor imitations of normal English speech. Viki seemed tragically doomed to a life without speech. Fortunately, Viki's parents were not totally surprised or alarmed by her failure to achieve speech or language, because Viki was a chimpanzee.

Chimpanzees are the closest living species to humans. Chimpanzees are closer to humans, in genetic and evolutionary terms, than they are to gorillas or other apes. The fact that a chimpanzee will not acquire speech, even when raised in a human home with all the environmental input of a normal human child, is one of the central puzzles we face when contemplating the biology of our species. For every normal child, anywhere in the world, will rapidly acquire the native language, or languages, in their local environment, and will do so even in the face of social, nutritional, and intellectual adversity far more severe than any difficulties Viki faced as an adopted child in her suburban home. In repeated experiments, starting in the 1910s, chimpanzees raised in close contact with humans have universally failed to speak, or even to try to speak, despite their rapid progress in many other intellectual and motor domains (Yerkes and Yerkes, 1929). This fact was already clear by the 1960s, and is undisputed by modern scientists, but the underlying *reasons* for this apparent inability remain contested even today. Each normal human is born with a capacity to rapidly and unerringly acquire their mother tongue, with little explicit teaching or coaching. In contrast, no nonhuman primate has spontaneously produced even a word of the local language. This difference between us and our nearest living cousins is made more striking by the fact that many more distantly related species easily and spontaneously acquire spoken words and phrases. Such speaking animals include parrots and mynah birds, and many other bird species, but also some mammals including harbor seals (the most famous example was Hoover, an orphaned seal raised by a Maine fisherman, who spontaneously learned to say his name, *hey!*, *get ova' here*, and produce a guttural laugh – all with a Maine fisherman's accent; Ralls *et al.*, 1985).

Apes improve significantly when offered a different medium of expression than speech: they achieve much more when trained on a manual rather than a vocal system. This is unsurprising, because ape gestural communication in the wild is more flexible and individualistic than their vocal production. Yerkes had already proposed training apes with a manual or signed language in 1910. The experiments, when performed in the 1960s, revealed far greater communicative competence: whether using a system like American Sign Language (ASL), plastic chips to be arranged on a tray, or poking at icons on a computerized keyboard, chimpanzees and other apes can acquire a substantial "vocabulary" including hundreds of symbols, and use these productively in a communicative situation. Despite their greater abilities in the non-vocal channel, however, such "language-trained" apes still plateau at a relatively modest level, with a small productive vocabulary of a few hundred symbols and very simple rules for combining vocabulary items that are dwarfed by a five-year-old child. Perhaps most tellingly, such apes mainly use their system to make requests for food or tickles. Unlike a human child, who seems to possess a drive to name the world, to express their inner world via questions, stories, and make-believe worlds, even the most sophisticated language-trained apes would make boring conversationalists. This is not because they have nothing to say: research on chimpanzee cognition reveals a complex and sophisticated mental world. Apes use tools insightfully, draw inferences about other individuals based on what they have and have not seen, solve novel problems on the first go based on causal reasoning, and in general would, one supposes, have plenty to talk about if they felt like it. For some reason, they don't.

Thus, the factors that kept Viki from acquiring spoken language were not simply consequences of an inadequate speech system, lack of intelligence, or an inability to learn, in general. They were more specific, and deeper, than any of these obvious possibilities. They were undeniable in Viki, and in all other chimpanzees and apes raised by humans. After three years of mothering this young chimpanzee, Cathy Hayes eloquently expressed the situation: "the only obvious and important deficit in the ape's innate intelligence, as compared with man's, is a missing facility for using and understanding language." Although we will discuss some amendments to this diagnosis later, this conclusion forms the basic factual starting point for this book. Any normal child will learn language(s), based on rather sparse data in the surrounding world, while even the brightest chimpanzee, exposed to the same environment, will not. Why not? What are the specific cognitive mechanisms that are present in the human child and not in the chimpanzee? What are their neural and genetic bases? How are they related to similar mechanisms in other species? How, and why, did they evolve in our species and not in others? My goal in this book is to address these questions, with a special focus on evolution.

1.1 A biological approach to the "hardest problem in science"

It has been suggested that the evolution of human language is "the hardest problem in science" (Christiansen and Kirby, 2003) and some skeptics have credibly concluded that scientists might spend their time more constructively on more tractable topics (e.g. Lewontin, 1998). Certainly, the scientific approach to language evolution faces unique difficulties. Language does not fossilize, and we lack time machines, so all of our data are indirect, and often several steps removed from the direct, conclusive evidence we might desire. But this is true of many problems in science that are considered legitimate pursuits, from the Big Bang to the origin of life, so this difficulty is not insuperable.

More problematic is the fact that understanding language evolution requires new insights in multiple, independent disciplines which lack a shared framework of terminology, problems, and approaches. For example, a complete understanding of language surely requires a clear understanding of "meaning" – but the nature of meaning is one of the most perennially controversial issues in philosophy and linguistics (cf. Jackendoff, 2002;

Hurford, 2007). A biological understanding of meaning would surely entail a full understanding of how brains generate, represent, and manipulate concepts, and such a broad understanding of cognitive neuroscience remains a distant hope today (some pessimistically suggest it is forever beyond the reach of the human mind; McGinn, 1991). Though aware of these (and other) difficulties, I am more optimistic. Indeed, I believe that recent, profound progress in the biological sciences, combined with insights from many other fields including linguistics, psychology, paleoanthropology, and philosophy, offer the hope that fundamental progress in understanding these questions will be made in the next few decades.

My optimism is tempered by a depressing sociological realization: the very breadth and difficulty of the problems often invites an amateurish attitude, where the strictures that accompany "normal" science (e.g. hypotheses should be testable, alternative viewpoints enumerated and discussed, and previous scholarly sources must be noted) are lifted. This is sometimes accompanied by a reliance on intuition and presumption, unsupported by rational argument, or by passionate denouncement of others' ideas (often based on misinterpretation) masquerading as "debate." All too often, the complexity of other disciplines goes unrecognized, and scholars well respected in their home discipline commit easily recognized howlers in the "foreign" discipline. This "anything-goes" attitude towards scholarship is common in the study of language evolution, and can be self-perpetuating (e.g. when a respected expert writes "I see no need at the moment to hold myself to a higher standard than the rest of the field"; p. 237, Jackendoff, 2002). This attitude also has a negative influence on depth of scholarship: a common attitude appears to be that "nothing very good has been done, so I don't need to read the literature" or "this field is just getting started so there's no need to read old papers." The running joke is that the Paris Linguistic Society banned discussion of language evolution in 1861, and the ban remained in force until 1990 (with the publication of Bickerton (1990) and Pinker and Bloom (1990)). In the interim, the story goes, all that happened was a comical series of silly unscientific hypotheses, nicknamed "bow-wow," "heave-ho," and "ding-dong" to expose their basic absurdity. *This view of the field is a myth.* Darwin himself, and subsequent linguists such as Jespersen, made important contributions to this literature after the famous ban, and there was a major, important revival of interest in the 1960s and 1970s when many of the issues under discussion today were already debated insightfully (e.g. Hockett and Ascher, 1964; Hewes, 1973; Harnad *et al.*, 1976). The fact that these works are rarely read or cited today seems explicable only by reference to the low scholarly standards tolerated by the field as a whole.

Sociological problems of this sort seem eminently avoidable, mainly requiring more serious attempts at interdisciplinary rapport and scholarship. The overview I attempt here maintains an attitude both critical and respectful towards colleagues past and present, and seeks the original sources for the hypotheses I discuss. Although I am sure that I have failed in many places, and I apologize to my colleagues in advance, I have found that this self-enforced attitude has deepened my understanding of language evolution. As we wend our way through these complex issues, and wrestle with the thickets of debate that surround virtually every question, let us keep the wise words of philosopher Suzanne Langer constantly in mind:

The chance that the key ideas of any professional scholar's work are pure nonsense is small; much greater the chance that a devastating refutation is based on a superficial reading or even a distorted one, subconsciously twisted by a desire to refute. (p. ix, Langer, 1962)

1.2 A comparative, pluralistic approach

With Langer's dictum in mind, I will examine theories about the evolution of human language from a biological and explicitly **comparative** viewpoint, using current understanding of vertebrate genetics, development, and evolution as the grounding framework. I will focus on empirical data, particularly our substantial recent gains in biology (especially molecular genetics, and research on animal cognition and communication) as well as linguistics. My reason for choosing a broad comparative biological perspective is that, first, the last decades have witnessed incredible empirical progress in our understanding of basic biology, including many discoveries that touch upon the biology and evolution of language. Today, biology can provide solid empirical anchors for linguistic approaches, where many issues are still in flux. Second, the biological sciences form my personal intellectual background and provided my initial training as a scientist, and I feel most comfortable and capable of critical judgment in this area. By grounding my discussion on clear, empirically demonstrated biological facts, I hope that this book can outlive the rise and fall of particular theoretical approaches, or hypotheses, concerning language evolution.

At the core of this book's comparative approach is the **multi-component approach to language**. Rather than viewing language as a monolithic whole, I treat it as a complex system made up of several independent subsystems, each of which has a different function and may have a different neural and genetic substrate and, potentially, a different evolutionary history from the others. There are many reasons to adopt this perspective, which I will illustrate throughout the book. For instance, neural lesions may cause irreparable damage to one subsystem (e.g. vocal production) while leaving another functioning at a nearly normal level (e.g. comprehension). Similarly, the ontogenetic time course may differ for different subsystems, with phonetic comprehension preceding production, and both maturing faster than syntax, in the developing child. Cleaving language into subcomponents also breathes new life into a comparative approach: although no other species possesses "Language" as a whole, we will see that many species share important subcomponents of language. Many aspects of conceptual structure, and thus components of semantics, are shared with primates and other animals. While primates have limited vocal control, many species (such as birds or seals) share our capacity for vocal imitation, and studies with such species can play an important role in understanding the mechanisms underlying vocal control. Even syntax, at least at a simple level, finds analogs in other species (e.g. bird and whale "song") which can help us to understand both the brain basis for syntactic rules and the evolutionary pressures that can drive them to become more complex. Indeed, once we break language into subcomponents, and cast our comparative net widely, we discover that most aspects of language are present in one species or another. Thus, the multi-component view goes hand in hand with the comparative method (cf. Koehler, 1954).

Unfortunately, the correct way to subdivide language remains a subject of considerable debate (cf. Pinker and Bloom, 1990; Jackendoff, 2002). One influential breakdown was provided long ago by the American linguist Charles Hockett (Hockett, 1960, 1963). Hockett conceived of language as a collection of "design features" suited to different tasks, some shared with animal communication and others unique to language. The original thirteen features, plus three additions made later, are listed in Table 1.1. Hockett wrote before it was widely acknowledged that signed language is comparable to spoken language, and he therefore placed undue emphasis (in features 1–5) on the vocal signal. He also listed as separate features many which were closely inter-related (e.g. arbitrariness or displacement obviously depend on semanticity), and accepted that animal signals were "semantic" in ways that would be questioned today. Hockett derived his features from a logical consideration of animal signaling systems, and his breakdown was far more influential in the field of animal communication than in linguistics. Nonetheless, Hockett isolated four features, in bold in Table 1.1, as features

Table 1.1. Hockett's (1960) design features of language

(1) Vocal auditory channel – Signal modality involves vocalization and sound perception.

(2) Broadcast transmission – Everyone in earshot can hear what is said.

(3) Rapid fading – Signals fade quickly, and do not "clog the airwaves."

(4) Interchangeability – Any speaker can also be a listener, and *vice versa*.

(5) Total feedback – Speakers can hear everything that they say.

(6) Specialization (speech as "trigger") – Linguistic signals accomplish their results not via raw energy (like pushing or biting) but by their fit to the receiver's perceptual and cognitive systems.

(7) Semanticity – Some linguistic units have specific meanings (words, or morphemes).

(8) Arbitrariness – Meanings are generally arbitrarily related to signals, rather than iconic.

(9) Discreteness – Each utterance differs from all others discretely (by at least a distinctive feature).

(10) **Displacement** – Meanings about past, future, or distant referents can be encoded and understood.

(11) **Productivity/Openness** – New utterances can be readily coined and understood.

(12) **Duality of patterning** – Meaningless units (phonemes) are combined into meaningful ones (morphemes), which can then be combined into larger meaningful units (sentences).

(13) **Traditional (Cultural) transmission** – Languages are learned, not genetically encoded.

Hockett (1963/1966): additional design features

Hockett (1963) (republished in a second edition in 1966) adds a few additional features:

(14) Prevarication – It is possible to lie.

(15) Reflexivity – It is possible to use language to talk about language.

(16) Learnability – It is possible for a speaker of one language to learn additional languages.

unique to human language. While Hockett viewed features 1–9 to be shared by other organisms, he argued that 10–13 were "key innovations" *en route* to language in its fully modern form. We will meet these, and other, design features frequently in this book.

My approach has been more traditional, and agnostic as to function or uniqueness. I classify the components along traditional linguistic lines such as "syntax" or "pragmatics." This approach will allow me to introduce linguistics to the outsider in a way that makes much closer contact with the current literature than the rather obscure approach Hockett chose (and which he already, by 1965, acknowledged as far from perfect; Hockett, 1966). I have no illusions that the componential analysis of modern linguistics, which I adopt in this book, is the best one, or even ultimately correct. Indeed, I suspect that traditional subdisciplines will prove at best to be related to the biological mechanisms that underlie them imperfectly. Nonetheless, *some* such division into separate components is necessary to correct a pervasive tendency to reify one or the other aspects of language as the "key" one (be it speech, or syntax, or theory of mind, or others). I believe that current knowledge forces us to acknowledge several separate mechanisms that, when combined, give us language. All are necessary, and no one alone is sufficient. It is surprising how often long-running debates can be resolved by the recognition that the two sides have selected different subcomponents of language as their explanatory focus. Ultimately, I foresee that the field will converge on a biologically driven decomposition of the human capacity to acquire language into a set of well-defined mechanisms, and the interfaces between them. It is crucial to recognize that there *are* multiple, critically important components, not to precisely define them. For now, then, traditional linguistic subdivisions – phonology, syntax, semantics, etc. – provide an adequate starting point.

1.3 The faculty of language: broad and narrow senses

In the summer of 1988 I was studying coral reef fish in Puerto Rico, and about to begin a PhD in marine biology. My attempts to learn Spanish and later German ignited an interest in language, and my background led me to consider language from a biological perspective. It was then, reading works by Philip Lieberman and Noam Chomsky, that I recognized the promise of a comparative approach to language evolution, and decided to switch fields. From the beginning, I found the rhetoric that typifies discussions of language evolution disconcerting: students of fish behavior and evolution certainly have their disagreements, like scholars in any discipline, but they typically remain amicable, and debates are often carried out among beers and laughter. Many of my early readings in language evolution revealed disputes that seemed deadly serious, and fiery denunciations of Chomsky were particularly common. This seemed surprising: Chomsky famously inaugurated the cognitive revolution with his (1959) review of behaviorist B. F. Skinner's *Verbal Behavior* (1957), and then went on to found an approach to theoretical linguistics which dominates the field today. Chomsky is one of the most famous living scholars, a champion of the cognitive revolution, and the first modern linguist to try to ground language in human biology. But I found Chomsky portrayed as being anti-evolutionary, based on various offhand comments interspersed throughout his massive published output (e.g. in Lieberman, 1984; Pinker and Bloom, 1990; Newmeyer, 1998b). Could this really be accurate?

When I finally met Chomsky personally, I discovered a scholar who was open-minded and interested in biology, evolution, and the kind of comparative work my colleagues and I were doing. Far from being "anti-evolutionary," he expressed a consistent commitment to seeing language as an evolved, biological object, shaped by both optimizing and constraining forces during its evolution. I began to recognize that much of the debate around language evolution paralleled a long-running debate in evolutionary theory in general, concerning the relative roles of natural selection as an optimizing force *versus* historical and physical constraints as hindrances to optimization (e.g. Gould and Lewontin, 1979; Maynard Smith *et al.*, 1985; Endler, 1986). Chomsky's perspective was clear: that only some aspects of language could be understood as adaptations for communication. Other aspects – including many of the minutiae of syntax or semantics – seemed more likely to result from cognitive, historical, or developmental constraints. This perspective seemed both congenial and diametrically opposed to the "Chomsky" caricature painted by the literature opposing him. Deep confusion was caused, it seemed, by some scholars using "language" to denote language *in toto*, while others like Chomsky used it to denote a far more circumscribed set of mechanisms: essentially the computational mechanisms central to syntax, which allow an unbounded set of structures to be formed by a finite set of rules operating on a finite vocabulary. It became clear, in discussions and correspondence, that much of the heated debate in the field was based on terminological misunderstandings, intertwined with a fundamental issue of ongoing biological debate (constraints *versus* adaptation).

Joint discussions along these lines finally led Marc Hauser, my colleague in the Harvard Psychology Department, to propose a collaborative paper aimed at bridging some of these terminological barriers, and encouraging a pluralistic, comparative approach to language. In it, we introduced the notion of the **faculty of language in a broad sense** (FLB) (Hauser *et al.*, 2002; Fitch *et al.*, 2005) as one over-arching conception of language (see Figure 1.1). FLB encompasses *all* of the mechanisms involved in language acquisition and use (many of which are shared with other animals, or with other human cognitive capacities such as music or vision). General processes of cognition, such as audition, vision, or short- and long-term memory, are part of the neural basis for language, but are widely shared among vertebrates, and underlie multiple aspects of human cognition. The term FLB refers to this broad and inclusive conception of language, spanning from the details of speech perception through mechanisms of word learning to context-dependent inference. The purpose of this term is to cast the net widely, and not prejudge the degree to which any mechanism is or is not "special to" language. If the primate color vision system, through its influence on color cognition and linguistic color classifiers, has a role in language, then it is one of the components of FLB. Many biologists

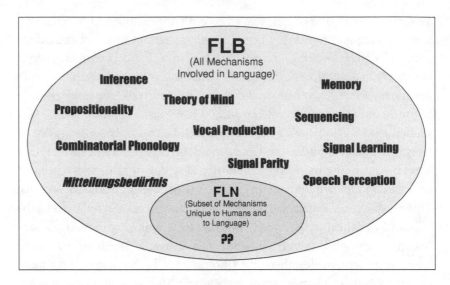

Figure 1.1 The faculty of language in broad and narrow senses: two ways in which the term "language" can be used. FLB (faculty of language in the broad sense) is the all-inclusive sense, incorporating *any* mechanism that is involved in language processing. FLN (faculty of language in the narrow sense) is the exclusive sense: by definition it includes only that subset of mechanisms that are both *specific to humans*, and *specific to language* within human cognition. Only a small subset of language-related mechanisms are expected to be in the latter category.

and psychologists find this broad notion close to the one connoted by the unadorned use of "language" in their fields.

In contrast, for many linguists "language" connotes a far more specific subset of mechanisms, which we dubbed FLN, for **faculty of language in a narrow sense**, meaning those mechanisms that are both unique to humans and special to language. We coined this term simply to clarify discussion and avoid confusion, once we realized that researchers (including ourselves) had been using the same word, "language," to talk about two different things (FLB and FLN) for many years, and thus had been talking past each other. While the term FLN itself is simply a matter of definition, the specific mechanisms that belong in the FLN category is a topic for empirical research. It could transpire that *no* subcomponent of the language faculty is truly unique, and that only the *combination* of linguistic mechanisms is unique to our species (though in my opinion this seems rather unlikely). From the multi-component perspective, the critical goal is to delineate the mechanisms involved in language in a biologically meaningful manner (that is, in a way that maps onto neural substrates and/or genetic mechanisms) and to discuss these mechanisms individually, in their own terms. Whether a mechanism is broadly shared (FLB) or narrowly specific (FLN) will have important ramifications for our abilities to study to it, but is not in itself the core question of interest. To the extent that some mechanism (e.g. phrase structure) is shared between language and music, we can use genetic or neural studies of musicians *versus* non-musicians as a powerful empirical probe to increase our understanding of that mechanism. If a linguistic mechanism is hypothesized to derive from visual cognition (e.g. Givón, 1995), we can use studies of language in the blind to test that proposition empirically. And so on. Because of the empirical difficulties of studying mechanisms unique to humans, biolinguists should be happy if most mechanisms involved in language do not fall into the FLN – the fewer its contents, the better.

Unfortunately, many scholars have misinterpreted these terms, apparently assuming that FLN refers to "true" or "core" language (the part we should be interested in), while peripheral aspects are "relegated" to FLB (see the critique by Pinker and Jackendoff, 2005). But to understand the biological basis for language, including its evolution, we need to first cast the net widely in terms of both mechanisms and species, and let the data tell us what is or isn't uniquely human. That is, we should assume a mechanism is shared until shown otherwise. In this book I argue that *most* components of the human capacity to acquire language are shared with other species, and open to a comparative approach. Some of these shared traits, like the capacity for vocal learning we have already discussed, are not shared with primates, but instead have evolved independently in other lineages like birds or whales. Because complex vocal learning evolved in humans, any complete model of human evolution must explain its origin and evolution. Far from "demoting" or denigrating it, the existence of this capacity in other animals allows us to explore both the mechanisms involved and the types of evolutionary forces that might drive it. Although there is no guarantee that vocal learning in birds and humans uses the same computational, neural, or genetic mechanisms, the molecular basis of development is highly conserved among living organisms (Carroll, 2000; Carroll *et al.*, 2001; Carroll, 2006). Therefore, in the vertebrate brain in particular, there are many good reasons to expect cross-species comparisons to yield deep insights, and even convergently evolved traits are often based upon shared genetic or developmental mechanisms (Shubin *et al.*, 1997; Gehring and Ikeo, 1999). For all these reasons, my working assumption in this book will be that most subcomponents of the language faculty are shared – components of FLB – unless there are good empirical reasons to suppose otherwise.

1.4 Debates and distinctions in language evolution: an overview

A newcomer to the field of language evolution is confronted with a bewildering variety of debates and distinctions (Botha, 2003). Technical terms such as "spandrel," "exaptation," "recursion," "subjacency," or "petalia" are profuse but often go undefined, and technical terminology from linguistics, genetics, evolutionary theory, or neuroscience appear frequently. Even ordinary words like "symbol" or "imitate" take on special technical meanings. In the course of the book we will meet, and I will define, many such terms. However, there are a number of cross-cutting distinctions, issues, and debates that are prevalent enough to deserve special treatment. I will now discuss some of these distinctions, particularly those that have been sources of confusion and misunderstanding in the past. Different scholars, particularly those from different disciplinary backgrounds, can interpret those same words in radically different ways. I will also try to make clear how, and why, I will use a particular word in this book. My goal is not to dictate proper usage, but to provide an example of how being specific about what one is discussing can help to avoid misunderstanding. I suggest that unspecified use of some terms, especially the word "language" itself, but also terms like "innate" or "instinct," is probably best avoided. Words with so many divergent interpretations often serve as a lightning rod for hot, but fruitless, debate.

1.4.1 Communication and language

A first crucial distinction is between communication and language. All animals communicate, some in rather simple ways (moths releasing a pheromone when they are ready to mate) and some in very complex ways (birds that learn, and then improvise upon, highly complex vocal songs). Many (probably most) animals communicate via multiple modalities – mammals such as dogs have a complex communication system that includes olfactory cues in urine, vocalizations of different types (barking, growling, whining), and visual displays ("play bowing" or "smiling"). Spotting a predator, vervet monkeys produce alarm calls differing according to predator type, and their calls allow other vervets to take evasive action. Cuttlefish communicate via rapid color changes, elephants via infrasounds we cannot hear, and electric fish via currents only they can generate and sense. All of these fascinating systems of communication, and many others, have been termed "language," but by the specific definition I will adopt in this book, none of them are. In order to motivate the view of language I will use, let us examine some forms of human communication that are not language.

Humans communicate through various distinct signaling modalities, and facial expressions make up a set of communication signals typical of our species. For example, smiling occurs in affiliative situations and is interpreted as a signal of happiness, pleasure, friendliness, or (sometimes) submission. Smiling is common to all human cultures, and is present in blind newborns who could never have seen this display (Eibl-Eibesfeldt, 1973). Smiling has parallels in many primates (Darwin, 1872b; van Hoof, 1972). Thus smiling is an excellent human example of an innate, evolved signal, whose evolutionary history we can understand using comparative data (Preuschoft, 1995). Similarly, both laughter and crying are species-typical vocal signals and require no experience for their expression (Eibl-Eibesfeldt, 1970). Such communicative signals can be termed "innate" because they are present at birth, but this could be misleading as they often have a learned component as well (we can learn to suppress crying or laughter in certain situations, and these are culture-dependent). Although such signals form an important part of human communication, they are not termed "human language."

Manual gestures make up a different set of human communication signals, more similar to languages in that they are learned and vary between cultures. A specific gesture can have very different meanings even between neighboring cultures (the "thumbs up" sign signifies affirmation in some European cultures and is a scatological insult in others). All human cultures have some such gestures, but their form and meaning are highly variable (Hewes, 1973; McNeill, 2000). This realm of human communication is sometimes called "body language" in the popular press, but students of signed languages have demonstrated the necessity of sharply distinguishing between gesture and sign language (Bellugi and Klima, 1978). Gestures, again, are an important and interesting component of human communication, but are not human language *per se*. Finally, music is a complex, learned form of human communication found in all world cultures (Nettl, 2000), and although some call music the "language of the emotions," common usage distinguishes between music and language.

Why, within our own species, do we typically distinguish between language and a variety of other signals used in communication, including innate signals such as smiling or learned signals like gesture and music? On what grounds? Because language represents and communicates meaning in a different, and much more flexible and detailed, way than these other systems. This is not to say, of course, that these other systems *lack* meaning: laughter certainly indicates happiness, music can convey a wide range of subtle moods and emotions very effectively, and an apt gesture can sometimes be far more communicatively effective than the "equivalent" words. But each of these other systems has a limited domain of expression, and none of them will allow one person to tell another what they did on their birthday two years ago, how stars formed in the early universe, or why it is wrong to steal someone else's toy. Indeed, virtually any thought we are able to think can be represented and communicated to another person's mind if we speak the same language. This combination of unlimited specificity of meaning, combined with a free flexibility to use language in novel ways (we easily understand sentences we have never heard, and express thoughts no one ever thought before), is the hallmark of language. Because signed languages possess this same open-ended expressive power, they are appropriately termed "languages" (in contrast to gestural "body language" or musical "emotional language"). Language is only one of the communication systems we have available to us, as humans, and its defining features are its scope and unbounded flexibility (extending to all we can think).

Returning now to animals, we can use the same basic criteria to ask if animal communication systems constitute "languages" in this same sense. This is a more controversial question. From a biological viewpoint, this question needn't have a stark yes or no answer, and we might better ask which subcomponents of language can be found in the communication systems of other species (following Hockett, 1960). I will discuss this approach to animal communication systems, and its results, in some detail in Chapter 4. But to cut to the chase, our best current evidence suggests that no other living species has a communication system that allows it to do what we humans do all the time: to represent and communicate arbitrary novel thoughts, at any desired level of detail. Indeed, our current data suggest that even a rudimentary version of this ability (to communicate *some* novel thoughts) is lacking in other species. As Viki's story illustrates, this is not because animals lack an ability to learn, and when brought into the laboratory many species can learn to understand and communicate at a level far exceeding that used in the wild. Rather, the lack of animal "language" in nature seems to reflect some deeper limitations, with a powerful biological basis that is not easily overridden. Our ability to express thoughts in a shareable form appears to make us unique among existing animals.

The distinction between communication and language is thus central to the study of language evolution. But this is a *distinction* and not a dichotomy: language is indeed one of the forms of communication available to us humans. But humans would be immeasurably poorer if we lacked laughter, crying, gesture, and music, and during its evolution language co-existed and co-evolved with these other systems. And acknowledging this distinction by no means renders the communication systems of other species irrelevant to human language. As a long-term student of animal vocal communication, who has often marveled at the richness, beauty, and complexity of animal sounds, I am often disappointed when I hear scholars dismiss such systems as uninteresting. But I am equally distressed when I see gullible portrayals of animal "language" in the popular press. The truth is not to be found at such extremes, but in treating each species on its own terms: all animals communicate, but do so in different ways, well suited to their particular social and ecological needs. Animals have their own rich suite of communication systems, distinct from language. But there is no reason to let our appreciation of these other systems lead us to foist the term "language" upon them inappropriately, or to blind us to the remarkable, and apparently unique, qualities of language *per se.*

1.4.2 Genes and environment: nature *via* nurture

The case of Viki nicely illustrates that a biological basis for acquiring human language is present at birth in a normal child, but not present in a chimpanzee. Nonetheless, no child is born knowing a language like English or Chinese: a long interaction with a suitable environment is needed to master any given language. A core fact of human nature is that any normal human can learn any of the 6,000 or so natural languages currently existing, if raised from birth in an environment where that language is used. A chimpanzee will not learn any of them. There is no evidence that populations of humans are genetically predisposed to learn the language of their community more than any other (though see Dediu and Ladd, 2007). In an important sense, our instinct to learn language is equipotential, supporting full mastery of any known human language. Although this fact has been realized for many years, its biological implications are still a matter of much discussion.

One could easily choose either the biological preparedness present in all normal children, or the great variety of languages a child can handle, as an interesting focus for a lifetime of research. Unfortunately, a tendency to focus exclusively on one or the other has generated one of the most persistently fruitless debates in science: the "nature *versus* nurture" debate. When posed in dichotomous terms – pitting innate biological factors in opposition to personal experiential factors – the distinction is dangerously misleading (Tinbergen, 1963; Lorenz, 1965). All known life forms require both the guidance of genes to develop and the presence of some permissive environment (e.g. with light, oxygen, nutrients, proper temperature, etc.) in which to execute their development. Development of most multicellular life forms requires more: interactions between cells and their local environment (within the developing organism) play a critical role in the self-organizing process by which each one of us went from a single-celled organism (a fertilized egg cell) to a complex body with trillions of cells.

This interactive process, termed **epigenesis**, is a well-established biological fact concerning both physical and behavioral development (Gottlieb, 1992; Gilbert, 2003). Epigenesis – nature *via* nurture – provides the unchallenged pathway out of unenlightening nature/nurture debates (cf. Ridley, 2003). Genes do not provide a blueprint of the body, or of the brain. Rather, the products of gene-expression regulate themselves, and those of other genes, in a complex cascade of interactions that depend upon, and are influenced by, certain aspects of the environment. Crucially, the "environment," from a genetic viewpoint, includes interactions within a cell (e.g. the local concentration of other gene products), within the body (e.g. the interactions between different tissue types during development), and in the environment as influenced by the individual's own actions (e.g. movements of the embryo within the egg, or of the babbling infant's own vocal tract). A notion of "environment" which includes only stimuli external to the body provides a hopelessly depauperate view of the role of experience in development. Conversely, a notion of "innateness" which lumps all of these types of developmental experience together as "innate" lacks the precision and specificity necessary for deeper understanding. The epigenetic perspective sees innate proclivities or constraints, and experiential input of many sorts, as equal partners in the developmental process. Any biological trait is 100 percent "innate" in the sense that it relies on pre-existing genetic and cellular mechanisms for its existence, but is 100 percent "environmental" in the sense that a specific environmental situation is required for its adequate development. This is as true for lung or hand development as it is for neural development and complex behavioral traits such as language.

Epigenesis does not cease at birth. Many organisms also respond to the environment in an active and adaptive manner after birth (or germination). For instance, the growth pattern of trees enables any individual tree to adapt to the pattern of light and nutrients it encounters (a tree growing between two houses, or in a dense forest, will have a different shape than a genetically identical sibling growing in the middle of a field). Such **phenotypic plasticity** is even better developed in animals with a nervous system. Brains allow individuals to make much more specific and detailed responses to their individual environment, which are often considered under the umbrella term "learning." Of course, there are huge differences between species in the neural bases of learning, from simple stimulus–response linkage (e.g. between a particular chemical odorant and noxious stimulation – a linkage that virtually any animal from worms to fish to humans will rapidly learn) to much more complex behavioral patterns that bear only an indirect relation to specific stimuli (for instance, the formation of a cognitive "map" of space from a sequence of traveled paths that only partially sample this space).

The fact of phenotypic plasticity in diverse organisms has important implications for discussions of nature and nurture in psychology. Any ability to respond adaptively to environmental circumstances, whether morphologically or behaviorally, itself rests on an ineliminable genetically guided biological foundation. Even a radical behaviorist acknowledges that "general learning mechanisms" must precede learning, and be biologically given. Because no system can be ideal for all imagineable tasks, there will be limits to this system, and these will often differ between species in a way that reflects that species' past evolutionary history (Garcia and Koelling, 1966). Some organisms are intrinsically more flexible than others: a fern's leaf structure is largely laid down before it unrolls, while many flowering plants change their form to suit their environment. In many insects, particular neurons, with specific connections and behavioral roles, reliably develop in the absence of any external environmental input, while the vertebrate nervous system seems in general to require specific types of environmental interaction to develop normally (Held and Hein, 1963). Even within a specific group (e.g. songbirds) we often find substantial differences between "specialist" species, with a variety of fine-tuned innate behaviors that suit them to their lifestyles, and "generalist" species which appear to rely more upon flexible individual adaptation to whatever environment they find themselves in. While humans are, in most ways, an extreme example of a generalist species (we eat almost anything, learn very flexibly, and can live almost anywhere), we are specialists in at least one domain: the early and rapid acquisition of language.

Box 1.1. Basic developmental biology and epigenesis

We all began life as a single cell: the fertilized egg cell, or **zygote**. This cell went through a repeated process of division to generate all of the trillion cells in our bodies. The zygote contains two sets of complementary genes, one from the mother and one from the father. Every cell in the body will receive these same genes. In addition to increasing in number, the daughter cells become specialized to different tasks and forms, a process termed **differentiation**. Because each cell contains the same genes, differentiation is determined by the activation of different subsets of genes in different cells: **differential gene expression**. Two broad classes of genes are involved: *structural* genes code for proteins such as enzymes or collagen that do work in the cell, while *regulatory* genes play a role in controlling the expression of other genes.

The process of development is an unfolding of a complex recipe. There is no "blueprint" of the future body encoded in the DNA, but rather a process in which cells interact with one another to produce coordinated outcomes. For example, in the developing eye, the future retina, an outgrowth of the brain, signals to cells in the overlying skin of the embryo, starting them down the path to becoming the lens, an interactive process called **induction** (Gilbert, 2003). The lens in turn later induces the skin above it to form the cornea. The complex interactive process by which cells induce other cells to differentiate, resulting in a well-organized three-dimensional embryo, is termed **epigenesis.** The local environmental conditions of each individual cell often play controlling roles in this epigenetic process, which unfolds in a reliable species-typical way. Because both genes and local environments are involved, every step of the way, a "genes *versus* environment" dichotomy fails to capture the essence of epigenesis (Gottlieb, 1992).

Recent breakthroughs in developmental biology have revealed that the regulatory genes underlying development are highly conserved, and in many case play identical roles in organisms that have been evolving separately for half a billion years. Thus in many cases there is a **deep homology** between similar structures in very different organisms: their development is controlled by the same, conserved genetic mechanisms. An example of this conservatism is Pax-6, a specific regulatory gene involved in eye development in flies, squid, mice, and humans (Gehring and Ikeo, 1999). A mutant mouse which would normally lack eyes, due to a breakdown in Pax-6 expression, can be "rescued" by injecting the Pax-6 protein of a fly! Thus, even convergently evolved traits, in widely separated species, may be based upon the same genetic information, inherited from a distant common ancestor.

1.4.3 Innateness and learning: language as an instinct to learn

Language is an art, like brewing or baking; but . . . it certainly is not a true instinct, for every language has to be learnt. It differs, however, widely from all ordinary arts, for man has an instinctive tendency to speak, as we see in the babble of our young children; whilst no child has an instinctive tendency to brew, bake, or write. (Darwin, 1872b)

Though the faculty of language may be congenital, all languages are traditional. (Müller, 1873)

Despite a frequent framing of debate in language evolution as one between "nativists" and "empiricists," all of these factors force us to recognize as misleading the question: "To what degree is language innate?" Whether language is learned wholly by general-purpose learning mechanisms, or acquired via a highly specialized and specific set of innate guidelines, language acquisition requires innate mechanisms present in our species and not in others. The answer to the converse question – "To what degree does language require learning from environmental input?" – is, again trivially, that language requires a huge amount of environmental input (even radical nativists agree that the lexicon of any particular language requires massive learning). So is language "an instinct" (Pinker, 1994b) or not (Tomasello, 1995; Sampson, 1997)? Framing the debate in these terms may be a good way to sell books, but is unlikely to increase our understanding of language.

The way out of this trap is to recognize that many, if not most, aspects of complex behavior, especially in vertebrates, are channeled *both* by environmental input *and* by genetically based constraints and predispositions (Tinbergen, 1963; Lorenz, 1965). We are born with "**instincts to learn**" (Marler, 1991b) about certain things. In the case of birds, it is an instinct to learn the song of their species; for humans it is an instinct to learn the language(s) in their environment. An instinct to learn may include predispositions to attend to certain types of cues and not to others, and constraints on what can be learned. A profitable way of rephrasing the "language instinct" debate is to ask: What are the constraints on language learning? What sorts of proclivities are babies born with (e.g. to attend to certain types of cues and not others)? The answers to these questions will almost certainly vary, depending on the component of language we are discussing. Finally, to what degree are these proclivities and constraints specific to language, rather than reflecting more general aspects of learning shared with other cognitive domains (e.g. music, motor control, social intelligence, vision, etc.)? This, I think, is the only really open question. To answer it, another type of comparison is crucial: comparison *between* cognitive domains in our own species. Such cognitive comparisons demand that we single out particular aspects of language acquisition for study (for example the learning of word meanings), and then compare it with acquisition in other non-linguistic domains like fact or motor learning (e.g. Markson and Bloom, 1997). A multi-component approach to language, biologically grounded in an understanding of epigenesis, allows us to supersede the oversimplistic nature *versus* nurture dichotomy, and to replace it with specific research questions.

By examining the nature of our instinct to learn language from a doubly comparative viewpoint, we can replace seemingly intractable philosophical debates with a range of more specific questions that can be examined empirically. Although this approach is only beginning to build momentum, it is already reaping rewards. These rewards, and the promise of accelerating progress within this perspective, provide fuel for my optimism, and for the approach pursued in this book.

1.4.4 I-language and E-language: cultural and biological evolution of language

Another confusion can be caused by two distinct uses of the word "language." "Languages" in the everyday sense include French, English, or Warlpiri. These are socially shared phenomena: they are cultural creations. More recently, many linguists and psychologists have focused on "language," conceived in at least two additional senses: first, as the complex cognitive system underlying language that is a property of an individual's brain, and second, as a general descriptor for the biological faculty or capacity that underlies and allows this system to develop. Although the seeds of this distinction can already be detected in Sausurre's langue/parole distinction (Saussure, 1916), the distinction was emphasized most clearly by Noam Chomsky (Chomsky, 1986). Chomsky argued that the proper focus for a biologically grounded theory of linguistics was the neural/cognitive system existing within an individual. He termed this system, a property of the mind/brain of that individual, "internal" language, or "I-language." In contrast, the "languages" studied by historical linguists, properties of populations of individual speakers, were termed "external," or "E-language." Chomsky argued forcibly that E-language provides a poor focus for linguistic study. E-language is simply an aggregate epiphenomenon, no more than the output of a set of I-languages, in which case we should study the more basic unit of I-language. It is clear that some historical linguists got a bit carried away in their fascination with E-languages as explanatory entities: the great German linguist August Schleicher believed languages are actual living things, and Jakob Grimm posited a *Sprachgeist* – an internal spirit of a language driving it to change along certain lines. Chomsky questioned both the ontological validity of E-language as a concept, and rejected it as

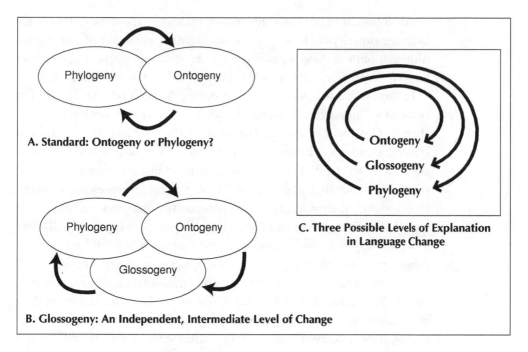

A. Standard: Ontogeny or Phylogeny?

B. Glossogeny: An Independent, Intermediate Level of Change

C. Three Possible Levels of Explanation in Language Change

Figure 1.2 Glossogeny denotes cultural change in languages (historical change), as distinct from ontogeny (development of language in the individual) or phylogeny (evolution of the language capacity in the human species). For most organisms, we need only to consider the influences of phylogeny or ontogeny (A). Glossogeny adds a third potential explanatory factor, concerning culturally transmitted change (B). The timescale of glossogeny is intermediate between the other two: much slower than language acquisition, but faster than genetic changes in the species (C). Each level of explanation will be useful for understanding certain aspects of language, and the interaction among levels may be complex [images after Kirby, 2002; Kirby *et al.*, 2007].

a useful focus of linguistic investigation. One might have expected that this would be the last mention of E-language, since Chomsky defined the term essentially to reject it. However, the term has been subtly redefined, and today receives widening use to denote a culturally shared set of utterances produced by some specific set of speakers (what Chomsky would call the "primary linguistic data," in what Hurford has aptly termed the "arena of use") (e.g. Kirby, 1999).

Both I-language and E-language (external, shared data) exist. But they are different phenomena, and considerable confusion can result from calling them both "language," particularly when the explanatory role of external-ized linguistic data is under debate. For example, it is common to find the term "language evolution" used *both* in the cultural sense, for example the historical change from Latin to French or Italian, *and* to language evolution in the biological sense primarily explored in this book: genetic change in the language capacity (FLB) during the phylogenetic evolution of our species. Although both of these types of change are obviously interesting and valid topics for scientific study, we will get nowhere if we fail to distinguish them.

In this book I will adopt a term proposed by evolutionary linguist Jim Hurford – "**glossogeny**" (Hurford, 1990) – to refer to *historical* linguistic change. This form of change follows from the core fact that language is culturally transmitted: simple copying errors will eventually lead to change. Glossogeny, although slow on the scale of individual lifetimes, is very rapid compared to phylogenetic change. Thus, glossogeny represents an intermediate level of change, interposed between the ontogeny and phylogeny typical of all living things (see Figure 1.2). Languages change so rapidly that, to a good approximation, we can assume that the biological basis for language remains fixed during substantial glossogenetic change. In 2,000 years, Latin has diverged into multiple mutually incomprehensible systems (e.g. French, Romanian, and Italian), while the genetic bases for acquiring these dialects has remained essentially unchanged. Similarities between historical linguistics and evolutionary theory have long been recognized: Darwin drew an analogy between biological evolution and the historical process by which one of two variant word forms disappear. Further implications of language change will be considered in later chapters (see also Hurford, 1994; Lightfoot, 1998; Kirby, 1999; Pagel *et al.*, 2007).

Which of these various uses of the term "language" should be the default? From an empirical viewpoint I concur with Chomsky's argument that scientists interested in the genetic and neural mechanisms underlying language need to focus on I-language, as instantiated in individuals' brains. I-language, and the capacity to acquire it, are the core systems we seek to understand biologically. I, along with many linguists, biologists, and psychologists, agree that I-language is the proper empirical starting point for this investigation. However, this is no argument against the study of glossogeny. Language change is a fact, and since the advent of writing we have a rich database documenting language change. These may provide further insights into the nature of the language acquisition system. Furthermore, it is becoming increasingly clear that glossogeny and phylogeny can interact in important and unintuitive ways (see Chapter 10 and Keller, 1995; Deacon, 1997; Kirby, 1999; Kirby *et al.*, 2004), and that language provides a prime example of what biologist Kevin Laland and colleagues have termed "cultural niche construction" (Laland *et al.*, 2001). Both the study of I-language and of historical change can be of value in understanding the biological underpinnings of the instinct to learn language.

2.1 Introduction

In this chapter I will discuss contemporary evolutionary theory as it relates to models of language evolution. I first attempt to give a brief, balanced overview of contemporary evolutionary theory, a condensed non-mathematical version of what one might receive in an undergraduate class on evolution, but tailored to questions concerning language evolution. I adopt a historical viewpoint because the history of evolutionary theory provides several nice examples of past success in the unification of warring disciplines – precisely what is needed, in the future, in biolinguistics. For those interested in the fascinating history of evolutionary theory, see Mayr (1982), Ruse (1986), Gould (2002), and Bowler (2003). For more detailed introductions to modern evolutionary theory, Dawkins (1987) gives an excellent popular introduction, and a good textbook is Ridley (1997), which also provides balanced overviews and detailed historical perspectives on some of the ongoing debates discussed below.

Second, I survey areas of controversy in language evolution. My guiding assumption is that evolutionary theory is general, applying to all living organisms: we neither need nor want a version of evolutionary theory specific to humans (Darwin, 1871; Hockett and Ascher, 1964; Pinker and Bloom, 1990). Language evolution is just another question for mainstream evolutionary theory, and special pleading about human evolution must be resisted unless clearly required by the data. Several major points of contention have yet to be resolved one way or another, and these will be my focus. I provide an overview of debates concerning gradualism in various guises, and the relative roles of adaptation and constraints (for a meticulous investigation of these debates see Botha, 2003).

2.2 Evolution: the beginnings

By the end of the eighteenth century, the voyages of discovery had covered the globe, and European ships had visited almost every corner of the world.

The specimens of plants and animals sent back to Europe had a profound impact on the biologists of the time. The first order of business was simply to name and classify the new specimens, and even this modest task posed serious challenges (Mayr, 1982). It suddenly became clear that the diversity of life was much greater than previously suspected: the discovery of mammals that laid eggs or of fish with lungs rendered the cut-and-dry classification systems of past centuries obsolete. As biologists groped for new classificatory principles, the French comparative anatomist and paleontologist Jean Baptiste de Lamarck was the first to clearly state the concept that would provide the ultimate solution to these problems: evolution (Lamarck, 1809). For Lamarck, evolution is the change of a species over long periods of time (that is, over multiple generations). The term, which means "unfolding," was already in wide use to describe individual development (the process whereby a seed becomes a tree, or a fetus an adult). Lamarck suggested that an analogous process could occur in species over generations. At the time, this notion that species could "transform" was radical, because to many it seemed a direct contradiction of the Bible, and controverted a notion of "the fixity of species" promulgated by leading biologists of the time, such as Cuvier and Owen. The idea was also considered intellectually distasteful, and politically dangerous, by many, threatening the whole idea of stable order and of the "rightness" of traditional social systems. Finally, if species could transform into one another, then any firm lines drawn between them might simply be convenient figments of our imagination, threatening *any* system of classification.

Yet without the concept of evolution, the fact that the wings of a bat and the legs of a cat should have precisely the same skeletal structure, right down to details of cartilages, nerves, and muscles, seems arbitrary. But from an evolutionary viewpoint, these similarities make perfect sense: bats and cats descended from a common mammalian ancestor, who had a five-digit forelimb with that structure, which was thus inherited by its descendents. While it is hard to understand why an omnipotent creator would be constrained in this way, it makes intuitive sense that organisms should be similar if they are related by descent. A vast array of anatomical similarities between diverse species suddenly became intelligible as resulting from common ancestry. But in addition to explaining *unity* as due to common ancestry, the idea of evolution also makes sense of *diversity*: differences between species that reflect their differing ways of life. Although the count of bones is the same in a bat's wing and a cat's forelimb, the many differences reflect the bat's adaptation to flight and the cat's to hunting. Other similarities occur when two unrelated organisms adopt similar ways of life: bats' and birds' wings are similar, superficially, because each is an excellent fit to the requirements of flight. A conceptual framework that could explain both similarity (due to common ancestry) and diversity (due to differing function and ways of life) was needed, and the idea of evolution offered a beautifully parsimonious solution to a core problem: understanding the unity and diversity of life

2.2.1 Natural selection

By 1831, evolution was a well-known idea, familiar to the young Charles Darwin as he set out on his famous voyage of discovery on the *Beagle*. But a core mystery remained: What force *drove* the close fit between the form of organisms and their way of life? The near-perfect correspondence between biological form and function seemed to demand some "intelligent designer," an invisible, guiding hand overseeing this process of evolution. Darwin's core insight was to realize that, if enough time was available, an ever better fit between a species' form and its way of life is *inevitable* and requires no guiding, sentient agent. Indeed, a close match between how organisms are, and what they do, is the logical consequence of three obvious characteristics of living things. The first is **variation**: individual organisms differ from one another. In a litter of puppies, each puppy will be somewhat different from its siblings. The second is **inheritance**: organisms resemble their parents. Although each puppy in the litter is different, as adults they will typically resemble their parents more than a randomly chosen member of the population. The third fact of life is **differential survival**: not all individuals that are born are lucky enough to live to adulthood and reproduce.

Variation and inheritance were the foundation for selective animal breeding, when humans preferentially select the prettiest flowers, the most productive corn, or the fastest horses as parents for the next generation. Darwin's core insight was that the struggle for existence *itself* can do the same job as a human selective breeder, because organisms that are better suited to their environment (in whatever way) are more likely to survive and reproduce than those who are less well suited. Offspring who inherit these characteristics will thus be disproportionately represented in the next generation. As long as there are differences in survival and/or reproduction, and these are influenced by heritable individual characteristics, a slow but non-random change will inevitably result, in the direction of a better fit between the environment and the population as a whole. By analogy to the "artificial selection" practiced by animal breeders, Darwin called this force **natural selection**. Natural selection is one of the most powerful ideas in all biology, because it provides a motive force driving evolution towards the observed close fit between organisms and their environments.

Natural selection is a logical consequence of everyday facts of life that any dog breeder or flower fancier could agree upon. Given that the three principles underlying natural selection are so obvious, and would have been acknowledged by scientists from Aristotle to Lamarck, why had no one before Darwin recognized the principle of natural selection as their inevitable logical outcome? Two facts provide partial explanations. The first is the matter of time: natural selection is a slow process, and huge amounts of time (millions of years) are required for any major observable changes to take place. Nineteenth-century Biblical scholars held that the earth was only about 6,000 years old, and while this might be enough time to turn a wolf into a chihuahua, it seemed inadequate to change a cat into a bat. But by Darwin's time a revolution in the science of geology had occurred, based on increased understanding of European sedimentary rocks and the fossils found within them, and most practicing geologists agreed that the earth's age must be measured in millions or billions of years, not in thousands. Darwin was well-schooled in the new geology, and so his imagination had already been opened to the idea that vast expanses of time were required to explain geological features such as mountain ranges or islands.

A second impediment to the idea of natural selection concerns the arithmetical magnitude of the struggle for existence. In Darwin's time, the majority of a European mother's children could be expected to survive to adulthood. In drastic contrast, a single female oyster, or a female cod, may produce millions of offspring in a single year, but only a few survive. In a good year a single oak tree will produce tens of thousands of fertile acorns. Only a tiny fraction will germinate, grow, and reproduce. Such intense struggle for survival is the norm in nature, and we humans are the exception. By Darwin's time, however, European populations were growing rapidly, and in 1798 Malthus had issued grim predictions about the impossibility of sustained European growth, predicting that populations would rapidly outstrip environmental capacities. This question was a much discussed concern in Victorian society, and a crucial spur to Darwin's thinking.

By 1858, natural selection was an idea whose time had come: when he first read Darwin's paper, Thomas Huxley is reported to have exclaimed: "How stupid of me not to have thought of that." Its timeliness is nicely illustrated by its independent discovery by biologist Alfred Wallace, which finally goaded Darwin to publish his long-nurtured idea. When Darwin conceived the idea of natural selection shortly after his return from the voyage of the *Beagle* in 1838, he set himself to the task of streamlining the argument and collecting supporting evidence. Although his ideas were well known among English biologists, Darwin hesitated to publish them for (justified) fear of the reaction of society and the Church, and he continued to amass an increasingly impressive body of data consistent with his theory (Darwin considered his 513-page *On the Origin of Species* an "outline"). Darwin's hand was forced when Wallace independently conceived the same idea, and mailed it in a concise ten-page letter. Darwin quickly wrote up a short précis, and both papers were presented to the Linnaean Society simultaneously in 1858. Had Wallace bypassed Darwin and published first, we might speak of Wallace's theory of evolution by natural selection, and Darwin would remain a poorly known documenter of Wallace's theory: a Victorian expert on barnacles, orchids, and earthworms.

In summary, Darwin's insight was not the idea of evolution itself, which had been widely discussed, but his concept of natural selection. Although initially controversial, the idea of natural selection was successfully combined with genetics in the first half of the twentieth century, a solid theoretical edifice today known as the **modern neo-Darwinian synthesis**. Despite the fact that the concept of evolution by natural selection is still misunderstood or rejected by some segments of society today, issues of debate in contemporary biology concern *not* the existence of natural selection nor its central importance to evolutionary theory, which are indubitable. Today, the debates focus on what additional elements are required to apply this simple, powerful, and in retrospect obvious, concept to specific biological problems.

2.3 Categories of selection: sexual, kin, and group selection

2.3.1 Sexual selection

Evolutionary theory has acquired two key additions since 1859, and both play an important role in contemporary discussions of language evolution. In *On the Origin of Species*, Darwin mainly focused on the adaptation of organisms to their physical environment in ways that aided individual survival. But he was well aware that some of the most obvious characteristics of living things, from the bright and beautiful colors of flowers to the elaborate plumage and song of birds, did not obviously aid survival directly, and indeed sometimes seemed likely to *hinder* survival. His solution to this problem was the idea of **sexual selection** – selection due to competition within a species for mates (Darwin, 1871). Darwin reasoned that survival was only the first step in the struggle for existence, and that reproduction was the crucial second step. If there is competition for mates for any reason, then traits which aid victory in reproductive competition may be selected and will appear preferentially in the next generation – even if they hinder survival. Consider the elaborate plumage of many birds. Bright coloration probably makes them easier for predators to spot, but if it helps increase attractiveness and boosts mating success, it can still be beneficial on average. For Darwin, female choice was a key driving force behind sexual selection, and the idea that females were more "choosy" about their mates than males directly explained the fact that, in most species, it is the males who are brightly colored and perform elaborate displays. Similarly, better weaponry or intimidating appearance might aid males in intraspecific competition, accounting for large antlers, manes, and the like.

Darwin's contemporaries had varying opinions of sexual selection. Wallace, for example, rejected the idea, and in male-dominated Victorian society the idea that female choice might drive evolution was seen as utterly implausible. For half a century the idea languished. Despite important and insightful work done on sexual selection by Fisher (1930), the topic was largely ignored until well after the modern synthesis. In the 1960s a number of important theoretical papers reopened the issue, and sexual selection is now seen as a major factor in understanding evolution, and has been a topic of both intense theoretical (Lande, 1980; Grafen, 1990b; Harvey and Bradbury, 1991) and empirical work (Bradbury and Andersson, 1987; Andersson, 1994). One of the explanatory virtues of sexual selection is that, under certain circumstances where female choice and male traits are self-reinforcing, very rapid and extreme evolutionary change can occur. Aware of this intuitively, Darwin suggested that many human-specific traits might have been driven by sexual selection (Darwin, 1871), and his idea has been resurrected with a vengeance today. Some commentators have suggested that most of the interesting aspects of the human mind result from sexual selection (Buss, 1994; Miller, 2001). Such ideas run into problems, however: unlike many polygynous mammals, the two human sexes are in fact relatively similar in both body size (we are less dimorphic than most primates) and intellectual ability. While there is little question that such sex-specific characters as beards or low-pitched voices have been driven by sexual selection, its role in human cognition, and especially language, remains controversial.

2.3.2 Inclusive fitness and kin selection

Both natural selection and sexual selection were understood by Darwin. But despite Darwin's remarkable breadth and depth as a thinker, a difficult problem remained that deeply troubled him to the end of his life: the evolution of "altruistic" behavior, when an individual sacrifices its time or even its life to help another. It was quite difficult for Darwin to see how his theory could explain, or even countenance, such self-sacrifice. The breakthrough required a better understanding of Mendelian genetics, and came with W. D. Hamilton's concept of *inclusive fitness* (Hamilton, 1963). The reconciliation of "altruistic" behavior with Darwinian theory required understanding a third subtype of selection, today often termed **kin selection**. The core notion was already grasped by Haldane (1955) when he acknowledged the selective advantage of saving, at risk to his own life, a drowning relative, because they were likely to share some of his own genes. Recognizing that there is a 50 percent chance of sharing any allele with a brother, and a 1/8 chance with a full cousin, Haldane is said to have quipped, "I would give my life for two brothers or eight cousins," thus recognizing the basic mathematical principle behind inclusive fitness. Haldane himself did not think such logic could account for altruism since (oddly enough) he had twice saved a drowning person, and in neither case stopped to think about their relatedness to him. But Hamilton realized that this argument was spurious, since it confused personal motivations and individual cognition with the ultimate "logic" of selection. Whatever the immediate motivation, if a "gift" of altruism ends up, on average, being bestowed selectively on relatives who share a good proportion of the donor's alleles, altruism may be favored. From a strictly genetic viewpoint, such "altruism" is selfish. By helping their kin, donors help their own genes, whether they know it or not.

For such an unconsciously "altruistic" act to be favored by selection, it need only satisfy Hamilton's famous inequality, $Br > C$ (the *B*enefit to kin, as diluted by the individuals' fractional relatedness r, must exceed the *C*ost to self). The basic logic behind this simple equation has been borne out both theoretically and empirically in recent decades and, like sexual selection, the theory of inclusive fitness now forms an important component of modern evolutionary theory. It has played a particularly central role in understanding social behavior, since there are many examples of apparent self-sacrifice in the social domain (E. O. Wilson, 1975; Dunford,

1977; Brown, 1978; Frank, 1998; Krakauer, 2005). I have suggested that kin selection and kin communication played a critical but typically overlooked role in language evolution, driving our unusual propensity to cooperatively share information (Fitch, 2004a).

An important caveat in using terms like "sexual selection" or "kin selection" is that these processes should not be seen as different in kind from natural selection. Darwin coined the term "natural selection" in opposition to the artificial selection practiced by animal breeders, and, in this context, kin and sexual selection are both examples of natural selection. For a population geneticist, evolution is simply changes in gene frequency in populations, and the non-random causal forces that influence this process are all just subtypes of natural selection (Frank, 1998). Nonetheless, because the evolutionary dynamics of these subtypes can be quite different and involve subtly different logic, it can be of considerable heuristic value to distinguish between them. I will follow the terminological convention that natural selection embraces all forms of individual or gene-level selection, and use the phrase "natural selection *sensu strictu*" to distinguish, as Darwin did, between selection for survival and selection due to competition for mates (sexual selection). This neat distinction is less applicable to kin selection, where in many cases the borderline is only vaguely drawn (Grafen, 1982), but I will use the term "kin selection" whenever inclusive fitness plays an ineliminable role over and above individual survival and reproductive success.

2.3.3 "Group selection" – a highly ambiguous term

No term in evolutionary theory seems as slippery as this one (for a concise and authoritative overview see Grafen, 1984). In principle, Darwinian logic applies wherever there is a struggle for existence among variable units that can replicate themselves. As Darwin recognized, this logic applies in principle to biological levels above and below the individual (Sober and Wilson, 1998; Burt and Trivers, 2006), and even to entities such as word variants in a language, or alternative ideas within culture (sometimes termed "memes"; Dawkins, 1976; Boyd and Richerson, 1985). Interest in selection at different levels has been increasing in recent years (Gould, 2002). However, since Williams's seminal work (Williams, 1966a) on adaptation, a recurrent mantra in evolutionary biology has been the rejection of "group selection" as a major force in evolution and, unlike sexual or kin selection, the status of biological group selection remains controversial (unlike *cultural* group selection (Boyd and Richerson, 1985), which is broadly accepted).

A naïve form of group selectionist thinking is captured by the oft-heard phrase "for the good of the species." This phrase is a *non sequitur* when applied to evolved behavior because modern evolutionary thinking relies on competition (among alleles, and between individuals) *within* a species and indeed within a population. If a male deer fights off a predator, it is not for "the good of the species" but for his own good, and perhaps that of his kin (still "his own good" in the genetic sense) but will certainly not be for that of "the species." This naïve form of sloppy evolutionary thinking, "group selection" in the original sense, is universally rejected as "mad, bad and dangerous to know" (Grafen, 1984).

A more subtle and sophisticated form of group selection is proposed to occur within small interbreeding social groups ("demes"). Because such groups may replicate (giving rise to other groups with a similar genetic make-up), and there may be competition between groups for resources, Darwinian logic applies in principle, and there could be selection at this group level. This logical possibility is universally accepted, and arguments concern not its possibility in principle, but its importance in practice. In a seminal article, John Maynard Smith introduced a "haystack" model to allow the relative roles of group selection and individual (kin and natural) selection to be evaluated (Maynard Smith, 1964). The basic idea was that small groups of individuals colonize individual haystacks (picture rodents in a vast barn), and successful groups can colonize new haystacks. Given some simplifying assumptions, we can then calculate the role of competition between *individuals* within a haystack, and the role of competition between *groups* in different haystacks. Maynard Smith found that the conditions under which group selection could overpower individual selection in this model were extremely restrictive, and unlikely to apply in real biological situations. This form of group selection was shown to be (and is still believed today to be) a weaker evolutionary force than individual or kin selection (Frank, 1998). Actual examples showing that group selection can override individual selection and kin selection have yet to be found.

A third variant of the term, introduced in Hamilton (1975), is a straight-forward extension of the concept of inclusive fitness into species that live in groups. This concept, which Grafen treats approvingly as "new" group selection, is particularly important for social species like great apes and humans. It is simply a specific form of kin selection where inclusive fitness, and Hamilton's rule, are intensified by the fact that organisms live in groups. If migration between groups is relatively low, relatedness will build up over time, to a theoretical maximum of $1/(2m+1)$, where m is the number of migrants per generation (Grafen, 1984), a measure which surprisingly is independent of total group size (Hamilton, 1975). Such situations give an extra edge to normal inclusive fitness because distant relatives "make up in multiplicity what they lack in close degree" (p. 399, Hamilton, 1975). Furthermore, such groups increase the importance of inclusive fitness in two ways. First, the mild inbreeding within the group raises the net relatedness of direct relatives. Second, non-zero group relatedness *decreases* the pressure for nepotism, by decreasing the contrast between neighbors and close kin (Hamilton, 1975). Hamilton argued that this combination of factors made inclusive fitness a particularly relevant concept in understanding the evolution of human sociality. The significance of this insight remains insufficiently appreciated, but we will return to it in Chapter 12.

Finally, in a recent book with a particular focus on human cognitive evolution, Sober and Wilson (1998) have resurrected what they call "group selection" in rather different, and I think confusing, terms. Sober and Wilson correctly point out that there is no reason why group-selective pressures should necessarily oppose individual selection: if both forces push in the same direction, group selection can help (at least a bit). This is perfectly correct, but Maynard Smith's arguments about their relative strength carry through. More radically, Sober and Wilson recast group selection as *any* form of selection between groups, *including kin groups*, and then proceed to use many of the classic cases of kin selection to support their arguments for "group" selection. Although mathematically equivalent to Hamilton's formulation, this terminological move seems more likely to confuse discussion than lead to any new insights (Grafen, 1984). As Maynard Smith said in a review of the book: "Read critically, it will stimulate thought about important questions. Swallowed whole, its effects would be disastrous" (Maynard Smith, 1998). Competition among groups of humans certainly occurs, and may have aided "standard" evolutionary processes of natural, sexual, and kin selection, formulated in terms of inclusive fitness. But there are no compelling grounds at present to think that group selection, when *distinguished* from kin selection, must be invoked in human evolution or in the evolution of language. These ideas remain an area of very active debate at present, but the use of the term "group selection" in this debate contributes to, rather than clears up, confusion.

2.4 The comparative method: the biologist's time machine

A central tool in the evolutionary biologist's intellectual arsenal is the **comparative method**: the use of studies on multiple related species to analyze the evolutionary history and adaptive function of a trait. The comparative method is the best substitute biologists have for a time machine (with fossils providing the only real competition). Darwin put this method to expert use to analyze a wide variety of questions, utilizing a host of different species in his comparisons. Although the mathematical and statistical techniques used by modern biologists engaged in comparative research have advanced considerably (the "bible" is Harvey and Pagel, 1991), the basic logic has changed very little.

Natural selection leads organisms to be well adapted to their way of life. Each individual species can therefore be seen as a natural evolutionary experiment, each solving the problems posed by their particular lifestyle. The process of speciation has led to the many millions of species that exist today (and many more that are now extinct), via a branching process that defines a natural "family tree" for species, termed a **phylogenetic tree**. Natural groups on this tree are termed **clades**. This term applies both to the end-most twigs representing species, but also to larger groupings of species. For example, dogs and cats are both members of the carnivore clade, and humans and chimpanzees are both in the primate clade. All four species belong to a larger grouping: we are all in the mammal clade. Clades at different levels have traditionally, since Linnaeus, been given specific names (from most inclusive to most specific: kingdom, phylum, class, order, family, genus, species), but today these traditional terms are recognized to have no objective meaning. In contrast, the more general notion of a clade remains a central notion in modern biology. Clades are natural units, and can be discovered using objective techniques from traditional morphology or, increasingly, molecular biology.

Together, existing clades offer a statistical sample of the evolutionary possibilities inherent in life. Because ways of life are so exceedingly varied, we see a great diversity of solutions, and this means that comparing different species can give us important clues into evolutionary problems, their solutions, and the mechanisms involved. By availing ourselves of such natural evolutionary experiments, that have been unrolling over millennia, we can gain insights into otherwise intractable questions.

There are two central aspects to the comparative method. The first focuses on **homologous** traits: traits that are related by descent from shared, ancestral traits. Fur is a homologous trait in mammals, and color vision is a homologous trait in chimpanzees and humans. Function is not a criterion for homology: a seal's flipper and a human hand are homologous despite their radically different uses (De Beer, 1971; Hall, 1994). By examining multiple homologous traits in a certain clade, we can reconstruct the common ancestor of that clade: although the last common ancestor of humans and chimpanzees is extinct, we can safely infer that it had fur (as a mammal) and color vision. No fossils (or time machines) are necessary. I shall use this logic to "rebuild" this last common ancestor, in detail, later in the book. The extinct last common ancestor of humans and chimpanzees plays such an important role in the book that I will henceforth abbreviate it as the **LCA**.

The second class of traits used in the comparative method are often termed **analogous** traits: a term which denotes characteristics that evolved *independently* in two separate lineages. For instance, color vision in humans and butterflies is an analogous trait. Wings in butterflies, birds, and bats are also all analogous, because each of these clades evolved flight independently. Such independent evolution of "the same" mechanism is termed **convergent evolution**, and "similarity" here refers to the *function* of the mechanism under discussion. From a statistical viewpoint, each of these separate flying clades is an independent data point, representing an independent evolutionary event. Thus we can use convergent evolution to test evolutionary hypotheses about function: a trait like color vision, which has evolved many times in animals, can be subjected to numerous insightful investigations that teach us about the function of vision (Carroll, 2006). Crucially, this is not the case for homologous traits. If an entire clade shares some trait due to its evolution in some common ancestor, this constitutes a single evolutionary event, and thus a single data point for evolutionary analysis, even if millions of descendent species share the trait (Harvey and Pagel, 1991). For these reasons, both homology and convergence are crucial aspects of the comparative method, and we will frequently discuss both in this book.

2.5 Controversies and resolutions in contemporary evolutionary theory

Having completed our whirlwind tour of areas of general consensus in evolutionary theory we shall now turn to areas of controversy – of which evolution has had more than its fair share. Many of these are also debated in the language evolution literature (cf. Pinker and Bloom, 1990). I focus first on the theme of gradualism and discontinuity: perhaps the oldest argument in evolutionary theory. **Gradualism** is the idea that evolution moves in small steps, not leaps. Darwin was a strict and unyielding gradualist, believing that the many discontinuities that we observe among living organisms result exclusively from selection acting on continuous variation in a population.

Although he was well aware of the existence of macromutations, or "sports" as he termed them, and also of the obvious fact that some variability is by its nature discrete (e.g. the numbers of fingers or bristles or flower petals), he was fully convinced that only small variations could underlie the process of adaptation by natural selection. The core argument against an *adaptive* role for major qualitative changes is that the macromutations we observe in nature disrupt adaptive function rather than enhancing it. Organisms are fine-tuned systems, and individuals born with large random changes have a very small chance of ending up fitter to survive. However, many of Darwin's colleagues disagreed with Darwin on this point. The role of macromutations, major phenotypic differences or "saltations," and discontinuities in evolution has been an issue debated ever since. There are at least three variants of gradualist debate, only one of which seems relevant to language evolution.

2.5.1 Mutation, saltation, and the modern synthesis

Despite its inexorable logic, the idea of natural selection faced heavy opposition in the early twentieth century. The reasons are of more than historical interest, because the central issue is one that still plays an important role today in debate about language evolution: continuity *versus* saltation. These early debates offer examples of the value of Langer's dictum in overcoming interdisciplinary strife (cf. Bowler, 2003). The resolution of the debate, discussed in any introduction to evolution (Futuyma, 1979; Dawkins, 1986), remains surprisingly relevant to ongoing debates about saltation in language evolution. The neo-Darwinian resolution of the modern synthesis occurred with the marriage of genetics and evolutionary theory starting in the 1920s.

The crucial mechanistic ingredient missing from Darwin's theory of natural selection was an understanding of inheritance. Mendel's experiments with peas, demonstrating the particulate nature of inheritance, went unnoticed until after Darwin's death, and Darwin's own theory involved blending the inheritance of acquired characteristics, a "Lamarckian" model now known to be essentially incorrect. The core difficulty is that natural selection "uses up" variation, apparently eliminating the precondition for its further operation. Darwin's model entailed that offspring should be phenotypically intermediate between their parents. But this means that as organisms attained a similar "good fit" to their local environment, variation would disappear and natural selection should quickly grind to a halt. Darwin's model thus seemed incapable of accounting for the origin of entirely new species, qualitatively different from their predecessors. This intuitive argument was advanced by Fleeming Jenkins, an important early critic of Darwin, and recognized as an important problem by both Darwin and the architects of the neo-Darwinian synthesis. For decades this problem kept many biologists (especially geneticists) from accepting Darwin's theory, and a battle raged between "**gradualists**" (who followed Darwin in accepting gradual, continuous variation) and "**saltationists**" (early Mendelians who saw the appearance of "sports" quite different from their parents as disproof of Darwin's theory).

By the early twentieth century, increasing evidence for particulate inheritance and for qualitative mutations, discontinuous between individuals, suggested that blending inheritance was an illusion. The descendents of crosses between white-eyed and red-eyed flies had either white or red eyes, not various shades of pink. Such findings set the stage for the modern reconciliation and synthesis of genetics and evolution.

The critical insight was one that many people still find non-intuitive: that evolution occurs in populations, rather than individuals. In his incisive exploration of these issues, Ernst Mayr refers to these two opposing viewpoints as "population thinking" *versus* "typological" or "essentialist" thinking (Mayr, 1982). The seeds for population thinking were planted by the great geneticist and mathematician R. A. Fisher, who recognized that even if two alleles (call them *a* and *A*) have discontinuous effects (e.g. red *versus* white eyes), the *distribution* of an allele in the population is an effectively continuous variable, ranging from 0.0 to 1.0, and calculated as simply $a/(a+A)$. In humans, for example, each individual has two copies of each gene. In modern terminology, "recessive" genes are those where an individual requires both copies (*aa*) in their genotype for the phenotype to be expressed. For example, the recessive trait "blue eyes" can remain unexpressed in either brown-eyed parent (both *Aa*) but can, if two *a*s combine in a child, lead to the "reappearance" of blue eyes. As the *a* allele becomes rare, it becomes ever less likely to be expressed phenotypically – and therefore less likely to be fully eliminated by natural selection. Fisher recognized that recessive genes could act as "reservoirs" for variation, and solved Fleeming Jenkin's "blending" problem. In the end, geneticists had their cake and ate it too: alleles could have discontinuous effects, as the saltationists claimed, but variation in populations could remain continuous, and Darwin's insights could apply. Fisher considered this his greatest intellectual achievement (Plutynski, 2006).

It is difficult to over-emphasize the importance of population-level thinking in the neo-Darwinian synthesis. For naturalists, ecologists, and population biologists this perspective seemed to come quite naturally, but geneticists, systematists, and developmental biologists before the modern synthesis often saw species as "ideal types" – Platonic perfect forms – and the variation seen in real life as simply error or noise. For such typological thinkers, the essence of speciation was the birth of a new individual, possessing a "macromutation." In contrast, the architects of the modern synthesis recognized that the generation of a mutant was only one precondition for the origin of a new species. That variant then had to spread through the population, until the population was different enough from some sister population that they could not, or would not, interbreed, and only then could a new species be said to have been born. Thus **population-level change in allele frequencies** was the key factor underlying speciation (Mayr, 1982; Gould, 2002).

To summarize in contemporary terms, gradual speciation and discrete mutation are not in conflict, but offer explanations at different levels of analysis. Mutations are always discrete: the digital nature of DNA guarantees that. A single base of DNA is one of just four possible bases, and a codon specifies one of only twenty amino acids. At the genetic level, evolutionary change is discrete and digital. However, population change will always be gradual: the birth of a novel mutant is not the birth of a new species, but simply one more entry in the "struggle for existence" who will have to make her way, survive, and reproduce like everyone else. From that point on, the fate of the novel allele will be determined by population-level dynamics. The new allele will be mixed into other genetic backgrounds by recombination, and in many cases novelties may disappear without a trace. If that mutant possesses some advantageous trait, her *descendents* may someday make up a new species, but that process of change requires a gradual change in the make-up of a population.

Box 2.1. Basic molecular genetics

DNA is the basis of Inheritance
DNA (deoxyribonucleic acid) is a double-stranded molecule. Normally, the two strands line up like train tracks. Each individual strand of the DNA is made up of sequences consisting of one of four **bases** (the nucleic acids adenosine, thyrosine, cytosine, and guanine – A, T, C, and G, respectively), which bind together in complementary **base pairs**: A with T and C with G. This complementarity means that the two strands of the DNA are informationally redundant with one another. If one strand has the sequence ACTG, the other strand will consist of TGAC. This redundancy is the basis of *replication*: you can divide a DNA strand

into its two strands, and each strand is capable of building up a new double-stranded molecule identical to the original. This duplication process (split and rebuild) is the basis for biological reproduction and inheritance, and occurs every time a cell divides. Every cell in the body shares the same DNA.

The genetic code

By itself, DNA can't do very much: it is a repository of information, but cells get work done by converting chunks of the DNA code into a single strand of RNA (**transcription**), via an isomorphic process of duplication (base to complementary base). Although RNA sometimes plays enzymatic roles in the cell, generally this RNA is processed and subsequently converted into protein by a non-isomorphic process called **translation**. In translation, a sequence of three adjacent bases called a **codon** is converted into a single amino acid (of which there are twenty). This is accomplished using the **genetic code**. Because there are 4^3 (64) possibilities for coding, but only twenty amino acids, the genetic code is redundant: there are several different ways to code a single amino acid. (Note that it would be impossible to build an adequate genetic code out of two-base codons, because 4^2 (16) possibilities could not code for all twenty amino acids.) This redundancy turns out to be very useful for molecular evolutionary biologists, because it means that a single **point mutation** in the DNA sequence, substituting one base pair for another, can either code for the same amino acid (a **synonymous** substitution) or change the amino acid. Since changes in amino acid sequence are typically the target of natural selection, we can use the ratio between these types of mutation to make an estimate of selection pressure on a particular chunk of DNA. If synonymous substitutions are common, but the amino acid sequence constant, this is evidence for strong purifying selection on that region of the DNA.

2.5.2 Resolution: evolutionarily stable strategies

A crucial evolutionary question therefore concerns the conditions under which such mutants can "beat the odds" and spread. Central to the modern synthesis was the application of mathematical tools to address this question involving notions of **optimization**: solving a set of equations for some stable "equilibrium" solution. In the 1970s, important extensions were made to population-level optimization thinking. These advances, led by evolutionary theorist John Maynard Smith, culminated with the application of game theory to behavioral evolution (Maynard Smith and Price, 1973; Maynard Smith, 1978, 1979). Game theory was originally developed to understand strategies and conflict among rational humans (Nash, 1996). Evolutionary game theory builds upon this theory, dropping the requirement for rational agents, and proceeds by first specifying different behavioral strategies in an idealized "game" involving others. The central goal is to determine whether one strategy constitutes an **evolutionarily stable strategy**, or **ESS**, able to outcompete one or more "mutant" strategies. Crucially, this approach requires the biologist to specify the phenotypic possibilities beforehand, and thus requires an understanding of the constraints on possible phenotypes. Even if a mutant is "better" in some ultimate sense, if it is unable to penetrate the population, no species-level change can occur. The body of theory that emerged from this work allows us to formulate, in mathematical terms, a crucial desideratum for any theory of evolutionary change:

Invasibility: To successfully penetrate a population, a mutant strategy must not only be "better" in some ideal or absolute sense, but must be demonstrably advantageous (receiving a positive differential payoff, on average) relative to the already established strategy or strategies. Invasibility (or uninvasibility) of an ESS can be evaluated using a game-theoretic closed-form solution in simple cases, or via computer simulations for more complex situations.

The notion of "optimization" used in this approach makes no "pan-adaptationist" assumption that natural selection always finds the theoretical optimum, nor that animals "know" what strategy they adopt, or why. After some debate, already resolved in the 1980s (cf. Maynard Smith, 1982; Parker and Maynard Smith, 1990), ESS/game-theoretic analyses have become standard tools in evolutionary research, whose utility is broadly accepted throughout biology (e.g. Maynard Smith and Szathmáry, 1995). However, invasibility analyses have been surprisingly rare in discussions of language evolution (exceptions include Nowak *et al.*, 2002; Zuidema, 2005).

2.5.3 Punctuated equilibrium and sudden evolutionary change

The influential evolutionary biologist Stephen Jay Gould was at the center of many recent controversies in evolutionary theory. For a brief, insightful, and balanced overview of Gould's many contributions see Sterelny (2001). The earliest debate sparked by Gould and his colleague Niles Eldredge concerned the rate of evolutionary change. Their starting point was a claim, supposedly embraced by the neo-Darwinian orthodoxy, that evolution proceeds at a fixed unchanging rate, a belief they dubbed "phyletic grad-ualism." In contrast, they argued that the paleontological data supported the view that evolution sometimes proceeds rapidly, and sometimes grinds nearly to a halt, a view they termed "punctuated equilibrium." The problem with this "debate" is that neither Darwin, nor the architects of the contem-porary neo-Darwinism, were "phyletic gradualists," and there is nothing in Darwin's theory that is incompatible with substantial variability in rates of evolutionary change. For example, two critical evolutionary variables are population size and the degree of mixing between populations. Ernst Mayr and other architects of the neo-Darwinian synthesis suggested that large well-mixed populations tend to slow evolution, in the sense that rare mutants are less likely to reach any appreciable frequency. In small, iso-lated populations (e.g. on islands) this problem is alleviated, and the effects of random genetic drift and *founder effects* (population differences due to chance variation in a small colonizing population) are also increased. Mayr suggested that rapid change and speciation events are only likely to occur in such isolated populations. This issue is relevant in human evolution because early hominid populations were probably quite small, and may have been relatively fragmented (Calvin, 2003). Furthermore, the explosive population growth characterizing our species since *Homo sapiens* left Africa provided the basis for founder effects in several human populations (e.g. in Australia, the Pacific, or the Americas), and similar effects might have also typified the early emergence of *Homo erectus* from Africa. Such ideas, con-sistent with punctuated equilibrium, are standard in modern approaches to evolution.

Unfortunately, "punctuated equilibrium" has often been misinterpreted as suggesting *instantaneous* evolutionary change: the idea of a lone mutant or "hopeful monster" whose birth ushers in a new species, presumably with the aid of some conveniently willing bride or groom, and some heav-ily inbreeding descendents. The heroic (indeed Biblical) connotations of this notion apparently catch the imagination of many, and hopeful mon-sters remain a persistent *leitmotif* in popular discussions of human evo-lution. But Gould himself, in discussions of this hopeful monster theory, was quite clear that this is a misunderstanding of punctuated equilibrium, which is "a theory about ordinary speciation (taking tens of thousands of years) and its abrupt appearance at low scales of geological resolution, not about . . . sudden genetic change" (p. 234, Gould, 1987). This is the first sense in which Darwin's gradualism is not in conflict with the paleontological record, nor with modern theory. Although different biologists have different estimates about the relative frequency of rapid change *versus* long stasis, clear examples exist of both (cf. Ridley, 1997; Pagel *et al.*, 2006), and virtually no one has ever defended a pure "phyletic gradualist" position. Variable rates of evolution pose no challenge to standard evolutionary theory, and punctuated equilibrium does not entail hopeful monsters. However, there is one further challenge to Darwin's gradualism to consider.

2.5.4 Macromutations and gradualism

Recognizing the importance of gradual changes in populations does *not* entail rejecting the importance of macromutation as an evolutionary force: the "size" of the phenotypic change caused by a mutation is a separate, independent dimension. This brings us to our final variant of the idea of discontinuity in evolution, the only one that remains an issue of substantive debate. The evolutionary model of pre-synthesis geneticists such as Goldschmidt required novel macromutations different in kind from gradual, continuous variables (such as body weight or length). Saltationists argued that such discontinuous, large mutants are the stuff of evolutionary change. While one component of their argument was the erroneous result of typological thinking, the factual basis for their argument did not thereby disappear: the existence of mutants with drastic phenotypic differences, particularly transformative macromutations, remained and remains unquestionable (Bateson, 1894). Furthermore, attention to such drastic "homeotic" mutations has led to some of the most important and exciting discoveries in modern biology.

Classic examples of homeotic mutants include such monstrosities as flies with an extra pair of wings, or with legs in place of antennae (see Figure 2.1). We now understand homeotic mutations as revealing the action of regulatory genes called **transcription factors**, genes which produce proteins that bind to DNA, and therefore effect the expression of other genes. In the particular case of homeotic mutants, the genes are the **homeobox genes** ("Hox genes"). Hox genes produce proteins which are expressed in a linear temporal and spatial sequence during development, from the front of an embryo to the back. Near the top of the regulatory gene hierarchy, Hox genes influence a huge variety of other genes: Hox gene expression serves as a kind of code telling a cell it is in a certain region of the body. This leads to a set of cascading genetic decisions which control subsequent cell fate and differentiation. Thus, if the Hox gene "code" tells a particular group of cells it is in the head region, they develop into antennae, while the same type of cell group in the thorax region will develop into legs. Homeotic mutations disrupt this code. If cells actually located in the head region receive a Hox

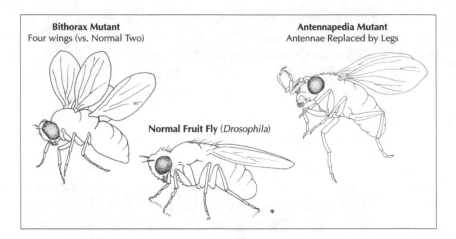

Figure 2.1 Homeotic mutants in the fruit fly *Drosophila melanogaster* – Small mutations in important genes, especially transcription factors like Hox genes, may have large phenotypic effects. In the examples illustrated, the "bithorax" mutant has converted the balancing organs of a normal fly into an extra set of wings, while the antennapedia mutant has converted the normally small antennae into an extra set of legs.

code that says they are in the thorax, the adult fly grows legs sticking out of its head (Figure 2.1).

Hox genes function similarly in widely different organisms (including humans, fish, and flies): like most other regulatory genes they are extremely conservative. They have remained virtually identical over huge spans of evolutionary time (McGinnis *et al.*, 1990; Coutinho *et al.*, 2003). However, small changes in regulatory genes certainly occur (*FOXP2* is an excellent example relevant to speech; see Chapter 10) and changes in regulatory gene expression appear to play a major role in the evolution of animal form (Carroll, 2000, 2003; Carroll *et al.*, 2005; Kirschner and Gerhart, 2005). One form of change in regulatory genes that has played an important role in the evolution of our own phylum, the vertebrates, is regulatory **gene duplication**. For example, Hox genes exist in a single series in insects and most other invertebrates. But in vertebrates, the entire set of Hox genes appears to have been duplicated twice, so that in many cases we (a fish, mouse, or human) have four Hox genes where a fly would have only one (Carroll *et al.*, 2005). Such gene duplications are increasingly seen as playing a crucial role in the evolution of development, for a simple and logical reason (Ohno, 1970). Most genes, particularly regulatory genes, will have multiple important roles in the body (termed **pleiotropy**), and a change that may be beneficial for one of these functions may well be deleterious to another. The greater the degree of pleiotropy, the more constrained the gene will be, because a change that is beneficial (or at least neutral) for all functions becomes increasingly unlikely. Gene duplication provides a way out of this bind: if two copies of the same gene exist, one copy can remain in the original state, doing the old jobs, while the other copy is free to vary or specialize.

This increasingly appears to be a core trick that evolution uses to generate new variation, and it strengthens biologist François Jacob's famous analogy of evolution as a tinkerer, making do with whatever variability becomes available, without planning or foresight (Jacob, 1977). Jacob presciently predicted that changes in regulatory genes would play a critical role in evolution, an idea receiving ever-increasing support as the genetic basis of development becomes better understood. Thus, the early geneticists' fascination with homeotic mutants has borne useful fruit. But what of the role of such macromutations in evolution? At first blush, current data suggests that virtually all such mutations are deleterious, and would be rapidly removed from real populations. When we search for living organisms that resemble homeotic mutants, we find little evidence that such mutants have gone on to form successful new species. There are no insect groups with legs on their heads instead of antennae, although one might construct adaptive scenarios in which a fly with legs in place of antennae might be favored. The key role for antennae as sense organs is probably one reason such macromutants have never been successful. However, particularly after gene duplication, rather drastic phenotypic changes might potentially be beneficial, and regulatory genes provide an unquestionable path by which minor genotypic changes can have a major phenotypic effect. Thus there is no *a priori* reason to reject a refined saltationist hypothesis of a relatively large phenotypic mutant playing a role in human evolution (the only variant of the non-gradualistic world view left standing). Importantly, however, there are no compelling examples of such changes at present.

2.5.5 Resolution: evo-devo and deep homology: genetic conservation down the ages

Resolution of the debates between early evolutionary biologists and geneticists played a central role in the neo-Darwinian modern synthesis in the 1940s. An equally long-running argument has characterized developmental and evolutionary biology until much more recently. Although the modern synthesis provided a link between genotypic changes in populations and evolutionary changes in species, it left unresolved the crucial link between phenotype and genotype. Recently, our understanding of the mechanisms of development has become sophisticated enough for a fertile new marriage between evolutionary theory and developmental biology, yielding a new discipline of evolutionary developmental biology – known as **evo-devo** to its friends (Gilbert *et al.*, 1996; Holland, 1999; Arthur, 2002; Wilkins, 2002; Carroll *et al.*, 2005). Development is relevant to the evolution of any biological trait, but becomes especially crucial in discussions of the nervous system, because the development of the brain and behavior is so richly intertwined with experience.

A central finding of evo-devo would have thoroughly surprised the architects of the modern synthesis: genes, and regulatory genes in particular, have been deeply conserved over evolutionary time. The Hox genes just discussed turn out to be shared, in terms of both gene sequence and patterns of expression, by insects and mammals who have trodden separate evolutionary paths for half a billion years. Conservatism now appears to be the rule, not an exception (Gerhart and Kirschner, 1997), and has important consequences. For reasons of convenience, biologists have long worked with "model organisms" like yeast, fruit flies, or mice, in the hope that principles of genetics, physiology, or behavior derived from them may retain some relevance for humans and other species. We now know, at the level of genes and development at least, that this hope is thoroughly justified: the principles of cell biology and genetic regulation are so conserved that identical mechanisms regulate wing growth in flies and hand growth in mice and humans.

Even more fundamentally, conservation of genetic mechanisms has important implications for the analysis of convergent evolution. For we now know that even if two traits or structures evolved convergently, the mechanisms underlying their development may nonetheless be homologous, a situation that has been termed "**deep homology**" (Shubin *et al.*, 1997). For example, the complex camera eye of vertebrates like ourselves and mollusks like squid or octopus evolved convergently: the common ancestor of these groups had little more than a tiny eyespot. Nonetheless, the genetic mechanisms underlying this development rely on the deployment of nearly identical genes such as Pax-6 (Gehring and Ikeo, 1999; van Heyningen and Williamson, 2002). The discovery of deep homology of this sort raises the previously inconceivable notion that the study of convergent evolution might reveal not just generalities about evolution, but actually unveil the specific mechanisms involved in both versions of the trait. For example, the Fox gene family, like Hox and Pax genes, includes highly conserved transcription factors present in all vertebrates. One Fox gene, *FOXP2*, has been shown to play a role in human speech production, specifically in the control of the tongue and lips: patients with a mutation in this gene suffer from extreme oro-motor dyspraxia and severe difficulties acquiring speech (Vargha-Khadem *et al.*, 1995). *FOXP2* is thus one of the first genes known both to play a role in human language and to differentiate humans from chimpanzees and other primates. Almost unbelievably, the same gene not only exists in birds, but plays a role in their vocal learning (Haesler *et al.*, 2004; Haesler *et al.*, 2007). Although vocal imitation has convergently evolved in humans and birds, the same gene is playing a closely analogous role, in the same brain regions. Although we shall hear more about this gene later, for now the point is clear: the possibility of deep homology adds an entirely new justification for comparative work that spans a wide variety of species, and a new rationale for investigating convergently evolved traits.

2.5.6 Selection and constraints: limits on adaptation and natural selection

Now we turn to debates concerning the roles of constraint and adaptation in evolution. In language evolution, a number of skeptical comments made by Chomsky over the years about *natural selection* have, I think, been misinterpreted as disdain for *evolution* (e.g. Pinker and Bloom, 1990; Newmeyer, 1998b). For example, acknowledging that "we know very little about what happens when 10^{10} neurons are crammed into something the size of a basketball, with further conditions imposed by the specific manner in which this system developed over time," Chomsky argues that "it would be a serious error to suppose that all properties, or the interesting properties of the structures that have evolved, can be 'explained' in terms of natural selection" (p. 59, Chomsky, 1975a). Properly understood, such comments take a natural and uncontroversial place in a larger debate about the role of constraints in evolution (Maynard Smith *et al.*, 1985; Endler, 1986; Gould, 2002).

Again, Gould has been an active participant in this debate, and the issue has been central to a number of recent debates concerning language (e.g. Hauser *et al.*, 2002; Fitch *et al.*, 2005; Pinker and Jackendoff, 2005). Much of this controversy can be resolved by recognizing that while natural selection is the only viable source of *adaptation*, it is only one of many forces involved in *evolution*. In the evolution of any complex structure, numerous other explanatory factors, such as historical and developmental constraints, or contingency, also play important roles (chapter 13, Ridley, 1997; Maynard Smith *et al.*, 1985). A conflation of evolution with adaptation can be a source of great potential misunderstanding. As soon as we recognize that not all aspects of an organism, and not all aspects of language, are adaptations (following Williams, 1966b), the question arises of what explanations are available for *non*-adaptive traits. As we shall see below, there are many different possibilities. Given the necessity for a multi-component approach to language, the question cannot insightfully be framed in monolithic terms of "Language," but must instead be asked of smaller subcomponents. There can be little doubt that language as a whole is beneficial to humans, but this by no means entails that every aspect of language (say, for example, phonological restrictions on syllable structure, or subjacency restrictions in syntax) is "an adaptation." This is a core argument in language evolution (cf. Pinker and Bloom, 1990), so I will now try to ground it in the broader evolutionary debates.

Organisms are not arbitrarily variable, and limits on variation act as constraints on the power and scope of natural selection. The relative roles of natural selection and constraints in explaining diversity have long been debated (Maynard Smith *et al.*, 1985; Ridley, 1997). This debate can be read in at least three ways. The first is a matter of taste: which of these components of the evolutionary process one finds most interesting. Gould has been a tireless advocate of the idea that the constraints on animal form and the historical contingencies by which they arise are fascinating aspects of biology, and I agree with him. Other biologists, including Maynard Smith or Dawkins, find equal delight in the ability of natural selection to discover optima, and marvel at the supreme fit of organisms to their environment. I find these topics equally fascinating: these two positions are complementary and there is no need to choose one over the other. There is no point arguing over such matters of preference.

A second interpretation of this issue is a mistaken dichotomy of adaptation and constraint, parallel to the "nature *versus* nurture" debate. If we pit constraints against selection, imagining that the structure of a given trait is 45 percent constraint and 55 percent selection, we overlook the crucial and complete role that both play in understanding animal form (Endler, 1986). Selection acts on the set of phenotypes that are actually present, and is clearly powerless to select beyond that set. If the only available phenotypes are red and white eyes, it makes no difference that green eyes might be optimal in some abstract sense. Evolution has no foresight, and selection must wait until a green-eye mutant appears by chance. If some constraints on pigments or eye function make this very unlikely, natural selection must simply wait. An understanding of such constraints is required to formulate the set of phenotypes available for optimization in the model, and there is no conflict between the standard optimization techniques used in evolutionary theory, as discussed above, and a wholehearted acceptance of the role of constraints in evolution: because this set of possibilities is limited by a panoply of constraints (see below), selection is completely constrained, at each step of the process, and there is no point asking how much it is constrained. Flipping the question around, each cycle of differential mortality and reproduction constitutes a cycle of selection, and the initial conditions of each subsequent cycle will be determined by selection on the previous cycle. Only in the hypothetical case where everyone survives and produces the same number of offspring is there "no selection" – a situation that will be vanishingly rare in the real world. Thus, selection plays an equally critical and ubiquitous role. Pitting selection against constraints creates an opposition between what are in fact both necessary components of the basic process of evolution.

The third version of the constraints controversy represents a real area of scientific debate in contemporary biology: the specific nature and power of limits on phenotypic variation, and thus on the power or rate of selection (cf. Kirschner and Gerhart, 2005). A bewildering variety of constraints affect living organisms. The most basic are constraints based on physics: there are certain arrangements of matter that are simply unstable or unworkable, and these apply to living things just as they do to mountains, bridges, or falling objects. A related and more interesting set of constraints follow from specific properties of biological materials. Certain systems may be physically workable in principle, but impossible for carbon-based life on an oxygen-rich planet. A subset of such principles will apply only to particular clades, or in particular habitats. For example, anaerobic bacteria, living in low-oxygen environments, are under different constraints than vertebrates, all of whom require oxygen for survival, and deep-sea sulfur-based communities represent yet another set of habitat constraints. Finally, at the molecular level, the chemical processes which determine protein structure (the process by which a simple sequence of amino acids folds into the complex three-dimensional structure which has an actual enzymatic effect) are crucially dependent upon both basic chemistry (properties of water, ionic concentrations) and the presence of other molecules that can aid or inhibit certain configurations (e.g. chaperonins, molecules that catalyze one or another configuration). Such physical and chemical limits on variation play a critical and undeniable role in evolution. However, biologists are continually amazed by the apparent "ingenuity" by which living things work around physical laws. An obvious example is flight: although birds or bats certainly obey the law of gravity, they do not fall to the ground when dropped, but fly away. Birds make use of muscle physiology and aerodynamics to evade the most obvious normal consequence of gravity. Similarly, the discovery of deep-sea organisms fueled by sulfur rather than energy from the sun has overturned many preconceptions about what life could or couldn't do (Boetius, 2005). Although living things must, of course, obey the laws of physics, biologists have learned to be cautious about blanket statements of the form "x is impossible as a way of life."

Another potential class of constraints are limits to natural selection, an area of much recent theoretical discussion. The oldest proposed limit on selection is variation itself: since selection in a sense "feeds" on variation, we might expect that it would quickly weed out all non-adaptive variants and leave itself nothing more to select from. Powerful sustained selection can lead to **fixation**, where one particular allele, outcompeting other genetic variants, becomes the only one left in the population. In such cases, genetic variability has dropped to zero. However, there is now a considerable body of empirical data indicating that the problem has been overestimated: natural populations seem to contain a surprisingly large amount of genetic variability, and artificial selection experiments typically discover considerable latent variability in quantitative traits (Lewontin and Hubby, 1966). Although a few experiments have, after intense selection, reached limits (e.g. after 20,000 generations of artificial selection in bacteria for larger size, a plateau was reached; Lenski *et al.*, 1998), in general the reservoir of variability in naturally occurring populations seems more than adequate to support ongoing natural selection. A variety of more specific, quantitative limits on the rate and power of natural selection are discussed in Barton and Partridge (2000).

Another important class of constraints on variation are solidly biological, and arguably central to detailed understanding of living things. Often termed "developmental" or "historical" constraints, they are at the center of evolutionary developmental biology, which provides multiple examples of constraints on biological form, harking back to some old proposals that sought to unify physical and biological forms of explanation (e.g. Thompson, 1948; Turing, 1952). Here I will explore only a few, but see Hall (1998) or Carroll *et al.* (2001) for more detailed tutorial overviews of this field.

Consider animal form from a mechanical viewpoint. For heavy objects, rolling on wheels provides an extremely energy-efficient solution to locomotion, yet there are no natural examples of animals that roll upon wheels. An *adaptive* story for the absence of wheels (e.g. wheels wouldn't be useful, because organisms need to negotiate uneven terrain) seems inadequate to explain the observed *total* absence of wheels (e.g. in a flat savannah or salt-pan desert wheels would work nicely). Most biologists would instead surmise that the absence of wheels results from physiological constraints (e.g. difficulties obtaining adequate circulation of nutrients through a rotary joint). But I can imagine ways around this constraint. For example, in arthropods (insects, crustaceans, and their allies), the outer surface of the body is dead skeletal tissue, and one can imagine an arthropod with rotary wheels that sheds the worn wheels and regenerates them with each new molt. Thus it seems more likely that there has been no suitable evolutionary pathway to reach a possible wheeled form. A set of intermediate variants, each of which is itself adaptive, needs to exist if an evolutionary path is to be viable. This requirement is an important constraining factor in language evolution.

A constraint closer to home concerns the difficulty in reconciling large brains, and thus large heads, with live birth. Almost all of the neurons present in an adult human brain are present at birth, apparently as a result of constraints on primate neural development: large brain size in adults seems to entail large brain size at birth. Unfortunately for us mammals, this interacts with the facts of live birth: that the young are gestated in the uterus, and must pass through the mother's pelvic opening during birth. This leads to the familiar fact that human birth is a difficult process, with unusually high perinatal mortality rates for both infant and mother compared to most mammals (similar problems afflict some other large-brained primates such as callitrichids or squirrel monkeys; Bowden *et al.*, 1967). It seems clear that these difficulties have played an important role in human evolution (Trevathan, 1987), and that pelvic size in mothers (which itself interacts with locomotion) has acted as a brake to ever-increasing brain size. Size has major developmental consequences: because of their large size, human brains must develop many of their connections, and grow substantially in size, after birth (Martin and Harvey, 1985). But this is not an absolute constraint. If humans were born from eggs, or if we were marsupials (where the young emerge from the womb at a much smaller and more immature rate, and complete development in an external pouch), this constraint would not apply. What appear to be purely mechanical constraints on form often turn out to be specific to a particular group, rather than blanket restrictions, and result from mechanical constraints interacting with developmental constraints that are specific and quirky traits of that particular clade.

To continue with brain evolution, consider the constraints on nerve conduction times. The basic functioning of nerve cells is common to all multicellular animals, from jellyfish and sea anemones to birds or humans. The rate at which an action potential propagates down the axon (neural conduction time) is pitifully slow compared to electrical signals carried by wires (Kandel and Schwartz, 1985). In general, fast conduction requires fat axons, and this is why some key model systems in neurobiology are components of fast-acting invertebrate escape systems (e.g. the giant axon of squid). This is a biophysical constraint applicable to all neurons. However, we vertebrates have evaded this by changing the rules: by wrapping the axon in myelin, a fatty insulator material, we can greatly accelerate signal conduction without a massive increase in axon diameter. This is quite an advantage in building big bodies, and big brains, but has certain drawbacks. In particular, the type of myelin generated in the central nervous system blocks further axon growth. Damaged areas within the brain cannot be "re-colonized" by new nerve growth, putting strict limits on neural regeneration. Aside from its depressing clinical implications, this means that the basic long-distance wiring plan within the brain needs to be completed before myelination can begin: substantial rewiring after myelination will be impossible. This is just one of several factors that might lead to the contrast between the great flexibility observed in the fetal or newborn nervous system relative to greatly decreased flexibility in adult brains (Liégeois *et al.*, 2004). The point is that purely physical constraints (on ionic conduction processes in tubes) interact with clade-specific evolutionary tricks (the evolution of myelin in vertebrates) to constrain the evolutionary paths available in a particular species. To understand the form and function of the human brain we will need to consider not only current selective pressures, or the hypothetical selective pressures experienced by Pleistocene hominids, but a whole suite of constraints that span a range from the basic laws of physics and chemistry, to general principles of neural function that apply to all multicellular animals, to quite specific details that characterize us as vertebrates, mammals, or primates. More generally, a complete description of any trait will include both constraints of these sorts and discussions of adaptive function. From this viewpoint, the quote from Chomsky (1975a) with which this section began is an uncontroversial statement that most biologists would readily accept (e.g. Szathmáry, 2001).

Summarizing, constraints can make it difficult or even impossible for the blind local search process of evolution to "consider" certain options, even ones that might be globally optimal. Such limits and constraints are as diverse as the biological problems that living forms face, and defy any neat system of categorization. The specific nature of particular constraints, and their relative role in the evolution of any particular species or trait, remain areas of active inquiry and debate (cf. Maynard Smith *et al.*, 1985; Endler, 1986). Developmental and historical constraints clearly exist, but their explanatory role relative to classical factors like natural selection or genetic drift remains controversial. A growing number of biologists are convinced that constraints on development, in particular, play an extremely important role in channeling the evolution of body form in metazoans, and research in the "evo-devo" context is widely seen as holding great promise to increase our understanding of such constraints on animal form and function (Kirschner and Gerhart, 2005; Carroll, 2006). After many years as being seen as opposing viewpoints about evolution, the mutually informative roles of selection and constraints are now accepted by most biologists as important aspects of biological and evolutionary explanation. The same attitude seems appropriate for language evolution. Stated more formally:

Constraints on evolvability: A successful theory of language evolution must, for each step of the proposed scenario, specify a continuous path of evolutionary changes from the LCA to modern language-ready humans. These proposed changes must be both *possible*, in the sense that they satisfy developmental constraints or other constraints on possible phenotypes, and *potentially successful* in the adaptive context in which they are hypothesized to occur.

2.5.7 Shifts in function: adaptation, preadaptation, and exaptation

A critical characteristic of Darwin's mechanistic explanation of adaptive evolution is that natural selection lacks any foresight. Random variability is generated via recombination and mutation without any relation to function, and is followed by immediate selection in the context of whatever immediate problems an organism finds itself. The fact that some mutation might be useful in the remote future has no bearing on its chances of becoming established in a population, and putting old parts to new uses is thus a frequent, and important, source of evolutionary innovation. Darwin gave many examples of change in the function of traits or organs, which he saw as strong evidence of natural selection, incompatible with any omniscient designer. For example, discussing the homology between the swim bladder in fish and the lungs of tetrapods, Darwin stressed "the highly important fact that an organ originally constructed for one purpose, namely flotation, may be converted into one for a widely different purpose, namely respiration" (Darwin, 1859). Such phenomena came to be termed **preadaptations**, and there are many clear examples in vertebrates. For example, two of the three mammalian middle ear bones derive from bones that formed part of the jaw joint in the synapsid ancestors of mammals (Hopson, 1966), and both these bones and the tetrapod vocal tract skeleton derive from the gill bars of the ancestral fish (Gaupp, 1904; Harrison, 1995). Once our ancestors became air-breathing and semi-terrestrial, gills were no longer of any use as respiratory organs and were free to be "re-used" as, among other things, the hyoid skeleton and the larynx (cf. Chapter 5). Such changes of function are ubiquitous in evolution over long evolutionary timespans.

Objecting that the term "preadaptation" connotes foresight, Gould and Vrba suggested a new term, **exaptation**, to refer to both the process of function shift and the end product of this process (Gould and Vrba, 1982). Subsequently, Gould stressed the importance of this concept for understanding human evolution, suggesting that shifts in function might play an even more important role in cognitive evolution than in morphological evolution (Gould, 1991). Unfortunately, although this term has become widespread, it is subject to various interpretations that have caused considerable confusion in the literature (e.g. Buss *et al.*, 1998). If exaptation were used to refer to *any* mechanism that served a different function at some point in the evolutionary past, then most adaptive traits would be exaptations, because most traits have experienced shifts in function at some point. We would have substituted one term, "exaptation," for another, "adaptation," with no gain in insight. This is not the way the term exaptation has come to be interpreted in the literature, where exaptation refers to the assumption of a new function (perhaps due to a behavioral innovation) and to the early stages of use of the trait in this new function. Once a variant of the trait is altered by selection for the new function, the trait becomes an adaptation again. Thus, I will reserve the term "exaptation" for the (typically brief) period during which an old trait is used in a new function, but before it has been honed by selection to suit this new task. "Adaptation" then retains its usual broad field of reference. "Preadaptation" remains useful in this regard, retrospectively, to refer to the trait that provided the raw material for the process of exaptation. Gill bars were preadaptations for both jaw bones and for mammalian ear bones, both of which were probably derived via exaptation (Chapter 5), but both of which are today adaptations because they have been selected for their new function.

A second term often mentioned in this connection is the term **spandrel**, which is an architectural term for the four tapered triangular spaces that result from mounting a dome atop four arches. In an influential and controversial paper, Gould and Lewontin (1979) generalized this term to refer to any biological structure that results, inevitably, from design constraints on some other set of structures. A student of art or architecture might suppose that the beautiful, richly symbolic paintings filling the spandrels in St. Mark's cathedral in Venice were the foreseen purpose for these spandrels, inspiring the architectural plan. This would invert the causal order of things: spandrels appeared, inevitably, due to the architectural plan, and some enterprising artist put them to expressive use. Gould and Lewontin suggested that biological innovations may often occur via an analogous process, when selection on one trait leads to the appearance of some new feature as an automatic, unselected byproduct. Such features are now commonly termed "spandrels" in the evolutionary literature (Gould, 1997), and provide an alternative to the model discussed above, whereby an organ designed for one function shifts to another, because spandrels originally had *no* function. Although the term is new, the idea that such unselected byproducts played a role in language evolution is an old one: "language was a corollary or epiphenomenon implicit in other evolutionary change" (p. 321, Orr and Cappannari, 1964). But again, once a spandrel is put to use, and subsequently modified to suit its new function (a second type of exaptation, according to Gould (1991)), the modified spandrel becomes an adaptation like any other.

In the "spandrels" paper, Gould and Lewontin suggested that pan-adaptationist biologists, fixated on the idea that every aspect of animal form is an adaptation, are forced by this belief to assert a function even for spandrels, and therefore concoct silly just-so stories to fulfill this need. Like Voltaire's Dr. Pangloss, who held that everything was precisely as it should be, and that noses were made for holding spectacles, such a claim would indeed be ridiculous. But Gould and Lewontin provided no examples of biologists making such silly errors (they had to turn to anthropologists), and few have been adduced since then. The portrait of a Panglossian adaptationist is a caricature, but the cautionary tale spun by Gould and Lewontin has been retold to generations of biology undergraduates, and there is little reason to fear pan-adaptationism among trained evolutionary biologists. However, there are strands of evolutionary psychology suggestive of a pan-adaptationist view of the human mind, and Gould and Lewontin's warning is perhaps relevant to some students of language evolution.

Spirited debate has surrounded the hypothesis that elements of language might represent *unmodified* spandrels (Pinker and Bloom, 1990). While Piattelli-Palmarini (1989) offers some compelling arguments that certain intractable elements of syntax might represent spandrels, linguist Frederick Newmeyer pronounces a "spandrel explanation for the design features of any significant aspect of the language faculty to be utterly implausible" (p. 315, Newmeyer, 1998b). From the multi-component perspective, the question "Is Language a spandrel?" is unlikely to have any simple answer: we should better ask, "Did component *x* of language (say vocal imitation, or syntactic constraints) arise as a spandrel, and if so, has it seen further fine-tuning by natural selection?" Thus reframed, Newmeyer's and Piattelli-Palmarini's conclusions may both be correct, but for different aspects of language (and perhaps differing conceptions of "significance"). It seems quite plausible that at least some details of the human language capacity reflect spandrels, given the number of different components that have been put to new use ("exapted") in this system over a relatively short time period.

No biologist would expect *every* aspect of a trait as complex as language to represent an adaptation. As stressed by Williams (1966a), adaptation is an "onerous" concept, to be demonstrated and not assumed. It would be absurd to suggest that every detail of organismic form or behavior is an adaptation, or even "adaptive" in the everyday sense of serving some useful function. Summarizing one of the central themes of Gould's long career – one to which I thoroughly subscribe – the only way to understand *evolution* is to adopt a pluralistic attitude towards the sources of evolutionary variability and the constraints on variability. At the same time, *adaptation* (meaning a close fit between innately guided complex form and complex function) is a process that at present admits of just one explanatory entity: natural selection (including sexual, kin, and in some cases perhaps group, selection as special cases). From the multi-component perspective, we start with the standard assumption that some aspects of some components of language are adaptations and others are not. From this perspective, which fully accepts the role of natural selection in language evolution, it is misleading to ask whether "language," as a whole, is an adaptation (e.g. Pinker and Bloom, 1990).

2.6 The evolution of behavior: constraints of the "four whys"

Humans are perennially fascinated by animal behavior: hunters, pastoralists, and pet owners have long sought to understand how and why animals behave. While the science of animal behavior got its start with Aristotle, the *evolution* of behavior has a shorter history (though we could date its beginnings to Darwin's monumental *The Expression of the Emotions in Man and Animals*; Darwin, 1872b), and remains a difficult topic. Because behavior, like language, doesn't fossilize, we have no clear fossil record for most behaviors (fossil footprints being an interesting exception). More importantly, there is an extra level of indirection between the genetic bases of behavior and the behavior itself: genes build brains, and brains then underwrite behaviors. Neither of these causal links is well understood. Finally, brains are very special organs: in most animals a core component of

brain design is its flexible adjustment to the local immediate environment –
its capacity to adapt and to learn. In vertebrates, the degree of epigenetic
adjustment of neural form is pronounced. All of these factors conspire
to make it much more challenging to attain a deep understanding of the
evolution of behavior than of morphology, and a detailed understanding
of the development and evolution of brain and behavior remains a distant
goal.

While evolution is central to virtually all branches of biology, its relevance to human psychology might be questioned, because in some ways
the flexibility of human behavior seems to free us from the confines of
our genetic heritage. While it would be silly to discuss the evolution of
video-game playing, there remains a central respect in which evolution
must be relevant even to learned behaviors with no evolutionary history,
such as flying jet planes or programming computers. Humans (and most
other vertebrates) possess learning mechanisms that enable us to master
novel tasks that never occurred in our evolutionary history. But these learning mechanisms themselves evolved. Furthermore, there can be no single
"perfect" learning mechanism, capable of mastering every task with equal
ease. We thus expect even the most "general" mechanisms to be shaped by
our evolutionary history, and to bear at least subtle marks of the selective
past, even if these are limited to what *cannot* be easily learned. Dobzhansky's
claim that "nothing in biology makes sense except in the light of evolution"
(Dobzhansky, 1973) is in this respect as valid for learned behavior as for
form or physiology.

Behaviorist psychology, which dominated American academia for at least
fifty years in the early twentieth century, was built upon a notion of "general learning rules" that would be the same for rats, pigeons, monkeys, and
humans. By assumption, such rules could thus be studied in any convenient
species because they were identical across all vertebrates. The first cracks
undermining this belief came from within the field, when psychologists
began studying avoidance learning. One of the more useful things a brain
can do is implement the simple rule, "if x had unpleasant consequences,
avoid x in the future," irrespective of what x, or the consequences, might be.
However, researchers on avoidance learning found that, in fact, the nature
of x often plays a crucial role in determining what rats can learn. A rat
can easily pair the taste of a food with an episode of vomiting hours later,
learning after a single trial to avoid that taste in the future. (Anyone who
has developed a taste aversion after suffering stomach flu will recognize this
mechanism at work – I still loathe mangoes because of such an episode.)

In sharp contrast, rats fail, even with hundreds of trials, to pair an auditory or visual stimulus with vomiting, or conversely to associate a taste with an electric shock (Garcia and Koelling, 1966). Thus behaviorists found that even "general" learning mechanisms are constrained, and these constraints make evolutionary sense. Such findings played a crucial role in the downfall of the simple hypothesis of unconstrained "general purpose" learning rules. Of course, the question of *how* general, or specific, a particular neural system is in its requirements must be determined on a case-by-case basis, empirically. But, once the questions are brought into focus, it hardly seems controversial that the "instinct to learn" language will be innately constrained in one way or another.

2.6.1 Explaining behavior: Tinbergen's "four whys"

The study of animal behavior had its birth as a separate field in the twentieth century. Or rather, as *two* separate fields, for in the 1950s animal behavior was essentially divided. In continental Europe, students of field biology, who used observation and experiments on animals in their natural environment, had developed a discipline they called "ethology." **Ethologists** studied a wide variety of species, and were steeped in the natural history of their study species. Concepts such as "instinct" and "innate releasing patterns" played a central theoretical role in this field. Across the Atlantic in the United States, **comparative psychologists** mostly worked in the laboratory with a few "model" species (especially rats, pigeons, rhesus macaques, and humans). Most of these scientists had a background in psychology, sought general "laws" of learning, and often were focused on questions of hormonal and neural physiology. For a number of reasons including geography, language, personal style, and philosophical viewpoints, these two disciplines did not see eye to eye, and by 1963 were engaged in public debates of increasing intensity. Fortunately, a resolution of these "behavior wars" was spearheaded by Niko Tinbergen, who in 1973 shared with Konrad Lorenz and Karl von Frisch (the only Nobel Prize ever given to researchers in ethology). Tinbergen stilled the waters of these debates in a now-classic paper (Tinbergen, 1963), still relevant to anyone interested in the evolution of behavior. A native Dutchman fluent in both English and German, he found himself in the middle of these battles, and was well suited to play a mediating role. Tinbergen spent most of his career at Oxford, and was less flamboyant, and more of an experimentalist, than Lorenz, earning him the respect of the behaviorists. But at his core he shared with the other European ethologists a desire to understand how animals behaved in their natural context, on their own terms, and a rich, insightful use of the comparative approach.

Tinbergen began by noting that biology is a multi-layered discipline, with many interacting causes underlying even the simplest behavior. A simple question, such as "Why do birds sing?," has multiple correct answers, each necessary for a complete understanding. At the most immediate level of causation, we find questions of **mechanism**: a songbird sings because it has a vocal organ (the syrinx) which produces complex song, because it has specific neural mechanisms devoted to controlling that song, and because hormone levels at certain times of year activate these mechanisms. Such *"proximate"* mechanisms were the focus of American behaviorists. At the other extreme we find answers to **functional** questions concerning evolutionary causation, termed *"ultimate"* causation: birds sing "in order to" attract mates or to defend territories. Put more precisely, a bird today sings because its past ancestors sang, and this singing increased their mating success, or the effectiveness of their territorial defense. The bird doesn't need to "know" this: at a proximate level he may sing because he's sexually aroused, or simply because it feels good to sing. Tinbergen observed that many disagreements between behaviorists and ethologists were caused by a failure to distinguish ultimate from proximate causation, and by viewing such answers as being in opposition. In fact, questions about mechanism are separate from, and complementary to, questions about function. However, the answers to one can influence our approach to the other, and both types of question can be addressed empirically via experiments. Lacking time machines, we cannot examine the function of singing in extinct ancestors, but we *can* investigate the function of birdsong in living birds today, for example distinguishing between mate attraction and territorial defense functions (e.g. Kroodsma and Byers, 1991). Tinbergen was a master experimentalist who excelled at addressing both proximate and ultimate questions. He saw clearly that both types of questions are valid and interesting, amenable to empirical investigation, and that both types need to be answered if we are to have a full biological understanding of any behavior.

Tinbergen also distinguished two additional, historical levels of description. At the relatively brief level of *individual* history are **ontogenetic** questions: How did an individual develop or learn the behavior in question? For birdsong, this would include the study of vocal learning (most songbirds need to be exposed to adults singing the song of their species in order to sing properly themselves) and phenomena such as subsong (a "babbling" process in which the bird sings softly to itself, a key component of song acquisition). On a far longer timescale of the history of populations and species, we have **phylogenetic** questions: How did this behavior originate and develop during the evolutionary history of the species? For behavior this is often the most challenging of Tinbergen's four types of questions to answer, since behavior typically does not fossilize, and the paleontological record typically provides little help in trying to reconstruct the behavior of extinct forms. Hence, ethologists turned to the comparative approach, comparing innate behavioral patterns in groups of related species. Augmented today by molecular techniques for discovering the evolutionary relationships among species, the comparative method provides a powerful way to reconstruct the physiology and behavior of past ancestors.

Tinbergen's pluralistic approach, and his four-way distinction (dubbed "Tinbergen's four questions" or "four whys") is now a classic conceptual component of evolutionary and behavioral biology. Awareness of this approach is not as widespread in psychology. In this book, I will take Tinbergen's pluralistic approach as a core component of the theoretical framework, rigorously distinguishing proximate, mechanistic questions from questions of function and phylogeny. However, as we shall see, language change demands an addition – a fifth "why" – to address questions specific to historical linguistic change (to answer "Why does English pluralize most nouns with -s?"). But the principles remain the same: multiple, interacting levels of causation and history must be understood to make sense of biological phenomena.

2.6.2 The role of behavior in evolution

If the evolutionary study of behavior is young, the study of the interactions between behavior and evolution is even younger. There are at least two different ways in which behavior can complicate evolutionary processes. First, behavior can help to lead evolution. An organism may act as an unwitting pioneer in some new niche by chancing upon it and then learning to exploit it. For instance, the first cetaceans feeding in the water lacked any particular specializations for an aquatic lifestyle. But once this clade began exploiting the abundance of fish in the sea, the increasingly aquatic lifestyle initiated by this behavioral innovation quickly began to have evolutionary effects on form as well. This idea, that behavior "drives" evolution in new directions, is well established in evolutionary theory (Mayr, 1963, 1974; West-Eberhard, 1989). Second, an associated idea, often called the **Baldwin Effect**, is that innovation initially driven by behavior could later be assimilated genetically, thus saving the young animal the trouble of learning (Hinton and Nowlan, 1987; Maynard Smith, 1987; Weber and Depew, 2003). This idea has been popular in discussions of cognitive evolution in recent years (Dennett, 1991; Deacon, 1997) and detailed evolutionary modeling has demonstrated its potential applicability to language evolution (cf. Briscoe, 2003).

However, the effects of behavior do not always drive innovation: behavior can retard or resist direct morphological or physiological adaptation as well (Huey *et al.*, 2003). For example, lizards' sun-seeking behavior, which enables them to maintain a higher-than-ambient temperature, can inhibit the evolution of enzymes with a lower ideal operating temperature. This example seems directly relevant to humans: when our ancestors emerged from Africa and entered cold-weather niches, it seems undeniable that a thick coat of fur would have been a useful adaptation. Given that humans have as many hair follicles as "hairy" animals like chimpanzees or gorillas, and the primary difference is in the fineness of our hair, it may seem surprising that Inuit ("Eskimos") and other cold-adapted populations lack thick pelts. The reason, of course, is that they wear clothing, and furs taken from other animals provided more than adequate shelter from any theoretical evolutionary forces driving human pelt evolution. Behavioral innovations, particularly the kind of radical innovation typical of humans, can inhibit as well as drive evolution. The relationship between behavior and evolution is rendered even more indirect if behaviors can be learned from others by imitation or other forms of cultural inheritance. Such phenomena again insert a cultural level of explanation between genes, brain, and behavior.

2.7 Summary

We thus end a brief flyover of the consensus and controversies in evolutionary theory. Despite its brevity, it should be abundantly clear by now that many debates in the evolution of language can be firmly situated within the findings and controversies of evolutionary theory in general. We have also seen several examples of scholars overcoming barriers to interdisciplinary communication, whose outcomes have led to such inspiring achievements as the neo-Darwinian synthesis, modern ethology, and "evo-devo" biology. However, in some places, including those just discussed concerning the relationship between cultural and biological evolution – between glossogeny and phylogeny – human language may provide our best model for understanding processes that evolutionary theorists are still grappling with. Fortunately, linguists and psychologists have spent generations characterizing language and its acquisition, and can offer many insights into the system whose evolution we will seek to understand in this book. Let us, then, switch gears and approach language on its own terms, through the eyes of a linguist.

3 | Language

On a fine spring afternoon in 1828, a shoemaker in the German town of Nuremberg encountered a strange sight: a young man waddling down the street with his arms outstretched, squinting and yelling incomprehensibly. When asked to explain himself, he stared uncomprehendingly, and only repeated his name – Kaspar Hauser – and the phrase "I want to be a horseman like my father." He vomited when fed anything other than bread or water, but was taken in by a kindly scholar, Georg Daumer, in the town. Kaspar Hauser's saviors quickly learned that, despite his lack of knowledge of German or any other language, and a total inability to clothe or feed himself, Hauser was perceptive and intelligent, and a remarkably fast learner. Over the several years that Hauser lived with Daumer, he acquired a considerable vocabulary, some basic syntax, and the ability to read and write – enough to write a crude autobiography – along with the basic skills necessary to survive in normal society. As Hauser's language abilities grew, the horrible story of his life became clear in outline. From a young age, for as long as he could remember, Kaspar Hauser had been kept in a dark dungeon, with absolutely no social contact. His entire existence was confined to a windowless room with an earthen floor and a few wooden toys, with no verbal or physical contact with other humans. Then, for reasons we will never know, he was released from captivity, pushed in the direction of the town, and abandoned by whoever had tended him all those years. In a mystery that remains unsolved (some still claim he was a kidnapped prince) he was murdered a few years later in 1833. Hauser did learn a fair bit of language (vastly surpassing Viki or other human-raised chimpanzees) but, despite his obvious intelligence, his verbal skills never even approached that of a normal German his age.

3.1 Sensitive periods for language acquisition

The strange story of Kaspar Hauser (Blumenthal, 2003), and various other "wild children" like him (Malson, 1964; Curtis, 1977), illustrate a number of important points about the biology of human language. First, and most obviously, an individual who is not adequately exposed to linguistic input will not spontaneously develop language. Although every normal human is born with the capacity to *acquire* language, considerable external input is necessary to activate and utilize this capacity. Second, human language-learning abilities are not as well developed in adults as in children: there is a **sensitive period** for fluent language learning that begins to wane after puberty (Lenneberg, 1967; Newport, 1991). Had Kaspar been an eight-year-old when released, there is little doubt that he would have developed normal German within a few years. As an adult, he developed only a halting, agrammatical communication system: useful, but lacking the expressivity of full language. Finally, Daumer and other onlookers continually remarked on Hauser's intelligence and the speed with which he picked up household tasks and many complex behaviors including writing, basic arithmetic, and chess (Feuerbach, 1832; Daumer, 1873). The fact that an individual has been deprived of the opportunity to acquire language does not entail lack of intelligence.

Although the story of Kaspar Hauser is a horrible one, his fate was in some sense happier than many other known cases of "wild children." Worse are severely deprived children of modern times, like the girl Genie, who spent her childhood strapped to a child's toilet in a back room, severely beaten by her father if she made any sound, until her rescue by social workers at the age of thirteen. Despite early signs of promise, Genie never developed language or communication skills, even to the level of Kaspar Hauser (Curtis, 1977). A recent example is John Ssebunya, a Ugandan boy who fled into the forest after watching his mother murdered, and lived with a group of vervet monkeys for about three years. When he was discovered, nearly dead, John ably imitated birdsongs and monkey alarm calls, but neither cried nor spoke. Fortunately, he was young enough that, once reintegrated into human society at age six, he mastered both Hutu and French, and now can fluently tell his tale (Blumenthal, 2003).

Sensitive periods for language acquisition are just one of many converging sources of data indicating that the instinct to learn language has a biological basis (Lenneberg, 1967). They demonstrate equally clearly the need for social and environmental input for this biological basis to be of any use. Unlike many instinctual behaviors among animals, the human instinct to acquire language is necessary but not sufficient: without the input of a spoken or signed language, a human child will not invent its own language. This was apparently not obvious to the ancients: several kings are reputed to have had children raised by animals to see what language the children would develop on their own. In the most famous "experiment," recounted by Herodotus

(1964 [450–420BC]), the Egyptian king Psammetichos had children raised among goats (Stam, 1976). They reputedly uttered a (bleating?) sound transcribed as "bekos" – Phrygian for "bread" – thus demonstrating Phrygian to be the original tongue. In contrast, modern natural "experiments" involving deaf children have clearly demonstrated that a social "critical mass" is required for a language to develop – again suggesting that language has an irreducible social component. Children deprived of a language model will coin words (or gestures) for objects and events, and even combine them, but do not construct a full language capable of expressing unbounded thoughts (Goldin-Meadow and Mylander, 1998). But deaf children clearly demonstrate that once these social conditions are in place, a true language, in all its syntactic glory, can arise in a very brief time (Senghas *et al.*, 2005). Thus a rich biological capacity for language learning *and* an appropriate social and cognitive environment are not alternative explanations for language. Both are absolute necessities.

This need for social input is by no means typical: in many mammal species the communication system can develop in the complete absence of communicative environmental input, as demonstrated by so-called "Kaspar Hauser" experiments. A squirrel monkey, raised alone or by a muted mother, hearing no vocalization from other conspecifics, will nonetheless produce the full range of complex vocalizations typical for its species, and in the appropriate emotional and social contexts (Winter *et al.*, 1973; Hammerschmidt *et al.*, 2001). Humans' need for rich input sets language apart from communication in most other mammals, and *all* other primates. But we are not entirely unique in this requirement, because some other mammals (especially marine mammals such as whales and seals) and many bird species (songbirds, hummingbirds, and parrots) require environmental input: like us, they must hear normal vocalizations to acquire the vocal communication system typical of their species. Young songbirds raised under Kaspar Hauser conditions typically produce highly aberrant song. Songbirds, like humans, require auditory input before a certain sensitive period in order to develop normal song (Catchpole and Slater, 1995; Marler and Slabbekoorn, 2004). Thus, the human system, while not unique, is very unusual, and apparently unique to us among primates. An important part of coming to grips with language evolution will involve understanding the conditions under which such unusual systems evolve.

In this chapter I will survey the generalizations discovered by contemporary linguistics, to provide insight into the biological mechanisms that underlie the human language capacity, in a broad sense. This will serve as the basis for the following chapter, which asks which of these many capacities are shared with other species, and which evolved in our more recent phylogenetic history.

3.2 Understanding linguists: an interdisciplinary dilemma

Scientists who study language face an unusual challenge regarding interdisciplinary communication. Every normal human acquires language easily, with little explicit tutoring, at a young age, and most of the "knowledge" thus acquired is implemented at an unconscious level. Language acquisition is literally "child's play," and the rich complexity of adult language is processed so automatically that it seems simple to us. *These facts mask the complexity of language.* Often, it is only when we try to learn a new language as adults that we appreciate the difficulty of the task. Linguists make it their business to explore such complexity in their own languages, and it doesn't take long before linguistics students are amazed by the complexity of their native language. Some find this mesmerizing. A certain type of mind characterizes most of the accomplished linguists I know: a rather rare proclivity for abstraction, combined with a delight in the hidden details of verbal phenomena. I have studied enough linguistics to know that I do not personally have this sort of mind, and have grappled unsuccessfully with tough linguistic problems long enough to develop a deep respect for people who do. My feeling about linguistics is parallel to my feeling about mathematics: I know enough in either field to be an educated consumer, recognizing a solid argument when I see one, but keenly perceiving my limitations regarding trying to do creative work myself. But while most people know that they don't understand advanced mathematics, and wouldn't dream of making broad pronouncements about a professional mathematician's theories, many people *do* believe that they know a lot about language. Uninformed opinions about language and linguistics are thus a dime a dozen. Linguists involved in interdisciplinary exchanges have often bemoaned these facts (Bickerton, 1990; Jackendoff, 2002; Newmeyer, 2003) and stressed that language is far more complicated than it appears superficially. Phonemes are just not speech sounds, syntax is not just word order, and semantics is not just word play on shades of meaning: each of these core linguistic concepts is far richer and more complex than this.

In this chapter I provide a condensed survey of the debates and findings of modern linguistics, with the goal of determining the multiple cognitive components that, working together, make up the human language capacity (FLB). After surveying some long-running debates and clarifying terminology, I will distill the many findings of modern linguistics down to a set of component mechanisms most linguists agree are required for human language: a provisional "shortlist" of candidate mechanisms involved in different aspects of language. These are collated in Table 3.1. This list will provide the foundation for the rest of the book, as we attempt to determine which of these many mechanisms are shared with other animals *versus* specific to humans and language (FLN). We will see in the following chapters that most mechanisms involved in language are shared with other animals. This investigation, in turn, will lead to a much shorter list of components that appear to have evolved recently in humans since our separation from chimpanzees, which any complete theory of language evolution must explain.

This survey will also try to convey the flavor of linguistic research – the kinds of problems that professional linguists grapple with. There is no denying that linguistics is a field full of controversy, and while I will survey several core debates in the field, I will highlight over-arching areas of agreement. For example, while there are major disagreements about how to characterize syntax (one sometimes gets the sinking feeling there are as many models of grammar as there are practicing syntacticians), there is virtually universal agreement that a theory of language must include *some* theory of syntax, and broad agreement about what sorts of phenomena, in a wide variety of languages, it must be able to explain. Linguistics as a field has thus agreed on a set of problems and has outlined a set of possible solutions. Although consensus solutions remain unavailable for many linguistic problems, this is no justification for ignoring the problems themselves. Because there are few accessible surveys of the areas of agreement (cf. Pinker, 1994b; Jackendoff, 2002; Hurford, 2007), and all of these are books in themselves, I will offer my own condensed version in what follows.

3.3 Modern linguistics and the interface with biology

I start with a brief overview of the aims and methods of modern linguistics, particularly the growth of biological approaches to language, and integrate these linguistic aims and terminology with those from biology and evolution, already surveyed above. We will see that certain concepts (such as "innate," or "Universal Grammar") have been unnecessarily divisive and that biological concepts like "instincts to learn" provide a way out. Others, such as the interaction between biological and cultural inheritance, necessitate changes to "standard" biological and evolutionary models, but are too often ignored. After such over-arching debates and terms have been clarified, I will begin the systematic survey.

3.3.1 Western linguistics: description not prescription

One can trace the birth of linguistics to the first prescriptive grammars of Sanskrit or Latin, or the Greek rules of logic (Seuren, 1998). Modern linguistics, however, makes a sharp distinction between attempts to **prescribe** language use (e.g. "*ain't* is not a word") and attempts to **describe** language. The modern descriptive endeavor has more recent roots, beginning in Europe with the discovery by William Jones in 1786 (Jones, 1798 [1786]) that the "classical" languages of Greek, Latin, and Sanskrit are related in specific rule-governed ways. As another example, English, Dutch, and German are closely related languages, with many cognate words. The differences in vowel pronounciation in modern English result from a comprehensive change in the speech habits of English speakers around 1500 called the Great Vowel Shift. The realization that such historical changes were *rule-governed* was surprising and fascinating, for it was clear that such changes were neither decreed by governments nor invented by a single individual. Such changes are "phenomena of the third kind," influenced by, but not directly created by, individual human minds (Keller, 1995). The discovery of "laws" of sound change suggested that the study of language could provide an indirect but nonetheless revealing window onto the nature of both the human mind and human culture, paving the way for the modern approach to language study.

Historical linguistics dominated the study of language for the next 150 years, and was itself dominated by phonology and phonetics. Although the study of semantic changes and word etymology was fascinating, changes in word meaning tended to be highly idiosyncratic. Syntax was barely even discussed. This began to change around 1900, when the diversity of the world's languages had become clear, and the many different ways languages have of structuring sentences became fully apparent. Linguists became increasingly interested in objective methods that could be applied algorithmically to languages to discover their structure (Sapir, 1921; Harris, 1951; Seuren, 1998). The dream was of a generalized "discovery procedure" that could first uncover the phonemic repertoire of the language, enabling a writing system that could then generate a dictionary, and then finally lead to a complete grammar describing the rules for combining words. The design of such algorithmic discovery procedures reached their apogee in the 1950s (Harris, 1951).

During this period, interest in the biological basis of language remained limited. Psychology in the US was dominated by a behaviorist quest for general-purpose learning mechanisms that applied to all animal species equally (see Chapter 2), and behaviorists showed little interest in those aspects of behavior that made a species unique. Most structuralist linguists shared the basic world view of the behaviorists, if they thought about psychology at all. Although the fact that apes raised among humans do not learn language was widely known (Yerkes and Yerkes, 1929), and many linguists around 1950 might have happily acknowledged some biological basis for language that was specific to humans, uncovering the nature of this capacity was not a focus of linguistic research. It was in this intellectual context that Noam Chomsky, Eric Lenneberg, and a small cadre of like-minded young scientists were to make their mark in the early 1960s.

3.3.2 Generative linguistics: mental, formal, and biological

Three keywords sharply distinguished the generative linguistics introduced by Chomsky and his colleagues from the then-dominant strains of structuralist and behaviorist thought: it was mental, formal, and biological. The idea that human behavior, and language in particular, could not be properly understood without postulating unobservable **mental** entities was obviously not a new one, but it nonetheless had a revolutionary flavor in the context of American behaviorism. It is hard for those of us who did not live through this "cognitive revolution" to imagine the excitement (and relief) it generated: finally it became respectable to talk about the mind again, and to use the full explanatory power of mental entities to understand human behavior. While "the return of the mental" was perhaps inevitable, and favored by the *zeitgeist* of the late 1950s, many scholars agree in giving Chomsky considerable credit for catalyzing the cognitive revolution with his skeptical review of Skinner's (1957) book *Verbal Behavior* (Chomsky, 1959; Gardner, 1985). From then on, linguistics embraced cognitive explanations, and has never looked back.

The **formal** aspect of Chomsky's ideas had its seeds in ideas that were already current in structural linguistics, but Chomsky's extension of these ideas into the domain of syntax opened many new doors. In particular, Chomsky adduced evidence of complexities and constraints on syntax that seemed impossible to explain in behaviorist terms of "general learning mechanisms." The core new idea was the mathematical notion of an infinite set of sentences that can nonetheless be **generated** by a finite set of rules. This core "generative" notion is central to all modern linguistics, and it built upon discoveries in mathematics successfully systematized by Turing, Post, and Gödel (Davis, 1965). The development of computers added to the interdisciplinary appeal and power of the generative approach to linguistics, which was absorbed into the foundations of computer science (see below). Another crucial formal insight from this early work was the notion of **syntactic structure**. Existing models of syntax posited rules for building sentence structures by manipulating individual words, but a closer look revealed that syntactic rules must be able to act on phrases. Chomsky and his students uncovered many syntactic phenomena that could only be understood by positing a level of abstract tree-like structure, placing structure at the core of syntax. Although a noun phrase can be, in simple cases, captured by a single word like *John*, a single noun phrase was more typically made of many words (*the big cat, John's wife's mother's best friend*), and it is these *structures*, rather than strings of individual words, that are at the heart of syntax. Despite the diversity of contemporary grammatical theory, all modern syntactic theories agree on this basic notion of structure-dependence, and even critics grudgingly admit Chomsky's central role in establishing this modern insight (e.g. Seuren, 1998).

Today, cognitive and formal approaches to language are widely accepted as necessary in linguistics, even if not fully sufficient to understand natural language. The final and most controversial innovation of the new wave of generative linguists was to stress the **biological** aspect of language. Directly inspired by the work of ethologists like Lorenz and Tinbergen, both Lenneberg and Chomsky suggested that the human capacity for acquiring language was as particular to our species as the echolocation systems of bats are to that group. This biological orientation of the new linguistics was clarified by Lenneberg (1967), who carefully considered many of the sorts of biological data (neural, developmental, genetic, and evolutionary) that we will discuss in this book. This biological aspect of generative linguistics, dubbed "biolinguistics" in the 1970s (Jenkins, 1999; Chomsky, 2005), remains controversial. Although nearly everyone will agree that there is *some* biological basis for language that is specific to our species (How else can we explain the difficulties apes experience mastering language, presented with identical input?), attempts to characterize this basis have been strenuously debated for almost forty years.

3.3.3 Biolinguistics: exploring the biological basis for language

Because the biological basis of language remains so controversial, I will briefly explore the various viewpoints on offer from a biologist's perspective.

To first distinguish terminological from substantive issues: the goal of biolinguistics is to gain an understanding of the biological nature of the human capacity for language. The simple fact that a dog or a cat or a chimpanzee raised in a human home will not acquire language, while a human child will, indicates the existence of *some* biological basis in our species. A dog raised in a human home can learn to recognize hundreds of words (Kaminski *et al.*, 2004), and a mynah, parrot, or a seal can learn to speak many phrases (Ralls *et al.*, 1985; Pepperberg, 1991). Great apes given access to a gestural or visual symbol system can also learn hundreds of vocabulary items and arrange them into meaningful novel strings (Savage-Rumbaugh, 1986). But none of these nonhuman animals has ever mastered a full language, with an unbounded capacity to express thought. Nonhumans never do what every normal human child in the same situation will spontaneously do by the age of four: invent a wide variety of multi-word sentences that they have never heard but which are nonetheless "correct" and interpretable, and use these utterances to describe past and future (or imaginary) events, to ask questions, to describe their own wants and needs, and to ask others about theirs. It is this biological difference that we seek to understand, if we are to understand a critical aspect of human nature. What, precisely, does this difference consist of, at the cognitive, neural, and genetic levels? What are its behavioral prerequisites and predecessors? How do these linguistic differences relate to other aspects of human and animal cognition?

Encapsulation

One approach to characterizing the human language capacity postulates that its biological basis is complex and highly specific to language: that it is **encapsulated**, to use philosopher Jerry Fodor's term (Fodor, 1983). (I avoid the term "modular" because it has received so many different interpretations in biology, linguistics, and cognitive science.) Encapsulated cognitive mechanisms have a specific task, defined by a set of specific inputs to which they are sensitive, and specific outputs that they produce. More importantly, an encapsulated mechanism has internal computational resources that are private to the mechanism – they can't be "exported" as part of the output of the mechanism. Such encapsulation is the core quality that, for Fodor, characterized both speech and syntax. Fodor contrasted these with "general purpose" cognitive mechanisms, such as working memory, consciousness, or attention, that are broad in their inputs and outputs, and open in their computational structure. Encapsulation is claimed by some evolutionary psychologists to be characteristic of *all* aspects of mind (Tooby and Cosmides, 1990a; Pinker, 1997). From their perspective, the mind is best understood as a "Swiss army knife," with many specific mechanisms dedicated to specific tasks, not as a general-purpose computer open to many different tasks. However, Fodor himself has strongly criticized this viewpoint as missing his core point: that some aspects of mind are, and some are not, encapsulated (Fodor, 2000), and pervasive encapsulation is rejected by many psychologists and neuroscientists.

An alternative perspective holds that a critical aspect of the language faculty is precisely that it is non-encapsulated. For example, Merlin Donald argues that language is "executive," in the sense of dominating, controlling, and unifying other aspects of cognition, and that it is precisely the power of language to "reach into" any aspect of cognition that gives it its power, sharply differentiating human language from other animal communication systems which have limited semantic scope (Donald, 1991). Donald grounds his perspective in neuroscience, offering a model of how this "executive suite" is implemented in prefrontal cortex, basal ganglia, and other neural subsystems. For Donald and many neuroscientists, this **executive** perspective on language highlights the similarity between other broad aspects of mind (attention, consciousness, "general intelligence," etc.) and linguistic function. The executive perspective leads to very different assumptions about how language is implemented in the brain and what its genetic basis might be.

This distinction between encapsulated and executive function defines a continuum, and from a multi-component perspective there is no reason to think that a complex function like language occupies a single point on this continuum. One can, without inconsistency, argue that "speech is special" and encapsulated (Liberman, 1996) but that semantics or pragmatics are executive and unencapsulated (Fodor, 1983). Indeed, almost by definition, semantic interpretation cannot be *fully* encapsulated to language since we can talk about anything we can think about. In principle, linguistic semantics seems to have access to the same computational aspect of our sensory or motor cognition, and lots more besides, as thought itself. The "internal" structure of these cognitive domains can be "imported" into language via semantics. In conclusion, the encapsulated/executive continuum is a useful one for classifying particular cognitive/neural functions, but we expect something as complex as language (FLB) to have elements at various places along this continuum, highlighting the importance of specifying particular mechanisms rather than using the broad term "language."

Innateness

To what extent are mechanisms of language acquisition "innate"? Some examples of truly innate behaviors can help clarify this question. Humans, like other mammals, are born with a suckling reflex: a newborn mammal will seek out a teat and begin sucking. Many hoofed mammals, including horses and wildebeests, are able to stand up and walk only minutes after birth. In such cases, uncontroversially, the organism is born with functional behavioral patterns in place. Such behavior is "innate" in the original etymological sense of "present at birth." The newborn did not learn to suck or walk from environmental input, or by being "taught" by its mother: there is neither adequate structure in the newborn's perceptual stimulation, nor adequate time, for sucking or walking to be learned. In contrast, by following its mother about, the young colt will learn its way between barn and field. From this broad viewpoint, everyone agrees that there are innate behaviors.

Now consider a more difficult example. Newborn ducklings distinguish their mother's voice from another female's, and newborn lambs also recognize their mother's voice at birth (Gottlieb, 1974). Human newborns recognize not just their mother's voice at birth, but can distinguish her native language from other languages (Mehler *et al.*, 1988). Newborn babies even recognize, and prefer, the theme song from their mother's favorite TV program over other songs (Hepper, 1991). These behaviors are "innate" in the sense of being present at birth, but they are nonetheless learned from environmental input. Many mammals and birds can already hear *in utero* or *in ovo* (humans have a functioning auditory system for about the last three months of gestation), and have processed and "imprinted" upon sounds perceived before they emerged into the world. Are, perhaps, other "innate" behaviors such as laughter or crying also learned *in utero*? No, because deaf infants, who have never heard anything, still make normal human laughing and crying sounds (Eibl-Eibesfeldt, 1970). In such cases, empirical data are required to sort out whether the behavior in question is innate in the ordinary, deeper sense: innate behaviors are those that reliably develop without relevant environmental input (Ariew, 1999).

Even trickier cases involve complex behaviors that develop well after birth. Birds are not born knowing how to fly. In some species, the young emerge from the nest long before they even have flight feathers, and walk or swim after their parents long before they can fly. In others, fledglings perch on the edge of the nest, jump, and fly away on their first attempt (though not always successfully, and never with full adult coordination). For a complex motor behavior like flight, there is little question of "learning" to fly from environmental input. Watching other birds fly does not give you the motor commands necessary to fly yourself, any more than watching Tiger Woods play golf gives you the ability to make a hole in one. Nonetheless, a process of "self-administered" learning is involved, which involves practice, failed attempts, and a tuning of the motor control system, and the young bird requires nothing more than time, wings, and air to develop this skill on its own. So, is flight innate or learned? The answer is both, or neither, depending on your interpretation of "learned," and this example illustrates the error of framing the question in either/or terms. A better way to ask the question is: To what extent is structured environmental input required for a trait to develop, *versus* innate reflex or self-generated activity?

Turning now to human language, it is clear that language on the whole is more like bird flight than like laughter or crying: the child is not born speaking and requires time and self-generated activity (e.g. babbling) before developing this skill. And certainly, many aspects of language must be learned. This is absolutely uncontroversial. Everyone agrees that the contents of the lexicon must be learned, in the most straightforward sense: the child must perceive and imitate environmental stimulation (speech or sign) in order to learn and produce individual words. Whatever innate endowment humans may have, it does not include English, French, or Japanese words: these must be learned. At the same time, a critical aspect of language is our ability to produce and understand *novel* sentences – stimuli that we have never before encountered. Thus, again uncontroversially, there must be deeper regularities in language that we are able to acquire and process despite the novelty of many sentences. It is here that the real arguments about innateness in language begin.

The poverty of the stimulus

Abstract regularities of sentence structure cannot be directly perceived in the environment. For example, an English speaker will recognize the novel sentence *Akbar bathed himself* as grammatical, while *Himself bathed Akbar* is not – despite the fact that most people won't have heard either sentence before. More interesting are the following examples:

(1)   (a) Akbar bathed himself.
     (b) Akbar bathed him. (*him* is not Akbar)
     (c) Akbar asked John to bathe him. (*him* may be Akbar)
     (d) *Akbar asked Maria to bathe himself.
     (e) Akbar asked Maria to help him bathe himself.
     (f) *Akbar asked Maria to help himself bathe him.

(Following linguistic convention, unacceptable sentences are marked with the "star" symbol *.) This series of sentences, all of which are presumably novel to most English speakers at the level of surface form, illustrates one of the core problems of syntax: there are quite detailed restrictions on syntactic structure and interpretation. This particular problem involves the binding of reflexive pronouns to their referent. The rules that determine which of the sentences above are acceptable, and which are not, are quite complex, and some restrictions seem to be based on syntax rather than semantics, since an English native speaker can still understand what (1f) means, despite recognizing it as ill-formed. A child is not born knowing these sentences, nor have such sentences been regularly available for reinforcement learning. Nor have the child's parents sat him down and explained the abstract rules governing reflexives (indeed, professional linguists are still arguing about what they are). The rules are not imposed by the linguistic environment (as words are) or the social environment (as table manners are). Nonetheless, by the age of five children both understand and produce such sentences, with the appropriate syntactic restrictions (Crain, 1991). The classic **argument from the poverty of the stimulus** suggests that, given the apparent lack of environmental input, such restrictions on syntactic form must be "innate," in the sense that bird flight is "innate": reliably developing in the absence of relevant external stimulation. Such rules develop epigenetically in the child, by virtue of human biology.

This argument is highly controversial, and one can distinguish several coherent positions. First, we might hypothesize that what we are observing here is a general-purpose **template learning** system: while the child has not experienced the specific words in sentences (1e) or (1f) before, they have heard the pattern in (1e), but have never heard the pattern in (1f). This is the hypothesis that was entertained by Skinner and other behaviorists interested in language. The problem with this hypothesis, in its simple form, is that it is rather easy to generate sentences where the pattern is quite obscure, and the template seems unlikely to have been presented enough for the child to learn by stimulus reinforcement, e.g.:

(2) (a) Akbar's request for Maria to bathe him was considered rude.
     (b) *Akbar's request for Maria to bathe himself was considered rude.

It is not obvious that, by the age of five, the child has sampled enough of the possible patterns in English syntax to build a "template"-based system to accept or reject such sentences. For those who still pursue this general-purpose pattern-learning hypothesis, e.g. some connectionists, the pattern-learning system must have the capacity not only to recognize and remember patterns, but also to combine them into more complex structures. But then, the distinction between (2a) and (2b) appears arbitrary – why should (2b) be blocked while (2a) is acceptable? Furthermore, the knowledge that (2b) is "wrong" is particularly inexplicable, since the fact that you've never heard a pattern provides no evidence that it is ungrammatical: it may simply be a very rare form. How is the template-based learner to distinguish these cases? Although one can certainly pursue this line of reasoning, and offer stipulations that block (2b), the system that is required begins to seem less and less "general-purpose," and not obviously suited to the other cognitive domains to which the system might apply (vision? music? motor control?). To be sure, the fact that something is "not obvious" is hardly a knock-down argument. But many contemporary linguists have found these considerations convincing enough to pursue one of the two remaining positions.

The next position has been most clearly articulated by Crain (1991), and asserts that restrictions on syntax (like the reflexive restrictions discussed above, and many others) are not present in the input, are not taught, and do not follow from other restrictions (e.g. in general pattern learning, or from semantic or pragmatic constraints). They are specific to linguistic syntax, and restricted to syntax – they are *encapsulated to syntax*. Such restrictions are seen to be part of the child's innate endowment, and necessary for a child to master the language to which it is exposed. The restrictions must be abstract, things like "syntax entails structure-dependent restrictions" (a gloss of course – no one imagines that the child consciously considers such options). Although this position is often simply called **nativist**, it should be clear that both this "encapsulated-to-syntax" view, and the "general-purpose pattern-learning" view, require an innate endowment, and the difference between the two concerns how specific to language or syntax this endowment must be.

A third coherent position on this subject agrees that there are innate restrictions specific to language and to humans, but questions whether they are encapsulated to syntax. In particular, it is possible that many of the restrictions originally recognized by generative linguists in syntax actually follow from broader semantic or cognitive principles (Tomasello, 1998a; Jackendoff, 2002). This position is thus sometimes termed **cognitivist** (Croft and Cruse, 2003). Other linguists argue that constraints or proclivities follow from the functional needs imposed on language as a communication system: the **functionalist** position (Newmeyer, 1998a; Givón, 2002). In the current context, what is important is that all of these different positions agree that a human-specific innate endowment exists that is necessary for language acquisition. That is, they accept the poverty of the stimulus argument in its general form. Again, these positions are not mutually exclusive: one could accept a functional explanation for one syntactic phenomenon, a cognitive explanation for a second, and a syntax-encapsulated explanation for a third. Some syntactic phenomena, such as the restrictions on reflexive sentences described above, seem difficult to account for in cognitive or functional terms. But as before, that something is "hard to imagine" is no argument that it doesn't exist. To me it seems reasonable that, if a linguistic phenomenon can be stated clearly in the syntactic domain but lacks any obvious functional or cognitive motivation, the burden of proof is on the cognitivist or functionalist to produce such an explanation. In conclusion, there is broad agreement among linguists that some innate mechanisms are required to learn many abstract aspects of language, that at least some of these necessary mechanisms are specific to humans, and that the nature of the whole system is of deep interest. The arguments center, then, around how specific to language (or syntax, or phonology) such mechanisms are.

3.3.4 The biological basis for language: terminology and "Universal Grammar"

With these terms in hand we can return to the controversy sparked by Chomsky's and Lenneberg's revival of questions about the biological basis for language in the early 1960s. We have seen that most contemporary linguists and psychologists agree that there is something innate in humans, not present in other animals, that enables us to master language in a few short years. There is, however, little agreement about what we call this "something." We could call this suite of mechanisms "pan-human language-learning principles," the "biolinguistic base function," the human cognitive toolkit, the "language bioprogram," or anything else, but the term chosen will make no difference to how we characterize these mechanisms. Chomsky, who takes an interest in the intellectual history of these issues, revived an old term – "Universal Grammar" – to denote this human capacity (Chomsky, 1965). The term was coined in the seventeenth century to cover all those aspects of language that would *not* be written in a "grammar" of Latin or French because they were *shared* by all languages: such obvious facts as "languages have words" or "words have meanings." Thus both the original historical meaning of the term, and Chomsky's revival of it, were quite agnostic about the detailed nature of Universal Grammar, or "UG."

Some biologists have approvingly interpreted UG in precisely this broad manner (Nowak *et al.*, 2001, 2002). Others have defended, or attacked, a far more specific notion of UG, in which UG is complex, innate, encapsulated to language (as opposed to shared with other cognitive resources), and specific to syntax (rather than semantics, phonology, or phonetics). Such a characterization has been defended most vigorously by Steven Pinker and colleagues (Pinker and Bloom, 1990; Pinker, 1997; Pinker and Jackendoff, 2005), but is assumed in some form or another by many contemporary linguists. But any of these characteristics can be relaxed to form a different characterization of UG. For instance, research within a minimalist framework seeks to simplify UG (perhaps down to a single operation, Merge), while retaining the assumptions of innateness, encapsulation, and syntax-specificity (Chomsky, 1995). A different move, but one with similar consequences, is to broaden the term "UG" to include non-syntactic aspects of language (Jackendoff, 2002), but again preserving encapsulation and innateness. Yet another approach is to recognize an innate core UG, with considerable complexity, but not to assume that this core is encapsulated or syntax-specific (Nowak *et al.*, 2002). This approach is taken by many proponents of cognitive and functional grammars (Bybee, 1998; Tomasello, 1998b; Givón, 2002) and neuroscientists (e.g. Donald, 1998) – although many such scientists dislike the term "UG."

Given this diversity of interpretations, there seems little point in asking whether UG "exists" (van Valin, 2008). The question is: What are its characteristics, and what, precisely, is its biological basis? Whether the *term* "UG" is an appropriate one will largely depend on the answer to these central questions, and to some extent is simply a matter of taste. We should not confuse the empirical questions with terminological ones. I conclude, in agreement with most contemporary scholars, that a human capacity for language exists, and has a strong biological basis. In either the original historical meaning of "Universal Grammar," or Chomsky's later restatement, UG clearly exists, and uncovering its nature is a fundamental project for linguistics and cognitive science. This statement by no means entails that *all* aspects of the human biological basis for language are encapsulated and specific to syntax, or many other propositions commonly associated with the term "UG." Because of the many conflicting ways of interpreting the term, I generally avoid using it, preferring to discuss innate constraints on the acquisition of syntax, phonology, or semantics, and leaving the question of encapsulation open for further empirical inquiry. Thus I will use the term "FLB" in this book, which I explicitly adopt to avoid controversial assumptions about encapsulation or species-specificity.

3.3.5 Historical linguistics revisited: glossogeny and natural selection

As we have seen, linguistics got its start as a historical science, focused on languages such as Latin or Sanskrit, and it took many years before biological questions about individuals' minds and brains were addressed. In an influential paper, Chomsky (1986) suggested that linguistics had traditionally, and incorrectly, focused on external "languages" (like English or Navaho). Instead, he argued, linguists should focus on the *internal* cognitive representations of language, which he termed "I-language." This remains, I think unnecessarily, a divisive issue among students of language. Many contemporary linguists accept Chomsky's argument, and consider an understanding of I-language their primary goal, and this meshes nicely with a biological conception of language. Certainly, reifying a collection of utterances, as if they were living organic entities (what Chomsky termed "E-languages") constitutes a fundamental error, a form of mysticism that some historical linguists such as August Schleicher were prone to. Nonetheless, historical linguists or corpus linguists have access, by necessity, only to externalized traces of language: such snippets of externalized language are their primary data. Equally important, utterances are the primary linguistic data available to a child learning language. Because a central fact about these external data is that *they change over time*, they constitute an additional complication in our understanding of language evolution in the biological sense. An important trend in contemporary historical linguistics is thus to reconcile the study of such externalized data, and the process by which they change over generations, with a goal of understanding I-language from a biological, generative perspective (Lightfoot, 1998; Niyogi, 2006): of reconciling cultural and biological change.

Contemporary evolutionary theory provides several promising ways of bridging individual and cultural levels of explanation. The first are Darwinian models of cultural change. Remember that *any* replicating unit that experiences differential survival can be a target of natural selection: the Darwinian notion of selection is not restricted *a priori* to individuals or genes. In recent years, Darwinian selection has been proposed as a model of "cultural" transmission of ideas and traditions, via imitation, between individuals (Dawkins, 1976; Boyd and Richerson, 1983; Avital and Jablonka, 2000). Ideas are learned, and thus replicated, with some error (variation). If there is a struggle for existence created by limited mental space for new ideas, cultural "evolution" can occur: standard Darwinian logic leads, inexorably, to selection among ideas (Dawkins, 1976; Mesoudi *et al.*, 2004). Dawkins dubbed units of cultural replication **memes**, and the term has been enthusiastically embraced by some scientists eager to broaden the scope of Darwinian thinking into the domain of culture and the history of ideas (e.g. Dennett, 1995; Blackmore, 2000). Although other theorists of cultural evolution are circumspect about the digital connotations of the term "meme," they affirm the value of Darwinian thinking for cultural phenomena (e.g. Richerson and Boyd, 2005). This is an area of very active progress in contemporary biology. Crucially, while such perspectives remain rather preliminary for most aspects of human culture, historical linguistics provides both the data, and well-understood analysis techniques, for detailed "memetic" studies.

Recently, evolutionary biologists have illustrated this promise by applying empirical techniques for DNA analysis to historical linguistic data. To date, such work has documented a phenomenon long suspected by linguists: that patterns of change depend strongly on the frequency with which words are used in discourse. For example, Lieberman *et al.* (2007) considered the cultural evolution of the English past-tense marker *-ed*. In Old English, this was just one of many different rules used to indicate past tense. Today, other once-widespread rules remain only as irregular residues, such as *fly/flew/flown*. Infrequent inflections like *help/holp* became regularized, while high-frequency English verbs retained their ancestral irregular state (*go/went* or *be/was*). Their disappearance rate was surprisingly orderly: a verb used one hundred times more often than another regularized ten times more slowly. In another study, Pagel *et al.* (2007) quantified the rate at which related words (cognates such as *water* in English and *Wasser* in German) have been replaced by other forms (like the French *eau*) during the cultural evolution of eighty-seven different Indo-European languages, and again found strong frequency-dependence: terms that occur with high frequency in Indo-European languages (such as *one*, *night*, or *tongue*) are resistant to substitution by new phonological forms. Despite significant differences in their methods, both studies documented the same general pattern: frequently used words are resistant to change. While an influence of frequency on language change has long been recognized (Zipf, 1949; Bybee and Hopper, 2001), such studies illustrate the potential of techniques developed in the context of biological evolution to be successfully applied to cultural "evolution," and specifically to change in externalized language.

Discussions incorporating language change (in this cultural sense) and biological evolution become confusing if we use the term "evolution" for both. To avoid such confusion, I will embrace a term introduced by the evolutionary linguist Jim Hurford: **glossogeny**, meaning historical language change (Hurford, 1990). Like ontogeny and phylogeny, glossogeny picks out a historical process by which an entity changes over time. While ontogeny refers to the individual and phylogeny to the species, glossogeny refers to a set of cultural entities close to what is called a "language" in the everyday sense. Glossogeny represents a complication to normal biological evolution, a fifth "why" to consider in addition to Tinbergen's four (Chapter 2), and an additional form of inheritance that we will need to address if we are to understand language fully (Deacon, 1997). The slow evolution of the "instinct to learn" language, combined with rapid change in language, may drive departures from ordinary evolutionary predictions: glossogeny may prevent certain kinds of adaptation while encouraging others.

For example, natural selection for children who are born knowing the meaning of *cow* will never occur, because words and their meanings change faster than gene frequencies in populations. Cultural change is too rapid for biological genetic change to "track" this level of detail. Nonetheless, if the biological instinct to learn is constrained in particular ways, the linguistic units of any given language will be "filtered" by this process. Thus, we can predict the **co-evolution** of cultural and biological systems ("co-evolution" refers to systems or species in which evolutionary change in one both influences, and is later influenced by, the other). Words that are easy to say, meanings that are relatively transparent, or rules that "fit" the learning system will be more easily acquired, and then preferentially passed on, than alternative words, meanings, or rules (Deacon, 1997; Kirby, 1999, 2000). If there are more items in the population than the average child will acquire – a "bottleneck" – we will have competition among these alternatives. Logically, then, this process can lead to an "evolution" in the population of linguistic units (in "language" in the ordinary sense, of English or Latin).

Glossogenetic evolution is related to immediate behavior in indirect ways, sometimes providing an illusion of intentionality or design where there is none. Models incorporating this insight have been dubbed **"invisible hand" models**, based on Adam Smith's metaphor of the invisible hand in economics (Nozick, 1974; Keller, 1995). An important characteristic of invisible hand explanations is an indirect relationship between the underlying causal principles of the system (e.g. an individual's purchasing decisions) and the behavior of the overall system (e.g. market price trends). Although the macro-level description may appear to be driven by some intentional agency (the "invisible hand"), the actual underlying causality is at the micro-level. The connection between these two levels may be very non-intuitive.

Linguist Rudi Keller explores a nice example of *perjoration*: the tendency of certain words to acquire negative connotations over time. For instance, many English words referring to women gradually acquire perjorative connotations. *Wench* once simply meant 'woman' but now connotes a low-status woman. *Lady* was originally a term reserved for noblewomen, but now is used merely as a synonym for *woman* (not necessarily a particularly polite one). The opposite trend often occurs with words for men (e.g. *knight* comes for the Old German *knecht* 'serving-boy,' but came to refer to noblemen). While it is tempting to see this phenomenon as a reflection of some underlying sexist tendency to see women as bad and men as good, Keller (1995) offers a non-intuitive but plausible alternative hypothesis. Whenever there is a contrast available between a pair of words, such as *wench* and *lady*, a micro-level tendency to be polite towards women will frequently lead to the choice of the nicer alternative. Over time, this previous high form will become the common, unmarked form, inexorably driving the previously unmarked "normal" term to have perjorative connotations. Keller provides convincing arguments that this indirect and often non-intuitive relationship between cause and effect is characteristic of historical change in language, as well as other similar cultural systems.

A growing theoretical literature on "gene-culture co-evolution" provides a foundation into which such observations can be married with contemporary evolutionary theory (Laland and Brown, 2002). Despite assertions to the contrary (Christiansen and Chater, 2008), the arrival of rapid cultural evolution does not cause biological, genetic evolution to cease, but rather changes and complicates the nature of selection (Feldman and Cavalli-Sforza, 1976; Feldman and Laland, 1996). Many studies reveal co-evolution of culture and genes to be theoretically plausible and potentially powerful (cf. Laland and Brown, 2002), and indeed such co-evolution can help solve puzzles about human cooperative behavior that might otherwise require explanations beyond a Darwinian increase in inclusive fitness (e.g. "cultural group selection": Boyd and Richerson, 1985). In addition there are several well-understood empirical examples of gene-culture co-evolution, such as the increase in lactase alleles among adults in cultures that previously evolved dairy farming (Durham, 1991). Thus, both in theory and practice, the existence of cultural transmission complicates but does not stop biological evolution. "Cultural selection" on linguistic elements and phenomena have been studied in computer simulations (e.g. Kirby, 2000; Briscoe, 2002) and most recently documented in the laboratory (Kirby *et al.*, 2008). It is thus surprising that the rich data of historical linguistics have, until the studies described above, received scant attention by theorists interested in gene-culture co-evolution.

The existence of an intermediate explanatory level of cultural evolution has interesting implications for the ongoing debates about evolutionary design and adaptation. Cultural/historical selection on linguistic units like words or rules, rather than on genes, provides an alternative explanation of a close fit between the instinct to learn and the system to be learned. First, the biological basis for learning may have evolved, through normal Darwinian processes, to suit the needs of language. This is only likely for aspects of language that are quite stable over time: universals of language that do not vary much, or at all. In contrast, for those aspects of language that *do* vary historically (word forms, specific inflections, or most other details of particular languages), any close fit may reflect glossogenetic change: a filtering out of hard-to-acquire and less-used items (Deacon, 1997). This second possibility means that a historical perspective on language change has an important role to play in discussions of "adaptiveness" in language evolution.

Components of language: a survey

In the next four sections I survey the multiple components involved in language from a linguist's perspective, following the traditional topics of phonology, syntax, semantics, and pragmatics. Inspired by Hockett (1960), I will break each of these components of language down into a set of mechanisms of which we can ask, empirically, the following questions: Is the mechanism specific to language or shared with other aspects of cognition? If specific to language, is it shared among components (e.g. between syntax and semantics)? Is the mechanism found in nonhuman animals? If so, does this appear to reflect homology, or convergent evolution? In this chapter I will focus on delineating the mechanisms, and their interaction within language and humans. Chapter 4 will focus on the comparative questions. Throughout, the goal is to appreciate the insights that many years of hard work by modern linguists have produced, without prematurely accepting any particular way of carving up the cognitive and computational systems underlying language (including Hockett's). Thus I have two goals: to explain, in a basic way, why linguists think that particular components of language exist and function the way they do, and to compile a menu of crucial mechanisms (assembled in Table 3.1 at the end of the chapter) which we can then evaluate based on comparative data.

3.4 Phonology

Phonology is the study of the sound structure of language, and the process by which a set of discrete phonemes (the *phonological inventory*) is organized into larger complexes (syllables, words, and phrases). Phonologists study the rules by which complex acoustic signals are generated *independent of meaning*. Phonology offers examples of many of the central characteristics of language, particularly the infinite use of finite means, the cultural transmission of complex signals, and the interaction between phylogenetic, glossogenetic, and ontogenetic levels of explanation, but avoids many complex and unresolved issues associated with meaning in language. Phonology shares some characteristics of syntax, such as generativity, but lacks self-embedded, recursively generated structures (see below). We can thus profitably think of phonology as "generative grammar level one" – hierarchy without recursion, and structure without meaning. While not entirely accurate (e.g. the most basic phonological unit, the phoneme, is diagnosed by changes in word meaning), this characterization encompasses the vast majority of phonological phenomena. Certain domains of phonology (e.g. metrical stress theory) have been successfully applied to a much wider variety of languages than is typical in syntax or semantics. Furthermore, much current activity in phonology focuses on unifying its theoretical constructs with lower-level constructs in phonetics and speech science, and there is a clear potential for the discovery of "bridging laws" between physics, biology, and this core aspect of language in the near future.

3.4.1 Phonology: a generative system

Phonology is at its core a generative system that can produce (or accept) arbitrary rule-governed signals. The signals generated by the phonological system form one layer of a two-level hierarchy of linguistic structure. At the bottom layer are the strings of meaningless phonemes arranged into well-formed phonological structures. At the overlying layer, a subset of these structures which are lexicalized ("words" or morphemes), have meaning in some sense, and are arranged into higher-order syntactic structures. The existence of these two levels appears to be a universal feature of human languages, and was considered one of language's core "design features" by Hockett (Hockett, 1960), who dubbed it **duality of patterning**. This two-level system helps provide a solution to a problem that must be faced by any communication system capable of expressing an arbitrary number of novel thoughts: such a system must be capable of generating an arbitrary number of discriminable signals. The biological acquisition of the capacity for such a generative process at some point in human evolution was a critical step in the evolution of language (Lindblom *et al.*, 1984).

Phonological structures are *constrained*: not all possible strings of phonemes are considered valid or acceptable by native speakers. In general, phonological constraints are quite varied among different languages and must therefore be culturally acquired by the developing child. Understanding such language-specific *phonotactic constraints* is a major focus of modern phonology. Strings that are well-formed phonologically, but are not actually used by a language are termed "possible words" or **pseudowords**, and play an important role in psycholinguistics. Thus, for example, letter strings such as SHRSTG or TRLA are not possible words in English (though they might be in some other language), while GRAP obeys English phonology and is thus a valid pseudoword. Native speakers have no problem distinguishing pseudowords from impossible nonwords, or in guessing how such pseudowords would be "correctly" pronounced. This indicates a rule-governed generative system with a scope beyond just those words memorized and stored in the lexicon.

The number of pseudowords in a language vastly outnumbers the actual words in a language. This is useful when new words are needed, as there is an unlimited store of them: marketers seeking new product names unconsciously obey the phonotactic constraints of their native language, but have little difficulty in finding novel candidate words to foist upon the lexicon. A quick calculation illustrates the vastness of this "potential" untapped lexicon. A language with ten consonants (C) and ten vowels (V), which allowed only simple CVC syllables, would have 10*10*10 (1,000) possible syllables. Assuming that any syllable can occur at any place in a word, the possible store of four-syllable words is $1,000^4$ ($= 10^{12}$, or one trillion) possible pseudowords. Of these, a small fraction (around 100,000) might actually be true words: roughly one in every ten million. This may be a high estimate, appropriate for a language like English with a rather large syllable inventory. Making the calculation more stringent, a language like Japanese has a highly constrained syllable structure (essentially allowing only CV syllables) – only a total of 46 syllables are needed in the Japanese "hiragana" script. Assuming 40 possible syllables, there are still 40^4 ($= 2,560,000$) possible four-syllable pseudowords (far larger than the vocabulary of any known language), and simply increasing the number of syllables to five gives us 100 million Japanese pseudowords, only one in a thousand of which is used in a 100,000 word lexicon. Obviously, although finite, the generative capacity of any human phonological system is more than adequate to generate as many words as could ever be needed for communication.

3.4.2 Blurry borders: phonetics, phonology, and syntax

Phonological structures occupy a level above that of the acoustic structure of individual speech segments ("phonetics"), but do not tie in directly with issues of meaning ("morphology" and "semantics"). Both of these bound-aries are in some ways based on an artificial distinction, since they are in fact crossed by bridging rules, or *interface constraints*. Much progress has been made in recent years in building robust links between phonetics and phonology (e.g. Browman and Goldstein, 1986; Goldstein *et al.*, 2006b). There is little doubt that, eventually, these two traditionally distinct dis-ciplines will be joined seamlessly by a set of bridging principles, much as physics and chemistry are today. However, as for chemistry, phonology has its own principles and units, and its own proper level of abstrac-tion, and will not disappear in the process. A more challenging set of bridging issues, looking in the other direction, concerns the relationship between phonology and syntax, semantics, and pragmatics (Jackendoff, 2002). The difficulty is that aspects of all of these higher-order compo-nents of language affect the phonological structure of the sound signal. In syntax, for example, the existence of phrase boundaries can block nor-mal processes of contraction or assimilation, so phonological rules must in some sense "see" syntactic phrase boundaries. Thus, in English the phrase *want to* contracts in most situations in ordinary speech to *wanna*, but this process is blocked if there is a phrase boundary between *want* and *to*, e.g.:

(3)　(a)　What do you want to do?
　　　(b)　What do you wanna do?
　　　(c)　Who do you want to go to the store?
　　　(d)　*Who do you wanna go to the store?

Similarly, **intonation** – the linguistic use of voice pitch as a cue to lin-guistic structure above the phonemic level – can be influenced by syntactic, semantic, or pragmatic constraints (Ladd, 1996). For instance, the following questions, identical in terms of segmental structure, are actually request-ing different information (capitalization indicates stress on the capitalized word):

(4)　(a)　Did MARY go to the store?
　　　(b)　Did Mary go to the STORE?

In (4a), the questioner is interested in (or surprised by) *who* went to the store, while (4b) focuses on *where* Mary went. Such use of stress indicates that possible options – a *contrast set* – is being implied, and is thus called *contrastive stress*. Such phenomena, among others, suggest that there is no strict "upper limit" to phonology, and that none of these subcomponents of language are strictly encapsulated.

3.4.3 Signals and the structure of phoneme inventories

The most basic requirement for a phonological system is a set of discrete elemental signals that can be combined into larger strings: **segments**. Segments are essentially meaningless perceptual units that can be combined into larger (potentially meaningful) units. A central requirement of segments, from the viewpoint of information transmission, is **parity**: signalers and receivers should share a representational framework in which to produce, or comprehend, them (what Hockett termed "interchangeability"). The framework may be essentially arbitrary: what is crucial is that both signaler and receiver share it (Liberman and Mattingly, 1989; Pinker and Bloom, 1990). We will see that achieving parity is not trivial in the evolution of communication (Chapter 13). Typically, linguistic segments are vocal signals, so I will focus on these, but signed languages accomplish the same functions with discrete, learned, manual actions.

Phonologists distinguish between *phones* – the observable speech sounds – and *phonemes*, which represent a more abstract specification related to meaning. This can easily lead to misunderstanding. Although phonologists are generally interested in phonemes, phones are the most theory-neutral phonological objects. Depending on phonotactic constraints in the language and one's theoretical predispositions, a quite rich system of phones might be analyzed as consisting of many fewer phonemes. For instance, Kabardian includes at least twelve vowels at the phonetic level, but can be analyzed phonologically as having just one, because each occurs only in conjunction with particular consonants (p. 23, Kuipers, 1960). But at the level of speaking and listening no one would claim that these phonetic differences between Kabardian vowels are unimportant. In articulatory phonology the elemental units are considered to be speech **gestures**, which are considered as abstract specifications of a closure and release at a particular vocal tract location (Browman and Goldstein, 1986, 1989). Either way, a basic set of elemental signals (phones, phonemes, or gestures) is a requirement for subsequent phonological operations of constrained hierarchical concatenation.

One can easily imagine a hodge-podge of signals (e.g. a belch, bilabial click, laughed syllable, and three different pitches of hoot) that might be adequate for effective communication from the viewpoint of information theory. But human phonological systems are never random assemblages. Instead, phonological systems are highly structured, and comparison of different languages reveals specific patterns of occurrence of different phones (Jakobson, 1968; Lindblom *et al.*, 1984). This patterning had already been extensively studied and catalogued (Trubetskoy, 1939/1969) when Roman Jakobson suggested, in a seminal book, that such patterns could be more richly understood by considering both the ontogeny of speech in children, and the pattern of breakdown seen in various types of aphasia (Jakobson, 1941, 1968). Based on his reading of the early child-language literature, covering many Indo-European languages and Japanese, linguist Roman Jakobson claimed that "the relative chronological order of phonological acquisitions is everywhere and at all times the same" (p. 46, Jakobson, 1968), and that this order reflected the *difficulty* of producing the individual phones. Furthermore, Jakobson argued that such universal patterns could sometimes be observed "in reverse" in aphasic patients, where increasing brain damage led to increasing loss of difficult phones. Jakobson argued that this same notion of difficulty could explain the distribution of phones in the world's languages. Like most attempts to specify "laws" for biological phenomena, Jakobson's proposals about comparative linguistics weakened in the light of subsequent research. But they remain surprisingly good statistical generalizations, enough that deviations from them are still considered interesting and surprising. His proposed laws of child language acquisition must be adjusted to the fact that the details of speech acquisition in normal children reveal a wealth of idiosyncratic pathways to a final mastery of their local language (Vihman, 1996). Nonetheless, the basic idea that there is a causal link between child language acquisition and the historically derived patterns observed in languages is one that has been explored from many different directions by subsequent workers. Jakobson may be seen as the first biolinguist, and both aphasiology and child language have been strongly influenced by his notion of production difficulty.

We can also understand the discreteness of phonemic inventories from a perceptual perspective. For many years, the phenomenon of **categorical perception** of speech sounds was viewed as the most powerful evidence of innate, human-specific mechanisms for language. Organisms tend to group similar stimuli together into categories, and this is as true for vision or smell as for sounds. Nonetheless, we can discriminate among different members of a category. Although in the supermarket you may categorize all the objects in one bin as "potatoes," you are still perfectly capable of distinguishing one potato from another. Categorical perception, originally discovered in the perception of speech sounds, is a more complex perceptual phenomenon than this "normal" type of simple categorization. In its purest form, categorical perception is when a listener is *unable* to discriminate between the different members of a category (Liberman *et al.*, 1957; Liberman and Mattingly, 1989). Speech scientist Alvin Liberman and his colleagues at the Haskins Laboratories discovered that an artificially generated continuum of speech sounds, each different from the others, does not *sound* like a continuum, but rather like a series of /ba/ sounds, followed by a series of /pa/ sounds. Even for the experimenters, who know exactly what is going on, it is difficult to hear the differences between two different sounds if both are categorized as "pa." The term "categorical perception" is used only for such situations, when the discrimination of stimuli within a category is significantly worse than that between categories.

Categorical perception is a striking phenomenon, and when discovered in speech, the close fit between speech categories and subject responses seemed to imply a specialization for speech perception. However, this hypothesis slowly unraveled as it became clear that categorical perception can also be seen for non-linguistic stimuli (e.g. Cutting and Rosner, 1974; Cutting, 1982; Etcoff and Magee, 1992). Furthermore, the initial hypothesis that it was specific to humans broke down as it became clear that animals both perceive their own vocalizations categorically (Zoloth *et al.*, 1979; Nelson and Marler, 1989; Fischer, 1998) and, more tellingly, perceive *human* speech sounds categorically (Morse and Snowdon, 1975; Kluender *et al.*, 1987; Kuhl, 1987). This phenomenon thus provides an excellent example of a mechanism which plays a crucial role in phonology – dividing the speech continuum up into discrete units – but is nonetheless widely shared with other species. Categorical perception, like many other aspects of the human capacity for language, was already present long before humans evolved language (cf. Hauser and Fitch, 2003).

3.4.4 Sequence memory, hierarchy, and the particulate principle

Phonological structures were initially considered simply as strings of phonemes (Jakobson *et al.*, 1957; Chomsky and Halle, 1968), but phonological structures also have a hierarchical structure, with syllables made up of one or more phonemes, phonological words made of one or more syllables, and phrases consisting of one or more words. Contemporary theories of phonology concern abstract hierarchical structures, such as metrical structure or syllable structure (Goldsmith, 1990), not just phoneme strings. Furthermore, studies of sign language "phonology" emphasize the existence of both sequential and hierarchical structure, with units analogous to phonemes and syllables, in the gestures that make up the linguistic "utterances" of signs (Brentari, 1996, 1998). Thus, modern phonologists are interested in the rule-governed arrangement of the smallest-level linguistic forms (be they speech sounds or handshapes) into larger complexes. This productive, combinatorial process is a necessity for the generation of the complex signals of speech or sign.

Given a small stock of indivisible elements, there are two essential processes for generating unlimited signal diversity. The first and more basic is **sequencing**. In principle, simple sequencing is adequate to generate an infinite number of signals from even the most depauperate set of elements, as nicely illustrated by the binary coding of numbers or letters used in all contemporary digital computer systems. A love letter, the Gettysburg Address, a picture of your mother, or your favorite song can all be encoded as a simple string of ones and zeros and sent zooming around the planet to be losslessly reconstructed by another computer. However, binary strings like "1010011010" are rather difficult to parse for a human being. We prefer larger sets of elements, arranged into more compact strings (e.g. the decimal version of the number above is "666"). Such parsability constraints (among other factors) lead to the second core generative process of *nesting*, or **hierarchical structure**. Although hierarchy is not, strictly speaking, necessary for signal coding, it is a ubiquitous aspect of cognitive structure (Simon, 1962). Hierarchy in phonology is nicely illustrated by the nesting of distinctive features (e.g. +labial, −voiced) into phonemes (/p/), phonemes into syllables, and syllables into words. Syllables themselves have a hierarchical structure, consisting of a *nucleus* with optional *onset* and *coda*. Some phonemes can appear only in restricted positions (e.g the "ng" sound at the end of *sing* cannot appear word-initially in English).

An important difference between the hierarchical structures found in phonology and those seen in syntax is that phonological structures are not *self-embedding*: we do not find syllables nested within syllables in the way that we find syntactic phrases nested within other syntactic phrases. Phonemes never contain other phonemes, and syllables never contain other syllables. Self-embedding hierarchies, often called **recursive structures** because they are most easily generated by a recursive algorithm, are central to syntax and will be discussed in the next section. But hierarchy *without* self-embedding is a basic aspect of phonological structure. Why?

There are a number of ways in which hierarchy seems to be a good thing in language. The first is that signals with hierarchical structure appear to be more easily remembered and accessed than those that lack such structure. The classic example is the phenomenon known to memory researchers as **chunking**: the reinterpretation of a string of elements as if it were a single element (Miller, 1956; Simon, 1974). Chunking facilitates memory because the capacity of short-term memory is apparently limited to between five and nine basic elements. If some overlearned and familiar strings may be treated as wholes that count as a single element, this fundamental limit can be transcended. Thus the string "BEEP BANG RING DING DONG" can be remembered roughly as easily as "X Z T R F," because the longer string can be "chunked" into familiar words. Such memory advantages may provide the most basic reason for organizing speech or sign into hierarchically structured signals: easy storage and lookup in the lexicon, or in a *mental syllabary* for rapid access during speech production and perception (Levelt and Wheeldon, 1994).

Another viewpoint on hierarchical structure is more abstract, but complementary. This principle – the **stability of hierarchical structure** (Simon, 1962, 1972) – applies to a wide variety of complex systems, including molecules in chemistry, the genetic code, and phonology. The core insight is that hierarchical structures are more stable than "flat" structures. Simon illustrates this point with a parable of two watchmakers, one of whom builds the watch out of independent "modules," while the other adopts a serial piece-by-piece approach, one step after another. If either watchmaker is interrupted, the ongoing work is undone. The modular watchmaker has a huge advantage if interruptions only disturb assembly of the current module. In contrast, a disturbance to the non-hierarchical watchmaker means the entire job is lost, and must be begun anew from step one. Simon argued that this simple constraint has powerful implications, and that the ubiquity of hierarchy in nature (and especially in human behavior) is driven in large part by this entropic advantage of hierarchical systems. From an evolutionary viewpoint, such modularity also frees natural selection to "tinker" with individual modules with less fear of disrupting the entire system, one reason that gene regulation may be organized along hierarchical lines (Kitano, 2002). Similarly, in motor control, the apparent ubiquity of hierarchical control may result from both stability and memory considerations. By breaking complex motoric planning into stable prelearned subcomponents, an organism can automatize individual subcomponents (by sequestering overlearned patterns to more peripheral control at the spinal cord or brainstem level) and then use higher-order neurocognitive resources to synchronize and coordinate these chunk-like patterns (Lashley, 1951; Lenneberg, 1967; Lieberman, 1984; Allott, 1989).

Combined with the production of sequences of discrete units, hierarchy solves a fundamental problem of signaling: the coding of an unbounded set of messages with a finite system. The alternative approach, observable in many animal communication signals, is to use *graded signals*, where the value of some signal parameter (e.g. amplitude or frequency) maps onto some message parameter (e.g. anger) in a direct, analog fashion. Unfortunately, as increasing numbers of potential messages are coded, this strategy rapidly runs into the problem of discriminability: each signal will grow more and more similar, and harder to identify (Nowak *et al.*, 1999). The alternative is to use a discrete code of easily discriminable elements and to code each message with a group of elements, a *coding chunk*. This is the approach used in the genetic code, where a group of three DNA base pairs codes for a single amino acid, and strings of these codons correspond to entire proteins. The virtue of this system is that it is robust against noise, because each element remains easily discriminable, but can nonetheless generate unlimited diversity. The existence of a parallel between linguistic hierarchy and the genetic code was recognized almost immediately as the nature of DNA became clear (Monod, 1971), and has more recently been dubbed the **particulate principle of self-diversifying systems** (Abler, 1989; Studdert-Kennedy, 1998; Studdert-Kennedy and Goldstein, 2003). That this principle typifies both multiple systems in biology and non-living systems such as chemistry suggests that it is a general principle. However, we shall see that it is not typical of primate communication systems, suggesting that the discovery of particulate, combinatorial phonology during human evolution was a major transition *en route* to language (Lindblom *et al.*, 1983; Zuidema, 2005).

3.5 Syntax

3.5.1 Introduction: the challenge and complexity of syntax

Take a sentence like this. It has five words, only one of which (*sentence*) has a directly identifiable referent that you could point to. *Take* is a verb, asking you to do something with that sentence. But what, exactly? Is 'taking a sentence' the same as 'taking' a cookie from the jar, taking someone prisoner, or taking something for granted? Apparently, whatever *take* means, it is dependent on the other words associated with it in a sentence. Similarly, what it means for something to be *like* something else depends on context: to say something *looks like* vs. *feels like* vs. *smells like* something else picks out for comparison quite different aspects of those things. Finally, *a* and *this* are even more dependent on the other words in the sentence, and indeed can't really be said to have their own meaning independent of those words. If we perform a similar analysis on any arbitrary sentence, we will find a similar continuum of words that seem to have relatively clear external referents (concrete nouns like *cat* and *Paris*) to words like *the*, *a*, and *that*, whose role in meaning is restricted to binding and coordinating the other words in the sentence into a whole. When put together into larger units, like *the artist formerly known as Prince*, or *the beauty of the sublime*, the referents of the resulting noun phrases can range the gamut from highly specific to extremely vague. This brief exploration only touches on the complexities inherent in the sentence that began this paragraph, but, when you first read it, you had no difficulty understanding it. Indeed, a crucial aspect of syntax, the study of sentence structure, is that syntax is very easy to *do*, as a language user (it is a highly automatic component of language processing), but extremely difficult to *understand*, as a scientist attempting to understand what is going on behind the scenes.

While we often "choose our words" carefully, connoting a degree of conscious volition over semantics and pragmatics, we rarely consciously "choose" the complex syntactic structures into which we arrange these words. Indeed (as every grade-school student of grammar learns), these syntactic structures are quite resistant to introspection and it takes serious mental effort to even begin to analyze their structure. This disjunction between our effortless use of syntax and the supreme difficulty of describing and understanding it has had important sociological and historical effects, many of which remain resonant today. Historically, it meant that syntax was the last major branch of linguistics to be addressed. Semantics was already discussed in some detail by the Greeks, and phonetics and basic phonology were both well-ploughed fields by 1900. But with few exceptions syntax tended to be neglected by linguists (e.g. Sapir, 1921; Bloomfield, 1933) until the modern era of linguistics was ushered in by Chomsky and his students, whose research put syntax at center stage.

3.5.2 What is syntax?

Syntax traditionally constitutes an independent level of description from either phonology or semantics. Syntax is often thought of as the arrangements of words into sentences, where word order determines meaning, but this conception is inadequate on several levels. First, what is a "word"? Chunks like *-ing*, *-ed*, or *-s* are not words *per se*, but attach to words, and serve to bind the sentence together into a hierarchically structured whole. Linguists refer to such stored bits of phonology as **morphemes**, and non-free-standing morphemes like *-ed* are called "bound morphemes."

In English, we also have a class of morphemes termed "function words" (*a, the, because, that,* . . .) which play a similar syntactic role. In English we consider such morphemes free-standing words, but the distinction is often quite arbitrary (is *nevertheless* one word or three?). Thus, syntax arranges morphemes rather than words, and many linguists today see arrangement of morphemes – "morphology" – as a core part of syntax. Second, syntactic structures are **hierarchical** (made up of parts, which are made up of sub-parts, etc.). What happens to the sentence *Fido has fleas* when we replace the noun *Fido* with the noun phrase *that black Labrador of Judy's*? Syntactically speaking, *nothing* happens, because noun phrases act just like nouns. So it is not really words *per se* that are the operative units in syntax, but **phrases**. A phrase can be made up of many words, or just a single word, but it is phrases that form the bread and butter of syntactic description. Furthermore, not all phrases can be stuck together willy-nilly: there are very specific restrictions on how different phrases can combine. Finally, what about meaning? Syntactic structure has a crucial relationship to meaning: the meaning of *John saw Mary* is not the same as *Mary saw John*, but the first sentence entails that *Mary was seen by John*. This simple example immediately shows us that "word order" is not enough to deduce meaning, because *Mary* and *John* appear in the same sequence in the second and third sentences, which nonetheless have different meanings. Meaning is thus dependent on the overall structure, which may be quite complex, and not simply on word order.

Syntax is thus the rule-governed combination of small meaningful units (morphemes) into hierarchical structures (phrases and sentences) whose meanings are some complex function of those structures and morphemes. Crucially, the syntactic system must allow for the unbounded generation of hierarchical structures, a capability nicely captured by Humboldt's phrase "making infinite use of finite means" or, more concisely, as **discrete infinity**. This capacity is necessary to express an unlimited number of thoughts. If we had a finite set of, say, 1,000 thoughts to be linguistically encoded, it would not be required (phonological generativity would then easily suffice). Syntactic structure goes beyond phonological hierarchy in at least two ways. First, the **structure dependence** of syntactic rules (their dependence on phrases, not words, and phrase structure, not word order) is a central aspect of all modern approaches to syntax. Second, syntactic phrases allow **self-embedding** (e.g. a noun phrase can have another noun phrase within it). Self-embedding requires *recursion*: an allowance for rules that, seemingly tautologically, refer to themselves in their own definition. Self-embedding is a powerful mechanism to generate an infinite set of syntactic structures, going beyond the simple hierarchy of phonological structures. While these formal aspects of syntax are clear, the mapping of syntactic structures onto meaning is highly complex, and a crucial open issue concerns the degree to which syntax can be insightfully discussed as a formal system *independent* of meaning. Let us start by exploring such formal approaches.

3.5.3 Many flavors of modern syntax

A non-linguist attempting to gain an overview of contemporary theories of syntax is in for a bewildering experience. Within the main line of generative grammar there have been numerous historical stages, from the original "transformational generative grammar" through "Government and Binding Theory" to "Principles and Parameters," and, finally, the Minimalist Program today. Each of these stages of generative grammar has spawned off-shoots and opponents: a short list includes generalized phrase structure grammar (GPSG; Gazdar *et al.*, 1985), head-driven phrase structure grammar (HPSG; Pollard and Sag, 1987), lexical functional grammar (LFG; Bresnan, 2001), role and reference grammar (RRG; van Valin, 1996), and categorial grammar (Steedman, 1996). Within computational linguistics, a wide variety of more "engineering" approaches have been developed (e.g. tree adjoining grammars; Joshi, 2002). In addition to such generative models, there are multiple models which differ in fundamental ways from the contemporary "mainstream" (cf. Sampson, 1980). I have spent a good part of the last five years trying to come to grips with all of these variants, and have reached the conclusion that most of them represent varying styles or attitudes more than fundamentally incompatible approaches (Borsley, 1996; van Valin, 2001; Carnie, 2002). Given our current state of understanding in biolinguistics, I feel that many of the hotly debated differences among syntacticians are not particularly relevant to questions in the biology and evolution of language. *All* of these models are generative, and incorporate structure-dependent operations as a core of modern syntax, and there are promising signs of convergence of a diverse set of grammatical formalisms to a particular, well-specified level of computational power (termed "mildly context sensitive"; see below). Many of them even focus on quite similar problems (such as unbounded dependencies) but simply use different formalizations to address these problems (e.g. "complex categories" in some systems do the work of "movement" in others). I think many such differences between models are unimportant in understanding the biology of syntax. However, the degree of separation between syntax and semantics remains a central concern.

3.5.4 The autonomy of syntax: formalism and functionalism

Because we currently lack anything like a complete, compelling theory of meaning, "formalist" approaches to syntax strive to separate the rules of syntax from meaning, when possible, while "functionalist" models stress the complex interdigitation of semantics and syntax, and see many syntactic phenomena explicable only in terms of semantic and communicative constraints (cf. Searle, 1969; Newmeyer, 1998a). **Formalist** theories attempt to treat linguistic syntax like the rules of mathematics or computer programming: as symbols with little intrinsic meaning, following explicit rules of combination and permutation. From the formal perspective, a syntactician's goal is to come up with an explict, mechanical algorithm that can generate all of the "well-formed" or "grammatical" sentences of a language and no others (or, given an input, to determine whether or not the sentence is part of this set). **Functionalist** approaches to syntax are heterogeneous, but have in common the recognition that most sentences have some communicative, semantic function, and the belief that scientific understanding of syntactic structure requires explicit attention to this function. The formalist/functionalist distinction defines a continuum, and few theorists occupy its extremes. No formalist denies that sentences have meanings and are often uttered with communicative intent, and no functionalist denies that there are regularities in sentence structure that can be summarized via formal rules.

The formal approach to syntax attempts as far as possible to leave meaning out of the picture. One good reason is practical: the state of the art in dealing with formal syntax at an explicit, mathematical level is well-developed, while our capacity to deal explicitly with questions of meaning remains rudimentary (illustrated by the lack of computer programs that can deal even vaguely intelligently with meaning). But there are other compelling reasons as well. The most prominent is that we are able to make syntactic judgments about grammaticality even when we can't understand the meaning. It is easy to see that a nonsense sentence like *The slar truffed several snarps into the twale* is syntactically well-formed in English, even if we can form no clear semantic picture of its meaning. Chomsky's famous sentence *Colorless green ideas sleep furiously* provides a classic example: even though each of these words is familiar, and the sentence is fully correct syntactically, it defies ordinary semantic interpretation in some obvious ways. The sentence is *syntactically* well-formed but semantically ill-formed. For these reasons, and despite the obvious fact that any complete model of language will have eventually to grapple with meaning and all its complexities, the formalist gambit regarding syntax has appealed to several generations of theoretical linguists.

These sorts of questions are at the heart of models of syntax, and because they are closely tied to questions of encapsulation, they have also been at the heart of biolinguistics. What specific types of (neurally instantiated) computation are required to process the structured sentences of human language? How do humans resolve ambiguity and use context to decide upon particular structural and semantics interpretations? How similar are these computations to those used by other species in processing their own species-specific signals? If there are differences (e.g. between us and chimpanzees), how are these differences instantiated neurally, how do they develop ontogenetically, and how did they evolve phylogenetically? At present, scientific answers to these questions seem far off, and even posing the questions empirically is a challenge. We need a set of terms and concepts that allow us to design experiments that even-handedly test humans against multiple animal species, and to make explicit predictions about the powers, and limitations, of specific computational systems or neural circuits. One such foundation can be found in the theory of computation.

3.5.5 Computability and the theory of computation

As already mentioned, generative linguistics had its beginnings in pure mathematics in the early twentieth century, in the work of such mathematicians as Gödel, Turing, Post, and Church (Davis, 1958). Practical interest in formal generative systems exploded with the dawn of the information era and the construction of digital computers: a solid, practical understanding of generative algorithms became a necessary component of computer science. As a result, the theory of computation was developed, clarified, and standardized, and one result – **formal language theory** – is now part of the standard computer science curriculum and theoretical computer science (Howie, 1991; Gersting, 1999; Hopcroft *et al.*, 2000; Nowak *et al.*, 2002; Parkes, 2002; O'Donnell *et al.*, 2005).

The theory of computation provides a road map through the infinite world of problems, classifying problem-solving algorithms by association with the abstract machines that are capable of implementing them. The most famous and powerful example of such an abstract machine is called a **Turing machine**, after the groundbreaking mathematician, and founding father of computer science, Alan Turing. Turing imagined a simple machine capable of implementing any computation. This imaginary machine consisted simply of a read/write head that could perceive, place, or erase symbols on an endless tape, and a finite "program" consisting of rules about when to move the tape and what to write. Such a Turing machine can be completely specified by its finite program and some initial state of the tape. We can further simplify this machine by stipulating that the symbols or marks may be of only two types: a 1 or a 0. Turing's remarkable claim is that *any algorithmic computation imaginable can be implemented on a Turing machine*. Because the notion of "imaginable" can hardly be cashed out formally or mathematically, this is a *thesis*, not a mathematical theorem subject to proof. What *has* been shown mathematically is that many superficially distinct computational systems are "Turing equivalent," in the sense that they can do what a Turing machine can do, and no more (cf. Davis, 1958). Computer scientists today accept the Turing machine model as synonymous with the outer limits of well-defined symbolic computations (for gentle introductions see Hofstadter, 1979; Berlinski, 2001).

We may also ask if there are other more restricted types of computations within this broad set. My laptop can do things that my pocket calculator can't, which in turn surpasses my digital watch's capabilities. More broadly, there are likely to be computations that a rat's brain can perform that the nerve net of a jellyfish cannot, and there are presumably at least some computations involved in human language that aren't available to the rat or jellyfish – otherwise the properly trained rat could learn human language. Pinpointing such limitations requires more specific computational landmarks: a broad classificatory system based on well-defined formal principles.

Formal language theory

For a brief period in the 1960s, foundational issues in linguistics were also discussed in this context, and linguists such as Chomsky played an important role in defining one standard classification of computational systems (Chomsky, 1956, 1957, 1975b) (thus often called the Chomsky hierarchy). This hierarchy also provided a foundation for some early psycholinguistics work (a brief and irreverent account is Miller, 1967). However, after some initial contributions (cf. Chomsky and Miller, 1963), Chomsky and many other theoretical linguists lost interest in this approach when it became apparent that the remaining open questions addressable within this formal framework had little relevance to the details of natural language and its implementation in human brains (Chomsky, 1990). The core difficulty is related to the structure-dependence of syntax discussed above: traditional formal language theory concerns sets of strings but *not* their structures.

Today, a student of computer science is far more likely than a linguist to be well versed in formal language theory. Nonetheless, this approach remains of considerable interest in formulating computational questions about how the human brain implements language, and for comparing human capabilities with those of other species (e.g. Hailman and Ficken, 1987; Fitch and Hauser, 2004; Gentner *et al.*, 2006), and I will discuss these findings in Chapter 4. The utility of the Chomsky hierarchy is that it provides a formally defined, widely accepted, and well-understood classification for computational systems less powerful than Turing machines (including, presumably, actual brains). It provides a road map including all possible symbolic computational systems (Nowak *et al.*, 2002).

The classification system developed in formal language theory provides a starting point for a more detailed exploration of the capabilities and limitations of rule-governed systems – including brains – that can generate and recognize discrete strings. I discuss them less because of their prominence in contemporary linguistics than because it seems likely that our attempts to "reverse engineer" brains of different species (Dennett, 1996) will be aided by some well-defined classification system along these lines. The human brain is presumably a mix of simple "quick and dirty" solutions, custom-designed for specific problems (e.g. color or movement detection in vision), and more general problem-solving systems. Since any such system will be limited in certain specific ways, it should prove useful to have a formal characterization of the computational subsystem under study. Although formal language theory had its origins in attempts to understand minds/brains computationally (e.g. Kleene, 1956), ultimately a mature field of computational neuroscience will devise its own road map of neural complexity. Such a system will eventually replace the stylized "machines" considered in formal language theory with real neural circuits. But the same sorts of considerations (e.g. understanding how the addition of certain specific forms of memory influences the power of the system) will almost certainly play an important role in constructing any such hierarchy. Some progress has been made in this direction via analysis of neural networks (Síma and Orponen, 2003), but this turns out to be as abstract as, and even coarser in grain than, the Chomsky hierarchy. Even a rather simple analog network, like a multi-layer feedforward perceptron, may be Turing equivalent (Siegelmann and Sontag, 1991), and the real problem is how to access this power via programming or "self-programmed" learning. Similarly, Bayesian models, information theory, or the branch of complexity theory based on Kolmogorov complexity and minimum description length may provide a promising complementary approach to these problems (e.g. MacKay, 2003). The main difficulty with such approaches is that, at the computational ("automaton") level, they are *too* powerful: they can do virtually anything. We need more fine-grained analyses of simple, less powerful systems if we are to understand the limitations of real brains.

For now, the hierarchy of formal language theory provides a finer-grained road map than these alternatives. It is well understood and provides a sensible starting point for classifying the computational power of different species in a way relevant to human language. An excellent example of the value of formal language theory as a foundation for empirical progress is provided by recent developments surrounding natural language. Chomsky's formal treatment of natural language proceeded by demonstrating that natural languages cannot be captured with finite-state systems, and went on to argue that context-free systems (see Box 3.1) are not adequate either (Chomsky, 1957). While there is no doubt on this first count, the latter issue was debated for many years (Pullum and Gazdar, 1982), before particular syntactic phenomena in Dutch, Swiss-German, and Bambara were clearly demonstrated to be beyond context-free grammars (Huybregts, 1985; Shieber, 1985). Since then, multiple independent groups of computational linguists seeking formal grammars of the appropriate power for human language have converged upon a class of formal languages slightly more powerful than context-free, termed **mildy context-sensitive**, or MCS, grammars (Joshi *et al.*, 1991). These systems include categorial grammar (Steedman, 1996), tree-adjoining grammar (Joshi, 2002), and minimalism (cf. Stabler, 2004). MCS systems encompass all known phenomena in natural language (Shieber, 1985), and provide at present the best-defined "target" for the formal complexity of the human language capacity available. We know that human brain evolution eventually arrived at this point: the question now is where do other species' abilities fit into this system? We shall return to this question in Chapter 4.

3.5.6 Formal language theory and music

A number of fascinating parallels exist between language and music (Fitch, 2006b). Both are systems found in all human cultures, and appear to have a biological basis. Both make infinite use of finite means, generating complex signals according to certain rules and obeying certain constraints. For example, melodies in all musical cultures are drawn from a relatively restricted set of notes (a **scale**), typically of five or seven possible frequency values and their integer multiples (Arom, 2000; Nettl, 2000), combined into sequences with particular statistical properties (Krumhansl, 1991), and they possess

Box 3.1. Formal language theory

Terminology: The term **formal** itself can be defined in terms of a set of desiderata: a formalized system should include algorithmically (mechanically) specifiable notions delineating representations, rules, and the links between them. Examples of fully formalized systems include the rules of logic, or computer programming languages like C or Java. No natural language has yet been fully formalized in this sense. Formal language theory makes use of the everyday terms "alphabet," "sentence," "grammar," and "language" in unusual ways: a **grammar** is a finite system of rules that can generate a (potentially infinite) set of sentences. **Sentences** are strings made up of symbols contained in a finite set called an **alphabet**. The set of sentences generated by such a grammar is termed a **language**. Typically, languages are constrained: if we imagine all of the possible combinations of the symbols (e.g. all possible word combinations) as one set, a grammar will typically generate only some subset of these possible sentences, which are thus said to be part of the language generated by the grammar. A language is said to be **infinite** if it contains an infinite number of sentences. *Each of the sentences of an infinite language is of finite length.* If the notion of an infinite language where sentences are finite in length seems intuitively odd (or even impossible), note that it is exactly parallel to the integers: the set of integers itself is obviously infinite, but each integer can be denoted by a finite string of symbols, and the whole series can be generated by the single rule "add one to the last one."

Automata: A core result in mathematical linguistics and computer science was the discovery of a one-to-one correspondence between grammars and automata, or "machines," which are specifications of devices that could implement or instantiate the rules of the grammar. "Machine" in this computer science sense has an abstract meaning: it is a theoretical specification of a certain type of device which is defined to have certain capabilities. Thus, a machine can be designed to **recognize** a particular formal language, or to **generate** it (that is, produce all and only the strings of that language). Such machines are useful abstractions for building intuitions and obtaining mathematical proofs, not to be confused with actual computers or the Intel chip in your laptop.

Taking the outer limits of "the computable" as Turing machines, we can start building our road map of computational abilities by considering simpler, less powerful systems. One class of systems powerful enough to be useful, and interesting, but which is nonetheless limited, includes the

finite state automatons (FSAs) and corresponding **finite state grammars** (FSGs). An FSA can be fully specified as a finite set of **states** (including a privileged start and end state) and a set of **transitions** between them, which depend solely upon the current **input**. When changing state, the machine can optionally emit some **output** symbol. Finite state systems have no equivalent of the endless tape in a Turing machine: they lack an extendable memory of past inputs and outputs. A finite state machine "lives in the moment." Because it can output strings of symbols, a finite state system is capable of producing **sentences** in the sense of finite "well-formed" strings of symbols. Finite state systems can also **accept** input strings if, given some particular input sequence, they can end up in a designated "end" state. The set of all the possible strings generated or accepted by any particular example of such a system is called a **finite state language**. Although the system itself is finite, the language it defines need not be: if there are loops, a finite state system can produce an infinite number of well-formed strings. Although this repetitive route to infinity is of a rather boring sort, it is nonetheless infinite, and this makes finite state systems interesting mathematically. Finite state systems were developed and explored in considerable detail in the mid twentieth century (e.g. Kleene, 1956), and are useful models for many practical devices or psychological capacities (Rogers and Pullum, 2009). Nonetheless, certain classes of strings are beyond their reach: and these include many of the sentences typical in natural language.

Consider the notion of a conversational aside: *John got fired* might be rephrased as *John, who works downstairs, got fired* or *John, who works (or I should say used to work) downstairs, got fired*. Each of these sentences conveys the same basic message, but the later ones include an "embedded" specification or clarification. Formally, forgetting about their meaning, sentence structures of this form can be captured by strings of embedded parentheses: (), (()), and ((())). Intuitively, we know that a string of parentheses with a form like (() or)() is incomplete or ill-formed, and that with time and patience, and paper and pencil, we could extend such "grammaticality" judgments to any number of parentheses. Our ability to do this with very long strings is limited only by extraneous factors like how long we can stay awake. Perhaps surprisingly, no FSA can be programmed to duplicate this feat. In formal terms, we say that the language of "balanced" parentheses (a "Dyck language") cannot be recognized by any possible FSA. The reason is that the only way an FSA can keep track of the past parentheses is via the current state it is in, and since (by definition) its states are limited, we can easily "break" any FSA by feeding it any finite, well-formed parenthetical expression that has more opening parentheses than our FSA has states. Another simple language that no FSA can recognize is the language composed of equal-length runs of two different symbols {ab, aabb, aaabbb, ... }. This language (which can be abbreviated a^nb^n) can also be shown to be beyond the capability of any FSA. (Note that a finite state language denoted a^*b^*, where $*$ means "repeat as often as you like," includes every string in a^nb^n, but includes a lot more besides, and thus won't do the job.) Given that we can specify these two languages algorithmically, they must be recognizable by a Turing machine. Thus we have discovered a class of languages that are computable, but are beyond the capability of any FSA.

Balanced parentheses, or the a^nb^n language, require (at least) a **context-free grammar** which has computational power beyond that of an FSA. Realistic examples in language abound. For example, in English *if/then* constructions, the word *if* must be followed by *then*, but there is no fixed limit to the number of words in between. This is beyond an FSA. The corresponding automaton that *can* handle such phenomena is called a **pushdown automaton**, or PDA, which supplements the finite states available to an FSA with an additional type of extendable memory. In the PDA, this additional memory is provided by an unbounded "stack" upon which items can be stored. This simple form of additional memory can store unlimited items but can only access them in first-in, last-out order (picture a stack of trays in a cafeteria). This is all that we need to deal with the languages above. Indeed, a pushdown automaton can be built to recognize or generate any context-free language (and any finite state language, as well). However, there are readily specifiable languages that are beyond this type of automaton as well: for example, the language $a^nb^nc^n$ can be recognized by a Turing machine, but not by a pushdown automaton. Thus we now have three systems: FSAs, PDAs, and Turing machines – each of which is made more powerful than its predecessor by adding some auxiliary form of memory to that available in an FSA. By adding one additional class (context-sensitive grammars, corresponding to a linear pushdown automaton) we reach the level of specificity outlined in the traditional Chomsky hierarchy (see Figure 3.1). Such reasoning can be continued as far as desired, to create an ever-more specific hierarchy: within each of the classifications discussed, scientists have isolated more specific types of grammars (Sipser, 1997). An excellent, non-technical introduction to formal language theory is Parkes (2002); more advanced texts are Sipser (1997) and Hopcroft *et al.* (2000).

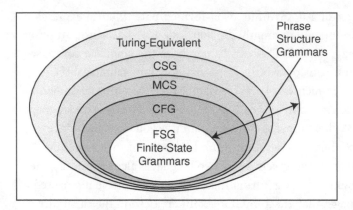

Figure 3.1 The formal language hierarchy, or "Extended Chomsky Hierarchy" – Formal language theory provides a framework for evaluating the complexity of different "grammars" or sets of generative rules. CFG: Context-Free Grammars; MCS: Mildly Context-Sensitive Grammars; CSG: Context-Sensitive Grammars; Turing Equivalent: Unrestricted Grammars that can include any possible computation. "Phrase Structure Grammars" denotes that set of grammars beyond the Finite-state level.

phrase structure that allows even untrained listeners to intuit that the end of a melodic phrase is approaching, or has been reached (for reviews see Seashore, 1967; Sloboda, 1985). Voice pitch is also frequently used as a phonetic cue in "tone languages" like Chinese or Thai, which comprise more than half of all languages, and again the frequency continuum is subdivided into a small set (between two and six) of categories (Crystal, 2002). These similarities are essentially between music and phonology (rather than syntax or semantics). As in phonology, musical signals are not typically used to encode complex propositional information, and the "meaning" of musical signals tends to be more affective than semantic. Thus, there are numerous interesting parallels between phonology and music worthy of detailed exploration. While the term "musical syntax" is in wide use, from a formal point of view the hierarchical structuring of music might better be termed "musical phonology," because music lacks the propositional meaning often connoted by the term "syntax" outside of formal linguistics.

The formal characterizations of musical "syntax"

At a formal level, there are direct correspondences between the alphabets, sentences, and grammars of formal language theory and musical scales, phrases, and styles. An obvious structural parallel between language and music is that both use a finite set of units to create an unlimited variety of structures (the set of permissible musical notes is an "alphabet" in the sense of formal language theory). A basic structural characteristic of musical performances is **repetition**. A "song" or a "piece" can be repeated, and such repetition is quite typical of human musical practice. Indeed, we have a much higher tolerance for repetition in music than in language. In music, repetition often occurs within a piece, and a chunk of music that is so repeated is called a **phrase**. Such phrases can be arranged hierarchically, so that short phrases built of a small number of notes can be combined into larger phrases, and these can in turn be combined into larger phrases (the themes, movements, etc. of classical music). Finally, musical phrases can be related to one another in specific ways, so that a musical style or form is characterized by higher-order structures of repetition formally similar to the rhyme schemes of poetry. Thus, musical styles can be characterized quite accurately by formal grammars at the context-free level (for discussion and examples see Balzano, 1980; Lerdahl and Jackendoff, 1983; Pressing, 1983; Sloboda, 1985; Cope, 1996; Temperley, 2001).

In spite of these striking similarities, the attitude of contemporary linguists towards music and musicology appears quite variable, and links between the two disciplines are by no means well developed. Although many authors have recognized the fact that both music and language are generative systems (Sundberg and Lindblom, 1976; Longuet-Higgins, 1978; Bernstein, 1981; Lerdahl and Jackendoff, 1983), far fewer have attempted detailed comparisons of the rules underlying music and language (Lerdahl and Jackendoff, 1983; Sloboda, 1985). In general, the two fields have gone their separate ways, pursuing different questions using different techniques. However, a recent surge of interest in the biology of music, both in terms of neuroscience (e.g. Zatorre and Peretz, 2001; Avanzini *et al.*, 2003; Patel, 2003; Peretz and Zatorre, 2003; Koelsch *et al.*, 2004; Koelsch and Siebel, 2005) and evolution (e.g. Wallin *et al.*, 2000; Fitch, 2005c; McDermott and Hauser, 2005), suggests that the time for a unification, for a biological approach that combines music and language, is ripe. Finally, there is recent progress in identifying the genetic bases for musical abilities that may end up shedding light on phonology as well (Drayna *et al.*, 2001; Peretz *et al.*, 2002). Such discoveries may provide important insights into the biology and evolution of language, discussed in Chapter 14.

3.5.7 Syntax summary: what needed to evolve

To summarize: a number of capabilities are required for a computational system to handle syntax in human language. First, and most important, the system must allow for the unbounded generation of hierarchical structures (**discrete infinity**). This capacity is necessary to express an unlimited number of thoughts. We have seen that from a mathematical viewpoint there is nothing magical about such a capacity: many finite systems have a capacity for discrete infinity (the ability to count via the repeated application of addition is a very simple one). But human syntax does more than count: it **combines** structures in a **structure-dependent** manner, and it allows recursive **self-embedding** of these structures. But building such structures is still not enough: they also need to be linked to signals (the phonological interface) and to concepts (the semantic interface). At the phonological level, this entails a **serialization** of complex tree structures, and it seems likely that this requirement places rather specific constraints on the nature of syntactic structures. What is most remarkable about language is that after this serialization, a listener can take the output signal and "rebuild" the syntactic, and then semantic, structures intended by the speaker. This "de-serializing" or unpacking process (called "parsing" for syntax) is remarkably effective, given that it is mathematically intractable, because a very large number of "unpackings" are theoretically possible. Nonetheless, we do normally manage to understand others and to make ourselves understood. Successful parsing therefore must involve **constraints** of various sorts, and probably a mixture of conceptual and linguistic constraints is used in normal conversation. This observation leads us to the remaining traditional branches of linguistics: semantics and pragmatics.

3.6 An appetizer: four hypotheses about the evolution of syntax

Unsurprisingly, given the many theories of syntax touched upon above, there are many notions about how syntax might have evolved. To offer some sustenance for the reader tiring of formal linguistics and hungry for evolution, here are four models that suggest the range of opinion. One line of argument, simply put, is that syntax *per se* did not evolve at all. That is, there is *no* biological adaptation for syntax itself, and the syntactic complexity of modern language is actually a culturally derived byproduct of other human adaptations (for semantic compositionality and social sharing of information). This "cultural origins" viewpoint has been advanced by Michael Tomasello (e.g. Tomasello, 1999). Far from reflecting innate dispositions or constraints, Tomasello argues that the syntactic features of human language develop by a purely cultural process of grammaticalization, under the constraints of communication. We can thus characterize Tomasello's stance on syntax as purely glossogenetic, with no remaining phylogenetic component. Similarly, Philip Lieberman has argued that syntax derives from speech motor control, and results from key changes in the basal ganglia driven by speech evolution (Lieberman, 2000). For Lieberman, speech control evolved, and is an adaptation, but syntax is an unmodified spandrel. Both authors strongly reject the very notion of a biologically based "Universal Grammar," but they seek its replacement in very different places (speech *versus* culture).

At the opposite extreme, other theorists argue for a very rich and complex set of adaptations specific to syntax. By this argument, Universal Grammar is a highly complex adaptation, the result of natural selection for increased communicative efficiency in language, and each of the individual components can be seen as part of this complex adaptation. This viewpoint has been defended clearly by Ray Jackendoff (Jackendoff, 1999, 2002) and Steven Pinker (Pinker and Bloom, 1990; Pinker and Jackendoff, 2005). Some arguments against this viewpoint are provided in the commentaries to Pinker and Bloom (1990) and by Tomasello (1995). Many other theorists find themselves somewhere between these extremes, arguing that there is *something* special about syntax, without accepting the elaborate innate UG of Pinker and Jackendoff, full of specific adaptations and syntactic rules. For instance, many scholars (Bickerton, 1998, 2000; Seyfarth and Cheney, 2005) have argued for an origin for complex syntax in social knowledge and understanding (citing data similar to those emphasized by Tomasello), but do not deny that this initial exaptation has been subjected to independent selection in the human lineage and thus constitutes a *bona fide* syntactic adaptation for language. Similarly, Givón (1995) seeks the origin of syntax in visual processing, but after this exaptive event postulates further natural selection. All of these hypotheses see syntax as a core capability which had to evolve in order to allow modern human language, and all constitute accounts of the evolution of syntax *per se*.

Although the "complex, adaptive UG" model is often associated with Noam Chomsky, we have already seen that since the early 1990s Chomsky's work on syntax has moved away from a notion of UG that includes a wide variety of different syntactic rules, classes, and constraints (Chomsky, 1995). Research within this more recent "Minimalist Program" takes as a disciplinary goal a description of syntax that has as few operators and stipulated constraints as possible. Minimalism implements Occam's razor as a research strategy in syntax: assume the system under study is as simple as possible until proven otherwise. We already know that phonology and semantics are complex, and that their complexities pervade language. To what degree is syntax itself encapsulated, but simple, with the apparent complexity "inherited" from these other domains? To the extent that this strategy is ultimately successful, it will have important biological implications: we should expect to find few specific mechanisms (neural subsystems or genetic regulatory mechanisms) that are "for" syntax specifically. This implication is of considerable interest for biolinguists, and for theories of the evolution of syntax (cf. Berwick, 1998). A specific evolutionary hypothesis along these lines has been offered by Hauser *et al.* (2002), who suggest that the evolved basis for syntax may be quite simple, perhaps limited to a single operation that can operate recursively (thus giving rise to unlimited structures). Most of the complexities of syntax then derive from the need for interfaces which bind syntactic structures to conceptual structures and phonological signals. A similar model, which finds precursors of syntax in social cognition, has been developed by Seyfarth *et al.* (2005; Cheney and Seyfarth, 2007); syntactic precursors from vision are discussed in Givón (1995) and from motor control by Lashley (1951). This evolutionary perspective has no particular ties to minimalism: similar goals are implicit in other research programs such as categorial grammar or tree-adjoining grammar, which also posit only a few, very powerful, syntactic operations. For example, adjoinment in tree-adjoining grammars, like Merge in minimalism (Berwick, 1998), provides a simple route to the recursive self-embedding typical of syntactic phrases (Joshi *et al.*, 1991; Abeillé and Rambow, 2000; Stabler, 2004).

Circumscribed models of syntax offer considerable hope for our ability to unravel its evolution. If many of the apparent complexities in linguistic syntax result not from the underlying complexity of an innate syntax module, but rather derive from much older mechanisms making up the subsystems for conceptual representation and signal generation/interpretation, much of this complexity was already present before human language evolution began. Because these are shared components of FLB, based largely on more ancient cognitive needs that predate language, their complexity may reflect ancient adaptations, or historical constraints having nothing to do with modern language. If this is true, it would be excellent news from a biologist's perspective. The evolution of one or a few pervasive and powerful operators in the short 500,000-year period of human evolution from *H. erectus* to modern humans will be more easily understood than that of a large suite of complex, interlocking, and evolutionarily novel mechanisms required by "complex UG" models. We shall revisit this idea in several places. For now, these hypotheses about syntax provide a taste of the issues under debate in language evolution more generally.

3.7 Semantics

3.7.1 The study of meaning in language

Semantics, broadly speaking, is the study of meaning in language. Words and phrases mean things: we typically express quite specific meanings with our linguistic signals. Behind this simple and obvious statement lie some of the deepest problems in the biology and evolution of language. What does it really mean for some signal "to mean" something? How are these apparent links between signals and meanings codified in languages, and acquired by children as they learn language? Why don't animal signals possess the combination of flexibility and specificity of meaning so typical of language? If phonetics is where linguistics makes contact with physics, and syntax is where linguistics meets mathematics and computer science, semantics is the branch of language study that consistently rubs shoulders with philosophy. This is because the study of meaning raises a host of deep problems that are the traditional stomping grounds for philosophers.

Utterances don't always mean anything, of course (think of nonsense rhymes or scat singing). One can also arrange real words into sentences which follow the syntactic rules of language, but which are still propositionally non-meaningful (as in *Colorless green ideas sleep furiously*). With such exceptions aside, the linguistic signals that we generate, and the syntactic arrangements into which we put them, are meaningful, and this is ordinarily why we generate them in the first place. Language without meaning would be like nonsense rhymes: complex and perhaps interesting, but not *really* language. Meaning is the *sine qua non* of language. It may be surprising, then, that scientists currently lack a complete theory of meaning, and that semantics remains a kind of "Wild West" of linguistic theory. Even more than syntax, semantics is full of rival approaches, and continued disagreement prevails, even about the basic question of what meaning is, or how it is to be defined. That such questions have remained in the domain of philosophy since the time of Aristotle is a testament to their difficulty: meaning can still be seen as the most important unsolved problem in the cognitive sciences.

Nonetheless, the study of linguistic meaning has a rich and complex history. Traditionally, the study of meaning is divided into two components – semantics and pragmatics – but the lines between the two are vaguely drawn (Stalnaker, 1972). Roughly speaking, the traditional remit of **semantics** is to describe what words and sentences mean, in and of themselves, while **pragmatics** is supposed to concern the meanings that speakers intended, or listeners infer, based on the current context and conversational needs. In formal semantics, which is the best-established component of this field, "the central problems in semantics have concerned the definition of truth, or truth conditions, for the sentences of certain languages" (p. 381, Stalnaker, 1972). From this perspective, semanticists study the conditions under which certain propositions expressed in natural language either are, or are not, true. **Propositions** are the abstract objects thought to provide the middle term in a link between "the world" and a truth value. Crucially, however, we often talk about things that aren't true now. Semanticists therefore think of propositions as functions that map *possible* worlds onto truth values: the sentence *It is raining outside* maps all the worlds in which rain falls outside the dwelling of the speaker/writer to "TRUE" and all the other worlds to "FALSE." Propositions must encompass possible worlds (in addition to the actual world) for the simple reason that we often want to talk about what "might" happen, or what "could have" happened, and thus discuss some possible world rather than the real one that exists. And if that sounds complicated, it is because meaning *is* complicated.

Recognizing the rampant complexity and ambiguity of natural language, a major thrust of **formal semantics** has been the creation of artificial model languages, formal systems such as predicate calculus that express propositions in some unambiguous manner approaching that of mathematical formulae. Building on traditional logic, mathematicians and philosophers have developed a rather arcane system to write down propositions explicitly (along the lines of *Principia Mathematica*; Russell and Whitehead, 1910). As a result, formal semantics is a quite complex and sophisticated field (e.g. Montague, 1974a) employing a technical apparatus that is formidably obscure to the uninitiated (the most accessible introduction I know is Portner (2005)). But such formal languages are just middlemen for the core abstract notion of proposition, which is supposed to describe thought itself, and thus to be independent of any language. "Semantics, then . . . has no essential connection with languages at all, either natural or artificial" (p. 382, Stalnaker, 1972). Semanticists study the bridge between the world of thought, of concepts and ideas, with the phonological and syntactic structures of language.

3.7.2 Formal semantics and propositional meaning

Formal semantics provides a well-established formal framework within which to formulate and solve various semantic problems (Montague,

1974b), and is thus a necessary component of the training of any semanticist (for a gentle introduction see Guttenplan, 1986). Although I will say little more about this framework here, it has an important virtue from a biological perspective: formal semantics allows us to clarify the notion of **propositional meaning**. A central distinction between language and other human communication systems (such as facial expression or music) is the ability of sentences to express propositions that have truth values. This is precisely what is formalized in formal semantics. In contrast, the far broader notion of "meaning" that applies to thought in general (e.g. including non-linguistic visual or musical cognition) has thus far resisted attempts at formalization. Thus, the apparatus of formal semantics allows us to define *linguistic* meaning more precisely. If you can't apply the referential variables of first-order logic, or the quantifiers of predicate logic, to a statement in some given "language," then it lacks the *propositional* meaning characteristic of human language.

Let us apply this test to music, which is sometimes termed a "universal language," a "language of the emotions," and so on. Music certainly possesses a "phonology" (the set of notes and rhythmic values considered permissible in any particular musical style) and a form of syntax (a set of rules for combining these into larger, hierarchical structures of essentially unbounded complexity). It is based on the same auditory channel as speech, and richly expresses emotions and moods (Juslin and Sloboda, 2001), as well as compellingly beautiful abstract relationships (Rothstein, 2006). Nonetheless, music is not "language" in the sense I will use it henceforth, because music cannot express propositional meanings. In particular, musical phrases or "statements" lack a propositional truth value: a set of possible words in reference to which it is true. A musical phrase may be sad, or beautiful, but it simply makes no sense to ask if it is true. One might correctly assert, in rebuttal, that the types of truths that music describes or expresses are abstract and relational (Rothstein, 2006), rather than referential and propositional. This may be true (at least for some composers, and some listeners), but at the simple practical level of making statements or asking questions about the world, language succeeds because of its capacities for reference, for predication, and for making nested statements with quantifiers (like *all* or *every* or *always*) that have scope to restrict or extend that whole statement. Thus the formal apparatus of contemporary semantics provides an acid test for meaning, in a core sense that neither music nor animal communication systems posesses it, but language does. Propositional meaning is another distinctive design feature of language: a central component of semantics that had to evolve for language in its modern sense to exist.

3.7.3 Mentalist semantics and the semiotic triangle

A long-running controversy in semantics asks whether sentences denote possible situations *directly*, the so-called "realist" view, or only indirectly (via the intervening action of a human mind: the "cognitive" view). This debate considerably predates the cognitive revolution, and I believe the combined data of modern cognitive science and animal cognition research leave only the latter option open: an adequate notion of meaning must be a cognitive one. That is, concepts occupy an irreducible intervening role between language and external meaning in the real world (Saussure, 1916; Bickerton, 1990; Jackendoff, 2002). Although this conclusion remains controversial among philosophers, it is now widely accepted among linguists and psychologists, so I will not belabor this point here (for detailed expositions see Jackendoff, 2002; Hurford, 2007). Briefly, contemporary formal semanticists often discuss proposition ↔ world mappings as if they are direct. From this viewpoint, propositional meanings are "out there" in the world, rather than depending on any individual mind that creates, or perceives, such links. This approach, perhaps for reasons of conceptual clarity and convenience, represents the model of meaning that dominates contemporary formal semantics, and much of philosophy, today.

Despite several virtues, truth-conditional semantics is inadequate as a complete cognitive model of meaning. Although understanding how *dog* can be inserted into a frame like *my dog is brown* or *all dogs are mammals* is useful, without an explicit model of how language users are able to identify dogs in the first place it is incomplete. This is sometimes called the **symbol grounding problem** (Harnad, 1990; Steels, 2002). Another major problem for this (or any "real-world" model of semantics) is created by imaginary referents. If I say *the unicorn in my dream last night was purple* or *Sherlock Holmes is an Englishman*, there is no obvious situation in the real world, or even *possible* real worlds, that could satisfy the truth conditions for this sentence. Cognitive models neatly solve such problems by hypothesizing that, first and foremost, "meanings are concepts." Cognitive models represent an ancient and intuitive model of meaning, dating back to the Stoics and Plato (Seuren, 1998). In cognitive models, understanding the word *dog* or *chien* involves generating a concept: a mental model or picture of a particular type of medium-size carnivorous mammal. Thus, concepts

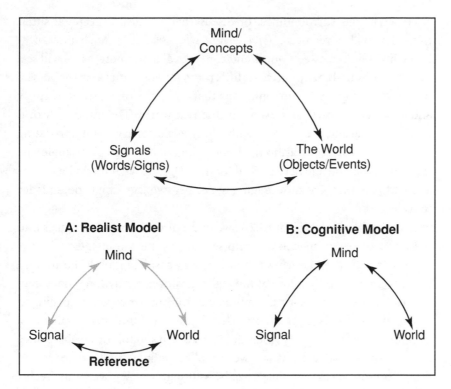

Figure 3.2 The semiotic triangle – Three possible components of reference are shown in the classic "semiotic triangle" of Ogden and Richards, in the top panel. At the bottom, two leading models of reference are diagrammed: Realist models of reference (A) focus on "direct" word <-> thing links, while Cognitive models (B) stress that words link to things in the world only via the intermediate step of mental concepts. See text for detalis.

exist prelinguistically: we can have concepts before we know words for them. By such a model, words and sentences denote concepts first (solving the "Sherlock Holmes" problem). These concepts then provide the foundation, in many cases, for real-world identification of the referents (using "ordinary" cognitive and perceptual processes that predated language biologically and are similar to those used, for instance, by a *dog* when it recognizes a dog). This crucial component of the symbol-grounding problem was solved long ago, by the evolution of vertebrate perceptual and cognitive systems.

These different conceptions of meaning can be nicely schematized by the famous "semiotic triangle" of Ogden and Richards (1923). Figure 3.2B shows the cognitive model we have just discussed, where only indirect word/meaning links, via the mind, exist. Each of these two separate links clearly exist. We often move directly between signals and concepts without reference to our surroundings, or discuss hypothetical conceptual situations that will never occur (*if I were a stickleback...*). Such utterances build direct links between words and concepts. Furthermore, as we will see, research in animal cognition leaves little room for doubt that animals possess non-linguistic mental representations that allow the organism to identify and cope with objects and events in the real world. The mind ↔ world link is a strong and ancient one, with a long evolutionary history predating language. In sharp contrast to the bottom link of the semiotic triangle, the top two legs are on a firm empirical footing. Despite what might be seen as a lack of parsimony, acknowledging the upper two legs simply does justice to reality.

In the realist model (Figure 3.2A) we find a direct arrow from signals into the world (or more specifically, into sets of possible worlds). Cognitivists argue, correctly I think, that we should be very suspicious of the bottom leg of the triangle, and therefore of the realist position, as anything more than a convenient shorthand for the more circuitous upper route. According to Ogden and Richards (p. 14), the model of 3.2A is a "fundamental fallacy"; a primitive "superstition." Portner (2005) argues in support of a realist stance for essentially practical reasons: we can observe links between words and things, but not ideas in people's heads. Although we may accept the realist model as a convenient shorthand for working semanticists, there are strong arguments against it as a biologically or cognitively meaningful model of linguistic meaning. For a detailed critique and argument, with answers to the standard philosophical objections, see Seuren (1998), Jackendoff (2002), and Hurford (2007).

Nonetheless, the model in Figure 3.2A is both intuitive and still defended by some contemporary philosophers. Why? A biological view of language provides a plausible developmental explanation for why the realist view is intuitively appealing. Consider the plight of the child exposed to words and phrases at whose meaning he must guess. While an adult may wonder what this *person* means, the young child acquiring language does not enjoy this luxury. Lacking *any* notion of the possible meanings, the child must simply guess "the" meaning, based on whatever context is available. Given the complexity of this process, the young child is far better off assuming that words point to meanings in the world *directly* rather than worrying about what the speaker means. By this argument, a simple (innate?) assumption that **words have meanings** is a heuristic device, a handy shortcut that helps the language user converge on the semantics of their local language(s). This process will have already proceeded quite far before the child even begins conceiving of pragmatic differences in word usage, or to comprehend the dual conceptual linkage that underlies the apparent direct link between words and meanings. This very propensity, the built-in assumption that "words mean things," is perhaps the most basic biological prerequisite of the semantic component of human language. It is this assumption, I suggest, that leads humans to attribute magical powers to names and words, and it is this same intuition that underlies the realist stance towards linguistic meaning. This stance seems indeed to be present in humans at or near birth, and perhaps necessarily so. The evolution of this referential assumption is one of our core *explananda* in a theory of the evolution of language.

3.7.4 Child language acquisition: the acquisition of word meanings

I will now briefly step aside from theoretical issues to sample another important branch of language study: child language research. Like work on animal communication, the literature on child language acquisition provides rich fodder for scientists interested in innate aspects of meaning (Brown, 1973; Bloom, 2000; Gleason, 2005; Peccei, 2006). In particular, studies of children's acquisition of word meanings provide strong arguments for innate constraints on human conceptual abilities. Perhaps surprisingly, there appears to be little disagreement as to *whether* some pre-existing constraints on word meaning exist (e.g. Clark, 1987; Markman, 1990; Gleason, 2005). Both theoretical arguments and abundant empirical data make the acceptance of constraints on word meaning seem almost inevitable, although the precise nature and number of constraints remains a topic of productive debate. A readable and incisive introduction to this literature is Bloom (2000). Furthermore, comparative work on *animal* word learning allows investigation of the similarities and differences between humans and animals in this domain.

Word meanings must be learned. The connection between their acoustic morphology and their reference is, with few exceptions, highly arbitrary. A child encountering a word for the first time thus has the dual task of memorizing its structure *and* guessing its referential significance. The latter task, despite the apparent ease with which children carry it out, is anything but trivial, and has generated a huge literature on child language acquisition. The theoretical problem was cast in sharp relief by Quine (1960), with his famous "Gavagai" parable. Imagine you are an anthropologist newly arrived among a group of monolingual hunter–gatherers, and in the course of the day's wanderings a rabbit hops by and the natives exclaim *Gavagai!* The normal referential interpretation of this utterance would be something like RABBIT, and we would expect any normal child (or anthropologist) to assume as much. Obviously, however, *Gavagai* could mean 'meat' or 'animal' or 'hopping' or 'long ears' or 'how cute' or 'Haven't seen one of those in a while!' or various other possibilities, and we wouldn't be terribly surprised if one of these alternatives turned out to be the correct meaning, as we master the language. But even these alternatives entail certain assumptions. Quine asked us to consider such assumptions more closely (imagine, if you like, that the anthropologist is from Mars, and has very different conceptual structures from our own). From a logical point of view, there is no reason that *Gavagai* couldn't have far stranger referents, like 'fuzzy + long legs' or 'intersection between rabbits and grass of a certain height' or 'undetached rabbit parts.' Indeed, there is an indefinite number of *logically* possible meanings for a word, uttered in a given context. While hearing the word repeated in various different contexts may help, it will not solve this logical "problem of induction" (Goodman, 1983): our ability to form correct generalizations in the face of an infinity of logically consistent options.

Quine's Gavagai problem is a theoretical problem, the kind it takes a philosopher to discover. But children and anthropologists muddle by perfectly well in spite of it, and a rich empirical literature on "fast mapping" (Carey, 1978; Markson and Bloom, 1997) shows that children can often correctly guess, and remember, the intended meaning of words after a single hearing. The child obviously does not unconsciously process all of Quine's various logical possibilities. Rather, the hypothesis space appears **constrained** in certain ways, and the child simply fails to consider many of these possible meanings. These constraints should develop early and reliably if they are to solve the problem (if constraints were learned based on external input, all the same logical problems would apply). This capacity to successfully extract word meanings from a given context is not limited to humans: animals are also capable of linking meanings to arbitrary sounds in human-like ways (see Chapter 4), suggesting that such constraints have a long evolutionary history.

While this argument has precisely the same form as the poverty of the stimulus argument (Crain, 1991) which has proved so controversial when applied to syntax, this conclusion is not particularly controversial in child language acquisition. Since Macnamara (1972), virtually all contemporary researchers take for granted that Quine's "Gavagai" problem is a real one, and that its solution entails some form of innate constraints on the child's attempts to map words onto meanings. However, students of child language acquisition remain divided over the degree to which such constraints are specific to word learning or to language. For example, Paul Bloom accepts the need for innate constraints but rejects the hypothesis that these constraints are specific to word learning (Bloom, 2000), and supports this suggestion with the fact that similar speed and accuracy are seen in children's non-linguistic concept acquisition (Markson and Bloom, 1997). Research on animals reviewed below supports this argument, suggesting that many of these constraints are older than the human species, and at least some reflect ancient conceptual biases and constraints on what "counts" as an object or event.

3.7.5 Constraints on guesses about word meaning

In reality, children virtually never make most of the errors that Quine highlighted as logical possibilities. Thus, in addition to the basic referential stance that leads the child to attribute meanings to words in the first place, the child's guesses about meanings seem to be constrained in various more detailed ways. Many possible constraints have been considered (concisely reviewed in Golinkoff *et al.*, 1994), and debates in this literature revolve around specific questions about the number and nature of these innate biases and constraints (e.g. Gathercole, 1987; Merriman and Bowman, 1989).

The most basic assumption children appear to make about novel labels is that they refer to whole objects, rather than their parts or qualities. This **whole object** assumption (Carey, 1978) goes a long way to solving the Gavagai problem, because we can safely assume that the child is already equipped with a language-independent visual object-recognition system. Thus, many of the extravagantly non-intuitive hypotheses suggested by Quine (e.g. 'undetached rabbit parts' or 'rabbits till 2001, and camels there-after') can be ruled out immediately by a prelinguistic conceptual system available to the child as a product of evolution of the visual and cognitive systems. The child doesn't induce such wacky concepts, for the same reason that a dog does not conceptualize "rabbit" in these ways, but rather as a medium-sized, fleet-footed potential prey item. This constraint thus may reflect what the child finds salient in the environment (namely whole objects) and conceives of, prelinguistically as a THING.

While the whole object assumption offers a first step to finding the meanings of nouns, it clearly leaves many problems unsolved. First, this assumption helps, in the moment of labeling, to find and conceptualize the referent – but how is this label to be applied in the future, in novel situations? What should the child take as the extension of the label (the set of other objects to which it might apply)? One very salient possibility is that the label refers to a general thematic relationships, categorizing whole situations in which multiple object types co-occur (in the way that the PLAY situation will typically include both children and toys). We know that young children are very attracted to this "thematic" hypothesis in many contexts: given a picture of a cow and asked to "find another one," four-year-olds will choose a picture of milk, rather than a pig, 75 percent of the time (Markman and Hutchinson, 1984), or they will sort a "boy" and "dog" together because the two might be going for a walk. Nonetheless, when given a novel *label*, such children switch strategies. Asked to "find another dax" they now choose the same type of object 65 percent of the time. This applies not only to known objects, like pigs and cows, but also to completely novel objects that the children are experimentally exposed to. Markman and Hutchinson proposed that such findings reflect a **taxonomic assumption** – given a label, children will apply it to other objects of the same type, overriding a prepotent bias to classify things along thematic lines.

A much stronger case can be made that this hypothesized taxonomic assumption reflects specifically linguistic constraints on the child's word learning, given the robust contrast between labeled and unlabeled conditions in these experiments. Even here, however, Markman has noted that this constraint might reflect a general conceptual distinction between whole events or *situations* (predicate/argument structures), to which languages typically refer with phrases or sentences, *versus objects* (arguments), which are the typical referents of words (Markman, 1990). **Syntactic bootstrapping** (the use of the syntactic frame of the sentence, and function words like *a* and *the* to guess word meanings) might suffice to bias the child towards one or the other. Thus it is equally possible that these experimental results reflect a more general conceptual constraint combined with broad syntactic notions of phrase and word (Bloom, 2000).

The whole object assumption allows children to pick out a particular referent in the moment it hears the word, while the taxonomic constraint provides restrictions on how this label/referent pairing will be extended in the future. The combination of the two goes a long way towards solving the Gavagai problem, but it raises another problem: human words don't exclusively refer to whole objects, and languages do generally have words for different levels of taxonomic hierarchies (both superordinate and subordinate levels). A third hypothesized constraint helps children solve this problem, helping them to acquire labels for attributes, qualities, and superordinate and subordinate categories. This constraint is termed **mutual exclusivity** (Markman and Wachtel, 1988) or **the principle of contrast** (Barrett, 1978; Clark, 1987), and entails avoidance of synonyms. Given a set of familiar objects ("cup" and "key") and some novel object, children assign new, nonsense, labels such as *glub* to the novel object: the child implicitly assumes a "new object ↔ new word" mapping. Furthermore, having once made this mapping, children can remember it weeks later (Carey, 1978).

In summary, principles like the whole object assumption and mutual exclusivity provide powerful constraints on children's attempts to guess word meanings, and thus solve the "Gavagai" problem. The value of such assumptions grows increasingly valuable as the child's lexicon grows. It may help explain the **word spurt** – the rapid apparent increase in the rate of word learning which often occurs at 16–19 months (Nelson, 1973; Markman, 1990). Diarists keeping track of a child's vocabulary growth typically find their job easy in the first two years of life, but eventually give up when the child appears to be acquiring words so rapidly that the parent's themselves are surprised by their child's understanding and/or use of new words. Although Bloom casts doubt on the value of reifying this phenomenon (which perhaps reflects a continuous process of accelerating learning, rather than any qualitatively new learning process; Bloom, 2000), there can be no question that children get better and better at learning words, and are able to use such phenomena as syntactic bootstrapping and mutual exclusivity to speed this process. In contrast, no animals learning words experience similar acceleration. However, we will see in Chapter 4 that comparative experiments suggest that some of these constraints are also available to nonhuman animals, suggesting that these are general cognitive constraints rather than language-specific ones.

3.8 Pragmatics

3.8.1 Pragmatics: context is everything

Imagine that Judy enters John's flat and says *I'm leaving*. After a long pause, John replies *Who is he?* In most possible contexts John's response is a *non sequitur*, and the exchange makes no sense. We nonetheless easily make sense of this depauperate string of phonemes, and the context, by filling in a richer context for it that *does* make sense: Judy and John are romantically involved, and John suspects Judy of finding a new lover. Now imagine that Andrew overhears a fistfight between Bill and Carl. Shortly afterwards he continues hearing Bill's taunting voice, but not Carl's. Andrew knows from past experience that he can beat Bill in a fight. So how should he react in the future if challenged by Carl? If Andrew is a bird, he will be more aggressive, and defend his turf more vigorously, after hearing the exchange above (Naguib and Todt, 1997; Paz-y-Miño *et al.*, 2004). Birds can use transitive inference (if A beats B and B beats C, then A beats C) to drive their future behavior. Thus, an ability to "fill in" a story to "make sense" of some sequence of signals is not unique to our species. Finally, imagine that Hermione looks intently towards some fruit. Harry helpfully grasps a fruit, and starts to hand it to her, only to see a displeased look in her eyes. He drops it, and hands her another piece, and they both produce a facial gesture that exposes their teeth. It may be surprising that, if Hermione and Harry are primates, they are almost certainly humans: this sort of cooperative exchange is typical of our species but rare or non-existent in most others.

All of these communicative exchanges are quintessentially social, and they hint at a mosaic of cognitive mechanisms underlying communicative exchanges. In communication, two or more individuals synchronize or "tune" their mental worlds to one another. **Pragmatics** as a discipline has many strands: communication is central to all of them. For humans there are at least three basic aspects of this phenomenon. First, humans are remarkably adept at combining context and world knowledge with short, ambiguous signals, to make inferences about what is going on in their social world. It turns out that such **context-driven inference** is an ability that we share with other species, especially primates. A second ability requires an individual to conceptualize what another individual knows. This capacity, often termed **theory of mind**, is far more complex, but recent data suggest that this, too, may be shared with other species, although in a far less developed form than in humans. Finally, we have a hypertrophied tendency, as producers of signals, to share our inner thoughts and feelings with others (a tendency denoted by the German word ***Mitteilungsbedürfnis***). This is the component of pragmatics that seems most distinctive of our species. While many species share a capacity for context-dependent inference, a number of more advanced cognitive abilities, often lumped together under the term "social intelligence," are characteristic of social birds and mammals, and especially primates. The most elaborate pragmatic

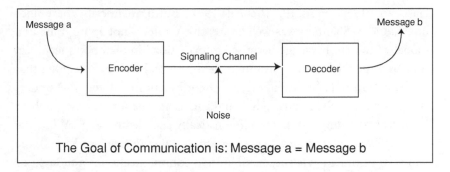

Figure 3.3 Shannon's model of communication – The standard model of communication in mathematical information theory, Shannon's model sees communication as an exchange of signals that "encode" messages. Relevance theory questions this model, see text.

abilities – advanced theory of mind and *Mitteilungsbedürfnis* – typify humans and perhaps only a few other species.

3.8.2 Pragmatic inference: context and interpretation

We will start by surveying a theory of pragmatics initiated by Grice (1957, 1975) and insightfully extended by Sperber and Wilson (1986). Sperber and Wilson draw a crucial distinction between two models of communication, which they call the *code* and *inferential* models. The **code model** of communication is the familiar model of signals and messages, formalized by Shannon and Weaver (1949), and widely accepted as *the* model of communication by most scholars today. Shannon's model, illustrated in Figure 3.3, is based on a telegraph or similar device, and involves two symmetrical communicators that share a code and signaling channel. This model entails a situation in which the signaler and receiver are cooperatively attempting to transmit a message by encoding and then decoding it. In addition to this cooperative intent (which remains implicit in Shannon's model), the two must share a signal (over a potentially noisy transmission line) and a code matching signals and "messages." Shannon's main goal in information theory was to devise a situation where perfect communication was possible, given a certain inevitable amount of noise in the signal. His model has been very successful: the entire digital world that we live in today was made possible as the result of his success (the term *bit* itself was introduced in Shannon's paper). It was not long before the updated Shannon code model of communication was adopted as a model of linguistic communication

(Jakobson, 1960; Lyons, 1977; Sebeok, 1977). But, as many critics have since noted, and as Shannon was well aware, this model is not appropriate as a model of human language because "information" in Shannon's technical sense is not equivalent to "meaning" in *any* sense. Having a computer that perfectly transmits "information" is not equivalent to a system that understands anything about this signal, and this is as true for a photograph or a musical recording as it is for a linguistically encoded message. While the "message" to be transmitted via telegraph is a text (a string of letters), the entity "transmitted" via successful human communication is a thought or concept. Imagine two telegraph operators, skilled in Morse code, but ignorant of the English language. Although they might convey an English text accurately, achieving "perfect" communication in Shannon's terms, neither operator has a clue about the *meaning* of the message transmitted. Thus, understanding a message requires more than an encoder/decoder pair. It requires interpretation, and a system capable of unpacking or expanding messages into concepts. In short, sharing meaning requires minds as well as codes.

3.8.3 Inferential models of communication

Accepting this fundamental limitation of the code model of communication, what are our further options? The central insight is that successful linguistic communication always requires the listener to draw *inferences* about the *intended* meaning of the speaker. We can see this easily by considering how we as listeners react to an unwitting slip of the tongue, or misuse of some word, by a speaker. In general, we discount the "actual" message transmitted, and instead build a representation of what (we think) the speaker intended to say. This is particularly true when talking to children, or to foreigners: we are always "looking through" the words into the intended meanings that lie behind them. And this is true even if the "actual" message (complete with slip of tongue) is perfectly well-formed and grammatical. It is not because of a coding violation that we reject such slips, but because of their inconsistency with a model we have built up, based on the previous discourse, about what the speaker is trying to say.

To make this code/inference distinction more concrete, consider two examples:

(5) *Inferential*:
    (a) Either Mary is early or Bob is late.
    (b) Bob is never late.

(6) *Encoded*: /meri Iz e:li:/

Presented with either (5) or (6), an English speaker will conclude that:

(7) Mary is early.

But the inferential process by which we arrive at (7) from the premises in (5) is fundamentally different from the way that (6) encodes the sentence in (7). The central insight of modern pragmatics is that human communication is largely such an inferential process. Our utterances *provide evidence about our thoughts*, and successful communication demands both that we intend them to do so, and that our listeners recognize this fact (Sperber and Wilson, 1986). Human communication in all of its forms is fundamentally cooperative in this respect, and the coding component of language would fail most of the time if this were not true. Put another way, coding is perhaps not a bad model of *speech*, but it fails to capture central aspects of *language*.

Considerable work in pragmatics, inspired by philosopher Paul Grice's work on cooperative maxims (Grice, 1975), has attempted to construct an adequate theory of how it is possible for such inferential communication to succeed. In the code model, we expect successful communication (and the main thrust of Shannon's information theory is in fact to *guarantee* success). By the inferential model, communication is never guaranteed, and the mystery is how it is that we are, so often, successful in communication. There are two fundamental assumptions of Gricean models in pragmatics. First, two interlocutors share knowledge about the world, both in terms of their immediate surroundings (e.g. both of them noticing that a dog is barking) and in terms of background knowledge (e.g. that dogs typically bark at something relevant, OR that a particular dog, Rolf, often barks at nothing at all). This **common ground** is a crucial component of successful inference. A key extension, due to Sperber and Wilson (1986), is the recognition that it is not mutual knowledge *per se*, but rather a shared world of possible inferences – what they call a shared "cognitive environment" – that is crucial for this notion to be successful. The second assumption is that we obey certain implicit rules – "Gricean maxims" – in communicating. The overall principle is **be cooperative!**, which entails maxims like "make your contribution as *informative* as required, but not more so" or "make your contribution *relevant* to the ongoing conversation" (see Box 3.2). Such relevance, and the cooperativity that underlies it, is a cornerstone of human language.

Box 3.2. Gricean maxims

Overall: Be cooperative. Be informative.

  I. Maxims of Quantity:
   1. Make your contribution as informative as is required.
   2. Do not make your contribution more informative than is required.
 II. Maxims of Quality: Supermaxim: Try to make your contribution one that is true.
   1. Do not say what you believe to be false.
   2. Do not say that for which you lack adequate evidence.
III. Maxim of Relation: Be relevant.
 IV. Maxims of Manner: Supermaxim: Be perspicuous.
   1. Avoid obscurity of expression.
   2. Avoid ambiguity.
   3. Be brief.
   4. Be orderly.

3.8.4 Symmetry of signaler and receiver: shedding a misleading intuition

Inference is a central aspect of cognition, and animal data suggest that we can take a well-developed "inference engine" for granted in our prelinguistic ancestors. This is not the case with cooperation: nothing like Gricean maxims or cooperativity on the part of signalers can be assumed in animal cognition or communication, where theorists agree that there are fundamental asymmetries distinguishing signalers and receivers (Dawkins and Krebs, 1978; Krebs and Dawkins, 1984). In general, animals produce signals because they need to get something done, and receivers attend if it is in their interests to do so. But, in the world of *human* communication, this asymmetry is muted, if not wholly balanced out. The "rules" of conversation that Grice and most subsequent pragmatists recognized presuppose an essential symmetry between speaker and hearer, an essential common interest in getting some point across. This constitutes a semantic type of parity in signal transimission, and it presupposes that interlocutors share the desire to communicate cooperatively.

  Because this is indubitably how humans typically operate, it is easy to overlook the degree to which the *speaker's* contribution to this process is anomalous in animal communication (Seyfarth and Cheney, 2003). This is a case where intuitions about communication based on human language are positively misleading. It seems intuitive to us humans that speakers naturally do their best to "get their thoughts across" to others. From the point of view of most animal species this is anything but "natural": animal communication, before language, largely involved signalers who generate signals either automatically (e.g. innate calls) or selfishly ("manipulation"), and thus obeyed no Gricean maxims. Listeners, on the other hand, have been processing these signals inferentially, fulfilling their half of the Gricean equation, for the entire history of communication systems, and this basic asymmetry has been the evolutionary norm for 100 million years of vertebrate communication. Pragmatics since Grice is based on a recognition that linguistic communication requires more than inference, and more than manipulation. The component of this Gricean model that demands special evolutionary explanation is, almost entirely, the *speaker's* contribution to this cooperative endeavor. "Going Gricean," then, required a fundamental change in the rules of animal communication on the part of signalers, and this step is a logical necessity before language could get off the ground (cf. Seyfarth and Cheney, 2003).

3.8.5 The evolution of inference: conceptual components

Animals can use the past behavior of others to influence their own future behavior. But humans do not stop with *behavior*. Humans *make sense* of behavior by positing a *mind* behind it. We are not satisfied with simple descriptions of what another individual does; we seek explanations about *why* they did it, and these explanations invariably involve such invisible constructs as goals and beliefs. We are less likely to think "A is chasing B" than "A is *trying* to make B go away, *because* A wants the food to itself." Seeing the world in this way – adopting what the philosopher Daniel Dennett has dubbed **the intentional stance** – seems to come to us naturally as humans. (We even attribute intentionality to clouds or machines, despite knowing this to be nonsensical.) Perhaps surprisingly, it is only recently that this core aspect of human cognition has been subjected to comparative analysis, prompted by a seminal paper by Premack and Woodruff titled "Does the chimpanzee have a theory of mind?" (Premack and Woodruff, 1978). In an equally seminal paper, a non-verbal experimental technique was introduced to ask the same question of children (Wimmer and Perner, 1983), with the surprising outcome that normal children, up to the age of four, are *unable* to represent others' beliefs, if they differ from their own beliefs. The clearest message from this literature is that it is a deep mistake to treat "**theory**

of mind" (ToM) as a monolithic whole that you either have or don't. Just like language, ToM is a complex of interdependent mental mechanisms that work together in most adult humans but that have separate times of appearance in ontogeny, and can be dissociated by brain damage or genetic defects. Again, a "divide-and-conquer" strategy must be adopted towards the intentional stance and ToM.

Dennett's evolutionary analysis of animal communication provides a conceptually clear starting point (Dennett, 1983) for this decomposition. At the lowest level in Dennett's system, we have systems that *lack* mental states (beliefs, desires, goals) entirely: *zero-order intentional systems*. This level includes a diverse range of natural objects, including rocks and clouds, but also potentially includes many living organisms. A sponge is "about" filter-feeding in some sense, but sponges don't have a mental state corresponding to filter-feeding, because they don't have a nervous system at all. Many other animals, including all vertebrates, do have mental states: this is the purpose of a relatively large brain. Modern cognitive ethology operates on the assumption that such animals are *first-order* intentional systems, with beliefs (and desires, goals, etc.). Such animals may, however, lack beliefs *about* beliefs: a dog may have no beliefs about what other dogs think. A first-order intentional explanation, in Dennett's terms, requires us to think that the system has a mind, but not a *theory* of mind.

Finally, human adults, at least, entertain thoughts about what other individuals think ("I wonder if she likes me"). This is a prerequisite to adopting an intentional stance, and it makes us at least *second-order intentional systems*. What's more, we frequently entertain higher-order levels, such as third order ("does she know that I know where the cookies are?"), and so on. A pragmatic analysis of communication such as Sperber and Wilson's (1986) demands that interlocutors have (at least) *third-order intentionality*. In order to strive to be informative, one must have second-order intentionality (thoughts about the other's lack of information, and a goal of rectifying the situation); and the listener must *know* that the informer has such thoughts. Humans are masters of this sort of higher-order intentionality, and strategic mentalistic maneuvering seems so natural and intuitive to us that it has taken many years to recognize how unusual it is.

3.8.6 Biological components of the theory of mind

What do children, and animals, know about others? Many animals can use the orientation of others to make a guess about what they are looking at ("gaze following"), and some animals (apes and corvids) can *use* such

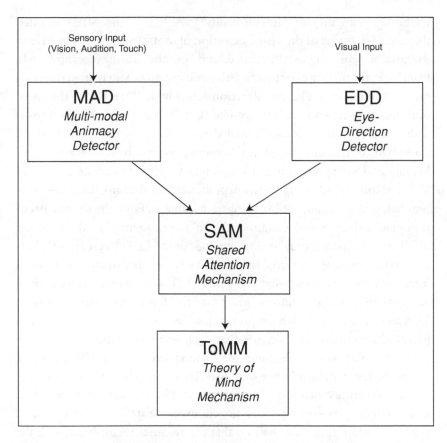

Figure 3.4 Components of theory of mind – Simon Baron-Cohen has proposed three basic mechanisms underlying the human capacity to represent other's beliefs, even when different from our own ("Theory of Mind"). The top three appear to be shared with other animals in some from; only TOMM may be uniquely human.

information to make inferences about their future behavior (infer that "seeing is knowing"). Based on current data, using *that* information cooperatively, to help others achieve their goals, may be a unique prerogative of humans. Developmental data on ToM in children suggests a complex developmental course, with multiple components that need to come together before adult-level competence is attained. Bearing in mind that the "natural" subdivisions are still debated, Figure 3.4 shows one breakdown of an overall "mind reading" system (following Baron-Cohen, 1995). The **multi-modal animacy detector** (MAD) is hypothesized to distinguish self-propelled activity (typical of animate beings) from other types of physical activity, and to attribute simple goals based on that motion (Baron-Cohen calls this the "intentionality detector," a term I avoid because of the already confusing ambiguity of "intentionality"). Although the MAD is often thought of in terms of the visual detection of motion, it also is sensitive to sound (distinguishing vocally created sounds, or the rustling of an approach, from background noise) or touch. This basic system is widely shared among (at least) vertebrates. The **eye-direction detector** (EDD) is tied to the visual domain, and seeks to analyze eye-like stimuli. Again, this mechanism is widely shared, and is certainly well developed in nonhuman mammals. These two components of the mind-reading system, then, have an ancient heritage and were present in our non-linguistic primate ancestors.

The second set of components hypothesized by Baron-Cohen are more unusual, and unusually well-developed in humans. First, the **shared attention mechanism** (SAM) combines the volitional agency "readout" of the MAD with the perceptual "seeing" readout of the EDD to create a higher-order representation, in a sense fusing what were before two separate types of information: "John sees (what I'm doing)." This mechanism might, given adequate processing resources, generalize to "John sees (that I see (that John sees the food))." Such a representation is not simply hierarchical, but potentially recursive, in the sense that we have two instances of the same complex "John sees . . ." in the same hierarchical structure. Thus, this is one of the few instances in non-linguistic cognition where there is a strong computational justification for moving from hierarchical embedding to a truly recursive embedding. Thus, the comparative status of the SAM is of particular interest, and we shall see that the evidence is consistent with the existence of SAM in chimpanzees, possibly with some restrictions on the contexts in which it is used.

The final mechanism in this quartet is the **theory of mind mechanism** (ToMM) itself. The crucial advance of this postulated mechanism over SAM is the ability to form representations that include both propositions and the other's stance or attitude towards those propositions. Thus, although similar in structure to the SAM's gaze-specific representations, the ToMM can represent *any* type of mental stance: believing, intending, pretending, hoping, etc. Such a generalized representation is a crucial prerequisite for second-order intentionality: to know something is false, while simultaneously knowing that someone else believes it to be true. Systematically successful deceptive communication obviously requires such a representation of another's false belief, as this is the goal of deception. Note that an animal might be capable of moving outside the field of view of a dominant in order to accomplish some desired goal, based on the SAM, while still not possessing a full-blown ToMM. The now-classic empirical test for such second-order representations are false belief tasks. The best known, sometimes called "the Sally-Anne task," was developed by Wimmer and Perner (1983).

The task involves enacting a story (sometimes with puppets, sometimes with real actors) of two characters, Sally and Anne. Sally hides a marble in a basket and then leaves the room. While she is gone, Anne moves the marble into a box. Sally then re-enters the room and the child is asked, "Where will Sally look for the marble?" (or, in some variants, "Where does Sally think the marble is?"). The results have now been repeatedly replicated: children under the age of three, consistently answer "the box," and it is not until 3–4 years of age that children appear able, in general, to separate *their* knowledge of where the object is from Sally's false belief. It should be noted that this test relies on correctly maintaining not only a representation of another's mind, but also correctly tracking it as false, and the latter operation may be considerably more taxing than representing another's belief when it is consistent with one's own representation. Thus, while *passing* the false belief task is widely accepted as clear evidence of "theory of mind" and second-order representations, failure on the task might still be consistent with a functional theory of mind that lacks the ability to inhibit a prepotent knowledge of how the world really is.

3.8.7 Autism and "mindblindness"

An important source of insight into the biology of ToM comes from studies of disorders in human clinical populations, in particular autistic children, who have been hypothesized to have a specific deficit in mind-reading. In the memorable terms of Baron-Cohen (1995), autistic children suffer from "mindblindness." Autism is a relatively rare congenital disorder involving a suite of symptoms that are typically noticed around age two. Autism is complex at every level: etiologically, neurally, and genetically, but the core symptom is a profound lack of interest in others, particularly as social, emotional beings. This symptom is most striking in the "high functioning" subset of autists with normal intelligence and language skills, who preserve an interest in the world, and facility in many practical and abstract matters. In a now-classic paper, Baron-Cohen *et al.* (1985) applied the Sally-Anne task to autists, and answered the title question of their paper – "Does the autistic child have 'a theory of mind'?" – negatively. While both normal children and retarded children with Down Syndrome generally passed false-belief tests, few of the autistic children did. This finding has now been repeatedly replicated (Frith, 2001), and although autists of normal intelligence eventually grow out of this and are able to develop second-order representations, they are severely delayed in this developmental time course (Happé, 1995). Although the genetic bases for autism remain undetermined, such data provide a clear indication that an innately based capacity for second-order ToM in humans can be selectively impaired. Because we will see that there is little evidence of this capacity in nonhuman animals, this is one more human-specific ability that needed to evolve in our recent evolutionary past.

3.8.8 *Mitteilungsbedürfnis*: the human need to share meaning

The process of inference involves a *listener* making inferences, and thus concerns "mind-reading" (Krebs and Dawkins, 1984). But even the most accomplished mind-reader can draw only limited inferences without the cooperation of the signaler. The last element of human pragmatic competence is the signaler's drive to share their thoughts and feelings with others. We humans give our mind-reading interlocutors plenty of help – we are a species that delights in sharing meanings and strives to do so (Sperber and Wilson, 1986; Dessalles, 1998). This last aspect of human behavior is absolutely central to human communication, but quite rare in the animal world. Perhaps because this drive to share meaning has no English name (*chattiness* might be the closest term), its importance has been noted too rarely. German has an excellent word for this drive – ***Mitteilungsbedürfnis*** (MtB) – which translates roughly as 'a drive or need to share thoughts and feelings,' and I will adopt this term in the present discussion. Biologists might categorize MtB as "manipulation," but this term doesn't quite to do justice to the drive. The point of MtB is not simply to get someone else to *do* something, but rather to get them to *share your thoughts* (Tomasello *et al.*, 2005). The MtB drive is not satisfied by someone simply nodding their head occasionally: an engaged listener is crucial (this can make sitting beside someone with a powerful MtB on a long journey quite taxing). Although the basic drive to share information is not unique to our species, I suggest that it is so hypertrophied in humans as to deserve careful consideration as a potential cognitive adaptation "for" language.

3.9 Chapter summary: multiple components of language

Thus we end our survey of language components, from the point of view of linguistics. Table 3.1 summarizes the conclusions of this chapter. This has been a general survey, and so the components I have isolated are also, in

Table 3.1. Components of the faculty of language (broad sense)

This table gives a preliminary breakdown, along traditional linguistic lines, of some of the core cognitive components of the instinct to learn language. As a mnemonic, we can think of these components as grouped under the "Three Ss" of signal, structure, and semantics, but each of these categories entails multiple separate but interacting mechanisms.

I Signal (speech or sign)
Signal learning: A large and extensible vocabulary of *learned* signals is required.
Parity: Signalers and perceivers can switch roles.
Signal categorization (discreteness): Desirable for rapid error-free processing.

II Structure (phonology and syntax)
Phonology
Sequencing.
Duality of patterning.
Combinatorial phonology/hierarchical chunking.

Syntax
Hierarchical phrase structure.
Structure-dependent rules.
Self-embedding (recursion).
Mapping to meaning and phonology (serialization).

III Semantics or meaning: formal semantics and pragmatics
Formal and lexical semantics
Propositionality.
Referential stance.
Constraints on induction of word meanings.

Pragmatics
Context-driven inference (pragmatic inference engine).
Theory of mind (ToM) – Gricean maxims.
Mitteilungsbedürfnis (MtB) – The drive to share meanings.

many cases, very general. We have seen that certain core concepts, such as the infinite use of finite means, pervade many aspects of language, while others, such as context-dependent inference, are particular to just one aspect of language. Furthermore, most of these broad components are not tightly encapsulated: there are broad interfaces between phonology and syntax, syntax and semantics, and semantics and pragmatics. Finally, I recognize that there are many far more specific components that might be proposed for each of the categories I have surveyed, and professional linguists might well slight this list for its superficiality ("Where is the obligatory contour principle?," ask the phonologists. "Where is subjacency?," ask the syntacticians). I offer this list as an overview, and a beginning, not an end, of attempts to decompose language into its functional, computational components (for alternatives cf. Koehler, 1954; Hockett, 1960; Jackendoff, 2002). Nonetheless, the virtues of some such list will be seen in the next chapters, as we try to ascertain which of the many components I *have* listed is present, in some form or another, in nonhuman animals. Many of the items in Table 3.1 will turn out to be shared, but a crucial few appear either unique to our species, or not present in our close primate cousins. These are the traits that needed to appear in language evolution, in the last five to six million years. Having *some* reasonably comprehensive shortlist of such mechanisms will be crucial in evaluating theories of language evolution later in the book.

Those who deny understanding to the higher animals, can have very little themselves. — Arthur Schopenhauer

At the turn of the twentieth century, a remarkable horse named Hans was paraded through Germany by his owner Wilhelm von Osten, a horse trainer and high-school mathematics teacher. Not only could "Clever Hans" understand complex questions put to him in plain German – "If Tuesday falls on the eighth of the month, what date is the following Friday?" – but he could answer them by tapping out the correct number with his hoof. Using this simple response, it appeared that Hans could add, subtract, multiply, and divide, tell the time, understand the calendar, and both read and spell words. Suspicious, the German board of education appointed a commission, including circus trainers, veterinarians, teachers, and psychologists, to investigate the situation. Surprisingly, they concluded in 1904 that no trickery was involved. This did not satisfy the board, and the case was passed to psychologist Oskar Pfungst for experimental investigation. Braving both the horse's and owner's notoriously bad tempers, Pfungst finally was able to demonstrate that Hans was no mathematician, but rather a fine observer of human behavior (Pfungst, 1911). In a story now told to countless "Intro Psych" students, Pfungst demonstrated that Hans could only answer questions correctly when: (1) the questioner knew the answer; and (2) Hans could see the questioner. It gradually became clear that human questioners (not just von Osten, but naïve individuals, and even Pfungst himself) made tiny postural changes as the correct answer approached, providing the cue for Hans to stop tapping. Hans, it turned out, excelled not at arithmetic, but at "reading" human behavior. Remarkably, even after Pfungst had unmasked this trick, he was unable to stop generating such cues himself. The "Clever Hans effect" revealed both the acuity of animal social perception, and the inability of humans to suppress unconscious cues – both highly significant findings.

4.1 Animal cognition: exorcising Skinner's ghost

Pfungst's research is a founding study in modern psychology, and helped stem the flow of increasingly fantastic and uncritical stories about animal minds that had become popular in the decades after Darwin. Unfortunately it also sparked a backlash against *any* form of research into animal cognition: in harmony with the behaviorist movement's opposition to the use of mental and cognitive concepts in humans, the discussion of internal mental processes in animals became virtually taboo. This neglect was aided by philosophers' long-standing association between thought and language, and the belief among many that thought of any complexity actually requires "inner language" (e.g. Langer, 1972).

The idea that animals *cannot* think has a long history, and was put most forcefully by Descartes, who argued that animals other than man are simply machines, their behavior governed by reflexes, but not animated by "spirit" or mind as are human behaviors. Although this argument was never particularly convincing or widespread, it still has its adherents today, enough for a book titled *Do Animals Think?* to be floated on the popular market (Wynne, 2004). The answer to this question of course depends on your definition of the word *think*, and a more relevant way of posing it is to ask, as Darwin did, what "mental" aspects of human behavior are shared with other animals (Darwin, 1871, 1872b). Darwin listed as shared features basic emotions (pain and pleasure, misery and happiness), a sense of curiosity, attention (as manifested in gaze), and memory. He devotes much attention to "reason," under which he gives many examples of animal learning, including tool use by monkeys and apes. Darwin ends by discussing self-consciousness, language, a sense of beauty, and a belief in God, which he doubts animals possess in human form, but in each case he cites possible animal precursors of these characteristics. It has taken many years for psychologists to catch up with Darwin's approach. While the cognitive revolution had already successfully thrown off overly restrictive conceptions of behavioral causation by 1970, this revolution left animals behind (Byrne and Bates, 2006). Not until eminent ethologist Donald Griffin's landmark book *The Question of Animal Awareness* (Griffin, 1976) were the questions seriously asked again: Do animals have thoughts, feelings, intentions, and awareness?

Today the tide has turned and animal cognition is once again a perfectly respectable subject among biologists, with multiple textbooks and reviews (Roitblat *et al.*, 1984; Vauclair, 1996; Tomasello and Call, 1997; Balda *et al.*, 1998; Shettleworth, 1998), popular treatments (Hauser, 2000), and a dedicated journal, *Animal Cognition*. It is now relatively uncontroversial that animals make and use tools, navigate using mental maps, remember the locations of stored food, nests, and other salient objects, engage in deception, and to some degree recognize the existence of themselves and others. Nonetheless, the cognitive revolution remains incomplete regarding animals. This is particularly true outside of biology, where, despite massive converging evidence from many carefully conducted studies, there are still those who take the idea that animals lack minds as self-evident. For example, linguist Roy Harris of Oxford recently denounced "current jargon" concerning animal cognition as "upmarket Mickey Mouse, decked out in pseudoscientific terminology" (Harris, 2007). Although this is unusually strong wording, it reveals a lingering discomfort with the very possibility of animal minds, feelings, or awareness. Skeptics often invoke **Lloyd Morgan's canon**: to avoid interpreting an action "in terms of higher psychological processes, if it can be fairly interpreted in terms of processes which stand lower in the scale of psychological evolution and development" (Morgan, 1903). The major difficulty with employing this application of parsimony to animal cognition is that we have no *a priori* grounds for ordering psychological mechanisms into a linear array from simple to complex. Are non-mental explanations always to be preferred to mental ones, however complex? Is an experienced awareness of pain "more complex" than a complex series of unconscious mental transformations leading to pain avoidance? Is "self-awareness" more or less complex than remembering the location of 10,000 stored seeds? Once we realize that such questions admit no simple answer, the utility of Morgan's canon for evaluating experiments in animal cognition is greatly reduced.

An example is provided by recent discussion of **episodic memory** (the ability to recall or mentally re-enact that past events happened to oneself). The term was introduced by a human memory researcher, Endel Tulving (Tulving and Thomson, 1973; Tulving, 2002). Based on introspection, Tulving suggested that episodic memory exists only in humans, and subsequent psychologists have argued that this "uniquely human" capacity is at the centre of human accomplishments (see review in Suddendorf and Corballis, 2007). But a stunning series of experiments in food-caching birds showed that they not only remember *where* they stored food but also *when*, as evidenced by their not retrieving food that would have spoiled (Clayton and Dickinson, 1998). These birds can use their memory of the past to predict the future and act accordingly, for example not caching food on the side of the cage where past experience shows the food will be unavailable (Clayton *et al.*, 2003b). Defenders of the human uniqueness position still argue that these experiments do not demonstrate an internally experienced, subjective sense of displacement in time. But no amount of behavioral evidence, other than the bird expressing itself via language or pantomime, could assault this position, and an assertion that is not falsifiable leaves the realm of science. Whether "subjectively experienced" or not, these birds clearly remember the past and use it to plan their future actions adaptively.

Another example of an *a priori* assumption of human uniqueness proclaimed in the absence of evidence from animals, and later demolished by experiments with animals, is the phenomenon of **categorical perception** (already discussed in Chapter 3). When first discovered, this phenomenon seemed so specifically tailored to the speech signal that Liberman *et al.* (1967) posited, before any comparative work was done, that it is uniquely human, and special to speech. It did not take long, however, for animal researchers to find clear evidence for categorical perception of speech sounds by animals (Kuhl and Miller, 1978; Kuhl, 1987).

Phenomena like categorical perception and episodic memory, unfortunately, are just a few of many cases where human uniqueness was initially claimed *in the absence of any relevant comparative evidence*: scientists seem remarkably ready to jump to the conclusion of uniqueness. Clearly, evaluation of human uniqueness must be founded not on presumptions or prejudice, but rather on objective, empirical comparative data. If we are to exorcise Descartes' old claims of human uniqueness, along with "Skinner's ghost," as it rears its head in discussions of animals, we should take comparative data as our starting point.

Conclusion: Valid claims of human uniqueness must be based on empirical data showing absence in multiple nonhuman species. If such a claim is intended as a scientific hypothesis, the claimant should specify how the trait in question could plausibly be demonstrated empirically in a nonhuman animal.

With this conclusion in mind, I will review what is known today about animal cognition, with an aim to understanding what we share, and what we don't, with other animals. I focus on relatively sophisticated abilities in nonhuman animal cognition, many of which are specific to particular species. I will be selective and review only those species, systems, and signals most relevant to language evolution. For a review that includes the large bodies of animal cognition that are more widely shared, see any neuroscience textbook (Kandel and Schwartz, 1985; Bear *et al.*, 2001) or comparative psychology compilations or textbooks (Hulse *et al.*, 1978; Roitblat *et al.*, 1984; Gallistel, 1990). Readers seeking more details of modern work in animal cognition will find a concise, reliable, and balanced guide in Vauclair (1996), more comprehensive coverage in Roberts (1998), Shettleworth (1998), and Bekoff *et al.* (2002), and a readable popular introduction in Hauser (2000). A comprehensive review of primate cognition is Tomasello and Call (1997), and introductions to comparable cognitive abilities in birds are Pepperberg (1999), Emery and Clayton (2004), and Rogers and Kaplan (2004).

4.2 Overview of animal cognition and communication

After a long period of assuming that primates reign supreme among animals in cognitive capabilities, the data emerging today from cognitive ethology suggest broadly comparable cognitive capabilities in many vertebrates. These data provide strong arguments against a *scala naturae* view of vertebrate evolution, with fish at the bottom, birds in the middle, and mammals and especially primates like us at the top. Instead, many nonhuman animals share a suite of complex cognitive capabilities, including impressive memories, motor control, transitive reasoning, basic numerical abilities, and hierarchical understanding of social structures. Furthermore, widely separated clades have convergently developed particular cognitive skills to a high degree. These cognitive data fit the branching pattern predicted by evolutionary theory. I will review several examples of the convergent evolution of cognitive abilities in mammals and **corvids** (the large-brained bird family including ravens, crows, and jays). These include tool use in apes, sea otters, and New Caledonian crows, and social intelligence in scrub jays, dogs, goats, and primates. Such examples of convergent evolution provide a valuable window into the nature of cognitive adaptation.

Compared to this increasingly rich and diversified picture of animals' cognitive lives, the scientific data for complexity in animal communication seem to have reached a plateau. When I was young, the media were abuzz with stories about "dolphin language," and apes raised with humans were learning language-like communicative systems with no clear limit to their attainments. The discovery of functionally referential signaling in vervet monkeys was thought to reveal an unsuspected complexity in animals' natural call systems. It seemed only a matter of time before some modern Dr. Doolittle would decode the language of an animal species, and this was (for me) part of the appeal of the field. Only fifteen years ago, biologist Jared Diamond predicted that further discoveries of referential complexity in animal communication systems, particularly those of chimpanzees, had only just begun (Diamond, 1992). Current data tell a disappointingly different story. Despite intense investigation, the natural communication systems of chimpanzees show a rich ability to convey emotional states and augment social interactions, and some limited referentiality, but not the unlimited ability to convey novel thoughts that characterizes human language

(Seyfarth and Cheney, 2005; Slocombe and Zuberbühler, 2005). Studies with captive animals have revealed considerable latent abilities not observed in nature: when guided by humans, chimpanzees, dolphins, and parrots can master arbitrary new symbols, match them with real-world referents, and use these pairings communicatively in a fashion far beyond what they do in the wild. But there are still clear limits on vocabulary size and syntactic complexity. No animal has yet displayed the vocabulary spurt typical of a human child, where new words are rapidly mastered from context, with little or no tutoring. Even the most enculturated animals do not attain the ability to freely express whatever they can remember, think, or imagine that typifies a human child at the age of four (Savage-Rumbaugh *et al.*, 1993).

The overall conclusion of this chapter, then, is that animals have surprisingly rich mental lives, and surprisingly limited abilities to express them as signals. Animals possess concepts (the "unnamed thought," or *unbennantes Denken*, of Koehler, 1954), but do not express them as signals. These conclusions are surprising to us humans, because we are a species born to express our thoughts. Something in our biology drives us to do what no other species apparently does – to freely (indeed incessantly) encode and express our thoughts – rendering our intuitions about animal communication untrustworthy. Humans tend to assume that an animal that is highly vocal, such as a singing bird or whale, "must be talking about something" – but all available data indicate that they are simply singing, making music for its own sake, rather than encoding thoughts into these sounds. People often think that an individual who says little has comparably little mental activity: hence the dual meanings of the word *dumb* – speechless and stupid. Abundant current data indicate that animals may be "dumb" in the first sense, but many vertebrates are anything but stupid. As stressed in Chapter 3, the species that is peculiar, from an ethological and biological viewpoint, is our own, and one can easily imagine that a scientist of a different species might be most powerfully struck by the unceasing chatter of humans, and our seemingly uncontrollable urge, even as children, to express our thoughts to one another. Our human *Mitteilungsbedürfnis* is bizarre, and we have to look quite hard to find systems in other animals that are even remotely comparable.

4.3 The study of animal cognition

The comparative study of animal behavior and cognition can be traced back at least as far as Aristotle, but it was Darwin who really initiated this field in its modern form (Darwin, 1871, 1872b). Darwin argued that animal behavior is genetically influenced, just like form or physiology, and thus could be encompassed by an evolutionary framework. He provided numerous examples of behaviors similar or identical in humans and other animals, arguing for the **continuity** of mental function during human evolution. His aim was to counteract the widespread idea that evolution could account for animal, and perhaps even human body form, but not for those mental aspects of our behavior that make us truly human (e.g. Wallace, 1905). However, Darwin was well aware of animal behaviors that were **discontinuous**, in the sense of being limited to a particular group of species: he cited human language or beaver dam-building as examples. Darwin had already realized that continuous evolutionary change over long periods can lead to radical differences among existing species: all that Darwinian theory requires is that constraints of evolvability and invasibility (Chapter 2) are satisfied. Nonetheless, a tension between continuity and species-specificity continues today, with different scholars tending to emphasize one or the other.

For most of the twentieth century, the study of animal cognition *per se* ceased, and only overt behavior was investigated. The cognitive revolution reopened the application of cognitive approaches to animal behavior, and many researchers today use **animal cognition** as an umbrella term incorporating both comparative psychology and ethology (e.g. Roitblat *et al.*, 1984; Vauclair, 1996; Balda *et al.*, 1998). Today, fieldworkers are often inspired by new findings and techniques from the laboratory, and are deeply interested in the mechanisms underlying behavior (Krebs and Davies, 1997), and laboratory workers take an increasingly ethological (evolutionary and ecological) perspective on their study organisms. Neuroscientists in particular have been quick to realize the advantages of the ethological approach (particularly workers who label themselves *neuroethologists*; Walkowiak, 1988; Marler, 1991a; Ghazanfar and Hauser, 1999), and the study of the neural mechanisms underlying species-specific behaviors (e.g. bat echolocation or birdsong) are major foci in contemporary neuroscience. An important factor binding all of these perspectives together is their explicit reliance on the comparative method.

4.4 Animal cognitive capabilities: the basic toolkit

Contemporary behavioral neuroscience focuses on mechanisms shared by many species. From a neural viewpoint it is the *similarities* among species that are most striking: nerve cells function in much the same way, using similar or identical ion channels and transmitters, in jellyfish, worms, fruit-flies, and people. Among mammals, the brain is remarkably conservative: detailed aspects of functional neuroanatomy and neural development remain constant. The main differences among species seem to depend more on the relative sizes and connections among brain regions than the presence or absence of qualitatively novel circuits or regions (Finlay *et al.*, 2001; Striedter, 2004). Short- and long-term memory, basic associative abilities, conditioning of various sorts, and basic navigation skills seem to be broadly similar among species, and rest upon similar neural mechanisms. Many aspects of cognition (e.g. learning, memory, categorization) are directly relevant to language acquisition. All of these capacities form a widespread "cognitive toolkit" shared by most vertebrates and at least some invertebrates. They include the following.

4.4.1 Categorization and learning

Animals can generalize from past experience to form general categories. For example, pigeons trained on photographs of trees can generalize a concept of "tree," such that they recognize novel pictures of trees, detect partially concealed trees, and silhouettes of trees. While one might think that "tree" is partly an innate concept for a bird, pigeons show similarly impressive competence for underwater pictures of fish, or for arbitrary shapes like the letter "A" (see review in Vauclair, 1996). While it is possible that some categories are innate (e.g. conspecific faces or calls), many are learned, and simple associative learning provides a precursor for some of the simple aspects of reference in human language that are shared among all vertebrates.

4.4.2 Memory

Animals can retain information about an object or a sequence after it has disappeared. Early work showed that monkeys and apes readily remember under which of several cups food had been hidden (Tinklepaugh, 1928). Pigeons can remember at least 160 meaningless "squiggles," or 320 natural scenes, for at least a year (Vaughan and Greene, 1984). In the so-called *delayed match to sample* task, monkeys presented with an object can correctly report whether a second object or sequence is the same or different (Fobes and King, 1982).

4.4.3 Time and planning

The adaptive value of memory is that it helps animals make decisions and plan future behavior. Animals can predict where a rotating clock hand should be after it has disappeared (Neiworth and Rilling, 1987). Humming-birds remember where nectar-rich flowers are, and keep track of how long it has been since their last visit (Healy and Hurly, 2004; Henderson *et al.*, 2006). Many animals can plan for the future: they hide or **cache** excess food when available, and retrieve it later. Mammals such as squirrels bury huge numbers of acorns, and foxes bury excess prey. Many bird species also cache food, and unlike mammals, which can often uncover hidden food using their acute sense of smell, food-hoarding birds have poor olfaction and must remember the spatial location of cached food. Thus, food-caching birds offer an ideal system for testing spatial memory and **anticipatory cog-nition** (planning for the future; e.g. Kamil and Jones, 1997; Clayton and Dickinson, 1998). Clark's nutcrackers store tens of thousands of seeds, and show excellent recall of their locations (Bednekoff and Balda, 1996). Food-caching scrub jays remember how long ago they hid food (Clayton and Dickinson, 1998; Clayton *et al.*, 2003a). In general, these data all support the idea that other vertebrates have memory capacities, allowing "mental time travel" like our own.

4.4.4 Inference and reasoning

Animals can also combine learned, cognitive representations and incorpo-rate them into novel behavior in useful ways. Take, for instance, a *transitive inference* task. If we know that A is bigger than B, and B is bigger than C, we can deduce that A must be bigger than C, without requiring a direct com-parison of A and C. Studies demonstrating transitive inference in animals might use colored containers with different amounts of food: the animal must first learn arbitrary associations between box colors and amounts of food (e.g. green has more food than red, red has more than blue). They are then tested with a comparison they have not previously seen (e.g. between green and blue). Spontaneous correct choices are considered evidence of transitive inference (these "test trials" are not rewarded, so success can't be explained away by reinforcement learning). Many species, including rats, several birds, squirrel monkeys, and chimpanzees, can perform successfully on such tasks (McGonigle and Chalmers, 1977; Gillan, 1981; Davis, 1992; Paz-y-Miño *et al.*, 2004). Although skeptics have been ingenious in devising non-cognitive explanations for such performance (Wynne, 2004), these can-not account for some of the more recent demonstrations (e.g. Paz-y-Miño *et al.*, 2004). Thus, numerous species can combine simple learned rules in new ways they have never experienced to successfully solve a novel task. By this cognitive definition of "thought," there can be little remaining doubt that animals "think," though perhaps unconsciously (those uncomfortable with the term unconscious "thought" can simply substitute "cognitive processing").

4.4.5 Number

A well-studied set of cognitive abilities is concerned with *number*. Both humans and animals appear to share two distinct numerical abilities, sometimes termed "small exact" and "large approximate," while only humans understand number terms which express a third ability, dependent on counting ability: "large exact" (see review in Dehaene, 1997). Thus, most animals tested thus far can distinguish between one, two, and three objects quite reliably. Furthermore, animals can make pairings between the numerosity of sets of objects (e.g. three grapes) and either a card with three marks on it, or (after more training) a card with the numeral "3" on it (Matsuzawa, 1985; Boysen, 1997). A parrot trained to speak the numbers up to the English word *three* can answer appropriately when presented with a tray of objects (Pepperberg, 1994). Finally, looking-time studies show that rhesus macaques have a basic arithmetic competence. In these experiments, objects are placed one after another behind a screen. When the screen is lifted, the subject sees either the correct number of objects or (by sleight of hand) an extra or missing object. Both human infants and monkeys look longer when the incorrect number of objects is revealed. Thus, the ability to represent small numbers of objects precisely is shared with other animals, and does not require language.

4.4.6 Cross-modal matching

It was long claimed that cross-modal matching – the ability to form multi-sensory cognitive representations – is a uniquely human ability tied to language evolution (Burton and Ettlinger, 1960; Cole *et al.*, 1961; Lancaster, 1968). Davenport and Rogers (1970) convincingly refuted this claim by showing that apes can match felt objects to their visually presented counterparts. More recent studies show that monkeys can match visual and auditory sequences for numerosity (Hauser *et al.*, 2002). Thus animals can both match sensory data directly, and match more abstract cognitive representations.

4.4.7 Serial order

Pigeons can learn to peck squares of four different colors in a particular sequence, and then correctly peck this sequence when the squares are spatially rearranged into novel locations. Furthermore, having learned the sequence A, B, C, D, they can correctly peck subsequences, such as A, C or B, D, that were not previously presented (Terrace, 2001). Rhesus macaques have shown even more impressive serial abilities, learning the sequence of up to nine photographs which are presented on a touch-screen in a different spatial constellation each time (Terrace *et al.*, 2003). Furthermore, various manual tasks suggest that nonhuman animals go beyond simple linear order to hierarchically subdivide motor sequences into "chunks" (Terrace, 1987; Greenfield, 1991; Byrne and Russon, 1998; Terrace, 2001). Because serial ordering of hierarchical structures is one important component of language production, these data suggest that some aspects of language are built upon ancient cognitive capabilities, widely shared with animals.

The abilities discussed above appear widespread among animals, most having been demonstrated in rodents, birds, and primates. Despite some ingenious rearguard defense by behaviorists, seeking to explain such abilities in terms of "simpler" laws of stimulus–response psychology, such explanations have grown increasingly baroque as the observed "cognitive" behaviors accumulate (Byrne and Bates, 2006). Today, most psychologists have concluded that it is simpler to accept that animals have basic cognitive (conceptual and representational) capabilities than to seek complicated behaviorist explanations, which at some point "seem to require more cognitive effort by both the human theorist and the rats" (p. 77, Walker, 1983).

4.5 Specialized forms of intelligence: physical and social intelligence

Are there more particular capabilities that are distinctive of primates, or apes? Two commonly cited possibilities are tool use (well developed in chimpanzees but not most other primates) and social intelligence (thought to typify primates as a clade). Both forms of more specialized intelligence have been plausibly suggested as primate precursors of language, and their existence in apes strongly suggests their presence in prelinguistic hominids. Therefore, I will now explore these data in more detail. Because many authors have suggested a tight link between tool use and language evolution (e.g. Holloway, 1969; Corballis, 1983; Davidson and Noble, 1993; Kimura, 1993), I will start there.

4.5.1 Animal tool use and "physical intelligence"

For many years, tool use was considered the hallmark of humanity, and the adoption of stone tools was considered to be a critical part of the complex of behaviors, including manual dexterity, bipedality, and carnivory, that launched our species on its unique path. Jane Goodall's reports of tool use by wild chimpanzees (Goodall, 1968, 1986) ignited a strong interest in the study of animal tool use (Beck, 1980; McGrew, 1992). It is now clear that numerous nonhuman species use **tools**, defined as detached objects, carried or held just prior to or during some goal-directed usage. For instance, sea otters use stones to break or pry open abalones (Hall and Schaller, 1964), and several bird species use spines or sticks as tools to spear grubs (Tebbich *et al.*, 2001; Hunt and Gray, 2003).

Chimpanzees use tools in a variety of ways, and the details provide important insights into the behavior of the LCA. There are three well-documented tool behaviors in chimpanzees. These include leaf sponging (the use of a wadded leaf to absorb water for drinking) and insect "fishing" (inserting and removing long sticks into insect nests, and then eating the attached insects; Goodall, 1986). Proper termite fishing requires chimpanzees to modify sticks or blades of grass to the appropriate width and length, and clearly constitutes tool manufacture. Third, some chimpanzee populations use stone tools to crack nuts. Although mentioned by Darwin ("the chimpanzee in a state of nature cracks a native fruit, somewhat like a walnut, with a stone"; Darwin, 1871), this behavior was "rediscovered" in wild chimpanzees in two different locations and has been intensively studied (Sugiyama and Koman, 1979; Boesch and Boesch, 1983; Boesch and Boesch-Achermann, 2000). Several aspects of nutcracking in chimpanzees are noteworthy. It is difficult, and takes considerable time and experience to master (Boesch, 1991). This may be one reason that nutcracking is not found in most chimpanzee populations. The stone tools used are as heavy as 3 kg, and often must be transported to the nut-bearing tree through dense forest, indicating spatial reasoning and planning (Boesch and Boesch-Achermann, 2000). Finally, the cracking of particularly hard nuts requires an anvil, which can be an already present tree root or another rock. Chimpanzees have even been observed using a third rock to level and stabilize the anvil ("meta tool use" – use of a tool on another tool). Recently, the use of digging sticks to uncover nutritious underground tubers has been documented in savanna-dwelling chimpanzees (Hernandez-Aguilar *et al.*, 2007). Given similar behavior in all human cultures, we can safely assume that tool use and toolmaking at approximately this level of complexity, using both stones and other materials, were present in our common ancestor with chimpanzees. Although tool use is at best rare in wild gorillas (Breuer *et al.*, 2006), it is occasionally observed in wild orangutans, who are also sophisticated tool users in captivity (Galdikas, 1982; van Schaik *et al.*, 1996).

Although chimpanzees have long been thought to be the most sophisticated nonhuman tool users (Beck, 1980), their supremacy has recently been challenged by a bird species, the New Caledonian crow (Orenstein, 1972; Chappell and Kacelnik, 2002; Hunt and Gray, 2004a; Kenward *et al.*, 2005). In their natural environment, these crows make a variety of plant-based tools, using sticks to probe crevices and to remove insect prey, but they also make hooks and stepped "saws" from leaves, which they use for similar purposes (Hunt and Gray, 2003, 2004a, 2004b). In the lab, one crow was videotaped making a hook-shaped tool from metal wire to hook the handle of an otherwise inaccessible bucket of food (Weir *et al.*, 2004a). Crows raised in the absence of bird or human models nonetheless learn to use sticks to probe for food, indicating that an inclination to use tools is innate in this species (Kenward *et al.*, 2005): another example of an "instinct to learn" a skill. In combination, the convergently evolved ability of New Caledonian crows to manufacture, store, and reason about tools rivals that of chimpanzees.

Because of the importance often attached to tool use in human evolution, and particularly in the evolution of syntax (Holloway, 1969; Corballis, 1983; Bradshaw and Rodgers, 1993; Kimura, 1993), it is worth pausing to consider what animal tool use reveals about their conceptual capacities in the absence of language. First, in order to make use of a tool, an animal must have a *goal* that it can keep in mind for at least long enough to find a tool and bring it to bear on the task. Animal toolmaking (as in chimpanzees or crows) requires more, since the animal must bear in mind the *sub-goals* involved in tool construction while still maintaining the main goal of food acquisition, implying a hierarchically structured goal system. Effective tool use requires various types of *physical knowledge*, depending on the task. Although this physical knowledge may be acquired through trial and error learning, the effectiveness with which mature tool users deploy this knowledge suggests that it is organized into a *causal model of the task*. Further, an animal with multiple tool possibilities (like the crow with a choice of spines *versus* leaves) can analyze the task at hand and choose the appropriate tool. All of these various tasks require *complex motor control*, but the crows' use of their beak shows that this needn't be tied specifically to the hands. In both chimpanzees and crows, tool use is consistently *lateralized*, so that a particular individual preferentially uses its right or left hand (or orients with its right or left eye) to performs the task (McGrew and Marchant, 1997; Weir *et al.*, 2004b). However, in neither species is a strong population-level bias found (comparable to the right-handed bias in humans), indicating that while lateralization *per se* may be important in effective tool use, lateralization shared by all members of the group or population is not necessary (but see Palmer, 2002; Hopkins and Russell, 2004). In summary, animal tool use and toolmaking indicate that a suite of complex, hierarchically arranged, effectively interconnected cognitive subsystems are possible in the absence of language, and were already present in our common ancestor with chimpanzees.

4.5.2 Animal interactions and "social intelligence"

The essentially ecological problems of finding one's way and accessing food pose one set of challenges to an individual organism. In a groundbreaking paper, primatologist Alison Jolly pointed out that many nonhuman primates live in complex social groups, and that behaving appropriately in these social groups poses another, independent, cognitive challenge (Jolly, 1966). First, a social animal must remember the identities of ten to fifty other individuals. More importantly, a social individual must remember the outcome of past interactions (whether friendly or agonistic) with other group members. Regarding aggressive interactions, it would be very useful to be able to observe interactions between two other individuals and integrate those indirect observations into a model of the group's dominance hierarchy (rather than risking injury through individual conflicts) (Bergman *et al.*, 2003). Furthermore, in many primates *coalitionary behavior* plays an important role, so a group of "subordinates" can vanquish a single "dominant." Coalitionary behavior between kin is common in many primates, and some primates also build non-kin coalitions (Bercovitch, 1988). Finally, many primate species exhibit *reconciliation* after fights (de Waal, 1989). Field primatologists quickly learn that combining all this information into a coherent mental model is not trivial, for humans or presumably the animals themselves.

Because group members are competing with other members of their own species, slight differences in cognitive abilities can have major effects on survival and reproduction, so the stage is always set for evolutionary arms races in a group-living species. Jolly suggested that the most important cognitive challenge facing many primates may be outsmarting their fellows, and that this provides a powerful adaptive explanation for primate intelligence. This hypothesis, extended by Humphrey (1976), has since become a major topic in studies of primate behavior and cognition, under the umbrella terms **"Machiavellian"** or **"social" intelligence** (Byrne and Whiten, 1988; Dunbar, 1993; Whiten and Byrne, 1997; Reader and Laland, 2002). Primate social cognition is directly relevant to the origin of pragmatic inference (Chapter 3), and social intelligence has been plausibly suggested to provide an important cognitive precursor for human language (Seyfarth *et al.*, 2005; Cheney and Seyfarth, 2007). These abilities therefore deserve detailed investigation here.

As the list above should make clear, "social intelligence" is a complex phenomenon, involving many different components. Within the broad category of social intelligence, as for language itself, we thus need to distinguish multiple separable capacities. For example, the ability to recognize another individual makes demands on long-term memory and perceptual generalization (recognizing the individual when it has grown or is wet, muddy, or wounded). Basic individual recognition, and recognition of kin, is widespread among both birds and mammals, and can be based on various cues including at least vision, audition, and olfaction (Barash, 1974; Cheney and Seyfarth, 1980; Walters, 1987; Rendall *et al.*, 1996; McComb *et al.*, 2000; Insley, 2001). This ability is necessary, but not sufficient, to accurately remember one's interactions with this individual, or its interactions with another animal. Several researchers have used the existence of dominance hierarchies in many animal species to show that information can be linked to individuals, and subjected to further cognitive processing: in at least two species, baboons and pinyon jays (Silk *et al.*, 1999; Paz-y-Miño *et al.*, 2004), individuals can reconstruct dominance hierarchies based on indirect third-party observations of conflict.

At the most challenging level, the ability to represent what another animal does or doesn't know – "theory of mind" – requires further capabilities. One classic experimental technique to probe animals' representations of other minds is *mirror recognition*. Many animals, from fish to squirrel monkeys, react to their image in a mirror with aggressive displays, as if it were another individual. However, great apes who have had experience with mirrors seem to recognize that the image is of themselves. This observation can be explored experimentally by sedating an individual and, while it is unconscious, placing a mark out of sight on its forehead (this is called the "Gallup test" after its originator, Gordon Gallup). Chimpanzees in this situation, given access to a mirror, look in the mirror and touch their forehead at rates much higher than when there was no mirror or no mark (Gallup, 1970). Chimpanzees will also use mirrors to explore otherwise invisible body parts (e.g. inside their mouths or genitals). Because this assay is simple, many other species have now been tested for mirror recognition, including various monkey species. While all apes "pass" the mirror test, most non-ape species have failed to show such behaviors; exceptions include dolphins (Reiss and Marino, 2001), parrots (Pepperberg *et al.*, 1995), and elephants

(Plotnik *et al.*, 2006). Gallup has suggested that mirror recognition indicates a concept of self (Gallup, 1991).

A more recent approach to evaluating theory of mind in animals concerns **gaze detection** and the ability to form inferences about others' minds based on what they can (or can't) see. A variety of species are sensitive to where other individuals are looking. For instance, house sparrows are sensitive to the direction in which an experimenter's head is pointing but not to eye direction *per se* (Hampton, 1994). A somewhat more complex ability is **gaze following**, when an animal detects the direction in which another individual looks, and itself looks in that direction (Tomasello *et al.*, 1999). This ability, too, is well attested in animals, including many primates (Tomasello *et al.*, 1998; Tomasello *et al.*, 1999), dogs (Call *et al.*, 2003), and goats (Kaminski *et al.*, 2005). For a social animal, gaze following can be highly adaptive, essentially enlarging the individual's visual "attention range" to that of the entire group. Thus it is unsurprising that basic gaze following is widely distributed in social animals.

Of course, knowing that someone is looking at you is not the same as knowing that they can *see* you. The latter is a mentalistic concept, and recognizing that "seeing is knowing" requires further cognitive resources. For many years, the work of Daniel Povinelli suggested that these resources were unavailable in chimpanzees (Povinelli *et al.*, 1990; Povinelli *et al.*, 1991; Povinelli *et al.*, 1999). In the most striking case, chimpanzees are familiarized with a begging situation, where holding their hands out to a human experimenter results in them being given hidden food (such begging comes naturally to chimpanzees, who show such behavior in the wild). Now, the chimpanzees are offered a choice of begging from two different humans: one who could see the food being hidden, and one who was blindfolded, or had a bucket over their head. The startling discovery in these experiments is that the chimpanzees distribute their begging *randomly* between these two. For a decade, the consensus based on these and similar experiments was that chimpanzees do *not* know that "seeing is knowing."

This consensus has been overturned, recently and spectacularly, with a new experimental paradigm introduced in Hare *et al.* (2000). Here the situation was competitive: a dominant and subordinate chimpanzee were both released into a central arena with food either visible to both animals, or visible only to the subordinate because it was behind a barrier. In normal conditions, dominants get all the food. But in situations in which only the subordinate could see the food, and particularly if it was given a small head start, it would rush preferentially to the *hidden* food. Various controls indicate that this capability is not due simply to reading the actions of the dominant animal, but involves integrating that animal's location, its gaze direction, and the location of the food relative to the barrier.

The discrepancy between the Hare and Povinelli results seems to be at least partially explained by the context: chimpanzees are much more able to exploit their knowledge of gaze and its underlying cognitive implications when they are put in a competitive situation than in the cooperative begging situation used by Povinelli (Hare and Tomasello, 2004). A cooperative situation that makes sense for humans (choosing a knowledgeable individual to provide aid) apparently does not compute for chimpanzees, whose social behavior tends to be far less cooperative than our own. Besides the clear importance of this particular finding, these experiments have an important general moral: we must be very cautious when interpreting negative experimental results concerning animal cognition. As David Premack said, discussing language training experiments: "Only when we know what constitutes proper training can we be certain who failed – teacher or pupil" (p. 821, Premack, 1971).

Data like these make the idea that primate sociality has driven the evolution of other aspects of primate intelligence compelling. Given the existence of highly developed sociality in most primates, we can assume that a strong basis for human social intelligence was already laid down earlier in our evolution, as primates. However, equally interesting examples of social intelligence are known in non-primates.

4.5.3 Dogs and gaze following: a simple trick?

Domestic dogs outperform chimpanzees, or dogs' wild progenitors – wolves, on cooperative tasks involving gaze, suggesting that their superior performance is due to recent, intense selection for cooperation with humans (Hare *et al.*, 2002). However, recent data show that experimentally domesticated foxes ("domesticated" for less than fifty generations and selected only for tameness, not cooperation) outperform normal foxes on such tasks (Hare *et al.*, 2005). This suggests that some rather basic change in cognition is adequate to develop improved gaze following abilities: perhaps simply a willingness to look into another individual's eyes without fear (Miklosi *et al.*, 2003). In most Old World primates and apes, direct gazing into others' eyes is avoided among adults, and locking gaze is interpreted as a threat. Although primates do look at others' eyes, they do so rapidly and surreptitiously, and adult apes virtually never stare directly into one another's eyes. It seems quite plausible that this **gaze prohibition** would impede the ability to derive detailed information about another individual's mind from their gaze. Is it possible that the willingness to look at another's eyes, and to let another individual look back, is enough to jump-start more sophisticated theory of mind abilities? The fox results make this hypothesis plausible, but more detailed studies on these and other domesticated species will be necessary before strong conclusions can be drawn (Kaminski *et al.*, 2005).

4.5.4 Avian social intelligence

In birds, corvids once again give primates a run for their money: scrub jays offer strong experimental evidence of social intelligence reminiscent of theory of mind (Emery and Clayton, 2004). One group of scrub jays are allowed to observe other birds hiding food, and then later granted an opportunity to pilfer the cache. These birds remember where the other birds hid the food (already impressive since it requires a viewpoint independent spatial map), and readily find the others' food and eat it. Later, these same birds are allowed to hide food themselves, with another bird watching through a glass partition. If they were observed hiding food, former thieves return when the watcher is removed and re-cache the food. Birds only do this if they have themselves had the opportunity to steal food: "it takes a thief to catch a thief." Naïve birds do not re-cache food, and experienced thieves do not re-hide food unless they were being watched (Emery and Clayton, 2001). Thus, these animals seem able to "project" their own experience of stealing onto another individual (one aspect of theory of mind) and use this knowledge to modify their own anticipatory behavior. This represents some of the most sophisticated behavior involving others' minds known in nonhuman animals. Similarly complex abilities have recently been documented in ravens, another corvid species (Bugnyar *et al.*, 2004; Bugnyar and Heinrich, 2005; Bugnyar, 2007), again suggesting that despite their smaller brains, the smartest birds are among the smartest of all nonhuman animals. Phylogenetic proximity to humans is not a reliable indicator of animal cognitive capabilities.

All of the data reviewed above suggest that pragmatic *inference* (drawing conclusions about others from their behavior) was well developed in primates long before humans evolved, and that "primate" social intelligence has deep roots in vertebrate social behavior. In a sense, then, the building blocks of pragmatics were in place long ago, with multiple features ready to be inherited or "exapted" by language as it evolved, including discreteness, hierarchy, open-endedness, and a basic form of propositionality (Cheney and Seyfarth, 2007). From another viewpoint however, these capacities are quite passive: animals draw pragmatic conclusions, but generally do not *help each other* to do so (though some evidence of animal teaching has recently been uncovered; cf. Thornton and McAuliffe, 2006). As discussed in Chapter 3, the full Gricean pragmatic package requires both a theory of mind and a propensity to use it to intentionally inform others. However, there is another way in which animal social behavior might be relevant to language evolution, and glossogeny in particular: if preservation of socially acquired behaviors provide an extended reservoir of capacity or knowledge beyond that of the individual. This brings us to the contentious issue of "animal culture."

4.6 Social learning, culture, and traditions: "animal culture"

In the early days of ethology, it was considered self-evident that animals are accurate imitators, and this is still a widespread assumption among non-ethologists. However, as the field matured it became increasingly clear that imitation, rigorously defined, is a highly demanding task that is relatively rare outside our own species. In contrast, other forms of "social learning" have taken center stage in our understanding of animal traditions and culture.

4.6.1 Vocal traditions

Today, the least controversial examples of true imitation, and imitation-based "cultural" traditions, come from *learned vocalizations* in birds and whales (Laland and Janik, 2006). Many birds learn their song by hearing others, and then practicing themselves, as demonstrated by experiments depriving young birds of either models or the opportunity to practice (Catchpole and Slater, 1995; Marler and Slabbekoorn, 2004). Such birds acquire only reduced, atypical songs. Furthermore, learned birdsong in a local area gradually differentiates from that in other areas, leading to bird-song "dialects" (Marler and Tamura, 1962; Baker and Cunningham, 1985b). Such dialects also are well documented in the songs of humpback whales. As in many birds, it is male humpbacks who sing during the breeding season, and the song may have both female attraction and male competition functions (Tyack and Clark, 2000). An intriguing difference is that, at any time and place, all breeding males sing the same song, which changes gradually throughout the season (typically a 40 percent change per year). Recently, however, a large scale "cultural revolution" was documented in Australia, where the group song off the east coast rapidly changed to match a (very different) song from the west coast (Noad *et al.*, 2000). This rapid change was apparently triggered by the movement of a few individuals from one coast to the other, but nothing is known about why the new variant was so successful or popular. Such examples provide the most clear and compelling evidence of "animal cultures" currently available, and we will therefore discuss vocal learning in detail in Chapter 9.

4.6.2 Non-vocal traditions

Non-vocal forms of social learning are often seen as more relevant to human cultural phenomena like toolmaking and foraging techniques. Again, the clearest examples come from non-primates: bluehead wrasses have been shown to learn their mating sites and migration routes from others, and these traditional routes outlast any individual fish: when entire groups are transferred from one reef to another, they devise different routes than their predecessors (Warner, 1988). Blackbirds fooled into thinking a conspecific was attacking a stuffed member of an unknown species went on to attack it themselves, and transferred this learned habit in a transmission chain over six individuals (Curio *et al.*, 1978). Many other examples of this sort are provided in Bonner (1983), and there can be little doubt that many species are able to pass learned traditions down over the generations.

Nonetheless, human culture involves far more than simple transmission, because humans not only remember and re-enact previous behaviors, but also can *improve* upon these past performances (Tomasello, 1990; Boyd and Richerson, 1996). Human culture is like a ratchet wrench, always moving in the direction of improvement. In recognition of this fact, students of animal social learning have sought to clarify the mechanisms that are needed to attain **cumulative cultural change**. Central to these mechanisms is **imitation**, which is operationally defined as the production of *novel* acts in response to seeing another individual perform very nearly the same act. If the "copier" previously produced this act (that is, if the act was in its pre-existing behavioral repertoire), then the term "imitation" is unjustified, and various other types of social learning are invoked (e.g. "local enhancement," where the observation of the place of the action increases the chance of copying, or "social facilitation," when observing some act – eating, resting – increases the probability of that action in the observer). By this widely accepted definition of imitation (Galef, 1988; Whiten and Ham, 1992), imitation is rare among animals. Reconsidering such classic cases of "imitation" in monkeys as the potato washing of Japanese macaques, combined with their own laboratory experiments with food washing and tool use, Visalberghi and Fragaszy (1990) concluded that imitation is infrequent or non-existent in macaques and capuchins. More recent data demonstrate simple forms of imitation in marmosets by this definition, for example removing a lid from a container (Voelkel and Huber, 2000). But complex motor imitation such as tool use remains undocumented in monkeys.

In apes, there is far stronger evidence of imitation. Although Kellogg and Kellogg (1933), who raised a baby chimpanzee and human side-by-side, already observed that humans' imitatative abilities are far more developed than chimpanzees', they saw many examples of novel behaviors apparently learned by observation, as did Hayes (1951) with Viki. Both field observations (Whiten *et al.*, 1999; Van Schaik *et al.*, 2003) and laboratory experiments (Whiten *et al.*, 2005) demonstrate that great apes can reliably transmit traditions over multiple generations, leading to what are termed "chimpanzee cultures." Nonetheless, careful experiments suggest that differences remain in the style of imitation: chimpanzees tend to "imitate" the *goal* of the action (sometimes termed "emulation") while children often slavishly imitate the action itself (Tomasello, 1990). The capacity of human infants and children (Piaget, 1962; Meltzoff and Moore, 1977; Meltzoff, 1988; Gergely *et al.*, 2002) to imitate motor actions (as well as vocalizations) remains unparalleled in its richness, despite clear homologs in ape behavior.

Thus, as for language itself, the question is not whether animals (or chimpanzees) have "culture," but *which* of the various mechanisms involved in social learning and culture in humans are shared with other animals. At present there can be little doubt that human culture differs sharply from anything known in the animal kingdom in its cumulativity (Richerson and Boyd, 2005). Psychologist Michael Tomasello has cogently argued, on the basis of abundant experimental data (Tomasello and Call, 1997; Tomasello *et al.*, 2003), that the advanced social/cultural intelligence of humans (particularly the capacity to share intentional states between individuals) is the primary difference between humans and other apes (Tomasello, 1999; Tomasello *et al.*, 2005). But it remains unclear whether this ability, and human cumulative culture more generally, can be disentangled from the possession of language itself.

In summary, many animals pass "traditions" over multiple generations, creating a second non-genetic form of inheritance parallel to human culture. The existence of rapid cultural change, independent of environmental and genetic change, has interesting and important evolutionary implications (cf. Odling-Smee *et al.*, 2003). But language, as it exists in humans, allows a degree of cultural cumulativity that is unparalleled in any nonhuman species (Laland *et al.*, 2001).

4.7 Inter-species communication: animals' latent abilities to use language-like systems

We now turn to what is probably the most controversial issue relating comparative work to human language: studies of "ape language" and similar communicative systems taught to other species (dogs, dolphins, sea lions, and parrots). I discuss these studies here, rather than in the next section on animal communication, because the capacity of an organism to master some human-invented system reflects their cognitive abilities, rather than those underlying their own species-typical communication system. These abilities are directly relevant to language evolution, because they clearly illustrate how "latent" capacities for language may be present in animals. These studies also unambiguously reveal features of human language that are *not* present, even in our nearest living relatives.

Controversy has unnecessarily polarized this area of research. For many of the researchers and commentators in this field, the crucial question has been "Do apes have language?," and the battle-lines are sharply drawn as soon as one answers "yes" or "no" to this question. This perspective on the research can be traced back to a paper controversially titled "Language in chimpanzee?" (Premack, 1971) – a question Premack was wise enough not to answer in his paper, though he expressed a "glass half full" opinion. A later paper, sharply critical of ape language experiments, was titled "Can an ape create a sentence?" (Terrace *et al.*, 1979), and their answer was an emphatic "no." This pair of titles captures the dichotomous essence of the debate, and indeed the whole controversy. Such questions are too broad to be usefully answered, and depend entirely on how one characterizes "language" or "sentence." Only after we subdivide these concepts into their component mechanisms can we hope to empirically address these questions.

Ape language experiments are particularly valuable for reconstructing the cognitive and communicative capabilities of our last common ancestor with chimpanzees (the LCA). They have helped to clarify both the severe limitations that needed to be overcome in hominid evolution (e.g. vocal learning) and, equally important, the considerable latent abilities that provided important prerequisites for the evolution of language. For example, everyone agrees that apes can learn a large number of referential signals with training (at least 125). Such data paint a rather surprising contrast to what apes do in the wild: nothing like this level of signal production has been observed in wild apes. Thus there is a latent cognitive ability in chimpanzees that apparently goes unexpressed in natural chimpanzee communication.

This ability presumably serves some other non-communicative cognitive function in the wild. Because such abilities were presumably present in the LCA, this finding is clearly relevant to models of language evolution, because we can assume that any mutations that increased referential signal *production* would already have found *listeners* able to make sense of these signals. Rather than argue about whether the learning of many arbitrary symbolic signals constitutes "language" (or not), we should simply accept it for what it is: one important prerequisite of human language that was already present in our LCA with chimpanzees. Perhaps surprisingly, however, work on non-ape species has been essentially congruent with the ape work. Acquiring a large referential vocabulary is not specific to apes: dogs and parrots readily master similarly large vocabularies (Pepperberg, 1990; Kaminski *et al.*, 2004).

It is important to note the potential difficulties in attempting to teach a member of another species to communicate using a system based on human language. The particular social situation of learning may be extremely important. Although many songbirds will learn song from a tape if they are raised in isolation, most will focus their attention on a live bird if one is available, even if that bird is a member of another species. A good illustration of this is found in parrots, which only learn to pair meanings with word forms when required to use a particular sound to obtain a favored object in a social situation (see below). This illustrates the need for caution in interpreting negative results: they may result from poor teaching rather than poor students.

One criticism sometimes leveled at studies of interspecific communication is that they are unfair, because learning another species' communication system is unnatural. More "ecologically valid" approaches study the species' own communication systems, as reviewed in the next section. While partially true, this is a weak criticism: interspecific communication is quite common in nature. Many species are known to listen to and correctly interpret the calls of other species (Hauser, 1988; Zuberbühler, 2000a; Rainey *et al.*, 2004). Certain alarm calls are shared, with largely the same form and meaning, among many different bird species (Marler, 1955). Growls, hisses, and other threat vocalizations are often directed at members of other species, who mostly interpret such calls appropriately (e.g. Morton, 1997). A rich example of "natural" interspecific communication is provided by honeyguides (Friedmann, 1955). Honeyguides are African birds that feed on beeswax and bee larvae, but are unable to open hives themselves. Honeyguides lead larger animals such as honey badgers, baboons, or humans to hives, by directing calls and conspicuous flight displays at these potential "partners in crime." After these large mammals open the hive and devour the honey, the honeyguides eat the wax and larvae left behind. This behavior is quite useful to human honey-gatherers: the Boran people of Kenya have an average search time of 3.2 hours when aided by honeyguides, and 8.9 hours on their own (Isack and Reyer, 1989). Thus, basic interspecific communication can be a normal, "natural" aspect of animal communication, posing no overwhelming cognitive challenge to many vertebrates.

4.7.1 Ape "language" studies

The most famous interspecies communication experiments have been performed with great apes. Following the failure of early attempts to teach chimpanzees speech (Yerkes and Yerkes, 1929; Kellogg and Kellogg, 1933; Hayes, 1951), an old suggestion by psychologist Robert Yerkes that use of gestural communication might work better was pursued. The first such attempt, training a chimpanzee with hand gestures borrowed from American Sign Language (ASL), was reported to considerable media fanfare by Gardner and Gardner (1969). The subject, a wild-caught infant named Washoe, had already mastered 30 recognizable hand signs by this first *Science* publication, and later estimates of her productive/perceptive vocabulary were as high as 250 items. A string of similar "ape language" projects followed with other apes, including Koko the gorilla (Patterson, 1978) and Chantek the orangutan (Miles, 1990), which also reported similar single-sign vocabulary sizes (e.g. 140 for Chantek). Although such claims are often treated skeptically (e.g. Pinker, 1994b), they are within the range well documented in dogs (200 spoken words; Kaminski *et al.*, 2004) or parrots (100 word–object pairs; Pepperberg, 1990). In most of these studies, careful precautions against "Clever Hans" effects have been taken. Parallel studies using plastic tokens rather than hand gestures also revealed considerable capacities in chimpanzees to perform arbitrary sign/meaning parings (Premack, 1971). There is little reason to doubt that Washoe, or other apes, can master arbitrary sign/meaning pairs numbering in the hundreds, and thus that this prerequisite for reference was already present in the LCA.

In contrast, animals' ability to combine individual words into larger meaningful wholes (syntax) remains highly controversial. This debate exploded in the 1970s with the work of Herbert Terrace and colleagues on another infant chimpanzee exposed to ASL signs, humorously named "Nim Chimpsky" (Terrace, 1979; Terrace *et al.*, 1979). Like Washoe, Nim seemed to master many signs, and sometimes to combine them into larger multi-unit "sentences." But careful analysis of the videotapes of Nim suggested that most of these were simply imitations of human strings produced just previously. These researchers concluded that, contrary to appearances, Nim had attained nothing even approaching human syntax. And neither, they implied, had Washoe or other apes. A roaring controversy ensued, from which this field has never fully recovered (cf. Wallman, 1992; Fouts and Mills, 1997).

The clearest new data since these early studies comes from the work of Sue Savage-Rumbaugh with common chimpanzees and bonobos, especially Kanzi (Savage-Rumbaugh, 1986; Savage-Rumbaugh *et al.*, 1993). These studies utilized a "Yerkish keyboard," named after Yerkes, covered with arbitrary meaningful symbols, and sometimes connected to a speech synthesizer to produce acoustic output. This work with Kanzi has provided several new insights. The most crucial finding was that attempts to teach bonobos like Kanzi's adopted mother, Matata, a simple communication system essentially failed. Meanwhile, her dependent young infant, sitting on her back or playing in the vicinity, picked up many aspects of the same system with no explicit training at all (Savage-Rumbaugh *et al.*, 1993). Kanzi acquired aspects of both Yerkish and spoken English spontaneously, without feedback, as an infant. Unlike the strict regimes and feedback that were used in most previous experiments, this result suggested a more human-like capacity to absorb significant information from context in young animals. Such age effects and context effects may be quite important in apes, just as Kaspar Hauser showed they are in humans.

Kanzi's understanding of spoken English is also considerable (Savage-Rumbaugh *et al.*, 1993), illustrating that apes' inability to produce speech is not a hindrance to their perception (a problem for motor theories of speech perception; e.g. Liberman and Mattingly, 1989). Finally, although Kanzi mainly produces single-sign "utterances," the occasional two- and three-sign productions do reveal regularities in order, and some of these appear to be generated by Kanzi rather than copied from his input (Greenfield and Savage-Rumbaugh, 1990). Kanzi uses word order in spoken sentences to disambiguate meanings (e.g. correctly enacting "make the doggie bite the snake" and "make the snake bite the doggie" with dolls). Equally significant, the same authors admit that "Kanzi had a much smaller proportion of indicatives or statements (4%) in comparison with requests (96%) than would be normal for a human child" (p. 567). Despite his unusual gift for communication, Kanzi uses it almost exclusively to ask for food or play.

Savage-Rumbaugh and colleagues argue that Kanzi has "grammar" at the level of roughly a two-year-old human. This suggestion makes many commentators bridle (e.g. Pinker, 1994b), because word order does not constitute "grammar" in humans, and indeed serial order abilities are well developed in many species. The middle way in this debate is to simply recognize that some aspects of language, components of FLB, *are* shared with chimpanzees, while others are not, and that the same is true for syntax (Premack, 1986; Deacon, 1997; Kako, 1999). From my perspective, Kanzi and other language-trained apes demonstrate an ability to acquire a sizeable lexicon, to use it in communicative interactions (though mostly, it must be admitted, to make requests for treats or tickles), and to produce and understand basic and non-random combinations of these lexical items. These communicative abilities do not constitute a language by the simple definition used in this book, because Kanzi cannot communicate all the concepts he can entertain. For example, Kanzi can successfully carry out quite complex motor actions, such as starting fires and making and using simple stone tools (Toth *et al.*, 1993), but his "linguistic" productions never even come close to the complexity required to describe these abilities. I believe that these experiments have been extremely valuable in revealing previously unknown capabilities of chimpanzees, and by inference the LCA. That apes do not attain full adult language is clear, and is agreed by all. Thus, "ape language" studies help to isolate and verify the factors that needed to evolve in our lineage on the way to language.

4.7.2 Communication between humans and other vertebrates

Some of the most important and surprising studies in interspecies communication have come from Irene Pepperberg's long-term study with African gray parrots, *Psittacus erithacus* (Pepperberg, 1999), in particular the now-deceased "Alex" and a number of conspecifics. Parrots can go beyond "parroting" (meaningless use of sounds) and learn to use spoken English meaningfully, correctly deploying words for objects, colors, shapes, materials, and numbers. The birds both understand these words when spoken, and are able to pronounce them clearly themselves. When shown a tray of objects and asked "How many red?," Alex can correctly respond "three." To the question "How many green?," he can correctly answer "none." When an object is held up with the question "What color?," the parrot can answer "red." The answers, though not infallible, are correct more than 80% of the time (far better than chance levels of 20–25%), and careful measures have excluded the possibility of unconscious "Clever Hans" cueing on the part of the experimenters. The most convincing approach taken has been to ensure ignorance on the part of the trainers (e.g. Pepperberg and Brezinsky, 1991). The test objects are placed in a box so that the experimenter could not see them, while the scientist responsible for placing the items in the box told the experimenter what question to ask. Alex's performance in these studies remained around 80%, and since no one in the room knew the correct answer it is difficult to explain this via cueing. Such control experiments have convinced most researchers familiar with this work to accept these results at face value (Kako, 1999).

The reason these results defy our intuition is that parrots normally treat their imitated utterances as "pure sound." Quite specific training paradigms are necessary to induce a parrot to learn the meanings of words. The basic approach is termed the "model/rival paradigm" (Todt, 1975), and the crucial ingredients are social: two human experimenters handle food or objects in which the bird is interested. One "dominant" experimenter controls the objects, and gives them to the second experimenter (the parrot's rival for attention) only if they correctly use the words being trained. Only in this competitive context do parrots learn to use their imitations of word forms in a meaningful fashion. Parrots will not learn to imitate from videos, any more than a human child will learn a foreign language from exposure to a TV broadcast in that language. The training procedure requires not just referentiality (a mapping between signal and meaning) and functionality (requests that achieve goals), but also a particular competitive form of social interaction.

These parrots are the only known nonhuman species that can actually engage in a simple spoken conversation with a human being. These abilities are instantiated in a brain which, as Pepperberg likes to point out, "is the size of a walnut – a *shelled* walnut." Thus, neither the ability to imitate sounds, nor to pair them with meanings, requires a large brain. Continuing work with other parrots provides no evidence that Alex was in any way extraordinary; Pepperberg's pioneering studies have only scratched the surface of their abilities. Although some fascinating work on "babbling" or solitary sound play in parrots has been reported, most of Pepperberg's attention has been focused on cognition, with speech being a means to an end rather than the primary focus of research. There is clearly much remaining to be learned about vocal communication in this species.

Similar findings come from work with dolphins or sea lions (Herman *et al.*, 1984; Schusterman and Krieger, 1984; Schusterman and Gisiner, 1988), suggesting that the cognitive apparatus necessary for understanding arbitrary signs and combining them into simple "phrases" is present in many different vertebrates. Questions such as the acquisition of syntactic patterns, or function words, remain unanswered. Studies on parrots reveal both commonalities with ape abilities (e.g. large vocabulary acquisition) and important differences (the use of speech) that are extremely informative. Unfortunately, unlike the uproar and debate surrounding the "ape language" studies, the work with parrots and marine mammals has often suffered a worse fate – being simply ignored – in the language evolution literature.

4.7.3 Are constraints on word learning adaptations "for" language?

I will give one further example of why research on a wide range of species is important for understanding language evolution. We have seen that there are certain constraints that children appear to bring to the problem of language acquisition, such as mutual exclusivity or the whole object assumption (Chapter 3). To what degree are such constraints on word learning specific to language, and to human beings? While one might see the rapid rate of child language evidence as *de facto* evidence of a human-specific adaptation (e.g. Pinker and Jackendoff, 2005), this conclusion is only warranted if similar abilities are not present in nonhuman animals. We saw that attempts to pit word learning skills against general fact learning skills shows no specific advantage for the former, providing no evidence that the mechanisms underlying word learning are specific to language (Markson and Bloom, 1997; Bloom, 2000). Perhaps surprisingly, multiple studies suggest that they are not specific to humans either. There is abundant evidence that animal learning, too, is constrained by biology (Garcia and Koelling, 1966; Gallistel, 2000), and that some of these constraints are widely shared.

Evidence for **mutual exclusivity** comes from an early study with "Rocky," a sea lion (*Zalophus californicus*) trained on a retrieval task. After considerable difficulty in learning a new color label for a known noun (a difficulty consistent with mutual exclusivity), the sea lion associated a novel color term to a novel shade correctly, immediately, and effortlessly (Schusterman and Krieger, 1984). While parrot research uncovered only inconsistent evidence for mutual exclusivity (Pepperberg and Wilcox, 2000), strong recent evidence for productive use of constraints on word learning comes from a pet dog, a border collie named "Rico." Rico had been trained by his owners to recognize verbal labels for over 200 objects (Kaminski *et al.*, 2004). After demonstrating this capacity unambiguously, by asking Rico to retrieve objects in a separate room (avoiding "Clever Hans" effects from the experimenter or owner), the experimenters presented him with a novel label. His choices included a set of familiar objects and a single novel object. In 70 percent of such trials, Rico retrieved the novel item; furthermore he showed evidence of remembering these labels one month later. The authors conclude, correctly in my opinion, that "some of the perceptual and cognitive mechanisms that may mediate the comprehension of speech were already in place before early humans began to talk" (p. 1683).

Much of the data considered here are consistent with a strong thesis: that the capacity for **reference** was already present in our ancestors before language evolved. Furthermore, the comparative findings are consistent with a broadly shared set of **innate constraints** or biases on what counts as a potential referent, and how labels to such referents are "naturally" applied. The problem of induction, correctly spotted by philosophers, is solved by constraints on the hypothesis space that are general components of the cognitive and perceptual machinery we are born with. Much of this machinery is shared to a significant degree with other animals, rather than constituting a specific cognitive adaptation to language or word learning, suggesting that Quine's "Gavagai" problem may be largely solved by cognitive biases that predated humans or language.

I conclude that the current data from humans and animals suggest that the impressive abilities of children to learn the meanings of new words overlap with animals general abilities to acquire new concepts. This conclusion is good news for biolinguistics, because it strongly suggests that work on animal cognition, and its neural basis, has much to teach us about the process of child language acquisition. This literature makes clear a crucial point that is often lost in the rhetoric surrounding nativist/empiricist discussions: a trait involved in language can be "innate" (reliably developing) without being specific to language, or to humans. Innate biases are needed to solve the logical problem of language acquisition, but this does not automatically make them adaptations that evolved *in order to* solve this problem. They are excellent examples of preadaptations for language. Constraints on concept acquisition *predated* the appearance of hominids on the planet, and played an important supporting role once the evolution of language got underway in our species.

4.8 Animal cognition: conclusions

In summary, a large body of experimental work demonstrates considerable cognitive abilities in nonhuman animals. Many different vertebrates have a surprisingly rich conceptual world and a broadly shared cognitive "toolkit" (Hauser, 2000), and the data reviewed above leave little doubt that sophisticated cognition is possible in the absence of language. Many capabilities that were long thought to be unique to humans have now been demonstrated convincingly in animals. These include cross-modal association, episodic memory, anticipatory cognition, gaze following, basic theory of mind, tool use, and tool construction.

With these data, we can answer the old question of whether animals think, and have concepts, affirmatively. If by "concepts" we simply mean "mental representations, not necessarily conscious," few scientists today question the notion that animals have concepts, at some level, and contemporary cognitive ethologists and comparative psychologists are providing an ever more impressive catalog of the types of concepts that non-linguistic creatures possess and manipulate. We can conclude that the basic functioning of the brain in nonhuman species supports an elaborate system of categories, concepts, flexible learning abilities, goals, and an ability to form novel sequences of actions in accord with knowledge and desires. The widespread notion that concepts and thought *require* language is indefensible: it either conceals a definition of "thought" that is based on human language (and is therefore tautological), or implicitly singles out and privileges a very small subset of human cognitive processes that are not shared with other animals as "thought." Neither of these moves seems well justified by the available data. A related gambit associates thought only with consciousness, and denies "animal thought" by denying that animals are conscious (Wynne, 2004). But "consciousness" remains a fuzzy concept, and remains difficult, if not impossible, to verify empirically even in humans, and such last-gasp efforts to deny animal cognition are essentially stipulative, with little other than long prejudice to recommend them (Griffin, 2001). Some remaining philosophical and linguistic objections have been parried, at book length, by Hurford (2007), which I recommend to anyone still skeptical of this conclusion.

Although many of these capabilities have been demonstrated in only one or a few species, it should be recognized that these experiments are quite difficult, often relying upon species-typical behaviors like food caching that are not present in all species. There are often few good species for research on a particular problem, where the questions can be posed experimentally (Krebs, 1975). Thus, absence of evidence for some cognitive ability (e.g. episodic memory) in a non-caching species should not be considered evidence of absence: we simply lack empirical methods to probe for such abilities. New empirical techniques in animal cognition research have initiated a new golden age of comparative cognitive research, and anyone who follows this literature rapidly develops a cautious attitude regarding suggestions that animals cannot do *x*, or that *y* is impossible without language.

Thus I conclude that concepts and ideas in the various senses described above both *predate* language in evolutionary terms, and are *independent* from language in contemporary neural terms. This will be a foundational observation for the rest of my discussion, with crucial implications for the evolution of language. The LCA had a rich suite of conceptual tools, forcing the conclusion that our shared ancestor could form concepts and memories, exhibit goal-directed behavior, draw basic inferences such as transitive inference, predict the movement of invisible objects, and learn complex serial orders, including at least some involving hierarchical tasks. Our prelinguistic hominid ancestors were sophisticated tool users. They lived complex social lives, requiring elaborate cognitive representations, and had well-developed concepts of space, time, and causality. Furthermore, some basic ability to quantify small numbers of objects and to perform mental operations upon the results was present before language evolved. Finally, they were able to link mental concepts to arbitrary signs, whether vocal or visual. In sharp contrast, as we will now see when we examine animal communicative capabilities in more detail, the communication system of modern primates, and thus of the LCA, are far more limited.

4.9 Animal communication

All animals communicate, but not all communication systems are language. A single-celled social amoeba on a rotting log secretes chemical substances that attract other amoebae to cluster together and reproduce sexually. A male bird sings from a treetop in early spring to attract a mate and defend his territory. A female ground squirrel makes a high-pitched whistle to warn her offspring of a coyote in the distance. A dog carefully doles out urine on each of many different landmarks to mark its territory. A mated pair of cranes engage in an elaborate "dance," with synchronized movements, to affirm and advertise their pair-bond. A male spider, one-tenth the size of the female, carefully vibrates her web with a species-specific pattern to encourage her to mate with, rather than eat, him. A chimpanzee, discovering a tree full of ripe fruit, issues a raucous, long-carrying pant hoot to attract others. A group of humans produces a staccatto vocalization called laughter, affirming their social bonds. This list could go on indefinitely. All of these behaviors are forms of animal communication, but none of them are language.

I define language as a system which bi-directionally maps an open-ended set of concepts onto an open-ended set of signals. Many researchers have noted that this open-ended ability to convey *any* thought imaginable contrasts sharply with animal communication systems, which typically have a small, closed set of signals for conveying particular, biologically critical meanings. As a longtime student of animal communication, with experience with a variety of vertebrate species, I tend to agree that human language has qualitative differences from other systems. Indeed, based on current understanding, *no* nonhuman animal communication systems are languages in the above sense (although we should keep an open mind concerning the many thousands of poorly studied species). Therefore, there is no logical or empirical basis for the common assumption that language *must* have evolved from some pre-existing communication system that existed in the LCA. After we examine primate communication systems closely, we will see that certain aspects of these systems do seem to provide potential precursor mechanisms to mechanisms involved in human language (e.g. the ability to interpret signals made by others as meaningful), while others do not (e.g. the innately determined structure of primate vocalizations does not appear to provide a cognitive precursor for the complex learned structure of human speech).

Animal communication represents a vast and fascinating area of research, one that has undergone quite rapid progress in the last decades due both to technological advances (e.g. recording devices, the sound spectrograph, and playback experiments) and theoretical advances in our understanding of how, when, and why animals communicate. One thing is made crystal clear by these observations: our intuitions as language-using humans are poor guides to what animals are actually doing with their communicative signals. We tend to assume both too much (e.g. that signalers and receivers are "mirror images") and too little (e.g. that innate "emotional" calls are necessarily involuntary). Unfortunately, such unwarranted intuitive assumptions frequently enter into models of language evolution, so it is important to look carefully at both contemporary theory and data.

But recognizing the uniqueness of language provides no justification for ignoring animal communication, for several reasons. First, even if novel aspects of language evolved from cognitive precursors having nothing to do with communication, they still had to *co-exist* with the set of innate signals that humans use for communication (cries, screams, laughter, smiles, frowns, etc.). Such signals are continuous with other primate signals, and still play a critical role in human social behavior. Thus a developing language system which was incompatible with such basic signals (e.g. by eliminating or distorting them) would be severely maladaptive. Second, although language is certainly useful in "private" form (for expressing thoughts in one's own brain), it is also used very effectively to communicate, and the evolution of the communicative aspects of language had to obey evolutionary constraints applying to communication in general. Finally, studies of animal communication clearly reveal that some critical aspects of language (e.g. simple pragmatic inference on the part of listeners) were already well established before language evolved in hominids. The study of animal communication provides the necessary context to appreciate the ways in which language really *is* different. It is only the long and detailed study of animal communication systems in the twentieth century that finally allowed scientists to recognize and document these differences. For all of these reasons, a basic understanding and appreciation of animal communication is a necessary component of biolinguistics. I will organize my review along the lines of the "three Ss" of signal, structure, and semantics (Chapter 3).

4.9.1 Continuity and discontinuity: a false dichotomy

A distinction is frequently made between "continuist" models of human language evolution, which seek the precursors of human speech and language in the communication of other primates, and "discontinuist" models that reject this possibility (Lenneberg, 1967; Bickerton, 1990). This is an excellent example of a false dichotomy of little value in understanding language evolution. Despite important areas of continuity between speech and primate calls (e.g. use of a mammalian vocal apparatus), there are good reasons to reject any wholesale continuity between primate calls and human spoken language. For example, the form of most (if not all) nonhuman primate calls is genetically determined, and will reliably develop in the absence of any relevant environmental stimulation. Human linguistic signals are learned, and indeed *must* be learned if they are to provide an open-ended, shared lexicon of signals appropriate for linguistic communication. For speech to evolve, humans thus needed to evolve a novel capacity: the ability to control the structure of vocal signals, copying previously heard sounds. Any adequate model of language evolution will have to grapple with this key discontinuity between human speech and primate vocalizations. In contrast, as we have just seen, many of the cognitive capacities that underlie the interpretation of the world, and of sounds, are probably continuous with those of other primates (or vertebrates more generally). These are crucial components of language apparently inherited in a rich form (though perhaps extended and modified) from our primate ancestors.

These components are all important in understanding language, in terms of both current mechanisms and evolution, and should be considered part of the human language capacity in a broad sense (FLB). Researchers who focus on non-shared mechanisms (FLN) often tend to favor discontinuous views of their evolution (e.g. Bickerton, 1990). But even a clear break between humans and other living animals does not imply an *evolutionary* discontinuity. The transition from flightless Triassic reptiles to the birds of today was gradual (as revealed by the fossils of feathered dinosaurs that could not have flown (e.g. Qiang *et al.*, 1998)), but bird flight is today discontinuous with the locomotion of reptiles, simply because intermediate forms have not survived. If only a few extinct hominid species had survived longer, we might today have a revealing series of intermediate protolanguages on hand. Present-day discontinuity does not imply evolutionary discontinuity.

4.9.2 Signals: a key distinction between innate and learned signals

A far more relevant distinction is between innate and learned signals. Consider domestic dogs: as everyone knows, the word for "dog" varies from language to language (*dog, Hund, chien, . . .*). Despite some onomatopoeia, even the word for the *sound* a dog makes varies (dogs are said to go *ouah ouah* in French, but *ruff* or *woof* in English). Crucially, however, the sounds that the dogs themselves make do not vary in this way. Dogs growl, whine, bark, howl, and pant in the same way all over the world. This is because such sounds are part of the innate behavioral repertoire that every dog is born with. This basic vocal repertoire will be present even in a deaf and blind dog. This is not, of course, to say that dog sounds do not vary: they do. You may be able to recognize the bark of your own dog, as an individual, and different dog breeds produce recognizably different vocalizations. But such differences are not learned; they are inevitable byproducts of the fact that individuals vary, and differences at the morphological, neural, or "personality" level will have an influence on the sounds an individual makes. Dogs do not learn how to bark or growl, cats do not learn how to meow, and cows do not learn their individual "moos." Such calls constitute an **innate call system**. By "innate" in this context, I simply mean "reliably developing without acoustic input from others" or "canalized" (cf. Ariew, 1999). For example, in "Kaspar Hauser" experiments in which young squirrel monkeys were raised by muted mothers, and never heard conspecific vocalizations, they nonetheless produced the full range of calls, in the proper contexts (Winter *et al.*, 1973). Hybrid gibbons produce intermediate calls, unlike anything they have heard from their parents (Geissmann, 1987). Cross-fostered macaques raised among a different species continue to produce calls typical of their own species. They do, however, learn to correctly *interpret* the calls of their new foster parents, and respond to them appropriately (Owren *et al.*, 1993).

The same regularity applies to important aspects of human communication. A smile is a smile all over the world, and a frown or grimace of disgust indicates displeasure everywhere. Although universally recognized today, this was actually disputed for many years (see Eibl-Eibesfeldt, 1970). Not only are many facial expressions equivalent in all humans, but their interpretation is as well (Ekman and Friesen, 1975; Ekman, 1992). Many *vocal* expressions are equally universal. Such vocalizations as laughter, sobbing, screaming, and groans of pain or of pleasure are just as innately determined as the facial expressions that normally accompany them (Scherer, 1985). Babies born both deaf and blind, unable to perceive either facial or vocal signals in their environment, nonetheless smile, laugh, frown, and cry normally (Eibl-Eibesfeldt, 1973). Again, just as for dog barking, individuals vary, and you may well recognize the laugh of a particular friend echoing above the noise in a crowded room (Bachorowski and Owren, 2001). And we have some volitional control over our laughter: we can (usually) inhibit socially inappropriate laughter. These vocalizations form an **innate human call system**. Just like other animals, we have a species-specific, innate set of vocalizations, biologically associated with particular emotional and referential states (Deacon, 1992; Jürgens, 1995). In contrast, we must learn the words or signs of language.

This difference between human innate calls, like laughter and crying, and learned vocalizations, like speech and song, is fundamental (we discuss its neural basis in Chapter 9). An anencephalic human baby (entirely lacking a forebrain) still produces normal crying behavior but will never learn to speak or sing (Lenneberg, 1967). In aphasia, speech is often lost or highly disturbed while laughter and crying remain normal. Innate human calls provide an intuitive framework for understanding a core distinction between language and most animal signals, which are *more like the laughs and cries of our own species* than like speech. Laughs and cries are unlearned signals with meanings tied to important biological functions. To accept this fact is not to deny their communicative power. Innate calls can be very expressive and rich – indeed this affective power may be directly correlated with their unlearned nature. The "meaning" of a laugh can range from good-natured conviviality to scornful, derisive exclusion, just as a cat's meow might "mean" she wants to go out, she wants food, or she wants to be petted. But the overall form of the signal remains the same, and most of the message is either expressed through direct, analog correspondence between signal and emotion, or inferred from the current context. Insightful observers of animals and man have recognized these fundamental facts for many years (Darwin, 1872b; Eibl-Eibesfeldt, 1970; Deacon, 1992; Jürgens, 1995).

Obviously, signals of "emotion" and signals of "linguistic meaning" are not always neatly separable. In myriad ways, but especially via vocal prosodic cues, facial expressions, and gestures, our linguistic utterances are typically accompanied by "non-verbal" cues to how we feel about what we are saying, many of them also aspects of our innate endowment as humans. One signal typically carries both linguistic, semantic information, intelligible only to those who know the language, and a more basic set of information that can be understood by any human being or even other animals. Brain lesions can lead to specific loss of one or the other of these aspects (with loss of the expressive component termed "aprosodia"; Ross, 1981, 1988). Non-verbal expressive cues provide a valuable cue to the child learning language, helping to coordinate joint attention and disambiguate the message and context. They also make spoken (or signed) utterances more emotionally expressive than a written transcription alone. Other than the exclamation mark "!" or "emoticons" like ":)," our tools to transcribe the expressive component are limited, but the ease and eagerness with which literate humans read illustrates that we can nonetheless understand language without this expressive component. This, too, reinforces the value of a distinction, though not a dichotomy, between these two parallel, complementary components.

As we discuss other species' communication systems, I invite the reader to compare these systems not only to linguistic exchanges, but also to the last time you had a good laugh with a group of friends, and the warm feeling that goes along with it, or the sympathetic emotions summoned by seeing someone else cry, scream, or groan in pain. The contrast between such experiences and linguistic expressions like *I find that extremely humorous* or *this causes me severe grief* helps us understand many of the communication systems we will discuss below. For each species, we should ask not, "Is this animal's communication system like human communication?" – a question which implies a false dichotomy between humans and other animals – but rather, "Is this call type more like human laughter and crying, or more like speech or song?" – a question that recognizes a crucial distinction within our own species-typical behavior. If innate calls seem somehow less valuable than learned vocalizations, try the following thought experiment: if forced to give up either language, or innate signals like smiling, laughter, and crying, which would you choose? Sympathetic reports of brain lesions that selectively destroy one or the other suggest that this choice should not be easy: the loss of normal emotional expressivity is extremely debilitating for patient, family, and friends (Sacks, 1985). While I would still choose to keep language, I would do so knowing that I was sacrificing a central aspect of what it is to be a human: the rich and intimate sharing of emotion with others, accomplished largely via our inborn system of vocal and facial signals. While other primates may not be able to discuss what they had for dinner yesterday, they are nonetheless woven into their social groups by an elaborate system of vocal and other signals, just like us, and it is no denigration to acknowledge that the structure, and to a large degree the meaning, of these signals is innately determined.

4.9.3 Emotional expression and "reflexive" communication in animals

Animal signals often express inner states of excitement or emotion. Since Descartes, this is often thought to imply an involuntary reflex action, where the animal lacks any psychological intent to signal, and the only "intent" is that of evolution, which built the signal into the animal as a reflex. This Cartesian conception of animal communication suggests that animals are simply automata, vocalizing when stimulated but not "experiencing" or "intending" anything, because animals lack minds. By such a model, a cry of pain is no more voluntary than the orange and black stripes on a caterpillar. Donald Griffin dubbed this view the "groan of pain" model (Griffin, 2001). Such a model of animal behavior is difficult to refute empirically, because we lack a way to objectively inspect the contents of animals' minds, and no one can conclusively demonstrate that animals *have* awareness or volition. Furthermore, most communication signals probably have an automatic component: just like laughter or crying in humans. However, three lines of data provide strong evidence that this reflexive view is incomplete.

First, in the laboratory, animals can control their emission of innate vocalizations. It is often stated in the language evolution literature that most mammals (including most primates) lack voluntary control over vocal production. The apparent source of this idea, though rarely cited, is Skinner's infamous *Verbal Behavior*, which states that "innate responses comprise reflex systems which are difficult, if not impossible, to modify by operant reinforcement. Vocal behavior below the human level is especially refractory" (p. 463, Skinner, 1957). Over time this "impossibility" has hardened into dogma. For example, "the point is generally accepted: the majority of primate calls are certainly involuntary" (Tallerman, 2007); "The lack of voluntary control . . . makes primate vocal calls ill-suited to exaptation for intentional communication" (Corballis, 2002a).

In fact, many experiments show that vocalizations *can* be brought under operant control in the laboratory in many mammals including cats, dogs, and guinea pigs (see review in Myers, 1976; Adret, 1993), as well as all primates tested so far including lemurs (W. A. Wilson, 1975), capuchin monkeys (Myers *et al.*, 1965), rhesus monkeys (Sutton *et al.*, 1973; Aitken and

Wilson, 1979), and chimpanzees (Randolph and Brooks, 1967). Although the acoustic *structure* of these vocalizations is innate, with proper training animals can learn to initiate or inhibit the *production* of such calls volitionally. Withholding is difficult, but possible, for chimpanzees in the wild, who may cover their mouths to avoid vocalizing (Goodall, 1986; Townsend *et al.*, 2008). Although Skinner was correct that it is far more difficult for most animals, and especially primates, to control vocalization than to control hand movements (e.g. lever pressing; Myers, 1976), and vocal operant studies take huge numbers of trials and many months of training before success (Sutton *et al.*, 1973), voluntary "gating" of vocalization is possible for essentially any mammal or bird. We will discuss the brain mechanisms underlying such control in Chapter 9. For now the key distinction is between **control of vocalization** *per se*, which is widespread, and voluntary control over the *acoustic structure* of vocalizations, which is absent in most terrestrial mammals, including apparently all nonhuman primates.

Further evidence against reflexive signaling comes from **audience effects** in animal communication. Many mammals will not produce alarm calls when no conspecifics are present (e.g. vervet monkeys; Cheney and Seyfarth, 1985) – the simplest form of audience effect, which already demonstrates that callers are not mere automata that call automatically upon sight of a predator. More complex effects are also attested, for instance calling only when relatives are present (e.g. ground squirrels; Sherman, 1977). Chickens demonstrate sophisticated audience effects (Marler *et al.*, 1991; Evans and Evans, 2007): males are more likely to produce alarm calls when with their mate, chicks, or other familiar birds than with unfamiliar birds, and only produce food calls when hens are present, not when alone with another cockerel (Evans and Marler, 1994). Such audience effects appear to represent the norm in vertebrate communication, not an exception (Marler and Evans, 1996). While the committed behaviorist can always construct more elaborate suggestions about the content of reflexive vocalization (e.g. "cocks have an innate food call reflex that requires food + hen as a releaser"), such non-cognitive explanations begin to look complex relative to the idea that animals are sensitive to and responsive to their audience when calling.

Finally, a number of avian species produce **deceptive alarm calls** when no predator is present, apparently to frighten away competitors (Munn, 1986; Møller, 1988), and similar behavior has been observed anecdotally in some primates (for review see Fitch and Hauser, 2002). The status of such calls as cognitive "deception" is questionable, but they certainly show that some animals can learn to produce calls when it benefits them. In summary, converging data from conditionability, audience effects, and deception suggest that most vertebrates have some voluntary control over the production of their innately structured calls.

Does this mean that such innate vocalizations do not, after all, reflect emotions? Not at all. The hypothesis that emotional cries actually correspond to specific emotional states receives strong support from self-stimulation studies. Electrodes placed in particular regions of the brainstem in most animals can reliably elicit particular calls. An animal with such an electrode implanted can then be given a choice to electrically stimulate itself or not. A series of studies by neurobiologist Uwe Jürgens showed that, in squirrel monkeys, calls normally associated with pleasurable stimuli and situations elicit self-stimulation, while the animal will work to avoid stimulation associated with "negative" vocalizations like screams (Jürgens, 1979). Humans and animals will voluntarily self-stimulate with electrodes implanted in centers that evoke subjective pleasure, and avoid stimulation of areas subjectively associated with pain (Olds and Milner, 1954; Heath, 1963), suggesting that stimulation not only elicits the vocalizations themselves, but also the subjective emotional state such calls normally indicate. This tight link suggests that many innate calls are indeed vocal signals of particular emotional states. In conclusion, the hypothesis of Darwin that many animal vocalizations can best be seen as expressions of internal emotional states appears to be well founded, and to encompass a broad range of innate animal signals (Darwin, 1872b). Nonetheless, animals have control over the production or inhibition of these signals, despite the facts that the structure of the signal, the ability to feel the emotion, and the link between the two are innately determined. An analogy for such calls is laughing when tickled: essentially a spontaneous response, but controllable voluntarily with some difficulty. But "innate" and "emotional" do not, as often thought, logically entail "involuntary."

4.10 Structure: phonological and syntactic phenomena in animal communication

One of the more divisive questions in animal communication is: "Do non-human animals have syntax?" There are various unenlightening ways of interpreting the question: if we mean "Do animals generate syntactic structures just like those of human languages?," the answer is a trivial "no." If we mean "Are there rules that govern the ways in which animals produce and process strings?," the answer is definitely "yes." The relevant question, then, demands some more specific characterization of the kinds of rules used by different species, where questions of semantics are left to one side. Formal language theory (see Chapter 3) provides one way of determining what kinds of computational resources are necessary to implement different kinds of animal signaling systems, and applies independently of what signals mean. This provides a good fit for many animal signaling systems, because the more complex ones (such as birdsong) have relatively simple, holistic meanings and the meaning of a signal does not change when the signal structure changes. Thus, a formal idealization focused on structural considerations, and abstracting away from semantic ones, is quite appropriate for language, music, and many animal signaling systems. There is a rather long history of considering animal signals from a structural viewpoint, and a virtue of the conceptual framework provided by formal language theory is that it can encompass all of these domains equally.

4.10.1 Non-random ordering

Even simple animal call sequences typically have a rule-based structure. For example, the "chickadee" call for which the black-capped chickadee is named follows a quite specific temporal pattern (Hailman and Ficken, 1987). There are four different syllable types, distinguishable by spectrographic analysis, that can be labeled from A to D. Of 3,479 calls analyzed, 99.7 percent occurred in the fixed order ABCD (e.g. ABCD, ABBCCD, ABCCCCD, etc.). The variant order BCB accounted for 9 of 11 remaining strings. Such regularities can easily be captured by a simple **finite state grammar**. Note that despite the simplicity of this system, the set of strings produced certainly qualifies as a "language" in the depauperate sense of formal linguistics: it is a set of strings formed by some set of rules. Thus, Hailman and Ficken are justified in claiming that "Chick-a-dee calling qualifies as 'language' by structural linguistics," but only in the trivial sense that chickadee calling is not entirely random. Regularities like those of chickadees also occur in the calls of capuchin monkeys, *Cebus nigrivitattus* (Robinson, 1984), and can also be captured by a very simple finite state grammar.

Of course, the fact that scientists can discover rules apparently governing strings of calls produced by an animal does not mean that the animals themselves perceive those rules: evaluating this requires further experiments. By creating birdsong stimuli that either followed or disobeyed the apparent rules of swamp sparrow song, and then examining the responses of listening birds, Balaban (1988) showed that the distinction between "own" and other grammars was noticed by conspecifics: females showed more solicitation displays to their "own" syntax, and males stayed closer to "other" syntax in a two-speaker choice paradigm. Similarly, young swamp sparrows will learn and imitate the experimentally stuttered, but still rule-governed, syntax of an older male (Podos *et al.*, 1999), showing that they perceive and store the underlying rule. Thus, in various species of birds and mammals, sequences of calls possess structural regularities, and conspecifics recognize and respond to them.

4.10.2 Phonological syntax and animal "song"

More complex examples of structure in animal vocalizations come from birds and whales, involving both learned signals and learned rules, but these appear to have little or no link to meaning. Many observers have noted that it may be more enlightening to consider the parallels between complex animal communication systems like bird and whale song with music, rather than natural language (Fitch, 2006b). An individual brown thrasher will know more than 1,000 specific syllables, and will arrange these in a species-typical order (Kroodsma and Parker, 1977). Furthermore, complex "songs" such as that of mockingbirds or whales are hierarchical, with multiple levels of structure: "notes" or syllables are arranged into short phrases which are repeated several times. Structure in such "songs" is best treated as phonological (or musical), because there is no evidence that these vocalizations convey complex propositional information: they are not meaningful sentences. Indeed, in birdsong, the message conveyed is typically very simple: "I am a male of species *x* and I am ready to mate." The extreme complexity seen in some birdsongs seems to represent a kind of vocal acrobatics, designed to impress potential mates or intimidate potential competitors rather than to convey any more specific information (Catchpole and Slater, 1995; Marler and Slabbekoorn, 2004).

The most complex animal "songs" rival human speech in their complexity, and appear to require context-free grammars. The mockingbird sings a mixture of species-typical and mimicked syllables, and arranges these into a hierarchical structure of phrases, themes, and longer strophes that provide a clear parallel to the hierarchical structure of phonological and syntactic phrases in language (Thompson *et al.*, 2000). Some species have songs which seem to require repetition of a particular syllable type for a modal number of times. For example, the song phrases of the Northern Mockingbird *Mimus polyglottos* can consist of any of a very large number of particular syllable types (including many that are imitations of other birds' vocalizations), but these are repeated three to four times on average, offering an intermediate level of phrasal structure in the song (Wildenthal,

1965; Thompson *et al.*, 2000). In this case, the role of such rule-governed structure may be in species identification, as the pattern differs between related *Mimus* species, and appears to be innate. For accomplished mimics such as mockingbirds, individual call syllables offer few cues for species determination, essentially forcing the species to use some higher-level patterning in species identification: another simple form of species-specific "grammar."

Our understanding of whale song is more limited, but similar clear hierarchical structure seems to be present in humpback whale songs (Payne and McVay, 1971; Suzuki *et al.*, 2006). Various phenomena in human phonology require similarities to be maintained between non-adjacent syllables. For instance, **rhyme** requires the nucleus+coda portion of a syllable at the end of a phrase to match that of a previous syllable, while **alliteration** requires onsets to match. Studies of the songs of humpback whales suggest that similar phenomena exist in some songs, perhaps serving as an *aide memoire*, for humpbacks (Guinee and Payne, 1988; Payne, 2000), in much the same way that rhyme is postulated to operate in oral transmission of long odes in many human cultures (Rubin, 1995).

The songs of a humpback whale or a mockingbird are vastly more complex than vocal sequences in primates. Such examples suggest that higher-order phonological structures (confusingly often termed "syntax" by ethologists) may not be uncommon in animal vocal signals, and that detailed phonological exploration of animal signals is a promising and largely open field for biolinguistic study (cf. Yip, 2006). Whale and bird "song" are clearly cases of parallel, convergent evolution, and do not provide evidence of *precursors* for syntax in the hominid line. They nonetheless provide important routes for investigating genetic and neural mechanisms (Chapter 9) and the adaptive value of complex vocalizations (Chapter 14).

4.10.3 Meaningful syntax

Among primates, there is good evidence that animals interpret not just individual calls as isolated units of meaning, but whole sequences of calls. Jane Goodall noted that the sequence of call produced by a group of interacting chimpanzees provides rich fodder for interpretation by a listener (pp. 131–132, Goodall, 1986), and this hypothesis has been affirmed by a number of playback experiments with primates (e.g. Silk *et al.*, 1996; Bergman *et al.*, 2003). While revealing a richer capacity for interpretation than might have been suspected (see below), the structure of these sequences is socially created, requiring two or more vocalizers. Nonetheless, from a perceptual/pragmatic viewpoint, interpretation of such social interactions involves several important ingredients of syntax (cf. Seyfarth and Cheney, in press).

There is far less evidence for meaningful call sequences produced by a single vocalizer. The best current data come from the work of ethologist Klaus Zuberbühler on the alarm calls of several species of African forest monkeys (genus *Cercopithecus*). Campbell's monkeys typically emit a low-pitched "boom" note in low-danger situations, followed by the alarm call itself. In more dangerous situations, the alarm calls alone are produced. Playback studies of these call sequences to a closely related species, Diana monkeys, indicated that listeners interpreted "boom" calls as modifiers, and reacted less to the following alarm calls than when booms were omitted. Crucially, this did not occur when Campbell's booms preceded Diana monkey alarm calls, thus ruling out the possibility that the booms have some non-specific calming effect (Zuberbühler, 2002). Similarly, putty-nosed monkeys have distinct alarm calls, "pyows" and "hacks," which are typically given to distinct predators. However, when arranged in a particular "pyow–hack" sequence of up to three pyows followed by up to four hacks, these same calls instigate movement in the complete absence of predators (Arnold and Zuberbühler, 2006). Arnold and Zuberbühler argue that this parallels the linguistic combination of two words (e.g. *hot* and *dog*) into a complex with a different meaning (*hot-dog*). These playback experiments currently stand as the best nonhuman evidence that call concatenation and rearrangement, by a single caller, can change meaning. However, it is important to note that these simple rules are "one-off" systems: they apply to specific, innately structured call types in a single context, rather than representing rules that are applied to all calls (or call classes), as syntactic rules in language are. Note also that such phenomena are currently known only in African *Cercopithecus* monkeys, and nothing similar is known in other well-studied monkey species or in any great ape. Thus, these provide little evidence of a "precursor" of syntax in the LCA.

In conclusion, animals which actually generate call sequences that appear random seem to be exceptional, and in many species there are rules (or constraints) upon vocal sequences that can reasonably be termed "animal syntax." However, the types of rules that govern these arrangements in primates are very simple compared to human linguistic syntax: they typically can be captured by trivial finite state grammars, and only the propositionally meaningless "songs" of birds and whales require more complex grammars. Thus, current data support the existence of a large gulf between animal "syntax" and that employed in any human language.

4.11 Semantics and the meaning of animal signals: reference and intentionality

This is by far the most difficult area of animal communication research, both because there is no over-arching theory of meaning as there is for signal or structure, and also because experimental work analyzing animals' interpretations of signals is challenging to conceive and grueling to carry out. Nonetheless, a dedicated cadre of animal communication researchers, often using computer-controlled playback experiments in the field, have greatly advanced our knowledge in this area in the last few decades.

4.11.1 Pragmatic inference in animal communication

Most animals have regular social interactions with other individuals, and many spend most of their time in large schools, flocks, or herds. Vertebrates, from fish to primates, can recognize and remember specific individuals, including their own offspring, mate, or competitors (e.g. White *et al.*, 1970; Cheney and Seyfarth, 1980; Myrberg and Riggio, 1985; Charrier *et al.*, 2001). Male birds defending territories recognize the song of their neighbors, who they tolerate unless established territorial boundaries are breeched. However, if an unknown bird appears (or if a novel song is played), all territory-holders react aggressively (the "dear enemy" effect; Temeles, 1994). Many vertebrates use "public information," interpreting the mere presence of others in a particular location as an "all clear" signal, or using their observations of others' feeding success to influence their own choices of feeding patches (Valone, 2007). Young female guppies watching the mating behavior of other females use this information in reaching their own mating decisions (Dugatkin, 1993). Experiments "staging" simulated social interactions for a focal listener demonstrate that simply observing social interactions can have a substantial effect on the listener's subsequent behavior: males observing fights between other birds adjust their own aggressive behavior accordingly (cf. Freeman, 1987; McGregor, 2005; Naguib and Kipper, 2006). Thus, many vertebrates make simple pragmatic inferences based on signals.

More complex inferences are also documented. "Staged" battles between pinyon jays revealed that observer birds both remember the outcomes of battles and perform transitive inference over the results (Paz-y-Miño *et al.*, 2004): if they watch A beat B and B beat C, they infer that A can beat C and behave accordingly. Playback experiments with baboon listeners elicit a stronger reaction to playbacks simulating a major group-wide dominance reversal than matched playbacks where only two individuals switched dominance ranks, suggesting that individual identity *and* group membership are represented (Bergman *et al.*, 2003). Thus, social vertebrates of many species and clades perform surprisingly complex reasoning over such representations, including transitive inference and more complex hierarchical inference. Thus, we can assume that the cognitive prerequisites fulfilling the *listener's* side of the Gricean bargain were already in place among our primate ancestors, long before the advent of language. Whether such conclusions are drawn "consciously" or not (or even whether birds or fish are conscious) is immaterial to pragmatics, as most of the inferences that make human pragmatic communication possible remain unconscious (Sperber and Wilson, 1986). Thus, social intelligence, in this specific receptive sense, is a basic building block of language that was present in animal communication long before our species began putting it to pragmatic use in language (Dunbar, 1998; Worden, 1998; Seyfarth *et al.*, 2005).

4.11.2 Functionally referential signals

The fact that animal signals often express the signaler's internal emotional state does not necessarily limit them to this function alone. In the last decades it has become clear that many signals can also provide information about external events, such as food or predators. Such calls are termed **functionally referential signals** (Marler *et al.*, 1992; Macedonia and Evans, 1993; Hauser, 1996; Zuberbühler, 2000b): "referential" because they convey information to a receiver, but "functional" because it is not necessarily the signaler's intent to do so.

It has long been known that many animals emit **alarm calls** when they see predators. Darwin reported an impromptu experiment where, on exposure to a stuffed snake, three monkeys (possibly vervets) "uttered sharp signal cries of danger, which were understood by the other monkeys" (Darwin, 1871). Experimental evidence that monkey alarm calls and food calls were "understood" was provided by the first playback experiments using an Edison phonograph, when playback elicited appropriate responses (Garner, 1892). These observations lay oddly dormant for nearly a century, until Dorothy Cheney, Robert Seyfarth, and Peter Marler performed some classic playback experiments on the alarm call system of vervet monkeys, which includes three well-studied call types (Struhsaker, 1967; Seyfarth *et al.*, 1980a, 1980b). When a male vervet sees a leopard (the most dangerous enemy) it begins making loud "barks"; other vervets quickly run into the

trees and themselves begin calling (female "leopard" calls are different –
a high-pitched squeal – but generate the same response). The calling is
typically taken up by the entire group, and continues until the predator
leaves. Large eagles (dangerous mainly to young animals) elicit a different
call: a double-syllable "cough." Other animals respond by looking up, and
often run for cover in bushes. Finally, large snakes such as pythons pose the
least risk to vervets, and elicit a low-intensity "chutter" call; other vervets
respond by standing on their hind legs, and may surround the snake making
"mobbing" calls. By concealing speakers and playing these sounds in the
absence of any predators, Seyfarth and colleagues found that vervet listeners
react appropriately to these sounds. Similar results have been documented
for other species in the same monkey genus (Struhsaker, 1970; Zuberbühler,
2000a) and a wide variety of other mammals (Macedonia and Evans, 1993;
Manser *et al.*, 2002) and birds (Munn, 1986; Evans *et al.*, 1993; Evans and
Evans, 2007).

Another functionally referential class of calls are **food calls,** produced by
many birds and mammals. For example, chimpanzees and rhesus macaques
produce loud calls that appear to convey precise information about food
(Hauser and Wrangham, 1987; Hauser and Marler, 1993; Slocombe and
Zuberbühler, 2005). Again, food calls lead reliably to predictable responses
on the part of listeners. But again, from the signaler's viewpoint, the call
could correspond to subjective excitement rather than an encoding of food
type or quality. Similarly, chimpanzee and macaque screams have been
suggested to convey information about the attacker (Gouzoules *et al.*, 1984;
Slocombe and Zuberbühler, 2007). Note that *none* of these functionally
referential signals have learned acoustic structure: these are all innate calls.
For example, vervets produce these calls from a young age and in the same
way all over Africa (there are no apparent "dialects" in vervet alarm calls).

Functionally referential call systems are often taken as evidence of language precursors: "we can already see many hallmarks of human speech
in the Old World monkeys. In the vervet's calls we have an archetypal
protolanguage. Quite arbitrary sounds are used to refer to specific objects"
(p. 141, Dunbar, 1996). But what do these alarm calls really signify? A behaviorist might simply argue that particular acoustic patterns "trigger" innate
behavioral responses (look up, run for the trees, etc.). Evidence against this
comes from habituation experiments, where a "leopard" call (for example)
is played repeatedly until listeners habituate and cease responding. Listeners
habituate quickly, suggesting that the response is under the listener's control and is not reflexive. To exclude the possibility that the vervet simply
surveyed the scene and decided that there was no predator, Cheney and
Seyfarth (1988) then played "eagle" alarm calls from the same individual,

and got an immediate response. Other playback experiments demonstrate both that vervets can recognize individual callers, and that they can react to two acoustically different calls similarly ("wrrs" and "chutters," which are given in the presence of rival groups). These and other playback studies strongly suggest that vervet listeners interpret alarm calls as indicators of the presence of the corresponding predator: they appear to interpret these alarm calls as representing events in the world.

4.11.3 Interpreting functional referentiality

A listener's ability to interpret calls produced by another animal as having "meaning" about events in the outside world does not necessarily imply that the caller "encoded" this information into the call (Seyfarth and Cheney, 1997, 2005). Observers may often infer valuable information in signals that did not evolve, and was not emitted, in order to provide that information. The isolation call of a primate separated from its group may be used by predators to locate it, but this is not the function driving the evolution of this signal. Interesting examples of unintended recipients are provided when animals learn to use the alarm calls of other species to make deductions about the presence of a predator. For example, vervets learn to be sensitive to the alarm calls of a bird, the superb starling (Hauser, 1988), while birds and several species of forest monkey in the genus *Cercopithecus* are sensitive to each other's alarm calls (Zuberbühler, 2000a; Rainey *et al.*, 2004). Various sources of evidence make it likely that these responses are learned by experience (see Hauser, 1988). Such "eavesdropping" provides a clear example of the need to distinguish between the information a receiver extracts from some signal and that "intended" (in a psychological or evolutionary sense) by the signaler. Indeed, such "overhearing" is an ever-present force working *against* the evolution of acoustic communication: it is often safer to be silent.

Playback experiments provide strong evidence that sophisticated inference is common among primates, as we have seen, but other studies are required to determine the signaler's *intent* in signaling. In the same way that a human hearing a particular well-known dog barking might infer the arrival of the postman, a knowledgeable animal listener, hearing an excited food call from an individual it knows well, may be able to make inferences about reality that are not "encoded" in the signal by its emitter. While playback experiments can show that a listener makes a correct inference about the world, they clearly cannot demonstrate that the signaler "encoded" that information into the signal.

A nice example of the difficulties involved in interpreting alarm calls comes from black-capped chickadees, small American songbirds. Chickadees live in social groups, which often react to predators by **mobbing**: surrounding the predator and calling loudly and repeatedly. These mobbing assemblages are often made up of multiple species, and are hypothesized to discourage sit-and-wait predators from hunting in the area (Curio, 1978). Alarm calling is one function of the "chickadee" call for which the species is named: it incites other birds to assemble for mobbing (Ficken *et al.*, 1978). Interestingly, there is a strong correlation between predator size and the number of "dee" notes in the alarm call (Templeton *et al.*, 2005). Smaller predators, which are more maneuverable and threatening, receive significantly more "dee" notes per call than larger predators. An observer can thus make a relatively accurate estimation of predator size by counting "dee" notes, and chickadees respond more strongly to calls with many "dees." But we still are left uncertain about the mental mechanism underlying the signaler's response. While it is possible that the signaling bird makes an estimate of predator size and "encodes" this information into the signal, it is just as plausible that the bird observes the predator, develops a state of alarm or excitement dependent upon its size, and that this emotional state is "encoded" in the signal. Given the wide variety of other circumstances in which this particular call is used, having nothing to do with predators (it is simply termed a "social" call by Ficken *et al.*, 1978), the latter interpretation seems more likely in this case.

Such questions immerse us in the complex issue of **intentionality**, a term philosophers use to mean the "aboutness" of a sign or signal, and not just volition or "intent." At the most basic level, so-called zero-order intentionality, the signaler has *no* intention psychologically, but the signal has nonetheless *evolved* to convey a message (Dennett, 1983; Maynard Smith and Harper, 2003). The coloring of an orange and black caterpillar informs potential predators of its nasty taste, but the caterpillar presumably has no psychological representation of this "meaning," any more than a red berry "knows about" its poisonous contents. Such signals mean something to a suitably intelligent observer, but not to the signaler itself. At the next level, an animal possessing mental representations of the outside world (e.g. of food or of a predator) may emit a signal when it encounters food or a predator. In such first-order intentionality, a link between a mental representation and reality justifies our psychological interpretation of the signal, but implies no specific intent to inform another (to modify the contents of another individual's mind). In the same way, a human might spontaneously laugh at a funny book without intending to inform anyone else of anything. In such cases, as before, a perceiver may correctly deduce something true about the world, without the signaler having encoded this information intentionally. The surprising conclusion of contemporary work on animal communication is that all communication by nonhuman animals appears to be in this category: informative of internal mental states, but not intentionally so. Despite this defying our most basic human intuitions about "communication," there are some rather convincing indications that animals do not go beyond such first-order intentionality (Cheney and Seyfarth, 1998).

In an insightful review, Macedonia and Evans (1993) suggest that alarm calls exist on a continuum from "risk-based" or "response-urgency" systems, at one end, to "referential" systems at the other, and provide some criteria for distinguishing between the two. But in fact there are two such continua, one for signaler and one for receiver. A call may be *functionally* informative about the outside world, from the listener's viewpoint, while for the signaler it is simply an expression of its current emotional state. Indeed, it remains possible that as far as the signaler is concerned, a vervet's alarm calls are expressions of different levels of alarm (high for leopard, medium for eagle, and low for snake), and that *all* of the interpretive work is done by the listener. Vervets attacked by a snake have been reported to produce high-intensity "leopard" calls, and vervets watching a snake eat another animal emitted "leopard" calls over a long period (Seyfarth and Hauser, reported in Macedonia and Evans, 1993). I have personally observed a captive vervet male, living in a skyscraper at Harvard, who consistently produced "leopard" calls upon sight of the Goodyear blimp over Boston. Thus, vervet "leopard" calls can be parsimoniously treated as being nearer the "risk-based" end of the continuum for signalers, even if they reliably produce "leopard-based" responses in listeners in the wild. Similarly, although the high-intensity "ground predator" calls of chickens are typically made to dogs, foxes, and the like, they also occasionally are made to hawks when the danger is great (Marler *et al.*, 1991); chickadee "zeet" calls, while normally made for aerial predators (and considered specific to them), are also made occasionally to mink (Ficken and Witkin, 1977). Similar comments apply to ground squirrel alarm call systems and some primate alarm calls (Macedonia and Evans, 1993). Clearly, then, correct interpretation of such calls does not imply intentional encoding of predator type.

4.11.4 Pragmatic signalers: are animals intentionally informative?

Human speakers typically do more than inform: we *intend* to inform. This requires, in addition to our own mental states, that we have a mental representation of our listener's mental states. Most of what we do with language relies heavily on a model of what our interlocutor knows and doesn't know, and a conversationalist with a faulty model is considered forgetful, impolite, or downright abnormal. The Gricean maxim "be informative!" is a core desideratum in human linguistic communication (Chapter 3). Do animals obey this maxim? The first requirement is that some animals know what others know, and we saw evidence for this in chimpanzees earlier. But being intentionally informative requires more than simply knowing what others know. It requires, additionally, the *goal* of changing this state of knowledge. Such **second-order intentionality** has not yet been demonstrated in any nonhuman animal, and several experts on animal communication have concluded that this represents an important gulf between linguistic communication and animal communication systems (Hauser, 1996, 2000). Indeed, it seems that "the inability of animals to recognize what other individuals know, believe, or desire constitutes a fundamental difference between nonhuman primate vocal communication and human language" (p. 249, Seyfarth and Cheney, 1997).

Many animal signals appear to be employed with the intent of modifying the *behavior* of other animals. Courtship and food begging signals in bird and primates are prototypical examples. The signaler has some goal, it produces the vocalization to increase the chances of achieving it, may increase the intensity depending on the listener's behavior, and finally stops when it either gives up or attains the goal. Such patterns are observed by any pet owner whose dog or cat whines or meows to be fed or let outside. Clear support for intentional deployment comes from use of **gestures** in great apes, who clearly deploy manual gestures voluntarily and take others' attention into account in choosing their signals. For example, apes are more likely to use auditory gestures (clapping or other sound-making movements) when their intended recipient is facing away from them (cf. Call and Tomasello, 2007). Apes whose begging gestures are "understood" by a human experimenter continue using the successful gestures. In contrast, unsuccessful gestures (that result in them getting undesirable food) lead to an increase in alternative gestures (Leavens *et al.*, 2005; Cartmill and Byrne, 2007). Most researchers in animal communication today therefore accept that at least some animal vocalizations are produced with intent to modify behavior (Hauser and Nelson, 1991; Griffin, 1992; Owren and Rendall, 2001).

An intent to modify the *thoughts* of another animal further requires that a signaler be able to represent absence of knowledge (ignorance) on the part of an intended recipient of the message. This seems such an intuitive and basic aspect of communication that it is quite surprising to find that this ability does not appear to be present in monkeys. Multiple lines of data converge on this conclusion, but the experiments that I find most telling concern food and alarm calling in two species of macaques (Cheney and Seyfarth, 1990a). The subjects were pairs of mothers and their young offspring (and in a few cases sibling pairs). Macaque mothers are cooperative and protective of their offspring, grooming, feeding, and defending them. Mothers were experimentally confronted with a "predator" (a veterinarian with a net) in an arena, in one of two situations: with their infant sitting beside them so it could see the predator as well ("knowledgeable"), or with the infant enclosed behind an opaque barrier ("ignorant"). The "predator" then hid, out of sight, while the offspring was released into the arena. Although the mothers were clearly distressed by the sight of the predator, often attempting escape, none of them changed their behavior in any way when their offspring entered the arena. In particular, no mothers alarm-called, although they often alarm-call to net-bearing technicians in other contexts. While offspring who observed the predator changed *their* behavior significantly (typically staying close to the mother), the mothers themselves did not alter their behavior when their child was unaware of the predator's presence.

In a second experiment, the same procedure was used with hidden food. Either the mother alone saw the food concealed, or she and her child both saw it. The mother produced food calls when seeing the food, but again there was no difference in the mother's behavior depending on whether the infant was knowledgeable or not. It is also unlikely that some more subtle cue (such as gazing or gesturing) was given, since the ignorant offspring took significantly longer to find the food than the knowledgeable ones. In conclusion, there were no significant differences in the mother's behavior depending on whether their offspring was ignorant or not. Although this negative result cannot be taken to demonstrate that mothers can't represent their child's ignorance, it does indicate that they don't act on such putative knowledge in any way that either the experimenters, or the offspring themselves, could detect. Similarly (and equally shocking to a human), in experiments where a baboon infant, separated from the group, emits "lost calls" (contact barks), baboon mothers do not answer its lost calls unless they are themselves separated from the group (Rendall *et al.*, 2000). Given the cooperative relationship of female primates to their offspring, and the strong potential evolutionary advantage in correcting a child's ignorance by sharing information in such settings, these studies strongly suggest a cognitive inability to be intentionally informative in these primate species.

Two important conclusions can be drawn from this work. First, intelligent interpretation of calls – a **pragmatic inference engine** – is well developed in nonhuman primates. Given some experience with calls, and the contexts in which they occur, primates turn out to be careful observers and insightful interpreters of others' behavior, including their vocal behavior. In sharp contrast, *intentional* informativeness in nonhuman animals is very rare, and perhaps non-existent. These data, together with data on "theory of mind" reviewed in Chapter 3, suggest that most and perhaps all animal communication that operates at an intentional level is intended to affect others' behavior, rather than the contents of their minds.

4.12 The evolution of "honest" communication: a fundamental problem

A fundamental problem in the evolution of communication was not recognized until the 1970s: why should signalers share reliable information with others? In the early days of ethology, this question remained unasked, and its importance still goes unrecognized by many in the field of language evolution. Ethologists like Lorenz and Tinbergen were focused mainly on the form of signals and how they evolved phylogenetically. But the functional question of *why* these signals had evolved remained in the background, perhaps because of an implicit intuitive assumption that reliable signals will benefit both signaler and receiver. It was not until the early 1970s, under the influence of an increasingly gene-centered and individualistic viewpoint, that evolutionary biologists began to question this assumption. In an influential paper, Dawkins and Krebs (1978) argued that signaling is best seen, not as the collaborative sharing of information, but as the **manipulation** of receivers by signalers. Perhaps because Dawkins and Krebs cast their argument as a refutation of a general ethological view, critics were quick to retort that this model only gets half of the equation. The other half consists of wily receivers, extracting information for their own benefit from the actions of unwitting signalers (Hinde, 1981). In response, Krebs and Dawkins crafted their now-classic article, which gave equal weight to both "mind-reading" and "manipulation" in animal communication (Krebs and Dawkins, 1984). Stressing the inadequacy of an assumption of communal sharing of information, the paper highlighted the tension between the roles of both receivers and signalers, and made the now standard point that for signaling to be evolutionarily stable it must provide net benefits to both parties. Although it will typically pay signalers to exaggerate their signals if they can, if signals do not reliably convey information, over the long term receivers will simply stop paying attention. The evolution of reliable signals (often called **"honest" signals**, with no connotation of conscious or intentional "honesty") is now seen as a core theoretical issue in animal communication (Hauser, 1996; Bradbury and Vehrencamp, 1998; Maynard Smith and Harper, 2003).

Such problems are particularly significant in language evolution (Maynard Smith and Szathmáry, 1995; Dunbar, 1996; Knight, 1998; Nettle, 1999b; Fitch, 2004a; Számadó and Szathmary, 2006). One route to honesty in animal signals involves costly signals. All evidence regarding human speech indicates, however, that speech is an extremely low-cost signal: speech is so cheap energetically that its cost is very difficult to measure with normal metabolic techniques (Moon and Lindblom, 2003). Although humans freely and continuously use language to share accurate information with unrelated others, we appear to have avoided any costly or "handicap" requirement for honest signaling. Indeed, human language appears, at least superficially, to have evaded *all* known theoretical routes to honest signaling. Evolutionary theory concerning "honesty" in animal communication thus provides strong constraints on plausible theories of language evolution, and has spurred numerous creative attempts to resolve this apparent contradiction (cf. Dunbar, 1996; Dessalles, 1998; Knight, 1998; Power, 1998).

4.12.1 How can "honest" signals evolve?

Several distinct, well-understood evolutionary processes can ensure signal reliability. Biologists distinguish between cues, signals, and indices (Maynard Smith and Harper, 2003). A **cue** is any aspect of an observed animal used by a perceiver. A predator may use the sound prey makes while foraging as a cue to stalk it, but these sounds are not emitted from the prey animal for this evolutionary purpose. **Signals** are the subset of cues emitted by the signaler *because* they affect a perceiver's behavior, or more precisely because, in the evolutionary past, perceivers' reception of the signal increased the fitness of the signaler's ancestors. The size of a spider is a cue, not a signal: size didn't evolve to influence others. However, the spider's web-vibrating behavior is a signal, and the receiver's response may depend on size information communicated by this signal. Finally, in many cases, there is a direct causal link between some important characteristic of the individual, such as size or condition, and specific aspects of the signal. Signals which directly transmit reliable information due to such causal connections are termed "indices." An **index** is a signal whose form is causally related to the quality being signaled, and which thus cannot be faked. Indices are an important potential source of reliability in animal signals, that result from inescapable physical and anatomical constraints on signal production. The spider's vibration frequency is controlled by its body mass, and is an unfakeable signal (at least until experimenters add weights to the spider and convert former losers to winners; Riechert, 1978).

An indexical signal relevant to human speech is the signaling of body size by formant frequencies (see Chapter 8 for more details). In many species, formant frequencies act as indices of body size (Fitch, 1997; Riede and Fitch, 1999; Reby and McComb, 2003; Rendall *et al.*, 2005), which leads to them being used by perceivers to judge body size. In one of the prototypical cases of "honest signaling" in animal communication, red deer roars convey honest, indexical information due to physical constraints on formant frequencies and vocal production (Reby *et al.*, 2005). However, not all acoustic cues convey accurate size information (Charlton *et al.*, 2008), and reliable signaling of size depends on correlations that may or may not apply to a particular call or species. More importantly, the types of information conveyed by indices are strictly limited (size, condition, sex, and the like) and provide no evolutionary route to flexible, arbitrary, linguistic communication.

Another potential source of honest signals has received much discussion in recent years: handicaps. A **handicap** is a signal whose reliability is ensured by its high cost. For example, the long elaborate tail plumage in many bird species may serve as an honest indicator of male quality, because only high-quality males can bear the cost of building and transporting the ornament. The term and concept were introduced by zoologist Amotz Zahavi (Zahavi, 1975). Zahavi's argument relied on intuition, and early attempts to evaluate it mathematically concluded that it would not work (Maynard Smith, 1976). Later theoreticians showed that the model *can* work (Grafen, 1990a), but only under a more restricted range of conditions than those put forward (then and today) by Zahavi himself. Zahavi argues that costly signaling is an almost unavoidable requirement for reliability, and sees his "Handicap Principle" as applying to nearly all animal signaling systems, with human language as a prominent exception (Zahavi and Zahavi, 1997). An influential article concerning mate choice and sexual selection by theorist Alan Grafen states that "if we see a signal that does signal quality, it must be a handicap" (Grafen, 1990a). Although technically correct in Grafen's context, this statement is deeply misleading for non-specialists, because Grafen does not consider indices, which he terms "revealing handicaps," to be signals at all. But most researchers *do* consider indices to be signals.

Indeed, the indexical roar of the red deer discussed above is a prototypical signal in the animal communication literature. Thus Grafen's statement is true only by semantic sleight of hand (cf. Maynard Smith and Harper, 2003).

The view of handicaps accepted by most evolutionary biologists today distinguishes two types of cost, termed "efficacy" and "strategic" costs. **Efficacy costs** are the costs involved in simply generating a signal so that it can be perceived effectively by its intended recipients. A signal intended to attract mates in a widely dispersed species must be able to travel long distances, or its purpose will remain unfulfilled. This may entail expensive or even exhausting signaling regimes, simply to reach the intended perceiver. Such efficacy costs must be distinguished from **strategic costs,** which are those costs over and above the costs of signaling itself, whose function, in one way or another, is to ensure honesty. The handicap principle deals only with the strategic costs. Repeated theoretical investigations have found that a handicap-based signaling system can be stably reliable *only* when the strategic cost for low-quality signalers is in some way *greater* than the cost for a higher-quality individual (Enquist, 1985; Pomiankowski, 1987; Grafen, 1990a; Johnstone, 1995). It is not enough that signals be costly, but they must be *differentially* costly for a handicap-based system to evolve. This drastically reduces the scope of the handicap principle, and indeed, solid evidence for such systems remains elusive. Although the *possibility* of handicaps guaranteeing reliability is now widely accepted, most theorists remain circumspect about its explanatory breadth (for a balanced appraisal see Maynard Smith and Harper, 2003), and even Zahavi admits that his handicap principle does not apply to spoken language (Zahavi, 1993).

The core realization from this literature is that reliable or "honest" sharing of information between individuals is not something we can assume "just happens" in the evolution of communication: where it occurs, it is something to be explained. There are many forces opposing the evolution of cheap, reliable signaling systems like language. On the one hand we have Machiavellian struggles between signalers and receivers. Typically, the interests of these two parties are not identical, and we can expect arms races, where each party is in a constant evolutionary struggle to "outsmart" the other. Such situations of conflict (that is, where signaler and receiver do not share each other's interests) can be seen as "evolutionary traps" blocking the evolution of language. One way to achieve reliable signals is to rely upon indices, where honesty is guaranteed by physics, but the types of information conveyed by such signals is limited to individual qualities like size, condition, or sex. While handicaps offer another route to reliability, they, too, in general will correlate with only quite general aspects of the signaler (quality, fitness, etc.) and don't provide open-ended reference. Regarding human language, costly signaling theory has limited applicability: modern language certainly is flexible, reliable, and cheap. Thus a key question in human language evolution is: How did we evade these dual traps?

4.12.2 Other routes to honesty: shared interests and communication among kin

One possible route to low-cost honesty in situations of conflict relies upon the **punishment** of cheaters (cf. Lachmann *et al.*, 2001). If reliable, punishment can be a potent evolutionary force (Boyd and Richerson, 1992). Unfortunately, examples of animal punishment remain very rare (e.g. Hauser, 1992), probably because punishers bear a potentially high cost if their targets retaliate. Indeed, punishment is itself a form of altruism, performed for the good of the social group, and it poses its own deep evolutionary problems (Boyd and Richerson, 1992). Once language already existed, cheater detection and punishment via gossip becomes viable, explaining the frequency of punishment for cheating in human societies (Dunbar, 1996; Deacon, 1997). But something that requires language to function cannot simultaneously be held up as a precondition for its initial evolution, and so this proposed route to honesty must be treated warily in theories of language evolution (cf. Chapter 12).

Fortunately, it is now well established that stable, reliably informative signaling systems can evolve without any strategic or handicap costs or punishment (Maynard Smith, 1991; Bergstrom and Lachmann, 1998b; Maynard Smith and Harper, 2003) *when signaler and receiver share a common interest*: when both members of a communicating dyad benefit from their signal exchange. This does not entail that signaler and receiver have *identical* interests, but only that they rank the outcomes of the interaction similarly. Some potentially relevant contexts of shared interests include communication between a mated pair, or among unrelated members of long-term social groups, but these situations typically involve multiple potential conflicts of interest. A far more common example is when signaler and recipient are related (e.g. parents and offspring). In such examples of **kin communication**, Hamilton's inclusive fitness theory comes to the rescue (Chapter 2), and provides a well-documented path to cheap, honest communication. Kin selection has broad explanatory power in understanding animal social behavior, particularly "cooperative" animal communication, because conditions fulfilling Hamilton's equation are common in social animals, particularly in communicative situations where the cost of signaling is low (Hamilton, 1975; Fitch, 2004a).

Such situations have been studied in some detail in the context of animal communication using the "Sir Philip Sidney Game" (Maynard Smith, 1991). In this model, an actor must choose whether or not to share some indivisible resource based solely on the reception of a signal from the potential recipient. The two individuals are related by some relatedness, *r*. When protagonists are related, cheap signaling can evolve and be stable (Maynard Smith and Harper, 2003). As with Hamilton's equation above, the relatedness of the two individuals serves as the guarantor of honesty, and if the cost of sharing information is rather small, any non-negligible benefit to the recipient can still lead to the evolution of cheap signaling among even quite distant relatives. This result has been extended and strengthened in many different variant models (e.g. Johnstone and Grafen, 1992; Bergstrom and Lachmann, 1998a, 1998b). Although communication among kin is not always without conflict (e.g. parents and offspring may have competing interests about how much food each offspring should receive; Trivers, 1974; Godfray, 1991), inclusive fitness theory provides a clear theoretical route to the evolution of cheap honest communication among kin.

4.12.3 Kin-selected communication systems

Many well-documented examples of kin communication among vertebrates appear to fulfill these conditions. The most famous are systems of alarm calls, especially ground squirrel alarms (Sherman, 1977, 1985). Ground squirrels are group-living rodents, where extended maternal families share underground burrows, but feed above ground. They are preyed upon by both aerial and terrestrial predators (e.g. hawks and coyotes). Their main survival tactic is to flee into their burrows when predators appear. Many ground squirrel species give two distinct alarm calls for these two types of predators, and some are thought to have more (Slobodchikoff *et al.*, 1991). Belding's ground squirrels follow several predictions for a kin-selected communication system. First, as is typical in alarm calling, animals produce no vocalizations when alone (this is an example of an audience effect, discussed above). Second, alarm calls are generally produced by females, when their kin are present. Third, newly immigrated males, who do not yet have kin in the group, do not produce alarm calls. Finally, after a tenure as a breeding male, and while *their* offspring are out of the burrow, these same males *do* produce alarm calls. Thus, this simple two-call alarm system obeys all the prerequisites for the evolution of a kin-selected communication system.

Excellent examples of kin communication are the elaborate communication systems that have evolved among eusocial insects, like ants and honeybees, including the justly famous **honeybee dance "language."** In eusocial insects, most individuals are female "workers" who do not themselves have offspring. Instead, they industriously tend the offspring of a "queen" who lays eggs at a prodigious rate and does little or no work herself. A worker bee never reproduces, and will give her life to defend the hive. How, Darwin wondered, could natural selection favor such a system? The answer is that all of the bees in a hive are sisters: they are all the daughters of the same mother, the queen. Due to a quirk of honeybee genetics, full sisters are often more likely to share genes than is a mother and her own daughter. Under these circumstances, honeybee workers are actually raising their own closest relatives. Although, by itself, this fact cannot explain the repeated evolution of eusociality in insects, it is widely agreed to play a facilitating role (cf. Wilson and Hölldobler, 2005; Foster *et al.*, 2006). Honeybees have evolved a complex system of at least seventeen distinct signals: an elaborate repertoire that appears to be fully innate. The most impressive component of this system is the *waggle dance*, a social behavior in which a returning "scout" female who has discovered some resource can share the location of this resource with her sisters in the hive (von Frisch, 1967). The waggle dance is typically done in the darkness of the hive. Under these conditions, the orientation of the "waggle" component, relative to gravity, corresponds to the angle of flight from the hive to the resource, relative to the sun. The length and intensity of waggling corresponds to the flight distance to the resource. This signal, clearly, is "functionally referential."

Several aspects of the waggle dance are worthy of comment because they share design features with human language. First, the system is *flexible*: although bees typically dance inside the hive, using gravity as the reference angle, they can also dance outside the hive on a flat surface, using the angle of the sun as their reference. Though bees typically dance about food or water, they can also use the waggle dance to communicate the location of a new nest site, so it is fair to think of the dance as a flexible system for "pointing" to anything of interest to bees. Another type of context dependence is seen by the fact that interest in a dancer is determined by the overall needs of the hive, as "judged" by individual workers. When the hive needs water, a scout dancing about nectar or pollen receives less attention than one returning with water. Crucially, since honeybees are communicating about something that is not currently present, the waggle dance provides an animal example of an otherwise very unusual aspect of human language: *displaced reference* (Hockett, 1960). The honeybee communication system thus provides a prototypical example of an elaborate kin-selected communication system.

In conclusion, both theoretical and empirical studies of animal communication show that signalers should be quite selective about the types of information they communicate and with whom they do so. Because signalers may often have conflicts of interest with receivers (who are not necessarily the intended recipients) we should often expect silence to be the best strategy. In cases of sexual selection or aggression, we expect bluffing, exaggeration, and costly signals to be common. Kin communication provides one of the most common ways for cheap, honest signals to arise. But we also expect perceivers to evolve sophisticated strategies to "see through" bluffs, and also to read much more from signals than is "intentionally" encoded (whether by natural selection or the individual), and such sophisticated signal interpretation is common in many species, especially primates. By contrast, signalers often seem quite unsophisticated in what they encode in signals: Cheney and Seyfarth's monkeys fail to obey the Gricean maxim to "be informative" that seems so intuitive and obvious to humans. One of the strangest of human traits is our propensity to communicate. Our unstoppable *Mitteilungsbedürfnis*, our need to share meanings, is as bizarre as our bipedality or hairlessness, and explaining it must be a central task for theories of language evolution. We shall return to it in Chapter 12.

4.13 Chapter summary

The basic conclusion of this chapter is that animals possess a rich cognitive world, but are quite limited in their ability to communicate their thoughts to others. Although all animals communicate, the "lines of communication" are typical tailored to specific needs, and shaped by evolution to these needs. The flexible ability that humans possess to communicate anything we can think via language appears to be unique among living things. This is definitely *not* because animals do not have thoughts – we can assume that a rich set of concepts was present in the LCA, and indeed long before. Furthermore, it seems that the capacity of nonhuman primates to *interpret* acoustic signals is far more sophisticated than their ability to *generate* relevant, informative signals. The limitations on nonhuman "theory of mind" mean that animals can only fulfill one half of the Gricean contract: they are well equipped for context-dependent pragmatic inference, but not for pragmatic expression. Finally, the rich body of evolutionary theory concerning the evolution of communication provides a clear indication of why humans are so unusual in this respect: there are diverse barriers to achieving cheap honestly-informative communication systems like spoken language. How humans overcame (or side-stepped) these limitations is thus a central question for theories of language evolution.

Meet the ancestors

5 | Meet the ancestors

As for me, I am proud of my close kinship with other animals. I take a jealous pride in my Simian ancestry. I like to think that I was once a magnificent hairy fellow living in the trees, and that my frame has come down through geological time via sea-jelly and worms and Amphioxus, Fish, Dinosaurs and Apes. Who would exchange these for the pallid couple in the Garden of Eden?
                                 — W. N. P. Barbellion

5.1 From a single cell to Miocene primates

Human evolution, in its full sense, begins with the origin of life on Earth, nearly four billion years ago. Most aspects of modern human biology were established long before we split off from chimpanzees, including many aspects of genetics, neuroscience, and cognition that are relevant to language evolution. It remains a regrettably common mistake to think of human evolution as "beginning" with our split from chimpanzees some seven million years ago – this simply marks the time we have been evolving independently of any other species that happens to be alive today. Had Neanderthals survived a few thousand more years to the present day, this arbitrary timespan would be greatly reduced. Were great apes to become extinct, it would be greatly increased. In this chapter, therefore, I examine the great sweep of human evolution from its beginning – the origins of life and the first single-celled organisms – focusing particularly on aspects of genetic control, neuroscience, and vocal communication that are relevant to language. For some aspects of this story our understanding has increased rapidly in the last decades, offering beautiful illustrations of the power of new molecular techniques and "evo-devo." Other subplots of this evolutionary narrative provide excellent examples of evolutionary principles such as preadaptation and exaptation, or the role of functional redundancy and gene duplication in paving the way to evolutionary innovations. Thus, this chapter will use vertebrate evolution to put some empirical meat on the theoretical bones outlined in Chapter 2.

The key message is that human evolution didn't begin and end in a Pleistocene "environment of evolutionary adaptedness" (EEA), as sometimes assumed by evolutionary psychologists (Barkow *et al.*, 1992). Rather, there are many "EEAs" – and the one which is relevant depends on the attribute in question. Certain key aspects of human biology, relevant to language, date back as far as the Urbilaterian common ancestor of vertebrates and insects, during which many genetic, cellular, and molecular-developmental aspects of human biology were established. Most of our brain organization was laid down in early jawed fish, and the beginning of our vocal apparatus appeared with the first tetrapods. Final aspects of brain organization (e.g. the addition of neocortex and auditory attributes) appeared with the first mammals no later than the Cretaceous. Finally, social propensities and color vision were established within our own order, the primates, long before our split with chimpanzees. Crucially, the common ancestors of each of these groups can be rebuilt in detail, based on a broad comparative database, allowing insights into their genetics, physiology, and behavior. In many cases, we also have fossil data to provide specific timing information. In this chapter I will discuss all of these traits. Chapter 6 describes our last common ancestor with chimpanzees (the LCA), based upon the application of the comparative method to humans and other apes alive today. Chapter 7 considers the last stretch of human evolution, from our divergence from the LCA and continuing to the present, the only period for which comparative data is unavailable. Sometime during this short period of six to seven million years, language evolved, constrained by and building upon all that went before. Fossils are all we have to go on for this last, relatively short phase of human evolution.

For reasons of space and focus, this evolutionary summary will be unapologetically oriented towards modern humans. This focus should not be misconstrued as reflecting any belief that humans are "the goal" or endpoint of evolution. We could perform the same exercise for any species – from earthworms to blue jays to mandrills – and the tale I tell here ends with humans only because it is we humans who evolved language. Critically, the story would be shared, to some extent, regardless of the species chosen as the endpoint, because the history of life on earth has the form of a vast tree where all living things share the same root: the original cell that was the ancestor of us all. Were a killer whale writing this book, its story would diverge from ours after the depiction of the proto-mammal. Only at the very end, at the branch tip that represents our own species, is the human evolutionary story ours alone. Thus, for the most part, as this chapter will make clear, our biology is shared with other species, all of whom are our relatives at some remove or other. Much of our basic cellular biology is shared with an amoeba, and the basic genetic toolkit for building multi-cellular bodies is the same in fly, fish, mouse, and man. Nearly *all* of our biology is shared with chimpanzees. Thus, isolating those aspects of biology underlying recent language evolution requires a process of elimination. Even if this human-oriented account can do little justice to the variety of life, it amply illustrates our kinship with other living things – from bacteria to blue whales.

In his recent book *The Ancestor's Tale*, Richard Dawkins inverts time, journeying backwards from modern humans to the first cell, "rejoining" the other descendents of each specific ancestor (chimpanzees, monkeys, dogs, birds, frogs, . . .) as he goes (Dawkins, 2004). I recommend this beautifully written book to anyone interested in a fuller picture of the tree of life than the sketch given here (cf. Cracraft and Donoghue, 2004). Here, I can only gesture towards the many other branches with whom we share each node of the tree of life. But it is important to bear in mind that the empirical database that goes into defining each of these nodes is made up of many species: we know what characterizes the proto-mammal, or the proto-primate, only by considering many mammals or primates.

It is equally important to realize that each species alive today has been evolving continuously. No species has statically retained the precise form, physiology, or behavior of the common ancestor. Furthermore, the fossils that we are fortunate enough to discover are unlikely to represent exactly the species that was the common ancestor (although they may sometimes be quite close). Thus, the process of reconstructing a common ancestor is always **inferential**: we cannot simply examine an existing species. The LCA *was not a chimpanzee*, and although it might have resembled a chimpanzee more than a human, its behavior and physiology were different. Indeed, a recent analysis comparing 14,000 matched genes in chimpanzees and humans suggests that chimpanzees have had *more* genes driven to fixation by selection than have humans (Bakewell *et al.*, 2007). Similarly, the last common ancestor of all existing mammals looked rather like a shrew, but despite this fact a modern shrew is no infallible guide to the nature of that ancestor. So-called "living fossils" – species whose modern morphology resembles ancient forms very closely – exist (examples include plants such as horsetails and mosses, or animals such as horseshoe crabs or lungfish), and they provide invaluable clues to physiology and behavior in long-extinct forms. However, they are not identical to them.

Many readers might be stymied by terms like "Cretaceous" or "Pleistocene." These are geological epochs, originally discovered by geologists on the basis of fossils found in characteristic rock layers, frequently named for specific places, often in England, where much of the original mapping was performed (Winchester, 2001). Thus, the Cambrian is named after rocks exposed in Cambria, the Roman name for Wales, while the Devonian refers to a geological layer characteristic of Devon. A critical breakthrough in modern geology was the realization that these rock layers were laid down over time in an orderly fashion, one over the other, so that superficial rock layers are recent, and deeper layers are progressively older. Thus, the names for the layers have been codified into a timetable which is now accepted and used by geologists around the world. The development of radioactive dating techniques in the twentieth century further allowed specific dates to be attached to the beginning and ends of these periods, which again are accepted worldwide. It is often easier to remember "mid-Devonian" rather than to remember the specific date attached to some fossil or geological event. I will also often give dates in millions of years (where MYA stands for "million years ago"). This universal system of geological nomenclature is given in Figure 5.1.

5.2 In the beginning: the first cells and the genetic code

The genetic code (by which nucleotides code amino acids) is shared among all living things, and has its origin at or near the beginning of life (more than 3.5 billion years ago).

The true origins of living things, from non-living matter to organisms that reproduce, remains a controversial topic. Darwin's theory of evolution does not kick in until *after* organisms could reproduce themselves, and can have little to say about this earliest and most crucial innovation. Darwin, recognizing this initial huge hurdle, implied that life's first origin might still require supernatural explanation – "life . . . having been originally breathed by the Creator into a few forms or into one" (Darwin, 1872a) – though this may have been added to appease religious readers. It has long been clear that inorganic processes on prebiotic Earth were adequate to create a "primordial soup" containing many of the essential compounds needed for life (amino acids, nucleotide bases, fatty acids, and others; Miller, 1953). But the mechanism(s) by which these raw materials became organized, self-replicating entities remain(s) highly controversial. One leading hypothesis involves an "RNA world," where RNA molecules play the role of both replicator and enzyme (because RNA has considerably greater enzymatic

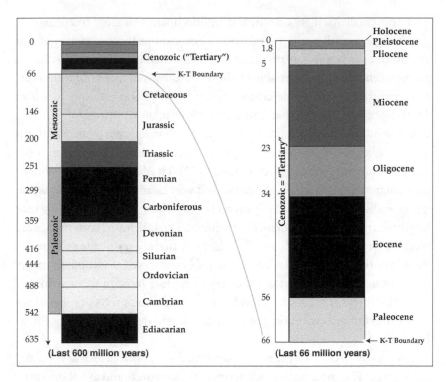

Figure 5.1 The geological timetable – Standard names for geological periods are given with their approximate dates in million years before present. On the left the period encompassing the evolution of multicellular life is shown; on the right is a close-up of the more recent period encompassing the evolutionary divergence of modern mammals including humans.

potential than DNA; Joyce, 2002), with DNA and protein taking on their current roles later. Various additional possibilities are being explored, such as the idea that random inorganic templates provided by clays or pyrites played a critical role (for reviews see Maynard Smith and Szathmáry, 1995; Knoll, 2003). For our purposes it suffices to say that various biochemical solutions have been proposed, none of them fully satisfactory at present, and this remains a very active area of inquiry. Crucially, although many variants on these processes were probably present early on, the successful version rapidly multiplied and dominated, such that all living things today derive from this singular event. We are all related – bacteria, plants, animals, and fungi – by descent from this original first common ancestor.

The evolution of life began in the form of single-celled organisms, and we spent the majority of our evolutionary lifespan in this state. Living things had already evolved around 3.5 billion years ago, roughly one billion years after the Earth itself was born, but multicellular animals ("metazoans") didn't appear until perhaps 600 MYA. Thus around three-quarters of our evolution as living things occurred in single-celled organisms. This fact is perhaps rendered less surprising by the fact that each of us, in our individual ontogeny, began as a single cell: a fertilized egg. This is one way in which Ernst Haeckel's dictum that "ontogeny recapitulates phylogeny" (that is, that our individual development re-enacts the evolutionary history of our species) is a reasonably consistent generalization (although by no means a "law," as sometimes thought; cf. Gould, 1977). The development of modern molecular and cellular biology has made it very clear that the processes that go on within a single-celled organism (a bacterium, yeast, or amoeba) are largely shared by the cells of all living things. Thus, although our bodies are made up of trillions of cells ($\sim 10^{13}$), the basic machinery inside each one of these is both highly complex and remarkably conserved. Fortunately, many excellent textbooks make it unnecessary to explore most of this machinery here (cf. Alberts *et al.*, 2008). Thus I can focus on two aspects of cell biology relevant to human evolution: the genetic code and the autonomy of cellular behavior.

Two classes of cells have traditionally been distinguished: prokaryotes and eukaryotes. The most ancient are termed **prokaryotes**, and are abundantly represented by bacteria. Prokaryotes lack a nucleus: their DNA is free-floating within the cell. It was in the stem prokaryote – the ancestor of us all – that the genetic code, and the processing machinery that "reads" it, developed and was perfected, such that it is shared, virtually identically, by all living things on the planet today (there are a few minor variants of the basic system). The genetic code is the system that allows DNA to code for proteins via an intermediary code of RNA (see Box 2.1). The combinatorics of this system are simple and important. Three base pairs per slot are used in the genetic code. Each three-slot "chunk" is called a **codon**, and there are 4^3 (64) possible codons to account for just 20 amino acids. This means, inevitably, that the genetic code is a redundant or "degenerate" system – many different codons can code for the same amino acid. For example, the codons TTT and TTC both code for the amino acid phenylalanine, while TGT and TGC both code for cystine. This redundancy gives the code a crucial property: some mutations in the DNA have no effect on the protein this DNA codes for. These so-called **silent substitutions** play a critical role in modern molecular phylogeny, because they are largely "invisible" to selection. Their accumulation over time thus provides a random mutational record of the history of that particular chunk of DNA. The more time that has elapsed since the divergence of two lineages, the more difference we expect in these silent positions: even if selection has rigorously maintained the specific protein composition coded by that gene. Thus we can roughly date ancient divergence times of lineages based on present-day DNA sequences.

5.3 Eukaryotes: the origins of cellular biology

Many basic biochemical pathways, including signaling pathways and processes underlying cell movement, are shared among all organisms whose cells contain a DNA-protecting nucleus.

The second main form of cells are the **eukaryotes**, a group including all metazoans, including humans, along with many single-celled organisms. While sharing the universal genetic code and a substantial amount of enzymatic and regulatory machinery with prokaryotes, we eukaryotes possess a nucleus in which most of the cell's DNA is sequestered, and various other components called "organelles" that make us considerably more complex than bacteria. The most prominent examples are **mitochondria**, which are characteristic of all eukaryotes (another important organelle, the chloroplast, is found only in plants). Mitochondria are possessed in large numbers by each cell, and generate the adenosine triphosphate (ATP) used throughout the cell as an energy source. It is now widely agreed that mitochondria originated via symbiosis (Margulis, 1992): the ancestral eukaryote cell absorbed (or was colonized by) a different species (the cousins of which are free-living bacteria which can still be found today). These two species became interdependent, and indeed most of the original **mitochondrial DNA** (or **mtDNA**) was transferred to the DNA of the host cell. However, some DNA remains in the mitochondria, and indeed retains the circular arrangement that characterizes prokaryote DNA. This turns out to be another useful quirk of molecular genetics, because the mitochondria (with their DNA) are passed independently of nuclear DNA from mother to child, inside the egg. Thus, while the nuclear DNA from mother and father is mixed together after fertilization (by a process called *recombination*), the mother's mtDNA alone is passed on intact (the father's, though present on the sperm, is cast aside at fertilization). This fact, along with the relatively small size of the mitochondrial genome and the fact that a single cell contains many thousands of copies of it, means that mtDNA has played an important role in molecular phylogeny in general, and in human evolution in particular (e.g. finally demonstrating the single, African origin of all living humans; Cann *et al.*, 1987; Cavalli-Sforza, 1997).

One of the most impressive traits of eukaryotic cells is their ability to change shape and locomote in response to their environment. This ability played a crucial role in the transition to multicellularity, and in development today, but was already well established in single-celled forms such as amoebae. Such flexible, autonomous behavior depends upon a complex **cytoskeleton**: a system of thin struts called *microtubules* which, when static, maintain the cell's shape, and when shortened, allow the cell to reshape itself and locomote, engulf food particles, adhere to the substrate, or release to float free. The cytoskeleton also moves intracellular material around internally, transporting nutrients and waste, and plays a role in gene expression. Because each individual cell is an autonomous individual, two genetically identical cells placed in different environments will display different behaviors that are adaptive in that local context.

It is worthwhile pondering the complexity of a single-celled organism for a moment, to provide a context for understanding the complexity of our own bodies, built up of trillions of cells of similar complexity. For example, a neuron in the developing human brain is in many ways similar to an amoeba: moving through its environment, sensing extracellular signals that guide its migration, and finally stopping somewhere to unfold its tree-like axonal and dendritic arbor. The cellular processes which guide this unfolding are often the same as those used by the free-living amoeba, sharing its essential autonomy and its dependence on its individual past and its present situation to determine future actions. The only difference is that the "environment" sensed by the developing neuron (or any other cell in the developing body) is one that is made up of other, genetically identical cells. But this crucial feature – the autonomy of the single cell – is shared by eukaryotes of both the solitary and social persuasion, and plays a critical role in the epigenesis characterizing metazoan (including human) development.

We don't know when the symbiotic event that gave rise to the first eukaryotic cell occurred (enigmatic fossils termed *acritarchs* suggest roughly 1.75 billion years ago). What we do know is that this new life form had an immense potential to diversify, and was thus a crucial transition in the history of life (Maynard Smith and Szathmáry, 1995). Prokaryotes typically group together only in amorphous assemblages, and their earliest fossils are mineralized remains of mats of blue-green algae (stromatolites, some dating to 3.5 billion years ago). But only eukaryotes have successfully experimented with multicellularity on a grand scale, in which different genetically identical cells differentiate into myriad different cell types, thus creating more complex tissues, and ultimately organisms. We are fortunate that a few intermediate forms representing the single-cellular to multicellular transition still exist today. In the best studied of these forms (the so-called "slime molds," or social amoebae, e.g. *Dictyostelium*), an individual spends most of its life as a single-celled amoeba, feeding on bacteria in damp forest environments. However, when times get hard, dispersed amoebae aggregate, communicating via cyclic AMP (an intercellular messaging substance that still plays a crucial signaling role in multicellular life forms), and reproduce sexually. Their spores are released into the environment where they will hatch into solitary amoebae, starting the cycle anew. Thus an existing species today recreates the crucial first stage of the transition to multicellularity, and shares with us a core signal used in intercellular communication in our own bodies.

5.4 Early metazoans: epigenesis, the Urbilaterian, and the developmental toolkit

A large collection of developmental mechanisms involving signaling molecules and tissue interactions are widely shared among multicellular organisms. Many critical genes are shared among all animals and so date back to before one billion years ago.

One of the deep aesthetic appeals of biology is the amazing variability of animal form. Antonie van Leeuwenhoek's microscope revealed an amazing diversity of form even in microorganisms, and more recently the molecular revolution has opened our eyes to the biochemical diversity of bacteria. Still, diversity of form is expressed most delightfully in the metazoan animals. From jellyfish to anglerfish, from lobsters to butterflies, and from snakes to seagulls, nature has run riot in her experimentation with animal form. Until recently, form has represented a major gap in our understanding of evolutionary theory: "a guest missing at the feast" of the modern synthesis (Maynard Smith and Holliday, 1979). Finally, in the last twenty years, findings in evolutionary developmental biology ("evo-devo") have opened this black box with a powerful combination of molecular techniques and the comparative method. We are rapidly learning more about the genetic basis of animal form, and the results are not just surprising, but revolutionary.

The two great groups of animals alive today (encompassing all of the animals above except jellyfish) share a highly conserved "genetic toolkit" for controlling and generating animal form. One is upside down relative to the other: our group has a dorsal nervous system and ventral digestive tract, while the other has the opposite arrangement, suggesting that one or the other did a "flip" in their early evolution (De Robertis and Sasai, 1996).

The recent discovery of this conserved developmental toolkit contradicts the old assumption that each phylum of animals has its own developmental program, controlled by genes unique to that species. Research in molecular development has shown this assumption to be spectacularly incorrect, revitalizing the study of comparative biology to an astonishing degree (Carroll, 2000, 2005a). We now know that systems and patterns of gene regulation discovered in fruit flies play similar roles in humans. When it comes to humans and mice, nearly every human gene has some rodent equivalent. This newly discovered conservatism of the genetic toolkit is a welcome boon for those interested in human evolution, since it means that a much wider spectrum of species (many of them far easier to study than humans or other primates) have direct relevance to the genetics, development, and evolution of our own line. Suddenly, against all odds, a broad and deep understanding the genetic basis of development appears to be within our grasp. The next twenty years promises advances in the understanding of animal form unimaginable when I was a young biology student in the 1980s.

One of the most exciting evolutionary advances made possible by these new techniques is that we can use our understanding of the genetic toolkit to reconstruct the body plan of the common ancestor of most living animals. The appearance of fossils that can be clearly linked to either vertebrates or arthropods is in the Cambrian period, around 530 MYA. However, these fossil forms are already identifiably different from one another: the common ancestor must have lived earlier. Modern molecular tools have allowed us to peer backwards into this mist to reconstruct this common ancestor. The two main groups of living organisms are the **protostomes** (including arthropods such as insects, spiders, and crustaceans – by far the most speciose animal group – as well as mollusks and various types of worms) and the **deuterostomes** (including vertebrates like ourselves, echinoderms like starfish, and various other lesser-known invertebrates). All of these forms share a bilaterally symmetrical body form at some stage of their existence (e.g. starfish have a bilateral larval stage), and can thus be termed **bilaterians**. Their common ancestor has thus been dubbed the **Urbilaterian** (De Robertis and Sasai, 1996). Although there are no known fossils of this creature (though *Kimberella*, an Ediacarian fossil from the pre-Cambrian Vendian period, may be close), the "genetic fossils" preserved in the DNA of its descendent species allow us to reconstruct its developmental genetic toolkit.

All existing bilaterians share a basic genetic "bodybuilding" toolkit, including a set of transcription factors that control further development. First a set of homeobox (or HOX) genes provides a basic coordinate system along the axes of the developing body. Second, a set of genes headed by

Distal-less (Dll) play a key role in developing appendages. Third, PAX genes play a critical role in eye development. Finally, a family of genes dubbed "tinman" (after the *Wizard of Oz* character) plays a critical role in heart formation. Together, the fact that both the genes themselves, and their role in development, are conserved among bilaterians suggests that the Urbilaterian was bilaterally symmetrical, with well-defined front/back, up/down, and left/right axes and a through-running digestive tract with mouth and anus. This creature probably had appendages (e.g. legs or mouthparts), though their detailed nature remains unclear. Although it probably lacked eyes in the modern image-forming sense seen in insects or vertebrates, it had some sort of light-sensing eyespot(s). Finally, it had some type of contractile, fluid-pumping organ that evolved into the heart of its descendants. Because the basic structure and function of neurons is identical among all living bilaterians, we can surmise that this creature possessed a simple central nervous system and most of the neurotransmitters and intracellular signaling pathways known today (indeed, most of the critical aspects of neurons themselves are present in jellyfish, so they predated the Urbilaterian and have been conserved ever since; Mackie, 1990). Roughly speaking, then, the Urbilaterian was a small, worm-like creature with a nervous system, heart, and eyespot, and perhaps primitive limbs, that probably moved about actively in its pre-Cambrian marine environment, roughly 600 MYA (De Robertis and Sasai, 1996; Erwin and Davidson, 2002; Carroll *et al.*, 2005).

5.5 Getting a head (and jaws): the first fish and the vertebrate nervous system

The overall structure of the vertebrate brain, including many details of nervous pathways and functional neurotransmitter systems, are shared with jawless fish, and thus date back to the early Cambrian. Vertebrate evolution provides excellent examples of the evolutionary roles of exaptation and gene duplication.

Our own clade shows some important changes relative to our nearest invertebrate relatives (Shubin, 2008). In addition to the traits already present in the Urbilaterian, we have a flexible rod-like structure running the length of the back called a *notochord*, which aids in swimming by allowing lateral wriggling movements. The presence of a notochord gives our phylum its name, the **Chordata**. Another chordate innovation was a branchial basket: a pumping system in the pharyngeal region (the "throat") that modern lancelets and sea squirts use to filter tiny food particles from the water, but which was put to work in respiration as the gills of fish, and later served diverse functions related to hearing and speech in mammals (after several rounds of exaptation, see below). On top of these chordate characters, early **vertebrates** evolved a crucial new tissue type: bone. This hard, mineralized substance played a crucial role in our further evolution (and also provided fossil traces which make vertebrate evolution well documented). Among vertebrates, only the cartilaginous fish (sharks, rays, and chimaera) lack bone, and possess a cartilaginous skeleton, but this is now thought to be a derived trait of this clade. An additional important structure built of bone in early vertebrates was the spinal column, which takes the place of the noto-chord in stiffening and strengthening the back. The spinal column is built of many vertebrae, which give the group its name. Vertebrae are one of many examples among animals of **serial homology**: the repetition of a similar structure in different places along the body. The duplication and subse-quent "re-use" of a similar part in different body regions, often specialized to different functions, provide economy in our genetic toolkit, an important factor in the evolutionary success of vertebrates (Carroll *et al.*, 2005).

The presence of an internal skeleton gives vertebrates a major advantage over the other main bilaterian group, the arthropods. The external arthro-pod skeleton (the *exoskeleton*) completely surrounds a lobster's, spider's, or insect's body, meaning that as they grow, they must periodically shed their skeleton, crawling out from inside it and generating a new one (a process called "molting"). During the post-molt period an arthropod's ability to move and feed is impaired, and it is quite defenseless against attack. In contrast, vertebrates' internal skeleton allows us to add muscle and tissue on top of our rigid skeleton, remodeling our skeleton by adding bone as we grow. This ability to quickly grow large provided a major advantage of early vertebrates over their arthropod prey (the largest arthropods – marine crustaceans like lobsters and crabs – are dwarfed by large vertebrates like dinosaurs, elephants, or whales).

A second crucial innovation of vertebrates was an entirely novel type of tissue called **neural crest**, particularly relevant to the anatomy of speech production and perception. This strip of cells runs down the back of early embryos, playing diverse roles in development. The neural crest is the source of many vertebrate-specific structures such as jaws, external ears, and many important neural, pigmentation, adrenal, and skin tissues (Le Douarin and Kalcheim, 1999). Vertebrates have considerably more types of cells than worms or flies, and many of these additional types derive from neural crest. It would be difficult to overestimate the importance of neural crest as a source of evolutionary novelty in our clade (Gans and

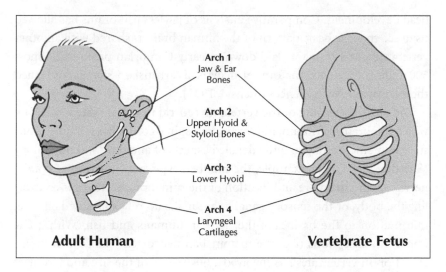

Figure 5.2 Branchial Arch Derivatives: from gills to vocal apparatus – Much of the human vocal apparatus is "exapted" from embryonic tissues which once gave rise to gills in our aquatic fish-like ancestors. This is true both of the production mechanism (larynx, hyoid skeleton, and jaw) and of important parts of the middle ear. The correspondence between gill arch number and adult skeletal components of the ear and vocal tract are shown. Adapted from Shubin (2008).

Northcutt, 1983; Northcutt and Gans, 1983). The neural crest led to the development of **complex gill bars**: serially repeated structures with a bony arch, attached muscles, and a dedicated circulatory system. When vertebrates emerged onto land and lost their gills, "left-over" branchial tissues were put to amazingly diverse uses, providing the embryonic origin for almost all of the vocal production system (the larynx, the hyoid, the jaw, and much of the face), as well as most of the external and middle ear (see Figure 5.2). The fact that human speech is expressed and understood via systems evolved from gills in our remote aquatic ancestors provides a concrete, language-relevant example of evolutionary "tinkering" and exaptation.

The origin of a true head – with a brain and sense organs protected by the bones of the skull – was another major step forward in vertebrate evolution (Gans and Northcutt, 1983; Northcutt and Gans, 1983). The primitive **jawless fish** that resulted were once abundant, but most disappeared long ago, outcompeted by their jawed descendants. A few jawless fish still remain, including hagfish and lampreys. These living species allow us to reconstruct, via the comparative method, many aspects of the earliest vertebrates' biology that would otherwise be lost forever to science, including their physiology, genetics, and behavior. Particularly important are the structure and function of the nervous system, and the genetic control of head development. Comparative analysis of jawless fish brains has allowed us to see that the basic pattern of the human brain is shared with all other vertebrates, and thus was laid down in early Cambrian proto-fish almost 500 million years ago. Anatomical analysis of early fish fossils has confirmed these comparative inferences (Stensiö, 1921).

The basic patterning of the vertebrate **central nervous system** (CNS) – with a forebrain, midbrain, hindbrain, and spinal cord – has remained constant ever since, down to quite detailed aspects of anatomy and physiology (Striedter, 2004). For example, the number, type, and function of cranial nerves, or the structure and location of the spinal motor neurons controlling the body, or the sensory ganglia that make up reflex arcs and channel information to the brain, are the same in humans and fish. With a few important exceptions (e.g. the mammalian neocortex), subsequent brain evolution in vertebrates has involved adjustments of the size and layout of these primitive brain circuits, rather than the addition of novel structures. These well-established facts contradict the widespread but incorrect idea of the "triune brain" (MacLean, 1990). MacLean suggested that the human brain was built up by an accumulation of new areas, during mammalian evolution, layering novel tissues on top of an ancient "reptilian" brain. In fact, homologs of all three of MacLean's areas were already present in ancient fish (cf. Striedter, 2004). Thus, many of the key constraints on brain evolution were already laid down long before vertebrates emerged onto land. Human brain organization has very ancient roots.

Although the earliest fish were quite successful and have left an abundant fossil record (Long, 1995), they lacked one crucial feature found in almost all living vertebrates: jaws. Quite soon after the diversification of early jawless fish in the Silurian, some fish found a novel use for the frontmost gill bar. The former gill muscles became enlarged to move the bar, and thus, strange as it sounds, our movable jaws were born from gills. This transformation of gill bar to jaw is re-enacted during development in living **jawed vertebrates,** and the evolution of jaws has also been well studied via a set of transitional fossils. More recently, the genetic basis of jaw formation has been explored in evo-devo studies (Forey and Janvier, 1993), confirming earlier findings from comparative anatomy and embryology. The subsequent evolution of a complex and powerful musculature, acting on a robust skeletal framework armed with teeth, was to play an important role in subsequent vertebrate evolution, and jaw oscillations are argued to be central to speech and phonology today (MacNeilage, 1998b). These early jawed fish rapidly evolved into large, successful predators. Teeth and jaws have been critical aspects of vertebrate evolution ever since, particularly in mammals, where teeth are extremely diversified and provide durable clues to past ways of life. The transformation of gill bars into jaws is one of many examples of an important evolutionary phenomenon: *serial homology provides a preadaptive basis for subsequent specialization.* The remaining gill bars could continue their "old" job as gills, allowing one pair to adapt to a new and spectacularly successful function: capturing and processing food.

A molecular parallel to serial homology in head and jaw development has become clear in recent years. In early vertebrate evolution the HOX genes present in the Urbilaterian ancestor were duplicated, twice, so vertebrates have four homologous HOX genes for each one present in an insect (Panopoulou *et al.*, 2003; Carroll *et al.*, 2005). This is but one example of another general evolutionary phenomenon: *gene duplication as a basis for gene specialization* (Ohno, 1970; Holland *et al.*, 1994). By creating two, initially redundant, copies of a gene, gene duplication allows one copy to change its function while the other continues to do the "old" job. In the case of vertebrate HOX gene duplication, the additional copies were free to make slight changes in the transcribed proteins and, more importantly, to be independently regulated in new times and locations during development. It is interesting that, after these two doubling events, the four-fold HOX gene complement was apparently adequate to provide the spatial coordinates for building a great diversity of bodies, from aardvarks to zebras – and modern humans. We have the same complement of HOX genes as these early fish.

Before continuing our story, as vertebrates move onto land, it is worth stopping to ponder the immense success of the fish who stayed behind. With more than 24,000 species, fish (meaning all non-tetrapod vertebrates) are by far the most speciose vertebrate group: birds have around 9,000 species, while reptiles, amphibians, and mammals each have less than 6,000. The vast majority of well-known fish (from anglerfish to swordfish and from trout to tuna) are the teleosts or "higher fish." This group is remarkably diverse in terms of morphology, physiology, and behavior. Interestingly, teleosts are unique in having undergone yet another gene duplication event (so, yes, some fish have more genes than you or me). Some groups, such as certain coral reef teleosts, have relatively large brains, complex social behavior including various forms of territoriality, complex courtship, and elaborate parental care (Bshary *et al.*, 2002). Many teleosts have independently evolved viviparity (giving birth to live young), the ability to breathe air, and warm-bloodedness (homeothermy) – all traits we normally associate with supposedly "higher" vertebrates such as mammals and birds. Many teleosts also have good underwater hearing and surprisingly diverse vocalizations, and provide a remarkable source of comparative data concerning vertebrate brain evolution that has only begun to be mined (Striedter, 2004). The recent discovery of conservatism in the genetic toolkit makes it likely that many lessons learned studying fish will have direct molecular relevance to humans and other terrestrial vertebrates. Unfortunately, many fish species are threatened by habitat destruction and wasteful, ecologically destructive fishing practices. Once-vast fish populations, such as North Atlantic cod, have collapsed completely because of overfishing (Kurlansky, 1997). So the next time you prepare to eat a fish, think twice. You may be eating an endangered species – check first at: www.msc.org – and those unblinking eyes are connected to a nervous system much like your own.

5.6 Onto the land: proto-tetrapods

New genetic and fossil finds have demanded rethinking of old ideas about the origins of lungs and fingers, illustrating the testable, empirical nature of evolutionary hypotheses.

Life evolved in the sea, and although the conquest of land began with bacteria, it wasn't until plants began to occupy the land that the potential of this initially unoccupied niche was heavily exploited. Plants produce organic carbon compounds upon which non-plant metazoans (animals and fungi) depend for life. The brighter light available in air makes the terrestrial environment highly productive, and land plants quickly evolved adaptations to suit life on land. By 370 MYA, in the Devonian, the first forests were forming, and these would blanket much of the earth during the Carboniferous (359–299 MYA) to lay down the vast coal beds for which that period is named (Niklas, 1997). The decaying leaves, branches, and trunks of the Devonian forests were already fed upon by the earliest land animals: arthropods such as millipedes and springtails. These in turn provided fodder for arthropod predators such as spiders and scorpions, and later dragonflies, some of which grew to colossal sizes. It was into this rich environment that our earliest terrestrial vertebrate ancestors emerged. Because they had four legs, the descendants are collectively termed **tetrapods**, including those like humans, birds, whales, or snakes, whose limbs have been heavily modified or lost. Tetrapod evolution provides nice illustrations of how new fossils can overturn previously accepted theories, and of how what once appeared to be universal constraints are in fact just contingent accidents.

The timing of the emergence of the proto-tetrapod is bracketed by fossil lobefin fishes from the late Devonian (e.g. *Eusthenopteron*), and diverse fossil amphibians from the Carboniferous. This places tetrapod origins at sometime around the end of the Devonian (about 350 MYA). Until recently, this crucial transition period was poorly documented by fossils, leading to many speculative hypotheses about precisely how, and why, the earliest tetrapods emerged from water. Perhaps the best-known scenario is the "drying pond" hypothesis promulgated by paleontologist Alfred Romer (Romer, 1941). Romer suggested that the early transitions from water-breathing, weak-finned fish to air-breathing, strong-limbed lobefins was driven by repeated escapes from drying ponds, and the need to find another pond to slide back into. Leaving their gill-dependent cousins drying and gasping in the sun, our lobefin ancestors dragged themselves along the mud, breathing air as they went, and slid happily back into new, wet homes. This scenario allows for a gradual Darwinian adaptation to dryer conditions. These early tetrapods perhaps snapped up a few insects as they moved along, longer stints on land were selectively favored, and the rest is history. Appealing in its simplicity, this provided the "standard" model of tetrapod origins for many years.

Recent discoveries, starting in the 1990s, have quite radically revised this viewpoint (cf. Zimmer, 1998; Shubin, 2008). It is now widely agreed that the earliest tetrapods were mainly or wholly aquatic, and that limbs with digits evolved *before* the transition to land. The critical discovery was that the earliest known tetrapod, *Acanthostega*, from 363 MYA in the late Devonian in Greenland, had skeletal grooves strongly suggesting functioning gills (Coates and Clack, 1991). It now seems clear that air-breathing **lungs**, rather than being tetrapod derivatives of a fish swim bladder (as thought by Darwin), already existed in early fish (teleosts later transformed lungs into a swim bladder; Liem, 1988). These discoveries paint a different, and much wetter, picture of tetrapod evolution than previously imagined: proto-tetrapods were shallow-water aquatic creatures who possessed *both* gills and lungs (the latter to help deal with the low-oxygen conditions that frequently affect warm shallow water). These early tetrapods were quite similar to modern lungfish, who are also "belt-and-suspenders" types possessing both gills and lungs. They were probably sit-and-wait predators, lurking in the shadows to lunge forth and snap up anything that moved – whether shallow-water fish and invertebrates or land-dwelling invertebrates. A tendency towards skull flattening (as seen in modern crocodilians) in our nearest lobefin cousins (e.g. *Panderichthyes*) suggests that some proto-tetrapods were already specializing on terrestrial prey. Thus it was probably hunger, rather than drought, that drew them onto land.

The origin of tetrapod hands and feet has provided more surprises. Except for occasional abberant forms, all living tetrapods have five or fewer digits, and abundant Carboniferous fossils show that this pattern, retained in modern humans, was already well established among early amphibians around 300 MYA. This regularity had already been noted by comparative anatomist Richard Owen, and provided a prime example of his idea of God-given homology (Panchen, 1994). The consistency of this five-fingered tetrapod "template" has long suggested that proto-tetrapods must have had five digits as well. Thus, the discovery of fossils showing that *Ichthyostega* possessed *seven* toes and *Acanthostega eight* fingers, and another early tetrapod, *Tulerpeton*, had six digits, came as a great surprise (Coates and Clack, 1990; Lebedev and Coates, 1995), and illustrates the caution required when interpreting reconstructed ancestors. It is now clear that there was considerable "experimentation," early in tetrapod evolution, with digit numbers. These paleontological findings have meshed nicely with the new evo-devo understanding of limb development (which re-uses the same gene code developed for Urbilaterian outgrowths for this new, tetrapod-specific function). This allows a deeper understanding of homology, in which homology of form is perhaps less telling than *homology in the developmental program*. All of the variable digit numbers in tetrapods, from *Acanthostega*'s eight, to our "normal" five, to a horse's single toe, result from different parameters input to the same developmental program. The same genes are deployed in a very similar way across all of these different species (Shubin *et al.*, 1997). Rather than resulting from a "blueprint" of a five-fingered limb, as Owen had imagined, the variety of limb development results from the same "recipe," implemented with different amounts and timing of ingredients. Tetrapod limb development provides one of the clearest cases of a conserved "bodybuilding" toolkit and deep homology, illustrating how insights from other vertebrates inform our understanding of our own five fingers.

5.7 Finding a voice: early tetrapods and vocal communication

Adaptations for auditory perception, and the structure of the vocal apparatus, are key innovations shared with all land-dwelling vertebrates, and many aspects of vocal communication thus date back to early tetrapods of the late Devonian (circa 350 MYA).

Two key innovations for vocal communication, closely linked to the transition to terrestriality, also occurred around the same time but are less clearly understood. These are the origin of an ear sensitive to airborne sound, and the evolution of a sound-producing larynx. Fish can sense underwater sound, using a mechanism directly homologous to our own hearing mechanisms. Called the **lateral line system**, it consists of grooves on the body surface containing hair cells just like those in our inner ear. Water movements cause these hair cells to fire, transmitting pressure or flow signals from the water to the fish's brain. Fish also possess an internal organ, within the skull, lined with these same hair cells, that is homologous to the *cochlea*: the sound-sensing organ in tetrapods. Because the cochlea is fluid-filled, it is the same density as the fish's body, and the water surrounding it, and so pressure waves can pass right through the body and stimulate the cochlea. Once the tetrapod head enters the air, however, this system is no longer effective: the great difference in density between water and air means that air waves simply "bounce off" the body. The key innovation that overcame this mismatch was the tetrapod **middle ear**. The basic system has two components: a lightweight membrane called the *tympanic membrane* (the "eardrum") – which because of its high surface area and low mass can be set into vibration by air waves – and a bone called the *stapes* that connects this membrane to the cochlea. This system compensates for the impedance mismatch in air and water, and allowed early tetrapods to hear airborne sounds. The stapes derives from a component of the jaw support which linked the jaws to the braincase in our fishy ancestors (called the *hyomandibular*). As the jaw became more directly and sturdily attached to the skull base, this bone became superfluous and shrank; in proto-tetrapods such as *Acanthostega* it was little more than a bony nubbin in the rear of the head, which may or not have functioned as a true stapes (Thomson, 1991; Clack, 1992, 1994). Either way, early amphibians clearly had already developed functioning ears with a stapes, and a notch in the back of the skull to support the tympanum, a few million years later. What were these early tetrapods listening to? Although listening for the sounds of insect prey might have been useful, the most likely function was the one served by ears in most amphibians today: listening to each other. This brings us to the second key innovation: the larynx.

Fish with lungs need a way to keep water out of, and air in, them. Modern lungfish accomplish this via a sphincter-like valve in the floor of their mouth; a primitive **larynx**. Not surprisingly, pressurized air passing through this sphincter can make a variety of sounds, including squeaks, hisses, and belch-like sounds, and lungfish apparently produce such sounds when provoked (M'Donnel, 1860). Lungfish laryngeal sound production is homologous to our own speech and song (most fish use completely different, non-homologous, mechanisms to produce sound; Demski and Gerald, 1974). Because the laryngeal cartilages do not fossilize, we do not have any good indication of when the two-part larynx of primitive tetrapods appeared, but comparative data from living amphibians suggest that it was already present in the basal tetrapod ancestral to both frogs and us. The larynx started out as a valve protecting the lungs, and it has retained this primary function ever since (Negus, 1949; Hast, 1983). But the heavy use of sound in territoriality and courtship in modern frogs and toads suggests that the early Carboniferous swamps may have already resounded with tetrapod vocalizations: the ancient precursors of modern human speech.

5.8 In the shadow of dinosaurs: amniotes and early mammals

Core aspects of human life history such as live birth, milk production, and maternal care, along with a highly developed auditory system and the six-layered neocortex, extend back to the earliest mammals, into (at least) the Cretaceous.

By the early Permian, about 300 MYA, terrestrial vertebrates were dominant predators. However, huge crocodile-sized amphibians such as *Eryops* needed to return to the water to breed (as do most frogs and salamanders today). But a new form of vertebrate had truly conquered the land, such that all stages of the life cycle could be completed out of water. This group was ancestral to modern reptiles, birds, and mammals, which are all called **amniotes**, after the crucial innovation that allows their egg to survive on land. The amniote egg has a membrane surrounding the developing embryo, the *amnion*, which, together with other membranes, keeps the embryo floating in fluid while allowing oxygen exchange and sequestering waste. These membranes still play this role in reptile and bird eggs (you can see them when you eat a boiled egg) and still protect and regulate the mammalian embryo *in utero* (the human medical procedure *amniocentesis* involves taking a sample from within the amniotic sac). It is difficult to say precisely when this key innovation occurred: organisms with skeletal features reminiscent of amniotes were already known in the Carboniferous by 338 MYA (Smithson, 1989), but the earliest fossil eggs that indisputably represent shelled terrestrial eggs are much later, in the Mesozoic. Regardless, amniotes were destined to play a dominant role in terrestrial ecosystems from that point on.

Very early on, the amniote clade was already split in two, as shown by certain aspects of skull morphology. One clade led to all of the existing reptiles (turtles, snakes, lizards, crocodilians) plus the birds, and the other led to mammals. This latter group, the *synapsids* (colloquially called "mammal-like reptiles"), were highly successful during the Permian and were top predators, preying on the smaller amniotes (like the diapsids who would evolve into dinosaurs, in a dramatic turning of the tables during the Mesozoic). Again, it is difficult to say when many key innovations that typify mammals evolved: milk, maternal care, fur, neocortex, additions to the larynx, and homeothermy ("warm-bloodedness") do not leave a reliable fossil record. However, the existence of all of these in egg-laying mammals suggests that they appeared very early. We are fortunate that at least one mammalian innovation, an elaborate middle ear, has a clear and well-studied fossil record (Hopson, 1966; Allin, 1975; Clack, 1997).

The clearest skeletal evidence for the origin of mammals comes from our distinctive middle ear bones: the **mammalian auditory ossicles**. Most amniotes have a single bone, the columella (homologous to our stapes, or "stirrup" bone), that transfers environmental vibrations from eardrum to cochlea. Mammals are unique in having two extra small bones, the malleus and incus ("hammer" and "anvil," respectively) interposed between the eardrum and the cochlea. These extra bones are derived from bones that formed part of the jaw joint in our amniote ancestors; homologous bones (the quadrate and articular) are still key components of the jaw joint today, in modern birds and reptiles. The process by which this unlikely transformation occurred – converting sturdy jaw bones into our delicate ossicles – has been nicely preserved in the fossil record (cf. Allin and Hopson, 1992). Early mammals such as *Morganucodon* had already completed this transformation, and can thus be unambiguously recognized from fossils as mammals by the late Triassic (Kemp, 2005). Other aspects of physiology remain questionable, however. Most experts agree that they were probably homeothermic, and had fur. Whether they already produced milk (like all surviving mammals) remains undetermined. Whether *Morganucodon* laid eggs (like the most primitive surviving mammals, the playpus and echidna) or gave live birth (like all other mammals, including marsupials and placentals) is harder to surmise. What is clear is that these stem mammals were in for a very long wait for the duration of the Mesozoic (from 251– 65 MYA), living in the shadows of the much more successful dinosaurs, before getting their chance at evolutionary radiation at the beginning of the Cenozoic. Much of mammalian evolution occurred during this long period.

A nice picture of the lifestyle of a Mesozoic mammal is provided by the small fossil mammal *Eomaia*, which lived 125 MYA in the early Cretaceous. *Eomaia* means "dawn mother" and is represented by an exquisitely preserved fossil found in China (Ji *et al.*, 2002). This fossil preserves the outline of fur – mammals had definitely evolved our characteristic pelt by this time (and probably long before). *Eomaia* was an active, agile climbing mammal, as revealed by skeletal characteristics of the wrist and shoulder girdle, and may have lived permanently in trees. The teeth are generalized and sharply pointed, suggesting an omnivorous diet biased towards insects and other small prey. At 25 grams, it was about the size of a mouse. Living during the peak of the age of the dinosaurs, this small size would have kept *Eomaia* from the attention of the many large and dangerous predatory archosaurs that dominated the carnivorous niche at that time. This lifestyle – small and scared – probably characterized mammals for the next 60 million years – half of the timespan from *Eomaia* to the present, although a few Cretaceous mammals achieved cat-like sizes (Hu *et al.*, 2005).

Besides fur and milk, a critical mammalian innovation was the origin of a new type of neural tissue, found only in mammals: the **neocortex**. The anatomical term "cortex" (meaning "bark of a tree" or "rind") refers to any layer of tissue that surrounds some inner core. In the vertebrate brain, a three-layered cortex is a primitive feature, clearly differentiated in living reptiles such as alligators (Striedter, 2004). The characteristic features of cortical tissue are its cell types – large pyramidal cells with well-developed dendritic and axonal arbors, along with smaller "interneurons" that form short-range connections between them – and the arrangement of these cells into layers. This arrangement is also found in the hippocampus, another highly conserved vertebrate tissue. However, mammals transformed this tissue by adding additional layers, to create a six-layered neocortex found only in mammals. Neocortex is a nice example of evolutionary tinkering, based upon a pre-existing layered cortical architecture. However, its importance in the evolution of mammals can hardly be over-emphasized: it is primarily the neocortex whose evolutionary expansion characterizes mammals in general, and primates in particular (Reader and Laland, 2002). The neocortex appears to represent a powerful, multipurpose computational architecture that can easily be expanded (by simply allowing precursor cells to go on dividing for a longer period), and subsequently specialized based on both intrinsic genetic markers and environmental input (Krubitzer, 1995; Allman, 1999; Striedter, 2004). The neocortex can form sensory maps based on visual, auditory, or somatosensory input. It can also create more abstract multi-modal or amodal representations in association cortex, or organize motor output into specialized somatotopic subregions. While we still do not understand the precise computational nature of the neocortex, it is apparently highly flexible (Braitenberg, 1977; Bienenstock, 1995), and represents a key cognitive innovation found in all later mammals. There have been no new neural tissue types added since then, and the main differences between mammal species consist of different gross brain size, different ratios of neocortex to non-cortical brain regions, and different proportions of sensory-motor to association cortex (Deacon, 1990a; Finlay and Darlington, 1995; Clark *et al.*, 2001): this basic "scalable architecture" has not undergone any obvious further evolution since the origin of mammals. Therefore, the evolution of the fundamental underlying neural architecture that was to support the evolution of language was complete by (at latest) 65 MYA.

5.9 The End-Cretaceous extinction begins the age of mammals

The ascendance of mammals is due not to any intrinsic superiority, but rather to a chance event which destabilized the pre-existing ecological system dominated by dinosaurs. This led to an explosion of mammalian diversity, and to the origins of primates.

After eons in the shadows, the abrupt extinction of the dinosaurs and other Mesozoic forms gave mammals our big chance. This occurred at 65 MYA, at the transition from the Cretaceous to the Tertiary (the "K–T transition"). A major extraterrestrial impact occurred at this time, wreaking havoc on all major biomes and blanketing large portions of the planet with iridium-containing debris, which can be detected at sites around the world. It is widely agreed that this K-T impact played a key role in the extinction of the dinosaurs (as well as dominant undersea predators like ammonites), though other ongoing geological factors probably also played a destabilizing role (Prothero and Dott, 2004). This event marks an abrupt transition in the ecology of our planet, and triggered a rapid and impressive diversification of birds and mammals (hence the traditional name for the Tertiary: "The Age of Mammals"). Previous to the K-T boundary, mammals were small and not very abundant creatures. A few million years later, a huge diversity of mammal species already existed, including large-bodied herbivores, primitive carnivores, and the primate-like arboreal plesiadapiforms. This explosion of mammalian diversity in the Paleocene filled most available ecological niches. By the beginning of the Eocene period at 56 MYA, many modern orders of mammals can already be recognized from fossils. Mammalian diversification was made possible by the mass extinction event, and the subsequent opening up of niches that had been successfully filled for the previous 150 million years by archosaurian reptiles. It did *not* occur because mammals were smarter, more efficient, or otherwise "better" than dinosaurs, and indeed mammal brains remained quite small during this first radiation (Jerison, 1973). The K-T impact is thus seen by most paleontologists as the canonical case of an external contingent event having a major irreversible effect on macroevolutionary patterns. Had it not occurred, humans and language might never have evolved.

5.10 Early primates: sociality, color vision, and larger brains

Sophisticated vision, complex and highly structured social systems, relatively large brains, and solicitous care for a single offspring at a time, are traits shared with most primates, which thus probably date back to the Eocene.

The first members of our own order of mammals, the primates, became clearly differentiated from other mammals quite early in the Cenozoic. Although certain archaic Paleocene mammals like plesiadapiforms have been linked to the primates, they lack the suite of derived morpohological features that distinguish primates from most mammals (such as having nails instead of claws). These traits appeared a bit later, during the Eocene, during which we have a relatively rich fossil record. Early Eocene primates had already split into two groups of true primates, the adapids (now extinct) and tarsiiformes (named for the tiny tarsiers, small nocturnal primates of South-East Asia). Both groups were forest-living arboreal mammals, mainly nocturnal and insectivorous (as are tarsiers today). The early Eocene was the warmest period Earth has experienced since the age of the dinosaurs, and the permissive climate helped spread the warm, moist forest habitat required by early primates nearly to the poles. This allowed early primates to spread widely over the globe. By the late Eocene a diverse primate fauna had evolved, one that is captured beautifully by fossils of the Fayum Depression in Egypt (Simons, 1995). Around 35 MYA, this site was a hot, wet tropical forest whose trees were inhabited by several distinct groups of primates. Two of these may represent the early precursors of modern apes and monkeys, respectively. Based on the almost complete prevalence of long-term and complex social groups in their surviving descendants, we can infer that these stem primates were already highly social. Thus **sociality** was an early, stable feature of the primate lineage, with implications continuing to modern humans. Coping with complex social groups has long been an important selective force for greater intelligence in primates (Dunbar, 1992; Foley, 1995; Byrne, 1997).

The smaller monkey-like primates are termed "parapithecids" ("beside apes"), and at around 3 kg were about the size of extant squirrel monkeys or capuchins. The larger primates are called propliopithecids, and they have several features placing them near the base of our own ape clade. Several specimens of *Propliopithecus* are known (sometimes placed in the competing genus *Aegyptopithecus*). They were the size of dogs (2–6 kg), with robust skeletons and grasping feet and hands, and well adapted to quadrupedal locomotion in trees. Their ape-like dentition suggests a diet consisting mainly of fruit. **Frugivory** represents a "cognitive niche" that poses interesting intellectual challenges relative to insectivory or leaf-eating (Clutton-Brock and Harvey, 1980). In tropical forests, tree fruiting times are staggered through the year, and a frugivore can thus potentially survive on fruit throughout the year. However, the fruiting time of individual trees is rather variable, and their location is distributed unpredictably over a large area of forest. Particularly for a species specialized to eat soft ripe fruit (as *Propliopithecus* probably was), remembering where in a large and complex jungle a tree is, and when its fruit is likely to be ready to eat, may have provided an important selective pressure, pushing early primate cognition towards increased memory, and perhaps more accurate storage of place and time information. Analogous forces may have operated on the most intelligent bird lineages, like crows and parrots, as well (Emery and Clayton, 2004).

Reliance on fruit also placed a premium on vision, and particularly on **color vision** (Carroll, 2006). Just as flowers are a plant's way of encouraging pollinators to help plants have sex, fruits are a plant's way of distributing its seeds. The fruit-eating animal deposits the eaten but still viable seeds (complete with fertilizer) further from the parent plant than would be possible by wind or gravity. Many plants that rely upon vertebrate dispersal advertise sweet or nutritious fruit with bright colors to attract particular species. Fruits "aimed at" birds often use the color red, because it gives excellent contrast against green foliage for an animal possessing color vision (as all fruit-eating birds do). Although full color vision (with at least three types of retinal cone cells) is a primitive vertebrate character (most fish, birds, and reptiles have better color vision than humans, with four cone cell types; Jacobs and Rowe, 2004), the long nocturnal existence of mammals in the Mesozoic led to a loss of this color system in our clade. Hence, most mammals today are still dichromats (or "color-blind" – relying on two, rather than three or four, cone types). However, many primate have independently reinvented color vision (by a process of gene duplication and divergence). Based on comparative data, this event seems to have occurred in the stem catarrhine, but after the split from other anthropoid primates (Vorobyev, 2004). An increase in red/green color contrast would have immediately benefited any fruit-eating primate, because brightly colored red and yellow fruits had already evolved bright colors to attract birds (and probably dinosaurs) during the Cretaceous (Beck, 1976). With dinosaurs gone, and other mammals being dichromats and thus disadvantaged at finding fruit, primates and some fruit bats became the only large fruit-eating mammals with color vision.

5.11 Early apes and the last common ancestor

Early apes were long-lived, large-bodied frugivores that had evolved by the Miocene, 20 MYA. One of their descendants was the LCA.

Unfortunately, the rich fossils of the late Eocene and early Oligocene are followed by a fossil desert: a nearly complete lack of primate fossils from the rest of the Oligocene. The Oligocene was a period of cooling and drying, and these climatic changes had powerful and sometimes catastrophic effects on many mammalian groups, including primates. The early Oligocene (starting at 34 MYA) in Europe presents such an extreme change in mammalian fauna that it is designated the "Grande Coupure" – the "great break" (Agusti and Antón, 2002). This period of cooler, drier climate was undoubtedly difficult for the forest-dwelling primates, but our fossil record, limited to a few scattered fragments, gives little clue as to how they reacted to this major stress. By the early Miocene, about 20 MYA, a clear group of "stem apes" had diversified. Fossil apes are distinguished from monkeys by their lack of a tail and certain features of the teeth and elbow. One long-known fossil ape is *Proconsul*, a relatively small frugivorous ape of the early African Miocene discovered in 1933. Most members of this genus remained relatively small (10–40 kg) and monkey-like in many ways (although the largest, *Proconsul major*, may have reached 76 kg – the mass of a modern human). *Proconsul* hand morphology looks strikingly human, and they were once incorrectly seen as initiating the specifically human line of ancestry. Today, even their status as *apes* is debated.

It is not until 15 MYA in the middle Miocene that undoubted apes such as *Aegyptopithecus*, a gorilla-sized species from Kenya, or the 12 MYA *Sivapithecus* from Asia can be found. The latter is of particular interest as it represents the only fossil form that can be clearly linked to a living great ape. The first remains of *Sivapithecus* were named *Ramapithecus*, and again thought to represent the earliest fossil ancestors of humans, but further finds indicated that this lineage led to the orangutans. This fossil species is thus often used to calibrate the molecular clock of ape evolution, and to date the divergence of humans from chimpanzees.

Debate about which of many fossil apes from the mid to late Miocene represent the common ancestor of the African great apes remains heated, with candidates including *Dryopithecus, Ankaropithecus*, and *Graecopithecus* (for a balanced discussion see Stringer and Andrews, 2005). It remains unclear which (if any) of these fossils represents the last common ancestor of humans, chimpanzees, and gorillas, or of just chimpanzees and humans. However, it is very clear that by the mid Miocene, a diverse set of ape species had evolved large bodies, relatively large brains, and thick tooth enamel, which characterize living apes and humans. Fossil apes are found in Africa, Europe, and throughout Asia, and were reasonably common. Thus, by the late Miocene apes were highly successful and widespread in the Old World. Dentition suggests that almost all retained a specialization for fruit-eating, and were probably arboreal. Relatively large bodies indicate that these apes were slow developing and long-lived; they possessed color vision and larger brains to help accomplish more challenging foraging tasks. In addition, the more general primate trend of sociality probably also selected for social intelligence (Dunbar, 1992, 1993). It has been suggested that large body size, combined with arboreality, provided another cognitive selective pressure for slow, careful arboreal clambering, and this led to the primitive self-concept characterizing apes, but not monkeys (Povinelli and Cant, 1995). We have reached the time of the LCA.

One of the many ways in which a *scala naturae* caricature of evolution can cloud evolutionary understanding is in the relationship between apes and monkeys. Because monkeys are thought to be lower on the "great chain of being," there is a tendency to assume that they dominated earlier in evolution. But the paleontological evidence suggests that this gets the facts backwards. About 15 MYA, dryopithecine apes (a general term for the ancestors of living great apes) were widespread throughout Africa and Asia, and monkeys were quite rare. But around the Miocene/Pliocene border, around 5 MYA, perhaps due to the climate changes and breakup of the once ubiquitous gallery forests into a mosaic of forest and grassland, the situation changed abruptly (Cameron, 2004). The fossil record does not allow us to reconstruct what happened in detail, but in more recent cases where the fossils are adequate (e.g. Pleistocene East Asia), monkeys succeeded during periods of ecological instability, while apes disappeared or were relegated to patches of stable rainforest (Jablonski, 1998). Today, the result of this difference is clear: monkeys are dominant primates ecologically, and modern apes are confined to pockets of isolated forest. Monkeys, with their high reproductive rates and generalist ways, have taken over in many regions where apes once dominated. Indeed, apes today can be thought of as relict populations of a once-dominant clade, hanging on in stable, welcoming environments. The monkeys' ecological "victory" is not due to greater intelligence, more efficient food use, or aggressive physical competition – in all of these respects apes outclass monkeys (Tomasello and Call, 1997). Apes (sometimes literally) "eat monkeys for lunch" (Stanford *et al.*, 1994b). So why are monkeys so successful today, compared to the once-dominant apes? The monkeys' clearest advantage is a much higher reproductive potential, particularly in situations of climatic variability, where high intelligence and large body size can no longer necessarily assure a long life. Competition from monkeys put a premium upon ensuring offspring survival, and we will see in Chapter 6 that this may have important implications for why language evolved in our lineage and not in others.

5.12 Chapter summary: from the first cell to the last common ancestor

We have reached the end of the vast sweep of human evolution from the dawn of life to the LCA. As I have emphasized, most aspects of human biology were already well established at this point, and no single "environment of evolutionary adaptedness" characterizes humans, or any other species. Instead, different traits have wildly different time depths and evolutionary histories. The LCA was already an unusual mammal in many ways: long-lived, large-bodied, and large-brained. However, the genetic toolkit used to build its body form and brain architecture was widely shared. It inherited a nervous system from the Urbilaterian ancestor of vertebrates and insects 500 MYA, and the structures of the brain had already been established in early fish, and codified in early mammals by (at the latest) 65 MYA. Thus, the last spurt of human evolution, which represents less than 1 percent of our total evolutionary history, was heavily constrained by this already well-established system. Because of these evolutionary facts, our ever-increasing understanding of the genetics of development in a diverse array of model species (including fruit flies, zebra fish, and mice) can be expected to place important constraints on theories of human evolution, including language evolution. During the last phase of our evolution, some relatively subtle genetic and neural tweaks led to major qualitative changes in human behavior, changes that will concern us for the rest of this book. To understand these it is necessary to reconstruct as much as we can about this LCA, since this is the last point in human evolution where comparative data concerning genetics, brain structure, physiology, and behavior is available. Thus, in Chapter 6, we use what is known about human and chimpanzee biology to reconstruct the biology of the LCA. Despite a lack of fossil evidence, the comparative approach allows us to paint a surprisingly rich picture of this extinct creature, the last great-grandmother we share with our nearest living relatives.

6 | The LCA: our last common ancestor with chimpanzees

6.1 Reconstructing the LCA

In the previous chapter we surveyed the vast sweep of evolution from the unicellular beginnings of life to the flourishing of primates in the Tertiary. We have arrived at a point crucial for our own evolutionary history: the evolution of hominids *sensu strictu* starting with our divergence from chimpanzees about seven million years ago (in the upper Miocene). This was the time of our **last common ancestor** with chimpanzees, or **LCA**, which was an African ape, probably confined to the forests stretching across the middle of Africa. These last seven million years have obviously been a period of considerable divergence of humans from chimpanzees and most other primates, with changes in locomotion, dentition, reproductive physiology, behavior, and brain size. We are fortunate to have a rich fossil record for later sections of this period for hominids (in striking contrast to our nearly non-existent record for chimpanzees or gorillas, who were living and evolving in Africa simultaneously). We have no fossils of the LCA, though new fossils from this time period give hope for such discoveries in the future (Brunet *et al.*, 2005). Thus, in order to reconstruct the lifeways of the LCA we need to turn to the comparative method, focusing particularly on the great apes (Wrangham, 1987; Foley, 1995). Thanks to decades of concerted efforts by field and laboratory researchers, our knowledge of chimpanzee behavior is now quite rich (Goodall, 1986; Tomasello and Call, 1997; Boesch and Boesch-Achermann, 2000). For brevity I will use the term "chimpanzee" to refer both to common chimpanzees (*Pan troglodytes*) and bonobos (*Pan paniscus*), and will use their Latin names when it is necessary to distinguish them. Likewise "gorillas" (*Gorilla*) and "orangutans" (*Pongo*) refer to all subspecies (or species, depending on your taxonomy) of each genus. For further terminology, see Box 6.1.

Apes ("hominoids") are relatively large-bodied primates, mostly vegetarian. Nonhuman apes are currently confined mostly to tropical forests in the Old World (although savanna-dwelling chimpanzees are known; Thompson, 2002; Pruetz and Bertolani, 2007). There are two main groups:

Box 6.1. Primate systematic terminology

The **Order Primates** represents a traditional order of mammals (other orders include bats, rodents, cetaceans, and carnivores). The sometimes confusing terminology is arranged here in terms of inclusive sets terminating with the hominid twig of the primate family tree.

Strepsirrhine: Prosimians Lemurs (Madagascar) and lorises and bush-babies (Africa/Asia) – "Lemuriformes"

Haplorrhine: tarsiers + anthropoids (non-Strepsirhhine primates)

Anthropoid: New World monkeys + Old World monkeys + apes

Platyrrhine ("wide-nosed" monkeys): New World monkeys (Central and South America)

Catarrhine: Old World monkeys + apes

Hominoid: Apes (including humans)

Hominid (often "Hominin"): humans + extinct fossil ancestors of humans after LCA split.*

---

* Many authors now adopt the term "hominin" for humans and their extinct fossil ancestors, to reflect the "demoting" of the (cladistically invalid) "family" Hominidae to a subfamily or "tribe" Homininae. Traditionally, the family Hominidae was reserved for the human lineage, in contrast to the family Pongidae, which included all other apes (an artificial grouping since chimpanzees are closer to us than they are to orangutans). Unfortunately this well-meant change wreaks terminological havoc, since in this new terminology the traditional term "hominid" now refers to the African Great Apes, contrary to the last century of usage, and a convention still used by many authors today. Because traditional Linnaean groupings like family and subfamily have no well-defined cladistic meaning anyway, I think this attempt at terminological reform risks doing more harm than good, and I retain the traditional terms in this book. Readers should have no trouble remembering that humans are members of the African Great Ape clade, without needing a reinterpreted Latin adjective to enshrine this relationship.

gibbons and great apes. The gibbons and siamangs (or "lesser" apes) form the smaller-bodied, more speciose, subgroup. **Gibbons** live in the rainforests of Asia, are highly arboreal, and generally form small territorial groups composed of long-term monogamous pairs and their dependent offspring. They exhibit long-term mating partnerships and male parental care, unusual behaviors that they share with humans. Despite gibbons' slightly greater phylogenetic distance, gibbon social and communicative behavior thus provides useful comparisons with human behavior, compared to other "great" apes, which show little or no pair-bonding or paternal care. The relative neglect of the "lesser" apes in discussions of human evolution is regrettable, as is the lack of attention to their long-term survival (many gibbon species are severely endangered in the wild). Like all apes, gibbons produce long, loud species-typical vocalizations called "long calls." These calls are complex, composed of multiple syllables, and recent data indicate that the arrangement of syllables into units distinguishes alarm calls from "normal" territorial calls (Clarke *et al.*, 2006). Unlike in the great apes, gibbon long calls are often produced as duets between mates, and are often termed "song." However, gibbon long calls are not learned: gibbons raised in acoustic isolation still produce normal song (Brockelman and Schilling, 1984; Geissmann, 2000), and hybrid gibbons produce hybrid vocalizations (Brockelman and Schilling, 1984; Geissmann, 1984; Mather, 1992). Thus, as for the other primate calls studied so far, learning plays at best a minor role in gibbon vocal production. There is no evidence for tool use in gibbons.

The other branch of the ape family, the larger-bodied **great apes**, includes the Asian orangutans and the African apes (chimpanzees, gorillas, and humans). Long debate about the precise relationships within this ape clade was finally resolved with molecular data (Wilson and Sarich, 1969; Carroll, 2003). Humans and chimpanzees are more closely related to each other than either is to gorillas. Orangutans are the most distant cousins in the clade. Because humans are nested within the chimpanzee/gorilla clade we are, biologically speaking, a form of African great ape. Great apes are relatively long-lived and have an unusually low reproductive rate, almost always giving birth to a single infant that develops slowly and has a very long dependent period. This fact has interesting implications for human evolution that we will explore below. Although all of the nonhuman apes are primarily vegetarian, all eat invertebrates, and chimpanzees, bonobos, and orangutans (like humans) enjoy vertebrate meat occasionally, when they can get it. Because chimpanzees are our nearest cousins they are of particular interest in reconstructing the LCA. Chimpanzees are classified into two species, the widespread "common" **chimpanzee** *Pan troglodytes*, which exists across a broad swath of equatorial Africa, and the **bonobo** or "pygmy" chimpanzee *Pan paniscus*, inhabiting the dense rainforests of central Africa and a bit of mixed woodland (Thompson, 2002). The two chimpanzee species appear to have split from each other only about 1.5 million years ago, and neither species is phylogenetically closer to humans.

6.1.1 Communication

Chimpanzees produce long calls called "pant hoot" sequences, with a complex structure that is species-typical and largely innate (Goodall, 1986;

de Waal, 1988; Arcadi, 1996). Chimpanzees and humans both produce a "laughing" vocalization in playful affiliative situations (Berntson *et al.*, 1990). Both chimpanzee species produce screams and cry vocalizations that are widely shared among primates and mammals (Newman, 1992), and both have a repertoire of grunts, hoots, and screams which play an important role in social behavior (Goodall, 1986; de Waal, 1988). The "pant hoot" is a long, loud, multisyllabic vocal display that is most idiosyncratically typical of chimpanzees (Mitani and Brandt, 1994; Mitani *et al.*, 1999). All of these vocalizations appear to have a powerful innate basis (Yerkes and Yerkes, 1929), and despite some recent evidence for some limited vocal learning abilities in chimpanzees, there is no evidence that chimpanzees (or any other nonhuman primates) can learn complex vocalizations like speech or song (Hauser, 1996; Crockford *et al.*, 2004). Chimpanzees raised in a human home will not learn to speak (Hayes and Hayes, 1951), and primates in general can be trained to control their vocalizations only with great difficulty (Larson *et al.*, 1973). Recent evidence suggests that some chimpanzee food calls may be "functionally referential" in that listeners can infer food type from call acoustics (Slocombe and Zuberbühler, 2005), but there is no evidence for referential alarm calls, like those of vervet monkeys, in apes, or thus in the LCA. Finally, chimpanzees often "drum" with the hands or feet on resonant structures at the end of pant hoot display sequences (Arcadi *et al.*, 2004). Drumming is a very unusual behavior in the animal world that, based on its similarities with gorilla chest beating and human drumming, was probably present in the LCA (Fitch, 2006b). Other than drumming, there is little indication that vocal communication in chimpanzees or other apes differs qualitatively from that in other Old World primates (cf. Seyfarth and Cheney, in press).

6.1.2 Sociality

Like most primates, African apes are quite social, living in relatively closed "communities" or large social groups. Chimpanzees spend much of their time in smaller foraging groups or "parties." In all three great apes, females typically emigrate from their communities when reproductively mature ("female exogamy"). This pattern contrasts with most other primates, where male emigration is the norm; the ape system provides a genetic basis for strong male bonds and alliances in chimpanzees (Wrangham, 1980, 1987; Wrangham *et al.*, 1994). Contact between communities is generally avoided, and can become violent (see below). Also unusually, all great apes build nests to sleep in, occasionally shared by adults for grooming or sex, so the

LCA almost certainly did the same (Yerkes and Yerkes, 1929; Fruth and Hohmann, 1996; Sabater Pi *et al.*, 1997).

6.1.3 Tool use, hunting, and medicine

A striking aspect of chimpanzee behavior shared with humans is their making and use of tools (Beck, 1980; McGrew, 1992). Cognitive aspects of tool use were already discussed (Chapter 4). Chimpanzee populations vary considerably in their use of tools, making this a prime example of "chimpanzee culture" (Whiten *et al.*, 1999). Ecologically, tool use may be quite significant for chimpanzees, particularly for females. Insects provide an important source of protein, often obtained using tools during termite and ant "fishing," and multi-part stone tools are used to crack open nutritious nuts in some chimpanzee populations (Boesch and Boesch-Achermann, 2000). Nutcracking is a complex task, difficult for young chimpanzees to learn. Both nutcracking and insect "fishing" are particularly typical of females. The use of digging sticks to uncover nutritious underground tubers has recently been discovered in savanna-dwelling chimpanzees (Hernandez-Aguilar *et al.*, 2007). Although *making* stone tools appeared much later in human evolution, the comparative data from chimpanzees in the wild clearly indicate that the LCA could *use* stone tools, setting the stage for one of the most striking human specializations.

Another interesting similarity between chimpanzees and humans is hunting, typically of monkeys, for meat (Goodall, 1986; Stanford *et al.*, 1994a; Boesch and Boesch-Achermann, 2000). Unlike tool use, hunting behavior is seen more often in males than in females (McGrew, 1979), often in groups, and sometimes incorporates strategies for herding and corralling prey. Recent observations suggest that chimpanzees "spear" small mammals for meat (Pruetz and Bertolani, 2007). Meat provides a rich source of protein for the otherwise mainly vegetarian chimpanzees. Meat may be shared with individuals who participated actively (Boesch and Boesch-Achermann, 2000), or with relatives or estrus females (Stanford *et al.*, 1994b). These comparative data allow us to conclude that the LCA used stone and other tools and hunted for meat, and the data from chimpanzees suggest that the former was primarily a female, and the latter a male, activity (cf. McGrew, 1979).

A third aspect of chimpanzee behavior was discovered most recently: chimpanzee self-medication (Wrangham and Nishida, 1983; Huffman, 1997). Like humans in most populations, chimpanzees are afflicted with various parasites, nutritional deficiencies, and infectious diseases. Sick chimpanzees seek out and ingest particular substances (mostly plants, but also soils with particular mineral composition; Huffman and Seifu, 1989; Huffman, 1997). Medicinal substances vary from location to location, and their effective use is probably learned to some degree. Thus there is a potential for cultural transmission of this information (McGrew, 2004). Even if learned individually, medicinal behavior is cognitively demanding, and might encourage a rich long-term memory, and perhaps episodic memory, and an ability to discover causal connections over hours. Combined with the variety of food plants exploited by chimpanzees, along with the tool use behavior already described, the generalist nature of foraging in our nearest cousins clearly provides the cognitive niche in which our own intelligence found its evolutionary beginnings.

6.1.4 Violence

A fourth behavior that seems to bind humans and chimpanzees is the most unsettling: a propensity to kill each other. Many primates (including gorillas and chimpanzees) are regularly seen to kill, and sometime eat, infants. Surprisingly common in mammals, infanticide is widely agreed to represent an adaptation to the relatively short period of tenure typically enjoyed by dominant males. By killing nursing infants, infanticidal males hasten the resumption of female cycling and increase their chances of fathering offspring that survive long enough to escape the next *coup d'état*. But chimpanzees go far beyond infanticide. The first and most destructive chimpanzee "war" was witnessed at Gombe by Jane Goodall, who was able to document a series of vicious inter-group encounters that led eventually to the death of all the males of the losing group, and the emigration of the remaining females to the victors (Goodall, 1986). Since then, similar fatal attacks have been documented in chimpanzees throughout Africa. Chimpanzees go on silent "border patrols," where a group of individuals (typically males) go to the edge of their territories and attack any lone individuals from other groups that they encounter. Multiple attackers hold down the victim while others bite and strike its face, body, and genitals, and the battered victim is left maimed and bloody, and sometimes dead. Recent playback experiments suggest that chimpanzees on border patrols make a careful calculation of relative numbers, and only attack when possessing a clear advantage (Wilson *et al.*, 2001). Despite its ubiquity in chimpanzees, there is no evidence for such attacks in bonobos. Although inter-group encounters in bonobos are typically tense, several remarkable peaceful encounters between bonobo groups have been documented (including both homosexual and heterosexual sexual intercourse among members of different groups). This has led many researchers to posit a much lower level of aggression in bonobos, who tend to resolve conflicts with sex rather than violence (Wrangham and Peterson, 1996). However, it is important to remember that bonobo field studies are still in their infancy, and the absence of observed bonobo "warfare" is not conclusive evidence of absence. Nonetheless, these data, combined with the relatively low inter-group aggression of gorillas, make a reconstruction of aggression in the LCA complicated. The LCA clearly had a *potential* for nasty inter-group aggression, but the bonobo observations raise the possibility that such violence had not developed to the brutal point seen today in chimpanzees and humans.

The brief introduction to ape behavior given above illustrates the many fascinating discoveries of the last fifty years (for more detail see Goodall, 1986; Boesch and Boesch-Achermann, 2000; McGrew, 2004). Despite decades of intensive investigation, we are still learning new things about chimpanzee behavior. Some behaviors, such as inter-group "warfare," are relatively rare, with decades of continuous study required to reveal them. Others seem to vary considerably from site to site – nutcracking with stone tools has never been observed in Gombe – and thus multiple long-term study sites are required to get a complete picture of chimpanzee potential (McGrew, 1992; Whiten *et al.*, 1999; McGrew, 2004). An excellent example is provided by a new savanna site in Senegal – Fongoli – that is only beginning to yield its secrets (Pruetz and Bertolani, 2007). Chimpanzees at Fongoli are the only chimpanzees known to take shelter in caves. Fongoli chimpanzees also bathe in water (most chimpanzees, including captive-raised chimpanzees, appear to be deathly afraid of water, and avoid even touching it). Obviously, we have not yet reached a full understanding of chimpanzee behavior, and further discoveries almost certainly await us (McGrew, 2007). Fascinating undiscovered customs may already be gone forever, their practitioners exterminated by humans to be eaten as "bush meat." This adds scientific force to the moral imperative to preserve the habitats of chimpanzees across Africa, and to halt their hunting.

In summary, many aspects of human and chimpanzee biology and behavior are shared, including important aspects of cognition, and these allow us to infer similar traits in the LCA. In particular, we share with chimpanzees both intense sociality, and propensities to use tools in foraging, to exploit a variety of plant foods for both food and medicine, to conduct group hunts for small mammals, and to kill conspecifics. Behaviorally transmitted practices – a basic form of culture – are also present in chimpanzees (Whiten *et al.*, 1999). All of these traits were very likely typical of the LCA. We share with all apes our relatively large body size, large brains, and long lives, and a long dependent childhood that leads to a very slow reproductive rate. In contrast, ape vocalizations are largely innate, involving poorly developed vocal control, suggesting that the LCA had similar vocal limitations. These aspects of cognition and behavior set the stage for the initial branching of our own clade (traditionally termed "hominid," or more recently and specifically, "hominin"). I will now discuss another aspect of ape biology that is less frequently recognized as centrally relevant to language evolution: the peculiarities of ape and human reproduction.

6.2 The ape's impasse: the hominoid mother's dilemma

Primates are unusual mammals from a reproductive viewpoint. In sharp contrast to the large litters of puppies, kittens, piglets, or mice, most primate mothers have just one child at a time (though twins are normal in some species). Furthermore, this one child has an unusually long period of dependence: in most monkeys the infant is completely dependent for a year, and then still associates with its mother in a protective relationship for years after that. Even by primate standards, apes are extreme. A chimpanzee infant is completely dependent on its mother for transportation and milk for at least two years, and more typically four, and the typical interbirth interval for chimpanzees is between five and six years. In the same time period a rhesus macaque female can already have grandchildren. The combination of low reproductive rates, long interbirth intervals, and a lengthy childhood (including a longer period to sexual maturity – ten years to sexual maturity for a female chimpanzee) puts apes at a reproductive disadvantage relative to virtually all mammals their size (although elephants or whales have equivalently long reproductive times). With powerful forces restricting her total lifetime reproduction, there is only one way a female ape can meet her reproductive potential: **offspring survival**. Thus it is not surprising that apes (like whales and elephants) are very solicitous parents. Only by living a long time herself, and ensuring that each of her precious children survive to reproduce, can the ape reproductive equation be balanced. The dilemma is illustrated in Figure 6.1. Increasing any of the factors on the right decreases reproductive potential, and only an increase in the mother's own

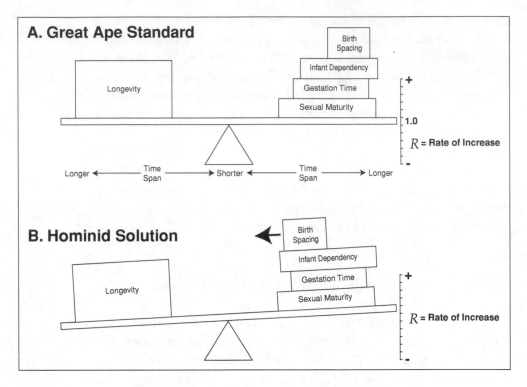

Figure 6.1 The great ape reproductive dilemma – A mechanical analogy illustrates the difficulty facing long-lived, slow-reproducing organisms such as great apes and humans (A). Lengthening interbirth interval, gestation period, the time to sexual maturity, or the period of infant dependency (equivalent to pushing their "blocks" outwards) decreases reproductive potential, R. Such changes must be balanced by a compensatory increase in lifespan (pushing "Longevity" to the left). Humans achieve a higher reproductive capacity than other apes mainly by decreasing birth interval to 2–3 years *versus* 5–6 years for chimpanzees (B). Adapted from Lovejoy (1981).

longevity can counteract them. Slow reproduction means that, even under ideal, protected conditions, ape populations grow very slowly (Boesch and Boesch-Achermann, 2000; Hill *et al.*, 2001). The long period of childhood dependence means a long interbirth interval, and there seems to be no way around this impasse. This is true for all apes.

But if we examine modern humans today, things have changed: we have a major advantage over our ape cousins (Locke and Bogin, 2006). Our unusual mating and reproductive system gives modern humans a much higher reproductive potential than a chimpanzee, gorilla, or orangutan (Hrdy, 1999). According to simple demographics, a typical human mother outreproduces any chimpanzee female through the simple expedient of having babies faster (Lovejoy, 1981). By shifting the birth interval to the left

(Figure 6.1B), and having babies every two to three years instead of every five to six years, we humans (including hunter-gatherer mothers) have found a way out of the ape's impasse. So why don't chimpanzee mothers simply wean earlier? Recent studies of chimpanzee demographics make the answer clear: earlier weaning means poor survival of the young, and ends up leaving the young smaller and less able to compete with other chimpanzees whose mothers have taken them up to their full potential body weight (cf. Kennedy, 2005).

It helps to look at the situation from a chimpanzee mother's perspective (Goodall, 1986; Hrdy, 1999). Your infant will ride on your back and nurse, deriving all of its protection and nutriment from you for its first year, much like a human infant. However, your infant will continue to nurse solidly till age two, when solid food becomes an appreciable component of its diet, and will continue nursing periodically until between four and six years old. Weaning at this point could be disastrous – if conditions change suddenly and no food is available for your child, it still lacks the reserves and skills to survive on its own. At age four, although it can locomote by itself, the child will still ride on your back for long voyages, and it is still mainly dependent on food you share with it. From the child's viewpoint, none of this is very different from the human situation. The big difference is that, because she has weaned her child from breast milk much earlier, the human mother has already given birth to another child, and is raising two (or more) children in parallel. In a situation of abundant, reliable food, and help with childcare, this is clearly an excellent solution. Unfortunately, this is not the situation that faces chimpanzees: although fruiting trees may present times of superabundance, they are interspersed with long periods of want, when difficult-to-learn skills like nutcracking or insect fishing may provide the main source of rich nutrition. Chimpanzee foraging practices offer no easy way that a chimpanzee mother can double her food intake, and early weaning is not an option (Kennedy, 2005).

6.3 Male parental care

Enter the male of the species. From the viewpoint of females and children, adult male apes are basically a waste of resources, useful as sperm donors and little else. Males eat a lot, often are behaviorally dominant, and can displace mother and child from food, while providing little childcare themselves. While male chimpanzees preferentially hunt for meat, they mainly eat it themselves. A mother carrying a dependent child is not much use in the acrobatics required to catch a monkey, and all she can hope for is a few scraps of meat, donated by the hunter, and perhaps nothing for her child. Despite its great *potential* value (Kennedy, 2005), the meat caught by male chimpanzees may contribute little to a mother's needs. Although male chimpanzees provide a degree of protection, both from predators and from potentially infanticidal males of neighboring groups, these defensive advantages accrue to all members of the group. From the viewpoint of feeding a particular baby, a mother chimpanzee can forget about males. Enticing males to contribute food to their own particular offspring would be an excellent solution, but in the free-for-all mating system that characterizes chimpanzees, paternity is typically unclear. Furthermore, because female chimpanzees emigrate out of the group, a male can't care for his sister's offspring either. What's a mother to do?

   In nature, the most reliable way to get males to help care for their children is to offer them paternity certainty: there is a striking overlap, in many species, between monogamy and paternal care (Kleiman, 1977; Clutton-Brock, 1991). Although uncommon in mammals, monogamy has evolved in parallel in many mammal clades, including various primates, most canids, and some rodents (Kleiman, 1977; Wickler and Seibt, 1981; Kinzey, 1987; Reichard and Boesch, 2003). It is the main mating system in birds, with over 90 percent of bird species showing monogamy (Reichard and Boesch, 2003). This, of course, makes perfect sense from an evolutionary viewpoint: a monogamous mating system (where a male and female pair off and stay together for the entire mating period) offers high paternity certainty. With highly dependent young, and high paternity certainty, the evolutionary balance tips, and it becomes more beneficial for a male to help care for his own children and help ensure their survival, than to abandon the mother after she is pregnant to seek another potential mate. A common spur towards monogamy is a short, synchronized breeding season (Brotherton and Komers, 2003), but this is uncommon in female primates. Chimpanzee females generally announce their own *private* breeding season – the estrus period – to all comers. This creates intense competition for breeding among males. Mating in chimpanzees typically occurs with multiple males (sometimes the entire group), yielding concomitantly low paternity certainty. However, there is another chimpanzee strategy, called "consortship," where a male and a female disappear into the woods together, alone, during her estrus period (Tutin, 1979). A similar alternative strategy may have been present in the LCA, offering a path to paternal care in the hominid line. By being more willing to enter into such consortships, thereby granting paternity certainty to her mate, a female ape could tilt the balance towards male parental care. This may have been a crucial initiating factor in the evolution of human mating and childcare practices.

6.4 Evolving paternal care and monogamy

Are humans monogamous? One needn't be a very perceptive observer of our species to realize that, in any strict sense, the answer is "no." Despite the cultural impostion of legal monogamy in many modern cultures, adultery is common (even in the face of extreme punishment). In most of the world's traditional cultures, polygyny is accepted: a man may have more than one wife at the same time. Thus, the notion that humans are biologically monogamous seems almost laughably naïve or Eurocentric, given the frequent exceptions to monogamy in both Western and other cultures. However, from a comparative perspective, it is now clear that many monogamous species have similar deviations from strict or pure *genetic monogamy* (where all offspring produced are from the pair) despite clear *social monogamy* (where males and females pair off socially beyond the mating period) (Reichard and Boesch, 2003). "Monogamy" turns out to be a rather diverse phenomenon, with a wide range of combinations of social, mating, and genetic monogamy possible. In many "monogamous" species, DNA paternity tests have revealed an unexpected amount of hanky-panky – demurely termed "extra-pair copulation" by biologists. Furthermore, many species practice serial monogamy: pairs mate and raise children cooperatively, but then choose new mates in future reproductive seasons. Biologists now realize that monogamy presents a continuum with polygyny, and a fairly high amount of infidelity is compatible with a behaviorally monogamous social system. By the definitions currently used by biologists, many human cultures, and most human sexual relationships, are typically socially monogamous, but genetic monogamy is less pervasive. But even social monogamy is quite rare in mammals (around 5 percent of all species) and demands an explanation (Clutton-Brock, 1991).

The more relevant, but closely related, question is whether humans, as a species, exhibit male parental care. The answer to this question is certainly "yes." Human males are expected to help care for children, particularly by providing food, in virtually all cultures, and even in cultures where the mating system leads to low paternity certainty, men often help care for their sister's offspring. The degree to which human males help care for children is striking to anyone who has spent time watching adult males of most primate species. This, of course, does not mean that *all* fathers care for *all* of their children: human males seem to employ mixed strategies in this regard. Given the high correlation between pair-bonding and paternal care among birds and mammals (Kleiman, 1977; Clutton-Brock, 1991), the undoubted existence of paternal care in humans itself suggests that pair-bonding is part of the biological "toolkit" of our species, not just a romantic modern creation.

Returning to the female ape's reproductive dilemma, it seems that the hominid line adopted increased male parental care as a way around the demographic impasse (Lovejoy, 1981; Diamond, 1992; Deacon, 1997; Mithen, 2005). Initially, based on hunting being a predominantly male activity in chimpanzees, paternal care may have been mainly initially through meat sharing (McGrew, 1979). Given that female chimpanzees who obtain more meat also have more surviving offspring (McGrew, 1992), it is likely that a simple shift in males' propensity to share meat with their previous consortship partners, and their own presumptive children, would be enough to start the ball rolling to the increased reproductive potential seen in modern humans. Fossils suggest that food sharing was probably well established by 2.5 MYA, before the genus *Homo* (Isaac, 1978; Plummer, 2004). However, once the interbirth interval decreases it is in everyone's benefit to help the weanling survive. This includes not only the presumptive father, but relatives like the mother's mother or brother(s) (O'Connell *et al.*, 1999), encouraging alloparenting by relatives as another component of this strategy (Hawkes *et al.*, 1998; Hrdy, 2005).

Male parental care has independently evolved numerous times among primates (Hrdy, 1981). Most prominently, the closest cousins to the great apes, the gibbons and siamang, all are behaviorally monogamous with some male parental care and provisioning. Behavioral monogamy, with paternal care, has evolved convergently in owl monkeys, *Aotus*. Solicitous support by fathers has also evolved in the callitrichids (marmosets and tamarins), allowing females to habitually give birth to twins, thus doubling their reproductive output at one stroke.

Biological factors underlying the change in human reproductive strategy include most prominently women's **concealed ovulation** and readiness to mate outside of fertile periods. There are many hypotheses for the precise function of concealed ovulation (for a humorous overview see Diamond, 1992), but one effect is clear – it tips the balance towards pair-bonding. Most primates copulate while the female is in estrus, and obviously fertile. A male who can either outcompete other males, or lure the female into solitary consortship, need only do so during this brief period in order to ensure his paternity. Because human females do not advertise their fertility, a more extended period of exclusive copulation is necessary to ensure paternity certainty. Well-concealed fertility, in the limit, "establishes mathematical parity between males restricted to a single mate and those practicing complete promiscuity" (p. 346, Lovejoy, 1981). Importantly, most apes are more like humans than chimpanzees: bonobos and chimpanzees are unique among apes in their prominent estrus swellings and promiscuous mating patterns. The LCA was probably more like humans, orangutans, and gorillas, with a relatively understated estrus with little swelling or obvious competition-inciting cues to her fertility. Humans have gone in one direction from this starting point, to unusually "invisible" fertility, while chimpanzees have gone in the other. The critical point is that, with concealed fertility, male *mating* success (the number of females mated with) is decoupled from *reproductive* success (the number of offspring fathered). Put crudely, even a human male who mates with a different woman every night for one month is not *guaranteed* higher reproductive success than a male who mates with a single woman for the same period. Unless they have some way of knowing when their mates are fertile, the two men may each conceive a single child. Of course, a woman is typically fertile for more than one day, so if the promiscuous male could keep up this performance, he would eventually outreproduce the monogamous male on average. But, crucially, reproductive success involves not simply conceiving offspring, but raising them to maturity, and the second monogamous male can gain a further advantage if he sticks around to help raise the child he has (conclusively) fathered.

6.5 Implications for language evolution: Why us and not others?

In conclusion, at some point in our evolution hominids diverged from the other great apes in our reproductive behavior, in a manner quite familiar among vertebrates: we adopted paternal care and alloparenting. Rather than the strongly dyadic relationship of mother and infant seen in most apes, hominid infants were born into a richer social environment, including other solicitous adults who provisioned, cared for, and played with them. Furthermore the dependent period of human children is actually *extended*, probably because of this extended "support network," with major implications for all aspects of human life history (Mace, 2000; Locke and Bogin, 2006). Given the centrality of reproductive success to all aspects of evolution, these changes had at least three important impacts on subsequent human evolution:

(1) it selected strongly for coordination and cooperation among adults, both mother and father (Deacon, 1997) and other related individuals (Hrdy, 2005);

(2) it selected for infants and children able to engage with, and learn from, multiple members of this extended social group; and

(3) this enhanced sociality further selected for sophisticated social intelligence, both in terms of pragmatic inference in receivers and intentional information sharing by signalers.

The LCA was already flexibly exploiting multiple sources of nutrition, and already supplementing this diet with meat from hunting, and sharing these innovations culturally. The changes surrounding infant care would thus have provided an important boost to any adaptations that helped transfer information from adults to the young, thus increasing their survival, and speeding their independence. I think these factors provide a compelling explanation for why hominids, in contrast to any other vertebrate clade, evolved a linguistic system capable of transferring thoughts from one individual's head to another's, once we acknowledge the importance of such a system in the survival and success of human children. Most animals deal with the problem of low infant survivorship by simply producing more offspring: increased litter size. This "easy way out" was not available to primates, and particularly not for the LCA, which had already reached a reproductive strategy with a nearly unique degree of infant dependency. The allomothering solution found by our specific hominid branch of the great ape clade is unusual, but by no means unique among vertebrates, and can be understood in a straightforward way by the application of life history theory and evolutionary thinking. By giving mothers a helping hand, other individuals in her social group allow humans a far greater reproductive potential than is found in any other great ape. This novel social environment, I suggest, was to provide a crucial context for language evolution. It remains to be determined whether this primarily affected sexual selection among mates (Deacon, 1997; Miller, 2001), or kin and natural selection among children (Falk, 2004; Fitch, 2004a), or (most likely) some combination of factors, but in either case changing hominid reproductive patterns played a crucial role.

When did these changes occur? While analysis of stone tools and bone accumulations strongly suggest food sharing by 2 MYA (Isaac, 1978; Plummer, 2004), there is obviously no direct fossil evidence of male parental care, so the timing of this particular behavioral change in our species remains open. However, two fossil indicators are compatible with increased monogamy. Both rely on the observation that polygynous species typically show increased sexual dimorphism relative to their monogamous relatives (Darwin, 1871; Andersson, 1994). The first indicator is the reduction in canine tooth size, and a near-loss of canine dimorphism between males and females. This change had already taken place in australopithecines (Johanson and White, 1979), compatible with the hypothesis that reproductive changes occurred very early in hominid evolution, well before expanded brains and increased tool use. Unfortunately these canine data are contradicted by body-size data, making the situation in *Australopithecus* impossible to resolve based on fossil data (Plavcan and van Schaik, 1997). Given the existence of consortships and meat sharing in modern chimpanzees, an early transition is certainly possible. The second indicator is a later reduction in body size dimorphism, thought by many authors to have arrived with *Homo erectus*. At this point it is likely that humans had shifted to something like our current system. I suspect that these reproductive changes occurred very early, playing a role in the hominid divergence from the LCA, but from the viewpoint of language evolution it makes little difference, since few commentators suspect australopithecines of having language. By the time human language evolution was well under way (in the genus *Homo*), humans were less dimorphic than other great apes, reflecting an increase in alloparenting, male paternal care, and the (admittedly imperfect) behavioral monogamy that goes with it.

6.6 Summary

We have now followed human evolution from the first cells to our parting of ways with our nearest living species, the chimpanzees and bonobos. Unfortunately, from this point on we can no longer apply the comparative method to living species. To reconstruct the last phase of human evolution, we must rely upon fossils and archaeological remains: a more tenuous source of data. Being limited to fossils means being almost entirely limited to skeletal remains (and a bit of relatively recent DNA), and since neither speech nor language fossilizes, these provide for the most part tantalizing clues, subject to varied interpretation, rather than solid data directly relevant to the evolution of language. Fortunately, because much of this last spurt of human evolution happened in relatively dry areas, the hominid fossil record is relatively rich (far more so than in other apes). Chapter 7 gives an overview of this material and discusses the inferences we can draw from it.

7 | Hominid paleontology and archaeology

7.1 What the fossils tell us

In broad outline, the post-LCA history of our species is becoming increasingly clear from a combination of fossil, archaeological, and genetic data. All hominid populations originated in Africa, but several waves of early hominids expanded into Europe and Asia. The last wave of migrants was our own species, *Homo sapiens* ("anatomically modern *Homo sapiens*," or AMHS), who left Africa in one or more migrations by 50 KYA (thousand years ago). These humans were accompanied by a wide range of technological and artistic innovations relative to all earlier hominids. They were capable of making difficult sea crossings to destinations beyond the horizon, and expanding along a "coastal express" route fringing the Indian Ocean, and had made it to the Andaman islands and Australia by around 45 KYA (Lahr and Foley, 1998; Mellars, 2006). AMHS witnessed (or caused) the complete extinction of all previously existing hominid lines, including *Homo erectus* in Asia and *Homo neanderthalensis* in Europe. Because all existing human populations have full and equal language abilities, this at least fifty thousand year divergence time marks the latest possible end to our species' evolutionary journey to language.

Although human paleontology is a highly controversial discipline, some crucial fossil finds since the 1960s allow us to make certain empirical statements with confidence. Our fossil record for hominids becomes rich around four million years ago, roughly two-thirds of our post-LCA evolution. We know that hominids became upright bipedal walkers *before* acquiring brains significantly larger than those of chimpanzees or other apes, well before any evidence of complex toolmaking beyond that seen in chimpanzees. Once stone tools appear, they are associated with cut-marked animal bones, indicating that these hominids were relying on meat far more than chimpanzees. In the next clade of hominids, sexual dimorphism decreased. Such facts from the fossil record allow confident deductions to be made, and are the topic of this chapter. I postpone discussion of hypotheses based on further extrapolation until later in the book.

7.2 Paleospecies: naming fossil hominids

Any detailed discussion of hominid paleontology runs into a problem that besets fossil interpretation in general: the delineation and naming of species. Species of living organisms can be delineated behaviorally as populations of potentially interbreeding organisms, or by measured genetic differences in DNA. The gold standard for differentiating two living species is that they cannot or will not interbreed (reproductive isolation): a solid criterion upon which most biologists can agree. Such certainty is obviously denied us with fossil species. Although breakthroughs in paleogenetics mean that DNA can be recovered from recent fossils, these techniques are unlikely to reach past about half a million years. The delineation of fossil species or "paleospecies" thus is and will probably remain a controversial domain. Typically, early fossil hominid finds were automatically given a new species name, and often new generic names as well, leading to a proliferation of fossil hominids with distinct Latin names through the 1950s (Mayr, 1951).

In reaction to this over-enthusiasm, many scholars stepped back to take stock of the situation, and by around 1970 the pendulum had swung in the other direction (e.g. Clark, 1971) with just two genera (*Australopithecus* and *Homo*) being widely recognized. This extreme of "lumping" was based on morphological criteria of bipedalism, brain size, and tooth structure. As recently as 1980 it was still possible to argue that *Homo sapiens* arose only about 40,000 years ago, and that all earlier members of the genus *Homo*, including Neanderthals, were *Homo erectus* in the direct line to modern humans (Krantz, 1980). Today, however, the pendulum has swung back, new fossils are being found at a rapid rate, and old generic names, unused for decades, are being resurrected once again. The result, today, is a highly confusing terminological profusion, where no universally agreed taxonomy exists, and even relatively widely accepted systems change on a yearly basis with new fossils or new analyses. The current literature in paleoanthropology thus poses serious challenges for non-specialist scholars.

Some justification of this recent proliferation of Latin names is a growing acceptance of an important fact about hominid evolution: that hominid evolution is "bushy" rather than linear. An old tradition, dating back to Darwin's time (Huxley, 1863), takes modern *Homo sapiens* as its endpoint, and seeks a starting point as far back in the fossil record as possible. For many years, human evolution was seen as the story of a steady, unstoppable progress along this line, towards bigger brains and increased technology. Despite its suspect intellectual basis, this linear model actually provided a reasonable fit to the fossil data for many years, when only a few fossils were known (*Australopithecus* species, *Homo erectus, Homo neanderthalensis,* and *Homo sapiens*). But with the discovery of the robust Australopithecines, and increasingly thereafter, it became clear that hominid evolution included many evolutionary experiments that ended with extinction (including most recently Neanderthals). Far from representing an unbroken succession of increasingly modern forms, hominid evolution exhibited the same tree-like branching pattern that characterizes other vertebrate lineages. It is pure happenstance that only a single morphological type, a single branch of the tree, remains alive today. This sea change in opinion explains the name proliferation that is the current fashion.

The widely acknowledged bushiness of the hominid tree does not, unfortunately, change the basic difficulties involved in delineating fossil species and genera. In particular, cladistics provides no logical justification for the traditional Linnaean hierarchy still used to name clades above the level of species (genus: family: order: class: phylum). Although one might theoretically use the time elapsed since evolutionary divergence to justify higher Linnaean categories (e.g. genera have been distinct for five million years, orders for fifty million, etc.), adoption of such a convention would require a major shakeup of all of systematics, not the sort of tweaking typical today. That all 400,000 diverse beetle species are traditionally placed in the "order" Coleoptera, or 500,000 species of Asteraceae in the daisy "family," makes a mockery of the Linnean tradition that would place 200-odd primates in their own order. Given such pervasive inconsistency, we must accept the Linnaean hierarchy as a quirky, historically contingent classification system, rooted in pre-Darwinian and pre-cladistic thought. This system is a valuable aid to communication among scholars, and is unlikely to disappear anytime soon, but it is futile to attempt to whip and cajole Linnaean categories into conformity with cladistic precepts. Thus, profligate coining or resurrecting of new generic names seems unjustifiable (Wood and Collard, 1999; Cela-Conde and Ayala, 2003), as does a recent suggestion to broaden the genus *Homo* to include chimpanzees, and the hominid "family" to all apes (Wildman *et al.*, 2003). The biological reality, and the words we use to discuss it, remain two separate things.

In an attempt to steer a path through this terminological morass, I will keep two principles in mind. First, it is the nature, age, and phylogenetic position of the fossils themselves that should be our main concern, not their names; and second, consistent names are needed to discuss these fossils and to read earlier discussion with comprehension. Most specific fossil finds have unambiguous museum labels (e.g. KNM-WT 15000, in the Kenya

National Museum, is fossil #15000 from West Turkana); famous fossils typically have nicknames as well (in this case, the "Turkana Boy"). Museum labels provide a terminological anchor for practicing paleoanthropologists, but can be rather daunting for an outsider. In the discussion that follows I will generally use the more traditional Latin names, following the general precepts laid out in Wood and Collard (1999). The Latin names of a number of important specific fossils are given in Table 7.1; for a beautiful and relatively complete introduction to these fossils see Johanson and Edgar (1996).

As an example, consider one of the best-known hominid fossils of all: the famous "Lucy," AL-288, from Hadar in the Afar Triangle, Ethiopia. Discovered by Donald Johanson in the late 1970s, this fossil was given the name *Australopithecus afarensis* (Johanson and White, 1979). The species name was new (as traditional), but the genus name followed that given by Raymond Dart to his famous "Taung Child" in 1925, named *Australopithecus africanus* (*Australopithecus* meaning "southern ape"). Johanson's "Lucy" was nearly identical to some previously discovered fossil fragments, from the same site, previously named *Praeanthropus africanus* by Weinert and Senyürek (found in the days when new fossil finds were typically given a new genus name as well), but Johanson and White argued that Lucy belonged to the same genus as Dart's fossil. This created an ambiguity in the specific name *africanus*, leading to the suppression of Weinert's "africanus" by the International Commission for Zoological Nomenclature in 1999. However, if one argues that Lucy in fact represents a *different* genus from the Taung Child, Weinert's genus name would still stand, and Lucy's name would be *Praeanthropus afarensis* (an increasingly common contemporary synonym of *A. afarensis*; see Stringer and Andrews, 2005). In order to spare the reader a blow-by-blow account of such debates, I have placed the information relating to the most crucial fossils in Table 7.1. When in doubt, I will err on the side of consistency with tradition, giving modern synonyms in parentheses where needed. In the text below I can then simply refer to Lucy (AL-288) as *Australopithecus* (= *Praeanthropus*) *afarensis*. It should be noted that this is *not* a correct Latin binomial designation, but a convention to designate a disputed taxon.

A final difficulty is brought into focus by the recent discovery of diminutive small-brained hominids, dubbed "hobbits," on the Indonesian island of Flores, which has been argued to represent a novel hominid species, *Homo floresiensis* (Falk *et al.*, 2005). With a brain size comparable to chimpanzees (~400 cc), but associated with sophisticated flaked tools known only from advanced hominids, this discovery might necessitate a wholesale rethinking

Table 7.1. Prominent fossil hominid specimens

Discoverer	Year	Location	ID	AKA	Original name	Synonyms	age (MYA)
Brunet	2002	Sahel, Chad			Sahelanthropus tchadensis		7–6
Senut team	2000	Tugen Hills, N Kenya			Orrorin tugenensis		6–5.8
Haile-Selassie	2004	Awash, Ethiopia			Ardipithecus kadabba		5.8–5.2
Asfaw	1992	Aramis, Ethiopia	ARA-VP-1/129		Ardipithecus ramidus	Australopithecus ramidus	4.4
Leakey/Nzube	1995	Kanapoi, Kenya	KNM-KP29281		Australopithecus anamensis		4.2–4.1
Johanson	1978	Hadar, Afar, Ethiopia	AL-288	"Lucy"	Australopithecus afarensis	Praeanthropus afarensis	3.2
Dart/Bruyn	1925	Taung, S Africa		"Taung Child"	Australopithecus africanus*		~2.3
Broom	1936	Sterkfontein, S Africa	TM 1511		Australopithecus (= Plesianthropus) transvaalensis		~2.5
Broom	1947	Sterkfontein	Sts 5	"Mrs Ples"	Australopithecus africanus		2.5
Broom	1950	Swartkrans	SK-48		Paranthropus crassidens*	Australopithecus robustus	1.5–2.0
M Leakey	1959	Olduvai	OH-5	"Dear Boy"	Zinjanthropus boisei	Australopithecus/Paranthropus	2–1.3
J Leakey	1960	Olduvai	OH-7	"Jonny's Child"	Homo habilis*		1.75
L Leakey	1972	Koobi Fora, Kenya	KNM-ER-1470		Homo rudolfensis*	Homo habilis	1.8–1.9
Kimeu	1984	Nariokotome	KNM-WT 15000	"Turkana Boy"	Homo erectus	Homo ergaster	1.6
Dubois	1891	Java, Indonesia	Trinil 2	"Java man"	Pithecanthropus erectus	Homo erectus*	0.5
Pei	1929	Zhoukoudian, China		"Peking man"	Sinanthropus pekinensis	Homo erectus	0.78
Zwigelaar	1921	Kabwe, Zambia	BH-1	"Broken Hill 1"	Homo rhodesiensis	Homo heidelbergensis	0.3
Unk/King	1856	Neander Valley, Germany Neanderthal 1	Neanderthal Man		Homo neanderthalensis*	Homo sapiens neanderthalensis	40,000 y
Schepartz	1983	Kebara, Israel	Kebara 2	"Moshe"	Homo neanderthalensis		60,000 y
Lartet	1868	Dordogne, France	Cro-Magnon 1	Cro-Magnon Man	Homo sapiens (sapiens)	"early modern humans"	34,000 y
Brown	2004	Flores, Indonesia	LB-1	"Flo," "Hobbit"	Homo floresiensis*	diseased Homo sapiens?	18,000 y

* Denotes the type specimen for this species.

of brain/intelligence assumptions. However, the species status of "hobbits" has been disputed, with some experts suggesting that the specimens are of diseased humans (e.g. suffering from congenital microcephaly) rather than an amazingly aberrant new species (cf. Martin *et al.*, 2006). As this book goes to press, the debate rages on.

7.3 A broad overview: major stages in human evolution since the LCA

For non-paleoanthropologists, the consensus view formulated in the late 1970s still provides a good starting point for understanding hominid evolution. Starting with the LCA, the first major innovation was the adoption of an upright bipedal stance. True bipedalism was already inferred from the anatomy of fossils such as Lucy, and confirmed by the discovery and painstaking excavation by Mary Leakey of a remarkable fossil trackway of hominid footprints in Laetoli (Leakey and Hay, 1979). These footprints from 3.6 MYA capture the behavior of two early hominids, presumed to be australopithecines, walking side by side through a fresh volcanic ashfall, and are almost indistinguishable from the footprints of modern humans except for their small size. In contrast, Australopithecine cranial vaults indicate brain sizes on a par with modern chimpanzees. Thus, bipedalism preceded brain expansion in hominid evolution. Additionally, there are no traces of stone tools from early Australopithecines that indicate clear progress in toolmaking skills beyond those still seen today in modern chimpanzees, and presumably present in the LCA. Thus, to a good first approximation, we can envision the earliest fossil hominids as bipedal apes. This initial stage of hominid evolution lasted for several million years, from about 4–2 MYA (most of the Pliocene), culminating with a well-studied "Oldowan" tool-making culture ("Mode 1" tools; see Figure 7.1). Such simple tools allowed butchery with sharp stone flakes, indicating clear advances in hominid lifestyle in late *Australopithecus*/early *Homo* (Isaac, 1978; Plummer, 2004).

The second stage, marked by an increase in body and brain size and a slightly later increase in the use and complexity of stone tools, is traditionally seen as the birth of the genus *Homo*. There is still considerable debate about which fossils best represent this transition (see below). Traditionally, this stage starts with *Homo habilis*, but recent commentators argue that the human genus starts later, with early African *Homo erectus* (= *Homo ergaster*; for discussion see Wood and Collard, 1999; Plummer, 2004). Shortly after the appearance of *H. ergaster* (by 1.9 MYA), we witness a very clear increase in

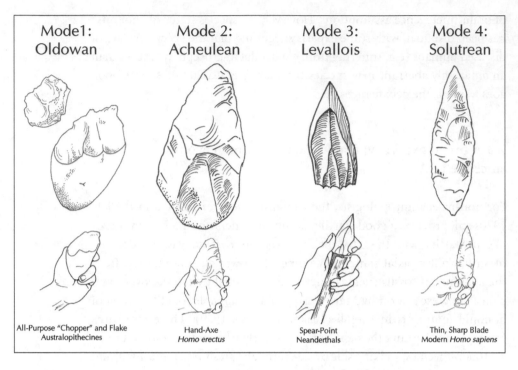

Mode1: Oldowan	Mode 2: Acheulean	Mode 3: Levallois	Mode 4: Solutrean
All-Purpose "Chopper" and Flake Australopithecines	Hand-Axe *Homo erectus*	Spear-Point Neanderthals	Thin, Sharp Blade Modern *Homo sapiens*

Figure 7.1 Examples of hominid tools – The three longest-lived stone tool types are shown on the left (Oldowan, Acheulean, and Levallois) along with one example from the more sophisticated toolkit typical of modern humans, a fine Solutrean knife blade.

toolmaking sophistication, characterized by the so-called Acheulean industry (by 1.5 MYA). The elegant and effective stone handaxes typifying this "Mode 2" level of technology were a remarkably long-lived invention, lasting more than one million years into the next stage of hominid evolution. *Homo erectus* was the first African hominid to leave our birthplace in Africa (the first *erectus* fossils discovered were found in Asia: "Java Man" and "Peking Man"), and these hominids clearly represented a major step forward in terms of their cognitive mastery of technology and the environment. Numerous scholars have sought the beginnings of language evolution at this *H. erectus* stage in hominid evolution, so we will discuss the relevant fossil evidence in some detail below.

The final stage in our path through the branching tree culminates with hominids traditionally called "archaic *Homo sapiens*," and encompasses AMHS, Neanderthals (*Homo neanderthalensis*), and an increasing variety of earlier "archaic" forms (e.g. *Homo helmei, Homo antecessor,* and *Homo heidelbergensis*). These forms all have in common large bodies and large brains, in the range of modern humans, and have a particularly rich (though still controversial) fossil record. An innovation of this period was the

Mode 3 technology, typified by the Levallois technique – longer flakes hammered off of a pre-shaped core, producing "blanks" which could then be further worked into blades, points, or other tools. Most of the relevant fossils are found in Africa, Europe, the Levant, and western Asia. By between 100–200 KYA, one branch of this bushy proliferation had arisen in Africa, that was to become the ancestor of all living humans, who produced a variety of sophisticated Mode 4 tools (harpoons, fishhooks, needles, . . .) illustrated by the Solutrean blade in Figure 7.1. These AMHS spread out of Africa successfully by around 50 KYA (Mellars, 2006). They witnessed (or perhaps caused) the extinction of all the other hominid lines, in particular *H. neanderthalensis* around 30 KYA. DNA recovered from Neanderthal, the last-surviving extinct hominids, opens the door to genetic analyses that are likely to remain impossible for earlier forms (Krings *et al.*, 1997; Krause *et al.*, 2007). The linguistic status of extinct hominids during this last branching stage, particularly of Neanderthals, remains extremely controversial, and may never be resolved. But we know that by the time AMHS left Africa, 50 KYA, language had evolved to its modern state.

Although the sketch above is oversimplified, it provides a conceptual road map for the detailed discussion that follows. For each of these broad periods of hominid evolution, I will discuss the different species that were present, focusing on the most informative fossil finds, and the solid data that allow us to reconstruct their lifeways. As before, for concision, I will focus unapologetically on the path that leads to modern humans, and say little about dead-end branches like the robust australopithecines.

7.4 The earliest hominids

So when did humans first diverge from chimpanzees? Very recent fossil finds have pushed the hard evidence for human ancestry back into the Miocene to near the 6–8 MYA split between chimpanzees and humans inferred from molecular data. The earliest discovered to date is *Sahelanthropus tchadensis*, a well-preserved skull from Chad (7–6 MYA). This is a peculiar specimen with a combination of features not seen in other fossil apes (or later hominids): small teeth with thick enamel, and a short face with prominent brow ridges. A slightly younger find, from Kenya, is *Orrorin tugenensis*, represented by a few teeth and some limb bones dated between 5.8 and 6 MYA. The femur is argued by its discoverers to indicate bipedalism, while its canines are large and pointed like contemporary apes. Finally, the youngest of these new fossils is *Ardipithecus* (with two species assigned, *A. ramidus* and *A. kadabba*), which is quite similar to *Orrorin*. Although each of these species has been suggested as representing the first steps onto the line of hominid evolution that leads to *Homo*, current evidence is too fragmentary for strong conclusions. Indeed, all three "genera" might well represent the same genus, or conceivably even the same species (Cela-Conde and Ayala, 2003; Stringer and Andrews, 2005). These finds are too new for any consensus to be formed among paleoanthropologists as to their proper systematic assignment, and such consensus may be a long time coming. Because these fossils are *older* than the genetic estimates of human/chimpanzee convergence, these finds may indicate that African apes at this time were more diverse, and less chimpanzee-like, than traditionally assumed. Thus, for an outsider, the best advice for now is to wait, and watch the debate.

One lesson that can be drawn from the new finds is based simply on the geographic location of the *Sahelanthropus* find, in Chad, near the center of the African continent in today's Sahara. This is far west of the Rift Valley that demarcates East Africa, where more African hominid fossils have been found. Earlier authors had argued that this restricted location allowed important ecological inferences about our beginnings, a hypothesis dubbed the "East Side Story" (Coppens, 1994). The Rift Valley is a result of the northern movement of Africa, and its collision with the Eurasian continent: an ongoing plate tectonic event that is pushing up the Alps and slowly closing the Mediterranean Sea. A bubble of magma underneath Africa pushed up the continent's center, and the subsequent collapse of the eastern portion created the Rift Valley, probably around 8 MYA (Prothero and Dott, 2004). This had a striking ecological consequence, clearly visible today. The uplifted western portion of Africa forces moisture-laden air to drop its rain on the dense rainforests that still thrive there. But the lower section, to the east, lies in the rain shadow of this plateau, with a much drier environment today characterized by grasslands and savanna, but initially containing a complex mosaic of mixed woodlands, grasslands, riverine forest, and swampy lowlands. It was in this drier mixed woodland environment that most of hominid evolution was played out. The East Side hypothesis (and many variants) put these ecological events at center stage in human evolution, suggesting that the ancestral LCA population was spread across central and southern Africa. The creation of the Rift Valley divided the population in two, and the western population stayed in the rainforest and evolved into chimpanzees, while the eastern population (our own ancestors) responded to the new challenges of the drier mixed woodlands by evolving bipedality. This hypothesis is weakened if *Sahelanthropus* is indeed on the *Homo* line, because it lived far to the west of the Rift Valley.

7.5 Australopithecines: bipedal apes

At about 4 MYA, our fossil record for Pliocene hominids becomes quite extensive. The first find, a child's skull recovered from a limestone quarry in South Africa, named by anatomist Raymond Dart as *Australopithecus africanus* ("Southern ape of Africa") and known as the Taung Child (Dart, 1925). This skull contains an unusual natural endocast: minerals entered the braincase of this skull and hardened into a limestone cast. This endocast was exposed in the specimen described by Dart, and he interpreted the pattern of sulci on the brain as ape-like. Based on further finds in nearby Sterkfontein, *Australopithecine* brain sizes were in the range of modern African apes. Dart noted the potential importance of a drier habitat in shaping this species, and suggested that *Australopithecus* was an accomplished hunter. Dart's discovery was not initially accepted as an early hominid, partly because the Piltdown skull (a fraudulent juxtaposition of a human skull and orangutan jaw) had skewed the conceptions of what an early hominid should look like. But many of Dart's ideas about his find, especially his claim that *Australopithecus* is close to the line leading to *Homo*, have held up well in the face of a rather rich fossil record for this genus.

In the 1970s two sites much further north, in Kenya and Ethiopia, yielded a clearer picture of a Miocene hominid: *Australopithecus* (= *Praeanthropus*) *afarensis*, including the famous find of Lucy already mentioned. These fossils have the large, thick-enameled teeth typical of later hominids, but their canines are reduced in size and sexual dimorphism relative to other apes (Johanson and White, 1979). *A. afarensis* was a fully bipedal hominid, but its brain size (adults around about 400 cc) was in the range of modern apes (Holloway, 1996). Average *Pan* brain volumes are around 400 cc, with *Gorilla* around 500 cc; humans average more than 1200 cc (Stephan *et al.*, 1981). Evidence for bipedalism includes an analysis of the pelvis and leg skeleton, particularly the form of the knee joint and foot. Such skeletal changes can be generated developmentally from habitual bipedal walking, without any genetic changes being necessary (monkeys, rats, or goats, forced to walk upright from a young age develop a bowl-like pelvis and human-like knee joints; Slijper, 1942; Kay and Condon, 1987). But regardless of their epigenetic origins, limb morphologies in *Australopithecus* clearly indicate habitual bipedalism.

The case for *Australopithecine* bipedalism is clinched by the remarkable 3.6 MYA fossil hominid trackways unearthed in Laetoli, Kenya (Leakey and Hay, 1979). These footprints were created by two australopithecines (and perhaps a third, smaller, hominid, walking in their tracks) who walked side by side through a fresh, wet ashfall generated by a volcano eruption (Hay and Leakey, 1982; White and Suwa, 1987). Because of the crystallization of dissolved salts in the ash, these footprints quickly hardened and were covered by another ashfall shortly afterwards, to be unearthed 3.5 million years later by Mary Leakey. The footprints extend almost 30 m, and but for their small size are virtually indistinguishable from modern human footprints. These hominids were joined by a variety of other creatures whose footprints were also preserved, from tiny millipedes up to a variety of large mammals. The trackways freeze a moment in time, when the two hominids stopped, turned to look at something, and then continued on their way (Day and Williams, 1980). Some critics have argued that these early hominids were not "fully bipedal," pointing out that australopithecine arms were longer, and legs shorter, than later hominids, making them less efficient bipeds than ourselves. Second, their curved hands are evidence of a retained proclivity for arboreality; many authors have plausibly suggested that these light-bodied hominids probably spent the nights in treetop nests, as do modern chimpanzees (e.g. Sabater Pi *et al.*, 1997; Mithen, 2005). But neither observation detracts from the very human-like bipedalism documented at Laetoli: as any child who has climbed a tree knows, modern humans remain well-adapted to arboreality compared to most other mammals.

The question of *why* these hominids were habitually bipedal has generated a wide variety of hypotheses (cf. Richmond *et al.*, 2001). First, bipedalism may provide locomotory advantages, either for more efficient walking, or more effective running for prey capture (cf. Carrier, 1984; Bramble and Lieberman, 2004). Another hypothesis, based on chimpanzee behavior, is that bipedalism is an adaptation to carrying (whether of food, tools, or babies) – modern chimpanzees sometimes walk bipedally when carrying food or rocks. Others have suggested that bipedalism enabled early hominids to look out above tall grass, again consistent with chimpanzees' frequent assumption of a bipedal stance to look above obstacles. More speculative hypotheses include the idea that bipedal stance was an adaptation to appear larger, for throwing stones, or that it was a way of avoiding the horizontal body "template" that supposedly triggers large carnivore hunting behavior. Finally, it has been suggested that upright posture is an adaptation for temperature regulation (Wheeler, 1984). In the hot tropical sun, only a biped's head is exposed to direct sun, while the rest of the body is available to shed heat by sweating, a process aided by having much of the body surface away from the ground and exposed to whatever breeze is available. This hypothesis is one of the few that provides a reasonable explanation of our peculiar hair pattern, with thick hair restricted to the head (providing a sun-shield) and the thin hair on the rest of the body aiding evaporative sweating. To the extent that the temperature-regulation hypothesis is valid, it suggests that this peculiar hair pattern would already have characterized australopithecines.

A final issue in understanding bipedalism concerns knuckle walking: the unusual quadrupedal terrestrial locomotory style seen in living great apes. Knuckle walking is very effective in forests, and upright posture is of little advantage when running on animal trails through dense tangled underbrush. Thus, any locomotory advantages of bipedalism hinge on the more open mixed woodland environment believed to characterize eastern and southern Africa during the Pliocene. For modern humans, bipedalism is an efficient way to get around in such unobstructed environments. The fact that efficient bipedal locomotion is almost universal among birds, and was common in dinosaurs, suggests that bipedalism has certain virtues in addition to the obvious one of freeing the forelimbs to specialize for other tasks (whether for predation in dinosaurs or flight in birds). One possibility is that a bipedal gait potentially frees the respiratory rhythm from that of the gait: in quadrupedal mammals, breathing rate is tightly coupled to running speed (Bramble and Carrier, 1983; Carrier, 1984), while in hominids and birds this strong coupling is broken. Bipedalism has thus been suggested to provide a preadaptation for sustained long-distance running, argued to be revealed by skeletal changes appearing in the genus *Homo* (Bramble and Lieberman, 2004).

Beyond bipedalism and brain size, other inferences drawn from the fossil remains of australopithecines are controversial. In particular, the issue of **sexual dimorphism**, which provides a possible indicator of social structure, has been difficult to resolve. A jumble of bones recovered from Hadar, including the remains of some thirteen individuals, has been interpreted as a hominid social group that perished together: the so-called "First Family." If these all represent the same species (*A. afarensis*), the find reveals a surprising degree of sexual dimorphism in body size in this genus. The diminutive Lucy, assumed female, was dwarfed by the male of her species, more than 50 percent heavier and nearly a foot taller (McHenry, 1994, 1996). Among the robust australopithecines (see below) dimorphism was even greater, with females estimated at half the body weight of males (Kappelman, 1996). This value approaches that of the highly dimorphic primates such as gorillas and orangutans, far different from the modest 20 percent difference in AMHS. Unfortunately, however, there is no way to be certain that these various australopithecine fossils in fact represent male and female of the same species, rather than two different species (as originally believed), and a recent re-analysis suggests that human-like levels of dimorphism were already in place in australopithecines (Reno *et al.*, 2003). In contrast, canine dimorphism had already dropped to very modest levels (Plavcan and van Schaik, 1997), consistent with a major reduction in intrasexual competition. These contradictory indicators suggest that conclusions drawn from Australopithecine sexual dimorphism must remain tentative.

Regarding tool use we have little evidence that early australopithecines were more sophisticated than contemporary chimpanzees. However, it is important to recognize that modern chimpanzees *are* tool users, arguably more sophisticated than any other nonhuman animal (though the competition from tool using crows is close; Weir *et al.*, 2004a). As an exhaustive survey by Beck points out, chimpanzees account for the vast majority of observations of diverse, flexible tool use in animals (Beck, 1980), and comparative inference thus strongly suggests that the LCA and australopithecines were equally flexible (McGrew, 1992; Boesch and Boesch-Achermann, 2000). Given the importance of tool use in increasing protein input in modern chimpanzees (whether by ant and termite fishing, or nutcracking), this is a prime case where the lack of definitive fossil evidence cannot be interpreted as evidence of absence. Termite fishing, the use of wooden digging sticks, or nutcracking with stone or bone tools, analogous to known chimpanzee behavior, would leave few archaeological traces. The safe assumption is that australopithecines at least used tools at the level of modern chimpanzees.

In addition to *A. afarensis*, widely thought to be on the line of hominid evolution leading to *Homo*, the genus *Australopithecus* has long been associated with a second set of hominids that appear to represent a long-lived but ultimately unsuccessful experiment: the "robust australopithecines." Although they have been traditionally assigned to the genus *Australopithecus*, many scholars now suggest this dead-end line deserves its own genus, *Paranthropus*. Two reasonably well-known species lived after *A. afarensis*, from 2–1.3 MYA, and thus overlapped with later hominids of the genus *Homo* (see below), only to die out without a trace. These are *Australopithecus* (= *Paranthropus*) *robustus*, and *Zinjanthropus* (= *Australopithecus* = *Paranthropus*) *boisei*. These hominids had powerful masticatory apparatus, with small front teeth and massive molars, a powerful jaw, and in some specimens a large saggital crest for the attachment of massive temporalis muscles, reminiscent of gorillas and orangutans. The modern human temporalis is tiny by comparison (see Figure 7.2). Such temporalis reduction is associated with the origin of the genus *Homo*, to which we now turn.

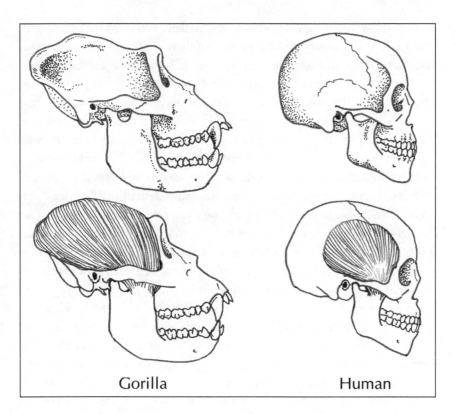

Gorilla   **Human**

Figure 7.2 Reduction of the temporalis muscle – Most mammals have a very large and powerful temporalis muscle for chewing. In humans this muscle is greatly reduced, partly due to a mutation in the MYH16 gene which codes for a protein component in this muscle. Such gene mutations can be roughly dated, allowing the order of occurence of different human-specific mutations to be estimated (see Chapter 9).

This change is associated with the genetic inactivation of a muscle component (MYH16) expressed in the temporalis muscle group, discussed in Chapter 9.

7.6 The Oldowan Industry and the genus *Homo*

The second stage of hominid evolution for which we have abundant evidence is marked by the appearance of a new class of stone tools: sharp stone blades, flaked from cobbles by hammering with a second stone. This new type of toolmaking is the first that can be unambiguously recognized in the fossil record, and is thus graced with its own name: the **Oldowan Industry** (named after the Olduvai Gorge in Kenya, where the first exemplars were found, also termed **Mode 1** technology; Leakey, 1966). More recent finds from Ethiopia securely date the earliest of these to 2.5 MYA (Semaw *et al.*, 1997). Although this was originally thought to be a diverse toolkit, some of the "tools" (e.g. choppers, bifaces, . . .) are now thought to simply represent the partially flaked remains of the cobbles, the raw material for the true tools. With the proper raw material, such flakes can be as sharp as a steel blade, and opened up a whole new world to the hominid forebears who invented them: the butchering of animal carcasses. Although chimpanzees tend to avoid dead animals, at some point in our evolution (perhaps already with early australopithecines) the nutritional potential of large dead animals killed by large predators or natural causes began to be exploited. In particular, stone hammers could be used to crack open long bones to extract the highly nutritious marrow (a rich source of proteins and fatty acids, precisely what is needed for building larger brains). A nimbly wielded stone blade can quickly cut the ligaments that bind marrow-containing long bones from the carcass, to be carried away to safer sites for leisurely cracking, and Oldowan sites with a preponderance of long bones and ample remains of both stone tools and cracked and cut bone suggest that this was a favorite activity of the new hominids (Plummer, 2004). Avoiding the large carnivores at a carcass must have been a powerful selective pressure favoring such "cut-and-run" scavenging. Stone blades also potentially open another richer resource: tough-skinned megaherbivore carcasses (elephants, rhinos, etc.). A dead elephant is potentially a huge nutritional windfall, but their thick tough skins make them inaccessible for some time after death until the skin is sliced or ruptured, after which they are rapidly defleshed by scavengers such as vultures and hyenas. Experiments have shown that stone blades can make quick work of such a carcass, with the potential to feed a large social group. Thus the origin of stone blades represented a crucial breakthrough in hominid toolmaking, reflecting an increase in meat-eating (fueling larger bodies and brains), and probably extensive food sharing, in hominid evolution. Similar stone blades have been used continuously since, up to today, with ever-increasing sophistication.

Interesting experiments with the bonobo Kanzi have demonstrated that living apes have the cognitive capacity to understand the value of blades, and how blades can be made by fracturing stone (Toth *et al.*, 1993). In experimental studies, Kanzi quickly realized that the easiest way to do this is to simply hurl an appropriate rock against a hard surface, and pick through the shards to find the sharp flakes that resulted (this is preferable to the inevitably thumb-bruising learning process necessary to master percussive flaking). Such an innovation would be nearly invisible in the fossil record, and so might represent a plausible precursor of Oldowan flaking. However, hurling is quite wasteful of the valuable raw material, and so the more controlled process would be preferable once mastered. Nutcracking with a stone hammer and anvils inevitably generates stone chips and the occasional stone flake (McGrew, 2004), and the first archaeological excavations of known chimpanzee nutcracking sites suggests caution in interpreting the earliest stone flakes – some might have been made by chimpanzees (Mercader *et al.*, 2002). Nonetheless, true Oldowan tools are more complex and intentionally shaped than these chimpanzee artifacts (D. Stout, p.c.).

It remains somewhat unclear just which hominids were making Oldowan tools (Plummer, 2004). When first discovered by Louis Leakey, only robust australopithecines were known from Olduvai; shortly thereafter the type specimen of *Homo habilis* ("handyman") was discovered at Olduvai, and immediately recognized as a more likely suspect. This is the main reason to grace this hominid with the genus *Homo*, and later scholars have pointed out that in many ways *habilis* is much more similar to an australopithecine. With an estimated body mass of 34 kg, this hominid was smaller than the robust australopithecines (around 44 kg), its limb proportions are australopithecine, and on average its brain is just a shade larger than previous hominids (the earliest *habilis* specimen, KNM-ER 1470, had an unusually large brain). Thus, the reputed association of the Oldowan toolkit with *Homo habilis* forms the main basis for dubbing this hominid the first member of our genus, and a number of contemporary commentators argue that this privilege should be restricted to our next hominid: *Homo erectus* (cf. Wood and Collard, 1999).

7.7 A major transition in human evolution: *Homo erectus*

Now we turn to the first universally accepted member of our own genus: *Homo erectus* ("upright man"). Today, this species is often subdivided, with earlier African forms known as *Homo ergaster* ("working man") and the original *erectus* moniker applied to later, mostly Asian, examples of the clade (but cf. Spoor *et al.*, 2007). The first *erectus* fossils discovered, found in Java by Eugene Dubois, are now dated to about 1.5 MYA, and the earliest fossils, from Africa and Java, suggest an origin at 1.8–1.9 MYA. The most striking exemplar of this group is provided by a remarkably complete skeleton, fossil KNM-WT 15000, recovered from Kenya, the famous "Turkana Boy" (or "Nariokotome boy"). This skeleton has been subjected to detailed analysis, and thus provides another "fixed point" in our hominid fossil record (Walker and Leakey, 1993). The fossil has been dated to 1.5–1.6 MYA; and is frequently assigned to the species *Homo ergaster*. The Turkana boy was a peripubescent boy around age 11 (range 8–13, depending on the skeletal measure used), remarkable for his already large body size – within the range of modern humans. Already over 1.5 m (about 5′ 4″), he might have grown to be 1.8 m (6′) tall if he had lived to adulthood. His brain size, 900 cc, is nearly double that of earlier hominid forms, and the range of *H. erectus* brain sizes (750–1250 cc) reaches the lower end of the modern human range (1,000–2,000 cc). *Homo erectus* was the first hominid to leave Africa (fossils from Dminisi in Georgia date to 1.7 MYA; Gabunia *et al.*, 2000), and enjoyed a long tenure in Asia, from some 1.5 MYA to about 100,000 years ago. However, these newer finds also suggest considerable variability in size, rendering long-accepted conclusions about large size and lack of sexual dimorphism less certain (cf. Spoor *et al.*, 2007). Despite such uncertainties, it remains clear that *Homo erectus* ushered in a great innovation in toolmaking, the Acheulean industry (see below) that was to last one million years. *H. erectus* represented a major breakthrough on many fronts, and is often thought to represent a key hominid in the evolution of language, possessing some form or other of "protolanguage" (see e.g. Hewes, 1973; Bickerton, 1990; Donald, 1991; Mithen, 2005).

Besides representing a major increase in body and brain size, and the first hominids out of Africa, what can we say about the lifeways of *Homo erectus*? Stone tools are among the least controversial source of evidence. In the earliest period, these hominids used the Oldowan toolkit already described above. But at about 1.4 MYA (Asfaw *et al.*, 1992), we see a qualitatively new form of stone tool appearing, culminating in the larger symmetrical handaxes of the **Acheulean industry (Mode 2)** (Gowlett, 1992). Named after the type site of Saint Acheul, in northern France, where the first examples were identified in the nineteenth century, Acheulean handaxes were worked symmetrically and on both sides. Handaxes, along with cleavers, are thus known as biface tools. Many authors see these implements as demanding a considerable increase in cognitive sophistication, involving a solid mental template of the end product to be kept in mind over a protracted process of toolmaking (Donald, 1991; Mithen, 1996). Acheulean handaxes were a ubiquitous, durable, all-purpose tool of hominids for a million years. In the latest periods, some exemplars showed astonishing size, symmetry, and beauty, and no signs of use as tools, suggesting that they may have played aesthetic or ritualistic, as well as functional, roles (Mithen, 1996). Successive generations of flint-knappers have scientifically reconstructed the process involved in making these tools, skill at which requires a protracted, diligent learning process. Making stone tools, using them at various tasks, and then studying the resulting microwear patterns microscopically (Keeley, 1980) has shown that the hand "axe" was indeed an all-purpose tool, used not just for hacking but for cutting and scraping as well. Similar tools, hafted and polished, were still is use by modern humans into the 1950s in the highlands of New Guinea, and implements resembling Oldowan tools were still used in Australia into modern times. Scholars who scoff at such implements as "clunky stone tools" (e.g. Bickerton, 1995) have probably never used, or attempted to make, one. These were artifacts revealing a high level of planning, motor control, learning, and cultural continuity that gave developing humans a unique advantage over any other living species.

Beyond the innovation of the Acheulean industry, many further aspects of *Homo erectus* lifestyle have been suggested but remain controversial. Perhaps the most significant is the use of fire. *Homo erectus* remains in the Zhoukoudian caves near Beijing in China offer a remarkable multi-layered record of hominid occupation, and clear remains of burnt bones have been offered as the first evidence of the control of fire by hominids (Weiner *et al.*, 1998), as much as 400,000 years ago. However, the degree to which these represent controlled fire (e.g. hearths) rather than the opportunistic use of wildfires remains uncertain, and we have to wait until much later for indubitable signs of hearths and controlled fire. The abilities that control of fire allows – to cook food, to harden implements, to generate warmth and light, and to repel predators – must have represented a huge advantage to the hominids who first developed it. Cooking, in particular, has been cited as a "key innovation" in hominid evolution, with evidence of improved nutrition in *Homo erectus* cited as evidence for its mastery at this stage (Wrangham *et al.*, 1999). Given its importance, it is unfortunate that archaeological clues to the timing of this innovation remain so controversial. Nonetheless, the apparently universal feeling of comfort inspired by an open fire in modern humans, in sharp contrast to the apparently innate fear of fire that typifies virtually all other animals, may reflect a degree of genetic adaptation to fire in our lineage, and the association of *H. erectus* camp remains with fire suggests that they shared this attraction, even if they did not themselves create fire.

A subtle but important aspect of *Homo erectus* anatomy and lifestyle was already mentioned: an apparent reduction of sexual dimorphism to the level of modern humans. Modern humans are only modestly dimorphic (males average 20 percent heavier than females). This small size dimorphism is to some extent compensated by other types of sexual dimorphism, such as the extreme and unusual dimorphism of our larynx, which leads the human male to have a pitch half that of females (Titze, 1989). But, viewed from a comparative perspective, the relatively low dimorphism in modern humans, and in *Homo erectus*, is consistent with the idea that these hominids, like us, displayed a tendency towards pair-bonding. Low dimorphism, combined with larger brains and prolonged childhood, leads many different scholars to conclude that a key transition to cooperative childcare has been made at this point, with multiple adults, including both related females and the father, necessary for successful child-rearing (Isaac, 1978; O'Connell *et al.*, 1999; Wrangham *et al.*, 1999; Aiello and Key, 2002; Hrdy, 2005).

7.8 Neanderthals: our large-brained sister species

The last well-defined hominid evolutionary branch is easily the best documented by fossils, but paradoxically even more controversial than the previous two. This stage is symbolized by Neanderthal man, *Homo neanderthalensis*, who is the epitome of the low-browed "caveman" for many people. For many years Neanderthalers were thought to be on the main line of modern human evolution, a subspecies of our own species termed *Homo sapiens neanderthalensis*. There is increasing consensus, however, that Neanderthals represent a separate branch of the hominid tree, our nearest cousins, but not our ancestors, and new paleogenetic data seem to clinch the case, providing no evidence of overlap or interbreeding between the two clades (Krings *et al.*, 1997; Lalueza-Fox *et al.*, 2007). Thus many contemporary authors now refer to Neanderthals as a separate species, *Homo neanderthalensis*. The common ancestor of these two species can therefore no longer be termed "archaic *Homo sapiens*," as was long the tradition, and there is considerable debate about which of several different earlier hominids represents the common ancestor of us and Neanderthals. For clarity, I will start with Neanderthals and work backwards.

Neanderthals were one of the first fossil hominids to be discovered, and were named after the Neander Valley (Neander "thal" in archaic German spelling, often updated to "Neandertal"), on the river Düssel, near Dusseldorf in Germany. Neanderthalers' similarity to modern humans is nicely illustrated by the fact that the skull discovered there was initially thought to be a Cossack soldier from a Russian invasion in 1814! Neanderthals had a brain size as large as or larger than the average for modern humans. Although shorter than your average *Homo sapiens*, they had massive, robust bones and were very powerfully built – on a par with the most muscular contemporary wrestlers. Early fossils thought to share Neanderthal features have been recovered from 100,000 years ago, but "classic" Neanderthals occupied western Europe from about 70 to 35 KYA. Fragmentary remains from about 200 Neanderthal individuals have been recovered (partly thanks to their apparent habit of burying their dead), and relatively complete skeletons for some 20 individuals have been found. Although some Neanderthal fossils are known from Israel, Turkey, and further east (to a limit in Uzbekistan), none are known from Africa or East Asia: they were a truly European hominid. European climate in this period was variable but cold, and the mammals associated with Neanderthalers – reindeer, wooly mammoths, and the like – were at home in cold, tundra-like conditions. Various skeletal features (very large nasal cavities and their stocky build) are thought to represent adaptations to the cold. It is an interesting bit of unconscious racism that "primitive" Neanderthalers are typically recreated as dark-haired and dark-skinned, while the later Cro-Magnon humans sport white skin and long blonde hair (both in popular books (Auel, 1984) and in textbooks (Stringer and Andrews, 2005)). In reality, the Neanderthals' long adaptation to the weak winter sunlight of Europe makes it likely that they were the lighter-skinned of the two species (since light skin allows crucial vitamin D to be synthesized with less light; Lalueza-Fox *et al.*, 2007). The Cro-Magnon *Homo sapiens*, freshly emerged from Africa, probably had dark skin and dark hair, like African populations today (Kurtén, 1987).

Neanderthals controlled fire, sometimes lived in caves, and were successful big game hunters, specializing in moderate-sized species like reindeer but capable of hunting woolly mammoths on special occasions. Their material culture, the **Mousterian**, shows an advance beyond the utilitarian handaxes of *Homo erectus* and involves a mastery of prepared core stone blades using the **Levallois technique (Mode 3 industry)**. However, there are few signs of less utilitarian products until quite late in their tenure, in an archaeological period termed the *Châtelperronian*. At this late period of Neanderthal evolution, some ornamental objects (pierced teeth and shells, and black pigments applied to skin or leather) can be found (D'Errico, 2003). These objects were possibly made under the cultural influence of the encroaching modern humans (for debate see D'Errico, 2003; Mellars, 2005). Their habit of burying the dead has led to much discussion, and a thick layer of pollen in a burial plot at Shanidar was used to support the claim that the deceased was covered with flowers. Some Neanderthal specimens lived to an old age (over forty), and some finds suggest that communal care for the elderly was present in some Neanderthal cultures. The use of pigment to adorn body or clothing is sometimes seen as a sign of "symbolism" based on modern human cultural use, but I know of no clear argument against a more functional use of pigments for camouflage or make-up. Perhaps the most evocative bit of evidence for culture is a recently discovered

Neanderthal artifact discovered in Slovenia, at Divje Baba. Thought by its
discoverers to be a flute, it is a cave bear bone with two well-preserved
holes and probably two more, that have been damaged through time, associated with Neanderthal remains and older than 35,000 years (Kunej and
Turk, 2000). However, few extrapolations from the hard evidence concerning Neanderthals go unquestioned: skeptics have concluded that the holes
represent the gnawing of a cave bear (D'Errico *et al.*, 1998).

Such tantalizing tidbits of information provide a screen upon which the
imagination can project a fully human creature, as intelligent as ourselves
and with a complex language, rich social structure, and detailed culturally
transmitted knowledge of its world (Auel, 1984). But the skeptic can cite
the lack of art and relatively static stone toolkit – along with their eventual
demise when modern humans moved into Europe – as evidence that they
were just as backward and unsophisticated as the common "caveman" image
portrays. Although the truth is probably somewhere in between, the basic
plausibility of the whole continuum is what makes the Neanderthalers such
a contentious topic for paleoanthropologists. My own attitude is agnostic,
but respectful. With a brain size comparable to our own, or slightly larger,
these hominids were no one's fool, and their tools appeared to be perfectly
adequate to make a good living in a very challenging environment (one in
which most contemporary humans would quickly perish, if unprepared).
They were successful big-game hunters, and were physically intensely powerful. It is unlikely that any modern human that tangled with a Neanderthal
one-on-one would come out a winner. Neanderthals successfully replaced
an early influx of modern humans into the Levant (D'Errico, 2003; Shea,
2003), though there is no evidence of interactions between them. Given
the absence of archaeological evidence for warfare (Shea, 2003), the notion
that *Homo sapiens* wiped out Neanderthals directly, in combat, seems less
likely than that some new disease brought along from Africa did the job –
as happened when Eurasians invaded the New World (Diamond, 1997).
But questions about Neanderthal culture, social structure, and cognition
remain unresolved by the available data. In particular, we simply don't know
whether Neanderthals had a form of language. I will discuss reconstructions
of the Neanderthal vocal tract in Chapter 8 to support this conclusion.

7.9 The common ancestor of Neanderthals and AMHS

Given the genetic data indicating that Neanderthalers were a separate branch
of hominid evolution from ourselves (Krings *et al.*, 1997), what can we say

about our common ancestor? Once termed "archaic *Homo sapiens*," the fossil data for this clade is widespread but controversial. The first exemplar found, from Germany, dates back to 1907: a jaw recovered from a sandpit and promptly labeled "Heidelberg man," *Homo heidelbergensis*. Shortly afterwards, in 1921, a mine in Zambia (then Northern Rhodesia) called Broken Hill yielded what remains one of the finest fossil hominid skulls ever discovered: Broken Hill 1, named "Rhodesian man," *Homo rhodesiensis*. Dating to around 300,000 years ago, this skull is clearly intermediate in form between *Homo erectus* and modern humans, with a brain size in the modern range but massive brow ridges like *erectus*. An associated shin bone suggests a tall individual in the modern size range. More recently, a number of fossils have been found that share these basic traits, though often with their own peculiarities, and arguments about naming these specimens remain lively. One find, 800,000 years old, from Atapuerca in Spain, has been given the name *Homo antecessor*, and may be the earliest European members of the clade (Bermúdez de Castro *et al.*, 1997). Another proposed name for the common ancestor of Neanderthals and modern humans is *Homo helmei*, distinguished from *H. heidelbergensis* by association with the Mode 3 prepared-core technology of the Middle Stone Age (Foley, 1998; McBrearty and Brooks, 2000). There appears to be some growing consensus to accept the original name of the Heidelberg specimen to name this whole group (or at least many of its members). I will adopt this convention, using *Homo heidelbergensis* to denote the post-*erectus* hominid who was the common ancestor of Neanderthals and modern *Homo sapiens*. This form arose in Africa, with Broken Hill *Homo heidelbergensis* (= *rhodesiensis*) being a representative of the line.

Some populations of *heidelbergensis* seem to have left Africa early, where they evolved into Neanderthals, by routes that remain unclear (the most realistic possibility is by land, through the Levant, but short water journeys could have bridged into Italy via Sicily, or Spain via Gibraltar). The others stayed in Africa to give rise to modern *Homo sapiens*, who would leave Africa much later. The transition to Neanderthal form is beautifully captured in a remarkable treasure trove of fossils from Spain, the famous "Sima de los Huesos" in Atapuerca, one of the richest fossil hominid sites ever discovered. Some 2,000 bones from more than 30 individuals have already been recovered, and more remain. These bones appear to capture, at about 350,000 years ago, the morphological transition from *H. heidelbergensis* to "classic" Neanderthal. Meanwhile, back in Africa, we have little evidence of the transition to modern humans, and it is not until about 250 KYA, from Florisbad in southernmost Africa, that we find evidence of a transitional form to our own species (*Homo helmei*: Lahr and Foley, 1998). Originally thought to be only 50,000 years old, the recent redating of the type skull to 260,000 years suddenly puts it at nearly the right time to represent the transition from *heidelbergensis* to modern humans. By 160 KYA these early modern humans could be found throughout Africa, from South Africa to Ethiopia to (a bit later) Morocco (Foley, 1998). Despite some suggestive claims about jewelry or symbolic activities in these hominids, the fossil record remains controversial.

What is clear about *H. heidelbergensis* is that they were accomplished big-game hunters, as shown by the large, exquisitely preserved throwing spears recovered from a coal mine in Schöningen, near Hanover in Germany. At 400,000 years old, these two beautifully made javelin-like projectiles are the oldest wooden spears, and are clearly made and balanced for throwing rather than thrusting (Thieme, 1997). These, and other less clearly identified wooden objects, and many "standard" flint tools, were found associated with large number of butchered remains of horse, red deer, and bear, along with elephants and rhinos. A productive and meticulously excavated *H. heidelbegensis* site in Boxgrove, in southern England, has revealed a similar set of species and pattern of butchery, including a horse scapula with a hole-like fracture suspected of being made by a spear point. The site is full of handaxes, mostly made on the spot from local flints, and in some cases the detailed shards were preserved as they fell, enabling a reconstruction of the toolmaking process.

Because all parts of the large mammals butchered at Boxgrove are present, it seems clear that the hominids killed these animals, and didn't just scavenge already dead animals. Although chimpanzee hunting behavior suggests that hominids preceding *Homo* may have been hunting and eating small animals throughout our evolutionary career, recent reinterpretations suggest that the large mammals butchered by australopithecines or early *Homo* were scavenged and not killed. But *Homo heidelbergensis* were hunting the largest and most dangerous animals, with all of the nutritional benefits (for big bodies and big brains) this entails. Thus, we have every reason to believe that both later clades of hominids – the Neanderthalers and ourselves – did the same thing. However, the preserved *heidelbergensis* toolkit still relied heavily on the same basic handaxe form as did *erectus*, making these Acheulean implements second only to Oldowan flakes as the most long-lived forms of human technology known. Later, these hominids developed the new Levallois technique, which was the key innovation of the Middle Paleolithic (Mode 3) appearing about 300,000 years ago.

7.10 Anatomically modern *Homo sapiens*: Out of Africa

Finally we arrive at our own species, *Homo sapiens*. Despite considerable superficial variation, all human populations share essentially identical cognitive capabilities. A child from Siberia, Patagonia, or the Australian desert can learn any of the world's languages with complete facility. In general, there is no evidence of average differences between contemporary human populations that are not dwarfed by much greater differences within populations. At a fundamental cognitive level, we humans are one species, each population possessing equivalent intellectual and linguistic capacities. This key fact enables us to infer with certainty that human linguistic and cognitive capacities were already fixed in our species by the time the first wave of human pioneers exited Africa and made it to Australia – at least 50 KYA (for a review see Mellars, 2006). This time point (which is still controversial) represents the last plausible moment at which human linguistic abilities like those of modern humans had evolved to fixation in our species. Subsequent migrations into the Americas (dates are still debated, but at least 18 KYA) confirm the same point. The obvious differences between living human populations are for the most part literally skin deep, with a variety of disease-resistant genes and some dietary adaptations being the only important exceptions.

An important contribution to contemporary paleoanthropology has been made by molecular genetics techniques, particularly studies of **mitochondrial DNA** (mtDNA). Mitochondria have their own genome, with a smattering of key genes arranged in the circular format typical of prokaryotes (see Chapter 5). This mtDNA is relatively short and conserved, and thus easily sequenced, and because each cell has thousands of mitochondria, mtDNA exists in vastly greater quantities than ordinary nuclear DNA. This is one reason that initial attempts to recover DNA from fossils focused on mtDNA. Finally, because mitochondria are inherited solely from the mother, it is much simpler conceptually to track the evolution of the mitochondrial genome than the scrambled nuclear genome.

By sequencing the mtDNA from human populations around the world, molecular geneticists have been able to finally resolve a long-standing debate in the evolution of modern humans. Early models of human evolution tended to see a progressive trend towards large-brained *Homo sapiens*, and early finds were consistent with the idea that this change had occured in parallel throughout the Old World. This **multiregional hypothesis** was also consistent, it seemed, with certain skeletal continuities that can be perceived in African, Asian, and European populations over more than a million years. However, increasingly detailed fossil data seemed to indicate the contrary: that all modern human populations stem from a single, ancestral population in Africa – the **Out of Africa hypothesis**. As long as only fossils were available, both of these hypotheses had their champions. But the molecular data provide resounding and unequivocal support for the latter hypothesis. Despite appearances, humans are actually less genetically variable as a species than most others (including, for example, gorillas or chimpanzees; Ruvolo *et al.*, 1993). Genetic data show that African populations hold most of the variability, possessing as much human genetic variation as the rest of the world combined. Specifically, when mtDNA is sequenced, and each different line of maternally inherited mitochondrial DNA, or **haplotype**, is placed onto a phylogenetic tree, the deep-rooted ancient haplotypes are all found in Africa. Furthermore, the haplotypes from the rest of the world can be mathematically organized into a tree with its root in Africa. Thus, human mtDNA can be traced back to Africa, to a single **mitochondrial Eve** who lived around 200,000 years ago. With this crucial genetic data in hand, the reinterpreted fossils are clearly consistent with the Out of Africa hypothesis (Foley, 1998; Mellars, 2006) which is now the model almost universally favored by paleoanthropologists (for a contrary view see Wolpoff *et al.*, 2001).

It is important to be clear about what this "African Eve" is *not*. Despite frequent misinterpretation (encouraged by calling her Eve), the fact that all modern human mtDNA haplotypes can be traced back to a single individual *does not* mean this single woman was the ancestor of us all. It is easiest to see why by imagining yourself in the sandals of a successful female contemporary of this Eve, who we might call Lilith. Suppose that Lilith, by chance, bore only male offspring, who went on to be highly successful fathers and grandfathers, and are ancestral to a significant proportion of the current human population. Because mitochondria are passed on only via females, none of Lilith's mtDNA made it to her granddaughters – who nonetheless carried one quarter of her nuclear DNA. Many of Lilith's genes (like those of many other female contemporaries of "Eve") live on – only those few genes carried by mitochondria didn't make it. Lilith, then, and not Eve, was the female ancestor in her generation of many living humans, and it is only the chance quirk that she bore only sons that left us bereft of her mtDNA. Any ancestral females whose line had one generation of solely male offspring suffered the same fate, and "Eve" is the female who just happens to have an unbroken female line of descent. Precisely the same argument applies to the Y-chromosome "Adam." Unfortunately the name "Eve" has encouraged a popular misconception of human evolution in which a *single individual*, a "hopeful monster" carrying some key mutation or set of mutations, went on to spawn the entire human race. There is no scientific basis for this idea; *populations*, not individuals, spawn new species, and there is no reason that "Eve" need have been either cognitively or anatomically modern.

The contributions of molecular genetics do not stop with mitochondrial Eve. Another clever use of the comparative method chose a surprising study species: the human body louse *Pediculus humanus* (Kittler *et al.*, 2003; Reed *et al.*, 2004). Lice are passed within a species, and very rarely between species. Thus, the louse genome represents an isolated population which tracks species, and chimpanzee lice are different from human lice. This in itself is not very helpful. The key fact is that humans, apparently uniquely, have *two* varieties of lice: head lice (which are good-old fashioned mammalian lice adapted to thick hair) and body lice (a novel louse form associated with clothing). Genetic analysis of this clothing-specific type indicated that they separated from their parent species 70 ± 40 kya: a maximum value thus associates these lice, and thus by inference clothing, with anatomically modern humans. This study, surprisingly, implies that clothing is a very recent development, uniquely associated with our own species. This is consistent with the archaeological finds: needles have only been found associated with modern human remains. If true, it suggests that Neanderthalers living in cold Europe either had thick pelts of their own or developed clothing independently. However, there is little reason to believe that body lice immediately colonized the new potential niche provided by clothing, or immediately specialized to that niche. Clothing may have been around for thousands of years before some intrepid head louse made its way downward onto the body. This example illustrates the power of modern genetic techniques combined with an understanding of organismic biology and evolution, to address questions about events that leave no fossil record.

7.11 AMHS and the Upper Paleolithic "Revolution"

So what of the archaeological record of our own species? Here we encounter striking testaments of cultures like our own. Finds include a wide variety of artifacts, most prominently artistic objects and evidence of body adornment, that together constitute the Upper Paleolithic "Revolution" (termed the **Aurignacian**, in Europe, representing the final stage of the Paleolithic), starting about 40 KYA (Mellars and Stringer, 1989; Mellars, 1991). In addition to a more elaborate toolkit, some of the earliest signs of truly modern cognition are semi-realistic statues, so-called Venus figurines, that are found throughout Europe about 40 KYA. Beautiful cave paintings, such as those at the Lascaux caves, are found throughout Europe and again dated to 35 KYA. Musical instruments make their appearance at about the same time, with some fine Aurignacian bone flutes from Geissenklösterle in Germany dated to 40 KYA. Mammoth bones, arranged into interestingly variable patterns at several homesites in Siberia provide the first indications of architectural "styles." At a practical level we find diverse bone tools, including needles, harpoons, and fishhooks. Skeletal remains of birds and fish suddenly appear in middens, rather than the exclusively mammal bones found in Neanderthal or *H. heidelbergensis* sites. As already mentioned, fine bone needles suggest the origins of carefully tailored clothing, and imprints on clay pots show that vegetable matter was being braided into ropes. Careful excavations show that a single animal was carved into chunks that were then devoured at three different campsites, early evidence of cooperative economic division. Even more striking is an extraordinary burial from 28,000 years ago, at the Sungir site in Russia, where a 60-year-old man (an age reached among hominids only by modern *Homo sapiens*) and two children are buried with amazing finery, including shirts made of 3,000 fine ivory beads. This rich burial contrasts strikingly with many other, plainer burials, suggesting that some level of social stratification was already present. The list goes on (cf. Tattersall, 1999; Mellars, 2005). For our current purposes, the point is clear: the archaeological record quite abruptly captures the behavior of beings that are unmistakably human, and who rapidly colonized the entire Old World.

However, this Upper Paleolithic explosion raises one of the deep puzzles in human evolution: the disjunction between the timing of *morphologically* modern humans about 200 KYA, with skeletons in the range of living *Homo sapiens*, and the kind of abrupt change in archaeological data that unambiguously indicates human culture – appearing about 40 KYA in Europe (Mellars and Stringer, 1989). The genetic and morphological data concur in placing the origin or our species much further back – at least 100,000 years earlier (Mellars, 1989). The existence of this difference is uncontroversial, but interpretations vary as to its significance. One viewpoint, recognizing that absence of evidence is no evidence of absence, suggests that the cognitive innovations that characterize our species did start 200 KYA, but that the technological *clues* that unambiguously indicate this new mind took their time accumulating, and early traces have been lost. Certainly, some extant or recent human populations, known to have sophisticated language and cognition, would have left few archaeological clues to this fact: the Australian Tasmanians had lost control of fire and wore little or no clothing, and many Amazonian tribes relying on wooden weapons or net-based hunting techniques would leave no archaeological traces of their sophistication. A nice illustration of this possibility are some baked Czech clay figurines from the Gravettian that predate any further evidence of baked clay pottery by 15,000 years. While this technology might have been lost and reinvented, it seems more likely that this long timespan simply reflects the incompleteness of the archaeological record.

Recent finds in southern Africa have succeeded in filling this gap to at least some degree, partially smoothing the transition to modernity. The most celebrated are those from Blombos Cave in South Africa, from at least 100 KYA (McBrearty and Brooks, 2000). These findings include a large collection of perforated shell beads, all from a particular species, with microwear patterns consistent with them having been worn on strings. Even more striking is a large accumulation of red ochre, which is widely used in ritualistic body ornamentation throughout Africa, thought to be consistent with some symbolic ritual in these humans. Finally, an engraved block of red ochre with incised crossing diagonal lines is often taken as the first unambiguous indicator of an artistic sentiment, preceding the Upper Paleolithic European sculptures just mentioned by some 60,000 years (Henshilwood *et al.*, 2002). These findings, while still difficult to interpret unambiguously as evidence for language (cf. Knight, 1998), suggest that the appearance of an abrupt revolution in Europe is misleading, and reflects a more gradual development of many of these traits in Africa (McBrearty and Brooks, 2000). An interesting suggestion is that the very sharp archaeological transition termed the "Upper Paleolithic Revolution" in Europe resulted from contact with the resident European Neanderthals, and that the humans who emerged from Africa at this time (Shea, 2003) used self-ornament as a way of emphasizing the differences between themselves and the (otherwise very similar) Neanderthals.

However, this still leaves a gap of some 100,000 years between morphology and archaeology. An alternative perspective on this gap is that it represents a true lag between the attainment of modern skeletal morphology and human cognitive capacity. Given our relatively rich fossil record, from many sites around the world, this hypothesis deserves serious consideration. It is possible that morphology and behavior were sometimes out of step in hominid evolution, such that morphological developments such as larger brains were permissive, setting up the preconditions for cognitive innovations to take place, without being directly causative. There is certainly no biological reason to suppose that all behavioral innovations go along with skeletal ones. Modern songbirds have remarkably similar skeletal form, despite great genetic and behavioral variety. There are no skeletal cues that indicate the mimicry ability of mockingbirds or the remarkable toolmaking abilities of New Caledonian crows. Thus, the simple fact that there were hominids who *looked* human 150,000 years ago does not entail that they acted human. It remains plausible that the fossil/archaeological gap is real, and that human body form and brain size were attained long before the critical *neural* changes that were required for modern human cognition, including language, took place.

Fortunately, this question does not have to remain unresolved forever. As our understanding of the genetic basis of human cognition progresses, we can expect important clues to the timing of various genetic events to be found "fossilized" in the genome. By examining silent mutations that have accumulated in or around key cognitive genes, using techniques pioneered in Enard *et al.* (2002), we can use variation in human populations to backtrack to the time of origin of particular alleles. Individually, such estimates will always have large margins of error (Perry *et al.*, 2004; Stedman *et al.*, 2004). But if, as most geneticists suspect, there are scores or hundreds of such genes, we will eventually have a large database of genes that can be *ordered* in time, if not precisely *dated*. Since the order of acquisition of different components of language is one of the central controversies in language evolution, this will be enough. Molecular data, integrated with increasing understanding of modern cognition and its genetic underpinnings, offer hope that cognitive events in human evolutionary history can be reconstructed more securely in the near future.

7.12 The evolution of human brain size

One of the few types of uncontroversial paleontological data concerns absolute brain size in fossil vertebrates including hominids (Jerison, 1973). A series of well-preserved fossil skulls with intact crania allows us to trace the increases in human brain size since our split from chimpanzees some 6–7 MYA with some certainty. Unfortunately, despite this solid empirical foundation, we will find that *interpretation* of brain-size data in cognitive terms is neither trivial or uncontroversial. For example, the degree to which these increases were relatively step-like or gradual remains contentious (e.g. Striedter, 2004; Holloway, 2008). I will only touch on the complexities of the issues here (cf. Jerison, 1973; Deacon, 1990a; Holloway, 1996). A short and sensible comparatively grounded analysis remains Jerison (1975), which emphasizes what can and can't be known based on fossil brain endocasts.

7.12.1 Absolute brain size

Chimpanzee brains average about 400 cc, and the brain sizes of early *Australopithecus africanus* were in the same size range: habitual bipedalism was not associated with any appreciable increase in brain size. Brain sizes began to increase as body size increased in some early lineages, but substantial increases in absolute brain size began in the genus *Homo*. With *Homo habilis* we see a mild increase to 550 cc. A rather substantial brain, twice the size of a chimpanzee's, is found in *Homo ergaster* (854 cc), the first hominids to create sophisticated stone tools and move out of Africa. There can be little doubt that at this point in human evolution, significant cognitive rearrangements had occurred which enabled these hominids to successfully colonize novel environments in a way that no other ape ever did. By the time we reach the common ancestor of Neanderthals and modern humans, who initiated the second "hominids Out of Africa" wave, bringing even more complex stone tools with them, we find absolute brain sizes within the low modern human range (*Homo heidelbergensis* at 1198 cc), and the average Neanderthal skulls have cranial capacities (1512 cc) well above the average modern human (1355 cc, males and females averaged). So over the course of human evolution, we see a tripling of brain size, in several punctuated stages. The most obvious changes were those that occurred at the *erectus* and *heidelbergensis* stages in the evolution of our own genus, each of which was accompanied by a considerable increase in behavioral flexibility, as evidenced by their migrations out of the African homeland. These are the facts of the matter that any paleoanthropologist will agree with, though debate surrounds the gradualness, or discreteness, of the changes.

Controversy starts when we begin to try interpret these brain-size data in functional terms. Let's start with some basic context from comparative brain data. First, there is no Rubicon of absolute brain size beyond which language, toolmaking, or other complex human abilities automatically appear (contra Keith, 1948; Tobias, 1965). Human microcephalics, with brains the size of chimpanzees, often have relatively normal language skills, and even learn to read and write (Lenneberg, 1967; Woods *et al.*, 2005). Further, many animals have brains larger than humans, but lack these abilities. An elephant brain at 4,780 cc is more than three times larger than a human brain, and although elephants are comparatively intelligent among mammals, they exhibit none of the cognitive features that set humans apart (Rensch, 1956). Nor is a brain size within a particular size range key: bottlenosed dolphin brains are in the human/Neanderthal range (1,500–1,600 cc), but dolphin communication lacks the sophistication of modern human language (Evans and Bastian, 1969; Tyack and Clark, 2000). While both of these species are undoubtedly quite intelligent, they illustrate that a large absolute brain size alone does not tell the entire story of human cognitive evolution.

7.12.2 Relative brain size

The largest brains, unsurprisingly, belong to the largest animals, the whales: a humpback whale has a 4.6 kg brain and a sperm whale 7.8 kg, six times larger than a human's. So a first step in a more detailed analysis of brain size is to attempt to control for body size. Let us therefore adjust for body size in the obvious way, to compensate for the whale brain-size issue, and examine *relative* brain size: brain weight/body weight ratios (Rensch, 1956). Unfortunately, we now run into a different problem, at the mouse end of the scale. Essentially, there appears to be a minimum brain size for mammals, and as body size gets very small, brain size does not shrink accordingly. Thus, in terms of relative brain size, a mouse has more brain per unit body than a human being! The inadequacy of this relative measure as an index of intelligence, at least over the entire mouse/elephant scale, is made most clear by considering relative brain size within a single species: dogs (Weidenreich, 1941). Brain sizes in domestic dog breeds are far less variable than body sizes, meaning that large-bodied dogs have relatively small brains. Small-bodied breeds such as chihauhuas have brain sizes that, relative to body size, are enormous relative to wolves or German shepherds. Thus, if relative brain size is key, we would expect chihauhuas and similar miniature breeds to be the Einsteins of the dog world (neuroscientist Terrence Deacon aptly dubbed this the "Chihuahua fallacy"; Deacon, 1997). In fact, there is no evidence that miniature breeds are more intelligent than "average" dogs, and some evidence to the contrary (Weidenreich, 1941; Rensch, 1956). Thus, even within a species, the use of relative brain size does not seem to provide an adequate measure of relative intelligence. Although domesticated animals are an atypical group from an evolutionary viewpoint, having undergone powerful recent artificial selection on body size, these facts must be kept in mind when we attempt to use relative brain size as a cognitively relevant measure.

A practical problem with using relative brain size is that we don't actually know the body weights of fossil humans. Although height can be estimated from leg bones, stature does not automatically translate into body mass.

Therefore, relative brain size for extinct hominids depends heavily on the equations used to estimate their body mass, another controversial issue, with some authors arguing for the use of measures such as skull length or eye size (estimated from the size of the orbit) as superior to measures of long bones (for discussion see McHenry, 1992). This adds to the uncertainty involved in using relative brain size as an index of conceptual abilities in fossil hominids.

7.12.3 Encephalization quotient (EQ)

Issues such as these led researchers to realize that some more sophisticated measure of relative brain size was needed (Dubois, 1897; Jerison, 1973). The approach almost universally used by researchers today involves some variant of the **encephalization quotient (EQ)** introduced by Jerison. The basic idea is rather simple: we calculate the overall curve relating body size to brain size for some group of species and then *subtract* this curve from the original data. We are left with *differences* from this average curve that are termed **residuals**. Because these mathematical operations are calculated on logarithmic axes (see below), the residuals give us the ratio of actual brain size to that predicted for a given body size. When this approach is taken, we find that humans have high positive residuals or EQ values, no matter which group we use as the comparison set (vertebrates, mammals, primates, . . .). Our brains are roughly three times larger than predicted for an ape of our size. Because we humans generally consider ourselves as smarter than both elephants and mice or chihuahuas, this outcome has the dubious virtue of providing a statistical measure that gibes with human prejudice. But given that either of the previous techniques leads to conclusions directly contradictory to what we know about animal cognition, some variant of the residual approach seems unavoidable. Thus, since Jerison's pioneering studies, most commentators have adopted the logic of EQ. Unfortunately, there are different ways to calculate EQ, and they lead to different conclusions about both living species *and* fossil hominids.

    To understand the many different approaches to EQ, we must first consider a bit more mathematics. As realized long ago by Galileo, variation in size tends to lead to variation in shape, because the mass of an object increases in proportion to a power of three of a linear measure of its size (such as height). If the larger of two cubes of the same material is precisely twice as long as the smaller, its *volume* will be 2^3 (8) times greater. This principle applies to any shape, with a proportionality constant that varies with the shape. Thus, as animals grow longer, they must adjust their shape to compensate for this increased mass. A mouse increased to the size of an elephant would be unable to support its own weight if it preserved its original shape perfectly (*isometrically*): the elephant needs thicker, more column-like legs to support its vastly increased mass. Shape change with different body sizes is termed **allometry** ("other shape"), and this term is also used to describe research on this topic. These basic insights, and the mathematics that go with them, go back to the work of Julian Huxley (Huxley, 1932).

The first step in allometric analyses is to "straighten" the cubic curve that results from an exponential function by using logarithms (as a reminder, the logarithm is the inverse of the exponential: taking a logarithm "undoes" the process of exponentiation). Allometric curves relating shape to mass can be "straightened" or linearized by taking the logarithm of the two measures. The slope of the line in logarithmic coordinates corresponds to the exponent of the function in normal linear coordinates. The first step in calculating EQ is thus to either stipulate or calculate this slope, and the proper choice here remains very controversial. In Jerison's original calculation of EQ, a power of 2/3 was observed to fit the overall data for vertebrates reasonably well, and Jerison argued on theoretical grounds that this derives from the fact that the size of the nervous system should scale with the *surface area* of the body (area, with a power of 2, relative to the overall mass scaling exponent 3). This leads to the "classic" EQ values ($EQ_{0.666}$). However, this stipulated exponent has been criticized by various authors (e.g. Martin, 1981; Holloway, 1996), who argue either for some other stipulated value (e.g. a 3/4 value that is argued to reflect the relation between metabolic rate and body mass; Martin, 1981), or for simply using the empirically derived exponent. The problem with this latter approach is that the exponent depends on which group is chosen as the "reference set." For example, if we calculate the curve for toothed cetaceans and anthropoid primates separately, the exponent is 0.7 for primates, 0.53 for cetaceans, and 0.72 for both samples combined (Marino, 1998), and Marino ended up calculating both this latter value and Jerison's 0.666 value. In general, there is enough noise in the samples used to calculate such values that the "correct" exponent remains uncertain (Pagel and Harvey, 1989), and we are left in a quandary about which variant of EQ to use. The debate is still unresolved after more than twenty years of discussion, remaining a matter of taste today.

Such issues have non-trivial implications when we consider the core issues of brain-size evolution (Deaner *et al.*, 2000). Jerison's original conception of his EQ value was that it provides a measure of "excess" neurons in the brain, and that these are related to the organism's basic cognitive adaptability or "biological intelligence" (Jerison, 1973), or ecological circumstances more generally (Pagel and Harvey, 1989). Jerison argued that a given body requires a certain volume of brain for maintenance, sensory processing, and motor control, and that neurons in excess of this value are available for more general, associative purposes, increasing intelligence. This seems sensible, and when we calculate EQ with the general mammalian curve, or with Jerison's 2/3 exponent, most primates come out with a positive value (possessing "excess neurons" compared to other mammals). But if we use an empirically derived primate value (e.g. 0.7 or thereabouts), about half of primates come out with *negative* EQs (*fewer* than predicted for the average). This outcome is an inevitable result of the statistics used and the choice of reference set, but is incompatible Jerison's justification of his measure. Indeed, Pagel and Harvey (1989) show that different groups of mammals show different scaling relationships, and that the choice of reference group is therefore irremediably debatable. We are forced to conclude that EQ is *always* a relative measure, strongly dependent on the reference set or exponent chosen. Straightforward calculations of "excess neurons" based on EQ values (e.g. Tobias, 1987) must thus be viewed with caution.

What does brain size tell us?

Given these inconsistencies in attempts to link brain size to cognition or "intelligence," why should we consider brain size at all? There are several good reasons. First, larger brains contain more neurons, which are the key information-processing units of the nervous system (Haug, 1987), and in general we expect more units to mean more capacity, by virtually any theory of brain function or computation (e.g. Rensch, 1956). Additionally, larger brains also tend to have larger neurons with more complex neuronal form, and this might increase the computational power of these individual cells, further boosting the processing power of large brains (Purves, 1988). Thus, computational theory suggests that bigger brains should have greater processing capacity. However, this postulated increase in computing power may or may not be harnessed behaviorally. Although the old canard that "we only use 5 percent of our brains" has no credible empirical foundation, we cannot therefore conclude that every organism continuously uses 100 percent of their available neural processing power. Much of our day-to-day activity probably uses far less than our full cognitive capacity, just as most of our locomotion is not at our peak running speed. However, neural tissue is extremely expensive metabolically, and thus we would expect processing capacity that was *never* used, over many generations, to be pruned away by natural selection rather quickly. Evidence in favor of this is provided by domesticated mammals and birds, all of which have smaller brains (absolutely and relatively) than wild-type members of the corresponding ancestral species (Darwin, 1875; Belyaev, 1969). Apparently, the decreased risk of predation and simplification of foraging needs that accompanied domestication relaxed the need for certain cognitive capacities (though perhaps human animal breeders also selected for decreased ingenuity).

Such arguments convince virtually all commentators that the increase in brain size during the course of human evolution had *something* to do with increased cognitive abilities, whether of very specific types (e.g. linguistic, social, or manipulative abilities) or of some more general type ("environmental" intelligence, IQ, or other such abstractions). Although this conclusion may seem like a truism, there are good reasons to be skeptical about any tight correlation between intelligence and brain size either across a wide range of species or within a particular species (Macphail, 1982). First, within humans, there is no universal measure of intelligence that applies across all ages and cultures (Gardner, 1983; Gould, 1996). Even if we narrow the sample to one culture and similar ages, empirically determined correlations between IQ tests and overall brain volume are rather weak, averaging $r =$ 0.33 in a recent meta-analysis based on MRIs of living subjects (McDaniel, 2005). This means that at best only 11 percent of the observed variance in intelligence can be linked to brain size. Furthermore, even these measures confound more indirect factors such as socioeconomic status, which might independently affect adult brain size (via childhood nutrition) and IQ test performance (via education). Thus the relationship itself is small, and the direct causal significance of even this small difference to cognition can be questioned.

Another ground for skepticism is found in the huge variability of brain sizes in people of equivalent intelligence. For example, there is no question that men on average have larger brains than women, by some 100 cc (Giedd *et al.*, 1997; McDaniel, 2005). However, there is no credible evidence for significant IQ differences between men and women and, regarding language skills, the evidence points if anything to the opposite conclusion: that women have superior verbal abilities to men (Hyde and Linn, 1988). Extreme variation in brain size is common in specific specimens of "normal" humanity. Two famous examples are the writers Anatole France, a prolific writer and Nobel laureate with a brain of 1,000 cc, and Jonathan Swift, similarly successful with a brain size of 2,000 cc (Holloway, 1996). Congenital microcephalics, some of whom develop adult brain sizes in the range of chimpanzees, typically suffer some degree of mental retardation, but may nonetheless have good command of spoken language (Weiden-reich, 1941; Holloway, 1966; Lenneberg, 1967; Woods *et al.*, 2005). Intact language in retarded microcephalic individuals (or in Williams syndrome patients; see Karmiloff-Smith *et al.*, 1995) points clearly to the importance of factors beyond simple brain size or general intelligence in determining language abilities.

The general conclusion is that the usefulness of brain size in testing theories is limited to broad comparisons among species or larger taxonomic groups (Jerison, 1975), probably because the forces that control variation within a population can be quite different from those operating between clades (Gould, 1975). Thus, the various apparent inconsistencies in this complex field should not lead us to ignore these data, but simply to remain circumspect regarding their interpretation. Like most data relevant to language evolution, they deserve a place in a larger interpretive picture, but by themselves warrant few strong conclusions.

7.13 Reorganization of neural connectivity

Brain size, while important, is not the only relevant variable in understanding animal behavior. Rearrangements of brain connectivity, and of the relative sizes of distinct brain regions, are also important in behavioral evolution (Striedter, 2004). Good examples of this are found when we compare the sensory "homunculus" that maps the body surface onto the primary somatosensory cortex. Monkeys with grasping prehensile tails have a larger tail representation than those with ordinary tails (Jerison, 1975). Mammals with sensitive snouts, like coatimundis, have larger snout representations than their more manually oriented cousins, the raccoons (Allman, 1999). Echolocating bats have larger auditory cortices devoted to the frequencies used in echolocation (Suga *et al.*, 1987). Such examples could be multiplied indefinitely: the brain "fits" the body in much more specific ways than simply scaling in size. It has more recently become clear that this fit is not wholly genetically programmed, but instead reflects an ontogenetic plasticity: the brain organizes itself to the demands of the body during development (Purves, 1988). Mammalian neocortex is particularly plastic, and the cortical maps observed in the adult animal actually reflect both the sensory complement on the surfaces of the body and the use to which they are put. This plasticity is clearly most pronounced in early ontogeny: it is possible to "rewire" auditory cortex to process visual stimuli experimentally in fetal ferrets (von Melchner *et al.*, 2000). But finger representations in sensory neocortex remain flexbile in adulthood in both man and monkey (Merzenich *et al.*, 1989; Schlaug, 2001). The conclusion is that ontogenetic plasticity plays a major role in the organization of connectivity in the adult, and does not need to be fully pre-specified. At least in mammals, evolution has created a brain that adapts itself to the organism's body and behavior.

Nonetheless, certain aspects of behavior are "pre-programmed" in the sense that they reliably develop *before* practice or environmental influences kick in. The propensity of infant humans (or young male songbirds) to "babble" or play with vocalizations is a nice example: such vocal play appears to be a biologically given propensity of humans that chimpanzees lack (Hayes, 1951). A simple propensity of this sort could interact with brain plasticity to create an adult brain with enhanced vocal motor control, and audio-motor connections, without any need for those connections to be genetically specified. Thus, we should be cautious when interpreting structure and connectivity in the adult brain as evolutionary adaptations *per se*, as they may reflect more indirect epigenetic responses to some other variable (cf. Deacon, 1997).

7.13.1 Fossil endocasts

Few clear inferences can be drawn from endocasts of fossil crania about hominid brain reorganization. This is both because functional changes are not typically reflected in gross morphological changes (e.g. there is no reflection of the tail enlargement of prehensile-tailed monkeys in their gross brain anatomy; Jerison, 1975), and because endocasts reflect even such gross changes only rarely and imperfectly. Therefore, Jerison advocated skepticism about attempts to interpret the finer details of fossil endocasts, while acknowledging the importance of brain reorganization in human evolution (Jerison, 1975). Thus, despite a long history of debate (Dubois, 1898), I will only briefly discuss these data. See LeMay (1975), Falk (1987), and Holloway (1996, 2008) for further discussion and details.

A long-lived attempt to link endocasts to brain reorganization is based on the position of the **lunate sulcus** (cf. Holloway, 2008). In apes, this sulcus provides an external indicator of the edge of the primary visual cortex, forming the border with the posterior parietal cortex. The relative size of visual cortex has decreased, due to expansion of parietal "association" cortex, and the lunate sulcus is thus pushed backwards in modern humans. Paleoanthropologist Ralph Holloway (1996) argued that a posterior location of this sulcus indicates early "hominization" of the brain in several Australopithecine skulls (e.g. the original "Taung Child" fossil discovered by Dart). These data, and Holloway's conclusions, have been contested by Falk (1983, 1987), while others have argued, like Jerison, that one simply can't tell (Tobias, 1987). In any case, the vast majority of hominid fossils bear no trace of the lunate sulcus, and its relationship to frontal and peri-sylvian areas remains quite indirect, so even if Holloway's arguments were fully accepted, their relevance to language evolution remains far from clear.

Holloway's fellow paleoanthropologist and longtime critic, Dean Falk, has, in contrast, focused on the frontal lobes and the region surrounding Broca's area (the lower portion of the posterior frontal lobes). Falk argues that Australopithecines retained a fundamentally ape-like frontal region (Falk, 1980). However, in the exquisitely preserved endocast of the famous *Homo habilis* specimen KNM-ER 1470, originally prepared by Holloway, the **third inferior frontal convolution** is "complex and modern-human-like" (Holloway, 1996). Because of the clear involvement of this region in both speech motor control and some aspects of syntax comprehension, this endocast has been used to argue that a fundamental step towards language had already been made in *Homo habilis*, at about 2 MYA (Tobias, 1987). While this appears to be one thing that paleoneurologists agree upon (Falk, 1987), and the association with Broca's area is suggestive, Tobias's suggestion that this expansion indicates full language capabilities has not been widely accepted. An alternative perspective is that changes in this region were linked with toolmaking (Holloway, 1969; Stout *et al.*, 2008), as the evidence for complex, right-hand-biased toolmaking becomes compelling at the same time (Toth, 1985).

A final area of discussion regarding endocasts is **hemispheric asymmetry**. Modern humans are functionally asymmetrical, in that most people are right-handed, and lesions to the left side of the brain are far more likely to produce severe, long-lasting aphasia than those on the right (Caplan, 1987). Some patients whose two cerebral hemispheres have been surgically disconnected appear to be able to speak only using the left hemisphere (Bradshaw and Rogers, 1993), though early loss of the left hemisphere is compatible with near-normal language (Liégeois *et al.*, 2004). From Broca's time up through the 1980s, it was widely believed that hemispheric asymmetry of this sort was uniquely human, and that the left hemisphere is the "seat of language." However, many humans show opposite lateralization without losing language, and modern brain imaging results have shown more extensive involvement of the right hemisphere in language and speech than had previously been suspected from traditional lesion studies. In particular, functional asymmetry in language dominance is not always reflected in overall volume differences (e.g. in planum temporale or Heschel's

gyrus); the only significant correlations between functional and morphological asymmetry are in Broca's area (Dorsaint-Pierre *et al.*, 2006). Thus,
the importance of left-brain dominance has been overstated.

Furthermore, comparative work has demonstrated that asymmetry, at an
individual level, is common in vertebrates (Bisazza *et al.*, 1998), and there
may be tenuous population-level asymmetries in some primates as well
(MacNeilage, 1991; Hopkins *et al.*, 2005). Studies of nonhuman primates
have revealed a degree of asymmetry in both anatomy and function (Gannon
et al., 1998; Poremba *et al.*, 2004). **Petalia**, or cranial impressions revealing
asymmetries in the relative shape of the two hemispheres, were the focus
of work by LeMay and colleagues (LeMay, 1976, 1985). In humans, right-
handers tend to have a wider occipital lobe on the left hemisphere, and wider
frontal lobes on the right (quite different from what the Broca's area hypothesis would predict). Petalias indicate such a torque is also present in KNM
ER-1470, initially buttressing the case for a modern-like brain morphology in this specimen. But again, further work showed similar asymmetries
in apes (LeMay, 1985; Holloway, 1996). Thus petalia appear to be only
marginally significant in language evolution. Despite several decades during which cerebral asymmetry was considered to be something of a "magic
bullet" for explaining the evolution of human language and other cognitive abilities (e.g. Corballis, 1991), current data strongly suggest that the
importance of asymmetry has been over-emphasized. I conclude, like Jerison (1973), that despite a large literature, there is little to be gleaned about
language evolution from the detailed study of fossil endocasts beyond the
simple facts of absolute brain size.

7.14 The brain as an expensive tissue

A novel, and promising, interpretive angle on brain size was introduced in
a seminal article by Martin (1981) and developed by Foley and Lee (1991)
and Aiello and Wheeler (1995). This line of inquiry starts with the fact
that neural tissue is extremely "expensive" from a metabolic viewpoint:
although the brain accounts for only 2 percent of body weight, it consumes
some 25 percent of overall metabolic resources. Neural tissue (along with
the digestive system, heart, and kidneys) is more expensive than muscle,
skin, or most other tissues. This suggests a tradeoff between different tissue
types during evolution. Thus, for example, leaf-eating monkeys have larger
guts but smaller brains than fruit-eating or insectivorous species; a response
to both the increased *digestive* demands of their low-nutrient vegetarian diet

and the decreased *cognitive* demands of finding leaves in a forest (relative to finding fruiting trees or catching insects; Clutton-Brock and Harvey, 1980; Allman, 1999). These facts have important implications for understanding brain evolution, suggesting that brain size can be used as a proxy for dietary input and foraging strategy. Put simply, the very fact that some extinct hominids could *afford* to have large brains tells us something important about their way of life: large-brained hominds, starting with early *Homo*, must have had some richer source of nutrition than their smaller-brained predecessors.

Recognizing the brain as a consumer of energy forces us to consider not only the "why" question of brain growth ("What selective forces drove the evolution of larger brains?") but also the "how" question ("What were those big-brained species eating to afford this luxury?"). Particularly important, the main determinants of brain size in the adult are the prenatal and perinatal resources available during the main period of brain growth (Martin, 1981). In humans, virtually all of the neurons in the adult brain are already present at birth; the considerable postnatal increase in brain size is a result not of new cells but of a size increase in those cells and non-neuronal tissue (glia, myelin, meninges, etc.). Brain growth demands high-quality nutrition, at first to the mother, and then to the child once weaned. The availability of meat, fat, and other animal foods (especially bone marrow) would provide an excellent source of the required nutrients, suggesting that pregnant and lactating women would have eagerly sought such foods by the time hominid brain growth had undergone its first spurt with the genus *Homo*, and especially given the additional increase in brain and body size in *Homo erectus* (Aiello and Key, 2002). Since a woman in late pregnancy or with a suckling infant is maximally disadvantaged as a hunter, this implies some degree of food sharing among these hominids (either among related females, between males and females, or more likely both). Before this, food sources such as marrow from long bones obtained by scavenging Australopithecines potentially provided a bonanza: a hominid able to crack open objects with stones would have found these to be a rich source of brain-building nutrients (Deacon, 1997).

Bigger brains also require longer maturation times. Progressive prolongation of childhood dependence during hominid evolution was probably a continuous process over the last two million years (Coqueugniot *et al.*, 2004; Hrdy, 2005; Locke and Bogin, 2006). Better nutrition enabled bigger brains, which enabled better hunting and foraging, which allowed better nutrition, and so on in a feedback loop. Heavy investments made in large-brained offspring, with their increasingly long dependence upon the mother and other caregivers, would have increased the value of sharing knowledge with these infants, decreasing their post-weaning mortality and perhaps increasing their immediate usefulness as additional foragers. This need for better nutrition thus provided an important driving force in the evolution of large brains, and part of the adaptive context for language. This life-history based approach to hominid evolution has considerable potential to enrich our understanding of extinct hominid lifestyles, with brain size providing an invaluable source of constraining data in this endeavor.

7.15 Integrating the strands: brain size and brain structure in human evolution

What can we conclude regarding hominid brain size? The first conclusion is that we have much to learn before firm statements can be justified. Our knowledge of brain function in relation to structure remains drastically incomplete even for living organisms, and is far too sketchy to support blanket conclusions about specific cognitive abilities in extinct species. Nonetheless, we are still left with data that are concrete and valuable when interpreted within the proper comparative context, and brain-imaging studies may provide important new advances in our understanding of structure/function relationships. The overall increase in hominid brain size since our separation from chimpanzees is clear, and links between enlarged brains and increased metabolic needs supports inferences about foraging and sociality in *Homo erectus.* These can be firmly embedded in a theory of mammalian life-history strategies that grows ever more solid and comprehensive (Mace, 2000).

At a more fundamental, computational level, brain size is increasingly recognized as a crucial parameter in the epigenetic processes that determine the wiring patterns of the mammalian brain (Purves, 1988; Deacon, 1990b; Striedter, 2004). The adult brain wiring diagram is best thought of as the outcome of a developmental process involving competition between groups of neurons for neural real estate and specific neurotrophic factors necessary for neuronal survival ("neural Darwinism"; Edelman, 1987; Purves, 1988). Rather minor relative changes in the relative size of brain to body, or of brain components to one another, can lead to major functional differences after this process has been played out. Size differences can indirectly influence the statistical processes that underlie neurogenesis. Because brain development is highly constrained within mammals (Finlay and Darlington, 1995; Finlay *et al.*, 2001), overall brain size may provide one of the major "handles" that natural selection can modify directly, to tweak the wiring diagram for a particular species. But in the process of selecting for some particular cognitive ability, this developmental conservatism means that there will be multiple other brain areas that also change, providing abundant room for cognitive "spandrels." It is therefore likely that selection for one or more specific types of intelligence (e.g. toolmaking, extractive foraging, social intelligence, etc.) might have led to the sorts of neural changes necessary for more complex semantics or syntax through such indirect means (Holloway, 1969; Deacon, 1997). Several concrete proposals of this sort have been advanced, but rigorous tests require a richer understanding of brain development and its genetic determination than is available today. But this situation is changing rapidly.

An exciting recent development is provided by research on a gene family clearly linked to the determination of brain size: the **MCPH gene family** (including *ASPM* and *Microcephalin*). Primary microcephaly (MCPH) is a congenital disorder characterized by severely reduced total brain size (400 cc), mild to moderate mental retardation, but normal brain structure and connectivity (Woods *et al.*, 2005). Recessive mutations at six known loci lead to primary microcephaly (labeled *MCPH1–MCPH6*). Two of these genes, named *Microcephalin* (*MCPH1*) and *ASPM* ("abnormal spindle-type microcephaly associated," *MCPH5*), have recently been subjected to detailed analysis. The evidence for *Microcephalin* suggests that this gene plays an important role in regulating brain size, affecting the cell cycle in the proliferative zone of the developing nervous system during neurogenesis (Jackson *et al.*, 2002). Evolutionary analysis of coalescent times, and comparison with other primates, suggests powerful selection beginning in great apes, and intensifying in the lineage leading to modern humans, about 5–6 MYA (Evans *et al.*, 2004). Strong selection continued during the course of human evolution: on average three advantageous amino acids were driven to fixation every million years, and these genes remained under selection at least until ~37 KYA (Evans *et al.*, 2005; Mekel-Bobrov *et al.*, 2005); however, such estimates must be treated with caution (Woods *et al.*, 2005).

Thus, MCPH loci have many of the characteristics predicted for genes involved in the three-fold expansion of human brain size since the LCA. Unfortunately, MRI investigations of brain size provide no evidence that these genetic variants influence brain size in non-clinical populations, nor are variant MCPH alleles associated with IQ differences (Woods *et al.*, 2006; Mekel-Bobrov *et al.*, 2007). Thus, despite the clear role of MCPH mutations in causing decreased brain sized in modern humans, the function (if any) of modern variation in these genes remains unclear. Intriguingly, there is a correlation between alleles of these genes and the frequency of tonal languages across the world (Dediu and Ladd, 2007). The causal significance, if any, of this gene/language correlation remains unknown. These brain-size genes illustrate both the potential power of molecular approaches to human evolution, and also the difficulties of moving beyond correlational findings to concrete, mechanistic hypotheses. MCPH genes have considerable potential both to reveal the mechanisms of brain growth and reorganization in the human lineage, and to provide intriguing clues about the timing of these changes in human phylogeny.

7.16 Summary: from the LCA to modern *Homo sapiens*

In summary, hominid evolution took the form of a bush: many experiments were tried, and most failed in the long run. Human evolution was not a process of steady increase in brain size, body size, and technological mastery occurring in a single unbroken population of interbreeding hominids. Instead, most of human evolution has been characterized by multiple species of hominids living simultaneously. How they interacted, if at all, remains unknown. Each of these species had different ways of life, and each was successful for a long period of time. Early hominids were small-brained bipedal walkers by 3.6 MYA. From the early australopithecines we see two major increases in brain size: first with *Homo erectus* (= *ergaster*), who had attained modern body size in some cases but had a brain size around 800 cc (roughly halfway between a chimpanzee and modern human), and later with *Homo heidelbergensis*, who had attained modern human brain sizes around 1,200 cc.

Each of these different lines of hominids were making and using tools in a way that no other species ever has. Hominids became increasingly reliant upon such tools, and began to supplement their diet with meat more than any other primate. We know that at some point our ancestors developed cooperative group childcare, including a propensity for pair-bonding and male parental care, and the fossil data, combined with neuroscientific and metabolic considerations, strongly suggest that these changes were in place by the time of *Homo erectus*. Regarding language, we can say less. As we will see in Chapter 8, the organs underlying speech production do not fossilize, and warrant few inferences about vocal production abilities (much less language *per se*) in fossil hominids. Together, these data allow us to conclude that *Homo erectus* marked a qualitatively new form of hominid, cognitively intermediate between that of modern humans and the LCA, suggesting some form of "protolanguage" with certain characteristics of modern human language, but not others. Those who favor an early appearance of symbolic language (e.g. with *Homo erectus*) have trouble explaining why the Upper Paleolithic explosion of artistic, symbolic, and musical behaviors came so much later. But those who favor a late appearance of full language, in modern *Homo sapiens*, face a similar problem (with a lag of 100,000 years instead of 1 million), and also need to explain what Neanderthals were doing with their large brains for all that time. Regarding the specific nature of the protolanguage(s) of all of these extinct hominds, the fossils remain mute.

The evolution of speech

8.1 Speech is not language, but is important nonetheless

Speech (complex, articulated vocalization) is the default linguistic signaling mode for all human cultures, except when the audio-vocal modality is unavailable, as for the deaf. Though speech is the default linguistic modality, it is not the only possibility. Signed languages of the deaf are full, complex, grammatical languages, independent of but equivalent to spoken languages (Stokoe, 1960; Klima and Bellugi, 1979), and this demonstrates that *speech is not the only signaling system adequate to convey language*. Writing is another example of a visuo-manual system of linguistic communication, but since writing systems are typically "parasitic" representations of spoken systems, they illustrate the multi-modality of language less convincingly. One of the first distinctions to be made in studying language evolution is therefore that between **speech** (a signaling system) and **language** (a system for expressing thoughts, which can incorporate any one of several signaling systems). Many languages use the same word to designate both speech and language (e.g. German *Sprache*), and in English one often finds the word *speech* used as an exact synonym for *language*, showing how close these concepts are in everyday use. Throughout this book, I will use "speech" only in the narrow sense of *complex articulated vocalizations*, where "articulated" implies tight coordination between the supralaryngeal vocal tract and the larynx. Besides linguistic speech, other examples of articulated vocalization include infant babbling, "speaking in tongues," nonsense speech, jazz scat singing, or Asian formant singing. All of these examples show that complex vocalization can sometimes be decoupled from meaning, and be treated as a signal, pure and simple. In this chapter we will consider the biology and evolution of speech in this sense, starting with its production, and then discussing perception.

If speech must be distinguished from language, why discuss speech in a book about language evolution? There are several good reasons. First, as already stressed, speech *is* the default signaling system for all human cultures, all over the world, and there is no evidence that this has ever been otherwise (it is unlikely that deaf individuals survived in adequate numbers to form communities until very recently in human evolution; Stokoe, 1960). The language faculty (broad sense) has thus traditionally relied upon the speech modality heavily, and was probably influenced by this modality. Second, many authors have discussed the "special" nature of speech, either at the level of speech production or speech perception, hypothesizing that various aspects of speech are part of the uniquely human component(s) of language. Third, a perennial hypothesis in language evolution is that speech is the critical "missing ingredient" keeping animals from language. The idea that some aspect of peripheral morphology allows (or disallows) speech has been discussed by numerous authors (Camper, 1779; Darwin, 1871; DuBrul, 1958; Kelemen, 1969; Lieberman *et al.*, 1969; Lieberman, 2007b), and thus is probably the oldest and most persistent hypothesis in the entire field of language evolution. Other researchers have taken human vocal tract reconfiguration as the key change that spurred other aspects of language, including syllable structure, syntax, or even semantic reference (e.g. Lieberman, 1984; Carstairs-McCarthy, 1999).

Finally, recent discussions of language evolution often focus on speech because it is the only aspect of language for which we have some hope of fossil evidence, based on reconstructions of vocal tract anatomy (e.g. Donald, 1991). I will argue in this chapter that comparative data make this hope appear increasingly tenuous, and that we cannot reconstruct the vocal tracts, or speech capabilities, of extinct hominids with any confidence. While this negative outcome may be disappointing (it certainly was to me), it nicely illustrates a basic theme of this book: a huge amount remains to be learned from empirical, comparative studies of living animals. The comparative physiology of vocal production allows rigorous, empirical studies, whose results fuel real scientific progress, but we will see that many central questions remain open.

Recent progress in understanding the evolution of speech has been helped considerably by our solid understanding of the physics of speech production. The field of speech science is perhaps the only language science where the core phenomena have been successfully analyzed and understood, through repeated cycles of theorizing and hypothesis testing, to a level of mathematical rigor that typifies the physical sciences. Researchers interested in the evolution of speech can stand on the shoulders of previous generations of researchers in speech acoustics and physiology, and base their hypotheses on well-understood physics. The evolution of speech is not only a key aspect of language evolution, but also illustrates the value of an empirical, comparative approach. For all these reasons I explore the evolution of speech in considerable detail here.

8.2 Vertebrate vocal production: basic bioacoustics

While the comparative anatomy of the vocal tract was already well understood by the 1930s (Gaupp, 1904; Schneider, 1964), a solid understanding of vocal acoustics had to wait until the mid-twentieth century (Chiba and Kajiyama, 1941; Fant, 1960; Titze, 1994; Ladefoged, 2001). This temporal mismatch had unfortunate consequences for our understanding of bioacoustics and animal vocal production: the anatomy was described before its acoustic functioning was understood. The older literature is filled with excellent descriptions of comparative anatomy accompanied by incorrect and antiquated ideas about acoustics. The result, today, is three largely disjunct literatures in anatomy, speech acoustics, and bioacoustics. The unification and reconciliation of these literatures is still ongoing (cf. Fitch and Hauser, 2002; Fitch, 2004b, 2006a). An understanding of these basics is a crucial prerequisite to evaluating possible fossil cues to speech.

Vocal production is based on the same acoustic principles in almost all tetrapods, including amphibians, reptiles, birds, and mammals. The basic anatomical components are illustrated in Figure 8.1. First, the source of energy that drives vocalization is provided by a respiratory **airstream** from the lungs. Second, this flow is converted to sound by tissue vibrations of the voice **source** (in humans, and most vertebrates, the vibrating vocal folds, or "vocal cords"). The rate of vocal fold vibration, called the **fundamental frequency**, determines the pitch of the vocalization. Third, this source sound is acoustically **filtered** by the air in the vocal tract (the pharyngeal, oral, and nasal cavities), which imposes a second distinct set of frequencies onto the vocalization, called **formant frequencies.** These formant frequencies are independently controllable by movements of the vocal tract (especially the lips, jaws, and tongue). Critically, ordinary vocalizations are characterized by *many different frequency components*, which have independent origins and are thus independently controllable. Thus it is meaningless to discuss "the frequency" of a vocalization – we must specify which frequency we mean. In particular, we need to distinguish the fundamental frequency and its harmonics (properties of the *source* that determine the pitch) from formant frequencies (properties of the vocal tract filter, and correlates of voice timbre). I emphasize this distinction at the outset because it is often

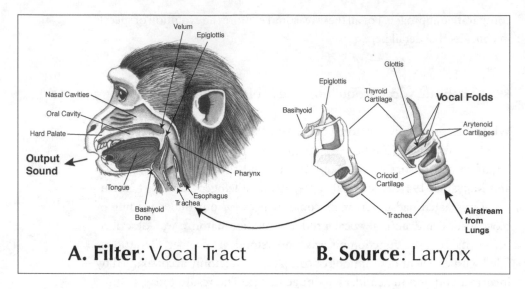

A. Filter: Vocal Tract   **B. Source**: Larynx

Figure 8.1 Basic mammalian vocal anatomy – The anatomy of a rhesus macaque illustrates the standard mammalian vocal production system, based on the principles of the source/filter theory. The basic anatomy, and the physical principles, are shared with humans. On the right, air from the lungs passes through the larynx. This makes the vocal folds vibrate, acting as the source of acoustic energy. On the left, the air contained in the vocal tract acts to filter the resulting sounds. The sound output incorporates aspects of both source and filter.

confusing, and sometimes mischaracterized even in the primary literature. Let us consider these components in more detail.

8.2.1 The pulmonary airstream

The energy driving vertebrate vocalization is provided by an airstream exiting (or, less frequently, entering) the lungs. The preponderance of expiratory vocalization is important, because expiration is mainly caused by the passive deflation of the elastic lungs. Because the active energy-consuming process of inhalation is required for respiration and is thus a necessity for life, the expiratory airstream is available "for free" and needn't have any additional physiological cost (Fitch and Hauser, 2002). People can talk all day without using appreciable energy (Moon and Lindblom, 2003). Although the energy needed for loud vocalizations (like opera singing in humans, or loud bird or frog vocalizations) may extract a noticeable physiological cost, simple quiet speech does not. Other ways to generate an airstream without using the lungs (e.g. creating a vacuum in the oral cavity to make a "click" or "tsk tsk" sound, or "lip smacking" in some nonhuman primates) are quiet, and rare in both human and animal vocalizations. The use of inspiratory vocalization is more common. Many mammal calls, such as donkey braying or chimpanzee pant hoots, have audible components on both exhalation and inhalation, and both human laughter and baby crying sometimes have inspiratory components. Finally, inspiratory vocalization during speech is rare but not impossible (the word for "yes" in both Swedish and French is sometimes produced during inspiration). Exceptions aside, the vast majority of human vocalizations are generated by an airstream exiting the lungs, and at a remarkably low physiological cost.

8.2.2 The voice source

The next step in vertebrate vocal production is the conversion of the airstream into sound. This occurs in the **sound source**, typically the larynx. A simple way to generate sound is to create an obstruction in the airflow that creates **turbulence**, which we hear as noise (an aperiodic sound with energy at a wide range of unrelated frequencies). The /s/ sound involves turbulence at the tongue tip, while turbulence during animal hissing or human whispering is generated by a constriction in the larynx. Interestingly, hissing is found in some form in all tetrapod groups, and even organisms that make no tonal sounds can hiss (such as some snakes). Hissing may thus be the most basic and primitive vocal sound. However, the evolution of the larynx as a protective gateway to the lungs provided the mechanism for a second, more common mode of sound production, termed **phonation**. In phonation, elastic tissue is set into motion by flowing air, and it is this tissue motion that generates sound. In most vertebrates, including frogs, alligators, dogs, or humans, the vibrating tissues are the **vocal folds** within the larynx. Birds have different sound sources: vibrating membranes housed in the *syrinx*, located at the base of the trachea, within the chest (see Figure 9.3). The syrinx is found only in birds, which have a larynx but do not use it in phonation (Marler and Slabbekoorn, 2004). The toothed whales (e.g. dolphins, orcas, or sperm whales) have evolved a different novel sound source, this time located in the nasal region below the blowhole (Tyack and Miller, 2002). These novel sound sources may have implications for the evolution of vocal imitation in these groups, discussed later. But in humans and terrestrial mammals, vibrating vocal folds in the larynx act as the sound source, just as in frogs or alligators.

This modern understanding of vocal fold physics and physiology is termed the **myoelastic-aerodynamic theory** of phonation (van den Berg,

1958; Titze, 1994). The first basic principle is that phonation is neurally passive: periodic vibration in the vocal tissue does not require periodic neural firing. Thus, normal phonation can be generated in a fresh larynx excised from the body. Once the vocal folds are brought close to one another, and air is blown through the glottis (the opening between them), they will vibrate at a frequency determined by their length, density, and tension. Thus, neural control of vocalization is generally limited to changing the "posture" of the larynx and vocal folds: opening and closing the glottis, modifying their shape, or increasing or decreasing their tension. There is no requirement for muscle contraction, or nervous firing, at the vibration frequency. This is in contrast to some fish sounds, where muscular excitation of the balloon-like swim bladder is used to generate calls (Bass and Baker, 1997), and thus requires active neural firing and muscle contraction at the vibration frequency. The neurally passive nature of vertebrate phonation allows us to produce vocalizations at far higher vibration rates than would otherwise be possible, including ultrasonic sounds, beyond the human hearing range, produced by some mammals like bats or rodents, involving frequencies of between 20 and 100 kHz (kiloHertz – 1,000 cycles per second) (Zimmermann, 1981; Holy and Guo, 2005).

The rate at which the vocal folds vibrate is termed the **fundamental frequency** (or F0) and it is the primary determinant of the perceived **pitch** of a vocalization. Voice pitch can be controlled by changing vocal fold length and tension. The fundamental is the lowest and often the strongest frequency component of a periodic signal, but most vocalizations also contain additional frequency components, termed overtones, or **harmonics**, that are directly dependent upon this frequency. Harmonics occur at exact integer multiples of the fundamental frequency. For example, a male voice with an F0 of 100 Hz will have harmonics at 200, 300, and 400, . . . Hz, while a high soprano sung note at 1 kHz will have harmonics at 2, 3, 4, . . . kHz. Thus, each harmonic is spaced from its nearest neighbors by an amount equal to the fundamental frequency. This mathematical fact has an interesting implication for pitch perception. Because both fundamental and overtones are direct results of the vibration rate of the source, they change in perfect synchrony, and thus provide redundant information: if you know the fundamental you can predict the other harmonics, and *vice versa*. Studies of pitch perception make clear that the auditory system takes account of this redundancy automatically, "inferring" a fundamental *even if that frequency is not present in the acoustic signal* (the "missing fundamental"; Moore, 1988).

Pitch is one of the most salient attributes of a voiced sound, and plays an important role in many aspects of vertebrate vocal communication, including human music and speech (e.g. Ohala, 1983a). Because F0 is determined by the length, density, and tension of the vocal folds, the lowest notes are made when tension is at a minimum, and their frequency is determined by the length of the vocal folds. An adult man's voice is lower than a woman's because the vibrating portion of the vocal folds are almost twice as long in males (Titze, 1989). This difference leads to male fundamentals around 110 Hz and females nearly twice as high, around 200 Hz. This elongation of the male vocal folds occurs at puberty, under the influence of testosterone, and is one component of the pubertal "voice change" (Kahane, 1982; Harries *et al.*, 1998). The non-overlapping voice pitch of men and women allows us to almost instantly identify adult gender by voice alone. This sexual dimorphism is a rather peculiar feature of the human voice: in many species (including chimpanzees and most primates) there are no such obvious dimorphisms in voice pitch. Sexual dimorphism in voice pitch represents one of several peculiarities of the human vocal apparatus that have evolved since our divergence from chimpanzees. Because of this sexually selected growth in the source at puberty, there is (counter-intuitively) *no significant correlation* between the pitch of an adult man's voice and his body size (van Dommelen, 1993). This is contrary to the widespread notion that F0 *must* be an indexical cue to body size (Morton, 1977). Oddly enough, human subjects still act as if there *is* such a correlation, and treat voice pitch, along with formants, as a cue to body size in perceptual experiments (Fitch, 1994; Smith *et al.*, 2005). This faulty perception may represent evolutionary inertia, or perhaps an inappropriate extension of learned experience.

8.2.3 The vocal tract filter

The sound generated at the source is already complex (with its fundamental frequency and harmonics), but an additional layer of complexity is laid on by the third component of the vocal apparatus: the supralaryngeal **vocal tract**. The vocal tract consists of the pharyngeal (throat), oral (mouth), and nasal (nose) cavities. The air within these cavities can vibrate at multiple different frequencies (the *normal modes* or *resonances* of the air column). (Picture a cube of jelly jiggling when smacked with a spoon for an image of how something can vibrate at multiple frequencies at once.) Each individual vibration frequency is called a **formant frequency**, and the overall vibration

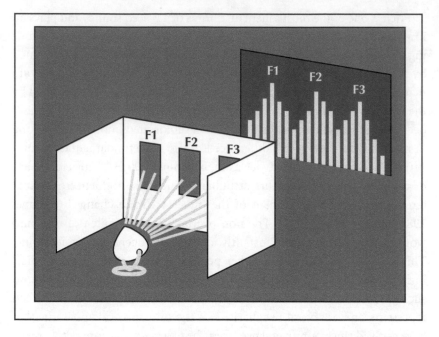

Figure 8.2 Formant "house" – A metaphor illustrating the source/filter theory of vocal production. Formants act as "windows" that allow certain frequencies to exit from the vocal tract. The source, like the lights within a house, determine what energy is available to escape. The formants filters these source frequencies, so the signal that escapes is strongest where the formants are located.

pattern of the air column is characterized by multiple formant frequencies, together called the *vocal tract transfer function*. The vibrating air in the vocal tract **filters** the complex signal traveling up from the source, thus imposing its formant frequencies onto this source signal. Each formant can be thought of as a "spectral window" that preferentially allows acoustic energy from the source to pass through it. The formants act as *band-pass filters*, letting some frequencies pass through and blocking others. Just as the type of light within a house (candlelight, neon disco ball, etc.) affects what is seen outside, the quality of the source affects the final output signal. The output sound combines the quality of the original source sound and that of the filter function (see Figure 8.2).

Vocal tract length (the distance the sound travels from the larynx out to the lips) is the single most important parameter controlling formant frequencies: longer vocal tracts have lower formant frequencies. This basic acoustic fact has some interesting implications for the information conveyed by vocalizations, discussed later in this chapter.

Formant frequencies are independent of the various frequencies that characterize the source. As already discussed, source frequencies (the fundamental frequency and its associated harmonics) determine the *pitch* of the voice. In contrast, formants have no effect on pitch, but are one important component of **voice timbre**. A voice with low formants will have a more baritone timbre, while high formants lead to a brighter or sharper timbre. There is unfortunately no colloquial word that specifically singles out the perceptual correlates of formants, but we are all intimately familiar with what formants sound like, because they are the most crucial acoustic cue in speech. If you sing at a constant pitch while producing different vowels (e.g. /i/, /a/, /o/, /u/), the difference you hear is entirely the difference in formant frequencies.

A vocalizing vertebrate can change its formant frequencies by changing the shape of its vocal tract. A mewing cat opens and closes its mouth, changing formant frequencies to create vowel-like "miaow" sounds (Carterette *et al.*, 1984). More subtle changes in formants can be generated by such maneuvers as pursing the lips to slightly lengthen the vocal tract, or retracting them to shorten it (Ohala, 1984). But even in the absence of such movements, the vocal tract imposes its formants upon the vocalization. Any time an animal vocalizes, even if it keeps its vocal tract fixed, its formant frequencies filter the vocalization. However, changes in the length and shape of the vocal tract play a central role in human speech production. The various organs and muscles that play a role in such shape changes in speech are called the **vocal tract articulators**, and include the lips, jaw, tongue, velum (soft palate), and pharynx. Several vocal tract articulators are uniquely well developed in mammals, including the lips, tongue, cheeks, and velum. Because these features are shared by most mammals, they must have evolved in ancestral mammals some 200 MYA, and they are thought to be key components of the adaptive suite surrounding suckling and lactation (Wall and Smith, 2001). Indeed, these articulators are tied to the highly complex reflex of mammalian swallowing, which involves some twenty-five muscles, controlled by five different cranial nerves, and already functions in a human embryo by three months gestational age. Because swallowing is the basic and primitive function of the vocal tract, both phylogenetically and ontogenetically, any changes in the vocal tract in human evolution must have been tightly constrained by the need to swallow, since speech is built upon this ancient neuromuscular system (MacNeilage, 1998b). Since these structures themselves are mostly derived from the gill bars of our ancient aquatic ancestors, we can see that the human vocal apparatus has gone through several cycles of preadaptation and exaptation during its evolution.

8.2.4 Independence of source and filter in vocal production

Summarizing, vocalizations are produced by a source, which converts air-flow into sound, modified by a filter, which filters or "sculpts" this signal with a set of formant frequencies. These two components are generated by two anatomically separate structures. The source determines the pitch of the sound, while vibrations of the air contained in the vocal tract determine the formant frequencies. The **source–filter theory of vocal production** holds that these two components are, to a good first approximation, acoustically independent (Chiba and Kajiyama, 1941; Fant, 1960). This simply means that you can generate any vowel at any pitch, and *vice versa*. Since its introduction in the field of speech science, this theory has been tested and verified repeatedly from many different empirical perspectives, and is accepted as a fundamental model for the production of human speech and song (Fant, 1960; Lieberman and Blumstein, 1988). More recently source–filter theory has been applied to other vertebrates, including a variety of frogs, birds, and mammals, where it appears to be equally typical (Paulsen, 1967; Fitch and Hauser, 2002). Thus, independence of source and filter appears to be a widespread feature of vocalization in vertebrates.

The significance of the source–filter theory is best illustrated by the broad class of acoustic systems to which it *does not* apply: musical wind instruments. Source and filter are not independent in a wind instrument. Wind instruments such as trombones or clarinets are structurally similar to a vocal tract: there is a vibratory "source" (the reed of the clarinet, or the trumpeter's lips) whose vibration rate controls the pitch of the sound played. The sound it generates then passes through the air contained in the body of the instrument. This air column is analogous to the vocal tract in that it includes several resonant frequencies, like formants, and these frequencies are determined by the length of the air column. But here the analogy ends, for in a wind instrument the frequencies of the air column feed back upon the vibratory source, controlling its rate of vibration. We say that source and tract are **coupled** in a wind instrument, and many details of wind instrument design enhance and stabilize this coupling (Fletcher and Rossing, 1991). This allows the instrumentalist to be rather sloppy in the control of the source signal, because the air tube, via its resonant frequencies, stabilizes the source vibration and the system as a whole generates a controlled, constant frequency tone. The instrumentalist can control this pitch precisely by changing the length of the air column or by drastically changing the tension of the source (this is how a wind instrument like the bugle, which has a fixed length, can produce several notes). In either case, though, the note ultimately produced is determined by the system as a whole, and resonances and source vibration are not independent.

Is it really true that all animal vocalizations lack source–filter coupling? Such a statement would be premature at present, given our very early stage of understanding, and I would be extremely surprised if there are not *some* species or call types in which strong source–tract coupling occurs. But accepting that source–tract coupling is rare in animal vocalization, why should this be? Why should virtually all wind instruments work one way, and all animal vocal systems another? One plausible reason is nicely illustrated by human speech: in uncoupled systems, the source and filter provide two different, and independently controllable, types of information. Also, the vocal tract is relatively inflexible compared to the larynx, and so the wide pitch range allowed by laryngeal control would be more limited if source–tract coupling were present. For whatever reason, the source–filter theory of vocalization accounts for all currently known animal vocalizations, and thus the principles that underlie human speech production rest upon a widely-shared and ancient acoustic and anatomical foundation.

8.3 The reconfigured human vocal tract

8.3.1 People are strange

Bioacoustics and the source–filter theory provide the necessary context for understanding a key peculiarity of human vocal anatomy, one that has been extensively discussed in the literature on language evolution: the **descent of the larynx** (see Figure 8.3). In most mammals, the tongue lies essentially flat in the oral cavity, with the tongue root anchored just below the bottom edge of the jaw, and the larynx just below that. The mammalian larynx is partially protected by the epiglottis, a hinged flap of cartilage that normally extends above the larynx, but closes over the opening of the glottis like a protective roof during the swallowing of solid foods (see Figure 8.1). But the rest of the time, during normal breathing, the epiglottis contacts the velum (sometimes extending quite far into the nasal cavity) to form a seal between the back portion of the nasal cavity and the larynx. This allows many mammals to breathe through their nose, while simultaneously swallowing saliva or liquids *around* the larynx and into the esophagus. The "breathing tube" (from nostrils, through the larynx, into the lungs) is separate from the "feeding tube" (from lips, around the larynx, into the stomach). This is

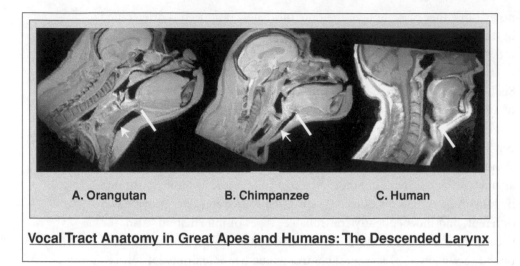

A. Orangutan   **B. Chimpanzee**   **C. Human**

<u>**Vocal Tract Anatomy in Great Apes and Humans: The Descended Larynx**</u>

Figure 8.3 Vocal tract anatomy in orangutan, chimpanzee, and human: MRI (magnetic resonance imaging) images illustrate the "descent of the larynx" and change in tongue shape that occurred at some point during human evolution. The two ape species on the left show the typical resting vocal configuration seen in most mammals, with the larynx high and the tongue resting mostly flat in the oral cavity. The white bar shows hyoid position; the arrows point to the air sacs in the two apes.

particularly important in infant mammals, for it allows them to suckle and breathe at the same time, and can be seen as an adaptation to lactation and suckling (Wall and Smith, 2001). Humans start life just like other mammals, with a high larynx, and a human infant can suckle and swallow while leaving the larynx in a high, sealed position, drastically decreasing its chances of choking on milk. But at about age three months, the larynx begins to slowly descend from this position, and by the age of four years has reached a low position where the nasolaryngeal seal is no longer possible (Sasaki *et al.*, 1977). In adult humans the larynx has descended to a position far below the hard palate, and we can no longer even touch the epiglottis to the velum, much less insert it to form a sealed breathing tube. If we adult humans inhale while swallowing, we choke (sometimes to death; Heimlich, 1975).

Given its centrality in many discussions of language evolution (e.g. Laitman and Heimbuch, 1982; Wind, 1983; Lieberman, 1984; Pinker, 1994b; Carstairs-McCarthy, 1999), this unusual human characteristic warrants detailed attention. Other aspects of human vocal anatomy have changed since our divergence from chimpanzees: we gained a sexually-dimorphic larynx and we lost the laryngeal air sacs present in all of the other great apes (Fitch, 2000b). But the issue of the "descent of the larynx" has played a far more central role in recent debates about language evolution.

The idea that peripheral anatomy allows, or prevents, speech is a very old one. Aristotle, noting the intelligence of dolphins, suggested that their inability to speak resulted directly from vocal anatomy: "its tongue is not loose, nor has it lips, so as to give utterance to an articulate sound" (Aristotle, 350 BC). Eighteenth-century Dutch anatomist Peter Camper suggested that the air sacs of orangutans prevented speech in great apes (Camper, 1779). The central question was framed nicely by Jan Wind: "let us assume that a whole chimpanzee vocal tract would be transplanted into a human individual, while its nervous system would remain human" (p. 626, Wind, 1976). What would be the speech output capabilities of such a hybrid? Wind himself concluded it would be little different from a modern human, a conclusion shared by Darwin (Darwin, 1871). Others have argued that a modern human vocal tract is necessary for modern human speech (Lieberman *et al.*, 1972; Laitman and Reidenberg, 1988), and many have found these arguments convincing (e.g. Donald, 1991; Pinker, 1994b; Carstairs-McCarthy, 1999). Today, the field is divided on the topic, but the majority of researchers accept the idea that a chimpanzee's phonetic potential is considerably reduced, purely due to its peripheral vocal anatomy – and would be even were a human brain in control. Of course, scientific truth is not determined by majority vote. My goal in the following sections is to review what is known, in enough detail to allow readers to reach their own well-informed opinion.

The adult human vocal tract has long been known to be unusual compared to other mammals: our larynx lies lower in the throat than that of a dog, cat, rabbit, or chimpanzee (Symington, 1885; Bowles, 1889). Indeed, until quite recently (Fitch and Reby, 2001), this descended larynx was believed to be unique to our species (e.g. Negus, 1949; Wind, 1970); it still appears to be unique among primates. Since Darwin, it has been remarked that having a lowered larynx should increase our chances of choking, since every food particle swallowed must pass over the glottal opening (Darwin, 1859). This apparent increased cost of choking should have quickly been selected out unless balanced by some countervailing selective advantage and, until quite recently, speech provided the only plausible advantage of the descended larynx. Specifically, the hypothesis is that the descended larynx increases the phonetic range of our vocal apparatus (Lieberman *et al.*, 1969). The reconfigured human vocal tract has thus long been seen, unequivocally, as an adaptation for human spoken language. This hypothesis raises an intriguing additional possibility: that we could infer something about the appearance of speech (and thus of language) by reconstructing the vocal tract of extinct hominids, using fossil cues to larynx position (Lieberman and Crelin, 1971; Lieberman *et al.*, 1972; Crelin, 1987).

Given the scarcity of alternative clues to language evolution in the fossil record, Lieberman's hypothesis has attracted considerable attention. There are few issues as widely discussed (and as often misunderstood) as this one in the contemporary literature on language origins. In understanding these debates it is necessary to distinguish the reconfiguration of the human vocal tract (which is an uncontested anatomical fact), and the significance of this reconfiguration for modern speech production (which is widely, but not universally, accepted), from attempts to pinpoint the timing of this change based on fossils (which remain highly controversial; e.g. Boë *et al.*, 2002). I will first discuss the anatomical changes and their significance for speech, and then review some of the recent comparative data that bear on the question, before turning in the last section to fossil reconstruction.

8.3.2 The role of the descended larynx in speech

To understand the significance of the reconfigured vocal tract for speech, we must return to the role of formants and vowels in human speech. The multiple formants in animal vocal tracts act as filters on the source signal. A simple uniform tube will have resonance frequencies evenly spaced in frequency, with the *length* of the tube determining formant frequencies. But any changes in the *shape* of the tube during vocalization will perturb this even spacing, shifting formant frequencies up or down depending on the shape. This principle is nicely illustrated by the first "speech synthesizer" built by von Kempelen in 1780 (Dudley and Tarnoczy, 1950). The machine used a vibrating reed to generate a source signal, rich in harmonics, but alone this signal simply sounded like a duck quacking. This source signal was then passed through a flexible rubber tube which acted as the vocal tract. By squeezing the tube and thus manipulating its shape, von Kempelen could generate different formant frequency patterns that sounded like the different vowel sounds. The device followed a principle precisely analogous to speech, except that we modify the shape of our vocal tract by moving our lips, jaw, and tongue around. By thus modifying vocal tract shape, we can change specific formant frequencies semi-independently. Speech consists essentially of rapid controlled movements of the vocal tract, and the corresponding rapid changes in formants.

Although formants are present in many animal vocalizations, and animals are sensitive to formant patterns, *rapid change in formant frequencies* is the distinguishing feature of speech, and is taken to an extreme in our species.

This is *not* because animals are anatomically incapable of changing their vocal tract shape. Many animals open or close their jaw in the course of a call (e.g. cats, as already mentioned; Carterette *et al.*, 1984), and changes in lip position are almost as common (Hauser and Schön Ybarra, 1994). But much more complex changes would, in principle, be possible (Fitch, 2000c). For example, the vocal tract goes through very significant shape changes during chewing, swallowing, and suckling, and if a dog or pig were to vocalize while making these movements, formant changes similar to speech would result. I have occasionally heard dogs, deer, or other animals vocalize while moving their tongue for other reasons (e.g. a dog growling while chewing) and audible formant changes result. But other mammals rarely make significant use of this latent capability in their communication systems. Thus, the simple observation that dogs do not speak tells us nothing about whether the cause of this is peripheral (vocal tract anatomy) or central (involving neural control of the vocal tract).

The tongue is a flexible structure, capable of changing its shape in extraordinary ways, but it is not infinitely flexible (Kier and Smith, 1985). In particular, there is no way to make abrupt step-like changes along the length of the tongue. This constrains the vocal tract shapes that a normal mammalian tongue, resting in the oral cavity, can make. The tongue can move up and down as a whole, but this will still generate an essentially cylindrical vocal tract shape with no significant changes to formants. By moving the tongue tip up while keeping the tongue root down (or *vice versa*), that animal could make a basically conical shape which changes formants to some degree (Carterette *et al.*, 1984); and adding changes in lip position gives additional flexibility. Indeed, with a human brain in control, even such a constrained vocal tract could most probably make a variety of consonants and vowels – considerably wider than the range actually observed in any nonhuman mammal. But Lieberman and colleagues argued that the one thing such a vocal tract could *not* do is produce the so-called "point vowels" – the vowels (/i, a, u/) that involve the most extreme formant values (Lieberman *et al.*, 1969). This observation is made more significant by the fact that such vowels are a human universal found in virtually every language of the world (Maddieson, 1984).

In order to make extreme changes in formant frequencies, we need to make extreme changes in the area of the vocal tube. Very abrupt changes (on the order of ten to one) are required to obtain the extreme values seen in vowels like /i/ or /u/ (Carré *et al.*, 1995). Such extremes are impossible to achieve with a stiff tube, or in a vocal tract where the relatively stiff tongue rests entirely in the oral cavity. The trick we use to achieve such abrupt changes is to permanently retract the tongue root downward, into the pharynx (which by necessity pushes the larynx downward as well). The front part of the tongue remains in the mouth opposite the palate, and up and down motions of the entire tongue can widen or narrow this portion of the vocal tract (for example, it is nearly closed for the vowel /i/ and wide open for the vowel /a/). But now, the retracted base of the tongue is further down in the throat, across from the posterior pharyngeal wall. This lower, pharyngeal portion of the vocal tract provides a whole new dimension: by moving the tongue backwards and forwards this lower tube can be *independently* modified (this arrangement is thus dubbed a "two-tube" tract). The pharyngeal tube is wide open in an /i/ vowel, and nearly closed for an /a/. Thus, the descent of the tongue root and larynx provides an additional degree of freedom, a new dimension of control, compared to the capabilities inferred for a normal mammalian tract. In particular, this reconfiguration crucially allows abrupt transitions in vocal tract area to be achieved at the junction between the oral and pharyngeal tubes, even with little deformation of the tongue, and changes of this magnitude are needed to produce the point vowels (Lieberman *et al.*, 1969; Carré *et al.*, 1995).

As this discussion should make clear, it is really the descent of the tongue root (and the basihyoid bone that serves as its support) that is the critical factor in speech production, rather than the descent of the larynx *per se*. The larynx could descend without a corresponding descent of the tongue root (indeed, this occurs in some deer species, as discussed below), and this would not have the critical effect on phonetic potential that we have just discussed. But because the larynx is suspended from the basihyoid bone, there is no way that the hyoid can descend without pushing the larynx down with it. In hindsight, then, it is more accurate to discuss the descent of the hyoid, or better yet, the descent of the tongue root, when discussing the critical factor in the evolutionary reconfiguration of the human vocal tract, and I will use the neutral term "reconfigured vocal tract" here. This first component of Lieberman's hypothesis is well grounded in empirical observations about speech in living humans. The next step attempts to apply these observations to fossil hominids.

8.3.3 Application to fossil hominids

Lieberman and colleagues argued, based on fossil reconstructions, that the larynx descended very late in hominid evolution, with *Homo sapiens*. Most controversially, they suggested that Neanderthals lacked speech like our own. But a change of this sort would not have any adaptive value in a species that does not already make use of formant changes in its vocalizations: without a formant-based communication system already in place, there would have been no point in reconfiguring the vocal tract. Thus, Lieberman and colleagues argued that hominids *must* have had some form of speech before the descent of the larynx. This point has often been misunderstood or misrepresented (Arensburg *et al.*, 1990; Boë *et al.*, 2002). The first paper on the topic was entitled "On the speech of Neanderthal man" (Lieberman and Crelin, 1971), and Lieberman *et al.* (1972) state that Neanderthals "lacked a well developed vocal mechanism but... undoubtedly must have had a 'language.' The remains of Neanderthal culture all point to the presence of linguistic ability" (p. 302). A footnote in the same paper makes the logic of this point clear: "Note that the prior existence of a form of language is a necessary condition for the retention... of mutations like the human pharyngeal region that enhance the rate of communication but are detrimental with regard to deglutition and respiration" (p. 305). As I will discuss below, the discovery of animals with reconfigured vocal tracts but no speech vitiates the force of this argument. But this provides no excuse to misstate the original claim: despite frequent misconceptions, Lieberman has never claimed that Neanderthals had no form of language (Lieberman, 2007b).

The specific claim was that "the speech of Neanderthal man did not make use of syllabic encoding" (p. 302, Lieberman *et al.*, 1972) and that "Neanderthal man's linguistic abilities were at best suited to communication at slow rates and at worst markedly inferior at the syntactic and semantic levels to modern man's linguistic ability." Understanding "syllabic encoding" requires some discussion of human speech perception (cf. Lieberman, 1984). The essential argument hinges around the hypothesis that, like speech production, speech perception is special (Liberman, 1996). Speech is distinguished from most other sound streams by its rapidity, and the rate of phonemes in ordinary speech appears to outstrip the rate of any other sounds we perceive (Liberman *et al.*, 1967). Early attempts to make reading machines for the blind employed arbitrary sounds like buzzes and beeps to represent individual letters. These machines were dismal failures: at a rate approaching that of speech, such sounds simply blur into a continuous cacophony (exceeding the fusion rate of the human auditory system). In contrast, when the sounds were played slowly enough to be individually perceptible, an ordinary sentence took so long to encode that its beginning had been forgotten before the end was reached. After producing the world's first electronic speech synthesizer, the Haskins researchers proposed that speech somehow overcomes this rate limit, and were the first to suggest that speech perception is somehow special. Further research suggested that speech achieves high information transfer rates via a "coding" process: the speaker "**encodes**" phonemes into syllables (which are produced slower than the rate of fusion of the auditory system). The listener then "decodes" syllables back into phonemes (or further, into distinctive features) by specialized speech perceptual mechanisms. Thus, the Haskins workers suggested, human speech production and perception, working together, exceed a hard limit set by our auditory systems. This is what is meant by "syllabic encoding" in the previous quote.

The other twist in understanding vocal tract reconfiguration has been emphasized by Lieberman in recent years: the special status of the vowel /i/. A skeptic of the hypothesis as discussed thus far might point out that there are many thousands of words in most languages that don't contain point vowels, and that any animal vocal tract should be adequate to produce all of these words. The fact that all humans produce such vowels doesn't make them necessary – they might just be accidental byproducts of a vocal tract lowered for other, independent reasons. To this Lieberman replies that one of these point vowels, /i/, is special (sometimes termed a "supervowel"; Nearey, 1978). This vowel is made at an extreme position of the vocal tract, with the tongue pulled as far forward and up as is possible without inducing turbulent airflow. Because of this, the /i/ vowel is uniquely identifiable in blind listening tests. More importantly, Lieberman argues, this vowel plays a central role in **vocal tract normalization**, the process whereby we adjust our perceptual expectations to the specific vocal tract length of a speaker. Because of the considerable variation in body size, people vary considerably in vocal tract length. This means that different-sized individuals producing the "same" vowel (the same vocal tract shape) actually produce acoustic signals that are quite different. Conversely, two identical signals will be perceived differently depending on the speaker from whom they emanate (Ladefoged and Broadbent, 1957; Fant, 1975). However, an /i/ vowel, being at the extreme edge of the phonetic space, does not suffer this confusion. Perhaps as a result, it seems to have a preferential role in cueing vocal tract length and body size judgments (Fitch, 1994). Lieberman concludes that the significance of the "supervowel" /i/, and the vocal tract that can produce it, goes beyond simply enlarging the phonetic repertoire somewhat, and that it in fact plays a central role in modern human speech perception.

It should now be clear why the reconfiguration of the human vocal tract relative to most mammals has played such a central role in discussions of the evolution of speech. Summarizing, humans have an unusual vocal tract, thought to increase our chance of choking. Lieberman and colleagues provided a carefully reasoned adaptive function for speech which could balance this negative selection. Not only does the descended larynx enlarge our phonetic repertoire, but it does so in a way that enhances speech encoding and decoding (thus allowing us to exceed the normal limit of information transfer in the auditory system), and it give us the point vowels that are found in all human languages, particularly the "supervowel" /i/, which plays a central role in vocal tract normalization. Assuming that the only apparent use for a descended larynx is in speech, this hypothesis provided grounds for analyzing the speech abilities of extinct hominids from their fossil remains. Every step of this argument makes logical sense, and is based on empirical data from rather diverse sources, including comparative anatomy, speech acoustics, and research on speech perception. In short, this was a hypothesis that seemed to move research on the evolution of spoken language from the domain of fairy tales to that of serious, testable, science, and was an important factor in reviving discussions of language evolution from fifty years of slumber. The only problem with this hypothesis, in hindsight, is that it was based on an inadequate comparative database. Despite some preliminary analyses of formants in primate vocalizations (Lieberman, 1968), very little was known about vocal production in other mammals until recently. We now turn to these studies. Because I was personally involved, I relate this work in a more narrative form.

8.4 The comparative data I: mammal vocal production

8.4.1 Dynamic reconfiguration of the mammalian vocal tract

Virtually all treatises on vocal anatomy and mammals have relied upon the dissection of dead animals (cf. Bowles, 1889; Negus, 1929; Kelemen, 1963). Discussions of vocal potential thus rested on the implicit assumption that the anatomy of a dead animal is an accurate guide to its function in the living animal. This assumption, we shall now see, is unjustified. In my own early work, X-ray movies (termed *cineradiography*) of the vocal tract in living, vocalizing animals, showed the vocal tract to be highly flexible and dynamic. In particular, the position of the larynx and tongue root in some mammals (such as dogs) changes actively and drastically during vocalization (Fitch, 2000c). This has clear, direct implications for speech evolution.

Our first successful cineradiographs of a vocalizing mammal came from a young goat kid, who was induced to vocalize by playing recordings of its mother's bleats from the next room. During resting breathing, the goat

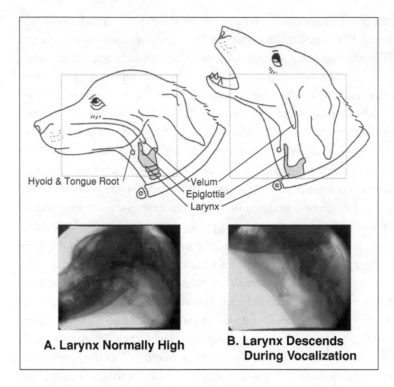

Hyoid & Tongue Root
Velum
Epiglottis
Larynx

A. Larynx Normally High

B. Larynx Descends During Vocalization

Figure 8.4 Dynamic descent of the larynx and hyoid during vocalizing –
These still frames from moving X-rays of a barking dog illustrate the
dynamic flexibility of the mammalian vocal tract. During vocalizing,
mammals temporarily retract their larynx, hyoid bone, and tongue root,
attaining a configuration similar to that typical of adult humans.

breathed through its nose, and its epiglottis remained firmly ensconced
behind its velum, in the "standard" mammalian configuration of a sealed
nasolaryngeal breathing tube (Fitch, 2000c). But what we saw during vocalization was a surprise: the larynx dropped from the nasal cavity, the velum
closed off the nasal passage completely, and the bleat was emitted entirely
through the mouth. This state persisted only briefly, during the vocalization, after which the goat returned to its normal state of nasal breathing.
This was already somewhat of a surprise, as some scholars had suggested
that animals lack the ability to seal the velum (Lieberman, 1984). The rapid,
coordinated change of the vocal tract configuration was also surprising: the
animal quickly went into a specific "vocalization" posture, just while vocalizing. This first subject already painted a rather different picture than what
we had expected. But the real surprise came when we X-rayed vocalizing
dogs (see Figure 8.4). During resting breathing, as for the goat, the epiglottis

and velum remained in contact. But just prior to barking, the larynx was pulled far down into the throat (presumably using the sternothyroid strap muscles, which exist in all mammals), pulling the tongue root down with it. Again, this position was maintained only during the bark. But during vocalization, the vocal anatomy of the dog became strikingly similar to that of a human, with the tongue root retracted far down into the pharynx. Further investigations of monkeys and pigs revealed the same pattern: they, too, lower the larynx out of the nasal passage during vocalization (though not as far as barking dogs). In summary, all of the mammals observed vocalizing show a dynamic reconfiguration of their vocal tract during vocalization, and all of the species examined so far lower their larynx, removing it from the normal breathing position, during loud calls.

The acoustic reason for this seems rather clear: sounds released through the absorbent nasal passages are much quieter than oral calls. In all the species above, the velum can be completely closed during vocalization, so that no sound leaks through the nasal passages and their calls are louder. These studies show beyond any doubt that the mammalian vocal tract is not a static structure, whose conformation during vocalization can be derived simply by post-mortem observations. In particular, the position of the larynx and tongue root is not fixed, and indeed is surprisingly dynamic during vocalization. A dog can adopt the two-tube conformation previously assumed to be uniquely human, and does so each time it barks. This renders attempts to reconstruct the details of possible articulatory movements from muscle angles in dead or anesthetized animals futile (e.g. Lieberman and Crelin, 1971; Crelin, 1987; Duchin, 1990). I conclude that a "two-tube" vocal anatomy, and thus many of the vocal tract conformations required for speech, are attainable by nonhuman mammals via dynamic vocal tract reconfiguration. Most, if not all, mammals have an ability to reconfigure their vocal tract during vocalization, including crucially an ability to retract the larynx and tongue root. This should be as true for chimpanzees, Australopithecines, or Neanderthals, as for any other mammal species. Therefore, even the earliest vocalizing hominids could attain a vocal tract configuration adequate for producing many clear, comprehensible phonemes by simply doing what all mammals do: reconfiguring the vocal anatomy while vocalizing (see Figure 8.5).

Given the significance of these observations for speech evolution, it seems surprising that they took so long to be discovered. X-ray exploration of speech production started in the 1930s (Holbrook and Carmody, 1937), and cineradiography had already been applied to human speech with great success by 1970 (Perkell, 1969). Human infants being born, taking their

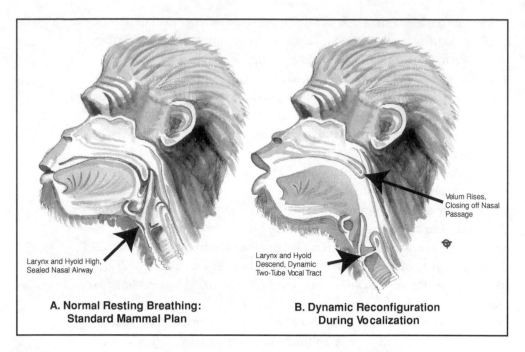

Larynx and Hyoid High, Sealed Nasal Airway

A. Normal Resting Breathing: Standard Mammal Plan

Velum Rises, Closing off Nasal Passage

Larynx and Hyoid Descend, Dynamic Two-Tube Vocal Tract

B. Dynamic Reconfiguration During Vocalization

Figure 8.5 Dynamic vocal reconfiguration in an extinct hominid – This reconstruction, based on X-ray observations of living mammals, shows the probable configuration of an extinct hominid during vocalization, assuming that hominids retained the basic vocal behavior typical of living mammals. During vocalization, the velum rises, closing off the nasal cavity, while the larynx and hyoid descend, pulling the tongue root down into a "two-tube" configuration.

first breaths, and making their first cries had been captured on X-ray in the mid-1960s (Bosma and Lind, 1965). The few mentions I have found of researchers using cineradiography on vocalizing mammals (Arvola, 1974; Laitman, 1977) mention nothing about vocal tract movements, and the only directly relevant publication I have found, an abstract by White (1968), is a report of laryngeal lowering during crowing in domestic fowl. During this period, scores of papers were published on the hominid vocal tract, and scientific battles raged about the speech capacity of extinct hominids, while vocal tract dynamics in everyday living mammals such as dogs and pigs went completely unexplored.

8.4.2 Permanently descended larynges in nonhuman mammals

The data just reviewed indicate that mammals can flexibly reconfigure their vocal tract anatomy into a conformation resembling that of humans. Static anatomy reveals little about phonetic potential. However, as quickly pointed out by Philip Lieberman when he first observed these videos, humans still differ in having a *permanently* reconfigured vocal tract. This difference might serve multiple functions in human speech. First, by stabilizing the tongue root, we may obtain more precise tongue control than would be possible in a dynamically reconfigured tract. Also, vocal tract length changes dynamically during a dog's bark, which might lead to problems in vocal tract normalization that would compromise speech perception (though the human larynx also moves up and down for different vowels; Fant, 1960). Thus, the core idea that the reconfigured vocal tract is a speech-specific adaptation remained plausible, with no alternative function available to explain permanent laryngeal descent.

Shortly after this conversation, I was contacted by David Reby, a French deer biologist and bioacoustician, asking my opinion about some odd throat movements he observed during vocalization in deer. The emailed video immediately reminded me of the laryngeal movements we observed in dogs, suggesting laryngeal movements during vocalization, with one excep-tion: the *resting position* of the larynx was halfway down the neck, in a position supposedly unique to human beings. Reby and I collaborated on a series of anatomical investigations, combined with detailed audio-video analyses of vocalizing stags, which confirmed our initial suspicion (Fitch and Reby, 2001). The resting position of the larynx is halfway down the neck, equivalent to its position in adult humans, in adult males of both red and fallow deer (see Figure 8.6a). *The permanently descended larynx is not uniquely human.*

Furthermore, red deer stags often retract their larynx as far as anatomi-cally possible, to the inlet of the chest cavity, attaining a vocal tract length approaching one meter (Figure 8.6b). During such roars, multiple, parallel formant frequencies move to a very low frequency, which is held for the remaining portion of the roar. However, the tongue root is prevented from moving this far. The deer hyoid remains bound to the skull, and the link between hyoid/tongue root and the larynx is highly elastic (unlike humans or most other animals, where the hyoid and larynx are tightly linked). Thus, deer vocal tracts resemble those of humans in one way, but differ in another. Although fallow and red deer are common European species that had been hunted and farmed for centuries, we were apparently the first to recognize the resemblance between deer and human vocal tracts, and its significance for human speech evolution (cf. Reby *et al.*, 2005).

Eyes opened, I began to look for other evidence of descended larynges in other mammalian species. In Australia, I dissected a koala and found a permanently descended larynx in this species, similar to that of humans or

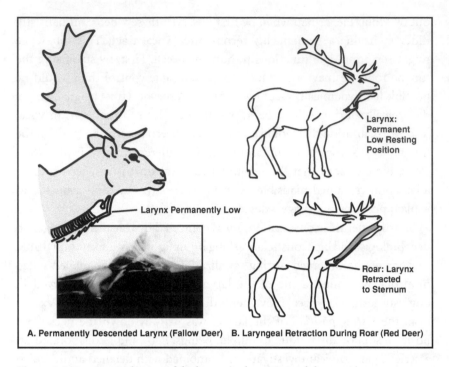

Figure 8.6 Permanent descent of the larynx in deer – Several deer species are now known to exhibit *permanent* descent of the larynx, equivalent to that seen in modern humans. Fallow deer bucks (A) have a larynx half-way down the throat, similar to the human position. Red deer stags (B) have a similar resting position, but retract the larynx further, nearly into the thorax, during intense roaring. In both species, unlike in humans, only mature males exhibit the descent.

deer, and I was able to find an oblique mention of this in the anatomical literature (Sonntag, 1921). Interestingly, although Sonntag subsequently published a comparison of ape and human vocal anatomy, he apparently did not recognize that the koala's vocal anatomy is closer than a chimpanzee's to humans'. The Mongolian gazelle has recently been shown to have an enlarged and permanently descended larynx, much like that of deer (Frey and Riede, 2003). Meanwhile, a Japanese team investigating chimpanzee vocal anatomy showed a slight but significant descent during maturation in chimpanzees (Nishimura *et al.*, 2003). Most significantly, all of the big cats in the genus *Panthera* (lions, tigers, jaguars, and leopards) also have a permanently reconfigured vocal tract (Weissengruber *et al.*, 2002). But in contrast to deer, where the larynx descends but leaves the hyoid in a relatively "normal" high position, the larynx and hyoid are tightly bound in big cats, just as in humans. Like us, big cats have a "free-floating" hyoid, attached only by an elastic ligament to the skull; this situation is unusual enough to have been noticed in Darwin's time (Owen, 1835). This entire apparatus descends permanently, pulling the elongated, elastic tongue root with it, giving big cats a vocal anatomy that corresponds quite closely to that of humans. Understanding the acoustic significance of this peculiarity had to wait nearly two centuries.

8.4.3 The function of the descended larynx: size exaggeration

The discovery that other mammal species have a convergently evolved, permanently descended larynx, much like our own, posed an evolutionary puzzle. None of these species produces speech, or even has unusually complex articulated vocalizations. Indeed, the "roar" vocalizations of red deer and big cat species, though impressive, are very simple acoustically, and show none of the complex, precise, rapid formant movements that typify human speech. Vocal tract reconfiguration in these species thus must serve some other function(s) than speech. *Therefore, there must be functions of a descended larynx other than increased phonetic versatility.* This basic point already has implications for fossil reconstruction, even without any further specification of what these functions might be, but exploring the possibilities provides some additional insights about human vocalization and speech evolution.

Several potential functions for elongating the vocal tract seem possible (cf. Fitch, 1999; Fitch and Reby, 2001; Fitch and Hauser, 2002). The intuitive idea that "low frequencies travel further" fails for terrestrial vocalizers due to destructive interference, leaving size exaggeration as the most plausible candidate explanation. The **size exaggeration hypothesis** for laryngeal descent holds that lowering formants (for example by the retraction of the larynx) functions to increase the impression of size conveyed by vocalizations. The factual basis for this hypothesis has been explored in considerable detail (Fitch, 2002). The basic idea is that the overall pattern of formant frequencies is controlled by vocal tract length, and that long vocal tracts produce low, narrowly spaced formants. Vocal tract length in most animals is essentially determined by the size of the skull, which is in turn tightly tied to body size. Thus, vocal tract length in most vertebrates should be closely correlated with overall body size (Fitch, 2000a). We can thus predict that formants should provide accurate **indexical** cues to body size (cf. Chapter 4). This prediction has been empirically tested, and borne out, in many mammal species including monkeys, dogs, pigs, and humans (Fitch, 1997; Fitch and Giedd, 1999; Riede and Fitch, 1999; Vorperian *et al.*, 2005). More recent data indicate that various animals also perceive formants, without training, in their own species-specific vocalizations (Rendall *et al.*, 1998; Fitch and Kelley, 2000; Hienz *et al.*, 2004; Fitch and Fritz, 2006). These data suggest that formants could serve as an honest cue to body size in many (probably most) vertebrates, including humans.

Furthermore, human and red deer perceivers *use* formants to estimate body size (Fitch, 1994; Reby *et al.*, 2005; Smith *et al.*, 2005; Charlton *et al.*, 2008). We can thus conclude that, long before the evolution of speech, the perception of formants played an important role in animal communication systems. Once formants are used as a cue to size by perceivers, the evolutionary potential arises for signalers to manipulate this cue to their own advantage (Krebs and Dawkins, 1984), providing the preconditions for size-exaggerating adaptations. Particularly for animals vocalizing at night, or in dense forest, any trait that increases the effectiveness of territorial vocalizations could provide significant adaptive advantages. There are at least three obvious ways to lower formant frequencies (not mutually exclusive): elongate your nose, protrude your lips, and retract your larynx. Although all of these tricks are seen in various animals, elongating the vocal tract via laryngeal descent has the advantage of being both invisible and flexible, and thus easily driven by gradual "escalation." The fact that, in deer and the Mongolian gazelle, the descended larynx appears only in post-pubertal males is consistent with a proposed territorial function. Because large males have longer necks than small males, the resulting signal, though exaggerated, is still a reliable "honest" indicator of size (Reby and McComb, 2003). In big cats, where both males and females exhibit territory defense, both appear to have a similarly reconfigured vocal tract. When we look beyond mammals, we find a number of anatomical peculiarities of the vocal tract that may represent size-exaggerating adaptations, such as tracheal elongation in birds, or hollowed nasal crests in dinosaurs (Weishampel, 1981; Fitch, 1999). The size exaggeration hypothesis thus provides a plausible explanation for vocal tract reconfiguration in nonhuman mammals, that is both theoretically and logically sound, and consistent with a wealth of data.

Interestingly, the principles underlying the size exaggeration hypothesis apply equally to humans. Indeed, in humans as in red deer, the larynx undergoes an additional descent, at puberty, but only in males (Fitch and Giedd, 1999; Lieberman *et al.*, 2001). This is a second acoustic component of the pubertal voice change mentioned above, and lowers male formant frequencies below those of women. After this additional descent, teenage boys show no corresponding increase in phonetic ability, and indeed girls appear to enjoy a slight advantage in speech ability over boys (Hyde and Linn, 1988; Henton, 1992). The only logical function for this male-specific pubertal descent of the larynx appears to be size exaggeration (Ohala, 1984; Fitch and Giedd, 1999). This secondary descent appears to be part of a suite of size-exaggerating traits that appear in males at puberty, including broad shoulders, beards, and the enlarged larynx already mentioned (which lowers voice pitch, and is acoustically and physiologically independent of laryngeal descent). Thus, in modern humans, there is solid evidence that laryngeal descent functions to exaggerate size, as for deer or lions, and does *not* imply additional speech ability.

These observations are important because it was previously believed that, if we discovered a descended larynx in an extinct hominid, we could safely conclude that they spoke. The existence of a clear alternative function for a descended larynx – size exaggeration – renders this assumption invalid. Discovery of a preserved Australopithecine with a low larynx would not prove this species had spoken language, any more than the lowered larynx of lions or koalas demonstrates their linguistic abilities. These observations force us to take seriously a different hypothesis: that the larynx descended originally, in prelinguistic hominids, for purposes of size exaggeration, and that laryngeal lowering served as a *preadaptation* for speech which occurred later.

Size exaggeration may provide a resolution to another mystery in the evolution of the human vocal tract: our loss of air sacs. All of the great apes, and many other primates and mammals, have inflatable air pouches connected to the larynx (between the skin and pectoral musculature; Guilloud and McClure, 1969; Kelemen, 1969; Abe *et al.*, 1977; Hewitt *et al.*, 2002). These sacs, which extend onto the chest, can hold a considerable volume of air (six liters in the orangutan) and almost certainly serve a vocal function. Little is currently known about the acoustic effects of these sacs, or their adaptive significance, and despite many hypotheses, there is inadequate data at present to discriminate among them (Gautier, 1971; Hewitt *et al.*, 2002). Recent investigations of formant frequencies in guereza monkeys suggest that air sacs may provide an alternative means of lowering formant frequencies and thus "faking" large body size (Harris *et al.*, 2006). If true, air sacs and a descended larynx may represent alternative ways of achieving the same formant-lowering function. Whatever their function, the fact that all great apes possess air sacs strongly suggests that they were also present in the LCA and earlier common ancestors, and thus that air sacs were lost during recent human evolution. The recent find of an Australopithecine basihyoid bone, with clear evidence for chimpanzee-like air sacs, suggests that this loss occurred early in the genus *Homo* (Alemseged *et al.*, 2006; see below). Unfortunately, without better information from living species, it is difficult to assess the significance of air sac loss in our hominid ancestors: a worthy topic for future comparative research (cf. Nishimura *et al.*, 2007). Nonetheless, this loss of air sacs is as striking, and as worthy of further investigation, as our gain of a descended larynx.

8.5 Comparative data II: Is speech *perception* special?

We saw in Chapter 4 that there is a fundamental asymmetry in most animals between call *perception*, which involves quite sophisticated inference based on social cognition, and call *production*, which is strikingly limited (Cheney and Seyfarth, 2007). The parity between vocal production and vocal perception in humans is quite unusual, and requires evolutionary explanation. We have just seen that human vocal production is not as different from that in other animals as long supposed. What of speech perception? The data suggest that, again, broad continuities in the perceptual realm are typical: the basic functioning of the vertebrate auditory system is broadly shared among terrestrial vertebrates. All mammals further share a three-bone middle-ear linkage, and a novel type of hair cell that actively "tunes" the cochlea to relevant frequencies. The brainstem nuclei that convey this acoustic information are also highly conserved among mammals (although the fixed ears of many primates have led to the loss of some brainstem structures involved in ear movements). Thus, any auditory differences between humans and other mammals must be interpreted against a broadly shared context (Webster *et al.*, 1992).

8.5.1 Frequency sensitivity

An obvious difference in hearing mechanisms among different mammal species is the absolute range of frequency sensitivity, which can be highly variable even among closely related species. The sensitivity to sound at different frequencies is summarized by an **audiogram**, a graph (or table) plotting frequency of a sine wave tone against its threshold (the amplitude at which this tone can detected). Humans hear frequencies from roughly 20 Hz to 20 kHz (Zemlin, 1968; Moore, 1988). Frequencies below this are termed *infrasonic*, and many large mammals such as elephants and whales can produce and perceive sound at these frequencies. Frequencies above 20 kHz are called *ultrasonic*, and most mammals can hear into this range. The top octave of human auditory potential, from 10–20 kHz, plays virtually no role in speech or music. The important information for speech can be squeezed into a much narrower frequency range, from 100 to 5,000 Hz (often called "telephone quality"). Some authors have noted that a broad peak of human spectral sensitivity, centered around 3,000 Hz, coincides more or less with the center of this speech bandwidth. Despite suggestions that this indicates a tight fit between our hearing and speech, the main cause of this peak appears to be the acoustic resonance of the ear canal, and this is the same in humans and chimpanzees (Kojima, 1990). Some potentially more interesting differences between humans and chimpanzees have been discussed (Elder, 1934; Kojima, 1990; Heffner, 2004). In general chimpanzees are more sensitive to frequencies above 8 kHz than humans (Elder, 1934), and slightly less sensitive to low frequencies below 250 Hz. Some chimpanzees also show an insensitive "notch" around 4 kHz. However, these studies used small numbers of subjects, and it is not clear that such relatively subtle changes in sensitivity would have important consequences for perceiving speech (chimpanzees hear perfectly well in speech range, and with training understand spoken words adequately; Savage-Rumbaugh *et al.*, 1993). In fact it is quite likely that this notch reflects noise-induced damage at the *most* sensitive region: such a 4 kHz notch is a common clinical sign of noise-induced hearing loss (McBride and Williams, 2001). In general, the comparative audiogram data suggests that the basic frequency range and sensitivity of humans is quite normal for a mammal our size (Heffner, 2004). This renders extrapolations about speech evolution based on fossil reconstructions of extinct hominid ears unconvincing (Martínez *et al.*, 2004).

8.5.2 Categorical perception

In Chapter 3, I mentioned the phenomenon of categorical perception: the loss of *discrimination* within a category, and an increase in sensitivity to between-category differences. We appear to perceive some speech sounds, particularly stop consonants, this way. This was a crucial discovery, suggesting that speech perception might be "special," and opened the door to a new and very productive line of research on auditory perception (Liberman, 1957). This hypothesis was falsified in its original form. First, categorical perception was documented in human subjects perceiving synthesized musical sounds along a "plucked/bowed" continuum (Cutting and Rosner, 1974). Although a re-analysis revealed some technical problems with this study (Rosen and Howell, 1981), a later study reconfirmed the essentials of the result (Cutting, 1982). Thus, the hypothesis that categorical perception is limited to speech was falsified. More important, animals show clear evidence of categorical perception of speech sounds (Kuhl and Miller, 1975; Morse and Snowdon, 1975; Kuhl and Miller, 1978; Kluender *et al.*, 1987) and conspecific vocalizations (Zoloth *et al.*, 1979; Nelson and Marler, 1989). These comparative studies together suggest that the formation of categories and heightened sensitivity to members of different categories is a general trait of auditory perception. Furthermore, the very specific pattern of consonant discrimination by chinchillas (Kuhl and Miller, 1978), which precisely matches that of humans, right down to details like a shift in the peak with different places of articulation, suggest that our use of the speech production apparatus has adjusted to fit pre-existing constraints of the mammalian auditory system. If any co-evolutionary "tuning" has occurred, speech production has adapted to the auditory system rather than *vice versa.*

8.5.3 Other potentially special aspects of speech perception

These data do not, of course, demonstrate that *all* aspects of speech perception are shared: numerous additional candidates for "special" status have been proposed. However, the history of categorical perception should represent a cautionary tale: do not hypothesize that a trait is uniquely human without first gathering some data from other animals (Hauser and Fitch, 2003; Fitch *et al.*, 2005). Unfortunately, perceptual phenomena are often claimed to indicate that speech is special, despite a lack of relevant data from animals. For example, as mentioned before, **vocal tract normalization** is the perceptual adjustment of a listener to the vocal tract length of different speakers. However, recent studies suggest that nonhuman animals, including birds and primates, spontaneously attend to formant frequencies, including the overall length cues that are critical for vocal tract normalization (Sommers *et al.*, 1992; Rendall *et al.*, 1998; Fitch and Kelley, 2000; Hienz *et al.*, 2004), suggesting that, at a minimum, the mechanisms underlying this ability have a long evolutionary history (Fitch, 1994; Lieberman, 2000). Other candidates include the McGurk effect (McGurk and MacDonald, 1976), duplex perception (Whalen and Liberman, 1987), or trading relations (Repp, 1982). There are far fewer comparative studies relevant to these issues. In general, laboratory studies using operant conditioning over thousands of trials reveal that nonhuman primates have speech perceptual abilities rivaling our own (Sommers *et al.*, 1992; Hienz *et al.*, 2004), although when examined at a fine enough level some differences are typically found (though see Sinnott and Brown, 1997; Sinnott and Saporita, 2000). For example, macaques can easily learn to distinguish among different stop consonants, but close examination of their patterns of errors and generalization suggests that they may fix upon different acoustic cues than humans (Sinnott and Williamson, 1999). But even human listeners seem to show fine-grained differences in their perception of such contrasts (Schwartz and Tallal, 1980; Tallal *et al.*, 1996).

A potentially "special" aspect of human vowel perception was proposed by Patricia Kuhl (Kuhl, 1991; Kuhl *et al.*, 1992), termed the **perceptual magnet effect**. This effect is closely related to categorical perception (indeed, some critics have suggested that it is identical; Lotto *et al.*, 1998). Prototypically "good" vowel sounds (synthetic vowels independently identified by listeners as particularly good exemplars of a vowel) appear to warp the neighboring perceptual space like a magnet, "pulling" less prototypical vowels towards themselves and making them less discriminable. If the sounds are drawn from different vowel categories, the effect is similar to a weak categorical perception (decreasing the salience of within-category differences), but the effect on exemplars within the category is different. Of the proposed "special" mechanisms for speech perception, this one is exemplary in that it was experimentally demonstrated in human adults and infants, and its absence documented in macaques, before it was held up as potentially unique to our species (Kuhl, 1991). However, starlings trained to discriminate vowels exhibit untrained generalization patterns closely mimicking those of humans (Kluender *et al.*, 1998). Thus, more data from a wider range of species will be necessary to determine whether this effect is broadly shared with other vertebrates (and the monkey results a "false negative") or has convergently evolved in humans and birds.

Thus, today, there are *no* convincing demonstrations of speech perceptual mechanisms that are limited to speech sounds and unique to human listeners, and the safe assumption at present is that speech perception is based on perceptual processing mechanisms largely shared with other animals. The fine differences that exist do not appear to represent a major impediment to perceiving speech sounds, or to be of a magnitude that would have posed a significant barrier to the evolution of speech in early hominids.

8.6 Implications of the comparative data

I conclude that auditory perception in nonhuman mammals is perfectly adequate to perceive speech, and that vocal tract anatomy in mammals would enable them to make a variety of perceptibly different sounds, certainly enough for a basic spoken communication system. Furthermore, a tiger's anatomy should allow it to produce the point vowels /i/, /a/, and

/u/. By process of elimination, the fact that mammals do not do so appears to result from differences in neural control of the vocal apparatus, rather than vocal morphology. These data strengthen and extend the conclusion reached by Darwin (1871): changes in the central nervous system, rather than peripheral vocal anatomy, were critical innovations in the evolution of speech.

Second, the fact that other animals have evolved similarly reconfigured tracts convergently, but do not produce speech-like sounds (or indeed sounds of any great complexity), provides an existence proof that *some* alternative function of laryngeal descent exists. The size exaggeration hypothesis, initially designed to explain laryngeal descent in animals, also turns out to apply to modern humans, and helps explain the otherwise curious fact that the human larynx descends a second time at puberty, but only in males. This raises the possibility that the *original* function of the descended larynx in early hominids might have been size exaggeration rather than speech: that the descended larynx was actually a preadaptation, later exapted into the complex articulation system we use today in spoken language. Does this mean that the descended larynx, today, is not an adaptation for speech? Of course not. The size exaggeration and speech-specific hypotheses are independent and mutually compatible, and to think otherwise would be to confuse current utility with original function, like saying that the bat's wings didn't evolve "for" flight because bats' ancestors used them "for" swimming or walking. Size exaggeration (or perhaps some other function) might plausibly have provided a precondition for the descent of the larynx, but it cannot account for the vocal tract reconfiguration seen in human infants at age three months (Fitch and Reby, 2001; Fitch, 2002). This hypothesis suggests that the use of our reconfigured vocal tract is a classic case of exaptation, where a pre-existing morphological structure was put to new use by a newly derived neural system underlying vocal control.

Besides their important implications for the evolution of speech, the comparative data just reviewed illustrate the value of a broad comparative approach. First, claims about human uniqueness were accepted uncritically for nearly a century, simply because no one looked at animals beyond primates. There remain many more such statements, common in the paleo-anthropological literature, that are rendered suspect by comparative data, but have not yet been conclusively researched. For instance, it is sometimes thought that human oral breathing is "special," because most mammals, including human infants, are "obligate" nose breathers. Neither claim is true: although initially resistant, human infants are quite capable of mouth breathing (Rodenstein *et al.*, 1985), and many mammals breathe through their mouths during panting, using evaporation from the wet tongue to cool the body (Schmidt-Nielsen *et al.*, 1970). Similarly, nasal closure by raising the velum has incorrectly been put forward as a capability restricted to humans, but physiological investigations show that the mammalian velum closes during both swallowing and vocalization (Fitch, 2000c; Wall and Smith, 2001). Finally, consider the oft-mentioned issue of the risk of choking mentioned earlier. The idea that the descent of the larynx in humans increases our risk of choking seems plausible, as every drop of fluid and morsel of food swallowed by an adult human must pass over the glottis *en route* to the esophagus. But the oft-cited figure of 3,000 deaths per year due to choking on food in the US (Heimlich, 1975) represents a very low death rate by comparison with other factors (Clegg and Aiello, 2000), and the critical comparison is of course with deaths due to choking in animals with "normal" vocal tracts. Animals can choke to death (e.g. young lambs occasionally die from choking on milk; Hight and Jury, 1970), but I have been unable to find reliable statistics on the rate of choking, or of death by choking, in nonhuman animals. Thus the comparative data gathered so far represent just the tip of the iceberg: empirical studies on living animals have much more to teach us about the evolution of the human vocal apparatus.

8.7 Reconstructing the vocal abilities of extinct hominids

I will now briefly discuss various attempts to reconstruct the speech capabilities of fossil hominids. Once the descent of the larynx caught the attention of paleoanthropologists, it didn't take long to find a possible skeletal cue to larynx position. The resulting controversy sparked a search for other possible fossil clues to vocal capability that has generated a fair number of creative hypotheses (see Figure 8.7). However, as should already be clear, the documented flexibility of the mammalian vocal tract bodes ill for this search, so I will not discuss all possibilities in detail (cf. Fitch, 2009).

8.7.1 The vocal tract skeleton

The roof of the vocal tract is provided by the base of the skull – the **basicranium**. Because most of the muscles and ligaments that make up the vocal tract are attached to either the basicranium or the hyoid apparatus, it provides the main skeletal support for the vocal apparatus. The basicranium is one of the most complex regions of the body, and its anatomy has reduced many an anatomy student to tears. It is a structure with very ancient

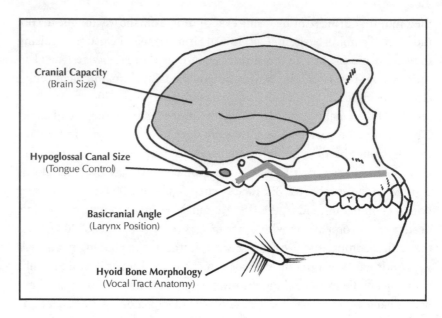

Figure 8.7 Proposed fossil cues to hominid vocal capacity. For cranial capacity, see Section 10.4.

affinities, with most components traceable to the earliest jawed vertebrates. The basicranium is pierced by many holes termed *foramina* (singular *foramen*) for blood vessels and nerves. The largest foramen (helpfully termed the *foramen magnum*) forms the passageway where the spinal cord enters the skull. This opening is flanked on either side by the uppermost joint between spinal column and skull, and it is on this *occipital joint* that the entire skull is balanced in an upright human being. The bone containing the foramen magnum and occiput is termed the "basioccipital bone," and moving forwards we find the temporal, sphenoid, ethmoid, and nasal bones, and finally the vomer, maxilla, and premaxilla, which make up the hard palate and upper jaw (see Figure 8.7). The human basicranium is unusually "buckled," compared to the relatively flat basicranium of a chimpanzee or most other mammals (Negus, 1949; DuBrul, 1958).

The **hyoid apparatus** provides a solid, bony anchor for the intrinsic muscles of the tongue, as well as most of the other muscles of the vocal tract, present in all mammals. It is a derivative of the branchial arches (homologous to the gill bars of fish; see Chapter 5), and it consists of several "loops" of cartilage or bone, the uppermost attaching to the basicranium much like the jaw. This upper *epihyal* portion of the hyoid apparatus is extremely variable between species. In some large herbivores (e.g. horses or sheep) it is extremely robust, resembling a jaw bone, and anchors the tongue root solidly to the skull base. In most carnivores, rodents, and bats, the epihyal is a chain of slim bones forming a more flexible link to the skull base. Finally, in primates and big cats, among others, this epihyal portion is reduced to ligament and muscle. The lower *basihyal* portion forms the functional core of the hyoid apparatus, centering on the U-shaped **basihyoid bone** (often simply termed "the hyoid" in humans, because only the basihyoid portion become fully ossified). In cases like primates or big cats, the basihyoid bone is essentially a free-floating bone, attached via a three-point suspension of non-bony tissues to the rest of the skeleton. The basihyoid is thus a quite unusual bone.

Because the larynx hangs below it, if we could reconstruct the basihyoid's position from fossils, we could determine when the larynx permanently descended (Lieberman and Crelin, 1971). The basicranial angle, a measure of the unusual buckled configuration of the basicranium, has long been held to provide such a clue (George, 1978; Laitman *et al.*, 1978; Crelin, 1987). The basicranial angle is measured from several well-defined cephalometric land-marks (the basion, opisthocranion, and nasion). Citing an apparent corre-lation between this angle and basihyoid position, all of these scholars con-curred in placing the hyoid, tongue base, and larynx of fossil hominids high in the throat, in the position found in apes, or in newborn humans. Unfor-tunately, the correlation between basicranial anatomy and hyoid height is at best imperfect. Careful developmental analyses of basicranial angle from longitudinal X-rays of growing children revealed no measures correlated with larynx height (Lieberman and McCarthy, 1999). Neither the initial descent of the infant hyoid, nor later pubertal descent, correlate with bas-icranial angle (Fitch and Giedd, 1999). Thus, even in our own species, the claimed relationship is weak or non-existent, as Philip Lieberman recently acknowledged (Lieberman, 2006, 2007a), although Lieberman now argues that neck length provides a fossil indicator of vocal tract morphology (cf. Fitch, 2009).

The comparative data reviewed above are equally problematic: species with descended larynges or hyoids exhibit no obvious changes in the bas-icranium, and it seems unlikely that the basicranium of a maturing deer stag could rearrange significantly so late in development. And the flexibility of the mammalian vocal apparatus during vocalization means that, even if the *resting* position of the hyoid could be calculated for a fossil species, this would not determine the actual position of the vocal tract during vocal-ization. Thus, a Neanderthal or Australopithecine might have had a high resting hyoid and larynx, but lowered these structures into a modern human conformation during vocalization. For all of these reasons, there appears to be no remaining empirical basis for reconstructing the phonetic abilities of fossil hominids (or other mammals) from their basicrania.

8.7.2 Other proposed fossil cues to vocal anatomy

Most other potential fossil indicators of vocal anatomy, unfortunately, warrant the same (negative) conclusion. An oft-repeated idea is that the simple attainment of upright **bipedalism** is alone enough to drive the larynx downward (e.g. Negus, 1949; Falk, 1975). This suggestion is implausible, as bipedalism and upright posture have evolved in parallel in many animal species, including all birds, kangaroos, and other species, without any concomitant descent of hyoid or larynx. Many nonhuman primates adopt an upright posture while feeding, and arboreal primates like gibbons or spider monkeys spend much of their lives in a fully vertical position. None of these species appears to have a descended larynx, indicating that neither upright posture nor bipedalism provide adequate explanations for hominid vocal tract reconfiguration.

Another possibility is that **facial shortening** during hominid evolution, combined with bipedalism, "pushed" the larynx and hyoid downward (DuBrul, 1958; Aiello, 1996). An important change in human skull anatomy relative to other apes, and most fossil hominids, is a retraction of the facial skeleton relative to the rest of the skull. The face and jaws of a chimpanzee or Neanderthal jut forward from the braincase, while those of modern humans are pulled backwards almost flush with the forehead. Facial flattening has far-reaching consequences for skull form, including mouth shortening (the main cause of our frequently impacted wisdom teeth) and a reduction of the space between the back of the palate and the front of the spinal column (Aiello and Dean, 1990). The latter change is exacerbated by the forwards movement of the foramen magnum and spinal column to the more "balanced" position associated with fully upright bipedalism. While a chimpanzee's foramen magnum points backwards (reflecting the forward-jutting head posture), ours points almost directly downward. Combined, these facts lead to the suggestion that there is no longer enough room in the posterior oral cavity for the nasolaryngeal seal to be formed. Although it is impossible to refute this hypothesis based on comparative data (I know of no nonhuman species that combines facial shortening and bipedalism), I find this idea unconvincing, because the "seal" is formed by the soft tissues of the velum and epiglottis, and is thus flexible. Neither the facial shortening already present in the human infant, nor that selected for in short-snouted dog and cat breeds, prevents a nasal/laryngeal seal. Thus there is at present no good reason to believe that bipedalism, alone or combined with other factors, would automatically drive a descended larynx or reconfigured vocal tract.

Another hypothesized clue to the vocal anatomy of fossil hominids was provided by the discovery of the basihyoid of a Neanderthal in Israel: the **Kebara hyoid** (Arensburg *et al.*, 1989; Arensburg *et al.*, 1990; Arensburg, 1994). The Kebara hyoid is quite robust (like the entire Neanderthal skeleton), but otherwise appears modern in structure, and was thus argued to provide support for the notion that Neanderthals had a modern vocal anatomy. But, as critics quickly pointed out (Laitman *et al.*, 1990), this argument is a *non sequitur*. The morphology of the hyoid bone does not itself determine its position in the vocal tract: this is determined by the muscles and ligaments that form its three-point suspension. If the sternohyoid muscles are tensed, the basihyoid moves downward (as seen during dog barking or other animal vocalization), while if the digastric and stylohyoid are tensed, it moves upward. The anatomically modern hyoid of a human infant is consistent with a high position, and no changes in hyoid structure are entailed by the secondary pubertal descent of the hyoid in human males. Thus, the modern morphology of the Neanderthal hyoid provides no indication of its position in the Neanderthal throat.

However, fossil hyoid bones *do* provide an interesting potential clue concerning air sacs. Based on their modern hyoid anatomy, Neanderthals had probably already **lost their laryngeal air sacs**. Chimpanzee, gorilla, and Australopithecine hyoids are very different from those of a modern humans or Neanderthals. In apes and early hominds, the basihyoid balloons into a thin-walled shell (a **hyoid bulla**), into which ape air sacs extend. Such bullae are often, or even typically, observed in primate species with large air sacs (Kelemen and Sade, 1960; Hilloowala, 1975), and a bullate hyoid was present in a recently discovered young fossil Australopithecine from Dikika in Ethiopia (Alemseged *et al.*, 2006). Unfortunately, the bulla/air sac correlation is imperfect: orangutans have very large air sacs, but do not have a hyoid bulla (Aiello and Dean, 1990). Nor does the occasional pathological appearance of laryngeal air sacs in humans (termed *laryngocele*) appear to entail any changes in hyoid structure (Micheau *et al.*, 1978). Thus, the non-bullate Kebara hyoid suggests, but doesn't prove, that air sacs had already been lost in Neanderthals, in turn suggesting that air sacs were lost in the intervening period of *Homo* evolution (see Figure 8.8).

8.7.3 Proposed neurally based cues to vocal control

Several authors have proposed alternative fossil cues based on the size of neural structures. The **hypoglossal canal**, the basicranial foramen through

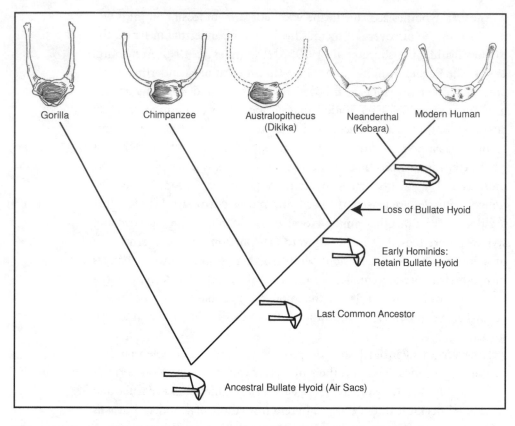

Figure 8.8 Hominoid hyoid bone evolution – The comparative method, combined with fossil hyoid bones, allows us to deduce the time at which the ancestral "bullate" (cup-shaped) basihyoid bone transformed into the modern non-bullate form: sometime between Australopithecines and Neanderthals. Because ape air sacs invade the hyoid bulla in living apes, this suggests that air sacs were lost during the same period of human evolution.

which the nerve supplying most tongue musculature passes, was proposed as an estimator of tongue control (Kay *et al.*, 1998). Given the central importance of tongue control in speech, and because tongue movements appear to play little role in most other mammal vocalizations, enlargement of this canal might indicate the onset of speech. Kay and colleagues' initial measurements suggested that humans have a much larger canal size than other great apes. However, later detailed measurements showed that there is in fact great variability in canal size in humans, along with substantial overlap between humans and other apes (DeGusta *et al.*, 1999). In a refreshing exception to the usual pattern of debate in this field, the authors of the original study now concur that there is no strong empirical basis for their original conclusion (Jungers *et al.*, 2003).

The final proposed fossil clue to hominid vocal control is the only one that appears at present to be plausible. This is the enlargement of the thoracic canal in modern humans (and Neanderthals), relative to other primates or earlier fossil hominids (especially *Homo ergaster*), that has been documented by comparative anatomists Ann MacLarnon and Gwen Hewitt (MacLarnon and Hewitt, 1999). Many of the muscles involved in breathing are fed by neurons in the thoracic spinal cord (especially the intercostals and abdominal muscles). Based on careful analyses of thoracic canal diameter in extant primates, MacLarnon and Hewitt found that the thoracic spinal cord and canal are significantly enlarged in modern humans. Because these muscles are implicated in the fine control of lung pressure during speech and singing (Ladefoged, 1967), these researchers suggested that the enlargement of the thoracic canal represents an adaptation to fine vocal control and speech. MacLarnon and Hewitt carefully examined several alternative hypotheses for why the thoracic cord might have expanded (e.g. increased control of throwing, or better breath control during walking) and convincingly rejected them. Thus, their hypothesis that thoracic canal dimensions provide a fossil cue relevant to vocal breath control seems plausible and well supported at present. Our fossil evidence for thoracic canal size is unfortunately quite limited, as vertebrae are not typically well preserved in the fossil record. The solid data come from living primates and modern humans, from the "Turkana Boy" *Homo ergaster* skeleton, and from several Neanderthal specimens, and indicate that thoracic expansion occurred sometime in the million-year period of evolution after *Homo ergaster* but before Neanderthals (e.g. later *Homo erectus* or *H. heidelbergensis*).

Accepting provisionally the hypothesized link between breath control and thoracic canal expansion, what further inferences can be drawn about speech and language? Interestingly, the breath control required for singing is as demanding as that for speech, and Johan Sundberg has convincingly argued that singing in fact requires finer respiratory control (Sundberg, 1987; Fitch, 2009). Thus, an increase in fine respiratory control would seem to be more important in singing (where, in modern practice, maintaining a constant and accurately controlled subglottal pressure for consistent amplitude and pitch is a necessity) than for speech (where pitch varies continuously over a wide range). This fact is particularly relevant to those hypotheses for the evolution of speech that, following Darwin, posit that true meaningful speech was preceded phylogenetically by a song-like system (Darwin, 1871; Livingstone, 1973; Brown, 2000; Marler, 2000; Mithen, 2005), as discussed in Chapter 14.

8.7.4 Summary

In this section I have discussed the various attempts that have been made over the years to reconstruct the anatomy of the vocal tract based on fossil remains. Because the key tissues of the vocal tract do not fossilize, possible reconstructions are based on indirect evidence, and most of these attempts fail to stand up to empirical scrutiny. The alluring dream that scientists can reconstruct the vocal anatomy of an extinct hominid from skeletal remains appears to be unrealistic. Furthermore, even if we were granted the extraordinary luck to discover a frozen Neanderthal in the melting ice of an alpine glacier, the mere presence of a descended larynx or tongue root would not necessarily demonstrate the possession of spoken language (any more than the reconfigured vocal tract of a lion shows language in that species). Nor, given the flexibility of the mammalian vocal tract, would a high laryngeal position demonstrate that the Neanderthal didn't speak: he or she might have lowered the larynx and tongue root dynamically during vocalization, as do many other mammals today. Although there seems, in principle, to be more hope of reconstructing potential neural control structures, even the most promising current example (MacLarnon and Hewitt's thoracic canal hypothesis) can only support limited phylogenetic inferences.

In a previous review of this literature, I concluded that "this line of inquiry appears to have generated more heat than light, and diverted attention from alternative questions that are equally interesting and more accessible empirically" (p. 263, Fitch, 2000b), and I stand by this conclusion today. Despite a large and daunting paleontological literature, few confident assertions can be made about hominid speech anatomy or speech motor control. Clearly, the significance of the descended larynx for speech and language has been overestimated, and the venerable hypothesis that limitations of peripheral morphology explain the inability of most animals to speak seems unsustainable. By a process of exclusion, the crucial changes in the evolution of speech appear to be neural rather than peripheral.

In conclusion, little can be said about the timing of the evolution of speech based on fossil cues, and it seems unlikely that valid new proposals will be forthcoming. It is worth emphasizing, however, that this negative conclusion represents real scientific progress, and that this progress is thanks directly to researchers like Lieberman, or more recently Cartmill and Kay, who were unafraid to put forth bold, creative hypotheses specific enough to be testable. Neither observations of vocal tract reconfiguration in other mammals, nor the discovery of mammals with a descended larynx, would *ever* have occurred if not for the seminal influence of Lieberman and colleagues' hypotheses concerning the descended larynx. When testable hypotheses drive scientists to notice otherwise obscure details, or to gather new data, science marches forward, even if a few beautiful theories get rejected by ugly facts. For the field of language evolution writ large, these data provide a model for how empirical progress can be made: via the generation and testing of strong, falsifiable hypotheses.

9 | The evolution of vocal control: the neural basis for spoken language

9.1 Neural control over speech: the central evolutionary event

The comparative data reviewed in Chapter 8 suggest that a normal mammalian vocal tract could generate many of the sounds of speech without reconfiguration and, by lowering the larynx, could presumably even create the point vowels. And yet, speech *is* special: it is a complex, learned signaling system involving rapid formant transitions, and the rapid movements of the tongue and lips used in speech have few apparent analogs in the animal world. These characteristics do not appear to result from differences in vocal morphology alone, strongly suggesting that some aspect of our neural endowment is critical to the evolution of speech. The ability that differentiates humans unambiguously from chimpanzees (and apparently all other nonhuman primates) is our capacity for **complex vocal imitation**, a cognitive and neural capacity that is crucial for human speech (Fitch, 2000b). Given the importance of this neural aspect of spoken language, I will explore it from all of Tinbergen's angles in this chapter: mechanism, ontogeny, phylogeny, and function.

9.2 Evolving learned vocalizations: phylogeny and function

From a comparative perspective, a number of distinctions are important in discussions of vocal learning (Janik and Slater, 1997). First, we can distinguish between "vocal learning" *per se*, which involves changing some acoustic aspect of the call itself (or "production learning"; Janik and Slater, 2000), and **call usage learning**, the ability to control the production of a pre-exisiting call, or to associate it to new contexts. As we saw in Chapter 4, an ability to produce a call on cue is generally present in mammals (e.g. Molliver, 1963; Burnstein and Wolff, 1967; W. A. Wilson, 1975). However, the calls thus produced are part of the innate species repertoire. A careful, controlled assessment of call usage learning has been performed for many different species of mammal (Schusterman, 2008). For example, while seals and sea lions are easily trained to produce vocalizations on command (Schusterman and Feinstein, 1965), such training is more difficult with dogs or monkeys (Larson *et al.*, 1973; Myers, 1976). Thus, the degree to which innate vocalizations are flexibly controllable varies considerably across mammalian taxa.

Speech requires much more than simply selecting among a pre-existing set of innate calls. A shared signaling system capable of labeling novel objects or events requires a flexible and open-ended generation of new signals, and thus requires vocal learning. **Vocal learning** is demonstrated when some aspect of call structure is modified due to specific experience with the environment (e.g. by imitating a perceived sound, or differentiating one's own vocalizations from it). While widespread in birds, vocal learning is quite restricted among mammals, with conclusive evidence currently present only for humans, marine mammals, and bats. In bats, the evidence for spontaneous vocal learning is limited to only a few species, and to the adjustment of a single call parameter of a species-specific call (Jones and Ransome, 1993). Similar aspects of call production (e.g. duration or amplitude) can, with difficulty, be brought under volitional control in the laboratory in nonhuman primates (Larson *et al.*, 1973). However, in neither case does this allow the generation of even a single novel signal. Such limited vocal learning capabilities are of little relevance to the type of neural control required for speech.

More relevant to speech is the capacity for **vocal imitation**, defined as the capacity to incorporate into one's vocal repertoire novel sounds that are perceived in the environment. For example, bottlenosed dolphins readily incorporate novel, computer-generated frequency contours into their own repertoire of vocal whistles, and then later use them spontaneously in communication with conspecifics (Reiss and McCowan, 1993). Empirically, the distinction between vocal imitation and vocal learning may seem slippery (Janik and Slater, 1997). Who is to say when changing the parameters of a call has created a "new call"? I think two lines of evidence are important. The most obvious is that a repertoire of discriminable signals is generated, and can be reliably reproduced. Thus, in the case of dolphin whistles, the subjects do not simply replace their pre-existing whistle with a new one, but add the new vocalization into a stable repertoire. Second, playback experiments enable us to ascertain whether conspecifics categorize calls as different or not (e.g. Nelson and Marler, 1989; Fischer, 1998), rather than relying on potentially faulty human judgments. Thus vocal imitation can be shown by demonstrating that a new vocalization has been added to the repertoire and that it is reliably and discriminably different, for conspecifics, from similar pre-existing vocalizations. This more complex level of vocal learning is currently known only in humans, birds, and marine mammals (and, new evidence suggests, elephants; Wemmer and Mishra, 1982; Poole *et al.*, 2005).

Finally, language requires both the ability to generate novel signals (vocal imitation), and a set of signals of comparable complexity to the concepts being expressed. The need to share a set of novel *complex* calls logically demands vocal learning abilities even more sophisticated than those underlying vocal imitation, including good memory for complex signals and an ability to differentiate their individual components (e.g. successive syllables). I will term this ability to imitate complex multisyllabic vocalizations **complex vocal imitation**. This capacity is the minimum necessary to support a system of spoken language. Such a capacity is most convincingly seen in animal species that imitate human multisyllabic speech, which include harbor seals (Ralls *et al.*, 1985) and many bird species (Darwin, 1871; Klatt and Stefanski, 1974; Nottebohm, 1976a). Although some of the toothed whales can probably imitate speech as well, the evidence remains limited (Eaton, 1979; Janik and Slater, 1997). Additionally, the well-attested abilities of humpback whales to imitate each other's complex songs provide convincing evidence for complex vocal imitation (Payne and McVay, 1971; Guinee and Payne, 1988; Payne, 2000). Similarly complex vocalizations that vary geographically and may indicate complex vocal imitation are seen in several other species of marine mammals, including several phocid ("earless") seal species and mysticete (baleen) whales (Janik and Slater, 1997; Fitch, 2006b).

9.2.1 Vocal imitation and song

Thus, complex vocal imitation has evolved convergently in several bird and mammal species. These data are almost certainly incomplete (Janik and Slater, 1997; Marler, 2000; Schusterman, 2008), and it would be very surprising if all imitating vertebrates have already been discovered. But taking the current data at face value, it is interesting to note that the only mammals capable of complex vocal imitation are those which, for independent reasons, are said to "sing." Ethologists, and students of birdsong in particular, typically draw a distinction between "calls" (rather simple monosyllabic vocalizations, often innate) and "songs" (complex, multisyllabic vocalizations, typically learned). Although complex innate vocalizations are sometimes termed "song," for example in suboscine birds or gibbons (Geissmann, 2000), innate "songs" are clearly exceptions to a general rule. Sometimes the term "song" is also used for any long vocalization produced by males to attract females (e.g. rodent courtship "songs" (Holy and Guo,

2005), frog or cricket "song," etc.), or even any animal vocalization deemed pleasant to human ears. Such extensions rob the term "song" of any empirical value, and I have suggested elsewhere that the term "song" be restricted to complex, learned vocalization (Fitch, 2006b).

The only primates commonly said to sing are the gibbons, who produce loud, distinctive vocalizations that appear to be involved in territorial defense; in many species these take the form of "duets" sung between members of a mated pair (Geissmann, 2002). There are clear differences in individual songs, and males and females in duetting species require a period of learning to synchronize their parts, so duetting involves vocal learning in the restricted sense. However, there is no evidence for vocal imitation in any gibbon species (or indeed any nonhuman primate). In fact, there is solid evidence that the structure of these complex gibbon long calls is innately determined (Geissmann, 2000). Gibbons raised in captivity away from conspecifics, or raised by foster parents of other species, nonetheless produce the long call of their own species. Furthermore, hybrid gibbons produce intermediate long calls differing from either parent species (Brockelman and Schilling, 1984; Geissmann, 1984). Thus, gibbons provide a clear example of complex mammal vocalizations that are genetically determined, and a warning to those who would assume that complexity alone indicates vocal learning (e.g. Holy and Guo, 2005).

9.2.2 Function and phylogeny of complex vocal imitation

As emphasized earlier, convergent evolution supports the most unambiguous insights into evolutionary function that are available (Harvey and Pagel, 1991; Pagel, 1992). Data on repeated convergent evolution of "song" in animals therefore provide a powerful source of potential insight into a critical aspect of the evolution of spoken language (cf. Koehler, 1951; Nottebohm, 1975, 1976b; Marler, 2000). What conclusions can we draw from this comparative database?

Complex vocal imitation is frequently manifested by male songs produced during the breeding season. Singing by males, only during the breeding season, typifies many (perhaps most) songbirds. Only male baleen whales sing (Watkins *et al.*, 1987; Clark *et al.*, 2002), and leopard seals may be the only seal species in which both males and females produce complex vocalizations (Van Parijs, 2003). Singing develops in these species as males approach sexual maturity, and is either absent or highly restricted in females. In some birds in which only the males sing, song can be induced experimentally in female birds by testosterone injections (e.g. Hausberger *et al.*, 1995a). All of these factors point to a strong involvement of **sexual selection** in the evolution of complex vocal imitation.

Male songbirds, seals, and whales sing their complex songs in order to attract and court females, and females are thought to choose males based on some aspect of their song (Kroodsma and Byers, 1991). Because "complexity" is always relative to other competing males, female choice can act as a powerful force to drive males towards complex song over evolutionary time. However, the need to preserve species recognition (another important function of song in many species) may make copying the vocalizations of other conspecific males the best solution to these dual constraints. Most songbird species appear to possess an innate, species-specific template that allows them to distinguish conspecific songs from others they may hear (Marler and Slabbekoorn, 2004), making birdsong the prototypical example of a constrained "instinct to learn" (Gould and Marler, 1987; Marler, 1991b). Song also often functions in **territory maintenance**, repelling other males from territories in many species. For example, if a male is removed from his territory experimentally, but replaced by a loudspeaker broadcasting song, the territory will be colonized by other males more slowly than when no song is played, and more complex songs may provide a stronger deterrent (Kroodsma and Byers, 1991; Catchpole and Slater, 1995). Singing male humpback whales are more widely spaced than non-singing individuals, suggesting a territorial function. Current data thus suggest that male song, in general, plays both an intersexual mate-attraction function and, simultaneously, an intrasexual male-repellent function. Either of these functions, or both, can drive the evolution of complex, learned song.

Despite the frequency of male song, females *do* sing in many species, a fact that, until recently, has been mostly overlooked (Ritchison, 1986; Langmore, 2000; Riebel, 2003). This is relevant to the evolution of speech because both human sexes are capable of complex vocal imitation. Often, female song in birds serves a territorial function, either in male/female duets, or by territorial females singing alone (Hoelzel, 1986; Ritchison, 1986; Yamaguchi, 1998). Duetting appears to be common in many tropical bird species, which tend to occupy long-term territories jointly defended by the pair. Because such species are both very numerous, and relatively poorly studied, there are potentially many unstudied species with female duetting (Langmore, 1998). When song functions to repel both sexes and plays no role in mating, it provides an example of natural selection *sensu strictu*, not sexual selection, driving birdsong.

Two groups of vocal learners exhibit comparable abilities among males and females: parrots and toothed whales. Parrots appear to use their abilities for complex vocal learning in very different ways than songbirds, to support **social bonding** between members of a pair, and also between members of families and groups more generally, but our understanding of the functions of parrot vocalizations remains quite limited at present (Bradbury, 2001). Shared songs in some songbird species, including starlings and grosbeaks, apparently play a role in social group maintenance (Ritchison, 1983; Hausberger *et al.*, 1995b). Among the toothed whales, research on the functions of shared vocalizations in bottlenosed dolphins and killer whales suggests that they support social bonding in both species (Sayigh *et al.*, 1990; Connor and Peterson, 1994; Janik and Slater, 1998). Thus, in species where vocal imitation is equally developed in males and females, some form of social bonding and/or group cohesion is commonly implicated as a function.

Recognizing the need for complex vocal imitation in spoken language, Darwin (1871) hypothesized that human speech evolved via an intermediate "protolanguage" similar to singing in birds (see Chapter 14), and argued that sexual selection on males drove this process. We know today that complex vocal imitation can have other functions, including non-sex-specific territoriality and social bonding. In songbirds, where male song is present in virtually all species, a two-stage scenario seems likely for the evolution of female song. First, sexual selection drives song evolution in males; and second, the mechanisms underlying song are later driven by functions of territoriality or social bonding to be expressed in females. Female birds share all genes possessed by males, so this evolutionary transition may be an easy one. In contrast, in species such as parrots or dolphins, there is no evidence that complex vocal abilities are either superior in, or evolved first in, males. These groups thereby provide evidence that such abilities can evolve directly, apparently driven only by selection for social bonding or similar functions. Either of these models provides a plausible evolutionary route for complex vocal learning abilities in our own species.

9.3 Ontogeny of complex vocal imitation

9.3.1 Sensitive periods

The comparative database also supports insights into the ontogeny of complex vocal imitation (cf. Doupe and Kuhl, 1999). "Kaspar Hauser" experiments show that songbirds need to hear conspecific song during a "critical period," or **sensitive period**. It has long been remarked that human language acquistion also seems to involve sensitive periods, with different sensitive periods for different aspects of language (Lenneberg, 1967; Newport, 1991; Johnson, 2005). Human sensitive periods never fully end (adults easily learn new words and can, with effort, master a new language). Similarly, some birds, so-called "open ended learners," retain an ability to learn new song syllables or phrases as adults (Nottebohm, 1999). Sensitive periods therefore represent an aspect of acquisition shared between humans and songbirds.

Why should such critical or sensitive periods exist? Two potential models are imprinting in mammals and birds, and critical periods in visual development. **Imprinting** is a form of learning in which dependent newborn animals learn to recognize and bond to their parents (Bateson, 1966; Bolhuis, 1991). Imprinting ensures that offspring recognize their parents, and later often influences the sexual partners chosen. An obvious functional reason this evolved learning mechanism should have an early, narrow, temporal window is that, with few exceptions, the first individual a newborn sees is its mother, and bonding with that individual should yield reliably positive parent and species identification. Other types of critical period phenomena have no such obvious function, and may result from mechanistic constraints on brain development. A well-studied example involves **critical periods in early visual development** (Held and Hein, 1963). Unlike primates, carnivores such as cats and dogs are born blind. A young kitten must receive adequate visual stimulation shortly after the eyes open, or the visual system malfunctions. Indeed, a normal cat raised in darkness during this critical period will spend the rest of its life "blind" (although its eyes are perfectly functional) because the higher neural circuits involved in vision do not develop. In this case, the critical period appears to result from the dynamics of neural development. The early vertebrate nervous system shows *exuberant branching*, where neurons destined to make contact with certain areas also send out axonal branches to other areas. These "excess" branches are later pruned by a process that depends upon perceptual stimulation and competition among different neurons: a beautiful case of epigenesis, where the brain develops via a "recipe" rather than a "blueprint," and requires a normal environment and peripheral anatomy (eyes or ears) to develop in the species-typical fashion (Striedter, 2004). Kittens must actively explore their environment visually to develop normal vision; the system depends on an active feedback loop between perception and action in order to develop (Held and Hein, 1963).

Sensitive periods can thus be thought of as time windows when certain types of information are required by the developing brain, either to help wire itself (as for visual critical periods) or to allow the organism to behave in an adaptive manner (as for imprinting). Sensitive periods for language acquisition could fulfill either, or both, of these functions. As already mentioned, the early sensitivity of the neonate to its mother's voice may play an important role in parental bonding (Mehler *et al.*, 1978), and rapid language learning later in childhood is clearly equally adaptive. However, it seems likely that epigenetic self-wiring development plays the more crucial role for most linguistic sensitive periods, simply because the later timing of such sensitivities has no apparent adaptive function. In particular, the "closing" of some sensitive periods with puberty appears positively counter-adaptive given human life history, since sexual maturity often marks the time when young adults join new groups with new dialects. This would seem a time when the ability to learn a new dialect or language would seem to be *most* favored, and it is puzzling that our language-learning abilities instead decrease at this stage. Thus, the slow closing of the sensitive period seems more likely to represent independent maturational processes, perhaps sensitive to rising levels of sex hormones, rather than a specific adaptation in itself.

9.3.2 Babbling and vocal imitation

Another fascinating similarity between human speech and birdsong is **babbling**. Human infants have a strong and apparently innate tendency to vocalize to themselves, and by the age of ten months this urge seems to be an overwhelming, self-absorbing activity (Menn and Stoel-Gammon, 2005). Infants engage in babbling without requiring feedback from others. Young infants "babble" with their hands as well as their mouths; and deaf infants gradually stop their vocal babbling, while hearing infants decrease manual babbling to focus on audio-vocal babbling (Stoel-Gammon and Otomo, 1986; Petitto and Marentette, 1991). Babbling appears closely linked to speech: the vocalizations produced late in the babbling stage have an influence on the first words the child produces (Vihman, 1986, 1991), and tracheostomized children, prevented from babbling for medical reasons, show a corresponding delay in their speech acquisition (Locke and Pearson, 1990). Thus, many authors have suggested that the babbling stage represents a necessary period for the infant to master the control of its vocal apparatus (Jespersen, 1922; Kuczaj, 1983; Locke, 1993; Menn and Stoel-Gammon, 2005). Similarly, young songbirds "babble": the subadult male sits by himself singing quietly, with no external rewards required. In a series of well-studied stages including *subsong* and *plastic song*, the young bird passes through a variable process of experimentation and selection of vocalizations (Marler and Peters, 1982). Talking parrots also engage in solitary "vocal play" that includes rearranging and permuting speech syllables (Pepperberg, 1999).

Early experiments with birds showed that the subsong period is a critical period for song learning: if a bird is temporarily deafened during this
period it can never learn "normal" song. An adult bird deafened later, after
the song has "crystallized," can in many cases go on producing normal song
indefinitely (Marler and Slabbekoorn, 2004). Many hypothetical functions
of babbling that remain speculative for humans have been demonstrated in
songbirds (Nottebohm, 1999; Tchernichovski *et al.*, 2001).

Complex vocal imitation, as defined here, may *require* a babbling stage,
during which the young animal develops and fine-tunes its neural control
over its vocal production system. By "closing the loop" between audition and
vocal motor control, a vocal imitator can develop the symmetry between
input and output required for imitation. For complex vocal imitation to
work, detailed aspects of the auditory signal need to be mapped onto equally
fine aspects of motor control. The process of babbling may be necessary for
such an abstract model, linking production and perception, to be discovered. This is a testable hypothesis: strongly predicting the necessity of a
babbling stage in other species capable of complex vocal imitation. Young
chimpanzees do not babble consistently (Hayes, 1951). The only primate
vocal behavior similar to babbling is seen in pygmy marmosets, which attract
and appease adults with highly variable vocalizations; these have not been
shown to serve as vocal practice (Elowson *et al.*, 1998a, 1998b). The story
of Hoover, a talking harbor seal adopted at birth by a fisherman, suggests
the possibility of a sensitive period for his speech acquisition, and informal
reports suggest that he did experiment with and improve these speech-like
vocalizations as he matured (Ralls *et al.*, 1985). I know of no data suggesting
solitary "vocal play" in marine mammals (Bowles *et al.*, 1988), and a well-
documented absence of babbling in such species would refute the epigenetic
hypothesis offered above, and demonstrate the possibility of other (perhaps
"pre-wired") routes to the type of detailed audio-motor matching required
for complex vocal imitation. For now, this remains a plausible hypothesis consistent with much comparative data, and suggests that the human
infant's innate predisposition to babble represents an "instinct to learn."
Babbling provides an "epigenetic playground," allowing the child to tune
its vocal production to its auditory perceptual mechanism, and providing
the route to the imitation of arbitrary signals later in life.

9.4 Neural mechanisms underlying complex vocal imitation

The neural mechanisms underlying complex vocal imitation are best understood, by far, for songbirds. Good recent reviews of this field are Nottebohm

(1999) and Marler and Slabbekoorn (2004). Virtually nothing is known about the neural mechanisms underlying vocal imitation in other vocal learners such as dolphins or seals. More surprising, we know little about these mechanisms in our own species: to my knowledge there is not a single brain-imaging study involving a vocal imitation task in humans (in contrast to a number of studies on visual/manual imitation). However, certain well-understood anatomical differences in the brains of humans and other primates may underlie our increased vocal control.

9.4.1 Shared mechanisms

The neural mechanisms for vocal control are quite conservative among mammals (Jürgens, 1998). Both the muscles of the larynx and vocal tract, and their primary nervous supply, are shared virtually identically among mammals, and many higher-order controlling structures in the brainstem and cortex are also apparently shared. We can distinguish between three different levels of control of the vocal apparatus (see Figure 9.1). The lowest and most conservative is the **brainstem chassis**, which consists of the motor neurons that actually drive the face, tongue, larynx, and respiratory muscles, and which is identical in humans and other mammals. At the next level, we find a **midbrain control center**, made up of the periaqueductal gray region and surrounding tegmentum, which serves to elicit vocalization and in some cases to control parameters. This control system is also shared among all mammals investigated, and many other vertebrates. It is only at the highest level, that of **cortical control systems**, that we find significant differences between humans and other mammals. I will now give a brief breakdown of these different levels of control. For more detailed descriptions, a brief but authoritative guide is Jürgens (1995); more details can be found in Deacon (1992) and Jürgens (2002).

The brainstem chassis

The cell bodies of the motor neurons controlling vocalization lie within the brainstem, and send their axons out to the various muscles via multiple *cranial nerves*. Briefly, the key motor neurons are in the facial and trigeminal nuclei (for the face and jaw), the hypoglossal nucleus (most tongue muscles), and the nucleus ambiguus (for the larynx and diaphragm). Destruction of any of these neurons will lead to complete paralysis of the associated muscles, and the details of the innervation patterns are thus very useful for the diagnosis of brainstem lesions and have been memorized by generations of medical students. The controlled structures have their primary

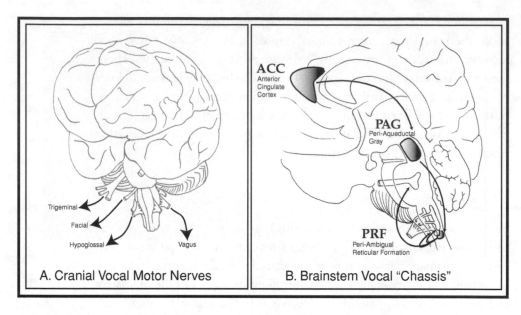

Figure 9.1 The brainstem "chassis" for control of vocalization in mammals – The cranial motor nerves that innervate the various muscles involved in vocalization in mammals are shown in A. The *Trigeminal* nerve provides motor control to the jaw, the *Facial* nerve to most facial muscles including the lips, the *Hypoglossal* to the tongue, and the *Vagal* nerve to the larynx and some respiratory muscles. A view inside the brainstem (B) illustrates the different control nuclei. The most important are the Peri-Ambigual Reticular Formation of the medulla (PRF) and Peri-Aqueductal Gray region of the midbrain (PAG); the Anterior Cingulate Cortex (ACC) is the only cortical region that plays a role in vocalization in most mammals, but it appears to have an on/off "gating" effect, with no direct control on vocalization structure.

functions in feeding and breathing, and thus damage to this region typically leads to severe health problems such as dysphagia (problems in eating and swallowing) and choking, in addition to speech problems. These critical functions make it unsurprising that their neural basis is highly conservative among all vertebrates. All of these muscles are branchial arch derivatives (see Chapter 5).

9.4.2 The midbrain control region

The core region involved in vocal control *per se* is a region in the brainstem called the *peri-aqueductal gray*, or **PAG**, which lies in the midbrain. Electrical stimulation of the PAG reliably elicits acoustically normal vocalizations in many vertebrate species, including all mammals and birds that have been tested (Jürgens, 1994). This region represents the primitive vocal control center for innate vocalizations. The connections of the PAG to the brain-stem chassis have been mapped in primates by Jürgens and Pratt (1979), who found direct connections onto or just surrounding three of the four key components of the brainstem vocal chassis: the trigeminal and facial nuclei, and nucleus ambiguus. However, no connections to the hypoglossal nucleus, which controls the tongue, were found. This is consistent with the observation that mammalian vocalizations generally involve laryngeal and facial components (jaws and lips), but *not* any active deformation of the tongue body (Jürgens and Ploog, 1976; Deacon, 1992).

The PAG is apparently enough, alone, to generate acoustically normal vocalizations in nonhuman mammals including cats and monkeys. Removal or disconnection of cortical centers does not impair vocal output (Deacon, 1992). This is also true for innate calls such as crying in humans: *anencephalic* babies, who lack the entire forebrain (cortex, thalamus, and basal ganglia, along with cerebellum), still react to painful stimuli with crying (Jürgens, 1995). A diffuse set of connections from other brainstem and limbic regions onto the PAG seem to link vocalization centers to the appropriate emotional or situational context for vocalizations, and stimulation of such regions leads to vocalizations with a much longer latency than stimulation of the PAG. Given this evidence, it seems appropriate to view the midbrain control centers as the basic command center for vocalization in vertebrates, which mediates between processing tied to sensory input (e.g. pain and pleasure, or surprising or dangerous visual stimuli), the affective reactions to these stimuli, and the vocal output mechanisms in the brainstem chassis.

9.4.3 Cortical control regions

When it comes to cortical centers, two separate systems play a role in controlling vocalization. The first and more primitive of these systems is again widely shared among mammals. This **medial cortical system** consists of the anterior cingulate cortex and neighboring areas (such as parts of the supplementary motor area) which appear to play a higher-order volitional role in exciting or inhibiting vocalization in most mammals, including humans (Myers, 1976; Jürgens and von Cramon, 1982). Electrical stimulation of this area can induce vocalization, and lesions to it induce mutism in animals and a loss of the ability to control vocalizations in an operant context; lesions to this area in humans also induce temporary mutism with a permanent loss of vocal affect expression (Jürgens and von Cramon, 1982). The neuroanatomical data are all consistent with a model which sees this medial system as the highest and most voluntary level of vocal control in most mammals, and as one which still plays an important role in vocalizations, including both speech and innate human "calls" like laughter and cries in our own species. This medial system appears to be solely responsible for the ability of most mammals to gate their vocalizations in an operant situation, but does not seem to allow the active modification of the acoustic structure of these vocalizations.

In all of the systems discussed up to now, humans appear to share the qualitative pattern of neural circuitry that is seen in other mammals and primates. However, a crucial difference in vocal motor circuitry between human and other primates does exist in the **lateral cortical system**. In particular, humans possess direct connections between the frontal motor areas of lateral neocortex and important brainstem motor neurons, especially those in the nucleus ambiguus involved in laryngeal control (Kuypers, 1958; Deacon, 1992; Jürgens, 1994). I will call these novel connections **cortico-laryngeal connections** (avoiding the more opaque but neuroanatomically precise term *cortico-ambigual connections*). While damage to this lateral cortical region causes prolonged voice loss in humans, damage to the same region in squirrel or rhesus monkeys has no effect on vocalizations, which remain normal in quantity and quality, but has a pronounced effect on control of the lips, jaw, and tongue, and thus greatly disturbs feeding (Jürgens *et al.*, 1982). This novel cortico-laryngeal connection is a robust, well-documented difference between human and other mammal brains that appears to be directly relevant to human vocal abilities (see Figure 9.2).

The distinction between this novel lateral system, and the shared, primitive medial system and midbrain control centers, is well illustrated by the frequency with which one can see a double-dissociation of speech and song on the one hand, and innate vocalization and emotional ejectives (such as cursing) on the other (Jürgens *et al.*, 1982). It is quite common for aphasic patients to have severely disrupted spontaneous speech, but to still laugh, cry, and curse normally. The fact that (learned) words involved in cursing can remain unimpaired after damage to the rest of the lexicon, and tend to segregate with innate calls, is quite interesting. It suggests that the linguistic system has in some sense partially "colonized" the older and more basic brain circuitry involved in emotional expression (Myers, 1976). However, the rest of the vocal output associated with complex vocal imitation is associated with these new, lateral connections. It is unlikely to be coincidence that the neurons that make these direct connections lie in the motor cortex immediately posterior to Broca's area, a spatial contiguity that will surface repeatedly in the rest of this book.

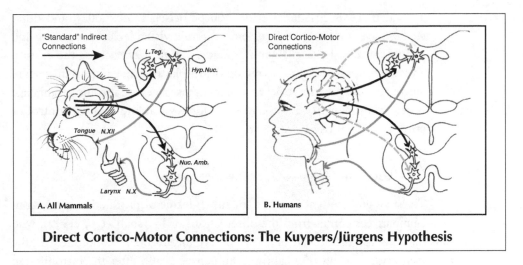

Direct Cortico-Motor Connections: The Kuypers/Jürgens Hypothesis

Figure 9.2 The Kuypers/Jürgens hypothesis of speech motor control – Direct connections between cortex and vocal motor neurons are hypothesized to underlie speech motor control in humans. On the left, the indirect connections from lateral motor cortex to brainstem interneurons are shown. These are typical of most mammals. Cortical neurons make no direct connections to the actual motorneurons that control the muscles of the tongue and larynx. In addition to such indirect connection, primates add direct connections from cortex to the motor neurons controlling the tongue, jaw, and lips (right top). Only humans, among primates, possess direct connections to the laryngeal motor neurons that control the muscles of the larynx (right bottom).

Broca's area is the inferior lateral portion of the premotor cortex, usually considered to encompass Brodmann's cytoarchitectonically defined areas BA44 and BA45. It lies just in front of the portion of the motor cortex that controls the face, jaw, and tongue (and which happens to lie just beneath the neurons controlling the hands and fingers). This region is thus, unsurprisingly, involved in the motor control of chewing and swallowing in mammals. More interestingly, it is implicated in the voluntary control of vocal production in humans, but lesion studies reveal no corresponding function in monkey vocalizations (Jürgens, 2002). Finally, some interpreters of endocasts of fossil hominids have suggested that this region has been a target of expansion during hominid evolution, starting at *Homo habilis* (e.g. Tobias, 1987). For all of these reasons, neural changes in the general region of Broca's area have been seen by many commentators as critical in the evolution of human vocal motor control. This view of Broca's area is consistent with the results of numerous imaging studies of vocal production, and the view of Broca himself, who saw it as the area controlling linguistic production only. However, Broca's region has also been implicated in both the production *and comprehension* of various aspects of syntax (Caramazza and Zurif, 1976; Friederici *et al.*, 2000; Koelsch *et al.*, 2002), and other studies have implicated this general region in visual lexical processing and phonological tasks (e.g. rhyming; Zatorre *et al.*, 1992). Thus the cortical areas encompassed by Broca's region clearly play multiple important roles in language, but it remains unclear whether these roles are specific to language or reflect more general aspects of volitional vocal and manual control or attention (Thompson-Schill *et al.*, 1997).

9.4.4 Vocal control in comparative perspective

The strongest evidence to date for some degree of production learning in chimpanzees comes from the observations of Marshall *et al.* (1999), who documented the spread of a "raspberry" or "lip buzz" component in the pant hoot displays of a captive chimpanzee group after the introduction of a male who produced such calls. This observation is strengthened by the arguments of Reynolds Losin *et al.* (2008) that such lip control is both voluntary and intentional in chimpanzees, and differently lateralized from normal species-typical calling. Accepting these observations at present as the only data consistent with production learning in chimpanzees, this has an interesting implication: that the core difficulty that keeps chimpanzees from learning speech is not vocal *tract* control, but *laryngeal* control. This is consistent with the observations of Hayes (1951) and Hayes and Hayes (1951) regarding their attempts to teach the chimpanzee Viki to speak: the few utterances she could control and shape with any facility were unvoiced: panted, rather than vocalized. These observations confirm that the crucial difference between humans and chimpanzees is control over the laryngeal musculature, consistent with the neuroanatomical observations that only humans have direct cortical-laryngeal connections.

A nearly direct test of the Kuypers–Jürgens hypothesis is provided by songbirds, which have convergently evolved complex vocal control. Unfortunately, the comparison is not totally straightforward, because both avian vocal production, and the structure of the avian brain, are quite different from those of mammals. Birds produce sound with a unique organ, the syrinx, at the base of the trachea (see Figure 9.3). They also lack a tissue comparable to the mammalian neocortex (see Chapter 5). But, bearing these differences in mind, birds clearly support the hypothesis: they possess direct connections from the forebrain motor areas to the neurons which control the syrinx (Iwatsubo *et al.*, 1990; Wild, 1993).

A peculiarity in the distribution of complex vocal imitation among mammals is that only aquatic mammals (whales and seals) clearly show complex

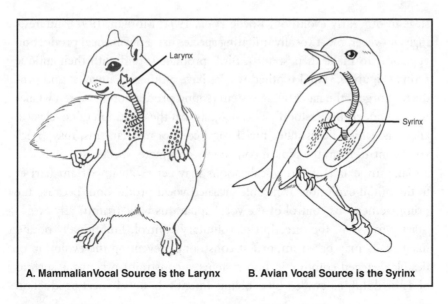

A. MammalianVocal Source is the Larynx   B. Avian Vocal Source is the Syrinx

Figure 9.3 Bird *versus* mammal vocal production – Mammals, like most terrestrial vertebrates, use the larynx to produce vocalization (A). Birds use a novel organ located at the base of the trachea, the syrinx, to produce vocalizations (B).

vocal imitation. If we relax our standards to include *all* vocal imitation, it will add additional seals, some bats, and perhaps elephants. Thus, virtually all nonhuman vocal imitators either fly or are aquatic (and adding the 4,000 or so bird species who vocally imitate just strengthens this pattern). Janik and Slater (1997) hypothesized that the mobility characterizing flying or swimming animals puts a premium on vocal communication and, perhaps, vocal imitation, and thus provides a possible functional basis for imitation. An additional functional constraint on marine mammals who vocalize underwater may be that the acoustic quality of the voice changes with depth, and may require more complex signals for recognition, or more complex control (Janik and Slater, 1997). I suggest a mechanistic hypothesis: that the requirements of flight or swimming demand increased voluntary control over the larynx and respiratory muscles, particularly for underwater breath-holding, which provided a preadaptation to complex vocal control. Interesting test cases for this hypothesis are provided by other aquatic mammals, including beavers, capybaras, otters, and polar bears. The vocal learning capabilities of any of these species could easily be studied, and should exceed those of closely related terrestrial species.

Humans represent an obvious exception to the "flying or swimming" rule (one valid reason given by enthusiasts of the "aquatic ape" hypothesis to support the idea that humans went through a semi-amphibious marine stage in our early evolution; Roede *et al.*, 1991; Morgan, 1997). Interestingly, however, most vocally imitating species use a novel vocal production apparatus to make their sounds. Birds produce sound with their unique syrinx (Figure 9.3) and toothed whales have a different novel sound production organ, the nasal bursa system (sound production in baleen whales remains poorly understood). This suggests that the evolution of novel vocal anatomy, which necessitates novel vocal control mechanisms, may "free" vocal control from the typical constraints on innate, species-specific calls. Socially important innate vocalizations may act as an important barrier to the initial evolution of flexible, learned vocal production, because the primitive nervous control of the vocal apparatus will "trump" any evolutionary forays in the direction of voluntary control. Emotionally bound innate calls may be an important constraint preventing the evolution of flexible, learned communication systems, a constraint organisms such as birds or dolphins evaded by evolving an entirely novel vocal production system.

Of complex vocal imitators, only humans and seals are known to produce their sounds with the typical mammal vocal production system: lungs, a larynx, and a vocal tract. Somehow, humans and seals have successfully "unbound" our vocal production system from its original role, and use it to produce flexible, learned vocal signals. This fundamental fact about complex vocal imitation has received surprisingly little attention from students of language evolution (though see Deacon, 1997). Unfortunately, we know little about how complex vocal imitation evolved among seals. The functions of seal song, like those of birdsong, may or may not have anything to do with the functions of human music or speech (Hauser and McDermott, 2003). But function aside, the neural and physiological mechanisms that underlie vocal production and vocal learning in seals are of great interest, as they provide the only analog currently known in which such mechanisms can be studied experimentally (Fitch, 2006b). The strong, testable prediction following from the review above is that seals should have direct corticolaryngeal connections. If so, seals would offer an ideal species to study the development and genetic determinants of this pattern, with many species kept in captivity in zoos and aquaria. Seals are readily trained, and quite manageable if raised in contact with humans. They are small enough to be scanned using non-invasive brain imaging technology developed for humans. There is no reason in principle why seal vocal production and neural control could not be studied in detail, as birdsong is today. Unlike birds, seals have a typical mammalian brain, like our own, and they use it to control a typical mammalian vocal system. They are also much closer genetically and neurally to humans than are songbirds. Thus, the door is open to a wide variety of comparative studies that could shed light on this crucial aspect of human speech production and control.

9.4.5 Implications of the novel circuitry in humans

Qualitatively novel cortico-laryngeal connections from the human motor cortex pose a serious problem for scholars who argue for continuity between primate calls and human speech (or song; Myers, 1976). Any theory for the evolution of human speech needs to account for the evolution of these novel circuits. While many authors have argued for continuity in primate and human vocal control (e.g. Lieberman, 2000, 2006), I know of only two scientists who have taken the challenge posed by these comparative neurological data seriously (Deacon, 1992; MacNeilage, 1998b). Both authors acknowledge an increased role of the lateral motor cortex in human vocalization. However, Deacon has suggested that this difference may be initially quantitative rather than qualitative, and that the quantitative differences seen in adulthood may result from epigenetic processes and the selective retention of neural connections (Deacon, 1984, 1992). MacNeilage has highlighted the role that the medial system continues to play in human vocalization, stressing a potential precursor role for the neural systems controlling the lips and jaw in primate lip-smack displays. These models will be discussed further in Chapter 10.

While I agree with these arguments, they do not in my opinion justify downplaying the importance of the novel lateral connections in humans, nor do they solve the continuity problem. While the vast majority of the anatomical and neural circuitry involved in human speech is shared with other primates, this does nothing to explain the core behavioral *difference* between humans and other primates: our ability for complex vocal imitation. The hypothesis of Jürgens *et al.* (1982) puts these novel lateral connections at center stage. Put simply, it suggests that our novel cortico-laryngeal connections provide fine voluntary control over the larynx, allowing us to coordinate phonation with detailed movements of the jaw, lips, and tongue (which were already under voluntary control for feeding in our earlier primate ancestors). In Jürgens' hypothesis, lateral cortical control is a neural prerequisite for complex vocal imitation, as seen in speech or song. While there are probably other important cortical or subcortical areas involved in complex vocal imitation, this hypothesis is both logical and consistent with a large body of detailed neuroanatomical data (Striedter, 2004).

9.5 The molecular genetic basis of complex vocal motor control

Ultimately, any speech-related neural differences between humans and chimpanzees must have some genetic basis. The 99 percent sequence similarity between these two species means that the search space is far more circumscribed than for most species whose genomes have been sequenced. Because both the human and the chimpanzee genome are sequenced (Chimpanzee Sequencing and Analysis Consortium, 2005) and available to all on the Internet, it might seem inevitable that the key functional differences will rapidly be isolated and traced to particular genes. Unfortunately, this assumption is incorrect, because most genetic differences are neutral and have no effect on the function or fitness of the organism (King and Jukes, 1969; Kimura, 1983). Those few changes that *are* adaptive, controlling critical phenotypic differences between organisms, are "buried" in the neutral, non-adaptive noise in the genome. Thus the search for those genetic differences that actually *make* a difference is like searching for a needle in a haystack. And 1 percent of the 10^9 base pairs in the human genome suggest that there are ten million base pairs to peruse: bad news for anyone contemplating a brute force approach to isolating the genetic differences critical to speech or language.

The first promising option is to look only at expressed portions of the genome. The human genome consists mainly of non-coding DNA (once called "junk" DNA, meaning that it is never transcribed into protein). Only about 2 percent of the human (or chimpanzee) genome are **coding genes**: DNA translated to proteins that play a role in the cell. This portion of the genome can be relatively easily located by computer (by searching for "start" and "stop" sequences). The vast majority of coding DNA appears to be nearly identical between the two species, with few differences having an apparent effect on protein function. Indeed, most human proteins are shared, with little change, with mice. Some interesting exceptions are known. Most of these are either olfactory genes, or genes expressed in the testis that play some unknown role in reproductive isolation or sperm competition (Clark *et al.*, 2003). However, some interesting changes in muscle proteins are known, such as the **MYH16** myosin gene, linked to the reduced human temporalis muscles (Stedman *et al.*, 2004). The *temporalis muscles* are chewing muscles in the temples, and in most mammals they are large and powerful. In adult apes, these muscles overlie almost the entire sides of the skull, creating a thick layer of muscle under the scalp, while in humans these muscles are very small and thin (see Figure 7.2). Temporalis reduction is linked to the silencing of the MYH16 gene, which codes for a form of myosin that is expressed only in these muscles. Comparative examination of the MYH16 gene in different primates allows researchers to estimate the time at which this key mutation arose during hominid evolution (Perry *et al.*, 2004). Hopefully, further research will reveal more such examples, but current data suggest that, to a reasonable first approximation, humans generally use the same proteins to build our bodies as chimpanzees. This suggests that it is changes in gene expression, rather than protein sequences, which play the primary role (Carroll, 2005b).

Regulatory genes play key roles in the complex epigenetic process underlying gene regulation. The most important class of regulatory genes are **transcription factors**: genes coding for proteins that bind to DNA, thus regulating the expression of other genes nearby. Transcription factors transcribed from one site on a chromosome can move to other areas, controlling multiple genes by "recognizing" particular sequences of base pairs, termed *binding motifs*, to which they bind preferentially. Binding to these sites may then increase or decrease gene expression in neighboring DNA. The stretch of DNA adjacent to the protein-coding portion of the genome is termed its "promoter region," and proteins binding to such regions are termed **cis-regulatory elements** (CREs – "cis" indicates the same strand of DNA). Typically, a single gene will have multiple different binding sites in its promoter region: imagine a set of locks on the door of a particularly well-secured urban apartment, where the CREs are the keys. In order to "open the door" and initiate gene expression, multiple transcription factor keys must be bound to the DNA (and other "blocking" CREs removed). Although the transcription factors themselves tend to be quite conservative, more and more evidence suggests that changes in the regulatory regions to which they bind play a crucial role in the evolution of organismic form and function (Carroll *et al.*, 2005).

Unfortunately, regulatory regions are more difficult to study than coding DNA because they have no clearly delineated start and end points. A promising approach for identifying crucial regions of non-coding DNA is to search for conserved regions of non-coding DNA in widely separated animal species (such as fish, birds, and mammals). Comparisons between mammals and "model organisms" such as the chicken or the fugu pufferfish (which has the smallest known vertebrate genome) suggest that another 2–3 percent of the vertebrate genome consist of highly conserved regulatory regions, and a detailed exploration of such regions promises further insights into the mechanisms underlying gene expression (International

Chicken Genome Sequencing Consortium, 2004; Vandepoele *et al.*, 2004), and the recent sequencing of the protochordate amphioxus reveals considerable conservation of such regions (Putnam *et al.*, 2008). These distant relatives will prove crucial in discovering, and understanding, non-coding motifs involved in gene regulation in the coming decade. For now, most genetic work has focused by necessity on protein-coding portions of the genome, but after this "low-hanging fruit" has been picked, the more difficult, and ultimately more significant, challenge of understanding the role of non-coding DNA in gene regulation will have to be faced (Carroll, 2003).

9.6 *FOXP2* and complex vocal motor control

To date, however, only a single regulatory gene has been isolated that has a clear relationship to a unique human ability: a gene called **FOXP2**, a transcription factor which is one member of the large forkhead box (*FOX*) transcription factor family (Carlsson and Mahlapuu, 2002). Deleterious mutations in this gene disrupt oral and facial sequencing (oro-motor praxis) in humans (Vargha-Khadem *et al.*, 1995). Furthermore, all human populations share a unique derived version of this gene, which differs in a few key places from that of all other primates. Thus, *FOXP2* is the only gene so far discovered that provides important clues to the evolution of speech.

The discovery of *FOXP2* provides some interesting insights into the difficulty of discovering such genes, and required a blend of diligent hard work by dedicated researchers (Faraneh Vargha-Khadem, Simon Fisher, and colleagues) and simple good luck (Marcus and Fisher, 2003). The central role in this saga is played by the **KE family** in Britain. Many members of the family suffer from an impairment of speech and language, the most prominent symptom of which is poor oro-motor facial control, but which also affects some aspects of speech perception and rhythmic motor control (Vargha-Khadem *et al.*, 1995; Watkins *et al.*, 2002). Early claims that these difficulties reflect a "language gene" whose effects were limited to morphosyntax (Gopnik, 1990; Pinker, 1994b) have now been thoroughly refuted (Vargha-Khadem *et al.*, 1995; Vargha-Khadem *et al.*, 2005). Although some affected members of the KE family also suffer from mental retardation, others have IQs in the normal range, and researchers have carefully controlled for this. Anatomical investigations revealed several differences in the cerebellum and basal ganglia (Vargha-Khadem *et al.*, 1998; Vargha-Khadem *et al.*, 2005). Functional imaging studies involving verb generation and word repetition tasks show a more diffuse and bilateral pattern of activity in affected members than in unaffected members of the same family (Liégeois *et al.*, 2003), with the putamen (part of the basal ganglia) and regions roughly corresponding to Broca's area being particularly affected.

Classical genetic linkage analyses were used to isolate this problem to a portion of chromosome seven bearing a number of candidate genes (Fisher *et al.*, 1998). The chance discovery of a second individual, with a very similar phenotype, allowed researchers to quickly pinpoint the affected gene as *FOXP2* (Lai *et al.*, 2001). This critical and most difficult advance opened the door to the full power of modern molecular biological techniques.

First, the *FOXP2* alleles of forty-four normal humans from around the world were sequenced. The amino acid sequence of the coded protein was found to be identical in all of them. In contrast, the human *FOXP2* protein was found to differ from that of chimpanzees (often designated as lowercase *FoxP2* for clarity) at several sites (Enard *et al.*, 2002). One difference – repeating sequences of the amino acid glutamine that vary in length – is considered to be unimportant because it is highly variable both within and outside of species, and does not co-segregate with the speech disorder in the KE family. If the polyglutamine stretches are disregarded, the human *FOXP2* protein differs at only three amino-acid positions from its ortholog in the mouse. The chimpanzee, gorilla, and rhesus macaque *FOXP2* proteins are all identical to each other and carry only one difference from the mouse and two differences from the human protein. Finally, the proportion of non-silent substitutions was significantly greater than expected by chance in humans, when compared to silent substitutions. This analysis is consistent with positive selection on the human allele. *FOXP2* fulfills the criteria for a genetic difference that *makes a difference in speech*: its disruption disturbs speech in a clinical population, the human version is different from chimpanzees and other primates, and the variant is shared by all human populations.

A second critical finding for *FOXP2* came from a more detailed examination of the non-coding intron sequences flanking the *FOXP2* exon in different human populations. Variability in these flanking regions allows a rough deduction of the time at which the novel human allele went from a novel mutational variant to become nearly universal in a population of early hominids: the "selective sweep." Significant evidence for a selective sweep is provided by an excess of rare alleles over common ones. Indeed, the metric for this analysis, called Tajima's D, was larger for *FOXP2* than for almost any other gene yet explored. Finally, and most importantly, variation in the human gene was used to estimate the time at which the new human version of the gene became fixed among humans: a range between 0 and

120,000 years ago. This range represents the 95 percent confidence interval, under assumptions of a constant population size. But because human population size has not been constant in recent history, the time at which population expansion began (10,000 to 100,000 years ago) must be added to this value in order to derive the true time of fixation. By these calculations, the maximum time at which the new human allele of the *FOXP2* gene reached fixation would be about 220,000 years: within the time range during which anatomically modern *Homo sapiens* (AMHS) arose in Africa, suggesting that the *FOXP2* genes arose in the last stage of human evolution. This is, of course, consistent with the hypothesis of a "great leap forward" in language and cognition, occurring with AMHS and unique to our particular lineage of hominids. However, more recent research with fossil DNA suggests that Neanderthals shared the modern human *FOXP2* variant, which would push this figure back at least to 300–400 KYA, to our common ancestor with Neanderthals (Krause *et al.*, 2007). These conflicting results show the need for caution in these early days: calibrating models like those used by Enard *et al.* (2002) is still quite difficult.

It is important to recognize that *FOXP2* is just the first gene to be discovered of many genes involved in speech and language. As more genes are discovered, an approach similar to that pioneered by Enard and colleagues will be crucial for testing hypotheses about language evolution. While providing specific dates for selective sweeps may always be difficult, *ranking* the order of selective sweeps on multiple genes will allow us to place different evolutionary events in their correct order, which is far more important than precise dates for discriminating between theories of language evolution.

FOXP2, like most transcription factors, is extremely conservative. It is found in nearly identical form in all mammals, and is shared with songbirds. Gene expression in humans and mice is broadly similar (Lai *et al.*, 2003). Thus, experimental organisms like mice, in which genetic engineering is possible, can be used to study the basic function of this gene. Two types of study are revealing. First, *FOXP2* has been subjected to a *targeted knockout* procedure in which the gene is inactivated (Shu *et al.*, 2005). Homozygous knockouts (where both copies of the gene are inactivated) show severe motor impairments and do not survive to adulthood. Heterozygous knockout mice with one functional version survive, but show major disruptions of cerebellar organization, and motor abnormalities. However, despite thorough examination, research on knockout mice has revealed no differences in the basal ganglia. Although vocal production is reduced in these knockout mice, the vocalizations that are produced appear to be normal.

The second set of results comes from so-called *knock-in* mice, which have had human versions of the *FOXP2* gene inserted into their genome. One set of mice has had the KE-family variant inserted into their genome (Groszer *et al.*, 2008). Again, homozygotes are quite impaired (but show normal vocalizations); heterozygotes are overtly normal, but show difficulties in motor-skill learning. *FOXP2* thus shows no connection to mouse vocal *control* in either of these datasets. This is perhaps unsurprising, as there are no data indicating that mice manipulate their supralaryngeal vocal tract during vocalization. Although male mice produce relatively complex courtship "songs" (Holy and Guo, 2005), complex courtship vocalizations are common in male rodents (Barfield and Geyer, 1972; Barfield *et al.*, 1979), and there is no evidence that they are learned. Finally, mice with the human version of the *FOXP2* gene have been created, by Svante Pääbo's laboratory in Leipzig (Enard *et al.*, 2009). These mice show some subtle differences in ultrasonic vocalizations and exploratory behavior. More importantly, significant changes are found in a certain class of neurons ("medium spiny neurons") which have increased dendrite lengths and increased synaptic plasticity. This genetically engineered model organism will be crucial in understanding the role of *FOXP2* in the nervous system. We can expect rapid progress on this front.

Equally exciting results have come from recent work examining *FOX* genes in songbirds. *FOXP2* exists in birds, along with other *FOX* genes, and is expressed in very similar tissues. Although there does not appear to be a particular mutation in the *FOXP2* gene in vocal learning birds (Haesler *et al.*, 2004; Webb and Zhang, 2005), the gene has been directly linked to vocal learning in songbirds (Scharff and Haesler, 2005; Haesler *et al.*, 2007). In particular, *FOXP2* expression increases during the song learning period in Area X, a basal-ganglia homolog known to be centrally involved in vocal learning. More impressive, *FOXP2* expression can be experimentally down-regulated using viral vectors in living birds; such birds show incomplete and inaccurate song learning (Haesler *et al.*, 2007). This change is already evident quite early on, during the subsong or "babbling" period, and strongly suggests a direct parallel between *FOXP2* in human and songbird vocal learning.

In summary, *FOXP2* at present represents the only genetic change that can be closely linked to uniquely human cognitive characteristic. *FOXP2* is presumably just the tip of a genetic iceberg: as a transcription factor it controls the expression of a branching cascade including many other genes. Thus, considerably more work is necessary before we understand what the minor changes in this gene do in the developing brain. The finding that only two amino acid changes in a transcription factor can lead to important effects on many brain regions is sobering, for it emphasizes the needle-in-a-haystack quality of our search for such genes. Furthermore, it remains uncertain whether these protein changes are the critical factor, because changes in the regulatory region of the *FOXP2* gene itself, and the upstream factors that control *its* expression, may be equally important. Thus, while the importance of this discovery should not be underestimated – it is historic – it should not be overestimated either. This gene is not a "magic bullet" that suddenly gave humans speech (or language), and considerably more work will be necessary to isolate the genetic mechanisms that underlie our unusual capacity for complex vocal imitation. *FOXP2* provides an important point of experimental access, but it is certainly neither the only, nor likely the most important, gene change related to spoken language (despite their early problems with speech, affected members of the KE family do, eventually, attain relatively normal language skills and communicate successfully. But *FOXP2* provides an excellent start for our search, illustrates the rich potential of the molecular approach, and is worthy of the close attention of all scholars interested in language evolution.

9.7 Summary: the vocal tract and its neural control

To briefly summarize what we have learned in the last two chapters: speech (complex, articulated, vocalization) must be distinguished from language, because signed language or the written word provide alternate signaling systems. Despite long interest and debate regarding the anatomy of the vocal tract in language evolution, investigations of vocalization in living animals have revealed the vocal tract and tongue to be dynamically reconfigured during vocalization in many mammals. This suggests that the importance of static vocal anatomy has been overemphasized in past discussion, and that early hominids could produce an adequate variety of vocal sounds for language. Therefore, as concluded by Darwin, the primary evolutionary changes required for spoken language were neural, not changes in vocal anatomy. Furthermore, the fact that other animals have a descended larynx and tongue root (a characteristic previously thought to be uniquely evolved for human speech), shows that human-like speech anatomy can serve non-speech functions, and thus cannot provide an unambiguous fossil indicator of speech. Most other proposed fossil indicators of speech do not hold up under comparative scrutiny, with the exception of an expansion of the thoracic canal, associated with increased breath control, sometime after early *Homo ergaster* and before Neanderthals.

Turning to the neural basis for speech, humans have direct connections from the lateral neocortex to the motor nuclei involved in phonation; such connections are lacking in most nonhuman primates or other mammals, and are the best candidates for the neural changes required for speech. Comparative data reveal that a number of different animal groups can acquire novel signals from their environment (including multiple bird clades and several groups of marine mammals). Humans and seals may be the only complex vocal imitators who use a phylogenetically ancient mammalian production system to imitate sounds. A human-specific variant of *FOXP2*, a gene involved in complex oro-motor control in humans, and differing from that of chimpanzees and other primates, is also involved in vocal learning of birdsong. Comparative molecular biological techniques suggest that *FOXP2* underwent a selective sweep recently in hominid evolution, and may have played an important role in the vocal control abilities expansion of our own species.

10 | Models of the evolution of speech and phonology

10.1 Evolving speech

In the previous chapters I first concluded that the vocal periphery, long emphasized in discussions of language evolution, played a minor role in the evolution of speech. A language-equipped brain could master, and communicate using, the vocal tract of a chimpanzee, or indeed a dog, quite adequately. Furthermore, the flexibility of the vocal apparatus attested in living mammals indicates that there is little hope of reconstructing the speech abilities of extinct hominids from their fossil remains. Finally, the discovery that several animal species possess a reconfigured vocal tract similar to our own, but do not use it in speech production, means that even if we *could* use fossils to determine when the larynx descended in hominid evolution, we could not necessarily deduce whether those hominids spoke. These relatively negative conclusions supported the positive conclusion that changes in the brain were crucial for the evolution of speech, and we then explored the neural and genetic bases that currently seem to be critical for vocal learning and imitation.

In this chapter, I will attempt to synthesize these diverse strands of evidence, and begin to investigate theories of the evolution of speech and basic phonology. I begin by considering models of speech evolution (often termed "theories," despite lacking the gravitas normally associated with this term in science). My goal will be to evaluate the central innovations and insights in each model. We will see that many open questions remain, but that considerable empirical progress has been made and can be expected in the future. Second, I will explore attempts at bridge-building which aim to unify levels of explanation from speech science, psychology, and phonology. Finally, I will evaluate a new and controversial methodological approach to the study of language evolution: computer simulations. These have been particularly useful in evaluating models of glossogenetic change in spoken language. I will conclude that, despite some problems, computer simulations are useful for evaluating hypotheses and testing intuitions, and that they will provide a crucial tool in evaluating broader hypotheses about language evolution.

By using the relatively solid basis of speech science, and the quite detailed models that have been proposed for the evolution of speech, I hope to lay the foundations for the integrative empirical approach to language evolution that we will pursue in the rest of this book.

Four models of speech evolution

10.2 Lieberman's model: beyond Broca's area

Philip Lieberman is one of the few scholars writing today who played an important role in the renaissance of interest in language evolution in the late 1960s (Lieberman *et al.*, 1969; Lieberman *et al.*, 1972; Lieberman, 1975, 2007b). Although he is most famous for his attempts to reconstruct the vocal tracts of extinct hominids (and his controversial conclusion that Neanderthals lacked full spoken language), his recent work has focused on the brain mechanisms underlying speech. In particular, Lieberman has emphasized the role of subcortical mechanisms, especially the basal ganglia, in speech and language, and has vigorously opposed the "traditional" model of a "language organ" located only in Broca's and Wernicke's areas. The recognition that language requires a network of brain regions beyond these traditional foci is now well established via brain-imaging studies (e.g. Bookheimer, 2002), and few contemporary researchers would support a simple Broca/Wernicke model today.

More controversial is Lieberman's claim of a special role for the basal ganglia in speech and syntax (Lieberman, 2000). Lieberman uses multiple strands of evidence, from brain-damaged and Parkinson's patients, and his own research on high-altitude speech and cognition deficits in mountain climbers, to argue that the basal ganglia play a critical role in speech timing (e.g. voice-onset time), as well as in some simple aspects of syntax. The **basal ganglia** (incorporating the striatum and globus pallidus) are important subcortical components of the motor control system, whose proper function is dependent upon a diffuse input of the neurotransmitter dopamine coming from the midbrain. In Parkinson's disease, these midbrain neurons degenerate, depriving the basal ganglia of dopaminergic input and leading initially to poor motor coordination, but progressing to severe motor difficulties and eventually dementia. Given their long-recognized role in motor control (Graybiel, 1994), it is unsurprising that the basal ganglia play a role in fine aspects of speech production as well. More surprising is their apparent role in some aspects of syntactic comprehension, as revealed by deficits in Parkinson's patients when their medically augmented dopamine levels are low.

Despite the virtues of Lieberman's broadening of the focus of neural interest to include subcortical structures, he has yet to provide a convincing case that *changes* in human basal ganglia from those of the LCA played a role in speech evolution. Nor does he justify his focus on the basal ganglia *versus* other subcortical structures known to be involved in language, such as the thalamus or cerebellum (Jonas, 1982; Dronkers and Baldo, 2001). It is one thing to acknowledge that the entire motor system is involved in speech production, and to accept the growing evidence from brain-imaging studies that traditional "motor" areas play a role in other aspects of cognition, including perception (Graybiel, 2005). But which changes in this system could underwrite the differences between human and chimpanzee vocal control, particularly our ability for vocal imitation? Although Lieberman cites the expression of *FOXP2* in the striatum as support for his arguments (Lieberman, 2007b), he never offers an account of the neural or computational differences that could underlie the differences in human speech and syntactic abilities (cf. Groszer *et al.*, 2008). Nor does he discuss the Kuypers/Jürgens hypothesis that direct cortico-motor connections were a key novelty required for human speech. Lieberman's model of subcortical precursors for speech – important components of the FLB – may thus be correct, but the neural changes, specific to our lineage, and required for complex vocal learning and vocal control, remain unspecified.

10.3 MacNeilage's frame/content model of vocal evolution

Peter MacNeilage has developed a model of speech evolution termed the "Frame/Content Theory" (MacNeilage, 1998b, 2008). MacNeilage suggests that the essential phonological structure of human speech, in all languages, can be captured by the distinction between periodic syllabic **frames**, akin to a series of "slots" which are then "filled" with differentiated **content** in the form of speech segments. He then proposed that, first, the phylogenetic origin of the periodic syllabic frames was in the cyclical jaw oscillations associated with feeding in mammals, and second, that these syllabic frames are still controlled today, in humans, by the separate and more ancient medial premotor control system.

The idea that phonological structure can be conceived of as a series of syllabic slots to be "filled" by phonetically distinguished segments is supported by a variety of **speech-error data** (e.g. Fromkin, 1973; Shattuck-Hufnagel, 1979). Phonetic analysis of speech errors, or "slips of the tongue," has long been recognized as providing a window into speech motor control (Lashley, 1951; Levelt, 1989). Although articulatory data suggest that listener's transcriptions provide an imperfect phonetic record (Mowrey and MacKay, 1990), it is nonetheless widely agreed that surprisingly consistent patterns can be observed in speech errors. Similar patterns are found in both spontaneous errors and those elicited by "tongue-twister" tasks or rapid repetition. There are five basic types of single-segment errors: exchanges, omissions, additions, substitutions, and shifts. The most revealing type are "exchanges" (or "Spoonerisms"), in which two different segments exchange places (e.g. *mell wade* or *bud begs*), because exchanges allow a determination of *where* the moved segment originated. The striking thing about such exchanges is that they almost always obey hierarchical syllabic constraints, with onsets going to onsets, nuclei to nuclei, and codas to codas (only 2 percent of exchanges violate this rule; Shattuck-Hufnagel, 1979). Other possible patterns, such as movements of whole syllables, are far less frequent, and segmental changes that move onsets into codas or *vice versa* are virtually unattested, despite existing in the lexicon (e.g. *eat/tea*). These data provide strong support for the phonological notion of the syllable as an abstract frame into which speech segments are inserted.

MacNeilage, correctly urging that this aspect of speech control needs to be explained evolutionarily, then adopts a comparative approach to its analysis. He suggests that repeated syllabic frames are relatively rare among primate vocalizations, and attempts to bridge this evolutionary gap by proposing that the preadaptive source for the syllable was provided by the motor control underlying feeding behavior: biting, chewing, suckling, and swallowing. At some level this hypothesis is obviously true: the mammalian vocal tract evolved for feeding, long before the advent of speech, and speech co-opts these organs and muscles to a new use. Thus speech control must be consistent with constraints imposed by the more basic and necessary activities of feeding. But MacNeilage goes further than this, suggesting that specific neural substrates involved in ingestive motor control in other primates have been exapted in speech. Specifically, central pattern generators originally evolved for ingestion were, he suggests, co-opted for speech cycles involved in the "frame" component. He further speculates that the lip-smacking, teeth-chattering, and "girney" displays seen in some Old World monkey species represent a "precursor to speech" that involves these same ingestive movements (normally without phonation).

MacNeilage's hypothesis that primate lip smacks represent precursors of speech is quite convincing. In chimpanzees, lip smacking is a common accompaniment to grooming behavior. Oral movements are under voluntary control in chimpanzees, and can be used intentionally to communicate (Hopkins *et al.*, 2007; Reynolds Losin *et al.*, 2008). The single documented example of "vocal" learning in chimpanzees – the apparent spread of a non-phonated "raspberry" lip buzz through a captive group (Marshall *et al.*, 1999) – suggests that such oral displays can be learned from others. The fact that both human speech and such primate displays are quiet, close-contact, affiliative vocalizations is intriguing, and may support MacNeilage's argument that these oral movements represent homologs to speech. This provides some behavioral and neural support for the notion that "vocal grooming" played some role in the evolution of speech (Dunbar, 1996; Mithen, 2005), discussed in Chapter 12.

Critics of the "ingestive preadaptation" hypothesis observe that mammalian vocalizations have been around for many millions of years, and the same arguments used to support ingestive precursors apply to vocal precursors (Andrew and Jürgens in MacNeilage, 1998b). Speech makes use of the vocal apparatus, may have co-opted many of its basic elements, and must have co-existed with other innate vocalizations during human evolution. Regarding syllabic cycles, MacNeilage overstates the differences between human syllabic structure and other mammalian vocalizations. A basic vocal gesture akin to the syllable exists in many loud vertebrate vocalizations: the mouth open–close cycle. This mandibular cycle is typical of bird and mammal vocalizations, and functions to increase call loudness. In mammals, at least, this cycle is accompanied by a rather complex set of vocal tract maneuvers, including a retraction of the larynx and closing of the velum (Fitch, 2000c). Further, many vertebrates oscillate the mandible in the course of a single vocalization, during a single exhalation (e.g. birds producing rapid syllable sequences; Westneat *et al.*, 1993; Podos, 1997). A striking example in primates is the very rapid jaw oscillation in the loud calls or "songs" of many gibbon species, during the climax portion of duets (Geissmann, 2000). Pervasive syllabicity in vertebrate vocalizations render MacNeilage's arguments in favor of ingestive precursors less convincing, providing a plausible alternative precursor that is already associated with vocalization and thus requires no change of function.

The need for any evolutionary precursor has also been questioned (Lindblom and Ohala in MacNeilage, 1998b). Cyclicity is required for any mechanical system to produce an extended output, and thus seems a general precondition for continuous operation in the physical world. An animal already possessing open–close gestures for vocalizations (e.g. any nonhuman mammal) would have little choice but to repeat this gesture cyclically if called upon to produce extended, diversified syllables. This conceptual necessity provides weak grounds for suspecting any particular neural function as "ancestral."

The neural element of MacNeilage's hypothesis concerns the role of cortex in phonological control. MacNeilage acknowledges the role of the inferior lateral prefrontal cortex (Broca's area) in speech organization, but sees it as limited to the specification of the "content" portion in his model: the specific identity of speech segments. He suggests that a different region is primarily involved in generating syllabic frames: the **supplementary motor area**, or SMA. This region has received little attention in discussions of speech motor control, or language evolution in general, and MacNeilage cites some interesting overlooked facts about this region. First, direct brain stimulation experiments on awake humans shows that SMA stimulation elicits repeated vocalizations like "da da da" or "te te te" (Penfield and Welch, 1951), and irritative lesions in this region can lead to similar productions in neurological patients. The SMA may be activated in brain-imaging studies of speech (Roland *et al.*, 1980). Destructive lesions may initially lead to mutism, but after recovery patients show excellent repetition, while spontaneous speech remains rare. MacNeilage sees all of these data as consistent with a hypothesis that syllabic frames are generated in SMA, part of the general medial premotor system involved with self-generated action. Thus the frame/content distinction is mirrored in anatomically distinct neural regions.

Several commentators have noted problems with this aspect of Mac-Neilage's proposal. Abbs and DePaul (in MacNeilage, 1998b) point out that the "medial system" is in fact a complex made of several distinct regions. The activation of the anterior regions in brain-imaging studies may have to do more with volitional motor control and speech initiation rather than speech motor control *per se*. The posterior portion ("true" SMA), in contrast, has no specific speech functions at all. Nonetheless, the SMA clearly does play a role in speech (Jonas, 1981), and aphasics with damage to both Broca's area and basal ganglia produce recurrent syllabic utterances such as "babababa." It thus seems that MacNeilage is right to call attention to this neglected component of the speech motor control system. MacNeilage also saw the involvement of the anterior cingulate both in primate vocal control and in brain-imaging studies of language suggestive of a link, but recent work reveals anterior cingulate activation in virtually any task with high attentional and motor demands (Paus, 2001), with no specific link to language. Hence, the allocation of the frame-generating component of syllabic phonology to the SMA and/or anterior cingulate region remains a weak component of MacNeilage's model.

10.3.1 Synthesis

An interesting aspect of phonetic "content" which has received little attention in the evolution literature is the important role of the tongue in human speech relative to other primate or mammal vocalizations. While cortico-hypoglossal connections exist in other primates (Deacon, 1992), these appear to play a role only in complex tongue movement underlying feeding behavior (chewing and swallowing). Humans are quite unusual, and perhaps unique among mammals, in producing large tongue movements during vocalization. The only other vertebrates known to utilize detailed tongue movements during vocalization are parrots imitating speech (Patterson and Pepperberg, 1994, 1998); parrots are also notable for their use of complex tongue control in feeding. The seemingly simple ability to coordinate complex tongue movements with phonation may be enough to allow humans to produce most of the vowels and many consonants of human speech. Because the range of tongue shapes assumed during chewing and swallowing encompasses those of speech (Hiiemäe and Palmer, 2003), the role of complex tongue movements as a potential primate precursor of speech might provide a richer preadaptation than simple jaw movements and cyclicity (cf. p. 92, MacNeilage, 2008). It seems relatively clear that complex, volitional tongue control was present in the LCA, based on the complexity of tongue movements seen during feeding in chimpanzees. If true, this would suggest that it is not so much increased tongue *control* that needed to evolve to subserve this aspect of speech, as increased *coordination* of a pre-existing high level of control with the vocalization system.

Synthesizing observations made by Jürgens, Lieberman, and MacNeilage, we can see speech motor control as consisting of both conserved primitive components of motor control (SMA and basal ganglia, as stressed by Lieberman and MacNeilage) and novel components evolved during human evolution (direct connections from lateral motor cortex to vocal motor nuclei, stressed by Deacon and Jürgens). The rather non-intuitive conclusion that falls out of this synthesis is that the *behaviorally* novel aspects of speech (lip, jaw, and tongue movements, controlling formant frequencies) are supported by neural structures shared with chimpanzees. Intentional motor control for all of these articulators was already present in our primate ancestors long ago, and was used both for ingestion and for some communicative acts (lip smacks, etc.), and it relies upon direct cortical motor connections seen in monkeys and apes (Deacon, 1992). In contrast, the *neurally* novel aspect of speech – direct connections from lateral cortex to the laryngeal and respiratory motor neurons in the nucleus ambiguus – control phonation and pitch, the acoustic aspects of speech most similar to nonhuman calls. This model is consistent, I believe, with all of the data currently available, and suggests that speech has been "tinkered" together from old parts, and one or a few novel additions. The question of what selective advantage(s) drove this amalgamation will be considered in later chapters.

10.4 Deacon's "leveraged takeover" model: Speech as spandrel?

Correctly recognizing the centrality of direct cortico-laryngeal connections to human vocal control, neurobiologist Terrence Deacon has proposed an intriguing hypothesis concerning their evolution in humans (pp. 247–253, Deacon, 1997). The model is based on the epigenetic process by which vertebrate brains "wire themselves" during embryonic development (Striedter, 2004). A neuron's contacts with other neurons are initially exuberant, involving rather diffuse, unspecific connectivity. These exuberant connections are then progressively "pruned" to their adult form, through a process involving competition between multiple neurons vying for the same target (Purves and Lichtman, 1980; Purves, 1988). Competition is based both on trophic factors released from the target, and on efficacy in activating that target ("neurons that fire together wire together"). Deacon suggests that cortico-laryngeal connections may initially be present in many mammals, especially primates (which have strong cortical connections to other brainstem areas), but that they are typically "outcompeted" during development by the prepotent connections underlying the innate call system: the midline PAG/reticular system which normally controls mammal vocalization (see Figure 8.7). The key factor tipping the balance in humans was our disproportionate increase in forebrain size, which led these cortical connections to be more numerous and thus more competitive. By this model, direct cortico-laryngeal connections are a developmental byproduct of increasing forebrain size: a spandrel occurring automatically as a result of brain growth (though elsewhere Deacon suggests that vocal control was *one* of the factors selecting for large brains). This model is an alternative to the more obvious idea that natural selection targeted these specific connections, and should eventually be testable as we learn more about how brains are wired up during development. Deacon's model also has a corollary: that we can estimate the speech abilities of extinct hominids based on their cranial capacities. Deacon suggests that hominid vocal skills were already beyond those of other primates by *Homo habilis*, roughly 2 MYA, but that cortical control increased steadily, as brain size increased, up to about 200 KYA.

Deacon's model provides an example of how neuroscientifically informed theorizing can provide testable hypotheses about language evolution. Because his model relies on general epigenetic processes typical of all mammals, its foundations are all testable by developmental neuroscientists. One can even envision lesion studies in fetal mammals that would test the competition hypothesis (cf. Sur *et al.*, 1988; Roe *et al.*, 1990). If projecting cells in the innate call system are selectively lesioned, or forebrain size increased using genetic engineering (or both), Deacon's hypothesis predicts that "normal" mammal species should preserve direct connections into adulthood (presumably displaying enhanced vocal control, e.g. in an operant task). Furthermore, Deacon's hypothesis admits a variant which I find more plausible: that the neural competition is "won" by cortical neurons not because they are more numerous, but because of coherent *activity*. Deacon mentions infant babbling as a product of direct cortical connections, a sign that these connections are maturing. But what if babbling instead plays a *causal* role in their preservation? That is, if the pleasurable activity of infant vocal play exercises these connections in parallel, and thus allows them to persist when they would normally (e.g. in a chimpanzee) be pruned away. It is interesting to note an observation by Hayes on the chimpanzee Viki, who one day "went Hawaiian with remarks like 'ah ha wha he'" (p. 63, Hayes, 1951). Hayes, suggesting that Viki's failure to speak was closely linked to her almost total lack of vocal play, initially derived false hope that these occasional outbursts might lead to more. But, just when a human child's babbling would take off (around five months of age), Viki became increasingly silent. Thus a variant on Deacon's hypothesis is that the self-reinforcing behavior of human infant babbling plays a causal role in the preservation of direct cortico-motor connections, and that this activity, more than increased forebrain size, underlies human adult connectivity. While studies of human infants prevented from babbling (for medical reasons) are rare (Locke and Pearson, 1990), they provide some support for this idea.

10.5 Carstairs-McCarthy: from speech to syllables to syntax

Several researchers have suggested that the simple form of non-recursive hierarchy observed in phonology may have provided an evolutionary precursor to recursive syntax (Garrett, 1988; Carstairs-McCarthy, 1999; Jackendoff, 1999). Linguist Andrew Carstairs-McCarthy has championed the importance of phonological hierarchy in language evolution (Carstairs-McCarthy, 1998, 1999). Suggesting that constraints on syllable structure follow automatically from the reconfiguration of the human vocal tract, he argues that syllabic structures are "linguistic byproducts of mundane physiological changes in the vocal tract" (p. 33, 1999). Carstairs-McCarthy suggests that vocal tract reconfiguration is derived automatically from bipedalism (citing Aiello, 1996) – an assumption that we have seen is unsupportable. He further elides the distinction between vocal anatomy and vocal control (p. 129), apparently accepting arguments by Duchin (1990) that these two are necessarily intertwined. But, as we have seen in the previous chapters, the fact that an organism has a reconfigured vocal tract is no guarantee that it will also have greater control over that system. Lions or deer with reconfigured vocal tracts do not use them to create syllable structures or a wider range of vocal signals. The argument thus starts on a weak foundation.

Carstairs-McCarthy's model of language evolution then turns to the expansion of potential vocabulary generated by our "more agile tongues": a vast potential lexicon of pseudowords (see Chapter 3). When combined with synonymy avoidance, this proto-lexicon created a dilemma for our ancestors: the enlarged vocabulary made possible by phonetic expansion "should be exploited rather than allowed to go to waste" (p. 131, Carstairs-McCarthy, 1999). The enlarged vocabulary thus generated, combined with constraints on memory, conspired to force the adoption of a hierarchical, syllable-based phonological system. I find the logic of this argument difficult to follow. Surely the mere fact of an expanded phonetic potential does not entail that the individual thus equipped should produce or remember all of these potential vocalizations. And the proposal that such an individual would need to assign *meanings* to all of these potential vocalizations seems even less compelling, given the large number of meaningless "pseudowords" that exist in modern languages (the *glubs*, *blicks*, and *flebbies* beloved of psycholinguists). Thus, these suggestions about the origin of syllabic structure, though interesting, seem unconvincing to me.

The remaining components of Carstairs-McCarthy's model are even more audacious: he seeks to account for the evolution of a crucial component of syntax (specifically the noun phrase/sentence distinction, which poses an interesting puzzle) and semantics (truth *versus* reference) from syllabic structure. The argument is an interesting one, but is only as strong as its weakest links and, as we have seen, the phonetic and phonological foundations are unconvincing. Thus, despite its commendably broad scope, and many interesting points made in passing, Carstairs-McCarthy's model as a whole seems deficient at numerous points (cf. pp. 81–91, Botha, 2003). However, I think the relationship he notes between hierarchicality in phonology and syntax represents an important insight, even if it cannot support the entire evolutionary edifice he erects upon it. The idea that a form of hierarchy rooted in motor control, and initially expressed in vocalization, might have provided a preadaptation to hierarchical syntax is implied in many authors' writings (Lashley, 1951; Orr and Cappannari, 1964; Lieberman, 1984; Allott, 1989; Studdert-Kennedy and Goldstein, 2003). This hypothesis is by no means far-fetched, and we shall return to it in later chapters.

10.6 Bridges from speech to phonology

Phonology provides a microcosm in which some core concerns of modern linguists, especially regarding how rule-governed structures are learned and can change through time, can be explored in relative freedom from the complications of meaning. At the same time, phonology is based on the relatively well-understood foundation of speech science and phonetics. Phonology thus provides a test-bed for exploring different levels of explanation in language evolution. Several contemporary strands of modern phonology strive for comprehensive explanations, in which laws of sound change are derived from biological foundations, iterated over generations, to explain generalizations applying to all languages, or a specified group of languages. Examples of these biological foundations include the articulatory constraints underlying coarticulation phenomena (Ohala, 1983b; Browman and Goldstein, 1992; Ohala, 1993), or the set of interacting perceptual and production constraints used to explain devoicing phenomena (Blevins, 2006). Phonologist Juliette Blevins terms this approach "evolutionary phonology," but it focuses squarely on glossogeny rather than phylogeny (Blevins, 2004). Today, we can begin to envision a compact but general framework of biologically grounded phonological principles and constraints that will accurately describe the phonological systems of the world's languages. This goal is still far off, but seems reachable, particularly in such focused domains as metrical phonology (Goldsmith, 1990; Hammond, 1995). The maturity of phonology makes such deeper explanatory enterprises feasible, and also paves the way to insightful comparisons with animal communication systems (cf. Yip, 2006). In this section, we will discuss some components of this approach.

10.6.1 Motor constraints on phonological structure

Two related properties of speech have received considerable attention in the evolutionary literature: coarticulation and syllabic encoding. Phonemes are not like beads on a string, but typically are fused together in syllables. Many phones, such as voiced stop consonants, cannot exist independently of a syllable: they require a vocalic nucleus to be pronounced. Furthermore, neighboring phones influence one another acoustically. This aspect of human speech is traditionally termed **coarticulation**, but has also been dubbed **syllabic encoding** to emphasize that it squeezes information concerning multiple phonemes into a single syllable (Liberman *et al.*, 1967; Lieberman, 1984). Lieberman suggests that such encoding, and the corresponding perceptual decoding ability, are crucial adaptive aspects of human speech (see Chapter 9). The case that syllabic encoding is an evolved adaptive feature of speech has never been convincingly argued. Indeed, it seems plausible that many coarticulatory phenomena result from simple, unavoidable biomechanical constraints operating on the vocal tract (Goldstein *et al.*, 2006a). Some articulators are relatively massive (particularly the jaw and tongue), and inertia prevents them from moving instantly from one gestural configuration to another. Thus, when producing the syllable /du/, the tongue must be relatively fronted to produce the /d/ and must be retracted to produce the /u/. There is an inevitable lag between these two endpoints, during which the vowel has a fronted /i/ quality. But such physical constraints, far from being uniquely human, would be expected in any mammalian vocal tract attempting to rapidly produce a sequence of articulatory targets. Current understanding of vocal tract dynamics in other mammals remains too incomplete to support strong statements about human uniqueness (cf. Fitch and Hauser, 1998). Thus coarticulation seems as likely to be an unfortunate byproduct of producing sounds with a massive tongue as a specially evolved "feature" of the human vocal tract.

A second source for coarticulatory phenomena may involve neural control (Lubker and Gay, 1982; Lieberman, 1984), and in particular the *coordination* of different articulators with the larynx. As an illustration, try producing /paba/ as rapidly as possible, while maintaining the distinctions between the unvoiced /p/ and the voiced /b/. The vocal tract maneuver here is very simple, requiring a simple oscillatory jaw movement (a "pure frame," in MacNeilage's terminology). While a /papa/ or /baba/ sequence can be performed very rapidly, the /paba/ sequence requires phonation to be turned on and off in close synchrony with jaw closure, requiring fine neural coordination. The difficulty is not the result of inertial constraints of the jaw or larynx, as either can independently oscillate at higher rates. Studies of infant babbling support the idea that the difficulty is neural. Reduplicated babbling, featuring repeated syllables like /babababa/, appears quite early (around six months). Variegated babbling, in which subsequent syllables are varied (/pabapa/, is a later achievement and does not become the more frequent type until about one year of age (Menn and Stoel-Gammon, 2005). Such neural coordination constraints may also be present in adulthood, e.g. in the phonological tendency for unvoiced intervocalic consonants to be voiced in casual speech (e.g. *letter* to be pronounced /ledr/ rather than /let'r/). This tendency is very common in the world's languages.

MacNeilage and Davis have proposed another production constraint on syllabic structure, based on patterns observed in babbling and infants' first words. Words are significantly more likely to begin with a labial–vowel– coronal (LC) combination (like *bud* or *pin*) than with a reverse CL pattern (MacNeilage and Davis, 2000). Interestingly, eight of ten diverse languages sampled by MacNeilage *et al.* (1999) also showed this LC constraint in adults. They argue that initiation of motor control is difficult for the child. Simpler /b/ or /m/ sounds are less problematic than the challenging coro- nals (/t/, d/, /s/, and the like), which can only be produced once vocalization has been initiated. But in this simple form, the hypothesis is inconsistent with the observation that during unconstrained babbling, babies in fact produce more coronals, suggesting that they are simpler. MacNeilage and Davis suggest that babies observe the LC constraint only when the additional challenge of interfacing to the lexicon occurs. This is consistent with Jakob- son's old idea that the pure motor activity of babbling may be relatively unconstrained. In late infancy, the cognitive challenge of integrating the phonological repertoire into a lexicon presents a difficult new task for the developing child (Jakobson, 1968). This hypothesis also explains the strange disjunction between the child's apparent mastery of the vocal organs dis- played during babbling, in contrast to the distinct and lasting limitations in early speech. Being able to produce a sound is one thing, but being able to use the sound clearly poses difficult problems for many children for years after their first words. This notion is underscored by MacNeilage and Davis, who cite the *interaction* of biomechanical, action initiation, lexical, and sociolinguistic constraints as the critical factor in the evolution of the LC preference. Thus this last constraint also concerns coordination, but now at a cognitive rather than purely motor level.

10.6.2 Perceptual constraints and phonological structure

There has been less interest in the role of potentially preadaptive perceptual constraints on phonology, but work on animals provides several interesting suggestions. One concerns distinctions between suprasegmental prosodic structure, captured informally by the term "speech rhythm." Phonologists distinguish **stress-timed** languages (such as English and most Germanic languages) from **syllable-timed** languages such as French (Ramus *et al.*, 1999). In the former, only *stressed* syllables are perceived as occurring at a roughly constant rate, while in the latter, *each* syllable is heard as equally spaced in time. Infants may use such suprasegmental cues to help them discriminate between different languages (Ramus, 2002). Interestingly, monkeys and rats are also able to discriminate between languages that differ in rhythmic type (Ramus *et al.*, 2000; Toro *et al.*, 2003; Tincoff *et al.*, 2005). This suggests that the perceptual mechanisms necessary to process these rhythmic differences are widely shared among mammals. Although useful in speech, they did not evolve specifically for use in phonological perception.

Various phenomena in phonology require similarities to be maintained between non-adjacent syllables. For instance, **rhyme** requires the nucleus+coda portion of a syllable at the end of a phrase to match that of some previous syllable, while **alliteration** requires onsets to match. Analyses of humpback whale songs suggest that a similar phenomenon occurs in these complex, learned vocalizations (Guinee and Payne, 1988), and Katy Payne and colleagues have suggested that this rhyme-like patterning acts as an *aide memoire* for humpbacks (Payne, 2000). Rhyme is postulated to aid in the oral transmission of long poems and songs in many human cultures, by providing redundant, self-reinforcing structural cues to content (Rubin, 1995). Similar higher-order phonological structures (often termed "syntax" by ethologists) are not uncommon in animal vocal signals, but whether listeners are sensitive to violations of such patterns, and whether they truly aid memory for singers, remains unclear. Detailed phonological exploration of animal signal perception provides a promising and largely open field for biolinguistic study (cf. Yip, 2006).

10.6.3 Vocal imitation, glossogeny, and dialect formation

Let us now return to the role of cultural transmission or glossogeny, discussed in the introductory chapters. Complex vocal learning inevitably allows an intermediate "cultural" level of change in the transmitted system, interspersed between the phylogenetic change and ontogenetic levels. Historical linguistic change in phonology provides an ideal model system to explore such changes. In phonology, simple underlying rules, applying over many generations, can sometimes account for broad patterns in the distributions of sounds in modern languages (e.g. Grimm's Law in Indo-European, or the Great Vowel Shift in English; Lass, 1997). The synthesis of such traditional diachronic generalizations with accurate *synchronic* (at a particular moment in time) descriptions of phonology is active but still in its early stages (Lightfoot, 1998; Blevins, 2004; Niyogi, 2006). Phonologists often describe the limits on the variety of languages based on a set of biological principles and constraints (e.g. McCarthy, 2002) that apply to each cycle of language acquisition, and that iterate to produce cumulative change over many generations.

To what extent can we find similar processes in nonhuman animals? In any system where organisms acquire behavioral patterns by copying others, a potential for a simple form of culture results (Bonner, 1983; Boyd and Richerson, 1983, 1985; Avital and Jablonka, 2000). While the degree to which non-vocal aspects of behavior such as foraging or migration support cumulative cultural change is still debated (Laland and Janik, 2006), one aspect of animal behavior is widely agreed to represent "animal culture": the learned songs of birds and whales (see Chapter 4). One effect is the appearance of geographically localized **dialects** within vocally learning species. Such dialects have been documented in countless birds and many marine mammals (e.g. Lemon, 1975; Baker and Mewaldt, 1978; Ford and Fisher, 1983; Thomas and Stirling, 1983; Baker and Cunningham, 1985a; Thomas and Golladay, 1996), and the generation of dialects by a system of vocal learning provides a clear parallel between human language (and music) and animal communication systems (Lachlan, 1999).

Variation between human dialects develops rapidly, and leads to audible differences in a few generations, and mutual unintelligibility in a few thousand years. Such differences may function as sociolinguistic "badges" of origin (cf. Nettle, 1999a; Dunbar, 2003). Are such differences adaptations? In principle, dialects should emerge automatically due to copying errors in any situation where geographic movement is restricted. Such random dialect variation would be expected to be selectively "neutral," the cultural equivalent of genetic drift in phylogeny (Kimura, 1983), so dialects may be an inevitable byproduct of the general adaptation for vocal learning. This neutral model must be rejected by anyone proposing an adaptive hypothesis (e.g. Dunbar, 2003). Although the function of bird or whale song dialects remains debated, a preference of females for males singing the local dialect suggests that finer comparisons are allowed when males sing similar songs (cf. Catchpole and Slater, 1995). The study of dialect, including explicit comparisons between humans and animals, seems another promising route for future biolinguistic exploration.

Another interface between glossogeny and animal vocal learning has only begun to develop very recently. This concerns the degree to which cultural transmission can sculpt a relatively amorphous starting system into a rule-governed, easily learned language (Deacon, 1997; Kirby, 2000). Creole languages have played an important role in this debate. In the last three centuries, humans speaking mutually unintelligible languages were thrown together (most notably on slave-based plantations), and often developed communication systems called **pidgins** that absorbed significant vocabulary from multiple sources, but lacked syntactic complexity. Such pidgins can become widespread and relatively stable, and provide a linguistic model for children growing up in pidgin-speaking communities. A repeated occurrence is that such systems can serve as a substrate for the formation of "true" languages, with all the syntactic complexities (phrase structure, function words, negation, and quantification, etc.) of other human languages. Such new languages are called **creoles**, and the process by which they develop "creolization" (Hall, 1966; Mühlhäusler, 1997). Strenuous debate surrounds the degree to which pidgins indeed "become" creoles, or whether the syntactic armature added by creolization is generated creatively, *de novo*, and the answer probably differs for different creoles (Bickerton, 1981; Singh, 2000; Mufwene, 2001). There are a number of interesting features that typify creole languages. First, they tend to show certain regularities irrespective of the substrate language(s). For instance, the basic word order SVO (subject–verb–object) is typical, along with the suite of more detailed sequencing constraints that go with it (Hall, 1966). Phonologically, creoles tend to have a simple CV structure, as do many of the world's languages. Perhaps most fascinating, there are specific regularities in the actual lexical items that come to serve grammatical functions, so (for instance) the number word 'one' becomes drafted for use as an indefinite article in many different creoles (Bickerton, 1995). Bickerton has argued that creoles are closer to the biologically based innate form of human language, and that regularities in creoles might therefore provide clues to Universal Grammar (Bickerton, 1984, 1990, 1995). However, it remains unclear whether such creole features reflect *de novo* creations, or are in fact absorbed from the surrounding or substrate languages (often due to the poor records available, combined with a frequent assumption that such languages are "simple" or "baby" forms of their parent languages). While most creolists would thus distance themselves from Bickerton's claim in its strong form, many remain intrigued by the possibility that similarities among creoles provide insights into the biological nature of human language.

A less controversial, and better documented, example of creolization is provided by **Nicaraguan Sign Language** (NSL). Prior to the mid 1970s, deaf people in Nicaragua lived dispersed throughout the country, with little opportunity to interact with other deaf individuals. While each individual would develop a "home sign" system adequate to communicate basic needs, these were not true languages. In 1977, a school for deaf children was founded in Managua and brought together fifty such children, later expanding to over 400 students. Although their teachers focused on lip-reading, these students quickly devised, among themselves, a pidgin sign system, and the succeeding generation creolized this system into a syntactically fully fledged language (Kegl, 2002). This ongoing process has been richly documented with video, and because older students only acquired the pidgin form, both forms can be studied in great empirical detail (Senghas and Coppola, 2001; Senghas *et al.*, 2005). The crucial conclusions from this work are, first, that isolated individuals do not, by themselves, spontaneously create languages, and a social critical mass is necessary. However, once a community is formed, a syntactically sophisticated language can develop with remarkable rapidity. This suggests that the instinct to learn language is indeed constrained by human biology, but that cultural transmission, and communicative need, play an important role in "triggering" this biological capacity.

Natural experiments in creolization such as NSL are extremely rare, and a few researchers have recently begun to bring certain aspects of glossogeny and cultural transmission into the laboratory. Laboratory copying experiments (Rubin *et al.*, 1993; Rubin, 1995) and iterated learning paradigms (Kirby *et al.*, 2008) show that important aspects of creolization can be replicated experimentally. As predicted by theorists (Deacon, 1997) and computer modelers (Kirby, 1999), repeated cultural transmission of initially haphazard communication systems can "filter out" difficult-to-learn items, and the end product of this selective attrition is a system that is more regular and consistent. Similar results are now being provided by laboratory studies of birds: recent work shows that a zebra finch group "seeded" with impoverished song developed by an isolated male will, after several generations of iterated learning, create a set of songs that are normal for that species (Feher *et al.*, 2008). Thus, again, there is exciting convergence in human and animal experimental work that promises insights into the precise nature of the biological constraints or predispositions underlying glossogenetic change. This work dovetails nicely with an older body of research using computer simulations.

10.7 Computer models of phonological change: simulating glossogeny

In addition to the comparative and experimental data just reviewed, evolutionary models of phonological evolution provide several nice examples of the value of computer modeling in understanding language evolution (cf. Cangelosi and Parisi, 2002). In computer modeling, all parameters of the system are under the programmers' control. But this power comes at a cost: all aspects of the hypothesis being tested must be specified explicitly, and this represents the great virtue of such models. While computer modeling has become extremely popular in recent years, some students of language evolution have been extremely skeptical of their value to the field (e.g. Bickerton, 2007). One reason may be confusion as to their goals. Most "artificial language" models deal with glossogeny, and not phylogeny, and the biological capacity to produce and perceive sounds is a built-in assumption of such models. Models of this sort cannot be interpreted as explanations of the biological basis for speech production or speech perception. Similarly, many models build in a process of imitation, whether overtly in a socially enacted game or covertly as a component of the optimization process that adjusts vowel production (see below). Imitation is assumed, not explained, in such models: the "biological" abilities and predispositions of the simulated agents do not change through the simulation. What these models can successfully show is that, given certain biological propensities, a community can develop communication systems with particular characteristics. Rather than providing an alternative, these models thus complement models that grapple with biological evolution (cf. Zuidema, 2005). When thus conceptualized, computer simulations can play a valuable role in testing intuitions about glossogeny. The assumptions and the rules of derivation implemented in computer code can be extremely complex, far beyond what can be logically or mathematically derived. Sometimes, a modeler finds the result of a simulation unsurprising, and the model functions to verify one's intuitions, as a "reality check." Less frequently, simulation results defy one's intuitions. If such results arise repeatedly, in different simulations, this is evidence that the result, however non-intuitive, in fact follows from the premises. Thus, the logical structure of research using computer simulations is directly analogous to more traditional deductive work in mathematics or physics, and provides a valuable tool for testing evolutionary hypotheses. I will now review several examples.

10.7.1 Modeling the development of phoneme inventories

An important early paper by Liljencrants and Lindblom (1972) examined the origins of vowel systems using computer simulations. In this seminal first example of an **artificial language** simulation, the authors sought to understand the origins of striking regularities in the vowel systems of the world's languages. Phonetically, all languages possess at least three vowels, and the modal number of vowels is five (Crothers, 1978; Maddieson, 1984). Germanic languages (English, Dutch, Swedish, etc.) have a comparatively large complement of vowels (10 to 15) but the upper limit on vowel count is much higher, at least 24 (in !Xu; Crystal, 2002). Despite this considerable numerical diversity in vowel systems, striking regularities in the distribution of vowels exist, as we move from simple three-vowel systems (almost always the "point vowels" /i/, /a/, and /u/) to systems with a larger selection. Liljencrants and Lindblom sought to explain these regularities. Their model involves the maximization of a quantity that roughly corresponds to the overall perceptual distinctiveness in the repertoire. The key values are the Euclidean distance between two vowels, represented as points in a two-dimensional space, with the first formant F1 on one axis and effective second formant F2E on the other. By summing over the inverses of the squares of these distances, an energy measure can be calculated that captures the perceptual quality of the vowel system. For each number of vowels, maximizing this measure provides a prediction of the optimal vowel space. These predictions show a strikingly good fit to the systems actually observed in human language. This result stands as one of the nicest examples of the power of an explicit mathematical approach to a problem in phonological evolution. A simple assumption, that vowel systems should maximize perceptual distinctiveness, provides an explanation for a considerable mass of linguistic data when placed in a rigorous computational framework.

However, the fit between this model and cross-linguistic reality is not perfect, and a number of researchers have extended this approach in recent years (cf. Zuidema, 2005). Bart de Boer implemented a model that involves a population of interacting individuals (referred to as **agents**; de Boer, 2001). Each agent has a built-in propensity for vocal imitation, and agents engage in multiple "imitation games" whose results influence their future behavior. Each agent strives both to imitate others, and to be imitated themselves, and each maintains a model of their current vowel repertoire which is adjusted based on the success of their interactions with other agents. Complex vocal imitation is thus a crucial built-in assumption of the model. Second, de Boer's agents have simplified but realistic built-in constraints on their perception and production of speech sounds. Despite these added complexities, all of which arguably make de Boer's model more realistic than its predecessor, the outcome is nearly identical. The simulation converges on vowel systems with essentially the same characteristics as real vowel systems, and several improvements over the Liljencrants results.

Pierre-Yves Oudeyer has also implemented agent-based simulations, relaxing several assumptions in de Boer's model, but again providing similar results (Oudeyer, 2005). Oudeyer's models do away with the "language game," and rely solely on perceptual and motoric maps, modeled on the self-organizing maps used in neural networks (Hopfield, 1982; Kohonen, 2001). An important extension is that vowels in Oudeyer's models are represented as vowel trajectories (akin to diphthongs), rather than the static points assumed in previous models. By *coupling* the perceptual and motor maps together (by analogy to babbling), many of the self-organization processes driven by interaction among *agents* in de Boer's models can emerge *within individuals* in Oudeyer's models. Oudeyer's models make the assumption that agents attempt to reproduce the sounds that they hear, thus also assuming a simple form of imitation. Again, despite important differences in assumptions, Oudeyer's model gives essentially the same results as the previous two models: the emergence of dispersed vowel systems with the essential characteristics of actual human vowel systems.

10.7.2 Commentary: explanation in computer simulations

Simulation models of this sort provide concrete examples of **"invisible hand" models** for language change (Keller, 1995). All three of these models take the same broad approach and, despite significant differences in assumptions and implementation, converge on similar results. Personal taste may render the simpler or the more realistic models more appealing, but it is the *convergence* of results that makes them convincing: given some basic assumptions, complex details of the phonological system emerge reliably, over time, through iteration of some optimization process. Taken together, the simulations show that once an imitative cultural transmission system is in place, and given any optimization mechanism that drives the system towards greater distinctiveness, a set of simulated vowel spaces will emerge that closely resemble the vowel systems of human language. Similar covergence can be seen in computer models of syntax (Steels, 1997; Kirby, 1999, 2002; Briscoe, 2003) to be discussed later. How do such modeling efforts fit into the broader field of language evolution?

The basic hope of explaining complex surface phenomena by virtue of simpler but more abstract principles underlies all science, and the examples above show that computer models can play a role in evaluating such principles. Obscuring this commonality, the terms "self-organization" and "emergence" have become buzz-words in the simulation community, emphasizing their difference from more traditional models. These terms denote situations where the iterated application of simple principles over time result in surprisingly complex structures, whose relationship to the underlying principles may be far from obvious. Again, such explanations are basic tools in understanding many physical processes, including crystal growth, e.g the formation of snowflakes, or the erosional processes that generate the shape of complex river valleys. However, such processes have particular relevance to biological and evolutionary systems which change significantly over time. Often temporally evolving systems are strongly influenced by the fine details of the starting point. Such "sensitive dependence on initial conditions" typifies chaotic systems (Lorenz, 1963; Ruelle, 1991). In contrast, many "self-organizing" systems tend to be robust to small perturbations, and most biological processes underlying gene expression or development exhibit such robustness. Robust systems can compensate for rather drastic changes in initial conditions: an early embryo can be cut in half and develop into two normal individuals, or an apparently crucial gene can be knocked out with no obvious effect on the phenotype. Robustness and self-organization are well-documented characteristics of diverse physical and biological systems (Glass and Mackey, 1988; Laurent, 2006).

Unfortunately, self-organization is sometimes held up as an alternative to natural selection in evolution, rather than a result of it (e.g. Goodwin, 2001). To choose an old example, the cells of honeycombs are perfect hexagons, representing a mathematically optimal solution to the problem of maximizing the volume of honey contained with a minimum of wax. Darwin discussed the problem of how honeybees can generate hexagonal forms in some detail, noting that "it seems at first quite inconceivable how they can make all the necessary angles and planes" (Darwin, 1859), but concluded after close observation and experimentation that bees shape their honeycombs volitionally, and instinctually. However, in a more frequently quoted passage, D'Arcy Thompson offered an plausible alterative explanation for hexagonal honeycombs in terms of self-organization: honeybees construct cylindrical chambers, and the physical process of distribution of tensions in slightly warm wax takes care of the rest (Thompson, 1948). Thompson's model suggests that physics does the hard part, and there is no need to posit an innate "instinct" for hexagonal construction in honeybees. Despite its plausibility, and its repeated use as an example in the literature on complexity and self-organization, Thompson's hypothesis is demonstrably incorrect. Beeswax cells do not, in fact, automatically assume hexagonal shape when warmed, and detailed experiments show that honeybees must shape each angle of the cell carefully. Honeybees sculpt their cells using gravity as a plumb line and small sensory hairs at each side of their head to evaluate the angles (von Frisch, 1974), and blocking these sensory hairs with glue makes bees produce irregular, circular cells. Honeybees have evolved an instinct for hexagons, and when this instinct is experimentally inhibited, physics and self-organization *does not* "repair" the resulting non-hexagonal cells.

This classic example provides an important lesson about the value of simulations. Given an explicit set of assumptions, simulations can provide demonstrations that, in principle, some factors may explain some observed pattern of data. When the observed pattern is optimal, invisible hand models of cultural "evolution" can provide an alternative explanation to adaptation by natural selection. In practice, however, the demonstration of a theoretical possibility does not, by itself, tell us how the pattern was "discovered" evolutionarily. Other forms of data (often direct observation of behavior in living organisms) are required to test such hypotheses. Both biophysical and biological constraints may play important roles in the final explanation, but such constraints are a component of evolutionary explanations, not an alternative to them (Maynard Smith, 1978). Thus computer models of phonological change successfully demonstrate that self-organization *could* generate vowel systems like those seen in human language, and potentially reduce the explanatory burden for theorists interested in the biological evolution of phonology. But the fact that vowel systems *could* develop based on such simple optimization principles does not necessarily demonstrate that they do so. An exploration of the specific mechanisms of vowel production and perception, and of the psychological processes underlying human vocal imitation, is a necessary source of evidence in such research, and complementary to simulations of this sort. Rather than serving as ends in themselves, computer simulations are best seen as one important empirical component of a multi-pronged, multi-disciplinary approach to language evolution. Their greatest value is when they challenge intuition, or serve to demonstrate the validity of lines of argument that might otherwise appear obscure or even impossible. Several examples of this will be discussed later in connection with syntax.

Evaluating phylogenetic models of language evolution

Humans are eternally fascinated by themselves, and cultures everywhere
have a story about how we came to be special (Long, 1963). Language often
plays a prominent role in these tales. Western scholarly debate about language origin blends seamlessly with such origin myths, and so I will start this
section with a short historical overview, beginning with the book of Genesis
and Plato's *Cratylus*, and moving rapidly through the seventeenth and eighteenth centuries to the views of Darwin, whose ideas on language evolution
I will consider more carefully later. This historical overview serves a dual
purpose. First, modern discussions of language evolution often present the
current revival since 1990 as the first serious scientific attempt to grapple
with the problem. This is both factually incorrect and leads to an unnecessary repetition of mistakes, the reinvention of theories, and the rehashing
of debates already explored by previous generations. Regarding language
evolution, there are very few new hypotheses under the sun, and current
debates can and should pick up where our scholarly predecessors left off.
The second, and more important, reason is that I believe there are real
insights in the older literature which remain unappreciated, particularly
those of Darwin and his contemporaries, but these require knowledge of
their historical context to be fully understood. Most prominently, it is easy
to forget that the pressing questions of one time may become *passé*, or even
entirely ignored, in another. Lacking a sense of the *zeitgeist* in which a given
scholar wrote, we risk misinterpreting, or completely overlooking, what
they saw as key points.

Nowhere is this more true than for various theories of word meaning traditionally given a cursory, derisive treatment in overviews of language (the
"bow-wow" theory, the "ding-dong" theory, etc.; Firth, 1930; Thorndike,
1943a; Pinker, 1994a; Aitchison, 2000). The tradition of giving derogatory
names to theories of language origin started with Max Müller (Müller, 1861,
1873), and was an important plank in his all-out campaign against Darwin's
then-new evolutionary theory. Appreciating Darwin's ideas about language
evolution requires an understanding of some of the long-abused ideas dismissed by Müller and his followers, and by most theorists today. I will not

attempt a full exegesis of these ideas (for further detail see Révész, 1956; Borst, 1957; Stam, 1976; Hewes, 1977; the Stam book is strongly recommended as an introduction to this mostly forgotten world of thought).

11.1 In the beginning: the first words

The oldest mentions of language origins in the Western tradition are in the Bible, in the book of Genesis. The first is worth quoting in full:

> And out of the ground the Lord God formed every beast of the field, and every fowl of the air; and brought them unto Adam to see what he would call them; and whatsoever Adam called every living creature, that was the name thereof. And Adam gave names to all cattle, and to the fowl of the air, and to every beast of the field. (Genesis 2, 19–20)

The concern here is obviously not where the *language faculty* came from – clearly God already had language, and man, who was made in his image, had it as well. The question addressed is the origin of specific *words* (the names of animals). The conclusion we are to draw from this passage, apparently, is that words are arbitrary – for God himself didn't know what Adam would come up with. If, in contrast, the origin of words was onomatopoetic, God might have confidently predicted that cows would be called *moo* and cats *meow*. Thus, the author of Genesis adopts a Saussurian stance on "arbitrariness." This issue was also the core debate in Plato's *Cratylus*. Do words have a natural relationship to their meanings, as in onomatopoeia, or are they instead wholly arbitrary coinages and purely conventional? Plato, through the character of Socrates, concludes that both notions have some truth.

Similarly implicit in the Biblical passage is the notion that concepts predated Adam's act of naming. This assumption is also typical of much modern thinking on language origin, and consistent with comparative data (see Chapter 4). It would be difficult to overestimate the influence that these Biblical ideas had on subsequent Western inquiry into language evolution. Until the twentieth century, virtually any idea about language origins would be evaluated, at least implicitly, with these Biblical preconceptions as a context. It would have been unnecessary, and probably dangerous, for an author to announce, "by the way, the theory I am advancing conflicts with the Bible." Knowledgeable readers would notice this immediately without prompting.

11.2 The onomatopoetic theory of word origins

Johann Gottfried Herder (1744–1803) came from a poor East Prussian family, and was self-educated until enrolling in 1762 at the University of Königsberg, where Immanuel Kant was professor. With Goethe, Herder was a founder of the "Sturm und Drang" movement in German literature. His famous *Essay on the Origin of Language* won a major European prize and catapulted him to fame. Against the Biblical backdrop, Herder's ideas about the origins of words in onomatopoeia, today often discarded as the "bow-wow theory," constituted a brave attempt to give a rational, non-religious, explanation for the origin of words (Herder, 1966 [1772]), and the prize he won for this essay indicates the willingness of contemporary judges to entertain such radical ideas. This theory was also seen in contrast to the "expression of emotion" theory that words developed from innate cries of pain and the like, another non-Biblical idea popular in those times. Thus, the onomatopoeia theory is characteristic of the earliest attempts to bring language and its origins under rational consideration. The core insight of his essay is thoroughly modern, concerning the importance of distinguishing between human language and animal communication:

> I cannot conceal my astonishment at the fact that philosophers...can have arrived at the idea that the origins of human language is to be found in...emotional cries. All animals, even fish, express their feelings by sounds; but not even the most highly developed animals have so much as the beginning of true human speech...Children produce emotional sounds like animals; but is the language they learn from human beings not an entirely different language? (p. 24, Herder, 1966 [1772])

But if the earliest words did not originate from innate cries, and they are not (as the Bible suggested) totally arbitrary, the theorist must seek *some* rational basis for their phonological form. Herder accepted that concepts predated, and formed the necessary basis for, words, and his core notion was that vocal imitation, once present, would allow our ancestors to signify all those natural sources of sound (animals, wind, etc.) in a way that would be readily understood by others. The theory of onomatopoeia thus solves, with one stroke, two crucial problems: how the crucial linguistic link between sound and meaning could be made, and how this link, once made, would automatically be understood by others. This idea is by no means absurd once seen in this context. Indeed, many onomatopoetic words exist in present-day languages, across the planet. But most words in modern languages are *not* onomatopoetic, and even words considered onomatopoetic are quite distant and imperfect imitations of the original (witness the sound supposedly made by a rooster crowing: *kikiriki* in German against *cock a doodle doo* in English). Herder clearly realized that onomatopoeia fails entirely as the source of all words in modern language, and proposed onomatopoiea only as a *bridge* between early non-linguistic humans and modern language. He thus proposed a candidate for a **protolanguage**: an intermediate stage between the communication system possessed by our non-linguistic hominid ancestors and modern fully evolved language. As such, it seems a thoroughly reasonable hypothesis about the origins of some early words.

11.3 The expressive or interjectionist theory

Expressive theories seek the origin of words and language in the innate cries of pain or pleasure produced by nonhuman animals. In contrast to the onomatopoetic theory, which emphasizes the importance of cognition in the relation between words and concepts, expressive theories seek to ground language in innate emotional expressions such as screams or laughter. Müller dubbed this, less memorably, the "pooh-pooh" theory, and dismissed it in the same breath as the onomatopoetic theory. But again, considered in historical context, this idea is a surprisingly modern one: that the seeds of speech are to be found in the various innate cries with which humans, like other animals, come equipped at birth. Thus the first word for 'pain' would be a simulated groan of pain, and for 'pleasure' a sigh of pleasure. As Herder noted, and modern neuroscience and ethology amply confirm, this notion seems to miss a central distinction between language and most mammal calls: the sounds of the former are learned, while those of the latter innately given. This is the core reason that innate animal cries in general, and non-human primate calls in particular, seem a poor start for modern spoken language. Innate emotional communication systems instead *contrast* with language in the sense of the term used throughout this book and in modern linguistics. By Darwin's time, the pioneering neurological research of John Hughlings Jackson and Broca, documenting patients who had lost speech but retained the capacity to cry in pain or laugh, was already cited as neural evidence against the expressive model (Müller, 1873).

Nonetheless, if we ask how a species *already* possessed of imitative skills could come to acquire specific word meanings, innate cries could provide fodder for a different category of words from onomatopoeia, including words for emotions, for reactions to events, and for individuals (e.g. by imitating their laugh). Thus one can reject the idea that innate calls form the seed of voluntary vocalization (see Chapters 4 and 9), while accepting that once imitation was present, such calls could form models for certain words, although they are not words themselves. Thus both Herder and Darwin saw these two theories as complementary, and suggested that both had some value for explaining word origins.

11.4 Alternative origins in sociality or song

A number of early theorists thought that the two dominant non-Biblical theories – onomatopoeia and expression – did not do justice to the communicative aspects of language (Stam, 1976). Taking it as self-evident that language originated as communication, Noiré suggested that "the most primitive impulse to the utterance of sound originated first of all in the feeling of sympathy . . . any one who on some important emergency has lent a helping hand to . . . pull ashore a ship in distress – will at once understand the truth of this remark" (p. 30, Noiré, 1917; an idea later dubbed the "heave-ho" theory). The idea that language is first and foremost a social tool was strongly championed later by Firth, who contrasted this idea sharply with the "rationalist" view of language as a vehicle first of thought and only secondarily of communication, again a debate which resonates today (Firth, 1930, 1937).

Another alternative to either expressive or onomatopoetic theories held that a learned vocalization system, more like birdsong than innate calls, formed a middle term in language evolution. This was briefly discussed by Lord Monboddo (James Burnet) in 1773, who criticizes the theory of an "ingenious acquaintance," conjecturing that "the first language among men was *music* and that before our ideas were expressed by articulate sounds, they were communicated by tones" (p. 313, Vol. 1, Burnet, 1967 [1773]). It seems clear from Burnet's description that birdsong provided an important impetus to this theory. Although Burnet himself avers that inarticulate cries are the only route to language, he finds it "highly probable, that the natural cries were varied by tones, before they were distinguished by articulation" (p. 321). In 1781, Rousseau also briefly mentions the idea of a musical precursor to language (Rousseau, 1966).

A third alternative was the idea that gestures provided a middle stage in language evolution. This had been discussed even earlier by Condillac, in 1747, who based his hypothesis on observations of deaf-mutes communicating in what today would be called signed language (Condillac,

1971 [1747]). Each of these ideas, in their modern guises, will be discussed in subsequent chapters. However, these variants played little role in the debates over language evolution sparked by Darwin's evolutionary theory.

11.5 Max Müller's attack on evolution and language origin theories

In 1859, when Darwin's *On the Origin of Species* was published (notably avoiding discussion of human evolution), Oxford Professor Friederich Max Müller was the most respected linguist in England, and perhaps in the world. As an acknowledged master of Indo-European philology, he was a leader in his field (which he termed "linguistic science"), and he used language frequently in his staunch resistance to Darwinism (Stam, 1976). Müller was a master of rhetoric, and wrote widely read and discussed popular articles. As an unabashed Christian, who saw the origin of language in the God-given human soul, Müller automatically enjoyed powerful religious backing. These factors combined to make Müller a formidable foe in the early battles concerning evolution, and he played a role in creating the historical chasm between linguistics and biology which is only being bridged today. Although Müller's name is largely forgotten today, several of his arguments continue to be important, and are unwittingly echoed by contemporary scholars. Müller's arguments thus must be considered carefully, if we are to understand Darwin's response to them when he finally addresses the question of language evolution in his 1871 *The Descent of Man.*

Müller's acolyte Noiré dubbed him "the Darwin of the mind" (p. 118, Noiré, 1917), considering Müller to be "the only equal, not to say superior, antagonist, who has entered the arena against Darwin." Anti-Darwinian scholars put Müller in "the front rank as a crushing argument, a mighty bulwark, entrenched behind which they could discharge their own feeble shafts against the great disturber of the public peace" (p. 73). Müller himself states that "in the Science of Language, I was a Darwinian before Darwin" (p. 175, Müller, 1873), due to his championing of the idea of a single common origin for all human languages. Müller accepted that animals have feelings, memories, emotions, and sensations, and that the human *body* might well have evolved from that of "lower animals," making him relatively forward-thinking for his time. In ceding all of these issues to Darwin, Müller made his argument that much stronger.

Müller's position was simple: "language is the Rubicon which divides man from beast, and no animal will ever cross it . . . the science of language will yet enable us to withstand the extreme theories of the Darwinians, and to draw a hard and fast line between man and brute." By placing "language" as the key feature of humans, which separates them clearly and distinctly from all animals, Müller effectively substituted "language" for the soul that played the key distinguishing role in earlier religion and philosophy. If Müller's position was clear, his specific arguments were considerably less convincing. First, he dismissed the onomatopoetic and interjection theories for word origins because they can't account for the vast majority of contemporary words. But his argument against them confuses two things – the origin of the language *faculty* and the origin of particular word forms – concepts Müller is at pains to distinguish elsewhere in his writings. Theorists such as Herder attempted to describe a *protolanguage*, not fully modern language. Probably aware of this inadequacy, Müller uses a rhetorical trick – giving the theories the "bow-wow" nicknames still in use today – because he "felt certain that, if this theory were only called by its right name, it would require no further refutation" (p. 189, Müller, 1873). This is a poor excuse for reasoned argument.

Müller's second line of argument is only moderately more convincing. He holds as the "most important discovery of the Science of Language the discovery of linguistic 'roots'" (reconstructed Indo-European root morphemes), and argued that the core of these roots is always a *concept*, not a thing (or a sound). "Every root is an abstract term" that marks "the beginning of rational speech" (p. 197, Müller, 1873). Müller believed that comparative linguists could reconstruct the *original shared language* of all mankind. This idea, even then, came under heavy attack by other linguists, who recognized the relative speed with which languages change. Today Müller's goal is seen as untenable because glossogenetic change is so much more rapid than the biological changes that gave us language (phylogeny). Even if the language faculty were only 35,000 years old, we would not be able to reconstruct the words of the first language.

The final and most important component of Müller's argument concerns the relationship between thought and language. According to Müller, "concepts" are impossible without language, and language impossible without concepts. By "concept" Müller means clear, conscious, realized thoughts, capable of being communicated, and he clearly distinguishes such concepts from the memories, sensations, and emotions that he accepted are shared between humans and animals. Thus, in modern terms, Müller has a strong Whorfian view (Whorf, 1964) of the necessary and intimate connection between word and thought, a viewpoint which remains common today. Although Müller's main support for this claim is a tedious recital of the arguments of Locke, Berkeley, Hume, and Kant, he does provide a potential empirical test by virtue of a claim that no animal can possess an abstract concept. For although the senses and intuitions of both humans or animals give them *particular* dogs or trees (equivalent to a proper name), he claims that only the human mind allows us to abstract over these sense impressions to form a true *concept* of dog or tree. Indeed, in Müller and Darwin's time, experimental demonstrations of "animal concepts" were nowhere to be found. Today, of course, the data of animal cognition clearly demonstrate animals' capacity for categorization and generalization of precisely the sort Müller denied (e.g. pigeons' capacity to form a general and extensible notion of 'tree' or 'fish' based on individual photographs of trees and fish), as well as birds and insects possessing far more abstract concepts such as 'insideness' or 'same/different' (Herrnstein *et al.*, 1976; Herrnstein *et al.*, 1989; Giurfa *et al.*, 2001).

Although Müller's specific factual claim is thus clearly refuted by abundant data, the underlying belief that the possession of language is necessary for some kinds of thought continues to be popular (Boroditsky, 2003; Gleitman and Papafragou, 2005). Its persistence is probably due to the underlying truth of the notion that language *affects* thought, or that certain types of thought are possible only with language. This milder notion is both reasonable and consistent with available data from animals. If one defines 'thought' in such a way that it denotes these particular effects, the proposition is (tautologically) correct. Nonetheless, modern research in animal cognition allows little remaining room for debate on the question of whether animals have *some types* of thought. Animals have feelings, concepts, memory, goals, and plans, and some of them make and use tools, while others have complex representations of their social milieu (see Chapter 4). Thus Müller's conceptual "Rubicon" has faded to insignificance in the light of modern research.

A final anti-Darwinian argument Müller invokes in several places is that the notions of difference and continuity are logically inconsistent. But, as his contemporaries were quick to point out, this is a fallacy easily refuted by the facts of development: the fact that an infant starts life without speech and gradually acquires it through a series of minor changes in no way negates the fundamental distinction between the emotional cries with which the infant began life and the complex language she will possess at age five (Farrar, 1870).

Despite Müller's fundamental anti-Darwinism and his repeated allusion to a special creation for the human mind, some of his arguments, *mutatis mutandis*, still play a role in modern discussions, even if his name is no longer attached to them. His dismissal of the onomatopoetic and interjection theories via his dubbing them with derogatory nicknames (Müller, 1861) has proven extremely robust (although Müller's role as inventor seems largely forgotten), and has become a trope in modern discussions. Although Müller himself saw the true beginnings of language as a saltation, just as unexplainable by scientific means or Darwinian argument as the origin of life itself, he did have his own theory for the origin of the "roots" in a somewhat mystical "resonance" between the vibrations all objects create when struck and the phonetic form of the roots. Turnabout being fair play, this notion was soon dubbed the "ding-dong" theory (Noiré, 1917), but Müller himself had already distanced himself from this speculation by 1873, preferring more abstract arguments from philosophy (Müller, 1873). But the crucial first volleys in the war of "language science" against Darwinism had already been fired by Müller (1861), and the echoes widely attended to, when Darwin himself finally advanced his own theory of language evolution.

11.6 Charles Darwin's theory of language evolution

Charles Darwin had developed his theory of natural selection by 1838, as evidenced by his unpublished notebooks, and he had privately applied it since then to human emotion, language, and cognition. The notebooks provide a fascinating view of the intellectual life of this broad and careful thinker, and their strong statements – "He who understands baboon would do more toward metaphysics than Locke" (M Notebook, 16 August) – are refreshing relative to the cautious statements in his published writings. Despite his private convictions, Darwin was aware of the sensitivity of discussing human evolution, and *On the Origin of Species* mentioned our own species only evasively: "light will be thrown on the origin of man" (Darwin, 1859). What *sort* of light remained, at that time, unclear. Some "Darwinians" such as Wallace argued that natural selection could account for all aspects of the animal world, and for the human body, but that the human mind could only be explained by reference to some "higher intelligence" (Wallace, 1864) – not very different from the modern Catholic position, which allows that evolution has been involved in human *bodily* evolution, but cannot account for the soul.

However, Darwin's trepidation regarding human evolution was not matched by all of his followers: Thomas Huxley published his *Evidence as to Man's Place in Nature* in 1863 precisely to address these issues. As "Darwin's Bulldog," Huxley made no concession to religious or metaphysical worries in his no-holds-barred statement of the Darwinian position: Man is an animal (an ape, to be exact) who evolved via exactly the same processes as all other species. Nor were Darwin's many opponents slow to jump on human mental powers, and language in particular, as the key weakness of his theory. Müller's dictum of language as an impassible Rubicon between humans and animals was seen as a powerful argument against all-encompassing Darwinism. Other linguists rallied in Darwin's defense, such as F. W. Farrar in 1865 (reprinted in Farrar, 1996). Thus, by the time Darwin was writing *The Descent of Man*, the battle-lines were clearly drawn.

Chapter Two of *The Descent of Man*, entitled "Comparison of the mental powers of man and the lower animals," is one of the most remarkable in the entire Darwinian corpus. The chapter is noteworthy for its concision, for its breadth of argument, and for the variety of evidence brought to bear in considering the evolution of the human mind. It is surprisingly, if not shockingly, modern in its conclusions, and mentions facts (e.g. that chimpanzees use stone tools to crack open nuts) that were long forgotten until rediscovered in the twentieth century. The first half of the chapter lays the groundwork of modern research in comparative cognition, arguing that animals have emotions, attention, and memory as well as many other mental traits in common with humans. But Darwin's opponents, notably Müller in his 1861 lectures, had already ceded that point: "If, with all these facts before us, we deny that brutes have sensation, perception, memory, will and intellect, we ought to bring forward powerful arguments for interpreting the signs which we observe in brutes so differently from those which we observe in men" (p. 14, Müller, 1861). Clearly language was a key issue, and one can imagine considerable anticipation of both pro- and anti-Darwinians as they turned to the section of the chapter simply titled "Language." In ten densely argued pages, Darwin lays out a three-stage theory of language evolution still worthy of serious attention today (we will revisit it in detail in Chapter 14).

Despite a few statements that, today, can be recognized as errors (e.g. the idea that some monkeys can imitate vocalizations), a reader today cannot fail to be impressed by the broad sweep of data Darwin considers (ethological, neural, physiological, and comparative/evolutionary), and his mastery of the logical and theoretical issues involved in language evolution. Summing his theory up in modern terms, Darwin recognizes the distinction between the evolution of the language *faculty* and of a particular language, seeing the former as crucial. He suggests that a crucial first step in language evolution was an overall increase in intelligence (consonant with the increase in brain size characteristic of the hominid line: data unavailable to Darwin). Considering and rejecting a gestural origin for language, he suggests that the first protolanguage was musical, and that this stage was driven by sexual selection (by analogy with learned birdsong). The bridge between such a musical protolanguage and true, meaningful, language would again have been driven by increased intelligence, and once this was in place, the origin of actual words would have been eclectic, including both onomatopoeia and expressive imitations. The most important missing piece of the puzzle was a better understanding of the complexity of language (especially syntax).

Darwin even discusses comparative and historical lingustics, and the distinct parallels between phylogeny and glossogeny, issues only very recently analyzed by modern thinkers. Surprisingly few scholars today even discuss Darwin's theory, much less recognize its many values (with the prominent exception of Donald (1991)). This is, to me, the saddest example of the unscholarly treatment of the topic of language evolution in the modern literature – for it can hardly be claimed that Darwin (1871) is an obscure or difficult-to-obtain book. Like many a classic, it seems to be frequently cited, but rarely read.

11.7 Protolanguage in theories of language evolution

As this brief historical review will have made clear, intelligent discussions of language evolution were already well underway in Darwin's time. Many of the relevant data (from animals, brain damage, deaf children and signed language, babbling, etc.), as well as many of the crucial distinctions necessary to make sense of language evolution, were already part of the debate. Darwin's own theory made broad use of such data and reached, in 1871, correct conclusions about questions that are still debated today. During the periodic re-awakenings of interest in language evolution that have occurred more recently (first in the late 1960s and again in the 1990s), these debates and conclusions have been too often ignored.

Before leaving this historical survey behind to examine modern theories of language evolution, I wish to highlight a crucial concept that became clear during this earliest stage of evolutionary discussion: the notion of **protolanguage** – a hypothetical stage of language evolution interposed between modern language and the ancestral system(s) of thought and communication present in the LCA. The term "protolanguage" is an old one, used in the eighteenth and nineteenth centuries to designate cultural, historical entities such as proto-Indo-European. Its use to designate a preceding *biological* stage of human evolution is relatively new (introduced by Hewes, 1973). However, the notion of a biological intermediate stage is implicit in the very notion of gradual evolution, and most of the early theorists before and after Darwin posited at least one such intervening stage (e.g. "pre-language" in Hockett and Ascher, 1964). Müller's attempts to refute the very possibility of language evolution therefore concentrated on, first, rejecting previously suggested intermediate stages, and second, affirming the all-or-nothing quality of human language. Müller denies the very possibility of protolanguage. Nonetheless, as we will see in the following chapters, the necessity for at least one intervening protolanguage stage in hominid evolution is nearly universally accepted today. However, the precise nature of such protolanguage(s) remains a central debate.

Using the concept of protolanguage to classify different hypotheses, we are finally ready to evaluate modern models of language evolution. We will start with models of "lexical protolanguage" (Chapter 12), in which protolanguage was made up of individual words unconnected by complex syntax. Next, we will discuss gestural origin theories (Chapter 13), which follow Condillac in suggesting that the communicative modality of protolanguage was essentially manual/visual, rather than the vocal/auditory speech mode. Finally, we will examine models positing a song-like protolanguage (Chapter 14). Such a musical protolanguage would have included both complex phonology and some aspects of syntax, but by hypothesis lacked the propositional meanings that give modern language its semantic power. Each of these broad sets of models has many variants, and both strengths and weaknesses, which we will now consider.

12 | Lexical protolanguage

12.1 Introduction

This chapter will discuss what is, to many, the most intuitive class of models for the evolution of language. Such models posit a "lexical" protolanguage, with a large learned lexicon of meaningful words, but no complex syntax. Words in a lexical protolanguage are not combined into complex syntactic structures, leaving modern syntax as the final step in language evolution. This "syntax-final" model of language evolution is shared by a diverse group of scholars who disagree about almost everything else (e.g. Lieberman, 1984; Bickerton, 1990; Givón, 1995; Jackendoff, 2002). A lexical protolanguage assumes, as prerequisites, an ability for vocal imitation (necessary to develop a shared spoken vocabulary) and a capacity and drive for referential communication. Although the idea of a lexical protolanguage is implicit in a number of distinct hypotheses about language evolution, it has been defended most explicitly by Derek Bickerton, especially in his book *Language and Species* (Bickerton, 1990). Bickerton's notion of protolanguage has since been adopted by various other theorists (Jackendoff, 1999, 2002) and criticized by others (Deacon, 1997; Lieberman, 2000). Bickerton's treatment draws on a wide range of data, and is relatively explicit, giving reasons (both data and argument) for most of his assumptions. He explicitly aims to build bridges between linguistics and evolutionary theory, taking both Chomsky and Darwin seriously, and thus provides a reasonable starting point for discussions of contemporary theories of language evolution. Bickerton's model of lexical protolanguage solves a number of problems quite neatly, while leaving several important evolutionary problems open. Various other theorists have offered solutions to these problems, thus extending and strengthening the lexical protolanguage hypothesis. But I will conclude that all of these hypotheses account adequately only for certain components of the FLB, leaving others (most prominently vocal imitation and phonology) unexplained.

12.2 The discontinuity between animal communication and language

A fundamental point of Bickerton's 1990 book *Language and Species*, and a recurring trope in his later writings, is that the field of language evolution has been dominated by non-linguists who don't recognize the complexity of language (cf. Lenneberg, 1967). "Syntax isn't simple, and does not reduce to word order" is a persistent theme. Bickerton insists that those who ignore the fundamental complexity of syntax also overlook the most fundamental discontinuity between animal communication and human language. Bickerton terms this the "continuity paradox": that the evolutionary continuity between humans and animals, in terms of both bodily and neural form, is in striking contrast to the sharp discontinuity in our communication systems. Bickerton considers, and rejects, the notion that "functionally referential" call systems, like the famous vervet alarm call system, provide a precursor for human language. He notes that such calls "refer" to *present events* in a holistic manner, while a crucial aspect of human language is precisely the way it breaks *concepts* (not necessarily in the here and now) down into subjects and predicates, and uses grammatical items to build complex *novel* phrases that are nonetheless readily intelligible. Thus Bickerton rejects the notion that human language evolved from an animal communication system, instead arguing that language evolved primarily as a system of **representation**, whose uses for communication are secondary. Bickerton bolsters this point by exploring data on animal cognition that indicate that animals have basic concepts, concluding that conceptual structure predates language by many millions of years: "Until we cease to regard language as primarily communicative and begin to treat it as primarily representational, we cannot hope to escape from the Continuity Paradox" (p. 16).

Bickerton thus starts by recognizing the gulf between animal communication systems and language, in terms of syntax, while affirming the continuity between human conceptual representations and those of animals. Vervet alarm calls are a red herring as precursors of language, because primate calls are unlearned and inflexible, and thus provide no foundation for the learned lexicon and flexible syntax that Bickerton argues are central to language. He accepts that the addition of language to the human mind changed the kinds of representation available (and later their importance for consciousness, culture, and technology), but the crucial first step in his solution to the continuity paradox is the idea that the prelinguistic precursors of protolanguage were conceptual, not communicative. He supports his conclusion with data from animal cognition and behavior, and although one can quibble over the details, the overall sweep of this part of Bickerton's book is quite consistent with the approach I have taken in this book. His basic conclusion – that a rich perceptual/cognitive world predated humans, and thus any form of human language – is consistent with the wealth of comparative data reviewed in Chapter 4 and with the conclusions of many other scholars (e.g. Pinker and Bloom, 1990; Newmeyer, 1991; Hauser *et al.*, 2002; Cheney and Seyfarth, 2007; Hurford, 2007).

Bickerton also argues that one's model of linguistic reference must be the referential triangle discussed in Chapter 3. In agreement with Jackendoff and my conclusions in this book, Bickerton argues that reference always requires the intervening existence of concepts. He briefly discusses interjection and onomatopoeia as sources of early words, rejecting the former while mildly affirming the latter. He correctly notes that the argument often given against onomatopoeia since Müller – that most words in most languages are not onomatopoetic – fails as soon as one distinguishes between protolanguage and full modern language. Nonetheless he concludes that "what form of signal was first used is relatively unimportant" – a fair statement of a near-consensus among modern theorists. Once the complexity of syntax is acknowledged, the specific form of early word–meaning pairs seems the least of our theoretical worries.

Bickerton reviews the fossil and archaeological evidence (see Chapter 7), concluding that Australopithecines were essentially bipedal chimpanzees, with wider-ranging and more catholic foraging habits, but with no obvious increase in neural, social, linguistic, or cultural complexity. In contrast, clear and drastic changes occurred with the genus *Homo*, most clearly in *Homo erectus*, with whom Bickerton, like many theorists, explicitly associates his protolanguage. Based on brain size, the migration out of Africa into much of the Old World, and the far more complex workmanship of the Achulean toolkit, Bickerton concludes that *erectus* was a new type of animal – something the planet had never seen before. Nonetheless, the million-year stasis of this toolkit suggests that *erectus* was not fully human, and Bickerton concludes that *erectus* provides the most probable paleospecies for an intermediate "protolanguage." This conclusion is in accord with a large body of fossil and archaeological data, and seems to be shared by many in the field (e.g. Donald, 1991).

12.3 "Living fossils" of protolanguage: contemporary windows onto protolanguage

While accepting Lieberman's account of vocal tract limitations in pre-sapiens hominids (that *erectus* lacked a modern human vocal tract and

Table 12.1. Elements of Bickertonian lexical protolanguage

Present in lexical protolanguage:
(1) Vocal learning and expression via the auditory/vocal modality (signal)
(2) Lexical items (individual form–meaning mappings) (semantics)
(3) Motivation/Drive to share information (*Mitteilungsbedürfnis*)

Missing – Modern syntax:
(1) Grammatical items (function words and inflectional morphemes)
(2) Phrase structure
(3) Obligatory expression of argument structure
(4) Readily identifiable null elements
(5) Varied word orders for varied semantic pragmatic functions

---

was thus phonetically limited), Bickerton rejects the notion that the language capabilities of extinct hominids can be adequately reconstructed from fossils. Indeed, he derides "fossilism" as the idea that the only relevant data for human evolution are "stones and bones." In their place, Bickerton uses various contemporary data as "living fossils" of past stages of our language evolution (an idea further explored by Jackendoff (1999)). Deacon has concisely stated the rationale for this idea: given that language does not fossilize, "we are forced to turn to modern humans for the first clues . . . Such a trick – one that no other species has hit upon – is not likely to have been cast away too quickly in the subsequent evolution of our species" (p. 384, Deacon, 1997). As far as our sources of information about protolanguage are concerned, I see this turn away from bony remains, and towards behaviors in modern humans (or animals), as an important step forward. Linguist Rudie Botha has dubbed such sources of evidence "windows" into language evolution (Botha, 2003).

As potential "living fossils" of protolanguage, Bickerton cites four: child language, pidgin languages and the pidgin/creole transition, the utterances of apes in various artificial languages, and the language behavior of Genie (Curtis, 1977). It is important to evaluate each of these potential "windows" onto protolanguage (Botha, 2008), because Bickerton uses these data to generate a quite specific model of what was, and was not, present in his hypothetical lexical protolanguage (see Table 12.1). To a first approximation, we can think of this as "modern language minus syntax." He is far less precise about what had to be *gained* for protolanguage to arrive on the scene, and seems to take the fact that chimpanzees and bonobos can, with training, acquire and use lexical items as evidence that the evolution of protolanguage was the easy step. Thus, in both his 1990 book and later,

Bickerton is mainly concerned with the later transition from protolanguage to language, and seems to assume a lexical protolanguage as essentially given in the LCA. As detailed below, this is not a safe assumption.

Regarding the behavior of language-trained apes (especially Nim, Lana, and Kanzi), Bickerton gives a thoughtful evaluation of the achievements of home-reared apes, and correctly notes the magnitude of their achievement, when given the proper tutelage. But because the main thrust of his argument is the difference between protolanguage and language, he seems ready (perhaps too much so) to grant such apes an *erectus*-like protolanguage. But while the ability to link signs with referents is clearly present in apes (and other vertebrates as well) this does not, by itself, constitute a protolanguage like that in a young child. Neither vocal control nor *Mitteilungsbedürfnis* characterize even highly trained apes, so there are important unshared elements between the "protolanguage" of a young human child and enculturated chimpanzees.

There are equally significant problems in using the data from a single "wild child," the unfortunate Genie, as examples of some previous state of human evolution. As we saw earlier, there is considerable variance in the linguistic achievements of abandoned children, and there are well-documented cases like that of the high-functioning "wild child" Kaspar Hauser that demonstrate a far more flexible and accomplished acquisition of language in later life (Blumenthal, 2003). In Genie's case, it is difficult to separate the effects of psychological and physical trauma, and congenital cognitive issues, from the language-specific aspects of her upbringing. Generalizations from this single, sad, case are thus unfounded (Curtis, 1977).

The more convincing data, then, concern normal human beings acquiring language. Bickerton dwells upon these, citing Haeckel's "law," that ontogeny (often) recapitulates phylogeny. But as he is aware, there is a major logical problem in using the output of modern human brains, possessed of all the genetic and neural mechanisms for language readiness, as a template for the brain and behavior of an extinct hominid. Human development does not, in any sense, recapitulate most aspects of human evolution from chimpanzees to moderns (Gould, 1977; Raff and Kaufman, 1983). For instance, newborn human infants have a unique fat layer, laid down in the last (extra) month of gestation, and are thus born in a state that does not recapitulate any stage of adult evolution in chimpanzees, or other primates. Instead, it appears to be a specific adaptation of the infant human form. More relevant to language, the extremely early and rapid acquisition of phonology, a lexicon, and syntax by infants in their first two years is unlikely to be recapitulatory. More likely, the rapid acquisition of language in human children reflects a powerful, recent selective pressure for early learning, exerted specifically on infants, after adult language already existed. We need to bear these caveats in mind when considering child language acquisition as a model of linguistic phylogeny. While Bickerton recognizes that recapitulation is not always the case, he takes it as a good first approximation for evolution, and perhaps the best we are going to get. Because beggars can't be choosers, let us see where these considerations lead.

According to Bickerton's interpretation, children between the age of one and two build a lexicon that is essentially grammar-free. In response to arguments about whether the child's internal representations of grammar resemble those of adults, or represent unique "child grammars," Bickerton proposes the radical solution that infants in this stage have *no grammar at all.* He thus see the rapid acquisition of grammatical morphemes and phrase structure that happens during the third year of life as a "catastrophic" acquisition of syntax from an essentially non-syntactic state, and he uses this "fact" in defense of a catastrophic model for the evolution of syntax. However, most child-language experts see syntax acquisition as occurring rapidly, but nonetheless gradually (for an overview see Gleason, 2005), and some suggest that the acquisition of syntax occurs in piecemeal fashion, verb by verb (for discussion see Tomasello, 2000; Fisher, 2002). The standard view, since Brown (1973), is of a slow, gradual climb to linguistic competence, starting at age two and proceeding in a quite regular way, morpheme by morpheme. Considerable evidence, starting with Chomsky (1969), indicates that this process is not complete by the age of eight years. Even strong nativists who posit innately given knowledge as the basis for child language acquisition (e.g. Crain, 1991) acknowledge that comprehension precedes production, and that evidence of overall grammatical competence appears gradually, not suddenly. Thus, child language data provide no real support for this aspect of Bickerton's argument.

Perhaps the most intriguing, if controversial, of Bickerton's "windows" comes from pidgin languages, and the transition to creoles. Pidgin languages seem indeed to be well characterized by a lexicon with little grammar: a contemporary stand-in for Bickertonian lexical protolanguage. Creoles, in contrast, are fully syntactic languages. The key phenomenon Bickerton cites is the sometimes very rapid transition, from one generation to another, between pidgins and creoles. There are now a number of well-attested examples where a pidgin language rapidly makes the transition to a cre-ole. The most compelling, because of its extensive documentation, is the case of Nicaraguan Sign Language (Senghas and Coppola, 2001; Senghas *et al.*, 2005), where the speakers of the two forms are still alive today, and thus can be interviewed in detail. While the process by which *individuals* acquire creoles when presented with pidgins is probably quite gradual, from a cultural glossogenetic viewpoint this transition is indeed sudden, even "catastrophic," going from a grammar-poor system to a richly syntactic system in a generation or two. Creole learners are, of course, fully modern, language-ready humans, so the suddenness of the pidgin/creole illustrates the possibility of "instant" syntax in a glossogenetic sense only.

12.4 Catastrophic syntax?

Bickerton thus posits a word-based protolanguage, arguing that complex modern syntax is the final, and most crucial, step in the evolution of language. Both of these suppositions are reasonable, and indeed intuitive. Bickerton's most controversial argument is thus that the transition to syntax was abrupt; in his words "catastrophic" (cf. Bickerton, 1998). This general notion has been both endorsed (Berwick, 1997) and sharply denied by others. Syntactic catastrophism is dismissed even by scholars who share many of Bickerton's assumptions about the nature of language and syntax (Pinker and Bloom, 1990; Newmeyer, 1998b; Jackendoff, 1999, 2002), although the critique is often framed as a response to Chomsky's vaguer quote concerning "a mutation" (Chomsky, 1988) than to Bickerton's specific proposal. Scholars who do not accept a generative linguistic framework are typically even less positive about this idea (e.g. Lieberman, 1986). What factual basis does Bickerton have in mind for this genetic and neural catastrophism?

While Bickerton's pidgin/creole transition example provides a reasonable argument that sudden change *could have* happened, it by no means demonstrates that it *did* happen. Indeed, the postulate that this cultural transition accurately reflects the biological evolutionary transition to language – that *glossogeny* recapitulates phylogeny – seems even less justified than the assumption that ontogeny does so. Far more support is required to make this argument compelling.

Bickerton sees the archaeological record as providing strong evidence for an abrupt post-*erectus* transition: "the argument that toolmaking and language co-evolved . . . comes up against the undisputed and massive facts of tool development . . . the original *erectus* toolkit . . . showed no significant improvement, or even change, over a period of approximately a million years" (p. 139, Bickerton, 1990). But Bickerton disputes such "facts" elsewhere in his book when discussing *modern* humans. Attempting to account for the 100,000-year lag between the advent of anatomically modern *Homo sapiens* and any evidence of a technological explosion, he notes that the development of an elaborate toolmaking culture in non-stone materials (baskets, nets, poison darts, etc.) would be forever lost from the fossil record. But this argument is, of course, equally applicable to *Homo erectus* culture. The failure of non-durable artifacts to fossilize could just as easily mask a slow, gradual increase in technology throughout the long tenure of *erectus*, and continuous with *sapiens* as a catastrophic transition between the two. I thus find this archaeological aspect of Bickerton's argument quite unconvincing.

Bickerton suggests that parsimony provides another potential argument for the catastrophic evolution of syntax, because single-stage models are simpler than those requiring multiple stages. But this argument is weak as well. Lacking foresight, evolution is not generally a parsimonious process. The simplest or most optimal "engineering" solution is unlikely to be found directly, if it is found at all. If complex syntax could be shown to result from a single genetic mutation, as Bickerton suggests in places, then this argument might go through, but there is no evidence that complex syntax of the sort Bickerton discusses is, or could be, caused by a single mutation.

Surprisingly, Bickerton gives little attention to aphasic data, despite the fact that cases where well-defined abilities are lost might be seen as a better model of pre-modern brains. He mainly cites a few utterances by Broca's aphasics to argue that they do *not* represent protolanguage. The wide variety of deficits seen in language after brain damage certainly makes it difficult to choose any single "syndrome" (e.g. Broca's aphasia) as exemplary of protolanguage. Nonetheless, the patterns of breakdown observed support inferences about how a brain lacking some neural mechanisms required for language behaves. One pattern is abundantly clear from the literature on neurolinguistics: deficits of surprising linguistic specificity can result from brain damage, spread across a wide variety of brain areas, suggesting that at least some computational aspects of language are pervasively distributed throughout the brain.

This leads to the most compelling of Bickerton's arguments for catastrophic syntax (perhaps the only one clearly in line with the neural and evolutionary facts). The basic hypothesis is that "the syntactic module consists not of an isolated brain area but rather of a particular type of nervous organization that permeates and interconnects those areas devoted to higher reasoning processes, concepts, and the lexicon, a type of organization that automatically sorts material into binary-branching tree structures" (p. 207, Bickerton, 1990). Although Bickerton's use of the term "module" to describe such an anatomically distributed system may seem odd, Fodor's notion of "module" does not imply a specific circumscribed chunk of neuroanatomy (as recently clarified in Fodor, 2000), so this usage is consistent with Fodorian modularity. However, from Bickerton's perspective, complex syntax results from a pervasive change occurring throughout the neocortex (more analogous to attention than, say, binocular vision). At some level, this idea *must* be right for conceptual aspects of language, since we are able to talk about anything we can think about (language can "reach into" all cortical sensory modalities and motor regions). Note that this hypothesis is *not* incompatible with the idea that some other aspects of language processing (e.g. speech parsing) are modular in both the Fodorian and neuroanatomical senses. These are separate hypotheses, about separate neural functions.

Reframed as a hypothesis about the neural mechanisms underlying complex syntax (cf. Berwick, 1997), the catastrophic hypothesis becomes more plausible, interpretable as a subtle but pervasive change in the micro-level wiring of the brain. Extending it somewhat, and framing it in more traditional neuroscientific language, I suggest the following scenario, simplified for the sake of clarity. Some continuously variable cellular trait (such as branching probability for neocortical pyramidal cells) is selected gradually to increase (either directly, because of increased storage capacity, or indirectly, by selection for a larger brain). Neurons become more branched, and in particular the density of (say) secondary dendritic branches increases. But at some point, the continuous variable of branching probability would lead to the appearance of tertiary branching: a qualitative change. Such a change could have major computational effects, effects permeating the entire neocortex, and yet be the result of continuous selection on a continuous trait, of a type to satisfy the most demanding gradualist. The sudden existence of a new class of neuronal connections, spread throughout the brain, could then lead to a "phase transition" in the types of computations possible in the brain, without any significant change in neural cell types, neurotransmitters, or overall connectivity. Although highly speculative, there is nothing "cryptocreationist" about such a hypothesis, and indeed it is compatible with current understanding of both neuroscience and evolutionary theory. I know of no micro-anatomical data directly supporting this hypothesis at present, but nonetheless this or similar ideas (cf. Szathmáry, 2001) deserve continued scrutiny (despite the fact that Bickerton himself devotes little space to the idea in his 1990 book, and seems to have moved away from it more recently; Calvin and Bickerton, 2000).

Overall, Bickerton's main arguments about catastrophic syntax hinge on debatable analogies and an unconvincing argument from parsimony, and on the claim that there is only one "syntax" or structure-building combinatorial system. This "syntactocentric" claim is itself based on weak evidence and considerations of parsimony, which have been questioned in a more recent extension of the lexical protolanguage model.

12.5 Jackendoff's model: protolanguage plus incremental evolution of syntax

Linguist Ray Jackendoff has extended Bickerton's basic notion of a lexical protolanguage in several ways (Jackendoff, 1999, 2002). Jackendoff shares many of Bickerton's basic presuppositions about the nature of language, as well as the pre-existing capabilities of our LCA with chimpanzees (based on studies of language-trained apes). Thus Jackendoff accepts that rich conceptual structures and a basic symbolic capacity to match sounds with arbitrary referents were present before language. Like Bickerton he assumes that all stages of language evolution were audio-vocal, but gives little attention to the evolutionary problem of complex vocal control. Jackendoff's proposals have three major differences from Bickerton's. First, he rejects the catastrophic evolution of syntax, and offers instead a detailed, multi-step process by which our species could have moved in incremental steps from a basic lexical protolanguage to full modern syntax. Second, he proposed new "windows" into protolanguage, based on examination of modern language in normal adults. Third, Jackendoff shares with many others the assumption that the key selective force driving language evolution, throughout human evolution, was communication: "I will argue that one actually can reconstruct from modern human language a sequence of distinct innovations over primate calls... each of which is an improvement in communicative expressiveness and precision" (p. 236, Jackendoff, 2002). He sees no reason to choose any particular communicative context as primary, but his list of possible communicative functions ("cooperation for hunting, gathering, defense... gossip, 'social grooming', or deception," p. 237) implies that communication among adults was critical, rather than pedagogy between adults and children.

The key extensions and advantages of Jackendoff's model relative to Bickerton's are intervening stages both before and after lexical protolanguage. Jackendoff justifies each of these, with contemporary data representing "fossils" of these stages. Before protolanguage, Jackendoff suggests a "one-word" stage, lacking any combinatoriality, where single holistic utterances were mapped onto holistic meanings. He sees this system as but a small step beyond standard primate capabilities, requiring only a novel capacity for vocal learning, and offers the interesting conjecture that interjections – e.g. English expressions such as *oops, tsk tsk, abracadabra,* and many others – are a holdover of this stage. He cites as evidence of their antiquity the preservation of such exclamations in very deep aphasics, and their frequent violation of the phonotactic constraints of the "host" language (e.g. *shh,* a fricative, serves as a syllabic nucleus, and *tsk tsk* is a tongue click not found in the phonemic inventory of English). Jackendoff is not, of course, suggesting that such "paleo-lexical items" are literally holdovers of an early stage of language evolution (i.e. that Neanderthals said 'ouch'), but that the capacity to learn and use such lexical items *is.*

Jackendoff observes the rather limited size of the vocabulary obtained by language-trained animals (in the range of hundreds of items, *versus* many thousands of items for a six-year-old), and suggests that the evolution of specialized innate "lexical acquisition tools" represented a further incremental step preceding Bickertonian protolanguage. Although plausible, there is considerable debate in the child language acquisition literature about whether the constraints children use to deduce word meanings, or the capacity for "fast mapping" (one-trial learning), are unique to either language or humans. Dogs' capacity to use mutual exclusivity and fast mapping in acquiring a novel label suggests that these capacities are not uniquely human (Kaminski *et al.,* 2004). Children appear to use similar cognitive resources for learning facts as for word meanings, suggesting that the cognitive capacities in question are not specific to language (Markson and Bloom, 1997). Although humans definitely learn more and faster than other animals, there is little data at present to suggest that this increased capacity represents a specifically linguistic adaptation.

A second important stage in Jackendoff's model is the combinatorial system of phonology: a generative system independent of meaning, providing an unlimited pool of word forms. He correctly sees this as a major advance over most primate call systems, arguing that the hypothesized existence of a "mental syllabary" (Levelt and Wheeldon, 1994) is a neural holdover of this stage. He also suggests that the ease with which children count syllables (*versus* phonemes) or recognize rhyme indicates the antiquity of this system and suggests a "cognitive primacy" of the syllable. Suggesting syllables as a unit of organization of an earlier stage of language, Jackendoff argues that the ability to concatenate such syllables provided a significant leap forward for generating large vocabularies (a basic form of generative combinatoriality). Curiously, although he recognizes combinatoriality (creative concatenation of meaningless elements) in birdsong, Jackendoff sees no "evolutionary link" between birdsong and phonology, because birds are not using this system to convey complex meanings (p. 245, Jackendoff, 2002). Here, Jackendoff seems to fall into a logical trap: having assumed (without argument) that all stages of language acquisition functioned to improve propositional communication, he rejects a potential evolutionary analog because it lacks this characteristic. But the same argument could be used to reject the possibility of evolutionary or computational parallels between music and phonology within our species, a possibility to which Jackendoff is quite open (Jackendoff and Lerdahl, 1982; Lerdahl and Jackendoff, 1983; Jackendoff and Lerdahl, 2006). I believe that this elision illustrates the danger of assuming that a single consistent evolutionary force drove all aspects of language evolution.

Jackendoff's model thus offers several intervening stages to reach a level that Bickerton, in the main, takes as a given: a lexical protolanguage with full vocal complexity and a large phonologically structured lexicon, used in a communicative context among adult members of some primitive hominid group. But Jackendoff's most important contribution comes after this protolanguage. Like Bickerton and many others, Jackendoff assumes that modern syntax, in all its generative and recursive glory, was the final crowning achievement of language evolution. Unlike Bickerton, however, Jackendoff suggests a series of incremental stages on the way to modern syntax. These steps include the concatenation of words and the use of word order to reflect semantic roles (such as "Agent First" or "Topic Last"). Phrases with heads are a major innovation: now a group of words can substitute for a single word (noun phrases for nouns, etc.). Although Bickerton agrees about the centrality of headed phrases, he suggests that the rest of syntax automatically appears with them.

Another, logically separate, innovation would be the invention of function words, and particularly relational words that allow phrases to be combined in more complex propositional structures ('if x then y,' 'while x, y,' etc.). Jackendoff cites as a "fossil" of this stage the mostly unconstrained ordering of adverbial phrases in English. Adverbial phrases can freely occupy several "slots" in English, so *Fred, with a sigh, left town* is as acceptable as *With a sigh, Fred left town* or *Fred left town with a sigh*. Similarly connectives like *with* seem to depend crucially on pragmatics for their interpretation: *got the ring with twenty dollars* and *got the ring with a crowbar* (or *with a gun*) imply rather different events, but the disambiguation of *with* must be semantically and pragmatically driven. Finally, Jackendoff suggests the very notion of "syntactic category" – the noun/verb *versus* the semantic entity/event distinction – as an important (and perhaps final) stage of syntactic evolution.

Jackendoff supports these hypothesized stages with data on simplified grammar in late second-language learners, what Klein and Perdue dub the "Basic Variety" (BV) (Klein and Perdue, 1997). This is an important contribution, given the ubiquity of late language learners in modern society, and the ease with which such subjects can be studied both psycholingusitically and neuroscientifically. Klein and Perdue and Jackendoff see the BV as revealing a basic subcomponent of UG: a robust core element of the human language capacity. Although "most robust" cannot necessarily be assumed to indicate "most ancient," the brain regions involved in various aspects of BV speech and comprehension might certainly be expected to reveal something about the brain regions involved in different ontogenetic endpoints of syntax acquisition of the same language, and the slightly different neural localization patterns that can result (Bates, 1999).

In conclusion, Jackendoff builds upon many of the same assumptions as Bickerton (1990) extended in several ways. However, he clearly rejects Bickerton's catastrophic model of syntax evolution, offering instead a gradualistic counter-proposal, based on a detailed examination of linguistic evidence. Bickerton's frequent critique of his critics as ignorant of linguistics cuts little ice in the case of Jackendoff – a card-carrying linguist whose work treats all aspects of language from phonetics through syntax through semantics and pragmatics in great detail. Together, these models provide good examples of linguistically motivated models of language evolution. However, both models fail to solve, or even consider, some quite serious difficulties posed for lexical protolanguage models by evolutionary and neuroscientific data. It is to these difficulties that I now turn.

12.6 The selective pressures underlying lexical protolanguage

Bickerton and Jackendoff both assume, with little argument, that it would be adaptive for early hominids to share information with one another. In places this seems to result from a confusion between population and species thinking: "the adaptations that are favored will be those that provide immediate and specific advantages to the creatures concerned . . . If these conditions are not met, the creature may fail to adapt and may become extinct, as have an overwhelming majority of species since evolution began" (p. 147, Bickerton, 1990). This sentence elides the distinction between competing individuals within a population and species-level extinction: at best, two very different levels of explanation. Later in the same chapter he seeks to explain the adaptive value for language in group-selective terms.

Bickerton's argument for the selective force behind the evolution of protolanguage is based explicitly on the adaptive value of sharing information within a group of adults. He argues that humans, as social animals feeding on a wide variety of omnivorous foods, "had a constant need for more and better information" (p. 153), and he suggests that this situation is relatively unique to our species ("social creatures are usually either herbivorous or carnivorous," p. 153). He suggests that the optimal foraging strategy for a wide variety of highly dispersed foods is to break into smaller foraging parties, and that "any find too large for a small group to consume is then reported to the band as a whole" (p. 154). Based on his well-argued conclusion that prelinguistic humans already had complex and detailed mental maps, Bickerton suggests that "all that was now needed was to put these two capacities together" (p. 154). At this point, the stage is set for separate bands of hominids to develop a handful of useful, shared words. "As long as the selective pressure was maintained – a need for information richer and more accurate and more swiftly delivered than that available to competitors – protolanguage would go on struggling to be born" (p. 155).

Bickerton's proposed selective force for protolanguage is explicitly group selectionist, positing that the more successful a group was at sharing information, the more likely it was to succeed against other competing groups. This solution – information-sharing arose to facilitate food sharing and communal foraging within a group, and was adaptive because it increased survival of that group relative to others – may seem plausible, but it raises a host of evolutionary problems that Bickerton does not confront in any serious way. As discussed in Chapter 2, most evolutionary theorists today still view group-selective explanations, other than those incorporating kinship and inclusive fitness, with suspicion. Certainly, most would rely on such explanations only if other, mainstream, adaptive forces of individuals increasing their inclusive fitness had first been carefully considered and found wanting. So let us consider the evolution of cooperative information sharing from the perspective of ordinary evolutionary theory.

12.7 The evolution of cooperative communication: solving a central problem

No instinct has been produced for the exclusive good of other animals, but... each animal takes advantage of the instincts of others. (Darwin, 1859)

As discussed in Chapter 4, a core issue in the evolution of language is that sharing detailed, truthful information involves a degree of **cooperation**. It seems perfectly obvious to humans that individuals "want" to share information with others, and often do so relatively freely. We now know that it is anything but obvious how such a system would evolve: the evolution of cooperation raises deep problems from the viewpoint of modern evolutionary theory. These problems are well known to biologists (see e.g. Panchanathan and Boyd, 2004), and Darwin already worried about them, but satisfactory solutions to his worries were not available until the 1960s (Hamilton, 1964; Trivers, 1971). Unfortunately, both linguists and anthropologists have tended to treat cooperation as an axiomatic aspect of human behavior, and failed for many years to recognize these as the central problems that they are (until e.g. Dunbar, 1996; Nettle and Dunbar, 1997; Hurford, 2007). This problem is far more general than human communication, and applies at all levels of biology (cellular to social) and to all taxa where cooperation has evolved (Axelrod and Hamilton, 1981).

The basic problem is that indiscriminate sharing with others is not an evolutionarily stable strategy (ESS), because a population of sharers can readily be invaded by a population of cheats who take the resource "donated" by the others, and then fail to reciprocate. Consider a population consisting of groups, each of which is made up of cooperating individuals who freely share food (or information, if you prefer). We may imagine that each individual has access to particular resources (types of food or information) and that each donates some of what she has gathered with her groupmates, and is shared with in kind. In this halcyon society, everyone is better off: in nutritional terms because of their more varied diet, and in informational terms because of a greater pool of shared information. But a "mutant" individual, who takes but does not give, is even better off, and can easily invade such a population – indiscriminate cooperation is virtually never an ESS against such a cheater. In a population that starts off uncooperative, a few cheaters are enough to keep cooperation from ever becoming widespread. Even if we start out with a cooperative situation, there is a continual threat of dissolution due to cheaters. Individuals who reap the benefits without paying the price will always be better off than cooperators, and will eventually replace them in the population.

Although the issue of cooperation and trust was traditionally raised in the context of some physical reward (food or nest sites), the problem looms just as large for cooperative communication (where the "resource" is truthful information about either the world, or one's own intentions). Since the seminal article by Dawkins and Krebs (1978), the traditional notion of animal communication as "information sharing" has become generally suspect, and models where animals signal to manipulate others, to their own selfish ends, are assumed today. The new outlook is one Dawkins and Krebs call "cynical": organisms signal, and attend to signals, when it is in their own best interests to do so. This view of communication is central to modern work on animal communication (Hauser, 1996; Bradbury and Vehrencamp, 1998; Maynard Smith and Harper, 2003). Although within-group punishment and restrictive reciprocity can help make cooperation more stable, the problem is exacerbated considerably if animals are mobile: a variant sometimes known as the "free-rider" problem (Enquist and Leimar, 1993; Nettle and Dunbar, 1997; Panchanathan and Boyd, 2004). When individuals have the option to move between groups, a "free-rider" can join a group, accept the gifts of others, and then move on without reciprocating. It is easy to see that, whether the gift is food or information, such an individual reaps greater benefits in sum than the cooperators, because free-riders have gained a benefit without paying any cost.

There are two main factors that contemporary theorists agree can solve this problem (following Krebs and Dawkins, 1984). The first, and by far the most common, is **kin selection**. An individual can pay an immediate cost, benefiting another, if that other is related to it and thus shares some of its genetic code (see Chapter 2). Today, kin selection is widely accepted as the main explanation for cooperation at all levels of biology (E. O. Wilson, 1975). The second factor used to explain cooperative behavior is **reciprocal altruism** (Trivers, 1971), and is typically invoked in situations where cooperation occurs between unrelated individuals. Reciprocal altruism is captured nicely by the phrase "I'll scratch your back if you scratch mine." The clearest examples of this are all from human beings. The scarcity of reciprocity among non-kin is probably the result of the free-rider problem, and grows more and more problematic as group size (the number of individuals interacted with) grows. In such situations additional mechanisms are required to enforce reciprocity. The best studied occurs when individuals interact repeatedly, in which case a simple rule, "tit for tat" – start out by being cooperative but stop sharing if your partner cheats you first – can sharply limit the costs paid by cooperators and the benefits reaped by free-riders (Axelrod and Hamilton, 1981; Axelrod and Dion, 1988; Axelrod, 1997). Again, the folk saying "fool me once, shame on you; fool me twice, shame on me," captures the logic of this concisely. Most-known examples of reciprocity among animals either occur among closely related individuals (e.g. vampire-bat blood sharing; Wilkinson, 1984, 1987) or support a very specific and limited form of cooperation rather than the wholesale cooperativity that characterizes our species (Packer, 1977; Seyfarth and Cheney, 1984).

Neither of these "normal" explanations of cooperation seems adequate to explain cooperation in modern humans. Humans cooperate with a wide variety of unknown, unrelated individuals, even when there is little chance of reciprocation. Unless seen as an "evolutionary error," such widespread cooperativity remains a prominent challenge in understanding human evolution (cf. Hurford, 2007). One solution to the problem of enforcing indirect reciprocity relies upon **punishment**. If inequalities among players (in dominance rank, fighting ability, and so forth) prevent effective retaliation by individuals (Boyd and Richerson, 1988, 1992), punishment by the group as a whole can serve to maintain reciprocity. But again, punishment at a sophisticated level appears to be common only in humans (for a possible exception see Hauser, 1992). The reason why is easy to see: in most cases punishment bears a potential cost to the punisher (who may themselves be injured in the process of punishing a cheater). Thus punishment itself is actually a form of cooperative behavior. Although there is no question that reciprocal altruism and punishment are important factors in modern human society, both arguably depend on sophisticated language for proper policing (via such factors as gossip and reputation; Dunbar, 1996; Dessalles, 1998). In conclusion, to be consistent with modern evolutionary theory, some other factor needs to be invoked if cooperation in general, or cooperative communication of the sort that typifies language, is to be an ESS. The cooperative sharing of information thus remains a central puzzle in language evolution.

12.8 Dunbar: grooming, "free-riders," and gossip

One contemporary argument that does away with the need for group selection is presented in Dunbar (1996, 1999), who offers an interesting take on the problem of cooperative communication, and particularly the "free-rider" (or "free-loader") problem. Dunbar uses comparative data and evolutionary theory to support an argument which is initially quite non-intuitive. His argument starts with the finding that free-riders can block the evolution of cooperation via reciprocal altruism quite easily, under a wide range of circumstances likely to apply to real organisms (Enquist and Leimar, 1993). What types of counter-measures are theoretically available to cooperators to exclude free-riders, or at least make their life difficult? Any method that increases the search time for a free-rider to find a victim will decrease the gains to free-riders. However, indiscriminate suspiciousness (e.g. waiting a long time before cooperating with anyone) also decreases the gains to cooperators. One excellent solution is captured by the notion of "reputa-tion," and Enquist and Leimar specifically suggest that **gossip** – a mechanism for generating reputations, based on sharing information about prospec-tive partners among group members – provides a potent defense against free-riders: "With gossiping cooperation can be stable even in very dense populations" (p. 751, Enquist and Leimar, 1993). Observing that anthro-pologists had remarked on the frequency of gossip in all human societies, they somewhat offhandedly suggest that this provides an explanation for the "impressive amount and diversity of cooperation between unrelated individuals in humans." Dunbar's book takes this basic argument and runs with it.

Dunbar's argument is grounded in the fact that most group-living pri-mates spend an inordinate amount of time **grooming** each other. Grooming is not, as sometimes thought, simply a foraging activity where individuals seek high-protein nourishment from parasites picked off others' bodies. In fact, grooming in extant primates is an important form of social bonding. Individuals pay careful attention to who grooms whom, and the patterns of dyads involved in grooming are far from random. "Social climbers" can raise their rank in the dominance hierarchy if they manage to groom high-ranking individuals, and grooming partners are more likely to sup-port one another in situations of conflict than randomly selected group members. Grooming "cliques" are subgroups characterized by high affilia-tion and mutual support, and although they typically involve closely related individuals, they extend beyond immediate family groups. Group living is a core feature of the primate lineage, and lone individuals often are at a selective disadvantage relative to those peacefully ensconced in a functional group. Once "trapped" into group living, as most individual primates are, an individual has no choice but to co-exist with others. Using these facts, Dunbar posits that grooming is a core behavioral mechanism for maintain-ing complex social groups, and that individual selection drives the evolution of grooming in most primates. This argument would be accepted by most primatologists.

The next step in Dunbar's hypothesis is also well grounded in data, and represents an extension of the "social intelligence" hypothesis discussed in Chapter 4. Citing relatively strong correlations between group size and mea-sures of brain size, Dunbar suggests that brain size provides a fossil measure of group size. Thus, the ever-increasing size of the brains of hominids since the LCA, he argues, implies an ever-increasing *group* size. As group-living primates, our lineage had to obey the same constraints as any other primate species, and to maintain group stability with ever-increasing grooming clique size. But the time required to groom this increasing number of partners in the "traditional" one-on-one fashion represented an ever-increasing load on each individual's time budget. Eventually, Dunbar suggests, the system reached a breaking point as groups exceeded a certain size. This, Dunbar argues, was the selective pressure that drove the evolution of complex vocalization as a form of "vocal grooming." The broadcast nature of sound, in contrast to hands-on stroking, picking, and biting, allowed one individual to "groom" multiple individuals simultaneously. This hypothesis provides an explanation for two empirical observations about human speech which Dunbar has documented: its incessantly social nature, and its frequent vacuousness regarding content. Low-content "phatic" speech ('nice weather today') seems explicable in these terms. It simply affirms social bonds, and nothing more.

Dunbar's treatment of grooming and gossip conflates several distinct problems. The first is the question of maintaining group stability, which primates do with grooming. But, as Dunbar himself points out, grooming generates endorphins but speech does not, so it is difficult to see why it should effectively cement social relationships. Indeed, Dunbar cites ritual and music as the means by which this necessary condition is satisfied, so this component of Dunbar's argument applies better to the evolution of music than to that of propositional speech. The second question is the evolution of propositional information exchange. As the original paper on free-riders made clear, the free exchange of specific information made possible by human language is a *prerequisite* of gossip as a defense against free-riders (Enquist and Leimar, 1993). Evolution lacks foresight, so this useful end product of an elaborate language cannot be used as its initial adaptive advantage for propositional information exchange. Indeed, I think the statement in Enquist and Leimar (1993) remains the only logical evolutionary sequence: once propositional information exchange has evolved, and becomes common among adults in a group for gossip, it becomes a very potent inhibitor of exploitation and cheating, and thus greatly enhances the possibility for reciprocal altruism in large groups. At such a point the stage is also set for the "selfish" use of language to show off how much the speaker knows, a phenomenon cited as central to current language by some authors (Dessalles, 1998; Miller, 2001). Thus it is language, and gossip specifically, I suggest, that underpins the hypertrophied reciprocity typifying our species. The lack of language in other species explains the rarity of nonhuman reciprocity. But attempts to use reciprocity as the driving force for propositionality put the cart before the horse, confusing the consequent with the antecedent.

To summarize, Dunbar's major contribution was in focusing on group dynamics as a crucial selective force in primates, one that has remained important (and indeed intensified) during the course of human evolution. He correctly recognized the problem of cooperative information exchange, and highlighted the difficulties posed by evolutionary theory for this problem. Finally, by collecting data on conversations – what people actually speak about today – and using this as a "living fossil" of earlier language usage, he (I think correctly) highlights the value of social information exchange in the evolution of a propositionally complex communication system. Nonetheless, the selective regime that he envisions fails to account for the leap to full propositionality. As Dunbar has acknowledged, many of his arguments provide as strong an argument for the evolution of music in our species as for a propositional component of language (we will return to this fact in Chapter 14). I see Dunbar's hypothesis as providing two different selective planks in the bridge between the primate call system of our LCA with chimpanzees to full modern language, but I do not think that the model is by itself adequate (cf. Power, 1998). Some additional selective element seems to be necessary to evolve propositionality.

12.9 Deacon: meat and monogamy; symbolism and group cohesion

One potential extension of Dunbar's model that tackles the particular problem posed by the evolution of honest symbolic reference is explored by Terrence Deacon (Deacon, 1997). Deacon's discussion is well grounded in both comparative data and evolutionary theory. He, like Dunbar but unlike Bickerton or Jackendoff, takes the evolutionary problems posed by cooperative propositionality very seriously, and indeed sees this as *the* crucial hurdle that needed to be crossed *en route* to modern language. And, like Dunbar, he sees the constraints of group living as critical factors. However, Deacon adds to this the peculiarity that sets us off quite sharply from chimpanzees: our propensity for pair-bonding and the bi-parental care that goes with it (see Chapter 6). Deacon highlights the rarity of species where multiple males in one group show preferential attachments to specific females. In most species, we see one of three patterns:

(1) polygyny, where a dominant male is the sole reproductive male in the group and has multiple female partners (the most common pattern in mammals);

(2) polygamy, where multiple females mate with multiple males and *vice versa*, often in a free-for-all where an estrus female may mate with many or even most of the adult males in a group (as in chimpanzees); or

(3) pair-bonding, where a single adult male and female are the only breeders, and the rest of the group is made up of subadult offspring of that pair, plus non-breeding adult "helpers" who may be reproductively suppressed.

Humans are unusual in sharing aspects of (2) and (3): multiple adult reproductive males co-exist in a group, and mate, but mating is preferential between particular pairs. Deacon suggests that this unusual aspect of human social behavior must play a central role in any selective explanation. The final component is nutritional: the need of growing young humans for nutrients provided by meat. Humans are unique among primates in our dependence on meat. Since at least the first members of genus *Homo*, the evolution of large brains necessitated a consistent and predictable source of protein and fat. In Deacon's model of the selective force driving propositionality, these three factors are woven together, with each strand playing a crucial part. Group living, and the need for stability and cooperation, was a continual force. But the evolution of larger brains simultaneously generated two contradictory demands: the degree of dependence of infants increased, while the need for meat and hunting also increased. Because a mother in late pregnancy or in the first two years of mothering is significantly hampered in obtaining meat for herself, Deacon argues, this forced humans into a situation favoring pair-bonding, and an essentially reciprocal relationship involving male provisioning (of mother and infant) and sexual fidelity. This "sex for meat" arrangement, by itself, might push pairs to become solitary and territorial (like gibbons, foxes, or many other pair-bonded species). However, the pressure for group cohesion and the over-arching need for large cooperative social groups prevented this more typical solution.

Deacon suggests that these pressures, together, were the crucial forces that drove the **symbolic** aspect of communication in our species. Deacon's use of the term "symbol" is somewhat unusual, and a potential source of misunderstanding. Bickerton and Jackendoff use this term in a very general way: any sign is "symbolic" for them. In contrast, following the philosopher Charles Peirce, Deacon has a more specific and idiosyncratic meaning in mind, based on Peirce's distinction between iconic, indexical, and arbitrary signs. For Deacon, neither icons nor indices are symbols: a "symbol" in his sense is a higher-order construct, an abstraction away from the iconic and indexical level. The first half of his book explicates this distinction from the viewpoints of philosophy, neuroscience, and animal learning (particularly chimpanzee experiments), and argues that this higher-level abstraction is both critical for human language (for propositionality, and thus for important aspects of syntax) and very difficult for chimpanzees to achieve. In the Peircean taxonomy adopted and extended by Deacon, a signal (a "token") functions as a symbol *only by virtue of its relations to other tokens*. The vocabulary of a protolanguage could include a large complex of indices – token ↔ referent mappings – and not have a *single* symbol. This is precisely what Deacon argues is normally acquired by chimpanzees or other animals in language-training experiments: a collection of indices. For Deacon, the crucial step towards making such a lexicon symbolic is the recognition of the relationships among different items, and a foregrounding of these relationships (rather than their relationships to their referents). It is precisely because of the ease with which animals can recognize and remember indices that the "aha" of truly symbolic thinking is so difficult for them to achieve. Thus for Deacon "symbolic" is closer to what I term "propositional" in this book.

Deacon recognizes the same evolutionary difficulties for cooperative communication as Dunbar. However, Deacon stresses the discontinuity between human language and animal communication systems, and specifically rejects "indexical" communication systems (e.g. alarm calls in vervets, or food calls in chimpanzees) as possible precursors of full "symbolic" or propositional communication. Indeed, Deacon cogently argues that the readiness with which primates master indexical signs serves to *block* fully symbolic/propositional communication, because a focus on concrete ties between signs and referents obscures the relationships between the signs themselves. Deacon argues that our peculiar combination of pair-bonding and male parental care with large multi-male groups is what drove our species over this symbolic Rubicon. Deacon advances "a scenario for ... how unique demands of reproductive competition and cooperation created the conditions that led to our unique form of intelligence" (p. 408).

Deacon argues that "regulation of reproductive relationships by symbolic means was essential for early hominids to take advantage of a hunting-provisioning subsistence strategy" (p. 401). If lactating females, and more importantly their highly dependent developing offspring, were to acquire the fats and proteins needed to support their large brains, they needed to rely upon someone else sharing meat with them. Deacon argues, based on both chimpanzee and hunter-gatherer data, that males were the main providers of such meat. To be evolutionarily advantageous, paternity certainty must increase, necessitating a drastic shift from the highly polygamous mating strategy observed in both chimpanzees and bonobos. Providing meat to another male's young is clearly not an ESS relative to eating it yourself (or sharing it with a non-lactating female in return for mating opportunities). This is the bind that a combination of multi-male groups and paternal care created, Deacon argues, in our species, and it is this that drove the evolution of true Peircean symbols: "This was the question for which symbolization was the only viable answer" (p. 401).

The essential idea is that only *unreal* or *invisible* referents would drive true symbolism, and that "social contracts" like promises and commitments are such referents. Essentially, the first symbols were like marriage contracts: indicators of a long-term pair-bond between a particular male and female, one that could recognized, respected, and enforced both by the individuals and by the group as a whole: "The need to mark these reciprocally altruistic (and reciprocally selfish) relationships arose as an adaptation to the extreme evolutionary instability of the combination of group hunting/scavenging and male provisioning of mates and offspring" (p. 401).

Deacon provides a well-argued case for this notion, but I see contemporary human behavior as posing problems for his hypothesis. For in fact, human pair-bonds are notoriously unstable. As playwrights and novelists love to remind us, extra-pair mating remains the most likely force to upset the social balance, even in today's highly regulated world, with the full power of language and gossip, and in some cases the threat of death. Deacon affirms elsewhere in his book that "such a trick – one that no other species has hit upon – is not likely to have been cast away too quickly in the subsequent evolution of our species" (p. 384). The frequency of adultery in present-day humans suggests that language has been unsuccessful at solving the core problem that Deacon rightly identifies. Certainly, however, language *helps* to stabilize groups and enforce shared norms, and perhaps this partial "solution" was good enough. Second, in a footnote, Deacon acknowledges that group condemnation for adultery seems rather one-sided (for females, punishments are far great than males, in many or perhaps most societies). While this makes sense in terms of paternity certainty, it does not fit with the other half of the reciprocal "bargain" between males and females that Deacon suggests is the central driving force of language evolution. Female fidelity is supposed to guarantee that she and her offspring obtain preferential access to the male's meat provisions, but in contemporary hunter-gatherers this half of the bargain is *not* enforced (indeed in most cases meat is shared with all members of the group). This seems a rather bad bargain from the female viewpoint. And if communication among adults, combining gossip and a social contract, is the core driving force accounting for language, what about babies? Why are infants so symbolic, so early in life?

Despite important differences between Bickerton's, Dunbar's, and Deacon's hypotheses, they share a focus on reciprocal information exchange, among unrelated group-living adults, as the crucial driving force underlying the evolution of propositional communication. Deacon's version is discontinuist, highlighting a very specific dilemma that characterizes humans, while Dunbar's continuist hypothesis sees human sociality as intensified primate sociality. Both theorists recognize the unusual cooperative reciprocity of modern human societies as an evolutionary exception, and both correctly see language as lying at the heart of this exception. But each version, it seems to me, fails to satisfactorily cross the crucial evolutionary bridge from selfish indexical communication to the honest, truthful sharing of propositional information characterizing language. This is a prerequisite of the gossip that maintains complex social groups in modern humans. In an offhand comment, Deacon suggests a potential role for kin selection: "Sociality . . . may also gain additional evolutionary support from kin selection" (p. 391). My own contribution to this debate (Fitch, 2004a, 2007) suggests that kin selection played not just a supporting role, but was the key stepping-stone to propositional communication. I suggest a two-step process, involving first kin communication, and then later reciprocal communication among unrelated adults, as the solution to the evolutionary puzzle posed by cooperative communication.

12.10 Fitch: the origin of information sharing via kin communication

To recap, all of the models of protolanguage discussed above face a similar problem in explaining cooperative information sharing. Sometimes this problem is acknowledged as important, as by Dunbar and Deacon, and sometimes it goes undiscussed, as for Bickerton and Jackendoff. Indeed, Bickerton states that "the immediate, practical benefits that hominids would have gained from communicating with one another in even the simplest form of protolanguage are obvious enough" (p. 156, Bickerton, 1990). Although it certainly may be beneficial *to the group* for all individuals to share their hard-won information, we need to show how this benefited individuals *within* the group. Stripped of "benefits for the group" reasoning, it is far from obvious why one individual should share their knowledge freely. While Dunbar's argument can explain why we should exchange pleasantries about the weather, or engage in otherwise meaningless greeting ceremonies, "gossip as grooming" does not provide an explanation for the detailed propositional information exchange that is a crucial distinguishing feature of human language. Far from being "obvious," it is one of the central oddities of our species from an evolutionary viewpoint; one that cries out for selective explanation.

I have suggested that the solution to this problem is to be found in kin selection: that information sharing evolved to help closely related individuals, and particularly dependent young (Fitch, 2004a, 2007). I posit that the free sharing of propositional information that language allows evolved, initially, in a context of transferring information from knowledgeable adults to their less-knowledgeable kin. A central observation supporting this idea is the speed and ease with which *children* learn language, and the frequency with which they use it with their parents: hard to explain by the models discussed above.

12.10.1 Stage 1: kin selection for information exchange

The core insight of this idea is that, from the viewpoint of contemporary evolutionary theory, sharing information with relatives (and particularly dependent offspring) is not "altruistic" at all. From a gene's-eye view, a parent who helps her offspring helps herself, and this logic extends to more distantly related kin as well (e.g. siblings, grandparents, aunts, etc.), though helping more distant kin accrues correspondingly decreasing benefits. Thus there is no evolutionary mystery in the propensity of honeybees to share honest information about food with one another: hivemates are each other's own closest relatives (Hamilton, 1964; E. O. Wilson, 1975). Similarly, the evolution of alarm calls is easily explained via kin selection, and experimental data are consistent with this hypothesis. Individuals who spot predators are more likely to call when kin are around than otherwise (Sherman, 1977, 1985; Cheney and Seyfarth, 1990b), and individuals without kin often do not call at all: they silently flee for cover. Even more extreme roles for kin selection have been demonstrated: subordinate male turkeys who never mate increase their inclusive fitness by aiding their dominant brothers in displays raising their reproductive output six-fold (Krakauer, 2005). Although there is a large literature and considerable debate about the details of kin-based explanations (Fitch and Hauser, 2002; Foster *et al.*, 2006), there is no argument about their fundamental logic. Thus, when we seek an evolutionary route to sharing (of food, information, or anything else), kin selection provides the most obvious and best-attested possibility. Indeed, even if a Bickertonian group-selected morph of our species *did* evolve, a mutant form which preferentially shared information with more *related* individuals would easily invade it: indiscriminate information sharing is not an ESS relative to selective sharing with kin (Nettle and Dunbar, 1997). Thus, the kin communication idea has considerable *prima facie* validity based on both evolutionary theory and comparative data from animal communication.

Because this idea is easily misunderstood, it is important to be clear that it concerns one specific component of language: our ability and propensity to share honest, propositional information. The hypothesis proposes a solution to the free-rider problem, and the evolution of propositional semantics, not to all components of language. Second, and more important, this hypothesis is focused on the evolution of *protolanguage*, not modern language. The fact that most contemporary human linguistic communication occurs between unrelated adults has not escaped my notice, and this is dealt with by positing a second, and logically separate, stage of human evolution. Kin communication cannot give us modern language, but it can drive the evolution of propositional information sharing.

Given that kin selection is an ever-present selective force, typifying all mammals and birds, how can it explain something as specific and unusual as language's capacity to encode propositional information? Note first that one asks of a valid evolutionary hypothesis that it can explain the existence of some trait, and where it is found, but not its absence in most other species. It might be very useful for vertebrates to have photosynthesis, but we do not ask botanists to explain why "solar feeding" has not evolved in humans or other animals. The kin communication hypothesis provides a logically and empirically valid explanation for information sharing in a diversity of clades (honeybees, ground squirrels, vervet monkeys, and humans) and for a "how possibly" explanation that should be virtue enough. Nonetheless, two aspects of our own clade are centrally important to explaining why inclusive fitness should play a greater role in our evolution than in other species. First, humans and other apes have a greatly extended childhood relative to other vertebrates. Combined with our very low reproductive output, this makes each individual child unusually valuable (see Chapter 6). Second, post-*erectus* hominids were generalist, tool-using omnivores, so individual adults possessed a vast store of hard-won information that could be profitably shared with relatives (in contrast, for example, to grass-foraging herbivores). Adults who could inform young relatives about cryptic or seasonal sources of food, water, or danger, the characteristics of materials for tools, the techniques for food processing and hunting, and a host of other valuable facts would be increasing their inclusive fitness with every proposition conveyed. The powerful selective pressures involved in child-rearing for all great apes, combined with a large store of knowledge worth sharing in humans, would have made honest information sharing with kin unusually valuable in some protolinguistic stage prior to modern language (Fitch, 2004a, 2007; Hurford, 2007). This combination is found in few, if any, other clades.

To complete the story, we need an explanation for the fact that we do not communicate with kin exclusively, or perhaps even preferentially, in today's world. One thing that takes the edge off this problem is that, for most of our evolution, humans lived in quite small groups, so intra-group relatedness has probably always been higher than that between groups. Thus selection between groups can often be reconceptualized in terms of inclusive fitness (e.g. Hamilton, 1975; Sober and Wilson, 1998). Second, there is evidence that adult humans still preferentially share valuable information with kin, and recent experimental evidence that adults' willingness to give depends on kinship, though this topic has not been carefully studied (Palmer, 1991; Madsen *et al.*, 2007). Finally, it is quite clear that modern humans *do* share a huge amount of information with kin, and particularly in the case of socializing offspring, this remains an absolutely indispensable role of language in our species, probably remaining a powerful selective force even under today's more relaxed selective conditions. Thus one could argue that we evolved as kin communicators in the "environment of evolutionary adaptedness" (Tooby and Cosmides, 1990b) and thus still *are* kin communicators at the mechanistic level. From such a perspective, our modern behavior is simply an overextension of this propensity, which there has been insufficient evolutionary time to "correct." But I personally find such an argument unconvincing, and have offered an alternative proposal that solves the problem without appeal to the inertia of past adaptation.

12.10.2 Stage 2: reciprocal altruism – no evolution needed

The second stage in the evolution of information sharing in this hypothesis is provided by **reciprocal altruism**, governing the regulated, reciprocal sharing of information among adults. I suggest that the biological adaptations required to get honest information sharing off the ground in the first place were kin selected, because this is the only initial path leading beyond the free-rider problem. However, once language in this form was in place, the subsequent broadening of the communication base to unrelated individuals (with ample attention to honesty, careful gauging of the value of information before sharing it, etc.) could take place without further biological adaptations *to language* being necessary. Indeed, the same sort of turn-taking and score-keeping that is already present in nonhuman primates may be sufficient to regulate information exchange among unrelated adults, once a linguistic system was in place. Now, gossip, social control, and group punishment can play their undoubted roles (Dunbar, 1996). Furthermore, competition to share *relevant* information, as a sign of one's quality, or as a way to increase status, could play an important additional driving role in this (Dessalles, 1998, 2000), as could information sharing during courtship, or among mated pairs of unrelated men and women (Deacon, 1997; Miller, 2001). The central point is that these hypotheses already require a capacity for propositional encoding to be in place. Kin communication thus provided a preadaptive basis for the system that we humans later evolved. Modern humans have generalized this to today's vastly broader (and consequently more powerful) system of less restricted communication. Crucially, reciprocal altruism, gossip, status seeking, and courtship would not have paved the way for pervasive parent–offspring communication, because offspring do not yet have much of value to contribute. The facts of contemporary language require an explanation of *both* child language and adult language, but non-kin models can explain only the latter.

This two-stage model – a stage of kin communication followed by the implementation of regulated information exchange among adults – does not, in principle, require *any* further biological adaptation during the second stage. That is, reciprocal regulation could evolve culturally, as a set of social norms, without any further biological specializations beyond those already present "for free" by virtue of our shared primate heritage of "Machiavellian intelligence." However, I find it quite plausible that some contemporary aspects of language use among unrelated individuals represent adaptations. Indeed, the "phatic communication" so typical of greetings can be conceptualized in this context as a way of checking the communication channels in preparation (potentially) for some real information exchange. An exchange like "Nice day, isn't it" followed by "Yup, not a cloud in the sky," carries no cost in terms of lost valuable information. But it carries considerable useful information about the interlocutors' dialect and their potential to exchange useful propositional information in an intelligible fashion. Furthermore, dialectal background might plausibly have served (and still serve) as a social marker of relatedness, and thus provide some proxy for individual identification (for further discussion see Nettle and Dunbar, 1997; Fitch, 2004a). This is an experimentally testable prediction: we should find that people's willingness to trust others should be correlated with the degree to which they share dialect (and other markers of group membership).

In summary, kin communication provides a way around the free-rider problem, and thus a viable route to an honest, propositionally unrestricted, protolanguage. The next stage of wider information sharing can be achieved with little specific biological change, but the converse is not true. Kin communication can thus solve a central puzzle in the evolution of language, and is consistent with both evolutionary theory and considerable empirical data. This hypothesis also provides a prediction regarding animal models of language evolution: exchange of honest information should occur in long-lived species with extended periods of childhood and parental care, and crucially a store of general purpose knowledge worth sharing. While these desiderata give us honeybees and other social insects as a retrodiction, it more constructively pinpoints species such as toothed whales (especially long-lived generalists like killer whales) and some bird species (particularly the long-lived parrots and corvids, some of which are generalists with complex foraging, and all of which have complex but poorly understood vocal communication systems). While kin communication by no means guarantees the evolution of language-like propositionality, it does suggest that some preconditions exist in vertebrate species that remain little studied.

12.11 Whence syntax?

We are still left with the question of complex syntax: why we humans, in all cultures and from a very early age, possess the ability and proclivity to arrange signals into larger, meaningful, syntactically structured wholes. This aspect of human biology sets us apart from other animals. By the time a child is four, she has (with imperfect input and little training) progressed significantly beyond the capacities of any nonhuman animal. Explanations for this fundamental aspect of human biology come in various flavors, distinguished along ontogenetic, glossogenetic, and phylogenetic lines. Since we know that each type of change occurs over very different timescales, each holds answers to the question "Where does syntax come from?" These different answers do not necessarily conflict with one another. Thus, the obvious first answer – children learn it from linguistic input data – is clearly true, but does not explain why a human infant does this and a chimpanzee infant exposed to the same data does not. Similarly, the fact that grammatical constructions change during glossogeny does not contradict the idea that constraints on such constructions have evolved over biological time.

Michael Tomasello argues that syntax does not rest on an evolved bio-logical basis, and that syntactic devices are derived culturally, while the human/chimpanzee difference reflects other innate differences, controlling the way humans use language culturally (Tomasello, 1999). Specifically, Tomasello argues that syntactic rules derive from a cultural process termed "grammaticalization" (Tomasello, 2005), whereby basic content words such as nouns and verbs are transformed, over historical time, into function words like prepositions and modifiers (for overviews see Heine *et al.*, 1991; Heine and Kuteva, 2002). Such changes are an important source for both specific function words in the lexicon and at least some more abstract grammatical constructions. Many independent researchers have observed similar processes in agent-based models, and agree that grammaticalization provides a plausible mechanism of generating grammatical constructions over historical (rather than biological) time (see e.g. Steels, 1997). How-ever, a focus on grammaticalization as a cultural process alone begs the question of why it takes the specific, highly constrained forms that it does (Christiansen and Kirby, 2003). For example, grammaticalization is almost always a one-way, irreversible process (Haspelmath, 1999), and only a small subset of imaginable transformations are actually attested in the histori-cal data. Ultimately, then, while grammaticalization lessens the need for specifically innate constraints that are purely syntactic, it does not dispense with the need for some kinds of human-specific constraints on language acquisition.

A second source of biological constraints on syntactic structures comes from conceptual constraints (Bickerton, 1990). The rich world of semantic complexity in higher vertebrates evidently evolved long before human lan-guage. Because the interface between syntax and these conceptual complexes must clearly play a role in structuring specific syntactic constructions, we might profitably seek the origins of some aspects of grammar (e.g. nouns and verbs) in pre-existing, innately determined concepts (e.g. objects and events). It is less obvious how such biological constraints could lead to the origin of function words, or explain the specific forms that grammatical changes tend to take, but approaches that posit a very rich set of univer-sal semantic categories may have considerable explanatory power in this regard (see Goddard and Wierzbicka, 2002). One virtue of this "conceptual constraints" approach is that it greatly lessens the explanatory load for the biological evolution of syntax. Assuming a post-Australopithecine starting point, two million years is not a lot of time, in evolutionary terms, for a complex suite of syntax-specific mechanisms to evolve and reach fixation. If much of the observed complexity in syntax derives from the pre-existing conceptual mechanisms involved in cognition, which began evolving in early vertebrates 200 MYA, we face far less difficulty in understanding how they evolved. This conception is shared by many biologically grounded theories of language evolution (Donald, 1998; Wray, 2000; Hauser *et al.*, 2002; Tomasello, 2003; Seyfarth and Cheney, 2005; Fitch, 2007). Some authors single out quite specific aspects of conceptual structure (e.g. Bickerton's ideas about social intelligence).

However powerful conceptual constraints might be in helping to explain the evolution of syntax, few scholars think that such constraints can shoulder the entire burden. One reason for this is that there are many aspects of syntactic categories that do not map transparently onto semantic/conceptual ones. Even the apparently simple category "noun" is by no means co-extensive with objects in any ordinary sense. We have abstract nouns like *truth* or *justice*, verb-like nouns such as *thunder* or *explosion*, and grammatical particles like *-ing* that convert between verbs and nouns. Thus, most theorists posit syntactic categories that are distinct from semantic categories. Also, although grammaticalization can account for the origin of function words or inflectional markers, the very notion of a syntactic marker seems quite specific to language, with no obvious parallel in non-linguistic cognition. Once language is off the ground, it is easy to see how grammaticalization provides grist for the syntactic mill, but it fails to address the basic questions of how the more general properties of syntax arose. Thus, such biological factors as innate semantic constraints or constrained cultural change seem to go only part of the way in explaining human syntactic competence.

A third possible source of constraints on syntax comes from the signaling side, and in particular from the motor control required to produce complex signals. This is an old, and I think very important, idea: that crucial aspects of linguistic syntax derive from what might be called **action syntax** – the highly structured cognitive systems underlying motor control (Lashley, 1951; Miller *et al.*, 1960). Crucial capacities of this system include hierarchical structures involving overlearned or "automatized" subroutines, and the parallel requirement that these be recombined in novel ways, rapidly and efficiently, to deal with novel situations. These two capacities characterize both motor control and aspects of syntax, probably by necessity (Simon, 1962), and thus offer a plausible third source of constraints that have been highlighted by many theorists (Orr and Cappannari, 1964; Lieberman, 1984; Allott, 1989; Kimura, 1993; MacNeilage *et al.*, 2000). However, to understand the precise means in which such constraints might play a role in language evolution, we must first understand the signaling mechanism used to produce linguistic utterances. The models of lexical protolanguage discussed above take for granted a signaling mechanism that can produce an unlimited number of shared linguistic signs. These previously discussed models all concern the "end game" of language evolution, in which such a system is already in place. We now turn to the evolution of the signalling system presupposed by lexical protolanguage models. Chapters 13 and 14 discuss the two most prominent models of the origin of signals: gestural protolanguage and musical (vocal) protolanguage.

13 | Signs before speech: gestural protolanguage theories

13.1 Introduction: From hand to mouth?

In Chapter 12, we discussed models of "lexical" protolanguage, involving utterances composed of single words, or multiple words combined without syntax. We saw that, despite a number of explanatory strengths regarding the "end game" of language evolution, such models take too much for granted in the earlier stages of human evolution, in particular the voluntary control of vocal expression. A further weakness of lexical models is their assumption that the posited protolanguage has essentially disappeared in modern human society, and protolinguistic "fossils" make their appearance only under extraordinary social circumstances (e.g. slavery leading to pidgins) or brief developmental periods during childhood. The other two major models of protolanguage posit more significant preservation of protolanguage in contemporary human cultures. In the first, "gestural protolanguage" is argued to be present not only during development, but also in the gestures that humans ordinarily produce while speaking, in pantomime, and in the signed languages of deaf communities. In the second, discussed in Chapter 14, music is seen as an ongoing exemplar of an earlier protolanguage. Both models of protolanguage have the virtue of explaining pervasive non-linguistic aspects of human behavior *in addition to* their posited role in language evolution. These hypotheses suggest that protolanguage is still with us, alive and kicking, thus making good on Deacon's argument that protolanguage "is not likely to have been cast away too quickly in the subsequent evolution of our species" (p. 384, Deacon, 1997) – what Merlin Donald calls the "principle of the conservation of previous gains" (p. 3, Donald, 1991).

This chapter reviews the arguments for a **gestural protolanguage**, in which a visual/manual communication system played a crucial intervening role in the evolution of our current vocally dominated system. This appears to be the first model where the term "protolanguage" was explicitly used to denote a phylogenetic precursor of language (in Hewes, 1973). Gesture meets certain crucial prerequisites of a theoretically viable protolanguage:

it is flexibly expressive, extensible from very simple to quite complex, and is within reach of our nearest ape cousins (and thus presumably of the LCA). Against these benefits, a significant disadvantage of gestural models is their difficulty in explaining the virtually complete transition to vocal, spoken language in modern *Homo sapiens*. Ironically, the existence of signed languages such as American Sign Language (ASL) provides an argument *against* the notion of a gestural protolanguage. Because such languages are full human languages, capable of efficient, boundless expression, they suggest that human language could have remained in the manual/visual domain, if it originated there. Whatever their virtues, models of gestural protolanguage are incomplete without a detailed and compelling model of the transition to spoken language, as most gestural proponents have recognized (Hewes, 1973; Corballis, 2002b; Arbib, 2005).

In this chapter I discuss gesture in modern humans, and clarify the all-important distinction between gesture and signed language. Then I will briefly review the older historical notions about gestural origins before considering in detail the proposals of Gordon Hewes, who provided the first modern theory of gestural origins in the early 1970s, building on the recognition of superior gestural capacities in great apes. After a brief consideration of the further contributions to this basic model, I will discuss the model of language evolution put forward by Michael Arbib and colleagues in detail, starting with neuroscientific data on "mirror neurons," and their significance for language evolution. Despite some shortcomings, I see Arbib's model as representing a sophisticated evolutionary framework for neurolinguistics, and thus a model that critics must seek to beat.

13.2 Gesture and speech

Humans around the world typically move their limbs and make faces while conversing. We do this largely unconsciously. In fact, effort is required to *suppress* these movements, even in cases where our interlocutor cannot possibly perceive them (e.g. speaking on a telephone). In common parlance the verbs "gesture" and "gesticulate" are often used interchangeably for such co-speech movements, but "gesture" has become the accepted scientific term. The study of co-speech gesture essentially started with the writings of David McNeill (McNeil, 1985, 1992), which remain excellent introductions. This is a fast-moving and somewhat contentious field, and many of the most basic issues remain controversial. A brief introduction to this research and some of these debates is Messing and Campbell (1999).

A crucial first distinction must be made between **signed languages** such as ASL (often abbreviated "sign") and **gesture** in its various senses. Sign is a full-fledged linguistic signaling system, with its own phonology, morphology, syntax, and semantics, and, despite superficial similarities, must not be confused with the gesticulations and pantomimes that all humans do. Everyday "gestures" can be divided into a number of categories, the most important being **pantomime** (in which objects and actions are "acted out" iconically, sometimes with no speech accompaniment) *versus* **co-speech gestures**. Among co-speech gestures, which occur alongside and in synchrony with spoken language, we find **deictic** gestures (most canonically, pointing to an object with the forefinger extended) worldwide. **Iconic** gestures are used to spatially represent some aspect of the spoken meaning ('the fish was at least this <gesture> big'). **Emblematic** gestures (such as the "thumbs up" sign, or the extended middle finger) have conventional, culturally determined meanings. **Beats** are gestures that accompany, and accentuate, the rhythmic aspects of an utterance. A large class of further co-speech utterances (referred to as **metaphorical** by McNeill, or **lexical** by Krauss and Hadar (1999)) accompany words in a manner more difficult to characterize: they can typically be linked to a particular word in the utterance (though they typically precede the spoken word, and never follow it) and can be highly idiosyncratic. While deictic, iconic, and emblematic gestures are generally shared by the speech community, both beats and metaphorical/lexical gestures may show no more similarity between speakers of the same language than those of different languages.

Quite a bit is known about the ontogeny of gesture (reviewed in Goldin-Meadow, 2003). Some of the first intentional communicative acts young humans make are gestural, and **declarative** gestures such as pointing or holding up objects are among the first acts that distinguish humans from chimpanzees (Call and Tomasello, 2007). In early development, gestures tend to substitute for (or be interchangeable with) spoken words or phrases: the child puts both arms in the air to signal 'up' (meaning 'please pick me up'). However, at a crucial point in development, coinciding closely with the onset of two-word phrases, children combine vocalizations and gestures in a more synergistic way: for example, denoting actions with words ("gimme") and objects with pointing. Such a division of labor between gesture and speech offers a good example of a potential scaffolding function of gesture in the acquisition of spoken language. Similar patterns, combining gesture and lexical tokens, are observed in language-trained bonobos (Savage-Rumbaugh *et al.*, 1993).

Later in development, speech takes on the dominant communicative role, but gesture does not disappear. Indeed, Goldin-Meadow and colleagues discovered that co-speech gestures can provide intriguing cues to the child's mental representation over and above that denoted by their words. Although gestures and speech are typically matched for meaning, these researchers have found that there are occasional mismatches between gesture and speech that signal high cognitive load or confusion. For example, in studies of children performing a Piagetian conservation task, children may state the incorrect answer verbally, while unconsciously signaling the correct answer with their hands. Most intriguing, it was these "mismatch" children who proved most able to learn, given adult guidance, the correct answer to the task (Goldin-Meadow, 2003). These observations suggest that gestures reveal our thoughts, conscious or not, consistent with the suggestion that gesture is a "living fossil" of some earlier communicative stage.

An important (and apparently still unresolved) question is the degree to which such gestures are communicative (cf. Messing and Campbell, 1999). Although their communicative function may seem self-evident, there are a number of facts arguing against this intuition. First, gesturing may express *different* thoughts from those being consciously communicated. Second, we gesture even when our interlocutor cannot see us (as when speaking on the phone, or in the dark). Although these gestures might simply be from force of habit, a more compelling observation comes from studies of gesture in the blind (Goldin-Meadow, 2003). Congenitally blind children gesture similarly to sighted children, despite the fact that they have never seen a gesture in their life, and gesture even while speaking to other blind people. The latter can't be *intentionally* communicative. Finally, empirical studies examining what viewers gain from watching a speaker gesture have provided equivocal results (Krauss and Hadar, 1999): the contribution of gestures towards understanding is weak, if present at all. Such observations have led virtually all informed commentators to agree that gestures play an important role, for the speaker, in structuring thought (McNeill, 1992; Krauss and Hadar, 1999; Goldin-Meadow, 2003), while leaving their communicative efficacy in doubt. Interestingly, the first "gestural origin" theory, that of Condillac (1971[1747]), explicitly considered gestures from this perspective: for Condillac the first problem was attaining private rational thought (which in his view required symbolic representations), and gestures were the crucial bridge to this. We shall return to this notion of "gesturing for thinking" below.

13.3 Signed language

In sharp contrast to gesture, there is no question about the communicative efficacy of the manually signed languages of the deaf ("sign" hereafter): they are fully functional languages, with all the communicative potential of spoken language (Stokoe, 1960; Klima and Bellugi, 1979; Armstrong, 1983; Emmorey, 2002). One can discuss past and future, imaginary worlds, mathematics and cosmology, and philosophy and morality, as readily with sign as with speech, and at essentially the same rate. Poetry is possible in sign, as is a high level of expressivity (via facial expressions and body posture) for powerful rhetorical or artistic effects. Sign is a hierarchically organized combinatorial system, and has all the levels of spoken language (from phonetics and phonology through to semantics and pragmatics). Sign "phonetics" involves handshape, location, movement direction, etc. rather than vocal sounds (note the etymological discord for *phon*etics or *phon*ology). Sign syntax allows all the richness of structure of spoken language, although it tends to use spatial location and facial expressions, in parallel with limb movements, in place of the temporal order, inflection, and agreement markers that typify spoken language. Signed languages such as ASL are conventionalized, culturally distributed systems with local dialects, and they exhibit historical change, much like spoken language. At every one of these levels, sign must be sharply distinguished from gestures of the sorts just discussed. Sign *is* language, in the fullest sense of the term, and gesture is not.

A crucial issue in sign language research, with considerable import for the gestural protolanguage hypothesis, concerns **iconicity**. While affirming sign as fully linguistic, scholars agree that it possesses considerably more iconicity than is typical of speech (where iconicity is limited to onomatopoeia or sound symbolism). Despite their use in "languages, denotative, arbitrary and digital," signs do not necessarily "lose their original analogic relation to what they 're-present'" (p. 42, Stokoe, 1974). These two aspects of gestural signs in signed language – arbitrary and iconic – seem almost paradoxical. But the paradox is easily resolved by looking more carefully at sign processing by native signers, rather than sign language dictionaries (which typically provide "iconic" glosses to signs as useful memory aids; cf. Klima and Bellugi, 1979). First, much of the apparent iconicity is illusory: the "icons" are actually arbitrary and highly variable from language to language (Stokoe, 1974), and of little aid in guessing the sign's meaning by naïve subjects. More importantly, even those signs that are, originally, iconic tend to be simplified, stereotyped, and "bleached" of iconicity over cultural time (Frishberg, 1979). Finally, and most significantly, native signers ignore (and indeed are often unaware of) the supposed iconic content in signs. Both verbal "slips of the hand" and recall errors suggest that sign processing occurs with respect to the "phonetics" of signs rather than by reference to iconic wholes. Signs, when used as a part of a full signed language by native speakers, are "bleached" of overt iconicity, and signed languages are as different from each other as spoken languages. As we shall see, these issues of iconicity and arbitrariness play an important role in discussions of gestural protolanguage.

On their face, these modern findings regarding signed language provide a strong argument against a gestural protolanguage. The problem sign poses for gestural protolanguage is simple, once detected. As Kendon has put it: "If language began as gesture, why did it not stay that way, especially if, as the deaf have demonstrated to us, it is perfectly possible to have a fully fledged language that is not spoken?" (Kendon, 1991). As we will see, the answers to this question are varied, but the most obvious ones will not work. In general, many scholars reject any equivalence between sign and gesture, and reject the gestural hypothesis as a result (Pinker, 1994b; MacNeilage, 1998a; Emmorey, 2002), with the prominent exception of William Stokoe, the founding father of sign studies, who was a consistent enthusiast of gestural protolanguage (Stokoe, 1974, 2001).

13.4 Gestural theories of language origin: a brief history

The notion of a gestural protolanguage is often credited to the French Abbé Éttienne Bonnot de Condillac (1715–1780), but Condillac's discussion was an elaboration of the discussion of language origin in Mandeville's *Fable of the Bees* (Mandeville, 1997 [1723]). Bernard Mandeville (1670–1733) is better known as a forerunner of modern economic theory, but the *Fable* also included some speculation on language origins. Remember that a divine origin of language was still the dominant assumption at this time. Accordingly, Mandeville structured his hypothesis around a situation of two children isolated from society, thus continuing in the long tradition of Psammetuchus as recounted by Herodotus (1964 [450–420 BC]). Condillac explored the same thought experiment, and despite an explicit introductory statement that God gave language to Adam, he concluded that humans could reinvent language, if isolated, and would do so via a language of gesture.

In Condillac's fable, a boy and a girl left to fend for themselves (a transparent allusion to Adam and Eve in the garden) would develop language spontaneously, due to their rational powers and sympathy for each other. This first language would be a language of action – body movements including facial expressions, manual gestures, and inarticulate vocalizations. Although these expressions would initially be private expressions of thought, social sympathies for the other would result in them being "codified" into communicative signs (what we today would call "ontogenetic ritualization"; see below), and eventually transformed into speech. This transition, he suggested, came about by a combination of "natural cries" with gestural signs: "They articulated new sounds, and by repeating them several times, and accompanying them with some gesture... they accustomed themselves to give names to things" (p. 174, Condillac, 1971 [1747]). However, Condillac suggested that the vocal tract was too inflexible to produce more than a few sounds, and that it took a long time before "articulate sounds became so easy, that they absolutely prevailed" (p. 175). He provides little indication of why this prevalence became so complete.

Condillac's idea was extremely influential on later Enlightenment scholars (cf. Aarsleff, 1976; Hewes, 1977), and his writings were probably partly responsible for the earlier, more sympathetic, treatment of the deaf in eighteenth-century France than elsewhere. His hypothesis provided an inspiration, or a foil, for many subsequent scholars. Maupertuis was largely sympathetic to his countryman's hypothesis, but went further by removing Condillac's biblical fig-leaf of divine creation, declaring language a human invention (Maupertuis, 1768). Like Condillac, Maupertuis placed natural cries and gestures at the root of language, later supplemented by conventionalized cries and gestures. Rousseau's *Essai* similarly affirmed the role of both gesture and vocal cries in early language (Rousseau, 1966 [1781]). The reason is relatively obvious: the spatial nature of gesture allows far more diverse possibilities for iconic communication and pantomime than is possible with speech. This greater capacity for iconicity is one leading reason to see gestures, rather than speech, as an easy route into a language-like communication system. While many later scholars affirmed a role for gestures in addition to vocalization (as did Herder and Darwin), few saw gesture as a central necessity as did Condillac, or modern proponents of the gestural origins hypothesis. However, in the twentieth century, two key discoveries – concerning ape gestural capacities and signed languages – breathed new life into these ideas.

13.5 Gordon Hewes: father of modern gestural protolanguage theories

The renaissance of gestural origins theories in modern times is due to anthropologist Gordon Hewes, whose contributions to this discussion are numerous and insightful (Hewes, 1973, 1975, 1977, 1983, 1996). The core contribution is Hewes (1973), accompanied by critical reviews and Hewes' response. The brevity and concision of this paper belies considerable scholarship and thought, and the paper remains a landmark among studies of language evolution. Hewes thoughtfully combined the best insights of previous generations with considerable new data about hemispheric asymmetry and the gestural abilities of great apes to paint a compelling picture of language evolution, and introduced the term "protolanguage" to refer to an earlier phylogenetic stage of hominid communication. There are three main strands in Hewes argument, which remain the main strengths of gestural theories today: ape abilities, semanticity, and neural data.

The first, and in my mind most compelling, of Hewes' arguments for a gestural stage of hominid communication is comparative: specifically, the relative ease with which living great apes master and use gesture (Call and Tomasello, 2007). In sharp contrast to their limited vocal control, great apes have excellent manual control, and they can easily be trained to exploit this control in artificial language experiments, using hand and arm shapes resembling those of signed languages (Gardner and Gardner, 1969). More significantly from an evolutionary viewpoint, apes' natural, species-typical use of gestures is volitional and intentionally informative, and gestures are made with close attention to the intended receiver's state of attention (e.g. Leavens *et al.*, 2005; Call and Tomasello, 2007; Cartmill and Byrne, 2007). The presence of these characteristics in all living great apes leaves little doubt that similar gestural capacities were available to our LCA with chimpanzees, and that these gestures share certain attributes of human language that ape vocalizations lack. Hewes suggests that gesture, as a signaling system, thus provides a "line of least biological resistance" into one of the most crucial aspects of language: its intentional semanticity.

This idea has recently received considerable empirical support from primatologists. Michael Tomasello and Josep Call, who have led a monumental 20-year comparative study on gesture among great apes, conclude their recent book by affirming and extending Hewes' argument (Tomasello and

Call, 2007). In addition to intentionality (both regarding manual control and attention to the other's attentional state), they cite the flexibility of gesture as an important similarity between ape gesture and human language, one that contrasts sharply with ape vocalization. While ape vocalizations are relatively stereotyped, involuntary, and innately linked to particular expressive needs, ape *gestures* are flexibly mapped to communicative needs. Ape gestures are flexible in two ways. First, many gestures can be used to achieve the same end (often in a way rationally connected to the intended receiver's orientation or response), and a single gesture may be used in a number of different contexts. Tomasello and Call argue that this bi-directional many-to-many mapping is more like the semantics of natural language than are ape calls. Equally fundamental is the new data on the *acquisition* of gestures by apes. While some gestures (like the hand out "begging" gesture) seem to be universal among chimpanzees, other's (e.g. the "arm up grooming" gesture) seem to arise via a much more idiosyncratic process of conventionalization, termed "ontogenetic ritualization." As noted initially by Plooij (1984), young apes seem to independently discover the communicative gestures that eventually compose their adult repertoires, which are thus both individually idiosyncratic and highly variable from group to group. Such observations typify gestures in all great apes, and thus very plausibly in the LCA. Thus, the link to ape gesture, cited by Hewes as the crucial new fact in support of gestural hypotheses, has grown even stronger in the light of subsequent research.

The second argument is focused on the ability of modern humans to use gesture and pantomime to communicate. Answering critics, who suggested that gesture's semantic range is strictly limited to simple "here and now" factors like food and water, Hewes collected records of the use of gesture and pantomime in communication between European explorers and native peoples, where extremely complex concepts were exchanged (e.g. concerning complex travel routes and terrain, or the political situation in neighboring tribes). One needn't be Marcel Marceau to express oneself richly and flexibly using body movements: this appears to be a pan-human capacity, available whenever circumstances demand it. Studies of "home sign" in deaf children of hearing parents corroborate this conclusion (Goldin-Meadow, 2003). Normally raised children are equally adept at using gesture: the pointing gesture is an example of a specific movement shared between humans and apes but with a far more sophisticated use in young humans. While chimpanzees (at least those in contact with humans) readily learn to use **imperative pointing** to demand food or other rewards, children (unlike chimpanzees) spontaneously use **declarative pointing** as a way of eliciting shared attention to objects. Gesture thus fulfills a crucial pragmatic prerequisite of word learning and language acquisition (cf. Tomasello, 1999). Again, gesturing offers a smooth pathway into this crucial component of language, compared with vocalization. Both observations (present-day existence, and the pan-cultural usefulness of gesture and pantomime) fulfill the desideratum that posited protolinguistic capacities should remain evident in modern humans.

Hewes also sees signed languages as support for his argument, but here he makes a number of assertions about sign, and ASL in particular, that would not be accepted today. For example, he suggests that sign is slower than speech (p. 10, para. 4, Hewes, 1973), that it has a limited vocabulary, and that it is essentially a back formation from spoken language. Such claims are rejected by modern studies of sign (Klima and Bellugi, 1979; Emmorey, 2002). Hewes asserts that chimpanzees can acquire "elementary" ASL with four years of training, an assertion that has been hotly contested (Terrace, 1979; Terrace *et al.*, 1979; Wallman, 1992). Finally, he suggests that an important selective drive in the switch from a sign-like gestural protolanguage to spoken language was the lack, in the former, of duality of patterning and phonemic structure (he saw ASL signs as largely iconic and holistic). Again, modern studies of sign phonology sharply reject these assertions (Brentari, 1998). Although Hewes' view of the nature and limitations of sign was reasonable at the time he wrote, few students of sign today would accept these limitations as intrinsic to signed languages. Therefore, what Hewes offered as an argument *for* gestural protolanguage has, with further understanding of sign, become the strongest argument *against* it. Given the essentially complete equivalence, as communicative systems, between sign and speech, why should speech have ever replaced sign as the innate default signaling system in our species? Hewes, like Bickerton and many others, underestimates the major neural changes required to evolve neocortical control over vocalization, and skates lightly over the fact that a mutation that allowed such vocal control would have no adaptive value in a fully gestural protolanguage of the sort he posits. Later accounts, especially Arbib's (see below), address this problem at the mechanistic level, but the lack of a plausible selective force to drive signed language into vocal language remains a compelling argument against a fully gestural, and fully linguistic, protolanguage.

13.6 Arguments against gestural protolanguage

Many subsequent commentators seek to answer this argument by suggesting advantages of the spoken modality. Three obvious, intuitive advantages of speech over sign are often cited as forces favoring the transition to spoken language (e.g. Corballis, 2002b), and some proponent of gestural protolanguage have concluded that together they provide an adequate explanation for the transition to speech: "These and similar advantages could easily account for such an hypothesized shift" (p. 232, Armstrong *et al.*, 1995). These advantages are:

(1) communicating in darkness (or other visually obscured environments);
(2) "freeing the hands" – speech allows communication while the hands were occupied;
(3) visual attention is freed for other tasks.

But as Hewes was aware, these intuitive arguments for the shift from gestural to spoken languages are rather weak. Each posited advantage can be paired with a similar selective force that would oppose them. Indeed, a careful consideration of each of these forces reveals them to be wholly inadequate to explain a wholesale shift from a gestural to a vocal protolanguage.

Consider, most prominently, the idea that a crucial advantage of spoken language is allowing communication in the dark (e.g. Corballis, 2002b). This is true – but signed language comparably allows efficient *silent* communication of a sort surely quite useful in hunting or intertribal warfare (not to mention selective gossip or the telling of secrets within a group). Sign shows a complementary utility for communication in the presence of noise (e.g. around moving water, volcanic activity, or in the midst of fire or migrating animals). Furthermore, in small foraging groups (especially those including children), the use of silent language would avoid attracting predators (or hostile humans), and constant verbal dialogue would surely entail disadvantages (Stephenson, 1974). Indeed, one of the most conspicuous differences between a group of human and chimpanzee young is the almost complete silence of the latter (or, from a chimpanzee's perspective, the unceasing din generated by the former). Among chimpanzees, sensibly, it is adult males – those least threatened by predation – who make the most noise. But if babbling is a requirement for speech, some child-generated sound may be irreducibly necessary for a speech-based system to evolve (see Chapter 9). This has led some scholars to suggest that human speech evolved only after our "dominance" over large predators: "ever since the development of the spear . . . human children have grown up in relative safety from predators" (p. 14, Kortland, 1973). But this is an illusion – leopards, the main predators on chimpanzees, still successfully kill humans today (while I was camping at Kruger National Park in South Africa, a park ranger *armed with a loaded rifle* was ambushed and killed by a leopard).

Single human-eating tigers have killed hundreds of humans in modern times (Mazak, 1981; McDougal, 1987), and bears, lions, and mountain lions still regularly claim human lives. The notion that humans have dominated large predators is profoundly Eurocentric, and quite incorrect. During most of hominid evolution a universal capacity for silent language would have had considerable selective value, as it still would today.

The arguments continue. Modern apes are diurnal, and spend their nights sleeping rather than communicating. Humans lack any nocturnal adaptations, providing few grounds for thinking ancestral hominids would gain any major advantage from communicating in darkness. The hominids posited by Hewes to use gestural protolanguage (*Homo erectus*) had probably already mastered fire. Thus, by the time gestural language existed, it could be seen by firelight, if necessary (Emmorey, 2005). Finally, although degraded, sign communication can occur in total darkness via contact: fluent signers signing onto the hands of others can still communicate. All of these points argue against any selective advantage of vocalizing in the dark, overwhelming enough to drive the complete replacement of sign with speech. Indeed, the counter-advantages listed should be enough to at least preserve fluent, propositional sign among hunters, soldiers, and predator-threatened foragers, if a gestural protolanguage once existed.

The second common argument is that gestural communication is impossible, or highly restricted, during tool use: that the switch from gestural to spoken language "freed the hands." But tool use occurred throughout hominid evolution, including particularly during the manually sophisticated *Homo erectus* stage. This was a constant force acting against gesture. Hewes notes that the intuitive notion that speech would allow toolmakers to be better teachers, by describing what they do as they do it, does not bear close scrutiny. Most manual learning appears to occur via observation and imitation rather than vocal descriptions (Hewes, 1973). Indeed, sign may even be superior for linguistic communication about such matters, due to its integration of space into the syntactic domain (Emmorey, 2005). Furthermore, native signers are quite flexible in their use of sign under adverse conditions: they can sign with one hand, while driving, cooking, or operating equipment.

Speech also has compensating disadvantages: mouths are used for things other than speech, both during feeding and as a tool. The ability conferred by sign to "talk with the mouth full" might be a surprisingly useful one, given the toughness of Pleistocene food sources and the amount of time our ancestors spent chewing, and the mouth's important role in tool use among both modern humans and, based on patterns of tooth wear, extinct hominids (Molnar, 1972). This suggests that a switch to oral language might have provided little net advantage, and suggests a *continuing* value of gestural communication during eating and working. If a larynx lowered during speech provides an increased risk of choking during swallowing, the often lethal effect of choking should provide another selective force against the evolution of exclusive reliance upon speech-based language (Emmorey, 2005).

Finally, the notion that visual communication requires more "attention" than vocal language ignores the fact that *auditory* attention is also important, and is occupied by speech. Indeed, during speech the auditory system as a whole becomes less sensitive due to the middle ear reflex. Again, in any context where silence is valued and hearing plays a key role (e.g. hunting, warfare) gestural communication would have considerable advantages over speech.

I conclude, as did Hewes, that the "standard" arguments could not account for a wholesale shift from sign to speech. Another, rarely discussed possible advantage of speech is that it is energetically more efficient than gesture. Indeed, speech is about as efficient as a motor action generating a perceptible signal could be, with energetic costs that only become *measureable*, using modern instrumentation, at loud volumes and effortful production (e.g. Moon and Lindblom, 2003). Although I know of no direct measures of the metabolic cost of gesture or sign, the mechanics (moving the large mass of the upper limbs with considerable acceleration) suggest costs at least an order of magnitude higher than speech. Unfortunately, the power of this argument to explain the transition to speech is clearly blunted by the fact that humans pervasively *gesture during speech* (McNeill, 2000). The real cost of spoken language, as it occurs outside the laboratory, is thus probably dominated by the gestural component, even today. If energetic cost was the selective force that drove a wholesale rearrangement of a hominid protolanguage, it seems strangely powerless in structuring today's multi-modal conversational displays.

The four forces listed above make intuitive sense, but on careful consideration their explanatory power is only skin deep. One can easily devise equally compelling counter-examples for each of them. It seems unlikely, in summary, that any of these factors, alone or in combination, would have been adequate to drive a complete switch to fully spoken language. It is intriguing that Gordon Hewes, a dedicated convert to the gestural protolanguage concept, had already reached this conclusion in 1973. Perhaps because Hewes did not spell out the objections as clearly as I have just done, subsequent gestural theorists have tended to rehearse these advantages as if they fully explained the transition (e.g. Armstrong *et al.*, 1995; Corballis, 2002b). Later scholars have also tended to turn a blind eye to Hewes' more compelling alternative hypothesis.

13.7 Arbitrariness, indexing, and duality of patterning as key advantages of speech

Given the inadequacy of the "standard" advantages of sign, Hewes suggests a far more interesting possibility founded on the relative iconicity of signed and spoken language. First, Hewes suggests that the potential iconicity of gestural communication – precisely the feature that hypothetically eased its initial evolution – would eventually cause problems for learning and the rapid processing of sign as vocabulary grew. If signs were essentially iconic wholes, he suggests, learning a vocabulary of more than a few thousand items might have become a significant cognitive burden. He cites as evidence the size of visual lexicons today: 1,500 *kanji* characters is a reasonable target for a high-school graduate in Japan (and Hewes claims that a lexicon of 2,000 signs typifies ASL or other signed languages). Thus, "gesture language may have reached the limits of its capacity . . . by the end of the Lower Paleolithic" (p. 11, Hewes, 1973). Hewes' hypothesized limit on vocabulary size in gestural protolanguage constitutes an interesting difference from many later theorists, who postulate a fully open, expansive gestural protolanguage (e.g. Corballis, 2002a; Arbib, 2005).

Hewes further suggests that the *processing* of semantically laden wholes would become slow and effortful beyond a certain vocabulary size (Hewes, 1983). Citing the literature on speech processing and lexical access (especially Fay and Cutler, 1977), he suggests "a large lexicon is only effective if its contents are readily accessible": a larger vocabulary would be of no advantage unless "accompanied by an efficient word-filing system" (p. 153, Hewes, 1973). Such efficiency requires the *elimination* of meaning in the filing system, Hewes suggests. As anyone who files documents by content knows, there are typically several possible categories for a given item, and retrieval often therefore involves going through several of these possible headings before the desired item is found. The solution is to use an unambiguous, semantically arbitrary system (e.g. alphabetization). Hewes suggests that phonemes in spoken words function in precisely this way: providing a single, unambiguous starting point for lexical search. He argues that this became a huge advantage of spoken language as vocabulary size increased, and that humans using a speech-based system accrued ever-larger gains in efficiency as vocabulary size grew. In other words, Hewes suggests that the iconicity of sign became a positive hindrance to the evolution of a large vocabulary (cf. Hurford, 2004).

This is an intriguing hypothesis, but it runs into problems when confronted with later work on sign processing. As already detailed by Klima and Bellugi (1979), the rate at which signers produce and process meaning, measured in propositions per unit time, is essentially identical to that of speakers. When fluent bilingual ASL signers and English speakers are asked to tell the same story in both modalities, they convey the same information over roughly the same amount of time. Although the rate of *signs* is much slower (perhaps due to the greater inertia of the limbs), this is compensated for by the use of space and face, in parallel, to convey distinctions that, in speech, must be coded into syllables. Hence, if Hewes' conjecture is correct, the signer's lexicon must also be organized via some arbitrary indexes. These are probably the "phonetic" components of sign (hand and finger shapes), equivalent to distinctive features in sign (cf. Pulleyblank, 1989). Thus, although Hewes makes an interesting point regarding the origins of arbitrariness and the duality of patterning, along with a plausible and relevant adaptive function, his proposal that this was a selective force adequate to drive humankind from a mainly manual to a mainly vocal system again seems inadequate.

Hewes cited some further, less compelling, possibilities smoothing the transition from gesture to speech: sound symbolism and the "mouth gesture" hypothesis of Paget (1930). Richard Paget was a physicist and acoustician who authored some important early work on speech acoustics (Paget, 1923). His book *Human Speech* (Paget, 1930) included a brief section on language origins. Paget quite correctly saw speech production as consisting essentially of vocal movements ("gestures"), predating modern accounts by more than fifty years (Browman and Goldstein, 1986). Upon this firm base he constructed one of the more precarious edifices in the field of language evolution: the "mouth gesture" theory. "Originally man expressed his ideas by gesture, but as he gesticulated with his hands, his tongue, lips and jaw unconsciously followed suit in a ridiculous fashion, 'understudying'... the action of the hands... In connection with the beckoning gesture – commonly made by extending the hand, palm up, drawing it inwards towards the face and at the same time bending the fingers inwards towards the palm. This gesture may be imitated with the tongue, by protruding, withdrawing, and bending up its tip as it re-enters the mouth and falls to rest. If this 'gesture' be blown or voiced, we get a resultant whispered or phonated word, like eda, eda or edra (according to the degree of contact between tongue and upper lip or palate) suggestive of the Icelandic hadr" (pp. 133–138, Paget, 1930). The complexity of signed language makes it unlikely that such reflexive processes could so effortlessly translate sign into speech. But Paget, in a later contribution (Paget, 1944, published in the journal *Science*, no less) went further, reconstructing many of these postulated word/gesture pairs, and finding them represented as word roots in reconstructed ancient languages like proto-Indo-European. Given an age of proto-Indo-European around 10,000 years at most (Gray and Atkinson, 2003), an attempt to use such reconstructions as evidence in favor of a theory of language origin can be confidently rejected today. Indeed, Paget's ideas gained little credence in his own time: "personally, I do not believe that any human being before Sir Richard Paget ever made any considerable number of gestures with his mouth parts in sympathetic pantomime" (p. 3, Thorndike, 1943b).

While Hewes agrees that "these attempts smack of certain nineteenth-century philological speculation," he suggests that we should not "brush them away as totally meaningless" (p. 10, Hewes, 1973). In further support, he suggests that onomatopoeia and sound symbolism might have been crucial additional factors in easing the transition to speech. Beyond the obvious advantage for vocalizations in rendering sounds in onomatopoeia (e.g. for representing animal calls), Hewes cites the existence of sound symbolism as another plank in the bridge from gesture to speech. **Sound symbolism** is the existence of non-arbitrary links between sounds and their meanings (Hinton *et al.*, 1994), and extends far beyond onomatopoeia. The best-documented example is size symbolism: the cross-linguistic association between high front vowels, especially /i/, with smallness, while low back vowels, such as /o/ and /a/, are associated with large size (Sapir, 1929). Hewes suggests that, by lowering the "arbitrariness hurdle," sound symbolism smoothed the transition from the obvious iconicity of gesture to the mostly arbitrary nature of speech. While this makes sense, it still goes only a small way in explaining the evolution of speech, and we are left concluding, as does Hewes himself, that this transition remains the greatest unsolved problem for gestural protolanguage theories.

13.8 The neuroscience of gesture: laterality and mirror neurons

Neuroscientific data provide another line of argument that has been pursued in the context of gestural origins. These data fall into two main categories: lateralization and mirror neurons. Neural lateralization was seen as a strong argument in the 1970s, but recent comparative data have raised deep questions about its relevance. In contrast, mirror neurons are frequently invoked in contemporary discussions, and have been seen by some as a key finding relevant to understanding the biological mechanisms involved in language.

13.8.1 Cerebral lateralization as evidence for gestural protolanguage

During the language evolution renaissance of the 1970s, human cerebral lateralization was seen as a central unusual characteristic of our species. At that time, population-wide cerebral asymmetries were considered a uniquely human character, and an explanation for their evolution was seen as a central requirement for any theory of language evolution. **Handedness** is the preferential use of one limb, and most humans show a strong right-hand bias (corresponding to the left half of the brain) for fine hand movements. **Cerebral laterality** – the neural basis for this behavioral side bias – is somewhat independent: even ambidextrous or left-handed humans are still likely to show a leftward brain bias for language. In contrast to these species-typical side biases, many mammals show similar paw or hand symmetries at the *individual* level that are essentially randomly distributed across the population, with roughly equal numbers of "righties" and "lefties" (Tsai and Maurer, 1930; Collins, 1970). The fact that both language and manual dexterity show a pronounced left-hemisphere bias in humans has long been cited as evidence of a connection between the two (Kimura, 1973, 1993), and was seen by Gordon Hewes as strong evidence in favor of the gestural origins theory. The basic notion is that manual dexterity initiated leftward cerebral asymmetry in early hominids, and that this provided a preadaptation for language asymmetry. The subsequent literature on laterality is full of variant hypotheses postulating some abstract computational difference between the hemispheres, including local *versus* global processing, rapid *versus* slow temporal processing, and various others (cf. Bradshaw and Rogers, 1993; Hellige, 2001). But despite a long-standing fascination with the question, neurolinguistics has yet to come up with any single widely accepted common explanation for this apparent association.

We can thus start our analysis of the putative link between dexterity and language dominance by asking whether it reflects a causal relationship or is due to chance. It is clear that there is nothing deeply special about the left hemisphere *per se*, as right-brained left-handers survive without difficulty in all human populations. Furthermore, while left-handers can have a right-hemisphere bias for language (thus representing "mirror images" of right-handers), they are actually more likely to have a left bias. Thus it is clear that the association between manual preference and language dominance is statistical and does not reflect a direct causal association. This alone is grounds for skepticism. Furthermore, because this is a statistical association, we should ask how statistically likely it is for two random traits to appear on the same side of the brain. The answer is the same as for two coin flips in a row coming up "heads": 0.5 * 0.5 or 0.25 (very far from the 0.05 level generally accepted as indicating statistical significance). Even three such associations (say, manual dexterity, language dominance, and rapid temporal processing) are perfectly likely to co-lateralize by chance (with a 0.125 probability, still not significant). When confronted with this argument in a powerful critique (Nottebohm, 1973), Hewes replied: "I find it almost unthinkable that this all happened on a '50% chance basis'" (p. 21, Hewes, 1973). Unfortunately, as always with "failure of imagination" arguments, Hewes' failure to accept this possibility is irrelevant to its basic and undeniable force. Without some more convincing hypothesis of an underlying causal connection between dexterity and language, the "statistical link" between the two (or with some third variable such as toolmaking) is, from an empirical viewpoint, completely unpersuasive.

Turning now to data, the force of lateralization arguments has been blunted by the now-pervasive evidence for population-level asymmetries in many animal species, from frogs to canaries. To the extent that cerebral asymmetries for communication are a pervasive feature of vertebrate brains, the need to invoke special selective forces, such as tool use, to explain asymmetry in language, disappears. This point was again raised by Nottebohm (1973), whose work on lateralization in songbird vocalization had already dethroned asymmetry as uniquely human. In songbirds, the sound-producing organ has two sides, each capable of producing an independent pitch (Greenewalt, 1968; Suthers and Zollinger, 2004). Nottebohm used lesions of the nerve on one side or the other to show that canaries, chaffinches, and some other species show an almost complete left dominance in song production (Nottebohm, 1971). Although mixed dominance now appears to be more typical, asymmetries of various sorts remain common in songbird vocal control (Suthers and Zollinger, 2004). These data suggested that "neural dominance may be associated with complex learned behavior, so that it can evolve in the absence of any concatenation of specifically human events" (p. 16, Nottebohm, 1973).

Further studies have strengthened the case for nonhuman asymmetries: fish, frogs, reptiles, and some mammal species also show left-sided biases for communication sounds (Bauer, 1993; Bisazza *et al.*, 1998), and this is increasingly seen as typical, rather than unusual to humans

(Bisazza *et al.*, 1999). Although primate handedness remains controversial, there is increasing evidence for subtle population-level asymmetries within our own order, since the seminal article reopening this question appeared (MacNeilage *et al.*, 1987). Most relevant in the current context is the data accumulating for apes that some aspects of gesture, including imperative pointing and facial movements, are biased towards the right side (Hopkins *et al.*, 2005; Liebal, 2007; Reynolds Losin *et al.*, 2008). Indeed, in his defense of the gestural origins theory, Michael Corballis inverts Hewes' arguments, and suggests that an ancient vertebrate asymmetry for *vocal* control drove the evolution of manual laterality (Corballis, 2002b).

Finally, modern brain imaging has weakened the very notion that one side is "dominant" for language: it is now clear that language is far more widely distributed in the brain than Broca's and Wernicke's areas (e.g. Lieberman, 2000; Scott, 2005), and language processing is by no means restricted to the left hemisphere. Today, right-hemisphere activations during language tasks are commonly found in brain-imaging studies, and accepted with little surprise (Bookheimer, 2002). Furthermore, in cases of early damage to, or even complete removal of, the left hemisphere, essentially normal language skills can develop in the right hemisphere (Smith, 1966; Vargha-Khadem *et al.*, 1997; Devlin *et al.*, 2003). Such developments have led this "central question" of the 1970s and 1980s to be seen today as less relevant as a core factor in human uniqueness (for a dissenting opinion see Gazzaniga, 2000). Left laterality is not necessarily a core aspect of language, gesture, or dexterity, nor a central feature of language evolution.

13.8.2 Cross-modal cognition

Another neural factor cited by Hewes has also fared poorly in the light of subsequent data: **cross-modal cognition**. In the 1960s, humans were thought to be uniquely proficient at transforming information from one sensory domain (e.g. tactile or auditory input) to another (e.g. vision). Spoken language relies fundamentally on the human ability to associate complex auditory with visual/tactile stimuli (Ettlinger and Blakemore, 1969; Geschwind, 1970). Despite demonstrations of tactile to visual transfer in apes (Davenport and Rogers, 1970), Hewes argued that apes had great difficulties integrating complex auditory information with visual or tactile knowledge. Hewes suggested that this inability necessitated a gestural origin of language. However, we now know that monkeys have far greater capacities to analyze and understand complex acoustic sequences than suspected at that time (see Chapter 4). Virtually all species tested thus far can associate "names with faces" (individually distinctive calls with the individual who produced it; e.g. Cheney and Seyfarth, 1980; Charrier *et al.*, 2001), and a baboon exposed to a sequence of calls from different individuals seems to readily interpret this as a social encounter (Bergman *et al.*, 2003). Although monkeys in the laboratory do find auditory tasks more difficult than visual ones (e.g. Brosch *et al.*, 2004), they often exhibit far better auditory skills in more natural conditions. Furthermore, lexigram-trained chimpanzees show sophisticated cross-modal transfer even when one of the dimensions is symbolically represented (Savage-Rumbaugh *et al.*, 1988). Thus, like lateralization, the notion that cross-modal transfer is uniquely human, or provides an argument for gestural origins, has evaporated with further comparative research. This does not, however, vitiate the basic insight that cross-modal integration is one of the crucial neural substrates for language. Instead, these comparative data push the origin of this neural substrate further back in time, indicating that these capacities were already present in the LCA. The same is true of our next topic: a class of cross-modal neuron termed "mirror neurons."

13.9 Cross-modal cognition and mirror neurons: Arbib and Rizzolatti's model

Neuroscientists Giacomo Rizzolatti and Michael Arbib have provided a new and influential neural argument for gestural origin theories, based on the discovery of mirror neurons in macaque monkeys (Rizzolatti and Arbib, 1998). **Mirror neurons** are motor neurons which normally fire while the monkey performs an action, but also fire when the monkey *observes* that action performed by another. In their most common form, these neurons fire during reaching and grasping actions of the hand, and during corresponding visual stimulation (Rizzolatti *et al.*, 1996). However, mirror neurons involved in oro-facial actions (grasping with the mouth) also exist, and neurons sensitive to auditory as well as visual stimulation have been documented in monkeys (Ferrari *et al.*, 2001; Kohler *et al.*, 2002). In humans, there is consistent evidence for a related neural "mirror system" (Iacoboni *et al.*, 1999; Iacoboni *et al.*, 2005), including a major auditory component (Gazzola *et al.*, 2006), but the rarity of single-unit recording in humans has prevented any direct demonstration of mirror neurons *per se*. This evidence suggests that mirror neurons might represent a shared primate mechanism that paved the way to a postulated gestural protolanguage.

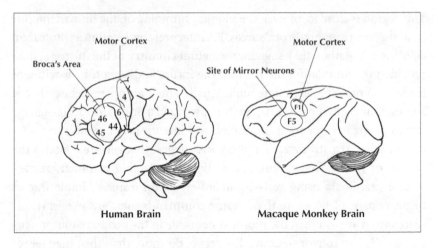

Figure 13.1 Mirror neurons in human and macaque brains – The diagram illustrates the similarity in location of the human Broca's area and area F5 in the macaque monkey, where motor neutrons are found.

Rizzolatti and Arbib's "mirror system hypothesis" for language evolution posits the following phylogenetic stages:

(1) primates (in general): manual grasping of objects;
(2) primates (LCA of macaques and humans): a mirror system for grasping;
(3) gestural communication system: providing an open signal repertoire;
(4) speech takeover (by "invasion" or "collateralization" of speech areas).

The novel contribution of mirror neurons to the gestural protolanguage hypothesis is to provide a neural substrate for **parity** in gesture understanding, predating language evolution and present in the LCA. Rizzolatti and Arbib (RA hereafter) note that parity, between acting and perceiving, is a prerequisite of communication (see Chapter 3). Based on the reasonable supposition that monkeys know, when watching another monkey feed, that feeding is occurring – that they can translate the visual stimulus into one with a specific and important personal significance – RA suggest that mirror neurons play a key computational role in this parity-establishing system. Interpreting an action, such as grasping, as meaningful requires a way for the brain to "tag" an *observed* action as equivalent to a *performed* action. The discovery of mirror neurons suggests this equivalence is reflected in single-neuron firing patterns, providing an abstract representation of actions.

The next component of RA's argument concerns the location of mirror neurons: in the monkey premotor region termed F5 (see Figure 13.1). F1 is the label for the primary motor cortex in monkeys, and F5 is in front of this, located just anterior to the hand and mouth regions of the motor strip.

This region is close to, or even the monkey homolog of, the human inferior frontal gyrus (roughly, Broca's area). RA interpret this location as more than coincidence. Rather, they suggest, the neural circuitry of the mirror system provided the foundation upon which the future audio-motor capacities of the human mirror system were built. Much of their argument echoes that of Hewes, namely that pre-human gesture provided a bridge to vocal language due to its greater openness, flexibility, and intentionality relative to vocalization. Like Armstrong *et al.* (1995), RA suggest that gesture contains the "seeds" of syntax, in the sense of a prelinguistic "action grammar" related to case grammars using verb argument-structure frames. Simple frames might consist of no more than motor commands like "grasp(raisin)," as represented anywhere in the motor systems, or in the ordinary motor neurons in F5. But mirror neurons, RA argue, do more than this: they represent a "declarative" structure including the agent of the action: or "grasp (John, raisin)" where "John" is another monkey, or a human experimenter. Perhaps, they suggest, these mirror neurons also represent the monkey's own grasp in a similar frame: "grasp (self, raisin)." Thus, just as Bickerton attempts to find the seed of syntax in social intelligence, RA find it in mirror neurons and motor control.

The link between mirror neurons and visual gestures is complicated by the discovery of "auditory mirror neurons" in both monkeys and humans (Kohler *et al.*, 2002; Keysers *et al.*, 2003a; Gazzola *et al.*, 2006). These are audio-motor neurons that fire both when performing an action, and when *hearing* the auditory result. A separation of oral and manual actions has been documented (Gazzola *et al.*, 2006), with oral actions located more ventrally (paralleling the mouth area in the primary motor cortex). These and similar motor activations during perception of auditory stimuli, either words or music (Martin *et al.*, 1996; Bangert *et al.*, 2006), support the idea that cross-modal audio-motor associations provided a precursor for perceptual/motor matching in speech (and music). Furthermore, tactile activation from visual stimulation has also been documented (Keysers *et al.*, 2003b). The discovery that mirror neurons are multi-modal, and code oral as well as manual action, removes much of the force of arguments using mirror neurons in the macaque as a justification for gestural protolanguage. Aptly dubbing auditory mirror neurons "echo neurons," Tomasello observed that "Unless we know that echo neurons do not exist, then mirror neurons do not provide crucial support for a gestural theory" (Tomasello, 2002). Now that the existence of such neurons is well documented, in both monkeys and man, this component of RA's argument for gestural protolanguage collapses. Indeed, recent brain-imaging findings in professional pianists, who show premotor activation both when hearing *and seeing* the piano played (Haslinger *et al.*, 2005), demonstrate that the mirror system is equally implicated in the evolution of instrumental music as gesture or speech, a theme we will revisit in Chapter 14.

The discovery of mirror neurons was not without precedent: Perrett and colleagues had discovered neurons which fire selectively to grasping and similar actions in the superior temporal sulcus (STS) years before (Perrett *et al.*, 1985), but without the motor component. Many organisms behave in a way suggesting that some "mirror" mechanism must be present to match one's own actions to the environment or to the actions of others, from the adaptive color mimicry of octopus (almost literally a mirror) to the social flocking of birds and the schooling of fish (cf. Hurford, 2004). Nonetheless, the discovery of a clearly defined, robust, single-cell mechanism underlying such capacities, in a primate, generated great excitement in neuroscience and beyond, and for several years mirror neurons were the *cause célèbre* of the behavioral sciences, and spawned a voluminous primary and secondary literature. A book about mirror neurons states that "it is hard to overestimate the importance of this discovery" (p. 1, Stamenov and Gallese, 2002). The distinguished neuroscientist V. S. Ramachandran predicted that "mirror neurons will do for psychology what DNA did for biology: they will provide a unifying framework and help explain a host of mental abilities that have hitherto remained mysterious," and argued that they underlay the "great leap forward" in human evolution (Ramachandran, 2006). But, particularly in the field of language evolution, the reaction has been far more mixed. Let us consider some of these criticisms.

13.10 Critiques of the mirror system hypothesis

Mirror neurons mean many things to many people, and even within Rizzolatti's own Parma group there is considerable debate about the specific role of mirror neurons in theories of human evolution. We can thus start by asking what, precisely, do mirror neurons do in macaques? Their function cannot be for imitation, because (despite the misleading saying "monkey see, monkey do") the imitative abilities of macaques are extremely limited (Visalberghi and Fragaszy, 1990). Even in apes, the degree to which there is imitation in anything like a human form remains controversial (Tomasello *et al.*, 1993; Byrne and Russon, 1998). But perhaps it is a very small neural step from a mirror system to full-blown imitation (e.g. mirror neurons are enough to support imitation, but this functionality is inhibited in most species). Some models of motor control, such as William James's (1890) "ideomotor" theory, suggest that a capacity for imitation is implicit in any brain, and should be a general phenomenon (cf. Prinz, 2002). From this viewpoint, the mystery is why imitation is so rare, particularly in species such as capuchins, with complex extractive foraging techniques, and thus with plenty in their social environment worth imitating (Fragaszy *et al.*, 2004). Similarly, we might expect evidence that lesions or pharmacological treatments would at least occasionally lead to **echopraxia** in macaques – the automatic imitation of observed movements. As far as I'm aware, this never occurs. Indeed, the only species in which echopraxia has been documented is *Homo sapiens*, where it occurs, often along with **echolalia** (the automatic imitation of speech), in a wide variety of clinical situations including autism, schizophrenia, and Tourette's syndrome (Berthier, 1999). This sharp human/monkey contrast suggests that any link between mirror neurons and imitation requires additional circuitry present in humans but not in macaques. Mirror neurons clearly do not give us imitation "for free."

In an important critique, Hurford (2004) builds upon the foundation of the Saussurian principle of the *arbitrariness of the sign* to interrogate putative links between mirror neurons and "meaning." While RA are careful to discuss "parity," not meaning, much of the subsidiary literature uses the term "meaning" to connote the "mirror" relation between seeing and performing an action. As Hurford points out (and Arbib concurs; Arbib, 2004), signal parity is orthogonal to the prototype of meaning in language: the arbitrary connection between signs and referents. Mirror parity allows a macaque to recognize (and, with additional machinery, us to imitate) a specific class of actions (grasping, manipulating, etc.) that are anything but arbitrary. The mirror neuron system is also limited by the fact that the class of "concepts" it can recognize is intrinsically circumscribed, applicable to the bodily actions of other animals, but not to trees, pathways, fruit, or other important concepts in the animal's world. This system cannot generalize to all concepts, as language can. Arbib points out that, at the neural level, the relation between patterns of motor firing and retinal ganglion firing is relatively arbitrary, but his own model of infants learning to grasp uses the highly specific relationship between ego's grasping and the resulting visual stimuli to master this relation. This type of experience, again, does not generalize to arbitrary referents. As Hurford concludes, a neural system that provides parity in a highly circumscribed and non-arbitrary domain seems to provide a poor precursor for a Saussurian system whose key properties are its arbitrariness and its openness to any and all concepts.

Perhaps in response, many recent discussions of mirror neurons have focused mainly on the role of the mirror system in empathy and understanding others, following Gallese and Goldman (1998). As discussed in Chapter 3, the capacity for perspective taking and "mind reading" is a crucial component of human language, so this view of the significance of mirror neurons is highly relevant to language evolution. However, the comparative data provide no evidence for empathy and mind reading in monkeys (Cheney and Seyfarth, 1990a), and even chimpanzees only show evidence of "mind reading" in constrained, mostly competitive, situations (Hare and Tomasello, 2004). Again, as for imitation, mirror neurons are seen as "precursors" for behavioral abilities absent in the species in which they were discovered. Mirror neurons were present in the common ancestor of humans and macaques, but their function was not as "precursors" of some function limited to humans. Thus both hypotheses beg the question of the function of mirror neurons in macaque cognition and behavior. These considerations raise significant problems for the notion of mirror neurons as the neural basis of the parity property of modern human language, either in the motor domain of imitation, or the broader domain of meaning or "mind-reading." While their role as *precursors* remains plausible, significant changes are required to the mirror neuron system, as known from macaques, to get either imitation or linguistic meaning. These problems are compounded with additional problems either directly inherited from, or parallel to, those of the gestural protolanguage more generally. Put succinctly, gestures and mirror neurons appear to provide a good way *into* a meaningful protolanguage – the problem is how to get *out* of such a system and in to the arbitrary, spoken signs that are the foundation of virtually all modern languages.

13.11 Arbib's move "beyond the mirror": the extended mirror system hypothesis (EMSH)

In a response to some of these criticisms, Arbib has extended the original RA "mirror system hypothesis" (MSH) in a direction he terms "beyond the mirror" (Arbib, 2002, 2005). Arbib recognizes (unlike some enthusiasts of "primate continuity") that the discovery of shared features between humans and nonhuman primates, by itself, is little help in understanding changes that occurred uniquely in human evolution, after humans separated from the LCA. Acknowledging the critiques above, Arbib extended the MSH by adding some caveats and a number of specific evolutionary stages to the original RA model (Arbib, 2005).

Arbib first three stages, within primates, lead to our LCA with chimpanzees:

S1: grasping;
S2: mirror system for grasping;
S3: simple imitation (shared with chimpanzees but not macaques).

The following four stages are hypothesized in the evolution between the LCA and modern humans:

S4: complex imitation (beyond chimpanzees);
S5: protosign (key innovation: open repertoire);
S6: protospeech (key innovation: neocortical vocal control via collateralization);
S7: modern language.

Arbib's new hypothesis is complex – too complex for me to do it justice here. The new hypothesis has many virtues: it is specifically mechanistic (trying to explain a putative link between mirror neurons in monkey F5 and the role of Broca's area in speech), and makes more testable predictions than many others in language evolution. It is a performance model, and well grounded in the modern literature on perception and action. Arbib's new model supports an analytic model of meaning, suggesting that "protosigns" mapped onto whole phrasal meanings (like "you are eating my food" rather than "food," "eat," or "you"). However, such models, to be discussed in Chapter 14, are not linked in any direct or necessary fashion to either mirror neurons or gesture. Acknowledging these virtues, I will concentrate below on how the new version differs from MSH, and on Arbib's response to critiques of his extended version.

Clarifying the imitation issue, Arbib acknowledges that macaques don't imitate, and that chimpanzee imitation abilities are limited. His first hypothetical stage of language evolution involved an extension of imitative abilities into an ad hoc pantomime-like system. Although Arbib still sees the mirror system as foundational, he pulls a number of additional cortical areas beyond the classic F5 premotor area into the "extended mirror system." These include regions around the supplementary motor area (SMA), a number of parietal regions, temporal areas responsive to biological motion including the superior temporal sulcus, and subcortical areas such as the basal ganglia. He correctly emphasizes the importance of gaining voluntary control over the communication system, and underscores the value of the manual modality for achieving this.

Arbib also offers a nuanced model of the gesture/speech transition, positing a gradual transition from a mainly gestural system, to a system augmented by limited vocalizations, to a mainly vocal system. He terms this gradual co-evolutionary transition an "expanding spiral." Noiré advanced a similar idea: "gesture was at all times accompanied by an inarticulate sound . . . Gesture, accordingly, is the main point; sound is only an accompanying subsidiary element" (p. 34, Noiré, 1917). From such a starting point, Arbib suggests, we can envision a gradual addition of vocalization, and a gradual move towards more arbitrary communicative referents. Arbib affirms a role for kin selection in driving this communicative process in the direction of greater complexity: "The ability to imitate has clear adaptive advantage in allowing creatures to transfer skills to their offspring" (p. 144, Arbib, 2005). The expanding spiral metaphor suggests a long period of selection on both systems, during which a gradual preponderance of vocal abilities evolved. However, Arbib provides no new selective forces driving this modality shift beyond those already in the literature, citing Corballis (2002b), and only briefly mentions the value of increased arbitrariness discussed by Hewes (1973, 1983).

Arbib's extended MSH also provides additional elaboration concerning the mechanistic basis for a shift from gesture to speech. This is based on the notion of "collateralization," a phylogenetic extension of the neural circuitry of the mirror system from the manual F5 to the neighboring oromotor areas involved (in humans) in vocal control. Arbib postulates that the type of neural circuitry underlying the manual/facial mirror system became duplicated in the ventrally adjacent tongue/larynx areas of motor and premotor cortex. In assessing this idea, as for laterality, we must first ask whether spatial contiguity in the brain is evidence of shared ancestry. If some novel capacity has evolved in a species, in a particular functional context, there is no reason that capacity could not be expressed in a different functional context in a completely different brain region: any neuron in the brain has the same DNA as any other. This makes neural homology a slippery concept (Striedter, 2004), and the observation that two neural regions are adjacent in the adult brain provides at best a weak argument for homology or other phylogenetic relationships. Nonetheless, this hypothesis makes specific, testable predictions. One possibility concerns the genetic determinants of architectonically defined cortical areas, which would be expected to be expressed in manual areas in monkeys, but in both oral and manual areas in humans. Arbib's "invasion" hypothesis suggests that the two neighboring areas (manual and vocal, including the larynx area, and not just the oral and facial areas) would share key aspects of their gene expression pattern in humans, but not in macaques or chimpanzees. This hypothesis is testable, using modern molecular methods across different species (cf. Sandberg *et al.*, 2000; Khaitovich *et al.*, 2004). The connective microstructure of different cortical areas must be regulated by different gene expression profiles during development or learning, and we can expect abundant information regarding the genes regulating development in area F5 in the macaque to be available in the near future (such information is already available in birds; Wada *et al.*, 2006).

However, cortical collateralization by itself seems inadequate to obtain the voluntary vocal control characterizing humans and not other primates. As discussed in Chapter 9, a crucial neural component of this appears to be direct cortico-medullary connections to the brainstem nuclei controlling the larynx; connections present in humans and not other primates (Jürgens, 2002). This well-documented difference requires long-distance connections, of a qualitatively different sort than Arbib is discussing. Given that direct cortico-motor connections to manual and facial motor nuclei exist in primates, but the crucial cortico-medullary connections do not (see Chapter 9), it is difficult to see how any purely cortical changes could be mechanistically adequate to result in the neocortical control of vocalization. However, it is possible that such direct connections exist early in development, and the issue is not with their creation but their preservation (Deacon, 1997). If true, the evolution of a vocal babbling stage in ontogeny, paralleling the known manual babbling of human infants (Petitto and Marentette, 1991), might be enough to preserve these connections epigenetically.

Second, Arbib claims that fully grammatical language is essentially a cultural invention, accruing over some half-million years of glossogeny, and requiring no accompanying biological, genetic changes. As he puts it, evolution gave us a "language ready brain" but not language; and true modern languages have evolved purely *culturally* over as many as 100,000 years. Arbib asserts that "agriculture, writing and living in cities provide evidence that being advantageous does not imply genetic change" (p. 156, Arbib, 2005). But human evolution did not start in the Pleistocene and end at the dawn of history, and modern humans are not, from a genetic viewpoint, identical to our African hunter-gatherer ancestors of 100,000 years ago. While cultural innovations do not *necessarily* force genetic change, the empirical fact is that population-level evolutionary change does frequently occur under such conditions, as variation among modern humans demonstrates. The classic genetic examples of lactose tolerance among adults in herding cultures (an evolutionary genetic change in response to agriculture), or the prevalence of the sickle-cell hemoglobin allele in malaria regions, are enough to refute any claim that human evolution has ceased. One can hardly imagine a stronger selective force than language learning in modern humans over at least the last 50,000 years, and the rapidity and certainty with which children acquire language, in contrast to most cultural innovations, suggests strong and consistent selection on language-learning abilities, continuing to the present. The fact that all human children can learn any of the world's languages does *not* entail that there has been no selective pressure on language acquisition since human populations diverged from the African common ancestor. There has almost certainly been parallel selection on all humans, regardless of language and culture, for rapid and accurate language acquisition. Arbib's argument also allows far more time than necessary for cultural "grammaticalization": creoles and modern sign languages have grammaticalized extremely rapidly (a period of about 200 years for ASL, and about 20 for NSL; Frishberg, 1979; Senghas *et al.*, 2005). These data suggest that a biological preparedness for a *grammatical* linguistic system is present in the "language-ready brain," and that an analyzed language can be created by children if it is not present in their environment. Thus millennia are not required to discover analyticity through cultural accretion. Arbib acknowledges that this aspect of his hypothesis is controversial, and that its truth or falsity is orthogonal to the extended mirror system hypothesis. Like Corballis's notion that the capacity for speech itself is a cultural invention (Corballis, 2002b), I see this argument as a diversion from the actual strengths of a gestural protolanguage hypothesis.

13.12 Critiques of Arbib's extended hypothesis

Three compelling critiques of Arbib's model, each of them voiced by several authors, emerged from the commentaries on his article. Two concern the weaknesses of his explanation of the evolution of speech, and the third concerns his dependence on an inadequate model of gesture and sign.

One criticism concerns Arbib's use of the term "speech" to refer to speech *production*, overlooking the considerable continuities between primate vocal *perception* and human speech perception (Rauschecker, 2005; Seyfarth, 2005). Citing field data on primate vocal perception, including his own lab's work on vervets and baboons, Robert Seyfarth argues convincingly for an unbroken continuity of perceptual abilities from the LCA to modern human speech perception (as we concluded in Chapter 4). Seyfarth's behavioral point (cf. Seyfarth and Cheney, 2005) is expanded at the neural level by auditory neuroscientist Josef Rauschecker, who

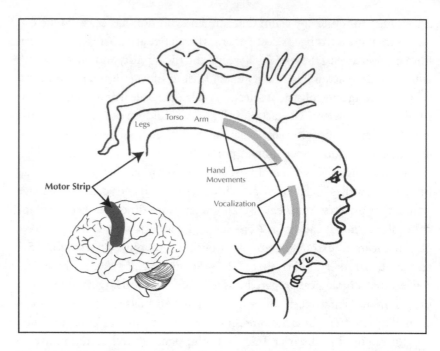

Figure 13.2 The motor "homunculus" – Control of contiguous body regions is mapped onto (mostly) contiguous regions of the motor strip in the frontal cortex. The hand area is directly beside the area controlling the facial and vocal musculature, which includes a large region that elicits vocalization when stimulated. This contiguity provides the spatial basis for Arbib's hypothesis that gestural control circuits "collateralized" speech control regions.

concludes that "the same anatomical substrate supports both the decoding of vocalizations in nonhuman primates and the decoding of human speech" (p. 144, Rauschecker, 2005). But these are oversights, not fatal flaws, and Arbib willingly concedes that his model has little to say about auditory perception, and that a clear distinction is necessary between auditory perception (where all parties acknowledge continuity) and vocal production (where the discontinuities are pronounced).

Turning to speech production, MacNeilage and Davis complain that gestural protolanguage hypotheses, including Arbib's, fail to explain the most salient features of speech, such as the phonological structure of consonant/vowel alternations (MacNeilage and Davis, 2005). These authors have suggested that the root of this basic phenomenon is found in mandibular cyclicities originally involved in chewing and other oral, ingestive phenomena (MacNeilage and Davis, 1990; MacNeilage, 1998a; MacNeilage and Davis, 2000). The neural details of oral control are critical in evaluating the EMSH. The primary discontinuity in the primate motor homunculus is between the thumb and neck (see Figure 13.2). This presents the major cortical leap for a manual gestural theory: from hand to face. Arbib finesses this leap by acknowledging both the existence of oral/facial mirror neurons, and the voluntary oro-facial control in monkeys, and by considering oro-facial motor control as a crucial bridge to full vocal control (incorporating laryngeal and respiratory control). MacNeilage and Davis suggest, in contrast, that rather than see these as "bridges," we can see such connections as the starting point for speech, and forget about the manual region entirely. As for gestural theories in general, and despite strengths regarding semantics, a chief stumbling block for Arbib's hypothesis remains the evolution of speech.

The final set of critiques concerns the nature of manual communication systems, including both gesture and sign, suggesting that Arbib conflates sign, gesture, and speech in a confusing manner. Once these systems are clearly separated, Arbib's case seems far less convincing. Starting with gesture, David McNeill and colleagues find that Arbib underestimates the degree to which modern co-speech gesture is part and parcel of a unified system of language output (McNeill *et al.*, 2005). This co-referential relationship suggests a continued co-existence of manual and vocal communication, throughout hominid evolution, rather than a "supplanting" of a mainly gestural system. Although Arbib's notion of an "expanding spiral" concedes this relationship, McNeill and colleagues feel he does not go far enough, and indeed argue that Arbib's hypothesis predicts for gesture "the evolution of what did not evolve instead of what did" (p. 139, McNeill *et al.*, 2005). While not hostile, this commentary reveals that scholars who have spent decades studying gesture do not necessarily favor gestural origins hypotheses. Turning to sign, sign expert Karen Emmorey is far more negative (Emmorey, 2005). The title makes her point clearly: "Sign languages are problematic for a gestural origins theory of language evolution." Emmorey stresses both the full linguistic equivalence of sign and speech, and the relative youth of existing signed languages, as points against gestural protolanguage and Arbib's notion of extended cultural evolution. She also cites the selective disadvantage of choking on food as a force opposing any transition from sign to speech. After weighing the advantages and disadvantages of modern sign and speech, and finding them essentially equivalent, Emmorey concludes that "there are no compelling reasons why the expanding spiral between protosign and protospeech proposed by Arbib would not have resulted in the evolutionary dominance of sign over speech" (p. 130). Again, the more closely one considers signed language, the less convincing gestural origin theories seem.

Summarizing, despite the important advances in specificity and testability that Arbib's new model provides, it remains in many scholars' minds inadequate in many of the same ways as earlier gestural origins proposals (Hewes, 1973; Armstrong *et al.*, 1984; Corballis, 2003), and a series of thoughtful critiques reveal major remaining difficulties explaining the evolution of speech. Arbib's response to these critiques further emphasizes a long, slow interdependence of sign and speech in his model. But this gradual expanding co-evolutionary spiral between protosign and protospeech, as well as the invocation of oral and facial gestures, blurs the boundary between an explicit, manually based gestural protolanguage (*à la* Hewes or Corballis) and a form of protolanguage that includes, but is not based upon, gesture (cf. Gentilucci and Corballis, 2006). Arbib's extended model provides a framework for appreciating the role that gesture might have played in language evolution, without drawing any sharp dividing line between vocal and gestural origins.

13.13 Summary: taking stock of gestural protolanguage

Our detailed consideration of gestural origins hypotheses, including the new additions of the mirror neuron findings, reveals both strengths and weaknesses. On the one hand gestural protolanguage provides a rather compelling hypothesis capable of explaining the evolution of voluntary, symbolic, open-ended communication in a rigorous, mechanistically grounded fashion. Gestural origins hypotheses are consistent with some important aspects of human language. The ease with which sign languages are acquired, and the existence of manual babbling in hearing infants, both make perfect sense, as vestiges of a past protolanguage. The ability of modern humans to communicate quite successfully via pantomime provides an existence proof of value: such a language would have been extremely useful in communication, and thus presumably favored among kin during human evolution. Gestural origins hypotheses are also consistent with comparative data from great apes, whose gestural capacities far outstrip their vocal learning abilities. Comparisons of human gesture with that of great apes make clear that gesture in our species has evolved beyond that present in great apes (Call and Tomasello, 2007). Gesture thus offers a smooth transition between the mostly imperative gesturing of apes and declarative, joint-attentional communication in humans. Furthermore, there can be little doubt that gesture has co-existed alongside vocal communication throughout the evolution of our lineage. Any broad theory of language evolution should incorporate the fact of sophisticated gesture in humans, not just the existence of speech.

But advocates of gestural protolanguage go beyond the mere co-existence and complementarity of speech and gesture to postulate that a *primarily* gestural communication system once existed in our lineage, and that its existence was a *necessary precondition* for the evolution of spoken language. From this perspective, several of these virtues transform into flaws. The most powerful flaw is the failure of gestural origins theories to convincingly explain the transition to spoken language – as some gesture advocates concur (e.g. Hewes, 1973). Many commentators have independently concluded that accepting modern sign as a fully adequate modality for linguistic communication makes it difficult to explain the virtually total transition, in modern humans, to spoken language (Kendon, 1991; Tomasello, 2002; Emmorey, 2005). Whether this flaw is seen as fatal clearly depends on whether one sees gesture and pantomime as the origin of language as a whole (in which case, I think, the problems are insurmountable), or whether one accepts the multi-component view advocated in this book. Seen as one of the evolutionary routes leading to specific components of modern language, its virtues stand on their own, and the "fatal flaw" is reduced to a previously unanswered question: How did our forerunners develop speech, including both the crucial vocal control underlying vocal learning, and the arbitrary referentiality built on top of it? For this vocal aspect of language, we need to turn to other, more compelling, hypotheses, which form the topic of Chapter 14.

*Denn der Mensch, als Tiergattung, ist ein singendes Geschöpf, aber
Gedanken mit den Tönen verbindend.*

(p. 76, Wilhelm von Humboldt, 1836)

*How did man become, as Humboldt somewhere defined him, 'a singing
creature, only associating thoughts with the tones'?*

(p. 437, Otto Jespersen, 1922)

14.1 Introduction: phonology remains puzzling

In the previous two chapters we have discussed models of the origin of
several key components of language. We saw how a lexical protolanguage
could provide a scaffolding for complex syntax, derived from pre-existing
conceptual primitives, and we saw how gesturally supported protolanguage
could provide one route to open-ended reference via iconic, intentional pantomime. However, both of these models have major difficulties explaining
human phonological competence. While Bickerton's model takes a capacity to intentionally generate complex vocalizations for granted, based on
the notion that chimpanzees have some cortical control over vocalizations,
we have seen that complex vocal control is not present in chimpanzees or
other apes, nor therefore was it present in the LCA, and it does not evolve
automatically as organisms get "smarter." Gestural theorists have grappled more earnestly with this problem, but most, including both Hewes
and Arbib, have had to postulate some separate selective story in order to
achieve the full *vocal* generativity of modern humans. This suggests that
the evolution of vocal control and phonology remains a major open issue,
and in this chapter we will discuss the ideas of theorists who have grappled
directly with this problem.

   In modern linguistics, vocal phonology is acknowledged to be a powerful generative system in its own right (to avoid circumlocution in this
chapter, I will restrict my usage of "phonology" to its original, audio-
vocal sense, explicitly excluding "sign phonology"). The phonological
subsystem, obeying its own rules, can generate a vast repertoire of

acoustically distinctive vocal signals by recombining a small set of sonic primitives. These primitives have no meaning themselves ("arbitrariness"), and open-endedness is achieved in phonology by combining them into larger structures ("generativity"). These key aspects of phonology combine to give "duality of patterning" – morpheme and words have meanings, but their phonological components do not. A crucial difficulty faced by gestural theories of language origin is how such duality can be achieved from an initially iconic, holistic, meaningful system. But such arbitrariness is almost automatic if you start with a vocal system, for the realm of the iconic is rather limited in vocalizations. Onomatopoeia can buy you some animal names, and some emotional expressions, via imitation, but not much more. But the flip side of this coin – too often overlooked – is that arbitrariness is a crucial step to a fully open field for semantic reference, and this is something that we gain almost automatically with the capacity to link meanings to vocal signals (Hewes, 1983). This provides an important virtue of models of language evolution that assume, throughout hominid evolution, a mainly vocal modality (e.g. Hockett and Ascher, 1964; Lieberman, 1984; Bickerton, 1990; Dunbar, 1996; Deacon, 1997; MacNeilage, 1998b; Wray, 1998).

Several scholars have also recognized the virtue (or even the necessity) of the second, generative, aspect of phonological systems. In particular, speech scientist Michael Studdert-Kennedy has championed the need for phonological generativity, based (following Abler, 1989) on the "particulate principle of self-diversifying system" (Studdert-Kennedy, 1998; Studdert-Kennedy and Goldstein, 2003). Studdert-Kennedy has rightly stressed the importance of the independence of a phonological representation from the semantic level, focusing attention on the crucial question of how such a system, including both complex vocal control, and vocal learning via imitation, could have evolved. To begin answering this question, it is useful to step back and consider phonology in its own terms, as a stand-alone system, rather than as subservient to syntax and semantics. What would "bare" phonology look like?

A phonological system generates a vast repertoire of structured sounds. In the case of most human languages, the potential output of the phonological system far outstrips the needs of the syntactic and semantic system. This is shown clearly by the existence of "pseudowords" like *grop*, *nax*, and endless others that are licensed by the English phonological system but don't happen to be used as morphemes and stored in the lexicon (in contrast to "impossible word" coinages like "stlar" or "ngopf," which violate English phonotactic constraints). The very existence of a category of pseudowords, which are easily processed and remembered, but are of absolutely no communicative use, encourages us to consider phonology as an independent generative system, whose neural basis and evolutionary history might be distinct from that of propositional, semantic language. They also illustrate that the output of bare phonology is meaningless: meanings are "attached" to phonological forms by processes independent of phonology.

Phonology generates this vast repertoire of meaningless signals by forming complexes from a small set of primitives (traditionally phonemes, or articulatory gestures (Browman and Goldstein, 1989), though it makes little difference to the argument if we choose features or syllables instead). These primitives are discrete, and categorically interpreted, rather than graded. The core generative process in phonology is the formation of larger units based on these primitives. This generative process is hierarchical, with syllables, phonological words, and phonological phrases being built up from them. There are constraints on these combinations: the system does not allow all possible combinations and permutations. Often, the system is highly constrained, for example only allowing syllables that start with a single consonant and end with a single vowel (such CV structure is a common phonological restriction). The primitives differ from language to language, as do the phonotactic constraints placed upon them, and thus the phonological system as a whole must be learned by the child, and is culturally transmitted. All these features must characterize "bare phonology" – and none of them entail any meaning being attached to the structures so formed. But why would an organism evolve such a system? Could such a system be of any use outside of language? Are there any parallels in non-linguistic domains, or in other species?

As the reader has no doubt surmised, the answer is "yes": "bare phonology" has an obvious non-linguistic parallel in humans in the form of music, particularly non-lyrical song (song that lacks meaningful words: think of jazz scat singing, the "doo wops" of fifties music, or children's nonsense songs). Music is a human universal, and although difficult to define, precisely because of its magnificent cultural variability, it involves a generative system, pumping out an endless set of "meaningless" structures, formed by hierarchically combining a small set of primitives (typically notes, but more generally tonal nuclei and syllable sequences in song, and acoustic events in instrumental music). Each culture has its own musical traditions, which involve both different sets of primitives ("scales") and constraints on the combination of notes into larger musical phrases ("styles"). These learned aspects of music directly parallel phonology, and are mastered very early in ontogeny (Trainor and Trehub, 1992; Trehub, 2003a; Trehub and

Table 14.1. Hockett's (1960) design features of language revisited

Design feature	Present in innate calls?	Present in music?
(1) Vocal auditory channel	yes	yes
(2) Broadcast transmission	yes	yes
(3) Rapid fading	yes	yes
(4) Interchangeability	yes	yes
(5) Total feedback	yes	yes
(6) Specialization	yes	yes
(7) Semanticity	?	no
(8) Arbitrariness	?	no
(9) Discreteness	no	**yes**
(10) **Displacement**	?	no
(11) **Productivity/Openness**	no	**yes**
(12) **Duality of patterning**	no	no
(13) **Cultural transmission**	no	**yes**

Design features of innate calls, music and language compared (see Introduction for details of each of Hockett's "design features"). Question marks for innate calls reflect the fact that some primate calls are "functionally referential" (e.g. alarm calls), but the existence of such calls in apes, and thus the LCA, remains unclear. The important differences between music and language on the one hand, and innate calls on the other, are that the former represent *discrete, generative* systems that are transmitted *culturally*, while innate calls are graded, closed systems transmitted genetically.

Hannon, 2006). From the point of view of Hockett's "design features" of spoken language, listed again in Table 14.1, there is a striking overlap (although Hockett himself evaded acknowledgment of several them by restricting his comparison to instrumental music; Hockett, 1960). Indeed, the main difference between spoken language and non-lyrical song is simply that the latter lacks specific, propositional meaning. Non-lyrical song thus automatically lacks the characteristics of duality and displacement that Hockett saw as central to language. More crucially, song possesses the characteristics of openness and generativity, as well as cultural transmission, that are needed for language. Of course, music and phonology are different in a number of ways as well (most obviously due to the discretization of time and frequency typical of most music), and music does not lack meaning entirely (see discussion below). Nonetheless, to a fairly good approximation, song *is* bare phonology: generative, arbitrary vocalization lacking discrete meaning (Fitch, 2006b).

These striking parallels between music and phonology, and the considerable overlap between design features of music and of language (Fitch,

2006b), provide a foundation for theories positing some form of "musical protolanguage" (Darwin, 1871; Jespersen, 1922; Livingstone, 1973; Richman, 1993; Brown, 2000; Merker, 2000; Mithen, 2005). These theories, particularly Darwin's, are the focus of the first part of this chapter. However, seen as one-stop solutions to the problems of language evolution, musical models remain incomplete. The problem of how meaning "infiltrates" such a system is discussed in the second half of the chapter. But from the viewpoint of the origins of phonology – the vocal generative component of language – the notion of a musical protolanguage is a powerful one, amply supported by data on the evolution of arbitrary, generative vocal systems in nonhuman species. In the same way that the homologies in ape gestural communication provide the most powerful comparative argument for gestural protolanguage, the repeated convergent evolution of song-like systems in at least six vertebrate lineages gives us numerous clues to the selective pressures and evolutionary circumstances that lead to music-like systems. Although vocal imitation was, indeed, a key innovation along the path to modern spoken language, repeated convergent evolution reassures us that, under the right circumstances, such systems readily evolve. We can thus posit a musical protolanguage without postulating a unique evolutionary process that occurred only once, in hominids. Finally, the existence of music, today, as a valued cultural artifact and a pervasive component in many people's everyday lives, is the best example so far of a hypothetical protolanguage that is "alive and kicking." Far from a "vestige," music remains an integral aspect of the human condition. All of these factors had already been carefully considered by Darwin when he finally offered his theory of the evolution of language, in *The Descent of Man, and Selection in Relation to Sex* in 1871.

14.2 Charles Darwin's theory revisited: "musical protolanguage"

As we saw in Chapter 11, Darwin sensitively avoided almost all discussion of human evolution in *The Origin of Species*, averring only that "light will be thrown on the origin of man" (Darwin, 1859). But Darwin's many opponents quickly pounced on human mental powers, and language in particular, as key weaknesses of his theory. Müller's dictum of language as an impenetrable Rubicon between humans and animals (Müller, 1861) was soon seen as a crucial argument against all-encompassing Darwinism, and indeed supported by Wallace (1871). By the time Darwin published his second magnum opus, *The Descent of Man* (Darwin, 1871), battle-lines were firmly drawn and language was widely seen as a crucial issue, not just for human evolution but for evolutionary theory itself. In a chapter simply titled "Language," in ten compact pages, Darwin laid out the impressive three-stage theory of language evolution reviewed here. The critical obstacle to understanding this theory is that the fundamental idea is non-intuitive: that the generative aspect of phonology might have emerged before it was put to any meaningful use. To consider this "speech before meaning" notion fairly requires a conscious effort to expunge ourselves of preconceptions of what early stages of language should look like. But, as Darwin made clear, there are plenty of phenomena to help us along this path and serve as "intuition pumps" – if only we are willing to consider them.

Starting by acknowledging that language "has justly been considered as one of the chief distinctions between man and the lower animals" (p. 53, Darwin, 1871), Darwin briefly discusses animal communication, including *Cebus* monkey alarm calls (today termed "functional referentiality") and dog barking (today's "emotional expression"), indicating that animals can sometimes communicate specific concepts and emotions to others. Despite these similarities, Darwin does not confuse such communicative calls with "articulate language," which he agrees is "peculiar to man." Then, in one sentence, Darwin deftly judges an issue that has consumed volumes in the contemporary literature on the evolution of speech: "It is not the mere power of articulation that distinguishes man from other animals, for as everyone knows, parrots can talk; but it is his large power of connecting definite sounds with definite ideas, and this obviously depends on the development of the mental faculties" (p. 54). The capacity for language is found in the brain, not in the vocal tract. Finally, Darwin observes that language "is not a true instinct, as every language has to be learnt. It differs, however, from all ordinary arts, for man has an instinctive tendency to speak, as we see in the babble of our young children" (p. 55). As Marler (1991b) has put it, language is not an instinct, but an "instinct to learn."

Darwin then turns to his primary analytic tool: the broad comparative method. He will exhaustively review the broad comparative database in ten chapters later in the book, so here he remains brief, concluding that "the sounds uttered by birds offer in several respects the nearest analogy to language," noting that song is learned and not innate, that, as in human babbling, young birds "continue practising" for months (today termed "subsong"), and that because of this learning process, birdsong in many species shows "provincial dialects." Darwin thus concludes that "an instinctive tendency to acquire an art is not a peculiarity confined to man." By distinguishing "articulate language" from vocal communication, by concluding that it is mental, rather than vocal, powers that are crucial, and by recognizing the parallels with songbirds' "instinct to learn," Darwin in 1871 not only provided a biological characterization of language which is thoroughly modern and, I believe, correct, but also supported this characterization with ample comparative data. His argument, up to this point, was not particularly controversial in his own time. He now comes to the heart of the issue – "the origin of articulate language" – and advances a three-stage scenario for language evolution that deserves serious consideration today. Unlike Darwin, I will present these stages in their proposed chronological order.

Darwin's first stage from an ape-like ancestor to modern human language was a greater development of proto-human cognition: "The mental powers in some early progenitor of man must have been more highly developed than in any existing ape, before even the most imperfect form of speech could have come into use" (p. 57). Elsewhere in the book, he makes clear that both social and technological factors may have driven this increase in cognitive power, which today would be associated with the genus *Australopithecus*. Next, Darwin outlines the crucial second step: the evolution of vocal imitation used largely "in producing true musical cadences, that is in singing" as do the "gibbon-apes at the present day." He suggests that this musical protolanguage would have been used in both courtship and territoriality (as a "challenge to rivals"), as well as in the expression of emotions like love, jealousy, and triumph. Based on his consideration of the comparative data later in the book, Darwin concludes "from a widely spread analogy" that sexual selection played a crucial role at this stage of language evolution (remember that Darwin invented the concept, and term, "sexual selection" in the same book). Thus he suggests that the capacity to imitate vocally evolved analogously in humans and birds.

The crucial remaining question is how an emotionally expressive musical protolanguage, which drove the origin of vocal imitation via sexual selection, could make the transition to true language. Here, he explicitly cites the previous writings of Farrar and Müller (and others), and concludes that articulate language "owes its origins to the imitation and modification, aided by signs and gestures, of various natural sounds, the voices of other animals, and man's own instinctive cries." In short, he embraces all three of the major leading theories of word origins of his contemporaries (see Chapter 11). Darwin's logic for this is clear: once proto-humans had the capacity to imitate vocally, and to combine such signals with meanings, any of the much-debated sources of meaningful words would be available, including onomatopoeia (an imitated roar for 'lion,' or whoosh for 'wind') and controlled imitation of human emotional vocalizations (mock laughter for 'happiness'). The attachment of specific and flexible meanings to vocalizations required only that "some unusually wise ape-like animal should have thought of imitating the growl of a beast of prey . . . And this would have been a first step in the formation of a language." Although, in contemporary terms, we might amend this as "formation of a protolanguage," the rest of the argument seems both clear and reasonable.

While Darwin thus derives a logically consistent scenario for spoken language from the comparative data, he does not suggest that the evolutionary process would stop there. For "as the voice was used more and more, the vocal organs would have been strengthened and perfected," and once in place, language would have "reacted on the mind by enabling and encouraging it to carry on long trains of thought" which "can no more be carried on without the aid of words, whether spoken or silent, than a long calculation without the use of figures or algebra." Comparing these two effects, on vocal organs and brain, he concludes "that the development of the brain has no doubt been far more important." Although Darwin was aware of the possibility of signed language (and indeed reminds us that using his fingers "a person with practice can report to a deaf man every word of a speech rapidly delivered at a public meeting", p. 58), he argues against gestural theorists, suggesting that the pre-existence in all mammals of "vocal organs, constructed on the same general plan as ours" would lead any further development of communication to target the vocal organs, not the fingers. Darwin is clear that this "power" is neural, and cites the aphasia literature as demonstrating "the intimate connection between the brain, as it is now developed in us, and the faculty of speech."

Although Darwin's summary contains a few statements that today can be recognized as errors (e.g. his belief in Lamarckian inheritance of acquired characteristics, or the idea that some monkeys can imitate sounds), a reader today cannot fail to be impressed by the broad sweep of data that Darwin brings to bear on the problem (ethological, neural, physiological, and comparative/evolutionary), and by his mastery of the logical and theoretical issues involved (his later discussion of historical linguistics, citing distinct parallels between phylogeny and glossogeny, presages modern "memetics" by a century). Summing his theory up in modern terms, Darwin recognized the distinction between the evolution of the language *faculty* and that of a particular language, seeing the former as crucial. He suggested that a crucial first step in language evolution was an overall increase in intelligence (consonant with the demonstrated increase in brain size in the hominid line: data unavailable then). Accepting a role for gesture, but rejecting a purely gestural origin for language, he suggests that the first protolanguage would have been musical, and that this stage was driven by sexual selection and has an apt analog in birdsong. The second bridge, between musical protolanguage and propositional, meaningful language was again driven by increased intelligence. Once meaning was in place, actual words would have been coined from various sources, encompassing any of the then-current theories of word origins.

14.3 Prosodic protolanguage: a contemporary update

Darwin's multi-faceted and self-consistent model for language evolution deserves, I think, serious consideration in future discussions of language evolution. All of the data cited by Darwin remain valid and relevant today, and new data have added considerably to the strength of Darwin's hypothesis. Comparative musicology has vastly broadened our notions of "music" from those of Victorian England, and confirmed Darwin's conviction that song is a universal (Nettl, 2000). The complexity of music as a generative system is also far better understood today (Lerdahl and Jackendoff, 1983; Jackendoff and Lerdahl, 2006). We now have a rich literature comparing music and language from both neural and theoretical viewpoints (cf. Avanzini *et al.*, 2005; Fitch, 2006b). Surprisingly, Darwin's model goes virtually unmentioned by many contemporary scholars (though see Donald, 1991), including those who themselves posit variants of a music-like protolanguage (e.g. Brown, 2000). Because Darwin's model has been so neglected, I will attempt here to reframe it in a modern light. First I will consider, from a modern perspective, evidence that strengthens Darwin's case, and then spotlight some aspects that he left out. The most important missing pieces of the puzzle in Darwin's time were a full understanding of the complexity of language (especially syntax), and an understanding of the neural bases of language and music. Then, after a brief discussion of Jespersen's important contribution to Darwin's model of musical protolanguage, we consider three modern versions, by Livingstone, Brown, and Mithen.

The core virtue of the musical protolanguage hypothesis is its logical explanation of the design features shared by song and spoken language, namely the use of the vocal/auditory channel to generate complex, hierarchically structured signals that are learned and shared across generations. Table 14.1 lists these features for language and song. Because these shared features do not involve meaning, this hypothesis can be simply stated as "phonology first, semantics later." But because the "bare phonology" postulated by this model provides sequences of units, arranged into phrases, and also rules for attributing phrase boundaries (e.g. phrase-final lengthening) and metrical structure (patterns of stress in words, rhythm in music), it goes far beyond simple phonetic segments to include some aspects of syntax. To make this song/speech equivalence explicit I have elsewhere suggested the term "prosodic protolanguage" as a near-synonym for "musical" protolanguage (Fitch, 2005b). Because the term "musical protolanguage" connotes discrete tones and beats (as does Brown's model of "musilanguage," see below), I introduced the term "prosodic protolanguage" to explicitly avoid this connotation. The term denotes a vocal system that was learned (rather than innate) and generative, but in which discrete tones (scales) and beats (regular rhythms) need not have been present. However, because this hypothetical system involved movements of the vocal tract (e.g. tongue and lips) it would have had proto-syllables which, by virtue of the shared mammalian capacity for categorical perception, would constitute a form of "syllabic discreteness" (also shared with modern phonology).

Given the difficulties other models have explaining precisely the learned, productive aspects of phonology, we must acknowledge the importance of Darwin's hypothesis for phonological evolution – even if it had nothing to say about other components of language. But this model of protolanguage has other virtues as well. Regarding syntax, prosodic protolanguage provides meaningless but hierarchically structured signals, which include phrases but lack many other syntactic complexities (restrictions on movement, pronouns, recursion, case marking and inflection, etc.) that are closely tied to semantics and conceptual structures. Put in other terms, this model delivers not just the generative aspects of phonology, but also some important parts of the syntactic interface. Nonetheless, there can be little question that hypotheses involving musical protolanguage require us to shed some of our core intuitions about language. Language involves propositional meaning right down to the core notion of "phoneme," and extracting the meaningless aspects of phonology demands us to rethink our contemporary linguistic notions of both phonology and syntax. More than other protolanguage models, musical protolanguage demands a radical rethinking of contemporary linguistic theory before it fits protolanguage. However, this is no criticism: we should not expect the theory of any exapted mechanism to provide an easy fit to precursor mechanisms which were its preadaptations.

The problems raised by meaning in this model are more difficult. Musical/prosodic structures are not *totally* devoid of meaning, but can indeed have powerful non-propositional associations. The ritualistic uses of music, typical of all human cultures (Nettl, 2000), exploit this form of meaning vigorously. Music has a kind of free-floating apparent "meaningfulness" that can attach itself, by force of association, to any type of repeated group activity and thenceforth both indicate and enrich events it accompanies (Cross, 2003). What would Christmas be without carols, a birthday without "Happy Birthday," or a church service without hymns? Personal associations of music with life events can be more idiosyncratic, but lose none of their power: songs can bring on a potent surge of memory or nostalgia when shared with a social partner. And for those who make music, communal performance of a shared repertoire of songs can have a profound unifying, barrier-dissolving effect. For these reasons, calling music "meaningless" would miss an important type of holistic, context-bound meaningfulness that makes so many people love music so deeply. Nonetheless, it is undeniable that music *lacks* a certain kind of meaning. Music lacks nouns, verbs, tense, negation, the embedding of meanings, and a host of other phenomena that play central roles in linguistic semantics. Thus, as discussed in Chapter 3, to be specific we can say that music lacks "propositional meaning." Musical meanings cannot be readily analyzed into words, representing correspondences between phonological structures and parts of semantic structures: the mapping from song to "meaning" is holistic, not compositional. With the exception of certain limited iconic devices, entire musical phrases or songs map onto whole contexts in music.

With these clarifications, Darwin's model can be neatly translated into modern linguistic terminology. Prosodic protolanguage was a system with phonological generativity, using a small set of elements to build hierarchical structures. These structures were vocally generated, voluntarily controlled, and learned, sharing core aspects of speech and song. Furthermore, they were culturally shared and infused with an ill-defined "meaningfulness," but lacked the atomic, decomposable, propositionally linked meaning that is the central feature of linguistic semantics. To the extent that there was a lexicon, it was a simple list of tunes or "riffs" – complex, multi-unit phrases linked to whole, context-bound events (e.g. recurring, socially shared events). The lack of propositional meaning entails that there was no duality of patterning (there is no "meaningful" layer on top of the meaningless signal structures) or explicit "displacement" (which would require tense, aspect, prepositions, and the like). In short, prosodic protolanguage possessed phonology, and parts of syntax, but lacked lexical, propositional semantics. Note that none of these positive features are imaginative fictions: they are easily observable features, today, shared by human music and phonology.

Most of the data that have become available since Darwin's time provide further support for his ideas. The comparative story has been strengthened by the discovery of new species, unknown to Darwin, which evolved vocal learning in the context of "song," including whales, seals, and hummingbirds (Fitch, 2006b). A recent boom in research concerning the neural basis of music, especially studies involving the functional imaging of musical tasks, provides strong evidence for processing resources that are shared between music and language (Patel, 2003, 2008). Although I will not attempt a detailed review of musical neuroscience here (cf. Zatorre and Peretz, 2001; Patel, 2008), the neural data that have poured in rapidly in the last decade are all consistent with Darwin's hypothesis: music and language have partially shared neural bases that are "intertwined" (Falk, 2000). While significant sharing of systems involved with sensory-guided motor planning (Zatorre *et al.*, 2007) may be unsurprising, "syntactic" aspects of music and language also have congruent neural foundations (Koelsch *et al.*, 2002; Koelsch and Siebel, 2005), as do some "semantic" components (Koelsch *et al.*, 2004). A right-lateralization of those aspects of music focused on fine pitch discrimination and harmonious tone combinations directly mirrors the left-biased linguistic network for phonetic and syntactic details (e.g. Zatorre *et al.*, 1992). This supports my suggestion below that discrete pitches are a recent addition, not present in protomusic. In general, a mixed pattern of shared networks for phonological and hierarchical processing, in contrast to independent networks for lexical access, phonetic detail, and propositional semantics, is what Darwin's hypothesis predicts, and what the current neural data reveal (cf. Fitch, 2006b; Patel, 2008).

Furthermore, the parallels between music and language also provide fertile, though mostly unexplored, fields for *testing* explicit evolutionary models of language evolution. For the experimentalist, music has a great empirical advantage over language: while every normal hearing person speaks and listens, and has vast experience producing and perceiving phonological structures, people vary considerably in their musical experience. We can easily find normal people who consider themselves unmusical, neither producing nor choosing to listen to music. In the same population (e.g. on a college campus) we will also easily locate highly musical individuals who began playing an instrument very early in life, spend many hours a day practicing, and who devote their lives to music. The possibility of conducting experiments contrasting expert and naïve subjects provides a clear advantage over language, because every normal human is an expert in speaking and perceiving their native language. "Natural experiments" involving children who grew up with little exposure to music, and no experience creating music, are commonplace, while in the domain of language such situations constitute child abuse. Studies of music thus provide a clear route for testing a specific model of language evolution, and will be of great interest in the future to explore the parallels between the neural bases for music and language.

Finally, an important testable prediction of the prosodic protolanguage model is that shared neural (and ultimately genetic) bases for phonology and song should lead to covariation among individuals in these traits, and independent variability in complex syntactic, or propositional semantic, processing systems. Although I know of no studies specifically designed to test this prediction, it is supported in a recent study examining musical and phonological skills in Finnish schoolchildren (Milovanov *et al.*, 2008). These authors found a good correlation between children's musical aptitude (as measured by the Seashore test of musical ability) and their capacity to produce foreign speech sounds. Event-related potential (ERP) data for these children suggest that this correlation is due to shared neural resources involved in these tasks. Although we cannot say at present whether such covarying individual differences have a genetic basis (they might reflect epigenetic changes due to experience with either music, foreign languages, or both), these findings point the way to rigorous tests of this prediction. As more information about the genetic bases for music and language becomes available, we should be able to test this hypothesis using individual genetic variability, exploiting single-nucleotide polymorphism databases. Eventually, as specific alleles involved in musical and linguistic brain networks are discovered, genetic variability can also be used to test the timing of selective sweeps, as for *FOXP2* (Enard *et al.*, 2002).

14.4 Prosodic protolanguage and modern music

Surprisingly few modern scholars have taken the musical protolanguage hypothesis seriously, often dismissing the "sing-song" theory in one breath with Müller's "ding-dong" or "heave-ho" theories. One possible reason is an overly literal application of the term "music" to this hypothesis, because several features found pervasively in modern music were not, by this hypothesis, present in musical protolanguage. Just as protolanguage was not identical to modern language, musical protolanguage was not identical to today's music. This "protolanguage" could be termed with equal validity "**protomusic**" – a

Table 14.2. Design features of music

Design feature	Present in language?	Present in innate calls?
(1) Complexity	yes	no
(2) Generative	yes	no
(3) Culturally transmitted	yes	no
(4) Discrete pitches	no	no
(5) Isochronic	no	no
(6) Transposability	yes	?
(7) Performative context	no	no
(8) Repeatable (repertoire)	no	no
(9) Non-referentially expressive	no	yes

Proposed design features of human music (from Fitch, 2005c).

hypothetical pre-musical precursor that existed in some extinct hominids. From this perspective, we can look at protomusic from the perspective of the "design features" of modern music (listed in Table 14.2), asking what features were *absent* from protomusic.

A prominent first candidate is instrumental music: the creation of complexly structured sound with parts of the body other than the vocal tract (typically, the hands). Although it is difficult to exclude the possibility that *Homo erectus* played drums (or at least clapped their hands – a behavior common in captive great apes), instrumental music is not necessary for the protomusic model. Thus, the general term "music" (which connotes instrumental music to many) is misleading – vocal *song* is the critical ingredient. When, precisely, instrumental music came into being is hard to say, though the archaeological record makes clear that sophisticated bone flutes were being made by *Homo sapiens* almost 40,000 years ago (Hahn and Münzel, 1995), and there is suggestive but highly controversial evidence that Neanderthals may have made or at least used flutes (Kunej and Turk, 2000). Thus, perhaps non-intuitively, this model stresses the alliance of song and speech, and emphasizes the difference between song and instrumental music.

Two further design features of music need not have been present in protomusic, both having to do with discreteness. Modern music, around the world, often uses a small number of discrete frequency units – "notes" – that together make up a "scale" (Nettl, 2000). A given song preferentially uses notes from one scale. Similarly, time is typically evenly subdivided into discrete "beats" which occur at a relatively regular tempo, and which are arranged according to a metrical structure of strong and weak events: the core ingredients of musical rhythm. Neither of these features are required in the model of protomusic we are discussing. Indeed, there are contemporary vocal styles of music lacking both forms of discreteness (Clayton, 1996). Thus, I think it is plausible that, although prosodic protolanguages/protomusics were syllabic and prosodically complex, they *did not* exhibit the discreteness typical of much modern music. The exaggerated intonation contours and repetitiveness of "motherese" (child-directed speech) may thus be a better model of protomusic than a modern song. However, despite being important for theories of *music* evolution, the phylogenetic timing of tonal or rhythmic discreteness is irrelevant to the evolution of language. For the purposes of this book, we can simply leave a question mark here, with no loss of explanatory power. Both of these factors emphasize the need to avoid an over-facile assumption of equivalence between protomusic and modern music: just as chimpanzees have continued to evolve since the split with humans, music has almost certainly diverged from protomusic in important ways.

However, one crucial feature of music that is not shared with language, or at least most uses of language, and that will play a crucial role in the discussions below is the design feature I call "**repeatability**." In most uses of language, a significant proportion of utterances are novel (e.g. almost every non-quoted sentence in this book). Pervasive novelty follows from combining the semantic use of language with the Gricean maxim of informativeness. If someone simply repeats the same phrase over and over, or their interlocutor repeats everything the first said, basic conversational conventions are violated. In music, in stark contrast, repetition is the norm. Within a piece, phrases are repeated (perhaps with some variations, but often exactly) and an identical piece may be performed over and over with no loss of satisfaction and no sense of boredom or maxim violation. Indeed, musical pieces typically require repeated listening to attain full satisfaction, and we happily subject ourselves to hundred or even thousands of rehearings of favorite songs. This striking difference between music and language has one exception: formulaic utterances such as greetings, niceties, ritualistic phrases, and such. Such formulaic uses of language may represent a "fossil" of a holistic stage of protolanguage, pervasively preserved in music but mostly lost in language (Wray, 2000, 2002). Again, we have abundant empirical evidence that such a stage is not just theoretically possible: it is *typical* of music, around the world, today.

Summarizing, modern data allow us to clarify and extend Darwin's musical protolanguage model somewhat, but in no way change its essential point:

musical protolanguage provided a preadaptation for spoken phonology and some aspects of syntax. The most crucial supporting evidence for the "song first" argument is the abundant comparative data on the evolution of vocal learning. Darwin knew only of parrots and songbirds as capable of vocal learning, but today we can add new species capable of complex vocal learning, nearly all of which use their vocal capabilities in a fashion more like song than meaningful language, and none of them have anything like a lexicon or propositional semantics. As Darwin recognized, these data strongly support the notion that something like a prosodic protolanguage can evolve rather easily in vertebrates in the service of non-linguistic but still highly adaptive functions. As a solution to the problem of the origin of vocal control and phonology, this hypothesis has few peers. What this model leaves problematic is meaning: How could a complex proposition–expression system have been bolted onto a system like musical protolanguage, that lacked such explicit, semantic capabilities?

14.5 Adding meaning to prosodic protolanguage: Jespersen's model and the origins of meaning

As already mentioned, Darwin's theory of musical protolanguage has had an oddly persistent tendency to be dissociated from its author's name, and to be rediscovered by later scholars. Many post-nineteenth-century champions of musical models fail to give proper acknowledgment to Darwin, even if they reference Darwin (1871) in some other connection (e.g. sexual selection; Jespersen, 1922; Mithen, 2005). Although surprising, such neglect might be viewed as a virtue: surely the repeated rediscovery of an idea, by multiple unconnected scholars, adds something to our confidence in its basic value. On the other hand, intuitiveness is no infallible guide to truth, and one might reasonably suggest that the repeated disappearance of an idea indicates its basic worthlessness. It thus seems worthwhile to evaluate each of what amount, in scholarly terms, to rediscoveries of Darwin's ideas, in their own terms.

The most significant advance over Darwin's model was offered by the linguist **Otto Jespersen**, in the final chapter of his comprehensive *Language: Its Nature, Development and Origin* (Jespersen, 1922). Jespersen was a forward-thinking linguist for his times, strongly affirming the complexity and adequacy of so-called "savage languages," and he incorporated his broad knowledge of comparative linguistics into his model for language evolution. After a brief review of earlier "speculative theories" (incorporating Max

Müller's nicknames, but dismissing Müller's own "ding-dong" theory with particular vehemence), Jespersen aims to try a new approach, using contemporary empirical data from child language acquisition and comparative linguistics as the starting point and working backwards in time. Jespersen's "inductive" approach is clearly consonant with the modern approach to language origins advocated in this book. Focusing on humans, he starts with the observation that bipedalism, pair-bonding, and the prolonged helplessness of human babies set us off from other primates, and provide conditions favoring vocal play (his model is unambiguously a "vocal origins" theory). While Jespersen cites animal communication as potentially relevant as well, he considers the field too immature at that point to be useful (though he does cite avian alarm calls in his discussion of the origins of meaning).

Jespersen's model is concisely summarized by his statement that language "began with half-musical unanalyzed expressions for individual beings and solitary events" (p. 441, Jespersen, 1922). His defense of the "half-musical" proposition is based on two important factors beyond those cited by Darwin. First, unlike Darwin, Jespersen had access to what had become a rather comprehensive literature on comparative musicology, and he cites Bücher's monumental *Arbeit & Rhythmus* in support of the idea that all cultures possess music, and indeed that music is much more pervasive and egalitarian in most societies than in the Western tradition of concert halls and professionals. He cites the Swedish peasant Jonas Stolt's reminiscence of his youth, when "young people were singing from morning till eve . . . both out- and indoors, behind the plough as well as at the threshing-floor and at the spinning-wheel" as evidence that even in Europe, music had played a much more integral role in daily life than it did in 1820, when Stolt could mourn "if someone were to try and sing in our days as we did of old, people would term it bawling" (p. 435). Jespersen noted that in many traditional cultures, "song" often lacks meaningful words, and can consist of totally meaningless syllables, or include "interspersed words suggesting certain ideas and certain feelings" but with incomplete sentences and no need for definite or complete propositions. "The mere joy in sonorous combinations here no doubt counts for very much" (p. 436). Both factors are consistent with modern comparative musicology.

Jespersen offered another argument that protolanguage was "half-musical" which seems considerably less convincing today. Observing that historical change in attested languages (e.g. Latin to French), and from reconstructed languages like Proto-Indo-European to their modern descendants, is relatively consistent, Jespersen argued that these changes, if extended backwards in time, would provide a picture of protolanguage. Since attested historical change works in the direction of tone loss (e.g. the shift from tonal accent in Latin or Greek to stress accent in their modern derivatives), Jespersen argued that "primitive language" (his term for protolanguage) was even more tonal. He also cites the preponderance of tonal languages outside of Europe as support for this, though he hastens to add it is weak support because such tonal languages are not "primitive" in any biological sense. Today, few believe that we can push the comparative method back 50,000 years, much less 500,000 years. However, there is another way of interpreting this aspect of Jespersen's argument: as an existence proof for a certain class of glossogenetic transformation. Attested transformations in modern language from tone languages, where pitch plays a central phonetic role, to languages where it doesn't, demonstrate that such transformation is possible, and neatly nullify any arguments from disbelief to the contrary. Surely, over the longer periods of time that language has been evolving, similar changes might have occurred, perhaps even more strikingly. In this sense, historical loss of tonality remains relevant to contemporary discussions.

Jespersen warns against a misinterpretation often raised in argument against any theory of musical protolanguage. "[W]e must not imagine that 'singing' means exactly the same thing here as in a modern concert hall. When we say that speech originated in song, what we mean is merely that our comparatively monotonous spoken language and our highly developed vocal music are differentiations of primitive utterances, which had more in them of the latter than of the former" (p. 436). Nor was Jespersen's hypothesized protolanguage itself an early form of "language" in today's sense: "[o]ur remote ancestors had not the slightest notion that such a thing as communicating ideas and feeling to someone else was possible. They little suspected that . . . they were paving the way for a language" (pp. 436–437). He emphasizes that despite our contemporary picture of "communication of thought as the main object of speaking, there is no reason for thinking that this has always been the case," or indeed for supposing utterances had any other purpose than "amusing oneself and others by the production of pleasant or possibly only strange sounds" (p. 437). This indeed is an important guideline in considering *any* model of protolanguage. Evolution lacks foresight, and any hypothesized intermediate form must have its own contemporary adaptive value for its bearers. There is no reason for supposing that such adaptive value(s) must be the same as in later forms: original and current functions might be quite different.

14.6 Analyzing holistic protolanguage

Jespersen's second core proposition in his model is that protolanguage used "unanalyzed expressions for individual beings and solitary events" (p. 441). In modern terms, Jespersen is claiming that protolanguage was **holistic** (the term used by Allison Wray, see below). Initially, just as in birdsong or music, meanings were attached to vocal phrases in a holistic, all-or-none fashion: a vocal phrase might be linked to a particular ritual (as for birthdays or Christmas today), a particular activity (working, playing, or drinking), or some individual person (as in the *leitmotifs* of opera). But in no case was there an articulated mapping between parts of the signal and parts of the meaning: a lexicon and syntax were absent, and the semantics was vague and non-propositional. Today's typical situation – where words mapping to objects and events (nouns, verbs), and serving other conceptual or grammatical functions (adverbials to mark tense and aspect, prepositions, and the host of inflections and other closed-class syntactic words and particles) – was absent. They were created, via a long analytic process spanning multiple generations.

Jespersen uses the same inductive form of argument to support this assertion as before. But in explaining how meaning could be linked to musical phrases, he enters his element, using considerable linguistic data to make a powerful case. His model goes beyond Darwin's vague suggestions about "increasing intelligence" to offer a specific path from irregular phrase– meaning linkages to syntactic words and sentences, offering examples of such transitions from attested language change. Pointing to the pervasiveness of both irregularities, and attempts (often by children) to analyze these into more regular, rule-governed processes ("over-regularization"), Jespersen suggests that hominids possessing protolanguage might readily form associations between certain meaningless songs and memorable events, or as proto-names for the people who sing them. He gives a detailed account for how such wholes can gradually be analyzed into something more like words (indeed, much of Jespersen's linguistic career was devoted to studying this process of *analysis*, which he termed rather unfortunately "secretion," in contrast to the *synthetic* accretion or coalescence of small units into larger ones).

Summarizing, Jespersen's model extends Darwin's basic notion of musical protolanguage by adding a credible explanation of the origin of meaning. His distinction between analytic and synthetic routes to syntax continues to play a central role in contemporary discussions (cf. Hurford, 2000). Interestingly, Jespersen rejects these terms as misleading: he prefers the term "entangled" for the more holistic end of the spectrum and "isolated" for the other, analyzed, pole. Jespersen pointed out that analysis of whole phrases into subcomponents occurs not just in language change, but is typical of child language acquisition as well. Children do not typically hear single words, but entire phrases, and one of the most basic and indispensable tools of language acquisition is an ability to segment words out of a continuous speech stream. This process is not always flawless, and mistakes provide a starting point for linguistic change. Although ontogeny in a modern language-ready brain does not demonstrate anything about phylogeny, the existence of this process occuring before our eyes weakens arguments that such segmentation is logically impossible (Tallerman, 2007, 2008). Jespersen's "holistic" model of meaning, augmented by an "analytic" stage which created modern language, remains a focus of discussion and debate today, to which we will return.

14.7 Modern versions of musical protolanguage theory

As with Darwin's musical protolanguage hypothesis, Jespersen's model goes largely uncited today (and indeed Jespersen himself made scant reference to Darwin's model). We now consider rediscoveries of musical protolanguage by later scholars. During the 1970s renaissance, Frank Livingstone briefly aired a musical model, in a short *Current Anthropology* article titled "Did the Australopithecines sing?" (Livingstone, 1973). Livingstone cites neither Darwin nor Jespersen – a lapse of scholarship noted in several responses to his article – and provides a far less convincing and wide-ranging case than either of his predecessors. His basic argument is that "singing is a simpler system than speech, with only pitch as a distinguishing feature" (p. 25). While this may be true, singing has its own complexities (as those who can speak perfectly well but can't sing will affirm), and this argument provides a poor foundation for an evolutionary theory. Livingstone cites the work of Marler and Nottebohm demonstrating that birds learn their songs, but his main focus is the speculative claim that song in proto-humans served a function of "individual and group recognition" and was used in a territorial context. But he rightly points out that "adaptation to this learned, open signal system" would have "preadapted the hominids to both speech and symboling" and thus grasps the central insight of musical protolanguage theories: their ability to account for phonological flexibility and generativity.

Another early adopter of the notion of musical protolanguage was Bruce Richman, whose long experience with the vocal exchanges of gelada baboons led him to see these "proto-conversations" as a primate model for the evolution of speech (Richman, 1976, 1987, 1993). Geladas (*Theropithecus gelada*) are an Old World monkey, related to the baboons of genus *Papio*. Geladas are unusual in several ways: they are specialized grass feeders who spend most of their time upright, using their unusually dexterous hands to bring seeds, grass blades, and rhizomes to the mouth. Probably in response to this typical position, they have evolved a wholly novel "sexual swelling" on their chest, whose color indicates sexual state in much the same way as the hindquarter swelling of baboons or chimpanzees. Geladas also form unusually large groups during feeding, and maintain social contact via elaborate vocal exchanges. Using geladas as an example, Richman finds fundamental similarities in the vocal production system of humans and other primates, and the use of vocalizations in what Dunbar later dubbed "vocal grooming." Similar traits can be found elsewhere, rarely, among primates (e.g. synchronization in gibbon song). Thus, from Richman's primate perspective, the crucial links between a musical protolanguage and a pre-existing communication system are their social functions (an idea also emphasized by later scholars such as Wray in discussion of "holistic protolanguages," see below).

14.7.1 Mithen's "Hmmmm" model

A very wide-ranging popular introduction to the musical protolanguage hypothesis is provided in paleoanthropologist Steven Mithen's tome, *The Singing Neanderthals* (Mithen, 2005). Mithen coins an acronym for musical protolanguage – "Hmmmm": holistic, manipulative, multi-modal, and musical. Unlike most previous theorists, Mithen attempts to outline several specific intermediate steps in the evolution of musical protolanguage (a postulated later version "Hmmmmm" adds mimetic to this list), and to align them with particular hominids using archaeological and paleontological data. Taking aim at the argument of Pinker (1997), that music is a non-adaptive byproduct of language (the "auditory cheesecake" hypothesis), Mithen cites numerous aspects of music that seem adaptive, and are difficult to explain as "spandrels" of language or as "technological innovations." He concludes that hominids since australopithecines have been steadily developing musical (specifically song) abilities, and that language *per se* is the recent innovation tied to the increasingly "fluid" or cross-modal intelligence that typifies our species. He hypothesized that the Neanderthals of his title were singing (and dancing) creatures, even more tied to, and in tune with, music than are modern humans.

I strongly recommend this book as a general introduction to musical protolanguage: Mithen reviews the relevant factual terrain in an enthusiastic and evocative fashion, knitting a remarkably broad array of evidence together into an accessible whole. However, this broad approach mixes the truly compelling aspects of Darwin's model with some less convincing arguments (cf. Botha, 2009), and often goes far beyond existing or even imaginable data. Two important insights of Mithen, among contemporary writers, is the value of a Jespersen-style conceptual marriage of Darwinian musical protolanguage with holistic models of meaning. Mithen also is the first since Darwin to grapple seriously with the questions about the nature of the selective pressures that would make a musical protolanguage adaptive, and to clearly recognize the value of kin communication in driving the evolution of music, via parent–offspring communication (see below).

14.7.2 Steven Brown's "musilanguage" model

A rapidly growing interest in the biology and evolution of music has followed the revival of interest in language evolution since 1990. In a major contribution to this literature, a group of scholars in Stockholm at the now-defunct Institute of Biomusicology organized a conference on the evolution of music in 1997, and produced a volume of papers with contributions from major players in animal communication and musicology (Wallin *et al.*, 2000). In one of these papers, musicologist/neuroscientist Steven Brown has again rediscovered Darwin's model, but with a few twists and a new label. Like Darwin and Jespersen, Brown posits a protolanguage that provided a common precursor for music and language, but which was identical to neither of these modern systems. Brown briefly discusses five possible models for the evolutionary relationship of language and music. In one of these, the "parallelism" model, the two systems evolved independently and have no intrinsic connection. In a second, the "binding model," the two have always been separate systems, but have interacted with one another evolutionarily, in a way reminiscent of Arbib's "expanding spiral" of speech and gestural communication, each scaffolding the other. Brown rejects these two models as unable to explain the "deep similarities" in music and language.

Brown then discusses what he considers three separate models positing a shared hominid communication system, in which the shared features of modern music and language are homologs deriving from this primitive precursor. In the "musical outgrowth" model, the precursor system is called "protolanguage," giving rise to language, and music is seen to derive from this main line. In its converse, the "language outgrowth" model, the tables are turned, and a mainly musical line of evolution from protomusic to music gave birth to language. Finally, Brown terms the compromise model, where the proto-system gives rise to both, the "**musilanguage model**." This final model, Brown asserts, is the major innovation of his paper (although he cites no previous scholars in association with any of these models). I personally see little merit in distinguishing these three models; from an evolutionary viewpoint they are entirely equivalent, and the difference hinges on a terminological distinction. Neither Darwin's model, nor Jespersen's, makes any commitments as to which "line of evolution" is primary, for to do so would be analogous to claiming that the line from LCA to humans is "primary," while chimpanzees are an off-shoot, or *vice versa*. Brown's stated reason for favoring his model is "that it greatly simplifies thinking" and "avoids endless semantic qualifications" (p. 277, Brown, 2000), and he aims to end such discussion by terminological fiat: "the common features of these two systems are neither musical nor linguistic but *musilinguistic*" (p. 277). I find all of these terminological choices equally unhelpful: rather than deciding whether some trait corresponds to "music" or "language," we need to specify its mechanistic structure and function, as I have tried to do above when comparing music and phonology. Terms are already available for many specific features (prosody in general, or rhythm, stress, accent and meter, intonational phrases, etc.) and their similarities (and differences) when employed in music and language should be our focus. I think Brown's account would have been strengthened by using well-established terms rather than creating a raft of new ones, especially since his paper often remains vague about which specific linguistic features it aims at (cf. Botha, 2008). Indeed, Brown pervasively conflates "language" and "speech." Nonetheless, some have embraced the term "musilanguage" (e.g. Mithen, 2005), so perhaps it does "simplify thinking," or at least simplify discussion in a desirable way.

Beyond these terminological issues, most of the ground covered in Brown's article has already been discussed above: the common traits of music and language are held to derive from a precursor communication system, possibly in *Homo erectus,* that possessed qualities of both, but was neither. What are these common traits? Here, I believe, Brown's reach exceeds his grasp, for he hopes to derive not just phonological generativity and phrase structure from his musilinguistic proto-system but also semantics. Specifically Brown suggests that a core feature of musilanguage was "lexical tone," the "use of pitch to convey semantic meaning" (p. 279, Brown, 2000). Correctly observing that the majority of the world's languages are tonal (Fromkin, 1978), Brown suggests that the first step in the evolution of musilanguage was the use of discrete level pitches – sung notes – as units of meaning directly parallel to the "referential expressive vocalizations" of vervet monkeys. The obvious objection – that modern tone languages do not use discrete, level notes as music does – is answered by the assertion that the underlying representation of Chinese or other tonal systems is theoretically discrete. After a discussion of this problem with reference to tone phonology, Brown concludes that "speech, like music, is based on scales consisting of discrete pitch levels" (p. 282, Brown, 2000). This claim seems Procrustean to me: better to assume a non-discrete system in musical protolanguage which remained this way in language, but became discrete in music (Fitch, 2005b). In any case, by fusing two mechanisms into a single evolutionary step, and thus seeking to evolve both the generative capacity of phonology, and an intentional, word-like form of basic reference in one step, Brown's model jettisons a core consideration that makes Darwin's musical protolanguage hypothesis attractive. Thus clarity requires that we distinguish Brown's musilanguage hypothesis from other musical protolanguage models, particularly that of prosodic protolanguage defined above, and not treat all of these as synonyms for "musical protolanguage."

14.7.3 Group selection

The other main distinction of Brown's musilanguage model is equally problematic. Based on "half a century of ethnomusicological research," Brown asserts that the principle function of music-making is the promotion of "group cooperation, coordination and cohesion" (p. 296, Brown, 2000). Although I agree with Brown that this is one important function, there are good reasons for skepticism concerning attempts to hold up any single function as driving the multi-step evolution of a complex trait (cf. Fitch, 2005b; Mithen, 2005). But Brown goes further, asserting that such group-binding functions are inexplicable from a neo-Darwinian viewpoint: "*Theories of individual selection must explain how these essentially group-cooperative musical devices evolved in the service of within-group competition.* I doubt that such models will be able to account for them" (his emphasis, p. 297, Brown, 2000). Brown then concludes that group selection is necessary to account for the group-binding function of music. But, as discussed in Chapter 12, this conclusion is unwarranted, and reflects a theoretical blind-spot: Brown, like many others, has missed the possibility of a role for kin selection in driving cooperation within groups. This is heralded by Brown's assumption that individual selection implies "within-group competition." But, as we have already seen, the concept of inclusive fitness obviates any such assumption:

there is no theoretical difficulty in understanding the evolution of group cooperation *if the cooperators are related.* Given that members of *Homo erectus* bands were almost certainly more closely related to each other than to members of competing bands (just like modern hunter-gatherers), there is no need to posit additional non-Darwinian forces to drive the cooperative aspects of modern human communication. Inclusive fitness does the job (Hamilton, 1975). While Brown's idea might be applicable to *cultural* group selection, as developed by Boyd and Richerson (1985), that model requires a biological predisposition for group conformity to already be in place, and cannot account for its origin. In conclusion, I find the two main innovations of Brown's musilanguage model (lexical tone and group selection) to be steps away from, rather than towards, plausibility, relative to Darwin's and Jespersen's models.

14.7.4 Sexual selection

A more plausible selective force for the evolution of music was championed by Darwin: sexual selection. The notion that complex, learned vocalization ("song") evolved in the service of territoriality, vocal competition, and courtship is abundantly supported by the comparative data on "singing" in other vocal learners. In most songbirds, in phocid seals, and in those baleen whales that sing (e.g. humpbacks and bowhead whales), it is the males who sing, and they do so before and during the mating period (Catchpole, 1980; Janik and Slater, 1997; Nowicki *et al.*, 2002; Van Parijs, 2003). A similar sexually selected function for human music and language has been championed by Miller (2000, 2001). As Darwin and Miller both note, sexual selection is theoretically attractive as a mechanism driving rapid evolution of unusual traits, because of the possibility of nearly unlimited selection strength (in highly polygynous species) and of runaway selection. However, sexual selection also poses a major problem due to inconsistency with some key empirical facts about human music (or language). Sexually selected traits in general, and song in whales, seals, and birds in particular, typically appear exclusively (or at least are far more pronounced) in males. The few exceptions prove the rule: in polyandrous birds, where females compete for male mates who brood the eggs (e.g. the Indian painted snipe *Rostratula beneglensis*, as discussed by Darwin), it is the females who have bright plumage, occupy territories, and have pronounced vocal adaptations (cf. Fitch, 1999). Furthermore, such sexually selected traits appear late in development, just before or during sexual maturity. In humans, in sharp contrast, both music and language are exceptional in appearing in infants, very early in ontogeny (at least a decade before sexual maturity) and equally *in both sexes*. The existence of musical abilities (and song in particular) in both babies and adult females raises a major objection against any model that relies exclusively on sexual selection to evolve such traits.

However, the phenomenon of female song in birds offers some instructive insights into this problem. Although we know far less about female birdsong than that of males, research in the tropics increasingly suggests that female song is more common than previously suspected (cf. Langmore, 2000; Riebel, 2003). Detailed data concerning both duetting species (where males and females co-defend their territories with interlocking vocal parts, often of great complexity), and of species where lone females sing (Langmore, 1998), suggest that female song has evolved, repeatedly, from ancestral clades with only male song. Although it seems likely that males are still by far the more vocal sex overall, it is becoming increasingly clear that duetting is more common in sedentary tropical (especially rainforest) birds – species which have received far less study than temperate species – and that female song is not as exceptional and non-adaptive as Darwin thought. Indeed, the assumption that "only males sing" became a self-fulfilling prophecy, because sex of monomorphic birds was determined by singing, presumed indicative of males. These recent data suggest a gradual transition is possible from male-only song to a sexually egalitarian distribution. Thus an early musical protolanguage stage could be driven by sexual selection on males, while later stages involved a shift to selection on both sexes.

Second (in line with Miller's hypothesis), a situation may arise in pair-bonding species where *mutual* mate choice occurs. In species with no male parental care (like most mammals), males may be quite indiscriminate about mating: females are a limited resource and thus the choosy sex. But if males contribute to child-rearing, as they do in many birds, and focus their reproductive efforts on a single female mate, they too have a strong interest in mate fertility and quality (cf. Trivers, 1972). In certain situations female competition for males can be as strong as male–male competition and complex female song can evolve in a sexually selected context. For example, females alpine accentors *Prunella collaris* (Langmore, 1996) sing complex songs that function in mate attraction, due to heavy competition in the short breeding season. In general, then, in accordance with evolutionary theory (e.g. Emlen and Oring, 1977), it is not the sex *per se* but the *operational* sex ratio and competition among a sex that determines which sex(es) will undergo sexual selection. Thus female song in birds offers two avenues of defense for Darwin's hypothesis that sexual selection drove the evolution of song in both sexes, even if it may be inadequate to drive the cooperative semantic aspects of language (cf. Fitch, 2004a; Zawidzki, 2006; Fitch, 2007).

14.7.5 Kin selection

However, as we already saw in Chapter 12, there is a third option as the selective force behind musical protolanguage: aiding relatives. This possibility has been explored in considerable detail by Ellen Dissanayake, an important pioneer in evolutionary aesthetics (e.g. Dissanayake, 1992). Playing off Darwin's comment that music is not "of the least use to man in reference to his daily habits of life," Dissanayake retorts that musical capacities are "of indispensable use in the daily habits of life of countless women, specifically mothers, and their infants, and that it is in the evolution of affiliative interactions" that we can discover their origins (p. 389, Dissanayake, 2000). She provides a long and compelling list of the functions quasi-musical interactions between mothers and infants serve in modulating infant arousal, strengthening the mother/infant bond, and socializing the infant. Interestingly, even the majority of mothers who profess to have no singing ability, nonetheless sing frequently to their babies, providing pleasure for both parties (Street *et al.*, 2003). This diverse set of highly useful functions, appearing very early in development, and universally found among human cultures, are hard to square with Pinker's "cheesecake" hypothesis (cf. Mithen, 2005).

Many of these ideas receive strong support from the child development literature, where the evolutionary relevance of these early interactions is becoming increasingly recognized (e.g. Fernald, 1992). Similar ideas have been advanced in the literature on music development, where the early sensitivity to, and indeed preference for, musical stimuli is a well-documented fact (e.g. Trainor, 1996; Trehub, 2000, 2003b). These ideas have been explored more recently, with peer review, by Falk (2004). Each of these scholars has specific arguments about both the structure and function of these early prelinguistic interactions between mothers and infants: Sandra Trehub and Laurel Trainor emphasize the usefulness of the specifically melodic component (lullabies and play songs), while Anne Fernald, Dean Falk, and Ellen Dissanayake all emphasize the more general rhythmic and tonally variable aspects common to child-directed speech ("motherese") as well as child-directed music. All of these researchers, however, concur on the fundamental utility of such interactions, on their cross-cultural ubiquity, and indeed on their important role in infant care.

The notion that the origin of music is to be found not in interactions between related adults, but in these earliest interactions between mother and infant, has considerable theoretical appeal (as well as far more empirical support than either sexual- or group-selection models; Trehub, 2003b; Fitch, 2005b). We know that major changes in parental care have occurred in the hominid line since the LCA, with important effects on all aspects of human sexuality (pair-bonding, concealed ovulation, male parental care, reduced dimorphism, . . . ; Lovejoy, 1981). We also suspect (though this is less certain) that habitual bipedalism created a problem for women, already faced by Australopithecines: what to do with your newborn baby. While most primate mothers carry their infants on their bodies during the altricial period of infancy, this is difficult for an upright biped. Carrying a baby on the shoulders may have been an option, and Australopithecine babies may have clung to their mother's head hair (or perhaps Australopithecines retained a chimpanzee-like pelt). However, the changes in foot anatomy due to bipedalism would already have reduced infant grasping capabilities, even at this early stage. By the time of *Homo erectus*, if not before, the need to "put down the baby" must have become a crucial issue for hominid mothers (Falk, 2004). As Falk has observed, mothers of many non-primate species, and a few prosimians, "park" their babies in some safe, secluded place while they forage. Over small distances the use of vocalization to remain in contact with, and calm, the distant infant could have represented a key innovation in mothering. By hypothesis, "motherese" in this broadest sense provides a compelling alternative explanation for the evolution of musical protolanguage, paralleling the arguments I have advanced about the role of kin selection in evolving honest, informative semantics (see Chapter 12). The strikingly early maturation of both musical and linguistic abilities in infants is perfectly consistent with both models.

It might seem that, in solving the "males only" problem of sexual-selection models, this "motherese" hypothesis creates a new quandary: Why can *males* sing in our species? But there are two obvious answers, not mutually exclusive. First, humans also evolved male parental care, and fathers also carry babies, sing to them, and speak with the exaggerated pitch contours of "parentese" to them (hence the growing use of the neutral term "infant-directed speech"). Second, as Dissanayake has emphasized, infant-directed vocalizations are not a one-way street. Instead they are highly interactive, with infants playing an important and active role (Trevarthen, 1999). Since both male and female infants require these capabilities, a lack of sexual dimorphism (rather than female bias) is predicted in infants by these models. Again, these variants on the "musical protolanguage" theme emphasize that protolanguage has not gone away in modern humans, but continues to play an active, vital role.

These factors provide an important additional virtue for kin-focused models of musical protolanguage, concerning the "key innovation" of semantics. In a pre-semantic protolanguage, children would be exposed to song from parents whose signals were "informative" only in personally idiosyncratic ways (perhaps as mnemonic devices to help remember the song). The "insight" that such utterances might have particular, composite meanings would then occur in children, who would in a sense "steal" ideas from songs that were not intentionally communicative. An innate tendency to interpret parental utterances as meaningful is both obviously present in children today, and a logical necessity for language acquisition, and this infant-first model for semantic evolution provides an adaptive context and function for this evolved feature. These considerations all make the kin communication models discussed earlier, applied to both musical and lexical protolanguage, both theoretically appealing and empirically well grounded.

14.8 Critiques of musical hypotheses

Despite their repeated reinvention, these variations on the "musical protolanguage" theme seem non-intuitive to many scholars, and have often been rejected in the strongest terms. For example, in response to the version of Livingstone (1973), Gerald Weiss complained that "anything is possible, but must we be subjected to speculation bordering on the absurd when no evidence in the primate line gives us any justification to entertain such a notion?," and concludes that "Livingstone's speculation . . . clearly did not come to him by any consideration of a body of evidence" (p. 103, Weiss, 1974). Weiss rejects the "speculation that mankind began its linguistic career by singing like the birds" as "pure quackery," concluding that "the trees destroyed to print this material were sadly wasted" (p. 104). Jespersen's version was treated equally derisively by his contemporaries. Müller's dismissal of Darwin's version seems positively courteous by comparison. But these are all variants on the "argument from disbelief," and the vehemence of a critique is no indicator of its scientific value. What serious objections have been raised to a "musical protolanguage"?

The most commonly offered scientific critique of musical protolanguage hypotheses is that the parallels between song in birds and humans "represent analogies rather than homologies, and are therefore irrelevant to the evolution of human speech" (e.g. p. 27, Steklis and Raleigh, 1973).

Mithen (2005) makes a similar critique. But they miss a main point of the analogy/homology distinction: homology allows the deduction of ancestral states, but analogy allows us to assess evolutionary likelihood and test hypotheses about function (Harvey and Pagel, 1991; Ridley, 1997). Examples of convergent evolution show *that* a specific trait can evolve, and allow us to test hypotheses about *why* such traits evolve. When multiple independent lineages have evolved the same capability, we have both an existence proof and a rough estimate of likelihood, of how great an evolutionary leap it is for a lineage lacking the ability to acquire it. For vocal learning in vertebrates, which has evolved independently in at least six different evolutionary episodes, the leap appears to be a rather small one that happens readily under certain circumstances. Similarly, Arbib responded to my arguments based on vocal learning in non-primates (Fitch, 2005a) that they are "irrelevant" to the mirror system hypothesis, "which asserts that humans had a particular history." This comment reflects a failure to appreciate the value of a broad comparative approach, incorporating both homology and analogy, for testing evolutionary hypotheses. In the same way, the repeated evolution of bipedalism in birds, marsupials, rodents, lizards, and dinosaurs allows us to better understand the evolution of this trait: as the copious insights thus gained demonstrate (DuBrul, 1962; Gatesy and Biewener, 1991; Carrano, 2000). Despite its regrettable frequency, this "critique" reflects anthropo- or primato-centrism, and a failure to comprehend the value of convergence in evolutionary arguments. When understood in this context, the repeated convergent evolution of mechanisms supporting complex vocal learning and phonological syntax for "song" in whales, seals, and multiple bird lineages is strong evidence in favor of the musical protolanguage hypothesis.

Another obvious critique of musical protolanguage mirrors one advanced previously, concerning the inability of gestural protolanguage to account for vocal imitation. Musical protolanguage leaves unexplained the existence of abundant co-speech gesture today, and the possibility of fully linguistic signed languages. While true, this is no critique: studies of living apes show that sophisticated gestural capabilities were *already present* in the LCA, long before language evolution began (Call and Tomasello, 2007). The proclivity for communicative gesture is a basal trait, one of many language-relevant traits we share with our primate cousins. That gesture persisted as language evolved is no more mysterious than the persistence of laughter or crying, and indeed could have "scaffolded" the addition of meaning onto vocal signals as suggested by Donald (1991) and Arbib (2005). The possibility of fully linguistic signed languages reflects the domain-general nature of syntax and semantics, but does not require the evolution of novel manual motor control (though sign *is* a problem for hypotheses like that of Lieberman (1998), that posit a direct relationship between speech and syntax).

A more justified complaint about musical protolanguage hypotheses is voiced in a penetrating recent critique of Brown's "musilanguage" hypothesis, in which linguist Rudi Botha calls attention to crucial examples of vagueness and confusion in existing expositions (Botha, 2009). As Botha observes, Brown's model pervasively confuses language with speech, and numerous aspects of Brown's argument that concern language are linguistically unsophisticated at best, or simply incorrect. Brown's model thus fails to recognize the crucial and specific explanatory role of a musical protolanguage for speech, independent of language. However, Botha clearly notes that his critique is specific to Brown's model, though he also notes similar areas of vagueness in some of Mithen's arguments. In my estimation, the model of prosodic protolanguage I have discussed above, based on Darwin's core insight and as extended by Jespersen, evades Botha's criticisms by making clear which specific aspects of modern language are being explained by the model, and which (especially semantics) are not. Thus, the process by which meaning, in its modern propositional, lexical sense, was combined with a musical protolanguage remains problematic. We now turn to modern solutions to this problem, which extend Jespersen's notion of a holistic protolanguage.

14.9 Holistic protolanguage today: Alison Wray's model of holistic protolanguage

As we have seen, Jespersen used Darwinian musical protolanguage as a foundation for meaning, which evolved from it in two additional steps. First, meaningless sung phrases, of complex phonological structure, came to be associated with events or people. Like birdsong or whale song, only broad, holistic meanings ('stay away,' etc.) were attached to such complex signals. Second, via a process of analysis, these "holistically mapped" meanings became subdivided, and linked to separate chunks of the already complex phonological signal. This notion of a holistic protolanguage, followed by a subsequent stage, where utterances were "analyzed" into modern compositional language, has recently been an area of major controversy and discussion (Wray, 1998; Kirby, 2000; Arbib, 2005; Tallerman, 2007). Discussion begins with linguist Allison Wray's proposal of **holistic protolanguage** (Wray, 1998, 2000). Wray's model assumes the pre-existence of phonology and semantics, and posits only the simplest form of link between the two.

Specifically, Wray envisions a protolanguage with a complex, culturally transmitted vocal repertoire (bare phonology) *plus* a simple, holistic mapping between meanings and whole phonological signals. The model is holistic because, although both the phonological structures and the meanings are complex, *there is no compositional mapping between the parts.* The model posits the existence of a complex generative phonology and a complex generative conceptual system, but only simple holistic/associative links between these two systems, linking wholes to wholes. Wray emphasizes that, in a functional sense, the proposed protolanguage is continuous with nonhuman primate communication systems. The proposed protolanguage existed for practical communication (speech acts like requests and commands), and posessed a simple, direct, and arbitrary link between call "meanings" (thought of as whole propositions, not words) and whole vocal signals. The highly non-intuitive consequence of this model is a protolanguage lacking words in the modern sense: there are no nouns and verbs, but simply whole phrases linked to whole meanings. This may seem a bizarre idea, until you consider such idiomatic oddities as *abracadabra* (which links to some vague meaning like 'now observe a magical surprise') or *gesundheit* (as often used in American English, meaning 'I acknowledge and forgive your recent sneeze'). Such "frozen phrases" or "formulaic utterances" are found in all languages, and are used surprisingly often in social contexts. Obviously, no part of *abracadabra* means 'magic' or 'see' any more than part of *gesundheit* means 'sneeze' (*Gesundheit* means 'health' in German, but this is unknown to most English speakers). But even phrases like *by and large* or *How do you do?* which *can* be syntactically analyzed are nonetheless stored as formulae: the knowledge that one should utter /haudjudu/ to politely acknowledge one's first meeting with someone does not follow from the meanings of the words as combined by the rules of syntax. Such formulae are simply learned, and "frozen" in the lexicon together with the appropriate pragmatics of use.

Wray considers such formulaic uses of language to be living reflections of the earlier protolanguage, and thus stresses continuity between the semantic/communicative function of holistic protolanguage with primate communication. She argues that, even today, much phatic communication and social manipulation is accomplished with a holistic system, in the form of pleasantries, stock phrases, ritual incantations, and similar speech acts. Wray stresses the discontinuity between holistic protolanguage and the analytic, rule-based, generative system that followed, taken by many linguists as the core of language. She suggests that true syntax derives not from such communicative needs but from its use in thought. She thus concurs with Chomsky (1980), Bickerton (1990), and many others in suggesting that the function of fully syntactic language is the expression of *thought*, in the most general sense, rather than communication *per se*. A limited, functional system with holistic qualities sufficed for the communicative needs of *Homo erectus*, and continues to do considerable work in the social domain even today. Holistic utterances in this model bear more resemblance to "words" in highly polysynthetic languages (such as Chukchi or Mohawk), in that each is composed of many syllables, but before they have been successfully analyzed into their component morphemes by the child.

Wray is quite clear that her model is compatible with numerous other proposals in the literature, including Bickerton's or Arbib's, and Arbib has indeed applied the holistic model to gestural protolanguage as well – holistic models need not be allied to a particular sensory-motor modality like voice or gesture. But the required notion of a complex signal structure that is already present, before any fractionation or analysis begins, is neatly accounted for by Darwin's updated theory of a prosodic protolanguage, as Jespersen recognized with his original holistic model. Despite this excellent fit between Wray's model and the musical protolanguage models just described, she herself makes little mention of music or song, and would not consider her idea wedded to such models. However, the virtues of a holistic model fit best with a "musical" notion of the preceding form, as Jespersen noted, and others (especially Mithen, 2005) have elaborated.

14.10 Critiques of Wray's holistic protolanguage

Wray's notion of a holistic protolanguage has recently been subjected to strong criticism by linguist Maggie Tallerman (Tallerman, 2007, 2008), attacking virtually every aspect of the holistic model. Her multiple criticisms fall into three groups. The first set of critiques, like Botha's, concerns vagueness: Wray has not fully fleshed out the process by which her proposed protolanguage evolved. Tallerman criticizes the notion of continuity between primate calls and Wray's holistic protolanguage, apparently missing the distinction between continuity in semantic mapping *versus* a sharp discontinuity in the phonological structure. It is true that Wray over-emphasizes *semantic* continuity over *phonological* discontinuity (Wray, 1998, 2000): the prosodic protolanguage of Darwin, Jeserpersen, or Wray is learned and generative, constituting a major break with other primate vocal systems. Tallerman's various criticisms, correctly affirming that the social, neural, and vocal tract basis of "primate calls" is very different from their basis in modern language, misses the main virtue of a musical protolanguage:

it provides one step in an evolving system which overcomes precisely that difference. Tallerman also correctly observes that an "analytic" stage could never be successful if protolinguistic utterances were monosyllabic: "the prior existence of discrete segments is taken for granted in this scenario" and thus that "the holistic approach is vacuous, since in effect we already have words" (p. 585, Tallerman, 2007). A similar critique seems implicit in the comments of Studdert-Kennedy and Goldstein (2003). These arguments overlook the distinction between phonology and semantics at the heart of the holistic model. What we have, in prosodic protolanguage, are phonological "words" which are just chunks of syllables, but not morphemes. In modern language, meaning runs all the way down through the system: the very term "phoneme" is a phonetic difference *that makes a difference to meaning*. Tallerman suggests that extraction and memorization of phonological units from a meaningless vocal stream would be impossible, without critical contrasts (read "semantic contrasts") to differentiate phonemes. But this simply reflects a failure of imagination, easily countered by the fact that birds learn their songs, and children learn melodies, without any semantic cues to guide them. To properly appreciate the notion of bare phonology we must conceptually separate all of these semantic elements from the phonological system. Once we do so, this class of criticisms lose their force.

A more telling line of criticism concerns Wray's assertion that massive periods of time – as much as 100,000 years – might be required for the analytic process to reach its modern stage, and that this would be a purely cultural process. As Tallerman correctly notes, phonological systems are in a constant state of flux (this is equally true for musical styles in humans, humpback whale song, and learned birdsong). Phonological systems change over small numbers of generations, if only because of the accumulation of errors ("random drift") as well as active forces (e.g. the desire for novelty). Thus we can't assume that a phonological system like that of prosodic protolanguage would provide a static target over 100 years, much less 100,000 years. Tallerman's critique here seems valid, but not damning: once a community has "pulled out" even a single meaningful chunk (the first proto-word) from the otherwise holistic stream, subsequent sound changes in that chunk will be no more problematic for protolanguage learners than they are for a child learning today's ever-changing languages. The cultural ratchet can keep turning, and more proto-words can be extracted as time goes by. Though Wray may overstate her case in suggesting 100,000 years as *necessary* for analysis, given one million years of *Homo erectus* evolution it is reasonable to suggest that such a timespan is *available*, if needed.

A final form of criticism of holistic protolanguage – often seen as most obvious, and telling, by critics – again seems to me to reflect a failure of imagination. Indeed, Tallerman specifically states that "by definition, protolanguage...has no syntax" (p. 88, Tallerman, 2008), as if the nature of past protolanguage(s) is a matter of definition rather than the open question being debated. The argument starts with the idea that Wray's and Jespersen's argument based on child language acquisition is misleading, because children are learning from adults who already have words. But "How can speakers ever agree on a set of meanings in the first place?" asks Tallerman (p. 590, Tallerman, 2007). These critics suggest that it would be impossible for speakers to settle on an agreed meaning when an utterance is holistic (cf. Bickerton, 2003). This argument seems to assume what holistic models explicitly deny: that the "meanings" of holistic phrases were like the highly articulated propositional meanings we express in modern languages. Although some of Arbib's examples do encourage this interpretation (e.g. Arbib's 'run over to the other side of that mammoth'), my impression was that these were given tongue in cheek, and Wray certainly uses much more simply holistic meanings (e.g. 'give it to me'). But, in a musical protolanguage, meanings can be even more vague and context-bound than this: simple associations between recurring events and the vocal phrase are adequate. No major cognitive skills are required to learn an association of this sort: a dog learns the association between "walk" and going for a walk quite readily, and there's no reason protolanguage learners couldn't do the same. We need only imagine food songs, hunting songs, rain songs, and the like as "proto-meanings" to recognize that there is no difficulty whatsoever in either agreeing upon meanings, or in children learning them.

The other side of this argument has more bite. How, given a parent whose phrases express only wholes, and do so without any regular structure mapping to meaning, could an analytic child discover even a single "proto-word"? Each regularity discovered by the child might be outweighed by examples that refute it. The force of this argument is blunted by the fact that children occasionally *over*-regularize their parents' speech: making up words that *are not present* in their parents' speech, or that of their local community. One need only extend this undeniable process over a far longer time period to recognize that children can and do "discover" words that, as far as their parents are concerned, are not there. Wray (1998) raises the additional possibility that children may simply ignore any counterevidence: once humans have decided on a "rule," however imperfect, they are loath to give it up. Another possibility highlights the *parents'* reaction to their children's "discoveries": we often find a child's over-regularizations delightfully humorous and charming. Indeed, in private, family speech, they may become lexicalized and used *as words*. All of these possibilities are attested in modern child language acquisition, suggesting that Tallerman's assertion (Tallerman, 2008) that a holistic protolanguage would require learning mechanisms far beyond those of modern humans overstates the case drastically. Clearly, children do (occasionally) over-analyze, and proponents of holistic protolanguage plausibly suggest that, over time, this is the thin end of the wedge into a fully analyzed modern linguistic system. But could such a process actually be adequate to convert a holistic protolanguage into a synthetic one (allowing for a remaining few irregularities and formulaic expressions around the edges)? Tallerman and Bickerton find this implausible, but this, as for many aspects of evolution, is a place where intuition is a poor guide. This makes it an apt problem for computer simulation.

14.11 Simon Kirby's simulations of holistic/analytic transitions

Linguist and computer scientist Simon Kirby has used computer simulations to address this issue (Kirby, 1999, 2000). Kirby and colleague's models are relatively simple, involving a community of agents who produce random but complex multisyllabic utterances heard by others. Hearers then learn these utterances, by rote, and produce them themselves later. Thus far, this is essentially a model of birdsong learning, and plausibly represents some variant of a musical protolanguage. However, the utterances are also holistic: meanings are holistically mapped onto whole complex signals, and there are no words. Meanings are assumed to be available, by inference over context, to the hearers. Thus Kirby has set up as his initial state a prosodic protolanguage, with a set of holistic signal ↔ meaning mappings: a protolexicon that simply lists pairings of complex signals with complex meanings. This is thus a semantic- and phonology-rich, but syntax-free, system.

Kirby's simulation allows gradual, but staggered, agent death and replacement. Surviving group members constitute a "cultural memory," implemented in what Hurford terms "the arena of use." Crucially there is *no natural selection* in Kirby's model: no rewards are reaped for accurate communication, nor penalties paid for continuing to generate absolutely random utterances. Despite this, cultural change occurs: over many generations, the agents converge, reliably, on a syntactic, analytic language, applying preexisting *conceptual* primitives onto chunks of signal. In the privacy of its own simulated mind, each agent attempts to "compress" or streamline its lexicon, storing partial semantic/phonology matches that happen by chance as a means of optimizing storage and retrieval. Ultimately, this produces a population-wide modern lexicon that associates *phonological words*, rather than whole utterances, with meanings. The process driving this cultural convergence is a simple frequency-based learning bias. Once one agent has made an analytic "mistake," it tends to produce that string more often. Subsequent agents remember this more regular aspect of the developing proto-lexicon simply because they hear it more frequently. This cultural evolution process reliably drives a random holistic system to become a compositional one, in all runs of the simulation (Kirby, 2000).

Kirby's model has been dismissed by some as falling into the trap of assuming what was to be proven (e.g. Tallerman, 2007). Critics suggest that by assuming the existence of discrete segments *and* of conceptual structure, Kirby's model "builds words in." But as we saw above, this criticism reflects a failure to appreciate the plausibility of a holistic model of musical protolanguage positing complex phonological structure ("phonological words") *without morphemes* or words in the modern semantic sense. The phonological complexes of prosodic protolanguage would be subunits without meaning – more like guitar riffs or small melodic phrases than modern words. Kirby's model demonstrates clearly that given such a generative phonological system, plus the articulated cognitive system assumed by most modern commentators, a lexicon which maps meaning subunit onto phonological subunits can, and indeed *will*, develop given some uncontroversial assumptions about the learning system.

While Kirby's model provides a proof of concept, the argument that further natural selection would cease once cultural change kicks in is unconvincing. Given the importance of linguistic communication to human children, and given a pervasive change in the nature of the ambient communication system, biological selection will still occur, favoring "segmentation-prone" infants who master the new analytic system more rapidly (in contrast to previous generations, where selection would favor the learning of holistic systems; Wray, 2000). The fact that languages still have both analytic and holistic (formulaic) components, combined with a large array of language-learning difficulties in human children, suggests the intriguing possibility that genetic variance in these capacities might still exist (with holistic tendencies revealing themselves, for example, in dyslexia), and provide a tool for future tests of the holistic hypothesis. Holistic models predict that any human-specific gene variants favoring analytic learning should be young, since they constitute the final step in the evolution of modern language. In contrast, a lexical protolanguage model predicts that the capacity for conceptual analysis, and mapping it to words, was the first, most ancient step in the evolution of language. Although, today, the idea of testing these models using genetic variation among living humans remains speculative, the analysis of genes like *FOXP2* (Enard *et al.*, 2002) or *MYH16* (Stedman *et al.*, 2004) provides proof of concept, and if widespread allelic variations turn out to correlate with subtle linguistic differences, as suggested by Dediu and Ladd (2007), genetic data may help resolve such debates in the coming decades.

14.12 Synthesis and prospects

In summary, Darwin's model of "musical" or "prosodic" protolanguage and Jespersen's notion of holistic protolanguage have been combined and extended by various scholars today. The multi-stage model below synthesizes many authors' writings, building on Darwin's core hypothesis that proto-song preceded language. The resulting model posits the following evolutionary steps and selective pressures, leading from the unlearned vocal communication system of the LCA to modern spoken language in all of its syntactic and semantic glory:

(1) *Phonology first:* The acquisition of complex vocal learning occurred during an initial song-like stage of communication that lacked propositional meaning. Based on comparative data, Darwin's proposal of a sexually selected function remains one plausible driving force, but the kin-selection model proposed by Dissanayake and others is an equally plausible contender, and these suggestions are not mutually exclusive. This system of "bare phonology" provided a learned, complex, generative vocal communication system, with multiple units being combined into a hierarchical, but propositionally meaningless, signaling system. Thus, the sharpest distinction between humans and chimpanzees – vocal imitation – arose first, along with simple "phonological" aspects of syntax (sequencing, hierarchy, and phrase structure). This innovation satisfies the "evolvability" constraint, as Darwin argued, because of its frequent convergent evolution in other vertebrate clades, including birds, whales, and seals.

(2) *Arbitrary, holistic meaning:* The addition of meaning proceeded in two stages, perhaps driven by kin selection. First, holistic mappings between whole, complex phonological signals (phrases or "songs") and whole semantic complexes (context-bound entities: activities, repeated events,

rituals, and individuals) were linked by simple association. This connection between arbitrary signals and concrete conceptual entities gives us Saussurian arbitrariness naturally (avoiding a problem faced by gestural models). The system was used communicatively to influence others, either among adults (as stressed by Darwin and Wray) or between parents and their offspring (as stressed by Dissanayake and Falk). At this stage, musical protolanguage was a manipulative, emotionally grounded vocal communication system (Mithen), not a vehicle for the unlimited expression of thought.

(3) *Analytic meaning:* During an extended "analytic" phase, these linked wholes were gradually broken down into parts: individual lexical items "coalesced" from the previous wholes. This is the step stressed by Jespersen and Wray, and modeled by Kirby. It requires no further genetic changes. Pre-existing conceptual primitives were the seeds for the semantic components of these proto-words and, as argued by Bickerton, for complex syntax. The mapping onto phonological components was arbitrary, driven by chance associations, gradually regularized by the "ratchet" of glossogenetic, cultural transmission. Even today, this fusion of analyzed conceptual structures to analyzed phonological structures remains incomplete. The unanalyzed "residue" forms a relatively peripheral component of spoken language but, as Wray stresses, one that remains in constant pragmatic use. Holistic protolanguage is still with us today. The mismatch between language as a successful vehicle for thought, and its frequently depauperate use in social intercourse, is intelligible by this model, due to the dual origin of the phonological and semantic components of language. Thus, Premack's paradox (that language is vastly more powerful than necessary for communication), and the apparent contradiction between the two uses of language (for communication *versus* thought) is resolved.

(4) *Modern language – genetic fixation of the analytic urge:* As the language of its community grew more analytic, pressure for rapid analytic learning by children became strong. This drove the last spurt to our modern state, where language is mostly composed of atomic meaning units (morphemes, or true words). As argued in Chapter 12, this last stage seems most likely to have been driven by kin selection, for the sharing of truthful information among close relatives.

By this model, some components of syntax evolved early, during the musical protolanguage stage (e.g. hierarchy and concatenation, as well as linearization). But the central aspect of syntax in many modern theories – the assembly of large, complex *semantic* structures that map in a compositional form onto such basically phonological structures – came later. Many of the complexities studied by modern syntacticians (variations in inflection and conjugation, different restrictions on order, agreement, and many other factors) would not, by such a model, be a biologically evolved aspect of language at all. Rather, they would represent various culturally discovered solutions to the ill-defined problem of mapping high-dimensional conceptual complexes onto simple hierarchical phonological representations, and out to the sensory-motor interface of speech or sign. As Chomsky has recently noted, "the problem of externalization can be solved in many different and independent ways" and those processes specific to individual languages are "subject to accidental historical and cultural events: the Norman conquest, teen-age jargon, and so on" (Chomsky, 2010). This is an idea supported in various forms, often under the heading "grammaticalization," by many contemporary scholars (e.g. Heine *et al.*, 1991; Tomasello, 1999; Steels, 2000).

A contemporary model that shares many virtues with this approach, but is not termed a "musical" model by its inventor, is the "mimetic protolanguage" model of psychologist Merlin Donald (Donald, 1991, 1998). Donald posits a cognitive stage reached by *Homo erectus* that was accompanied by a "mimetic" communication system much like the holistic systems we have discussed here. But, while accepting an important role for facial and vocal expression (essentially the prosodic protolanguage I have described above), Donald additionally stresses the role of gesture (and by extension dance) in such a system. As we have already seen in Chapter 13, there can be no doubt that hominids have been gesturing since the LCA, and that the human gestural system has grown more complex, iconic, and intentional during hominid evolution. Thus, like Arbib's model, Donald's emphasizes the importance of a multi-modal communication stage, rather than a purely vocal flexibility. This emphasis is shared by Dissanayake and Mithen, who stress that mother/infant communication is a rich, multimedia affair, and that the common denominator in motherese, child-directed song, and other aspects of interaction is *rhythm* and the shared, intentional, proto-conversational temporal dimension of human sociality. But these extensions are easily absorbed by the term "musical protolanguage," if we allow our notion of music to be informed by all of the world's cultures, rather than the active performer *versus* static listener of most Western music. Thus enriched, I see musical protolanguage models as strong contenders, which easily incorporate the valid insights of both lexical protolanguage models and gestural models.

Having outlined a series of "how-possibly" models (Brandon, 1990), we see that in principle there are many possibilities. One can construct a number of different "evolutionarios" that move, step-by-step, from the reconstructed capabilities of the LCA to those of modern humans. However, as they become more specific, these models can be tightly constrained by current knowledge of language, brain development, and evolution: it is by no means trivial to come up with a complete model that can account for all that is currently known. However, to move beyond plausibility, we must inquire whether such models can be tested, empirically. I believe that the answer is "yes." Let us consider some testable predictions of the musical protolanguage model, for example.

The core hypothesis of musical protolanguage models is that (propositionally) meaningless song was once the main communication system of prelinguistic hominids. This suggests that the mechanistic bases of song production and perception should show many signs of being adaptations: they should involve reliably developing neural mechanisms, and the genetic basis for these should show the signature of past selection to fixation. We would also expect listeners to show strong biological reactions to, and developmental readiness for, musical stimuli. Because the neural mechanisms underlying song were precursors of phonological mechanisms in spoken language, we expect considerable overlap between phonological and musical abilites (within individuals) and mechanisms (across individuals). However, other mechanisms specific to language (in particular all those associated with propositional semantics) should be disjunct from those involved in music, except to the extent that listeners assign meanings of some sort to musical stimuli (e.g. restful *versus* exciting, or associations such as weddings or birthdays). Finally, because language has today superseded music as the primary communicative medium of our species, we expect language-specific mechanisms to bear the genetic signature of more recent selection. For the same reason, we expect musical mechanisms to have experienced relaxed selection, which may again leave genetic traces, and will also be reflected in increased variability among individuals in musical, as opposed to semantic, abilities and mechanisms. All of these predictions are testable, and indeed most of them already find considerable empirical support in the contemporary musicological and brain-imaging literature. The main exceptions are the genetic predictions: because we have not yet isolated phonological- or music-related genes, analysis of genetic variability or amino-acid substitution ratios has not yet been possible. However, recent progress in the search for genes involved in phonology (e.g. Fisher and DeFries, 2002) and music (e.g. Drayna *et al.*, 2001) suggests that such genes will be discovered soon enough. Thus, we have a number of strong and testable predictions which, if confirmed, will provide substantial support for musical protolanguage hypotheses (and note that none of these predictions follow from lexical or gestural protolanguage hypotheses).

15 | Conclusions and prospects

The reader, reaching these final pages, might understandably feel a sense of frustration that I have neither specified which of the many hypotheses discussed in the book I believe to be correct, nor laid out a theory of language evolution I believe to be true. Instead, I have stressed both the weaknesses and strengths of many different hypotheses, approaches, and perspectives on language evolution. The book may seem inconclusive as a result. Such a frustration is natural, and inevitable, given the goal of this book. My aim was to provide readers with the intellectual framework and empirical data to draw their own conclusions about language evolution, and further to generate their own hypotheses (perhaps quite different from any reviewed here). I have stressed the need for a research program in language evolution that sympathetically considers multiple hypotheses, in parallel, derives contrasting predictions from each, and tests these predictions empirically. Given this goal, it would be inconsistent for me to conclude by defending my own favored theory of language evolution: my argument was for an overall approach, not for any particular model.

There are enough books proffering strong opinions about language evolution, vigorously defending each of the hypotheses we have discussed (Donald, 1991; Bickerton, 1995; Calvin and Bickerton, 2000; Lieberman, 2000; Burling, 2005; Mithen, 2005). My intent here was not to add to this list, but to integrate their arguments into a larger framework. The fact that so many serious scholars have reached conclusions that are, in some cases, diametrically opposed indicates, I think, that we do not yet have fully convincing answers. My suspicion is that creative combinations of many approaches will be needed to find a satisfactory resolution to current debates, and that future progress will depend more on testing existing hypotheses than on developing new ones.

For example, each of the three main approaches to protolanguage has strengths and weaknesses. The strengths typically concern features seen as central to human language by the theorist in question, such as the signaling medium in gestural or musical models, or syntax for lexical theorists. Within these broad categories, we find important differences among theorists focused on continuity (e.g. the similarity between apes and humans in their use of gestures) or discontinuity (e.g. the sharp divide between apes and humans with respect to vocal learning). But, as emphasized throughout this book, each of these perspectives is valid for different components of language, and a complete model must incorporate them both. The discontinuity among primates in vocal learning demands an adaptive explanation, and I argued above that Darwin's "musical protolanguage" model, suitably updated, provides such an explanation. But it would be foolish to overlook the continuity in ape and human uses of gesture. Apes use gesture meaningfully, as do modern humans in all cultures, and we have every reason to believe therefore that gesture played an important supporting role in communication throughout hominid evolution. Thus, I endorse Arbib's notion that speech and gesture interacted during the evolution of language, perhaps during what Donald terms a "mimetic stage" of human evolution. I see these combined models as providing the signaling prerequisites for a later "lexical protolanguage," rather than as three conflicting models.

But accepting that different models of protolanguage have their strengths does not entail a bland "everyone's a little bit right" conclusion, and I believe that dispassionate comparison of the virtues and weaknesses of such models will lead to much stronger scientific conclusions in the coming decades. The key factor in reaching such conclusions will be *converging data* from many different disciplines, used to test multiple, specific hypotheses. A key source of data will be genetic: as our understanding of the genetic bases for unique human cognitive traits grows, we will have an invaluable window back into our evolutionary history. The genetic data will help to resolve debates that no fossils ever could, by allowing us to analyze the order in which different cognitive capacities and proclivities appeared during hominid evolution. The stunning discoveries of evo-devo, and the deeply conservative nature of vertebrate development, mean that we can avail ourselves of a much wider range of species than previously suspected. This broad comparative approach will help us understand how cognitive processes work, at a mechanistic level, and how they evolve, at the phylogenetic and adaptive levels. Although at present we simply don't know the answers to many central questions, I conclude that eventually we can know, *if* the field adopts a data-driven, hypothesis-testing approach. In this book I hope to have illustrated many open questions and testable predictions, and the kinds of data that are needed to adjudicate among the various approaches currently available.

I hope to have convinced the reader that an empirical, data-driven approach to language evolution is possible, but will require far more interdisciplinary collaboration and understanding, and respect for differences of opinion and perspective, than has been typical in the past. A pluralistic multi-component perspective on language is a prerequisite for such progress, and I hope that the parable of the blind men and the elephant will come to the reader's mind immediately if, in the future, they encounter arguments that some feature *x* is the core or "essence" of language. Each part of the large and complex "elephant" that comprises language plays a role, and immediate progress will be based not on grand theories of language evolution, but rather on specific testable hypotheses about the biology and evolution of particular clearly defined mechanisms.

A broad comparative approach will be a key to further progress. The many components of spoken language are shared variously among the many different clades of which we are part. We inherit our genetic code by virtue of being living things, our neurons as animals, our eyes as vertebrates, our maternal care as mammals, and our dexterous hands as primates. In evaluating theories of language evolution, no one of these clades has priority over the others, and the appropriate clade must be determined on a case-by-case basis. Although often overlooked, convergent evolution in distant clades can provide a powerful tool for testing hypotheses about adaptation and constraints. I have carefully considered the available data from chimpanzees to help deduce the nature of the LCA, but I have also advocated looking beyond primates to diverse species like deer, seals, birds, or honeybees for further insights into language evolution. Evolution, in its modern form, is an all-encompassing theory, applicable to all living creatures. The fact that each given species is unique, including our own, provides no justification for inventing evolutionary principles applicable only to a specific species or clade. The long and unfortunate tradition of human exceptionalism in discussions of language evolution has no place in the far broader program of comparative research that I envision for the future.

If we hope to ever reach a scientifically based scholarly consensus about the evolution of language, the first step is to admit our ignorance about key questions. These questions include, most basically, the neural and genetic bases for language in the human brain. Each of the many different mechanisms involved in language requires different forms of neural computation, probably implemented in different ways and/or in different regions of the human brain. Although brain imaging in normal subjects has already proved useful in unveiling this diversity, we still have a long way to go. Ultimately we need more sophisticated theories of neurolinguistics, specified at a computational level, if we are to isolate the specific differences in human and animal brains required to learn, process, and produce language. While available data allow us to reject simplistic models placing "language organs" exclusively in the left hemisphere, or in Broca's and Wernicke's areas, this work merely clears the way for the difficult task at hand of specifying how the much larger network involved in language processing does its job. Even accomplishing this major task is only a beginning, for a central goal must be to understand how these neural circuits are generated at the developmental and genetic levels. Ultimately, I believe, molecular geneticists will uncover language-related differences between many human genes and their coun-terparts in non-linguistic primates. We will soon have a suite of genes like *FOXP2* that are directly implicated in core aspects of human language, are found in all normal humans, and differ in sequence or expression pattern from those in other animals. These will provide crucial tools for testing evolutionary hypotheses, providing a window into the evolutionary past and allowing us to determine the relative order in which such variant alle-les became fixed in the human genome. I believe that such breakthroughs will, in the coming decades, help resolve issues that have been debated for centuries.

It would be foolish indeed if we were to squander this opportunity by allowing traditional assumptions or disciplinary biases to blind us to valid arguments that, however non-intuitive, might conceivably be correct. What is "conceivable" varies from person to person, and discipline to discipline. My approach in this book has been to follow Langer's dictum: if serious scholars have defended an idea with logically valid arguments, then it prob-ably counts as "conceivable" regardless of my, or anyone else's, contrary intuitions. The perceptive reader will no doubt have noticed my sympathies for musical and holistic models of protolanguage. One important reason for defending them is precisely because so many opposing scholars have dismissed them with arguments based essentially on opposing intuitions, or an unwillingness to accept certain of their premises. Intuition is of con-siderable value in initially generating scientific hypotheses, but it is of little use in deciding among the many hypotheses currently on the table. I do not feel at present that a convincing-enough scientific case, based on both rigorously developed theory and abundant converging data, has been made concerning any proposal about language evolution. Building such a case will be an important focus of my own future research. But for now skepticism is well justified about them all.

Once language is conceived of as a suite of different, but inter-related, mechanisms, the "problem" of language evolution becomes a suite of dif-ferent, inter-related problems. All of the hypotheses considered in this book (and others I did not have space to discuss) offer plausible "how-possibly" solutions to one, or sometimes a few, of these problems. But I know of no single author who has offered a "how-possibly" solution for all of these problems that is fully consistent with all available data. My suspicion is that any such solution will partake of certain aspects of each of the different protolanguages we have discussed, and that many such solutions can be developed. Generating more of them is left as an exercise for the reader. But such hypotheses are the beginning, not the end, of our task: good hypotheses make predictions about relevant data that have not yet been gathered. The hypotheses discussed in this book make predictions about the neural mechanisms involved in each characteristic of language, about their genetic bases, and about the timing whereby novel variants of genes became fixed in hominid evolution. *All* of these crucial data are being gathered, right now, and we can confidently expect them to flood in over the next decades. Having a more rigorous theoretical edifice in place to deal with these data will allow us to move to a truly empirical stage, where predictions are made and tested, and the "how-possibly" models are winnowed down to a few, or perhaps one, consistent with all of the data.

In conclusion, the body of theory and data relevant to language evolution is large and growing rapidly. Although I have attempted to capture something of this developing field, as it stood in 2009, this is a field in flux, chock-full of hypotheses and perspectives, but allowing precious few firm conclusions. Nonetheless, I believe that an empirical, hypothesis-testing approach, embracing a comparative, multi-component view, offers realistic hopes for real scientific progress in the next twenty years or so. Working together, researchers in this field face the realistic prospect of resolving some of the deepest and most ancient questions humans have asked about themselves and their origins. If this book helps hasten such progress, I will be very pleased.

Glossary

allele – a variant of a single gene, inherited at a particular genetic locus (chromosomal location).

amniotes – the vertebrate clade including reptiles, birds, and mammals, characterized by a protective membrane around the embryo called the amnion.

analogy – in evolutionary biology, a character shared by two species that was not present in their common ancestor; analogies result from convergent evolution.

biology – (Greek *bios* "life" + *logia* "study of") the scientific study of living organisms (introduced as a scientific term in 1802 in French by Lamarck).

clade – a natural grouping of animals, linked by descent from a common ancestor. Species are clades, and so are families (like the cat family) or classes (like mammals).

codon – a triplet of nucleotides (or "bases") in DNA that codes for one particular amino acid. The entire code mapping nucleotides to amino acids is called the genetic code.

corvids – (biology) the large-brained bird family including ravens, crows, and jays (corvids are oscine passerines, and thus "songbirds").

cue – (biology) in animal communication, any information an organism makes available to perceivers. Signals (q.v.) are a subset of cues.

deep homology – while "standard" homology refers to traits themselves, deep homology denotes the sharing, by descent from a common ancestor, of the underlying genetic and developmental mechanisms that generate traits. Deep homology can exist even if the superficial traits themselves evolved convergently.

endocast – (biology) a cast of the internal volume of the braincase of a skull; often used as a proxy for the brain itself in studies of fossil skulls.

epistasis – (genetics) an interaction between two different genes (at different loci) which leads to a phenotype different from that expected if the genes were expressed independently.

ethology – (biology) the study of animal behavior, especially as it occurs in the wild, and focused on a comparative study of specific behaviors of specific species rather than general study of animal learning, conditioning, and the like.

evo-devo – a widely used abbreviation of "evolutionary developmental biology": the new marriage of neo-Darwinian evolutionary theory with classical embryology and molecular developmental biology.

evolutionario – an "evolutionary scenario" or model of how a trait evolved phylogenetically (sometimes derided as "fairy tales" or "just-so stories" by detractors, and often termed "theories" by their originators).

exon – (genetics) the coding portion of a gene: exons are translated into amino acid sequences, and introns are not.

fixation – (biology) in population genetics, fixation refers to the elimination of variant alleles from a population, either because of founder effects or drift, or due to powerful natural selection. After fixation has occurred, only a single allele is left.

formant – (speech) a resonance of the vocal tract; formants act as frequency "windows" (band-pass filters) that allow certain frequencies to pass through the vocal tract relatively unhindered. Formants are the central acoustic cue separating different vowel sounds.

founder effect – (biology) in population genetics, "founder effects" are caused by the reduced amount of genetic variability carried when a few individuals start a small, isolated population (e.g. by colonizing an island or new environment).

fricatives – (speech) speech sounds produced by turbulence in a constriction of the vocal tract, such as an "s" produced with the teeth.

fundamental frequency (F0) – (speech) the lowest frequency in a periodic waveform; central determinant of voice pitch.

genetics – the subdiscipline of biology dealing with heredity and heritable variation in living things.

genotype – the set of two gene alleles at a particular locus in a particular individual (e.g. *aa, Aa,* or *AA*).

glossogeny – (linguistics) historical change in a language or language family (e.g. the change from Latin to French, or Old English to Modern English). Sometimes confusingly termed "language evolution," but assumed to involve no biological or genetic change.

handicap – (biology) in animal communication, handicaps are signals whose costs are higher than required to simply convey the information (the term was introduced by Amotz Zahavi in 1975). Also called "strategic costs."

harmonic – (physics) in acoustics, a harmonic sound is characterized by a set of energy components or "partials" that are related as integer multiples of some fundamental frequency (e.g. 100, 200, 300). Can be used as a synonym for "overtone", in which case the "first harmonic" is the partial *above* the fundamental (as in this book); a variant usage considers each partial a harmonic, in which case the "first harmonic" is the fundamental frequency.

homozygous/heterozygous – individuals having two copies of the same allele at a given locus are homozygotes (*AA* or *aa*). Individuals having a mixture are heterozygotes (*Aa*).

hominid – the traditional term denoting the clade encompassing humans and all of our extinct ancestors and relatives (e.g. the genera *Australopithecus* and *Homo*) since our split from chimpanzees. Since the 1990s the term "hominin" is often used to denote this clade.

homology – a trait or characteristic in two related species, where the trait's similarity is by virtue of inheritence from a common ancestor. Homology can exist despite differences in function, and is used in contrast with analogy (q.v.).

homoplasy – a grab-bag term for similarities that are *not* homologous. These include "analogy" or convergent evolution, and parallelism.

hyoid bone (also "basihyoid") – in humans, a horseshoe-shaped bone that "floats" above the larynx and serves as the skeletal support of the tongue and larynx.

index – (biology) in animal communication, signals which contain information because of a physical law (e.g. formants as an indexical cue to body size). Contrast with handicaps (q.v.).

innate – reliably developing or "canalized." Innate traits are those whose development shows a high robustness in the face of environmental variation; this does not imply that they are necessarily inflexible or that environmental information does not play a role in their development. As used in this book, the term "innate" carries no connotation that a trait is an adaptation.

instinct – an innate behavioral pattern; a trait may be instinctual and yet involve learning, such as the "instinct to learn" birdsong.

invasibility – in evolutionary game theory, a population is said to be "invasible" if a mutant strategy is able to invade it. An invasible strategy is not an ESS, or evolutionarily stable strategy.

isomorphism – (Greek "same form") having a similar shape, organization, or formal arrangement. Two triangles are isomorphic despite having different colors or sizes, and the sentence "the bottle fell, shattered, and glass flew everywhere" has a temporal isomorphism to the event described.

larynx – the "voice box"; an organ of the body, situated in the neck at the top of the trachea, that houses the vocal folds. Vocal sounds are produced, in most species, by vibrations within the larynx.

last common ancestor (LCA) – the extinct common ancestor of two existing clades. The nature of an LCA can be reconstructed, using the comparative method, by examining shared homologous traits in descendent species. The notion of an LCA plays a central role in all aspects of evolutionary theory and phylogenetic inference; in this book the abbreviation "LCA" is used as a short-hand for "the LCA of humans and chimpanzees."

lexicon – (linguistics) the cognitive inventory of morphemes, words, and expressions of a particular language; the "mental dictionary".

locus – the location on a chromosome, within the DNA, occupied by a particular gene.

macromutation – a mutation of large phenotypic effect, especially if the phenotype is highly unusual in the current population.

metazoan – a clade encompassing all multicellular animals; the large group of eukaryotes colloquially termed "animals."

morpheme – the smallest meaningful component of language; simple words like "dog" or "house" are morphemes while composite words like "hot-dog" or "greenhouse" contain two morphemes. Grammatical particles like "-ed" or "-s" are termed "bound morphemes."

morphology – (1) (biology) the study of animal form; "functional morphology" relates form to function in terms of biomechanics and physiology; (2) (linguistics) the branch of linguistics which studies the formation and structure of complex words from separate morphemes (like "dog" + "house", "turn" + "ing", or "re" + "turn") and various related processes. Today often considered as part of syntax: "morpho-syntax"; (3) (biacoustics) "call morphology" refers to the acoustic structure of a particular animal vocalization.

mutual exclusivity – in logic, two statements are mutually exclusive if it is impossible for both to be true simultaneously. In the study of child language acquisition, "mutual exclusivity" is the principle that words are not perfect synonyms, as displayed when a child correctly infers that a novel word refers to a novel object.

ontogeny – (biology) (1872, coined from Greek *on* (gen. *ontos)* "being" + *-geneia* "origin") the development of an individual, from fertilized egg to adulthood. Both embryology and individual growth (developmental biology), and intellectual development and maturation (developmental psychology) are covered by this term. One of Tinbergen's four levels of causal explanation in biology.

paleontology – (biology) (Greek *palaios* "old, ancient" + *on* (gen. *ontos*) "being" + *-ology* "study of") the study of fossil remains, which, together with an understanding of geological history, allows us to reconstruct the form, ecological environment, and sometimes behavior of extinct life forms.

petalia – (biology) impressions on the inner surface of the skull, or on cranial endocasts, revealing asymmetries in the relative shape of the two hemispheres. In humans, for example, the right frontal lobe often extends beyond the left one.

phenotype – the morphological or behavioral characters of an individual organism, whether due to genetic or environmental variation (compare "genotype").

phonetics – (linguistics) the detailed nature of speech production and perception; closely linked to "phonology."

phonology – (linguistics) the study of speech sound systems or the cognitive faculty which generates and interprets them. The term has also been extended to the study of non-vocal movements in "sign language phonology."

point vowels (also "corner vowels") – [a], [i], and [u]; vowels at the corners of a vowel triangle; they necessitate extreme placements of the tongue.

phrase structure – (linguistics) the structural dependencies of the morphemes in a sentence, illustrating how they group together in a tree-like form (also, a diagram illustrating such structures).

phylogeny – (biology) (coined in 1866 by German biologist Ernst Heinrich Haeckel from Greek *phylon* "race" + *-geneia* "origin," and first used in English by Darwin) the origin and subsequent sequence of long-term historical changes describing the evolutionary trajectory of a phylum (clade or species) through time. Also used for the tree-like diagrams representing the ancestral relationships among a set of species.

phylogenetic tree – a diagram representing the relationships among a set of species in terms of common descent: closely related species are linked by short paths, while more distant relatives have longer paths. The existence, and importance, of phylogenetic trees was a central insight of Darwin. Today, they are often generated using gene sequences.

pitch – (psychology) a perception of how high or low a sound is on a musical scale.

pleiotropy – (genetics) the common situation in which a particular gene has multiple phenotypic effects and thus influences multiple different traits.

polymorphism – (genetics) existence, in a population, of more than one allele at a given genetic locus.

pragmatics – (linguistics) the branch of linguistics concerned with the proper generation and interpretation of linguistic utterances in a communicative context.

semantics – (linguistics) that branch of linguistics concerned with the propositional meaning of words and sentences (or the cognitive faculty with the same remit). Formal semantics is often focused on the truth or falsity of statements, considered from a purely logical viewpoint.

signal – (biology) in animal communication, signals are perceptible cues produced by an organism because of their past evolutionary effects on perceivers.

source–filter theory – a theory that assumes the time-varying glottal airflow to be the primary sound source and the vocal tract to be an acoustic filter of the glottal source.

spandrel – in architecture spandrels are components of domes supported by columns; in biology the term has been used since Gould and Lewontin (1979) to refer to biological structures that exist as an automatic consequence of some other trait, but were not themselves selected for.

species – (biology) a central classificatory category in biology, most commonly defined by the "biological species concept," which defines a species as a set of potentially interbreeding organisms. Species are referred to with a Latin binomial name, comprising the genus (always capitalized) and species (*never* capitalized), e.g. *Homo sapiens* or *Canis familiaris*.

spectrum – (physics) short for "spectrum of frequencies"; a display of relative magnitudes or phases of the component frequencies of a waveform.

subjacency – (linguistics) a constraint on sentence structure, which prevents pronoun references from spanning arbitrary phrase boundaries. Often conceived as a constraint on movement of elements over certain phrase boundaries, subjacency has been hypothesized to constitute a universal restriction in human language.

synapomorphy – a derived character shared by some related group of organisms. Synapomorphies are homologies which differentiate one group from others (e.g. feathers in birds or lactation in mammals): other more widely shared traits are called symplesiomorphies.

syntax – (linguistics) the study of hierarchical phrasal and sentence structures in linguistics; or the name given to the cognitive component that builds or manipulates such structures.

syrinx – the sound source in birds (which plays the same role in birdsong as the larynx in most other vertebrate vocalizations). All birds have a syrinx, though it varies greatly in complexity in different groups. No living non-bird species have a syrinx.

tetrapods – the vertebrate clade including amphibians, reptiles, birds, and mammals (roughly, terrestrial vertebrates; more accurately "non-fish vertebrates").

thyroid cartilage – the largest cartilage of the larynx; it is comprised of two plates joined anteriorly at the midline. Its anterior prominence is called the "Adam's apple."

transcription factor – a protein which binds to specific regions of the DNA in the same organism to control gene transcription (transcription is the process of decoding the gene from DNA to RNA, which may later be translated to protein). Examples include HOX genes and FOXP2.

vertebrate – the clade of animals which possess a spinal column made of vertebrae. Humans are vertebrates, and the clade includes fish, amphibians, reptiles, mammals, and birds.

vocal folds (also termed "vocal cords," but *not* "chords") – a pair of tissue layers within the larynx that can vibrate to produce voiced sound.

vocal tract – the airway between the glottis and the mouth; also called the "upper respiratory tract" or "supralaryngeal vocal tract."

zygote – the single cell formed by the fusion of male and female gametes (sperm and egg).

Appendix: list of species names

Insects

Honeybee (domesticated)	*Apis mellifera*

Primates

Chimpanzee	*Pan troglodytes*
Bonobo	*Pan paniscus*
Gorilla	*Gorilla gorilla*
Orangutan	*Pongo pygmaeus*
Humans	*Homo sapiens*
Squirrel monkey	*Saimiri sciureus*
Capuchin monkey	*Cebus spp.*
Baboons	*Papio spp.*
Vervet monkey	*Cercopithecus aethiops*
Campbell's monkey	*Cercopithecus campbelli*
Diana monkey	*Cercopithecus diana*
Guereza monkey	*Colobus guereza*

Domesticated mammals*

Wolf/Dog	*Canis lupus/C. familiaris*
Goat	*Capra hircus*
Pig	*Sus scrofa*
Horse	*Equus caballus*

Cetaceans

Bottlenosed dolphin	*Tursiops truncatus*
Humpback whale	*Megaptera novaeangliae*

Other mammals

Rat (Norway/laboratory rat)	*Rattus norvegicus*
Sea otter	*Enhydra lutris*
Red deer	*Cervus elaphus*
Fallow deer	*Dama dama*
Lion	*Panthera leo*
Tiger	*Panthera tigris*
Leopard	*Panthera pardus*
Jaguar	*Panthera onca*

Birds

Chicken	*Gallus gallus*
Duck	*Anas spp.*
Honeyguide	*Indicator indicator*
European robin	*Erithacus rubecula*
Mockingbird	*Mimus polyglottos*
House sparrow	*Passer domesticus*
Swamp sparrow	*Melospiza georgiana* s
African gray parrot	*Psittacus erithacus*
Black-capped chickadee	*Parus (=Poecile) atricapillus*
Indian Painted Snipe	*Rostratula benghalensis*

Corvids

New Caledonian crow	*Corvus moneduloides*
Raven	*Corvus corax*
Scrub Jay	*Aphelocoma californica*

Fish

Fugu pufferfish	*Takifugu (=Fugu) rubripes*

* Domesticated animals are sometimes considered separate species, particularly in the older literature, e.g. *Canis familiaris*, but today are typically considered subspecies of their wild progenitors, e.g. *Canis lupus familiaris*.

References

Aarsleff, H. (1976). "An outline of language-origins theory since the Renaissance," *Annals of the New York Academy of Science* **280**, pp. 4–17.

Abe, H., Hasegawa, Y., and Wada, K. (1977). "A note on the air-sac of the ribbon seal," *Scientific Reports of the Whales Research Institute* **29**, pp. 129–135.

Abeillé, A. and Rambow, O. (eds) (2000). *Tree Adjoining Grammars: Formalisms, Linguistic Analysis and Processing* (Stanford, CA: CSLI Publications).

Abler, W. (1989). "On the particulate principle of self-diversifying system," *Journal of Social & Biological Structures* **12**, pp. 1–13.

Adret, P. (1993). "Vocal learning induced with operant techniques: An overview," *Netherlands Journal of Zoology* **43**, pp. 125–142.

Agusti, J. and Antón, M. (2002). *Mammoths, Sabertooths, and Hominids: 65 million years of mammalian evolution in Europe* (New York, NY: Columbia University Press).

Aiello, L. C. (1996). "Terrestriality, bipedalism and the origin of language," *Proceedings of the British Academy* **88**, pp. 269–289.

Aiello, L. C. and Dean, M. C. (1990). *An Introduction to Human Evolutionary Anatomy* (London: Academic Press).

Aiello, L. C. and Key, C. (2002). "Energetic consequences of being a Homo erectus female," *American Journal of Human Biology* **14**, pp. 551–565.

Aiello, L. C. and Wheeler, P. (1995). "The expensive tissue hypothesis: The brain and the digestive system in human and primate evolution," *Current Anthropology* **36**, pp. 199–221.

Aitchison, J. (2000). *The Seeds of Speech: Language origin and evolution* (Cambridge: Cambridge University Press).

Aitken, P. G. and Wilson, W. A. (1979). "Discriminative vocal conditioning in Rhesus monkeys: Evidence for volitional control?," *Brain and Language* **8**, pp. 227–240.

Alberts, B., Johnson, A., Walter, P., Raff, M., and Roberts, K. (2008). *Molecular Biology of the Cell* (New York, NY: Garland).

Alemseged, Z., Spoor, F., Kimbel, W. H., Bobe, R., Geraads, D., Reed, D., and Wynn, J. G. (2006). "A juvenile early hominin skeleton from Dikika, Ethiopia," *Nature* **443**, pp. 296–301.

Allin, E. F. (1975). "Evolution of the mammalian middle ear," *Journal of Morphology* **147**, pp. 403–438.

Allin, E. F. and Hopson, J. A. (1992). "Evolution of the auditory system in Synapsida ('mammal-like retiles' and primitive mammals) as seen in the fossil record," in *The Evolutionary Biology of Hearing*, ed. D. B. Webster, R. F. Fay, and A. N. Popper (New York, NY: Springer-Verlag, pp. 587–614).

Allman, J. M. (1999). *Evolving Brains* (New York, NY: Scientific American Library; distributed by W. H. Freeman and Co.).

Allott, R. (1989). *The Motor Theory of Language Origin* (Sussex: The Book Guild).

Andersson, M. B. (1994). *Sexual Selection* (Princeton, NJ: Princeton University Press).

Arbib, M. A. (2002). "The mirror system, imitation, and the evolution of language," in *Imitation in Animals and Artifacts*, ed. C. Nehaniv and K. Dautenhahn (Cambridge, MA: MIT Press, pp. 229–280).

(2004). "How far is language beyond our grasp: A response to Hurford," in *The Evolution of Communication Systems: A comparative approach*, ed. D. K. Oller and U. Griebel (Cambridge, MA: MIT Press, pp. 315–321).

(2005). "From monkey-like action recognition to human language: An evolutionary framework for neurolinguistics," *Behavioral and Brain Sciences* **28**, pp. 105–167.

Arcadi, A. C. (1996). "Phrase structure of wild chimpanzee pant hoots: Patterns of production and interpopulation variability," *American Journal of Primatology* **39**, pp. 159–178.

Arcadi, A. C., Robert, D., and Mugurusi, F. (2004). "A comparison of buttress drumming by male chimpanzees from two populations," *Primates* **45**, pp. 135–139.

Arensburg, B. (1994). "Middle Paleolithic speech capabilities: A response to Dr. Lieberman," *American Journal of Physical Anthropology* **94**, pp. 279–280.

Arensburg, B., Schepartz, L. A., Tillier, A. M., Vandermeersch, B., and Rak, Y. (1990). "A reappraisal of the anatomical basis for speech in middle Paleolithic hominids," *American Journal of Physical Anthropology* **83**, pp. 137–146.

Arensburg, B., Tillier, A. M., Vandermeersch, B., Duday, H., Schepartz, L. A., and Rak, Y. (1989). "A middle paleolithic human hyoid bone," *Nature* **338**, pp. 758–760.

Ariew, A. (1999). "Innateness is Canalization: In defense of a developmental account of innateness," in *Where Biology Meets Psychology: Philosophical essays*, ed. V. G. Hardcastle (Cambridge, MA: MIT Press, pp. 117–138).

Aristotle (350 BC). *The History of Animals* (London: Heinemann).

Armstrong, D. F. (1983). "Iconicity, arbitrariness, and duality of patterning in signed and spoken languages: Perspectives on language evolution," *Sign Language Studies* **38**, pp. 51–69.

Armstrong, D. F., Stokoe, W. C., and Wilcox, S. E. (1984). "Signs of the origin of syntax," *Current Anthropology* **35**, pp. 349–368.

(1995). *Gesture and the Nature of Language* (Cambridge: Cambridge University Press).

Arnold, K. and Zuberbühler, K. (2006). "Semantic combinations in primate calls," *Nature* **441**, p. 303.

Arom, S. (2000). "Prologomena to a biomusicology," in *The Origins of Music*, ed. N. L. Wallin, B. Merker, and S. Brown (Cambridge, MA: MIT Press, pp. 27–29).

Arthur, W. (2002). "The emerging conceptual framework of evolutionary developmental biology," *Nature* **415**, pp. 757–764.

Arvola, A. (1974). "Vocalization in the guinea-pig, C. porcellus L.," *Annales Zoologici Fennici* **11**, pp. 1–96.

Asfaw, B., Beyene, Y., Suwa, G., Walter, R. C., White, T. D., WoldeGabriel, G., and Yemane, T. (1992). "The earliest Acheulean from Konso-Gardula," *Nature* **360**, pp. 732–735.

Auel, J. M. (1984). *The Clan of the Cave Bear* (New York: Bantam).

Avanzini, G., Faienza, C., Minciacchi, D., Lopez, L., and Majno, M. (eds) (2003). *The Neurosciences and Music* (New York, NY: New York Academy of Sciences).

Avanzini, G., Lopez, L., Koelsch, S., and Majno, M. (eds) (2005). *The Neurosciences and Music II* (New York, NY: New York Academy of Sciences).

Avital, E. and Jablonka, E. (2000). *Animal Traditions: Behavioural inheritance in evolution* (Cambridge: Cambridge University Press).

Axelrod, R. (1997). *The Complexity of Cooperation: Agent-based models of competition and collaboration* (Princeton, NJ: Princeton University Press).

Axelrod, R. and Dion, D. (1988). "The further evolution of cooperation," *Science* **242**, pp. 1385–1390.

Axelrod, R. and Hamilton, W. D. (1981). "The evolution of cooperation," *Science* **211**, pp. 1390–1396.

Bachorowski, J.-A. and Owren, M. J. (2001). "Not all laughs are alike: Voiced but not unvoiced laughter readily elicits positive affect," *Psychological Science* **12**, pp. 252–257.

Baker, M. C. and Cunningham, M. A. (1985a). "The biology of bird song dialects," *Behavioral and Brain Sciences* **8**, pp. 85–133.

(1985b). "The biology of bird-song dialects," *Behavioural Processes* **8**, pp. 85–133.

Baker, M. C. and Mewaldt, L. R. (1978). "Song dialects as barriers to dispersal in White-crowned sparrows, *Zonotrichia leucophrys nuttali*," *Evolution* **32**, pp. 712–722.

Bakewell, M. A., Shi, P., and Zhang, J. (2007). "More genes underwent positive selection in chimpanzee evolution than in human evolution," *Proceedings of the National Academy of Sciences* **104**, pp. 7489–7494.

Balaban, E. (1988). "Bird song syntax: Learned intraspecific variation is meaningful," *Proceedings of the National Academy of Sciences* **85**, pp. 3657–3660.

Balda, R. P., Pepperberg, I. M., and Kamil, A. C. (1998). *Animal Cognition in Nature: The convergence of psychology and biology in laboratory and field* (London: Academic Press).

Balzano, G. J. (1980). "The group-theoretic description of 12-fold and microtonal pitch systems," *Computer Music Journal* **4**, pp. 66–84.

Bangert, M., Peschel, T., Schlaug, G., Rotte, M., Drescher, D., Hinrichs, H., Heinze, H. J., and Altenmüller, E. (2006). "Shared networks for auditory and motor processing in professional pianists: Evidence from fMRI conjunction," *Neuroimage* **30**, pp. 917–926.

Barash, D. P. (1974). "Neighbor recognition in two 'solitary' carnivores: The raccoon (*Procyon lotor*) and the Red Fox (*Vulpes fulva*)," *Science* **185**, pp. 794–796.

Barfield, R. J., Auerbach, P. A., Geyer, L. A., and McKintosh, T. K. (1979). "Ultrasonic vocalisation in rat sexual behaviour," *American Zoologist* **19**, pp. 469–480.

Barfield, R. J. and Geyer, L. A. (1972). "Sexual behaviour: Ultrasonic post-ejaculatory song of the male rat," *Science* **176**, pp. 1349–1350.

Barkow, J., Cosmides, L., and Tooby, J. (eds) (1992). *The Adapted Mind* (Oxford: Oxford University Press).

Baron-Cohen, S. (1995). *Mindblindness* (Cambridge, MA: MIT Press).

Baron-Cohen, S., Leslie, A., and Frith, U. (1985). "Does the autistic child have a 'theory of mind'?," *Cognition* **21**, pp. 37–46.

Barrett, M. D. (1978). "Lexical development and overextension in child language," *Journal of Child Language* **5**, pp. 209–219.

Barton, N. and Partridge, L. (2000). "Limits to natural selection," *Bioessays* **22**, pp. 1075–1084.

Bass, A. H. and Baker, R. (1997). "Phenotypic specification of hindbrain rhombomeres and the origins of rhythmic circuits in vertebrates," *Brain, Behavior and Evolution* **50**, pp. 3–16.

Bates, E. (1999). "Plasticity, localization and language development," in *The Changing Nervous System: Neurobiological consequences of early brain disorders*, ed. S. Bronan and J. M. Fletcher (New York: Oxford University Press, pp. 214–253).

Bateson, P. P. G. (1966). "The characteristics and context of imprinting," *Biological Reviews* **41**, pp. 177–220.

Bateson, W. (1894). *Materials for the Study of Variation Treated with Especial Regard to Discontinuity in the Origin of Species* (London: Macmillan).

Bauer, R. H. (1993). "Lateralization of neural control for vocalization by the frog (*Rana pipiens*)," *Psychobiology* **21**, pp. 243–248.

Bear, M. F., Connors, B. W., and Paradiso, M. A. (2001). *Neuroscience: Exploring the brain* (Baltimore, MD: Lippincott Williams & Wilkins).

Beck, B. B. (1980). *Animal Tool Behavior: The use and manufacture of tools by animals* (New York, NY: Garland STPM Press).

Beck, C. B. (1976). *Origin and Early Evolution of Angiosperms* (New York, NY: Columbia University Press).

Bednekoff, P. A. and Balda, R. P. (1996). "Social caching and observational spatial memory in Pinyon Jays," *Behaviour* **133**, pp. 807–826.

Bekoff, M., Allen, C., and Burghardt, G. M. (eds) (2002). *The Cognitive Animal: Empirical and theoretical perspectives on animal cognition* (Cambridge, MA: MIT Press/London: Bradford Books).

Bellugi, U. and Klima, E. S. (1978). "Two faces of sign: Iconic and abstract," *Annals of the New York Academy of Science* **280**, pp. 514–538.

Belyaev, D. K. (1969). "Domestication of animals," *Science Journal*, January, pp. 47–52.

Bercovitch, F. B. (1988). "Coalitions, cooperation and reproductive tactics among adult male baboons," *Animal Behavavior* **36**, pp. 1198–1209.

Bergman, T. J., Beehner, J. C., Cheney, D. L., and Seyfarth, R. M. (2003). "Hierarchical classification by rank and kinship in baboons," *Science* **302**, pp. 1234–1236.

Bergstrom, C. T. and Lachmann, M. (1998a). "Signalling among relatives I: Is costly signalling too costly?," *Philosophical Transactions of the Royal Society B (London)* **352**, pp. 609–617.

  (1998b). "Signalling among relatives III: Talk is cheap," *Proceedings of the National Academy of Sciences USA* **95**, pp. 5100–5105.

Berlinski, D. (2001). *The Advent of the Algorithm: The 300-year journey from an idea to the computer* (San Diego, CA: Harcourt).

Bermúdez de Castro, J. M., Arsuaga, J. L., Carbonell, E., Rosas, A., Martínez, I., and Mosquera, M. (1997). "A Hominid from the Lower Pleistocene of Atapuerca, Spain: Possible ancestor to Neandertals and modern humans," *Science* **276**, pp. 1392–1395.

Bernstein, L. (1981). *The Unanswered Question: Six talks at Harvard (Charles Eliot Norton lectures)* (Cambridge, MA: Harvard University Press).

Berntson, G. G., Boysen, S. T., Bauer, H. R., and Torello, M. S. (1990). "Conspecific screams and laughter: Cardiac and behavioral reactions of infant chimpanzees," *Developmental Psychobiology* **22**, pp. 771–787.

Berthier, M. (1999). *Transcortical Aphasias* (London: Psychology Press).

Berwick, R. C. (1997). "Syntax facit saltum: Computation and the genotype and phenotype of language," *Journal of Neurolinguistics* **10**, pp. 231–249.

  (1998). "Language evolution and the Minimalist Program: The origins of syntax," in *Approaches to the Evolution of Language*, ed. J. R. Hurford, M. Studdert-Kennedy, and C. Knight (New York: Cambridge University Press, pp. 320–340).

Bickerton, D. (1981). *Roots of Language* (Ann Arbor, MI: Karoma Press).

  (1984). "The language bioprogram hypothesis," *Behavioral and Brain Sciences* **7**, pp. 173–221.

  (1990). *Language and Species* (Chicago, IL: Chicago University Press).

  (1995). *Language and Human Behavior* (Seattle: University of Washington Press).

  (1998). "Catastrophic evolution: The case for a single step from protolanguage to full human language," in *Approaches to the Evolution of Language*, ed. J. R. Hurford, M. Studdert-Kennedy, and C. Knight (New York, NY: Cambridge University Press, pp. 341–358).

(2000). "How protolanguage became language," in *The Evolutionary Emergence of Language: Social function and the origins of linguistic form*, ed. C. Knight, M. Studdert-Kennedy, and J. R. Hurford (Cambridge: Cambridge University Press, pp. 264–284).

(2003). "Symbol and structure: A comprehensive framework for language evolution," in *Language Evolution*, ed. M. Christiansen and S. Kirby (Oxford: Oxford University Press, pp. 77–94).

(2007). "Language evolution: A brief guide for linguists," *Lingua* **117**, pp. 510–526.

Bienenstock, E. (1995). "A model of neocortex," *Network: Computation in Neural Systems* **6**, pp. 179–224.

Bisazza, A., Rogers, L. J., and Vallortigara, G. (1998). "The origins of cerebral asymmetry: A review of evidence of behavioural and brain lateralization in fishes, reptiles and amphibians," *Neuroscience and Biobehavioral Reviews* **22**, pp. 411–426.

(1999). "Possible evolutionary origins of cognitive brain lateralization," *Brain Research Reviews* **30**, pp. 164–175.

Blackmore, S. J. (2000). *The Meme Machine* (Oxford: Oxford University Press).

Blevins, J. (2004). *Evolutionary Phonology* (Cambridge: Cambridge University Press).

(2006). "A theoretical synopsis of evolutionary phonology," *Theoretical Linguistics* **32**, pp. 117–166.

Bloom, P. (2000). *How Children Learn the Meanings of Words* (Cambridge, MA: MIT Press).

Bloomfield, L. (1933). *Language* (New York: Holt, Rinehart & Winston).

Blumenthal, P. J. (2003). *Kaspar Hausers Geschwister* (Munich: Piper Verlag).

Boë, L.-J., Heim, J.-L., Honda, K., and Maeda, S. (2002). "The potential Neandertal vowel space was as large as that of modern humans," *Journal of Phonetics* **30**, pp. 465–484.

Boesch, C. (1991). "Teaching among wild chimpanzees," *Animal Behavavior* **41**, pp. 530–532.

Boesch, C. and Boesch, H. (1983). "Optimization of nut-cracking in wild chimpanzees," *Behaviour* **83**, pp. 265–286.

Boesch, C. and Boesch-Achermann, H. (2000). *The Chimpanzees of the Taï Forest* (Oxford: Oxford University Press).

Boetius, A. (2005). "Microfauna–macrofauna interaction in the seafloor: Lessons from a tubeworm," *PLos Biology* **3**, pp. 375–378.

Bolhuis, J. J. (1991). "Mechanisms of avian imprinting: A review," *Biological Reviews* **66**, pp. 303–345.

Bonner, J. T. (1983). *The Evolution of Culture in Animals* (Princeton, NJ: Princeton University Press).

Bookheimer, S. (2002). "Functional MRI of language: New approaches to understanding the cortical organization of semantic processing," *Annual Review of Neuroscience* **25**, pp. 151–188.

Boroditsky, L. (2003). "Linguistic relativity," in *Encyclopedia of Cognitive Science*, ed. L. Nadel (London: MacMillan, pp. 917–921).

Borsley, R. D. (1996). *Modern Phrase Structure Grammar* (Oxford: Blackwell).

Borst, A. (1957). *Der Turmbau von Babel: Geschicte der Meinungen über Urspring und Vielfalt der Sprachen und Völker* (Stuttgart: A. Hiersemann).

Bosma, J. and Lind, J. (1965). "Cry motions of the newborn infant," *Acta Paediatrica Scandanavica* Suppl **163**, pp. 61–92.

Botha, R. P. (2008). "On modelling prelinguistic evolution in early hominins," *Language & Communication* **28**, pp. 258–275.

(2009). "On musilanguage/'Hmmmmm' as an evolutionary precursor to language," *Language & Communication* **29**, pp. 61–76.

(2003). *Unravelling the Evolution of Language* (New York, NY: Elsevier).

Bowden, D., Winter, P., and Ploog, D. W. (1967). "Pregnancy and delivery behavior in the squirrel monkey (Saimiri sciureus) and other primates," *Folia Primatologica* **5**, pp. 1–42.

Bowler, P. J. (2003). *Evolution: The history of an idea* (Berkely, CA: University of California Press).

Bowles, A. E., Young, W. G., and Asper, E. D. (1988). "Ontogeny of stereotyped calling of a killer whale calf, *Orcinus orca*, during her first year," *Rit Fiskideildar* **11**, pp. 251–275.

Bowles, R. L. (1889). "Observations upon the mammalian pharynx, with especial reference to the epiglottis," *Journal of Anatomy and Physiology, London* **23**, pp. 606–615.

Boyd, R. and Richerson, P. J. (1983). "The cultural transmission of acquired variation: Effects on genetic fitness," *Journal of Theoretical Biology* **58**, pp. 567–596.

(1985). *Culture and the Evolutionary Process* (Chicago, IL: University of Chicago Press).

(1988). "The evolution of reciprocity in sizeable groups," *Journal of Theoretical Biology* **132**, pp. 337–356.

(1992). "Punishment allows the evolution of cooperation (or anything else) in sizable groups," *Ethology and Sociobiology* **13**, pp. 171–195.

(1996). "Why culture is common but cultural evolution is rare," *Proceedings of the British Academy* **88**, pp. 77–93.

Boysen, S. T. (1997). "Representation of quantities by apes," *Advances in the Study of Behavior* **26**, pp. 435–462.

Bradbury, J. W. (2001). "Vocal communication of wild parrots," *Journal of the Acoustical Society of America* **115**, p. 2373.

Bradbury, J. W. and Andersson, M. B. (eds) (1987). *Sexual Selection: Testing the alternatives* (Berlin: Springer-Verlag).

Bradbury, J. W. and Vehrencamp, S. L. (1998). *Principles of Animal Communication* (Sunderland, MA: Sinauer Associates).

Bradshaw, J. L. and Rodgers, L. J. (1993). *The Evolution of Lateral Asymmetries: Language, Tool Use, and Intellect* (San Diego, CA: Academic Press).

Braitenberg, V. (1977). *On the Texture of Brains* (New York, NY: Springer-Verlag).

Bramble, D. M. and Carrier, D. R. (1983). "Running and breathing in mammals," *Science* **219**, pp. 251–256.

Bramble, D. M. and Lieberman, D. E. (2004). "Endurance running and the evolution of Homo," *Nature* **432**, pp. 345–352.

Brandon, R. N. (1990). *Adaptation and Natural Selection* (Princeton, NJ: Princeton University Press).

Brentari, D. (1996). "Sign language phonology," in *The Handbook of Phonological Theory*, ed. J. A. Goldsmith (Oxford: Blackwell, pp. 615–639).

(1998). *A Prosodic Model of Sign Language Phonology* (Cambridge, MA: MIT Press).

Bresnan, J. (2001). *Lexical–Functional Syntax* (Oxford: Blackwell).

Breuer, T., Ndoundou-Hockemba, M., and Fishlock, V. (2006). "First observation of tool use in wild gorillas," *PLOS Biology* **3**, p. e380.

Briscoe, T. (ed.) (2002). *Linguistic Evolution through Language Acquisition: Formal and computational models* (Cambridge: Cambridge University Press).

(2003). "Grammatical assimilation," in *Language Evolution*, ed. M. Christiansen and S. Kirby (Oxford: Oxford University Press, pp. 295–316).

Brockelman, W. Y. and Schilling, D. (1984). "Inheritance of stereotyped gibbon calls," *Nature* **312**, pp. 634–636.

Brosch, M., Selezneva, E., Bucks, C., and Scheich, H. (2004). "Macaque monkeys discriminate pitch relationships," *Cognition* **91**, pp. 259–272.

Brotherton, P. N. M. and Komers, P. E. (2003). "Mate guarding and the evolution of social monogamy in mammals," in *Monogamy: Mating strategies and partnerships in birds, humans and other mammals*, ed. U. H. Reichard and C. Boesch (Cambridge: Cambridge University Press, pp. 42–58).

Browman, C. and Goldstein, L. (1986). "Towards an articulatory phonology," *Phonology Yearbook* **3**, pp. 219–252.

(1989). "Articulatory gestures as phonological units," *Phonology* **6**, pp. 201–251.

(1992). "Articulatory phonology: An overview," *Phonetica* **49**, pp. 155–180.

Brown, J. L. (1978). "Avian communal breeding systems," *Annual Review of Ecology & Systematics* **9**, pp. 123–155.

Brown, R. (1973). *A First Language: The early stages* (Cambridge, MA: Harvard University Press).

Brown, S. (2000). "The 'Musilanguage' model of music evolution," in *The Origins of Music*, ed. N. L. Wallin, B. Merker, and S. Brown (Cambridge, MA: MIT Press, pp. 271–300).

Brunet, M., Guy, F., Pilbeam, D., Lieberman, D. E., Likius, A., Leon, M. P. D., Zollikofer, C., and Vignaud, P. (2005). "New material of the earliest hominid from the Upper Miocene of Chad," *Nature* **434**, pp. 752–755.

Bshary, R., Wickler, W., and Fricke, H. (2002). "Fish cognition: A primate's eye view," *Animal Cognition* **5**, pp. 1–13.

Bugnyar, T. (2007). "An integrative approach to the study of 'theory-of-mind'-like abilities in ravens," *The Japanese Journal of Animal Psychology* **57**, pp. 15–27.

Bugnyar, T. and Heinrich, B. (2005). "Ravens, Corvus corax, differentiate between knowledgable and ignorant competitors," *Proceedings of the Royal Society B* **272**, pp. 1641–1646.

Bugnyar, T., Stöwe, M., and Heinrich, B. (2004). "Ravens, Corvus corax, follow gaze direction of humans around obstacles," *Proceedings of the Royal Society, B* **271**, pp. 1331–1336.

Burling, R. (2005). *The Talking Ape: How language evolved* (Oxford: Oxford University Press).

Burnet, J. (1967 [1773]). *Of the Origin and Progress of Language* (Menston: Scholar Press).

Burnstein, D. D. and Wolff, P. C. (1967). "Vocal conditioning in the guinea pig," *Psychonomic Science* **8**, pp. 39–40.

Burt, A. and Trivers, R. L. (2006). *Genes in Conflict: The biology of selfish genetic elements* (Cambridge, MA: Belknap Press).

Burton, D. and Ettlinger, G. (1960). "Cross-modal transfer of training in monkeys," *Nature* **186**, pp. 1071–1072.

Buss, D. M. (1994). *The Evolution of Desire* (New York: Basic Books).

Buss, D. M., Haselton, M. G., Shackelford, T. K., Bleske, A. L., and Wakefield, J. C. (1998). "Adaptations, exaptations, and spandrels," *American Psychologist* **53**, pp. 533–548.

Bybee, J. L. (1998). "A functionalist approach to grammar and its evolution," *Evolution of Communication* **2**, pp. 249–278.

Bybee, J. L. and Hopper, P. (eds) (2001). *Frequency and the Emergence of Linguistic Structure* (Amsterdam: John Benjamins).

Byrne, R. W. (1997). "Machiavellian intelligence," *Evolutionary Anthropology* **5**, pp. 172–180.

Byrne, R. W. and Bates, L. A. (2006). "Why are animals cognitive," *Current Biology* **16**, pp. 445–448.

Byrne, R. W. and Russon, A. E. (1998). "Learning by imitation: A hierarchical approach," *Behavioral and Brain Sciences* **21**, pp. 667–684.

Byrne, R. W. and Whiten, A. (1988). *Machiavellian Intelligence: Social expertise and the evolution of intellect in monkeys, apes and humans* (Oxford: Clarendon Press).

Call, J., Braeuer, J., Kaminski, J., and Tomasello, M. (2003). "Domestic dogs (Canis familiaris) are sensitive to the attentional state of humans," *Journal of Comparative Psychology* **117**, pp. 257–263.

Call, J. and Tomasello, M. (2007). *The Gestural Communication of Apes and Monkeys* (London: Lawrence Erlbaum).

Calvin, W. H. (2003). *A Brain for All Seasons* (Chicago, IL: University of Chicago Press).

Calvin, W. H. and Bickerton, D. (2000). *Lingua Ex Machina: Reconciling Darwin with the human brain* (Cambridge, MA: MIT Press).

Cameron, D. W. (2004). *Hominid Adaptations and Extinctions* (Sydney: University of New South Wales Press).

Camper, P. (1779). "Account of the organs of speech of the Orang Outang," *Philosophical Transactions of the Royal Society of London* **69**, pp. 139–159.

Cangelosi, A. and Parisi, D. (eds) (2002). *Simulating the Evolution of Language* (New York, NY: Springer).

Cann, R. L., Stoneking, M., and Wilson, A. C. (1987). "Mitochondrial DNA and human evolution," *Nature* **325**, pp. 31–36.

Caplan, D. (1987). *Neurolinguistics and Linguistic Aphasiology* (New York, NY: McGraw Hill).

Caramazza, A. and Zurif, E. B. (1976). "Dissociation of algorithmic and heuristic processes in language comprehension: Evidence from aphasi," *Brain and Language* **3**, pp. 572–582.

Carey, S. (1978). "The child as word learner," in *Linguistic Theory and Psychological Reality*, ed. M. Halle, J. Bresnan, and G. A. Miller (Cambridge., MA: MIT Press, pp. 264–293).

Carlsson, P. and Mahlapuu, M. (2002). "Forkhead transcription factors: Key players in development and metabolism," *Developmental Biology* **250**, pp. 1–23.

Carnie, A. (2002). *Syntax: A generative introduction* (Oxford: Blackwell).

Carrano, M. T. (2000). "Homoplasy and the evolution of dinosaur locomotion," *Paleobiology* **26**, pp. 489–512.

Carré, R., Lindblom, B., and MacNeilage, P. (1995). "Acoustic factors in the evolution of the human vocal tract," *Compte Rendu Academie des Sciences, Paris, IIb* **320**, pp. 471–476.

Carrier, D. R. (1984). "The energetic paradox of human running and hominid evolution," *Current Anthropology* **25**, pp. 483–495.

Carroll, S. B. (2000). "Endless forms: The evolution of gene regulation and morphological diversity," *Cell* **101**, pp. 577–580.

(2003). "Genetics and the making of Homo sapiens," *Nature* **422**, pp. 849–857.

(2005a). *Endless Forms Most Beautiful* (New York, NY: W. W. Norton).

(2005b). "Evolution at two levels: On genes and form," *PLOS Biology* **3**, p. e245.

(2006). *The Making of the Fittest: DNA and the ultimate forensic record of evolution* (New York, NY: W. W. Norton).

Carroll, S. B., Grenier, J. K., and Weatherbee, S. D. (2001). *From DNA to Diversity: Molecular genetics and the evolution of animal design* (Malden, MA: Blackwell Science).

Carstairs-McCarthy, A. (1998). "Synonymy avoidance, phonology, and the origin of syntax," in *Approaches to the Evolution of Language: Social and cognitive bases*, ed. J. R. Hurford, M. Studdert-Kennedy, and C. Knight (Cambridge: Cambridge University Press, pp. 279–296).

(1999). *The Origins of Complex Language* (Oxford: Oxford University Press).

Carterette, E. C., Shipley, C., and Buchwald, J. S. (1984). "On synthesizing animal speech: The case of the cat," in *Electronic Speech Synthesis: Techniques, technology, and applications*, ed. G. Bristow (New York, NY: McGraw-Hill, pp. 292–302).

Cartmill, E. A. and Byrne, R. W. (2007). "Orangutans modify their gestural signaling according to their audience's comprehension," *Current Biology* **17**, pp. 1345–1348.

Catchpole, C. K. (1980). "Sexual selection and the evolution of complex songs among warblers of the genus *Acrocephalus*," *Behaviour* **74**, pp. 149–166.

Catchpole, C. K. and Slater, P. L. B. (1995). *Bird Song: Themes and variations* (New York, NY: Cambridge University Press).

Cavalli-Sforza, L. L. (1997). "Genes, peoples, and languages," *Proceedings of the National Academy of Sciences* **94**, pp. 7719–7724.

Cela-Conde, C. J. and Ayala, F. J. (2003). "Genera of the human lineage," *Proceedings of the National Academy of Sciences, USA* **100**, pp. 7684–7689.

Chappell, J. and Kacelnik, A. (2002). "Tool selectivity in a non-primate, the New Caledonian crow (Corvus moneduloides)," *Animal Cognition* **5**, pp. 71–78.

Charlton, B. D., Reby, D., and McComb, K. (2008). "Effect of combined source F0 and filter (formant) variation on red deer hind responses to male roars," *Journal of the Acoustical Society of America* **123**, pp. 2936–2943.

Charrier, I., Mathevon, N., and Jouventin, P. (2001). "Mother's voice recognition by seal pups," *Nature* **412**, p. 873.

Cheney, D. L. and Seyfarth, R. M. (1980). "Vocal recognition in free-ranging vervet monkeys," *Animal Behavavior* **28**, pp. 362–367.

(1985). "Vervet monkey alarm calls: Manipulation through shared information?," *Behaviour* **94**, pp. 150–166.

(1988). "Assessment of meaning and the detection of unreliable signals by vervet monkeys," *Animal Behavavior* **36**, pp. 477–486.

(1990a). "Attending to behaviour versus attending to knowledge: Examining monkeys' attribution of mental states," *Animal Behavavior* **40**, pp. 742–753.

(1990b). *How Monkeys See the World: Inside the mind of another species* (Chicago, IL: Chicago University Press).

(1998). "Why monkeys don't have language," in *The Tanner Lectures on Human Values*, ed. G. Petersen (Salt Lake City: University of Utah Press).

(2007). *Baboon Metaphysics: The evolution of a social mind* (Chicago, IL: University of Chicago Press).

Chiba, T. and Kajiyama, M. (1941). *The Vowel: Its nature and structure* (Tokyo: Tokyo-Kaiseikan).

Chimpanzee Sequencing and Analysis Consortium, The (2005). "Initial sequence of the chimpanzee genome and comparison with the human genome," *Nature* **437**, pp. 69–87.

Chomsky, C. (1969). *The Acquisition of Syntax in Children from 5 to 10* (Cambridge, MA: MIT Press).

Chomsky, N. (1956). "Three models for the description of language," *I.R.E. Transactions on Information Theory* IT-2, pp. 113–124.

(1957). *Syntactic Structures* (The Hague: Mouton).

(1959). "Review of 'Verbal Behavior' by B. F. Skinner," *Language* **35**, pp. 26–58.

(1965). *Aspects of the Theory of Syntax* (Cambridge, MA: MIT Press).

(1975a). *Reflections on Language* (New York, NY: Pantheon).

(1975b). *The Logical Structure of Linguistic Theory* (New York, NY: Plenum Press).

(1980). *Rules and Representations* (Oxford: Blackwell).

(1986). *Knowledge of Language: Its nature, origin, and use* (Westport, CT: Praeger).

(1988). *Language and Problems of Knowledge: The Managua lectures* (Cambridge, MA: MIT Press).

(1990). "On formalization and formal linguistics," *Natural Language and Linguistic Theory* **8**, pp. 143–147.

(1995). *The Minimalist Program* (Cambridge, MA: MIT Press).

(2005). "Three factors in language design," *Linguistic Inquiry* **36**, pp. 1–22.

(2010). "Some simple evo devo theses: How true might they be for language?," in *The Evolution of Human Language: Biolinguistic perspectives*, ed. R. Larson, V. Deprez, and H. Yamakido (Cambridge: Cambridge University Press.

Chomsky, N. and Halle, M. (1968). *The Sound Pattern of English* (Cambridge, MA: MIT Press).

Chomsky, N. and Miller, G. A. (1963). "Introduction to the formal analysis of natural languages," in *Handbook of Mathematical Psychology*, ed. R. D. Luce, R. R. Bush, and E. Galanter (New York, NY: John Wiley & Sons, pp. 269–322).

Christiansen, M. and Chater, N. (2008). "Language as shaped by the brain," *Behavioral & Brain Sciences* **31**, pp. 489–509.

Christiansen, M. and Kirby, S. (2003). "Language evolution: Consensus and controversies," *Trends in Cogntive Science* **7**, pp. 300–307.

Clack, J. A. (1992). "The stapes of Acanthostega gunnari and the role of the stapes in early tetrapods," in *The Evolutionary Biology of Hearing*, ed. D. B. Webster, R. F. Fay, and A. N. Popper (New York, NY: Springer-Verlag, pp. 405–420).

(1994). "The earliest known tetrapod braincase and the evolution of the stapes and fenstra ovalis," *Nature* **369**, pp. 392–394.

(1997). "The evolution of tetrapod ears and the fossil record," *Brain Behavior and Evolution* **50**, pp. 198–212.

Clark, A. G., Glanowski, S., Nielsen, R., Thomas, P. D., Kejariwal, A., Todd, M. A., Tanenbaum, D. M., Civello, D., Lu, F., Murphy, B., Ferriera, S., Wang, G., Zheng, X., White, T. J., Sninsky, J. J., Adams, M. D., and Cargill, M. (2003). "Inferring nonneutral evolution from human-chimp-mouse orthologous gene trios," *Science* **302**, pp. 1960–1963.

Clark, C. W., Borsani, J. F., and Notarbartolo-di-Sciara, G. (2002). "Vocal activity of fin whales, *Balaenoptera physalus*, in the Ligurian Sea," *Marine Mammal Science* **18**, pp. 286–295.

Clark, D. A., Mitra, P. P., and Wang, S. S. (2001). "Scalable architecture in mammalian brains," *Nature* **411**, pp. 189–193.

Clark, E. V. (1987). "The principle of contrast: A constraint on language acquisition," in *Mechanisms of Language Acquisition*, ed. B. MacWhinney (Hillsdale, NJ: Erlbaum, pp. 1–33).

Clark, G. (1971). *World Prehistory: A new outline* (Cambridge: Cambridge University Press).

Clarke, E., Reichard, U. H., and Zuberbühler, K. (2006). "The syntax and meaning of wild gibbon calls," *PLOS ONE* **1**, p. e73.

Clayton, M. R. L. (1996). "Free rhythm: Ethnomusicology and the study of music without metre," *Bulletin of the School of Oriental and African Studies, University of London* **59**, pp. 323–332.

Clayton, N. S., Bussey, T. J., and Dickinson, A. (2003a). "Can animals recall the past and plan for the future?," *Nature Reviews Neuroscience* **4**, pp. 685–691.

Clayton, N. S. and Dickinson, A. D. (1998). "Episodic-like memory during cache recovery by scrub jays," *Nature* **395**, pp. 272–278.

Clayton, N. S., Yu, K. S., and Dickinson, A. (2003b). "Interacting cache memories: Evidence of flexible memory use by scrub jays," *Journal of Experimental Psychology: Animal Behavior Processes* **29**, pp. 14–22.

Clegg, M. and Aiello, L. C. (2000). "Paying the price of speech? An analysis of mortality statistics for choking on food," *American Journal of Physical Anthropology* **111**, p. 126.

Clutton-Brock, T. H. (1991). *The Evolution of Parental Care* (Princeton, NJ: Princeton University Press).

Clutton-Brock, T. H. and Harvey, P. H. (1980). "Primates, brains and ecology," *Journal of Zoology (London)* **207**, pp. 151–169.

Coates, M. I. and Clack, J. A. (1990). "Polydactyly in the earliest known tetrapod limbs," *Nature* **347**, pp. 66–69.

  (1991). "Fish-like gills and breathing in the earliest known tetrapod," *Nature* **352**, pp. 234–235.

Cole, M., Chorover, S. L., and Ettlinger, G. (1961). "Cross-modal transfer in man," *Nature* **191**, pp. 1225–1226.

Collins, R. L. (1970). "The sound of one paw clapping: An inquiry into the origins of left handedness," in *Contributions to Behavior-Genetic Analysis: The mouse as a prototype*, ed. G. Lindzey and D. D. Thiessen (New York, NY: Appleton-Century-Croft, pp. 115–136).

Condillac, É. B. d. (1971 [1747]). *Essai sur l'origine des connaissances humaines* (Gainesville, FL: Scholar's Facsimiles and Reprints).

Connor, R. C. and Peterson, D. M. (1994). *The Lives of Whales and Dolphins* (New York, NY: Henry Holt).

Cope, D. (1996). *Experiments in Musical Intelligence* (Madison: WI: A-R Editions).

Coppens, Y. (1994). "East Side Story: The origin of humankind," *Scientific American* May, pp. 88–95.

Coqueugniot, H., Hublin, J.-J., Veillon, F., Houët, F., and Jacob, T. (2004). "Early brain growth in Homo erectus and implications for cognitive ability," *Nature* **431**, pp. 299– 302.

Corballis, M. C. (1983). *Human Laterality* (New York, NY: Academic Press).

(1991). *The Lopsided Ape* (Oxford: Oxford University Press).

(2002a). "Did language evolve from manual gestures?," in *The Transition to Language*, ed. A. Wray (Oxford: Oxford University Press, pp. 161–179).

(2002b). *From Hand to Mouth: The origins of language* (Princeton, NJ: Princeton University Press).

(2003). "From hand to mouth: The gestural origins of language," in *Language Evolution*, ed. M. Christiansen and S. Kirby (Oxford: Oxford University Press, pp. 201–218).

Coutinho, C. C., Fonseca, R. N., Mansurea, J. J. C., and Borojevic, R. (2003). "Early steps in the evolution of multicellularity: Deep structural and functional homologies among homeobox genes in sponges and higher metazoans," *Mechanisms of Development* **120**, pp. 429–440.

Cracraft, J. and Donoghue, M. J. (eds) (2004). *Assembling the Tree of Life* (Oxford: Oxford University Press).

Crain, S. (1991). "Language acquisition in the absence of experience," *Behavioral and Brain Sciences* **14**, pp. 597–650.

Crelin, E. (1987). *The Human Vocal Tract* (New York, NY: Vantage Press).

Crockford, C., Herbinger, I., Vigilant, L., and Boesch, C. (2004). "Wild chimpanzees produce group-specific calls: A case for vocal learning?," *Ethology* **110**, pp. 221–243.

Croft, W. and Cruse, D. A. (2003). *Cognitive Linguistics* (Cambridge: Cambridge University Press).

Cross, I. (2003). "Music, cognition, culture and evolution," in *The Cognitive Neuroscience of Music*, ed. I. Peretz and R. J. Zatorre (Oxford: Oxford University Press, pp. 42–56).

Crothers, J. (1978). "Typology and universals of vowel systems," in *Universals of Human Language*, ed. J. Greenberg, C. A. Ferguson, and E. A. Moravcsik (Stanford, CA: Stanford University Press, pp. 93–152).

Crystal, D. (2002). *The Cambridge Encyclopedia of Language* (Cambridge: Cambridge University Press).

Curio, E. (1978). "The adaptive significance of avian mobbing I: Teleonomic hypotheses and predictions," *Zeitschrift für Tierpsychologie* **48**, pp. 175–183.

Curio, E., Ernst, V., and Vieth, W. (1978). "Cultural transmission of enemy recognition: One function of mobbing," *Science* **202**, pp. 899–901.

Curtis, S. (1977). *Genie: A psycholinguistic study of a modern-day "wild child"* (New York, NY: Academic Press).

Cutting, J. E. (1982). "Plucks and bows are categorically perceived, sometimes," *Perception & Psychophysics* **31**, pp. 462–476.

Cutting, J. E. and Rosner, B. S. (1974). "Category boundaries in speech and music," *Perception & Psychophysics* **16**, pp. 564–570.

Dart, R. A. (1925). "Australopithecus africanus: The ape-man of South Africa," *Nature* **115**, pp. 195–199.

Darwin, C. (1859). *On the Origin of Species* (London: John Murray).

(1871). *The Descent of Man, and Selection in Relation to Sex* (London: John Murray).

(1872a). *On the Origin of Species* (London: John Murray).

(1872b). *The Expression of the Emotions in Man and Animals* (London: John Murray).

(1875). *The Variation of Animals and Plants under Domestication* (London: John Murray).

Daumer, G. F. (1873). *Kaspar Hauser: Sein Wesen, seine Unschuld* (Leipaig: Dornach).

Davenport, R. K. and Rogers, C. M. (1970). "Intermodal equivalence of stimuli in apes," *Science* **168**, pp. 279–280.

Davidson, I. and Noble, W. (1993). "Tools and language in human evolution," in *Tools, Language and Cognition in Human Evolution*, ed. by K. R. Gibson and T. Ingold. (Cambridge: Cambridge University Press, pp. 363–388).

Davis, H. (1992). "Transitive inference in rats (Rattus norvegicus)," *Journal of Comparative Psychology* **106**, pp. 342–349.

Davis, M. (1958). *Computability and Unsolvability* (New Yorl, NY: McGraw-Hill).

(ed.) (1965). *The Undecidable: Basic papers on undecidable propositions, unsolvable problems and computable functions* (Hewlett, NY: Raven Press).

Dawkins, R. (1976). *The Selfish Gene* (Oxford: Oxford University Press).

(1986). *The Blind Watchmaker* (New York, NY: W.W. Norton).

(2004). *The Ancestor's Tale* (New York, NY: W. W. Norton).

Dawkins, R. and Krebs, J. R. (1978). "Animal signals: Information or manipulation?," in *Behavioural Ecology*, ed. J. R. Krebs and N. B. Davies (Oxford: Blackwell Scientific Publications, pp. 282–309).

Day, M. H. and Williams, E. H. (1980). "Laetoli Pliocene hominid footprints and bipedalism," *Nature* **286**, pp. 385–387.

Deacon, T. W. (1984). "Connections of the inferior periarcuate area in the brain of *Macaca fascicularis*: An experimental and comparative investigation of language circuitry and its evolution." Unpublished PhD thesis, Harvard University, Cambridge, MA.

(1990a). "Fallacies of progression in theories of brain-size evolution," *International Journal of Primatology* **11**, pp. 193–235.

(1990b). "Problems of ontogeny and phylogeny in brain-size evolution," *International Journal of Primatology* **11**, pp. 237–282.

(1992). "The neural circuitry underlying primate calls and human language," in *Language Origins: A multidisciplinary approach*, ed. J. Wind, B. A. Chiarelli, B. Bichakjian, and A. Nocentini (Dordrecht: Kluwer Academic, pp. 301–323).

(1997). *The Symbolic Species: The co-evolution of language and the brain* (New York, NY: Norton).

Deaner, R. O., Nunn, C. L., and van Schaik, C. P. (2000). "Comparative tests of primate cognition: Different scaling methods produce different results," *Brain Behavior and Evolution* **55**, pp. 44–52.

De Beer, G. (1971). *Homology: An unsolved problem* (Oxford: Oxford University Press).

de Boer, B. (2001). *The Origins of Vowel Systems* (Oxford: Oxford University Press).

Dediu, D. and Ladd, D. R. (2007). "Linguistic tone is related to the population frequency of the adaptive haplogroups of two brain size genes, ASPM and Microcephalin," *Proceedings of the National Academy of Sciences of the United States of America* **104**, pp. 10944–10949.

DeGusta, D., Gilbert, W. H., and Turner, S. P. (1999). "Hypoglossal canal size and hominid speech," *Proceedings of the National Academy of Science, USA* **96**, pp. 1800–1804.

Dehaene, S. (1997). *The Number Sense* (Oxford: Oxford University Press).

Demski, L. S. and Gerald, J. W. (1974). "Sound production and other behavioral effects of midbrain stimulation in free-swimming toadfish Opsanus beta," *Brain, Behavior and Evolution* **9**, pp. 41–59.

Dennett, D. C. (1983). "Intentional systems in cognitive ethology: The 'Pan-glossian paradigm' defended," *Behavioral and Brain Sciences* **6**, pp. 343–390.

(1991). *Consciousness Explained* (Boston, MA: Little, Brown).

(1995). *Darwin's Dangerous Idea* (New York, NY: Simon & Schuster).

(1996). *Kinds of Minds* (New York, NY: Basic Books).

De Robertis, E. M. and Sasai, Y. (1996). "A common plan for dorsoventral patterning in Bilateria," *Nature* **380**, pp. 37–40.

D'Errico, F. (2003). "The invisible frontier: A multiple-species model for the origin of behavioral modernity," *Evolutionary Anthropology* **12**, pp. 188–202.

D'Errico, F., Villa, P., Llona, A. C. P., and Idarraga, R. R. (1998). "A Middle Palae-olithic origin of music? Using cave-bear bone accumulations to assess the Divje Babe I bone 'flute,'" *Antiquity* **72**, pp. 65–76.

Dessalles, J.-L. (1998). "Altruism, status and the origin of relevance," in *Approaches to the Evolution of Language*, ed. J. R. Hurford, M. Studdert-Kennedy, and C. Knight (New York, NY: Cambridge University Press, pp. 130–147).

(2000). "Language and hominid politics," in *The Evolutionary Emergence of Language: Social function and the origins of linguistic form*, ed. C. Knight, M. Studdert-Kennedy, and J. R. Hurford (Cambridge: Cambridge University Press, pp. 62–80).

Devlin, A. M., Cross, J. H., Harkness, W., Chong, W. K., Harding, B., Vargha-Khadem, F., and Neville, B. G. R. (2003). "Clinical outcomes of hemispherectomy for epilepsy in childhood and adolescence," *Brain* **126**, pp. 556–566.

de Waal, F. B. M. (1989). *Peacemaking Among Primates* (Cambridge, MA: Harvard University Press).

   (1988). "The communicative repertoire of captive bonobos (Pan paniscus), compared to that of chimpanzees," *Behaviour* **106**, pp. 183–251.

Diamond, J. (1992). *The Third Chimpanzee* (New York, NY: HarperCollins).

   (1997). *Guns, Germs and Steel* (New York, NY: W. W. Norton).

Dissanayake, E. (1992). *Homo Aestheticus: Where art comes from and why* (New York, NY: Free Press).

   (2000). "Antecedents of the temporal arts in early mother–infant interaction," in *The Origins of Music*, ed. N. L. Wallin, B. Merker, and S. Brown (Cambridge, MA: MIT Press, pp. 389–410).

Dobzhansky, T. (1973). "Nothing in biology makes sense except in the light of evolution," *American Biology Teacher* **35**, pp. 125–129.

Donald, M. (1991). *Origins of the Modern Mind* (Cambridge, MA: Harvard University Press).

   (1998). "Mimesis and the executive suite: Missing links in language evolution," in *Approaches to the Evolution of Language*, ed. J. R. Hurford, M. Studdert-Kennedy, and C. Knight (New York, NY: Cambridge University Press, pp. 44–67).

Dorsaint-Pierre, R., Penhune, V. B., Watkins, K. E., Neelin, P., Lerch, J. P., Bouffard, M., and Zatorre, R. J. (2006). "Asymmetries of the planum temporale and Heschl's gyrus: Relationship to language lateralization," *Brain* **129**, pp. 1164–1176.

Doupe, A. J. and Kuhl, P. K. (1999). "Birdsong and human speech: Common themes and mechanisms," *Annual Review of Neuroscience* **22**, pp. 567–631.

Drayna, D., Manichaikul, A., de Lange, M., Snieder, H., and Spector, T. (2001). "Genetic correlates of musical pitch recognition in humans," *Science* **291**, pp. 1969–1972.

Dronkers, N. F. and Baldo, J. V. (2001). "Neural basis of speech production," in *International Encyclopedia of the Social & Behavioral Sciences*, ed. N. J. Smelser and P. B. Baltes (Amsterdam: Elsevier, pp. 14875–14879).

Dubois, E. (1897). "Sur le rapport du poids de l'encéphale avec la grandeur du corps chez mammifères," *Bulletin et Mémoires de la Société d'Anthropologie de Paris* **8**, pp. 337–376.

   (1898). "Abstract of remarks on the brain-cast of Pithecanthropus erectus," *Journal of Anatomy and Physiology* **33**, pp. 273–276.

DuBrul, E. L. (1958). *Evolution of the Speech Apparatus* (Springfield, IL: Thomas).

   (1962). "The general phenomenon of bipedalism," *American Zoologist* **2**, pp. 205–208.

Duchin, L. E. (1990). "The evolution of articulate speech: Comparative anatomy of the oral cavity in Pan and Homo," *Journal of Human Evolution* **19**, pp. 684–695.

Dudley, H. and Tarnoczy, T. H. (1950). "The speaking machine of Wolfgang von Kempelen," *Journal of the Acoustical Society of America* **22**, pp. 151–166.

Dugatkin, L. A. (1993). "Sexual selection and imitation: Females copy the mate choice of others," *American Naturalist* **139**, pp. 1384–1389.

Dunbar, R. I. M. (1992). "Neocortex size as a constraint on group size in primates," *Journal of Human Evolution* **20**, pp. 469–493.

(1993). "Coevolution of neocortical size, group size and language in humans," *Behavioral and Brain Sciences* **16**, pp. 681–735.

(1996). *Grooming, Gossip and the Evolution of Language* (Cambridge, MA: Harvard University Press).

(1998). "Theory of mind and the evolution of language," in *Approaches to the Evolution of Language*, ed. J. R. Hurford, M. Studdert-Kennedy, and C. Knight (New York, NY: Cambridge University Press, pp. 92–110).

(1999). "Culture, honesty and the Free Rider Problem," in *The Evolution of Culture*, ed. R. I. M. Dunbar, C. Knight, and C. Power. (Edinburgh: Edinburgh University Press, pp. 194–213).

(2003). "The origin and subsequent evolution of language," in *Language Evolution*, ed. M. Christiansen and S. Kirby (Oxford: Oxford Unviersity Press, pp. 219–234).

Dunford, C. (1977). "Kin selection for ground squirrel alarm calls," *American Naturalist* **111**, pp. 782–785.

Durham, W. (1991). *Coevolution: Genes, culture, & human diversity* (Stanford, CA: Stanford University Press).

Eaton, R. L. (1979). "A beluga whale imitates human speech," *Carnivore* **2**, pp. 22–23.

Edelman, G. M. (1987). *Neural Darwinism: The theory of neuronal group selection* (New York, NY: Basic Books).

Eibl-Eibesfeldt, I. (1970). *Ethology: The biology of behavior* (New York, NY: Holt, Rinehart & Winston).

(1973). "The expressive behaviour of the deaf- and blind-born," in *Social Communication and Movement*, ed. M. Von. Cranach and J. Vine (London: Academic, pp. 163–194).

Ekman, P. (1992). "Facial expressions of emotion: An old controversy and new findings," *Philosophical Transactions of the Royal Society of London* **335**, pp. 63–70.

Ekman, P. and Friesen, W. V. (1975). *Unmasking the Face* (Englewood Cliffs, NJ: Prentice-Hall).

Elder, J. H. (1934). "Auditory acuity of the chimpanzee," *Journal of Comparative and Physiological Psychology* **17**, pp. 157–183.

Elowson, A. M., Snowdon, C. T., and Lazaro-Perea, C. (1998a). "'Babbling' and social context in infant monkeys: Parallels to human infants," *Trends in Cognitive Science* **2**, pp. 31–37.

(1998b). "Infant 'babbling' in a nonhuman primate: Complex vocal sequences with repeated call types," *Behaviour* **135**, pp. 643–664.

Emery, N. J. and Clayton, N. S. (2001). "Effects of experience and social context on prospective caching strategies in scrub jays," *Nature* **414**, pp. 443–446.

(2004). "The mentality of crows: Convergent evolution of intelligence in corvids and apes," *Science* **306**, pp. 1903–1907.

Emlen, S. T. and Oring, L. W. (1977). "Ecology, sexual selection and the evolution of mating systems," *Science* **197**, pp. 215–223.

Emmorey, K. (2002). *Language, Cognition and the Brain: Insights from sign language research* (London: Lawrence Erlbaum).

(2005). "Sign languages are problematic for a gestural origins theory of language evolution," *Behavioral and Brain Sciences* **28**, pp. 130–131.

Enard, W., Gehre, S., Hammerschmidt, K., Holter, S. M., Blass, T., Somel, M. *et al.*, (2009). "A humanized version of Foxp2 affects cortico-basal ganglia circuits in mice," *Cell* **137**(5), pp. 961–971.

Enard, W., Przeworski, M., Fisher, S. E., Lai, C. S. L., Wiebe, V., Kitano, T., Monaco, A. P., and Paäbo, S. (2002). "Molecular evolution of FOXP2, a gene involved in speech and language," *Nature* **418**, pp. 869–872.

Endler, J. A. (1986). "The newer synthesis? Some conceptual problems in evolutionary biology," *Oxford Surveys in Evolutionary Biology* **3**, pp. 224–243.

Enquist, M. (1985). "Communication during aggressive interactions with particular reference to variation in choice of behaviour," *Animal Behavior* **33**, pp. 1152–1161.

Enquist, M. and Leimar, O. (1993). "The evolution of cooperation in mobile organisms," *Animal Behavior* **45**, pp. 747–757.

Erwin, D. H. and Davidson, E. H. (2002). "The last common bilaterian ancestor," *Development* **129**, pp. 3021–3032.

Etcoff, N. L. and Magee, J. J. (1992). "Categorical perception of facial expressions," *Cognition* **44**, pp. 227–240.

Ettlinger, G. and Blakemore, C. B. (1969). "Cross-modal transfer set in the monkey," *Neuropsychologia* **7**, pp. 41–47.

Evans, C. S. and Evans, L. (2007). "Representational signalling in birds," *Biology Letters* **3**, pp. 8–11.

Evans, C. S., Evans, L., and Marler, P. (1993). "On the meaning of alarm calls: Functional reference in an avian vocal system," *Animal Behavior* **46**, pp. 23–38.

Evans, C. S. and Marler, P. (1994). "Food-calling and audience effects in male chickens, *Gallus gallus*: Their relationships to food availability, courtship and social facilitation," *Animal Behavior* **47**, pp. 1159–1170.

Evans, P. D., Anderson, J. R., Vallender, E. J., Gilbert, S. L., Malcom, C. M., Dorus, S., and Lahn, B. T. (2004). "Adaptive evolution of ASPM, a major determinant of cerebral cortical size in humans," *Human Molecular Genetics* **13**, pp. 489–494.

Evans, P. D., Gilbert, S. L., Mekel-Bobrov, N., Vallender, E. J., Anderson, J. R., Vaez-Azizi, L., Tishkoff, S. A., Hudson, R. R., and Lahn, B. T. (2005). "Microcephalin, a gene regulating brain size, continues to evolve adaptively in humans," *Science* **309**, pp. 1717–1720.

Evans, W. E. and Bastian, J. R. (1969). "Marine mammal communication: Social and ecological factors," in *The Biology of Marine Mammals*, ed. H. T. Andersen (New York, NY: Academic Press, pp. 425–475).

Falk, D. (1975). "Comparative anatomy of the larynx in man and the chimpanzee: Implications for language in Neanderthal," *American Journal of Physical Anthropology* **43**, pp. 123–132.

(1980). "A reanalysis of the South African Australopithecine natural endocasts," *American Journal of Physical Anthropology* **53**, pp. 525–539.

(1983). "Cerebral cortices of East African early hominids," *Science* **221**, pp. 1072–1074.

(1987). "Hominid paleoneurology," *Annual Review of Anthropology* **16**, pp. 13–30.

(2000). "Hominid brain evolution and the origins of music," in *The Origins of Music*, ed. N. L. Wallin, B. Merker, and S. Brown (Cambridge, MA: MIT Press, pp. 197–216).

(2004). "Prelinguistic evolution in early hominins: Whence motherese?," *Behavioral and Brain Sciences* **27**, pp. 491–450.

Falk, D., Hildebolt, C., Smith, K., Morwood, M. J., Sutikna, T., Brown, P., Jatmiko, Saptomo, E. W., Brunsden, B., and Prior, F. (2005). "The Brain of LB1, Homo floresiensis," *Science* **308**, pp. 242–245.

Fant, G. (1960). *Acoustic Theory of Speech Production* (The Hague: Mouton).

(1975). "Non-uniform vowel normalization," *Speech Transactions Laboratory Quarterly Progress and Status Report* **2–3**, pp. 1–19.

Farrar, F. W. (1870). "Philology & Darwinism," *Nature* **1**, pp. 527–529.

(1996). "On language," in *The Origin of Language*, ed. R. Harris (Bristol: Thoemmes Press, pp. 42–80).

Fay, D. and Cutler, A. (1977). "Malapropisms and the structure of the mental lexicon," *Linguistic Inquiry* **8**, pp. 505–520.

Feher, O., Mitra, P. P., Sasahara, K., and Tchernichovski, O. (2008). "Evolution of song culture in the zebra finch," in *The Evolution of Language: Proceedings of the 7th International Conference*, ed. A. Smith, K. Smith, and R. Ferrer i Cancho (Singapore: World Scientific Press, pp. 423–424).

Feldman, M. W. and Cavalli-Sforza, L. L. (1976). "Cultural and biological evolutionary processes, selection for a trait under complex transmission," *Theoretical Population Biology* **9**, pp. 238–259.

Feldman, M. W. and Laland, K. N. (1996). "Gene-culture coevolutionary theory," *Trends in Ecology and Evolution* **11**, pp. 453–457.

Fernald, A. (1992). "Human maternal vocalizations to infants as biologically relevant signals: An evolutionary perspective," in *The Adapted Mind*, ed. J. Barkow, L. Cosmides, and J. Tooby (New York, NY: Oxford University Press, pp. 391–428).

Ferrari, P. F., Fogassi, L., Gallese, V., and Rizzolatti, G. (2001). "Mirror neurons for mouth actions in monkey ventral premotor cortex," *Society for Neurosciences Abstracts* **27**, No. 729.4.

Feuerbach, P. J. A. (1832). Kaspar Hauser: Beispiel eines Verbrechens am Seelenleben des Menschen (Ansbach: Dolfuss).

Ficken, M. S., Ficken, R. W., and Witkin, S. R. (1978). "Vocal repertoire of the black-capped chickadee," *Auk* **95**, pp. 34–48.

Ficken, M. S. and Witkin, S. R. (1977). "Responses of black-capped chickadees to predators," *Auk* **94**, pp. 156–157.

Finlay, B. L. and Darlington, R. B. (1995). "Linked regularities in the development and evolution of mammalian brains," *Science* **268**, pp. 1578–1584.

Finlay, B. L., Darlington, R. B., and Nicastro, N. (2001). "Developmental structure in brain evolution," *Behavioral and Brain Sciences* **24**, pp. 263–308.

Firth, J. R. (1930). *Speech* (London: Ernest Benn).

(1937). *The Tongues of Men* (London: Ernest Benn).

Fischer, J. (1998). "Barbary macaques categorize shrill barks into two call types," *Animal Behavioe* **55**, pp. 799–807.

Fisher, C. (2002). "The role of abstract syntactic knowledge in language acquisition: A reply to Tomasello (2000)," *Cognition* **82**, pp. 259–278.

Fisher, R. A. (1930). *The Genetical Theory of Natural Selection* (Oxford: Clarendon Press).

Fisher, S. E. and DeFries, J. C. (2002). "Developmental dyslexia: Genetic dissection of a complex cognitive trait," *Nature Reviews Neuroscience* **3**, pp. 767–780.

Fisher, S. E., Vargha-Khadem, F., Watkins, K. E., Monaco, A. P., and Pembrey, M. E. (1998). "Localisation of a gene implicated in a severe speech and language disorder," *Nature Genetics* **18**, pp. 168–170.

Fitch, W. T. (1994). *Vocal tract length perception and the evolution of language* (UMI Dissertation Services, Ann Arbor, Michigan).

(1997). "Vocal tract length and formant frequency dispersion correlate with body size in rhesus macaques," *Journal of the Acoustical Society of America* **102**, pp. 1213–1222.

"Acoustic exaggeration of size in birds by tracheal elongation: Comparative and theoretical analyses," *Journal of Zoology (London)* **248**, pp. 31–49.

(2000a). "Skull dimensions in relation to body size in nonhuman mammals: The causal bases for acoustic allometry," *Zoology* **103**, pp. 40–58.

(2000b). "The evolution of speech: A comparative review," *Trends in Cognitive Science* **4**, pp. 258–267.

(2000c). "The phonetic potential of nonhuman vocal tracts: Comparative cineradiographic observations of vocalizing animals," *Phonetica* **57**, pp. 205–218.

(2002). "Comparative vocal production and the evolution of speech: Reinterpreting the descent of the larynx," in *The Transition to Language*, ed. A. Wray (Oxford: Oxford University Press, pp. 21–45).

(2004a). "Kin selection and 'mother tongues': A neglected component in language evolution," in *Evolution of Communication Systems: A comparative approach*, ed. D. K. Oller and U. Griebel (Cambridge, MA: MIT Press, pp. 275–296).

(2004b). "Vocal production system: Evolution," in *MIT Encyclopedia of Communication Sciences and Disorders*, ed. R. D. Kent (Cambridge, MA: MIT Press, pp. 56–59).

(2005a). "Protomusic and protolanguage as alternatives to protosign," *Behavioral & Brain Sciences* **28**, pp. 132–133.

(2005b). "The evolution of language: A comparative review," *Biology and Philosophy* **20**, pp. 193–230.

(2005c). "The evolution of music in comparative perspective," in *The Neurosciences and Music II: From perception to performance*, ed. G. Avanzini, L. Lopez, S. Koelsch, and M. Majno (New York, NY: New York Academy of Sciences, pp. 29–49).

(2006a). "Production of vocalizations in mammals," in *Encyclopedia of Language and Linguistics*, ed. K. Brown (Oxford: Elsevier, pp. 115–121).

(2006b). "The biology and evolution of music: A comparative perspective," *Cognition* **100**, pp. 173–215.

(2007). "Evolving meaning: The roles of kin selection, allomothering and paternal care in language evolution," in *Emergence of Communication and Language*, ed. C. Lyon, C. Nehaniv, and A. Cangelosi (New York, NY: Springer, pp. 29–51).

(2009). "Fossil cues to the evolution of speech," in *The Cradle of Language*, ed. R. P. Botha and C. Knight (Oxford: Oxford University Press, pp. 112–134).

Fitch, W. T. and Fritz, J. B. (2006). "Rhesus macaques spontaneously perceive formants in conspecific vocalizations," *Journal of the Acoustical Society of America* **120**, pp. 2132–2141.

Fitch, W. T. and Giedd, J. (1999). "Morphology and development of the human vocal tract: A study using magnetic resonance imaging," *Journal of the Acoustical Society of America* **106**, pp. 1511–1522.

Fitch, W. T. and Hauser, M. D. (1998). "Differences that make a difference: Do locus equations result from physical principles that characterize all mammalian vocal tracts?," *Behavioral & Brain Sciences* **21**, pp. 264–265.

(2002). "Unpacking 'honesty': Vertebrate vocal production and the evolution of acoustic signals," in *Acoustic Communication*, ed. A. M. Simmons, R. F. Fay, and A. N. Popper (New York, NY: Springer, pp. 65–137).

(2004). "Computational constraints on syntactic processing in a nonhuman primate," *Science* **303**, pp. 377–380.

Fitch, W. T., Hauser, M. D., and Chomsky, N. (2005). "The evolution of the Language Faculty: Clarifications and implications," *Cognition* **97**, pp. 179–210.

Fitch, W. T. and Kelley, J. P. (2000). "Perception of vocal tract resonances by whooping cranes, *Grus americana*," *Ethology* **106**, pp. 559–574.

Fitch, W. T. and Reby, D. (2001). "The descended larynx is not uniquely human," *Proceedings of the Royal Society London, B* **268**, pp. 1669–1675.

Fletcher, N. H. and Rossing, T. D. (1991). *The Physics of Musical Instruments* (New York, NY: Springer-Verlag).

Fobes, J. L. and King, J. E. (1982). "Measuring primate learning abilities," in *Primate Behavior*, ed. J. L. Fobes and J. E. King (New York, NY: Academic Press, pp. 289–326).

Fodor, J. A. (1983). *The Modularity of Mind* (Cambridge, MA: MIT Press).

  (2000). *The Mind Doesn't Work That Way* (Cambridge, MA: MIT Press).

Foley, R. A. (1995). "The adaptive legacy of human evolution: A search for the environment of evolutionary adaptedness," *Evolutionary Anthropology* **4**, pp. 194–203.

  (1998). "The context of human genetic evolution," *Genome Research* **8**, pp. 339–347.

Foley, R. A. and Lee, P. C. (1991). "Ecology and energetics of encephalization in hominid evolution," *Philosophical Transactions of the Royal Society of London, B* **334**, pp. 223–232.

Ford, J. K. B. and Fisher, H. D. (1983). "Group-specific dialects of killer whales (Orcinus orca) in British Columbia," in *Communication and Behavior of Whales*, ed. R. Payne (Boulder, CO: Westview Press, pp. 129–161).

Forey, P. L. and Janvier, P. (1993). "Agnathans and the origin of jawed vertebrates," *Nature* **361**, pp. 129–134.

Foster, K. R., Wenseleers, T., and Ratnieks, F. L. W. (2006). "Kin selection is the key to altruism," *Trends in Ecology and Evolution* **21**, pp. 57–60.

Fouts, R. and Mills, S. T. (1997). *Next of Kin* (New York, NY: Harper).

Fragaszy, D. M., Visalberghi, E., and Fedigan, L. M. (2004). *The Complete Capuchin: The biology of the genus Cebus* (New York, NY: Cambridge University Press).

Frank, S. A. (1998). *Foundations of Social Evolution* (Princeton, NJ: Princeton University Press).

Freeman, S. (1987). "Male red-winged blackbirds (Agelaius phoeniceus) assess the RHP of neighbors by watching contests," *Behavioral Ecology and Sociobiology* **21**, pp. 307–311.

Frey, R. and Riede, T. (2003). "Sexual dimorphism of the larynx of the Mongolian Gazelle (*Procapra gutturosa Pallas, 1777) (Mammalia, Artiodactyla, Bovidae)*," *Zoologischer Anzeiger* **242**, pp. 33–62.

Friederici, A., Meyer, M., and von Cramon, D. Y. (2000). "Auditory language comprehension: An event-related fMRI study on the processing of syntactic and lexical information," *Brain and Language* **74**, pp. 289–300.

Friedmann, H. (1955). "The honey-guides," *Bulletin of the United States National Museum* **208**, pp. 1–292.

Frishberg, N. (1979). "Historical change: From iconic to arbitrary," in *The Signs of Language*, ed. E. S. Klima and U. Bellugi (Cambridge, MA: Harvard University Press, pp. 67–87).

Frith, U. (2001). "Mind blindness and the brain in autism," *Neuron* **32**, pp. 969–979.

Fromkin, V. A. (1973). *Speech Errors as Linguistic Evidence* (The Hague: Mouton).
(ed.) (1978). *Tone: A linguistic survey* (New York, NY: Academice Press).

Fruth, B. and Hohmann, G. (1996). "Nest building behaviour in the great apes: The great leap forward?," in *Great Ape Societies*, ed. W. C. McGrew, L. F. Marchant, and T. Nishida (Cambridge: Cambridge University Press, pp. 225–240).

Futuyma, D. J. (1979). *Evolutionary Biology* (Sunderland, MA: Sinauer Associates).

Gabunia, L., Vekua, A., Lordkipanidze, D., Swisher, C. C., Ferring, R., Justus, A., *et al.* (2000). "Earliest Pleistocene hominid cranial remains from Dmanisi, Republic of Georgia: Taxonomy, geological setting, and age," *Science* **288**, pp. 1019–1025.

Galdikas, B. M. F. (1982). "Orang-utan tool use at Tanjung Puting Reserve, Central Indonesian Borneo (Kalimantan Tengah)," *Journal of Human Evolution* **10**, pp. 19–33.

Galef, B. G. (1988). "Imitation in animals: History, definitions, and interpretation of data from the psychological laboratory," in *Social Learning: Psychological and biological perspectives*, ed. T. Zentall and B. G. Galef (Hillsdale, NJ: Lawrence Erlbaum Associates, pp. 3–28).

Gallese, V. and Goldman, A. (1998). "Mirror neurons and the simulation theory of mind-reading," *Trends in Cognitive Science* **2**, pp. 493–501.

Gallistel, C. R. (1990). *The Organization of Learning* (Cambridge, MA: MIT Press).
(2000). "The replacement of general-purpose learning models with adaptively specialized learning modules," in *The New Cognitive Neurosciences*, ed. M. Gazzaniga (Cambridge, MA: MIT Press, pp. 1179–1191).

Gallup, G. G., Jr. (1970). "Chimpanzees: Self-recognition," *Science* **167**, pp. 86–87.
(1991). "Toward a comparative psychology of self-awareness: Species limitations and cognitive consequences," in *The Self: An interdisciplinary approach*, ed. G. R. Goethals and J. Strauss (New York, NY: Springer-Verlag, pp. 121–135).

Gannon, P. J., Holloway, R. L., Broadfield, D. C., and Braun, A. R. (1998). "Asymmetry of chimpanzee planum temporale: Humanlike pattern of Wernicke's brain language area homolog," *Science* **279**, pp. 220–222.

Gans, C. and Northcutt, R. G. (1983). "Neural crest and the origin of Vertebrates: A new head," *Science* **220**, pp. 268–274.

Garcia, J. and Koelling, R. A. (1966). "Relation of cue to consequences in avoidance learning," *Psychonomic Science* **4**, pp. 123–124.

Gardner, H. (1983). *Frames of Mind: The theory of multiple intelligences* (London: Heinemann).
(1985). *The Mind's New Science: A history of the cognitive revolution* (New York, NY: Basic Books).

Gardner, R. A. and Gardner, B. T. (1969). "Teaching sign language to a chimpanzee," *Science* **165**, pp. 664–672.

Garner, R. L. (1892). *The Speech of Monkeys* (London: William Heinemann).

Garrett, M. (1988). "Processes in language production," in *Linguistics: The Cambridge survey, Vol. III: Language: Psychological and biological aspects*, ed. F. J. Newmeyer (Cambridge: Cambridge University Press).

Gatesy, S. M. and Biewener, A. A. (1991). "Bipedal locomotion: Effects of speed, size and limb posture in birds and humans," *Journal of Zoology, London* **224**, pp. 127–147.

Gathercole, V. C. (1987). "The contrastive hypothesis for the acquisition of word meaning: A reconsideration of the theory," *Journal of Child Language* **14**, pp. 493–532.

Gaupp, E. (1904). "Das Hyobranchialskelet der Wirbeltiere," *Ergebnisse der Anatomie und Entwicklungsgeschichte* **14**, pp. 808–1048.

Gautier, J. P. (1971). "Etude morphologique et fonctionnelle des annexes extra-laryngées des cercopithecinae; liaison avec les cris d'espacement," *Biologica Gabonica* **7**, pp. 230–267.

Gazdar, G., Klein, E., Pullum, G. K., and Sag, I. (1985). *Generalized Phrase Structure Grammar* (Oxford: Basil Blackwell).

Gazzaniga, M. S. (2000). "Cerebral specialization and interhemispheric communication: Does the corpus callosum enable the human condition?," *Brain* **123**, pp. 1293–1326.

Gazzola, V., Aziz-Zadeh, L., and Keysers, C. (2006). "Empathy and the somatotopic auditory mirror system in humans," *Current Biology* **16**, pp. 1824–1829.

Gehring, W. J. and Ikeo, K. (1999). "Pax 6: Mastering eye morphogenesis and eye evolution," *Trends Genet* **15**, pp. 371–377.

Geissmann, T. (1984). "Inheritance of song parameters in the gibbon song analyzed in 2 hybrid gibbons (*Hylobates pileatus* s *H. lar*)," *Folia primatologica* **42**, pp. 216–225.

(1987). "Songs of hybrid gibbons Hylobates pileatus x H. lar," *International Journal of Primatology* **8**, p. 540.

(2000). "Gibbon song and human music from an evolutionary perspective," in *The Origins of Music*, ed. N. L. Wallin, B. Merker, and S. Brown (Cambridge, MA: MIT Press, pp. 103–123).

(2002). "Duet-splitting and the evolution of gibbon songs," *Biological Reviews* **77**, pp. 57–76.

Gentilucci, M. and Corballis, M. C. (2006). "From manual gesture to speech: A gradual transition," *Neuroscience & Biobehavioral Reviews* **30**, pp. 949–960.

Gentner, T. Q., Fenn, K. M., Margoliash, D., and Nusbaum, H. C. (2006). "Recursive syntactic pattern learning by songbirds," *Nature* **440**, pp. 1204–1207.

George, S. L. (1978). "A longitudinal and cross-sectional analysis of the growth of the post-natal cranial base angle," *American Journal of Physical Anthropology* **49**, pp. 171–178.

Gergely, G., Bekkering, H., and Király, I. (2002). "Rational imitation in preverbal infants," *Nature* **415**, p. 755.

Gerhart, J. and Kirschner, M. (1997). *Cells, Embryos, and Evolution* (Toronto: Blackwell Science).

Gersting, J. L. (1999). *Mathematical Structures for Computer Science* (New York, NY: W. H. Freeman).

Geschwind, N. (1970). "Intermodal equivalence of stimuli in apes," *Science* **170**, p. 1249.

Ghazanfar, A. A. and Hauser, M. D. (1999). "The neuroethology of primate vocal communication: Substrates for the evolution of speech," *Trends in Cognitive Science* **3**, pp. 377–384.

Giedd, J. N., Castellanos, F. X., Rajapakse, J. C., Vaituzis, A. C., and Rapoport, J. L. (1997). "Sexual dimorphism of the developing human brain," *Progress in Neuro-Psychopharmacology and Biological Psychiatry* **21**, pp. 1185–1201.

Gilbert, S. F. (2003). *Developmental Biology* (Sunderland, MA: Sinauer).

Gilbert, S. F., Opitz, J. M., and Raff, R. A. (1996). "Resynthesizing evolutionary and developmental biology," *Developmental Biology* **173**, pp. 357–372.

Gillan, D. D. D. (1981). "Reasoning in the chimpanzee II: Transitive inference," *Journal of Experimental Psychology: Animal Behavior Processes* **7**, pp. 150–164.

Giurfa, M., Zhang, S., Jenett, A., Menzel, R., and Srinivasan, M. V. (2001). "The concepts of 'sameness' and 'difference' in an insect," *Nature* **410**, pp. 930–933.

Givón, T. (1995). *Functionalism and Grammar* (Amsterdam: John Benjamins).

   (2002). *Bio-Linguistics: The Santa Barbara lectures* (Amsterdam: John Benjamins).

Glass, L. and Mackey, M. C. (1988). *From Clocks to Chaos: The rhythms of life* (Princeton, NJ: Princeton University Press).

Gleason, J. B. (ed.) (2005). *The Development of Language* (Boston, MA: Pearson, Allyn & Bacon).

Gleitman, L. and Papafragou, A. (2005). "Language and thought," in *Cambridge Handbook of Thinking and Reasoning*, ed. K. J. Holyoak and R. G. Morrison (New York: Cambridge University Press, pp. 633–661).

Goddard, C. and Wierzbicka, A. (eds) (2002). *Meaning and Universal Grammar: Theory and empirical findings* (Amsterdam: John Benjamins).

Godfray, H. C. J. (1991). "Signalling of need by offspring to their parents," *Nature* **352**, pp. 328–330.

Goldin-Meadow, S. (2003). *Hearing Gesture: How our hands help us think* (Cambridge, MA: Harvard University Press).

Goldin-Meadow, S. and Mylander, C. (1998). "Spontaneous sign systems created by deaf children in two cultures," *Nature* **391**, pp. 278–281.

Goldsmith, J. A. (1990). *Autosegmental and Metrical Phonology* (Oxford: Blackwell).

Goldstein, L., Byrd, D., and Saltzman, E. (2006a). "The role of vocal tract gestural action units in understanding the evolution of phonology," in *From Action to Language via The mirror neuron system*, ed. M. A. Arbib (Cambridge: Cambridge University Press, pp. 215–249).

Goldstein, L., Whalen, D. H., and Best, C. T. (eds) (2006b). *Laboratory Phonology 8* (Amsterdam: Walter de Gruyter).

Golinkoff, R. M., Mervis, C. B., and Hirsh-Pasek, K. (1994). "Early object labels: The case for a developmental lexical principles framework," *Journal of Child Language* 21, pp. 125–155.

Goodall, J. (1968). "The behaviour of free-living chimpanzees in the Gombe Stream Reserve, Tanzania," *Animal Behaviour Monographs* 1, pp. 161–311.

(1986). *The Chimpanzees of Gombe: Patterns of behavior* (Cambridge, MA: Harvard University Press).

Goodman, N. (1983). *Fact, Fiction and Forecast* (Cambridge, MA: Harvard University Press).

Goodwin, B. C. (2001). *How the Leopard Changed its Spots: The evolution of complexity* (Princeton, NJ: Princeton University Press).

Gopnik, M. (1990). "Feature-blind grammar and dysphasia," *Nature* **344**, p. 715.

Gottlieb, G. (1974). "On the acoustic basis of species identification in wood ducklings (Aix sponsa)," *Journal of Comparative Physiology and Psychology* 87, pp. 1038–1048.

(1992). *Individual Development and Evolution: The genesis of novel behavior* (New York, NY: Oxford University Press).

Gould, J. L. and Marler, P. (1987). "Learning by instinct," *Scientific American* **256**, pp. 74–85.

Gould, S. J. (1975). "Allometry in primates, with emphasis on scaling and evolution of the brain," in *Approaches to Primate Paleobiology*, ed. F. Szalay (Basel: S. Karger, pp 244–292).

(1977). *Ontogeny and Phylogeny* (Cambridge, MA: Belknap Press).

(1987). "Integrity and Mr. Rifkin," in *An Urchin in the Storm: Essays about books and ideas*, ed. S. J. Gould (New York: Norton, pp. 229–239).

(1991). "Exaptation: A crucial tool for evolutionary psychology," *Journal of Social Issues* **47**, pp. 43–65.

(1996). *The Mismeasure of Man* (New York, NY: W. Norton & Co.).

(1997). "The exaptive excellence of spandrels as a term and prototype," *Proceedings of the National Academy of Sciences* **94**, pp. 10750–10755.

(2002). *The Structure of Evolutionary Theory* (Cambridge, MA: Harvard University Press).

Gould, S. J. and Lewontin, R. C. (1979). "The spandrels of San Marco and the panglossian paradigm: A critique of the adaptationist programme," *Proceedings of the Royal Society, B* **205**, pp. 581–598.

Gould, S. J. and Vrba, E. S. (1982). "Exaptation – a missing term in the science of form," *Paleobiology* **8**, pp. 4–15.

Gouzoules, S., Gouzoules, H., and Marler, P. (1984). "Rhesus monkey (Macaca mulatta) screams: Representational signalling in the recruitment of agonistic aid," *Animal Behavior* **32**, pp. 182–193.

Gowlett, J. A. J. (1992). "Tools: The Paleolithic record," in *Cambridge Encyclopedia of Human Evolution*, ed. S. Jones, R. D. Martin, and D. R. Pilbeam (Cambridge: Cambridge University Press, pp. 350–360).

Grafen, A. (1982). "How not to measure inclusive fitness," *Nature* **298**, pp. 425–426.

(1984). "Natural selection, kin selection and group selection," in *Behavioural Ecology*, ed. J. R. Krebs and N. B. Davies (Sunderland, MA: Sinauer Associates, pp. 62–84).

(1990a). "Biological signals as handicaps," *Journal of Theoretical Biology* **144**, pp. 517–546.

(1990b). "Sexual selection unhandicapped by the Fisher process," *Journal of Theoretical Biology* **144**, pp. 473–516.

Gray, R. D. and Atkinson, Q. D. (2003). "Language-tree divergence times support the Anatolian theory of Indo-European origin," *Nature* **426**, pp. 435–439.

Graybiel, A. M. (1994). "The basal ganglia and adaptive motor control," *Science* **265**, pp. 1826–1831.

(2005). "The basal ganglia: Learning new tricks and loving it," *Current Opinion in Neurobiology* **15**, pp. 638–644.

Greenewalt, C. H. (1968). *Bird Song: Acoustics and physiology* (Washington: Smithsonian Institution Press).

Greenfield, P. M. (1991). "Language, tools, and brain: The ontogeny and phylogeny of hierarchically organized sequential behavior," *Behavioral and Brain Sciences* **14**, pp. 531–595.

Greenfield, P. M. and Savage-Rumbaugh, E. S. (1990). "Grammatical combination in Pan paniscus: Processed of learning and invention in the evolution and development of language," in *"Language" and Intelligence in Monkeys and Apes: Comparative developmental perspectives*, ed. S. T. Parker and K. R. Gibson (New York, NY: Cambridge University Press, pp. 540–578).

Grice, H. P. (1957). "Meaning," *Philosophical Review* **66**, pp. 377–388.

(1975). "Logic and conversation," in *The Logic of Grammar*, ed. D. Davidson and G. Harman (Encino, CA: Dickenson, pp. 64–153).

Griffin, D. R. (1976). *The Question of Animal Awareness* (New York, NY: Rockefeller University Press).

(1992). *Animal Minds* (Chicago, IL: Chicago University Press).

(2001). *Animal Minds: Beyond cognition to consciousness* (Chicago, IL: Chicago University Press).

Groszer, M., Keays, D., Deacon, R., de Bono, J., Prasad-Mulcare, S., Gaub, S., Baum, M., French, C., Nicod, J., Coventry, J., Enard, W., Fray, M., Brown, S. D. M., Nolan, P. M., Pääbo, S., Channon, K. M., Costas, R. M., Eilers, J., Ehret, G., Nicholas, J., Rawlins, P., and Fisher, S. E. (2008). "Impaired synaptic plasticity and motor learning in mice with a point mutation implicated in human speech deficits," *Current Biology* **18**, pp. 354–362.

Guilloud, N. B. and McClure, H. M. (1969). "Air sac infection in the Orang-utan," *Proceedings of the Second International Congress of Primatology* **3**, pp. 143–147.

Guinee, L. and Payne, K. (1988). "Rhyme-like repetition in songs of humpback whales," *Ethology* **79**, pp. 295–306.

Guttenplan, S. (1986). *The Languages of Logic* (Oxford: Blackwell).

Haesler, S., Rochefort, C., Geogi, B., Licznerski, P., Osten, P., and Scharff, C. (2007). "Incomplete and inaccurate vocal imitation after knockdown of FoxP2 in songbird basal ganglia nucleus area X," *PLOS Biology* **5**, p. e321.

Haesler, S., Wada, K., Nshdejan, A., Morrisey, E. E., Lints, T., Jarvis, E. D., and Scharff, C. (2004). "FoxP2 expression in avian vocal learners and non-learners," *Journal of Neuroscience* **24**, pp. 3164–3175.

Hahn, J. and Münzel, S. (1995). "Knochenflöten aus dem Aurignacien des Geissenklösterle bei Blaubeuren, Alb-Donau-Kreis," *Fundberichte aus Baden-Würtemberg* **20**, pp. 1–12.

Hailman, J. P. and Ficken, M. S. (1987). "Combinatorial animal communication with computable syntax: Chick-a-dee calling qualifies as 'language' by structural linguistics," *Animal Behavior* **34**, pp. 1899–1901.

Haldane, J. B. S. (1955). "Population genetics," *New Biology* **18**, pp. 34–51.

Hall, B. K. (ed.) (1994). *Homology: The hierarchical basis of comparative biology* (San Diego, CA: Academic Press).

(1998). *Evolutionary Developmental Biology* (London: Chapman & Hall).

Hall, K. and Schaller, G. B. (1964). "Tool using behavior of the California sea otter," *Journal of Mammalogy* **45**, pp. 287–298.

Hall, R. A. (1966). *Pidgin and Creole Languages* (Ithaca, NY: Cornell University Press).

Hamilton, W. D. (1963). "The evolution of altruistic behavior," *American Naturalist* **97**, pp. 354–356.

(1964). "The genetical evolution of social behavior," *Journal of Theoretical Biology* **7**, pp. 1–52.

(1975). "Innate social aptitudes of man: An approach from evolutionary genetics," in *Biosocial Anthropology*, ed. R. Fox (New York, NY: John Wiley, pp. 133–155).

Hammerschmidt, K., Freudenstein, T., and Jürgens, U. (2001). "Vocal development in squirrel monkeys," *Behaviour* **138**, pp. 1179–1204.

Hammond, M. (1995). "Metrical phonology," *Annual Review of Anthropology* **24**, pp. 313–342.

Hampton, R. R. (1994). "Sensitivity to information specifying the line of gaze of humans in sparrows (*Passer domesticus*)," *Behaviour* **130**, pp. 41–45.

Happé, F. G. E. (1995). "The role of age and verbal ability in the theory of mind task performance of subjects with autism," *Child Development* **66**, pp. 843–855.

Hare, B., Brown, M., Williamson, C., and Tomasello, M. (2002). "The domestication of social cognition in dogs," *Science* **298**, pp. 1634–1636.

Hare, B., Call, J., Agnetta, B., and Tomasello, M. (2000). "Chimpanzees know what conspecifics do and do not see," *Animal Behavior* **59**, pp. 771–785.

Hare, B., Plyusnina, I., Ignacio, N., Schepina, O., Stepika, A., Wrangham, R. W., and Trut, L. (2005). "Social cognitive evolution in captive foxes is a correlated by-product of experimental domestication," *Current Biology* **15**, pp. 226–230.

Hare, B. and Tomasello, M. (2004). "Chimpanzees are more skillful in competitive than cooperative cognitive tasks," *Animal Behavior* **68**, pp. 571–581.

Harnad, S. (1990). "The symbol grounding problem," *Physica D* **42**, pp. 335–346.

Harnad, S., Steklis, H. S., and Lancaster, J. (eds) (1976). *Origin and Evolution of Language and Speech* (New York: New York Academy of Sciences).

Harries, M. L. L., Hawkins, S., Hacking, J., and Hughes, I. (1998). "Changes in the male voice at puberty: Vocal fold length and its relationship to the fundamental frequency of the voice," *Journal of Laryngology & Otology* **112**, pp. 451–454.

Harris, R. (2007). "Concepts where there are none," in *Times Higher Education* (London).

Harris, T. R, Fitch, W. T., Goldstein, L. M., and Fashing, P. J. (2006). "Black and white colobus monkey (Colobus guereza) roars as a source of both honest and exaggerated information about body mass," *Ethology* **112**, pp. 911–920.

Harris, Z. S. (1951). *Methods in Structural Linguistics* (Chicago, IL: University of Chicago Press).

Harrison, D. F. N. (1995). *The Anatomy and Physiology of the Mammalian Larynx* (New York, NY: Cambridge University Press).

Harvey, P. H. and Bradbury, J. W. (1991). "Sexual selection," in *Behavioural Ecology*, ed. J. R. Krebs and N. B. Davies (Cambridge, MA: Blackwell Scientific Publications, pp. 203–233).

Harvey, P. H. and Pagel, M. D. (1991). *The Comparative Method in Evolutionary Biology* (Oxford: Oxford University Press).

Haslinger, B., Erhard, P., Altenmuller, E., Schroeder, U., Boecker, H., and Ceballos-Baumann, A. O. (2005). "Transmodal sensorimotor networks during action observation in professional pianists," *Journal of Cognitive Neuroscience* **17**, pp. 282–293.

Haspelmath, M. (1999). "Why is grammaticalization irreversible?," *Linguistics* **37**, pp. 1043–1068.

Hast, M. (1983). "Comparative anatomy of the larynx: Evolution and function," in *Vocal Fold Physiology: Biomechanics, acoustics and phonatory control*, ed. I. R. Titze and R. C. Scherer (Denver, CO: Denver Center for the Performing Arts, pp. 3–14).

Haug, H. (1987). "Brain sizes, surfaces, and neuronal sizes of the cortex cerebri: A stereological investigation of man and his variability and a comparison with some mammals (primates, whales, marsupials, insectivores, and one elephant)," *American Journal of Anatomy* **180**, pp. 126–142.

Hausberger, M., Henry, L., and Richard, M. (1995a). "Testosterone-induced singing in female European starlings (Sturnus vulgaris)," *Ethology* **99**, p. 193.

Hausberger, M., Richard-Yris, M.-A., Henry, L., Lepage, L., and Schmidt, I. (1995b). "Song sharing reflects the social organization in a captive group of European starlings (Sturnus vulgaris)," *Journal of Comparative Psychology* **109**, pp. 222–241.

Hauser, M. D. (1988). "How infant vervet monkeys learn to recognize starling alarm calls," *Behaviour* **105**, pp. 187–201.

(1992). "Costs of deception: Cheaters are punished in rhesus monkeys," *Proceedings of the National Academy of Sciences* **89**, pp. 12137–12139.

(1996). *The Evolution of Communication* (Cambridge, MA: MIT Press).

(2000). *Wild Minds: What animals really think* (New York, NY: Henry Holt).

Hauser, M. D., Chomsky, N., and Fitch, W. T. (2002). "The Language Faculty: What is it, who has it, and how did it evolve?," *Science* **298**, pp. 1569–1579.

Hauser, M. D., Dehaene, S., Dehaene-Lambertz, G., and Patalano, A. L. (2002b). "Spontaneous number discrimination of multi-format auditory stimuli in cotton-top tamarins (*Saguinus oedipus*)," *Cognition* **86**, pp. B23–B32.

Hauser, M. D. and Fitch, W. T. (2003). "What are the uniquely human components of the language faculty?," in *Language Evolution*, ed. M. Christiansen and S. Kirby (Oxford: Oxford University Press, pp. 158–181).

Hauser, M. D. and Marler, P. (1993). "Food-associated calls in rhesus macaques (*Macaca mulatta*) I: Socioecological factors influencing call production," *Behavioral Ecology* **4**, pp. 194–205.

Hauser, M. D. and McDermott, J. (2003). "The evolution of the music faculty: A comparative perspective," *Nature Neuroscience* **6**, pp. 663–668.

Hauser, M. D. and Nelson, D. (1991). "Intentional signaling in animal communication," *Trends in Ecology and Evolution* **6**, pp. 186–189.

Hauser, M. D. and Schön Ybarra, M. (1994). "The role of lip configuration in monkey vocalizations: Experiments using xylocaine as a nerve block," *Brain and Language* **46**, pp. 232–244.

Hauser, M. D. and Wrangham, R. W. (1987). "Manipulation of food calls in captive chimpanzees: A preliminary report," *Folia primatologica* **48**, pp. 24–35.

Hawkes, K., O'Connell, J. F., Blurton Jones, N. G., Alvarez, H., and Charnov, E. L. (1998). "Grandmothering, menopause, and the evolution of human life histories," *Proceedings of the National Academy of Sciences, USA* **95**, pp. 1336–1339.

Hay, R. L. and Leakey, M. D. (1982). "The fossil footprints of Laetoli," *Scientific American* **246**, pp. 50–55.

Hayes, C. (1951). *The Ape in Our House* (New York, NY: Harper).

Hayes, K. J. and Hayes, C. (1951). "The intellectual development of a home-raised chimpanzee," *Proceedings of the American Philosophical Society* **95**, pp. 105–109.

Healy, S. D. and Hurly, T. A. (2004). "Spatial learning and memory in birds," *Brain, Behavior and Evolution* **63**, pp. 211–220.

Heath, R. G. (1963). "Electrical self-stimulation of the brain in man," *American Journal of Psychiatry* **120**, pp. 571–577.

Heffner, R. S. (2004). "Primate hearing from a mammalian perspective," *Anatomical Record* **281A**, pp. 1111–1122.

Heimlich, H. J. (1975). "A life-saving maneuver to prevent food-choking," *Journal of the American Medical Association* **234**, pp. 398–401.

Heine, B., Claudi, U., and Hünnemeyer, F. (1991). *Grammaticalization: A conceptual framework* (Chicago, IL: University of Chicago Press).

Heine, B. and Kuteva, T. (2002). "On the evolution of grammatical forms," in *The Transition to Language*, ed. A. Wray (Oxford: Oxford University Press, pp. 376–397).

Held, R. and Hein, A. (1963). "Movement-produced stimulation in the development of visually guided behavior," *Journal of Comparative and Physiological Psychology* **56**, pp. 872–876.

Hellige, J. B. (ed.) (2001). *Hemispheric Asymmetry: What's right and what's left?* (Cambridge, MA: Harvard University Press).

Henderson, J., Hurly, T. A., Bateson, M., and Healy, S. D. (2006). "Timing in free-living rufous hummingbirds, Selasphorus rufus," *Current Biology* **16**, pp. 512–515.

Henshilwood, C., D'Errico, F., Yates, R., Jacobs, Z., Tribolo, C., Duller, G., Mercier, N., Sealy, J., Valladas, H., Watts, I., and Wintle, A. (2002). "Emergence of modern human behavior: Middle Stone Age engravings from South Africa," *Science* **295**, pp. 1278–1280.

Henton, C. (1992). "The abnormality of male speech," in *New Departures in Linguistics*, ed. G. Wolf (New York, NY: Garland Publishing, pp. 27–59).

Hepper, P. G. (1991). "An examination of fetal learning before and after birth," *Irish Journal of Psychology* **12**, pp. 95–107.

Herder, J. G. (1996[1772]). *Essay on the Origin of Language* [*Über den Ursprung der Sprache*], trans. John H. Moran (Stuttgart: Verlag Freies Geistesleben).

Herman, L. M., Richards, D. G., and Wolz, J. P. (1984). "Comprehension of sentences by bottlenosed dolphins," *Cognition* **16**, pp. 129–219.

Hernandez-Aguilar, R. A., Moore, J., and Pickering, T. R. (2007). "Savanna chimpanzees use tools to harvest the underground storage organs of plants," *Proceedings of the National Academy of Sciences* **104**, pp. 19210–19213.

Herodotus (1964 [450–420 BC]). *The Histories* (Baltimore, MD: Penguin).

Herrnstein, R. J., Loveland, D. H., and Cable, C. (1976). "Natural concepts in in the pigeon," *Journal of Experimental Psychology: Animal Behavior Processes* **2**, pp. 285–311.

Herrnstein, R. J., Vaughan, W., Jr., Mumford, D. B., and Kosslyn, S. M. (1989). "Teaching pigeons an abstract relational rule: Insideness," *Perception & Psychophysics* **46**, pp. 56–64.

Hewes, G. W. (1973). "Primate communication and the gestural origin of language," *Current Anthropology* **14**, pp. 5–24.

(1975). *Language Origins: A bibliography* (The Hague: Mouton).

(1977). "Language origin theories," in *Language Learning by a Chimpanzee: The Lana Project*, ed. D. M. Rumbaugh (New York, NY: Academic Press, pp. 5–53).

(1983). "The invention of phonemically-based language," in *Glossogenetics: The origin and evolution of language*, ed. É. d. Grolier (New York, NY: Harwood Academic Publishers, pp. 143–162).

(1996). "A history of the study of language origins and the gestural primacy hypothesis," in *Handbook of Human Symbolic Evolution*, ed. A. Lock and C. R. Peters (Oxford: Clarendon Press, pp. 571–595).

Hewitt, G., MacLarnon, A., and Jones, K. E. (2002). "The functions of laryngeal air sacs in primates: A new hypothesis," *Folia Primatologica* **73**, pp. 70–94.

Hienz, R. D., Jones, A. M., and Weerts, E. M. (2004). "The discrimination of baboon grunt calls and human vowel sounds by baboons," *Journal of the Acoustical Society of America* **116**, pp. 1692–1697.

Hight, G. and Jury, K. (1970). "Hill country sheep production II: Lamb mortality and birth weights in Romney and Border Leicester × Romney flocks," *New Zealand Journal of Agricultural Research* **13**, pp. 735–752.

Hiiemäe, K. and Palmer, J. B. (2003). "Tongue movements in feeding and speech," *Critical Reviews in Oral Biology and Medicine* **14**, pp. 413–429.

Hill, K., Boesch, C., Goodall, J., Pusey, A. E., Williams, J., and Wrangham, R. W. (2001). "Mortality rates among wild chimpanzees," *Journal of Human Evolution* **40**, pp. 437–450.

Hilloowala, R. A. (1975). "Comparative anatomical study of the hyoid apparatus in selected primates," *American Journal of Anatomy* **142**, pp. 367–384.

Hinde, R. A. (1981). "Animal signals: Ethological and games-theory approaches are not incompatible," *Animal Behavior* **29**, pp. 535–542.

Hinton, G. E. and Nowlan, S. J. (1987). "How learning can guide evolution," *Complex Systems* **1**, pp. 495–502.

Hinton, L., Nichols, J., and Ohala, J. (eds) (1994). *Sound Symbolism* (Cambridge: Cambridge University Press).

Hockett, C. F. (1960). "Logical considerations in the study of animal communication," in *Animal Sounds and Communication*, ed. W. E. Lanyon and W. N. Tavolga (Washington, DC: American Institute of Biological Sciences, pp. 392–430).

(1963). "The problem of universals in language," in *Universals of Language*, ed. J. Greenberg (Cambridge, MA: MIT Press, pp. 1–29).

Hockett, C. F. and Ascher, R. (1964). "The human revolution," *Current Anthropology* **5**, pp. 135–147.

Hoelzel, A. R. (1986). "Song characteristics and response to playback of male and female robins Erithacus rubecula," *Ibis* **128**, pp. 115–127.

Hofstadter, D. R. (1979). *Godel, Escher, Bach: An eternal golden braid* (New York, NY: Basic Books).

Holbrook, R. T. and Carmody, F. J. (1937). "X-ray studies of speech articulations," *University of California Publications in Modern Philology* **20**, pp. 187–238.

Holland, P. W. H. (1999). "The future of evolutionary developmental biology," *Nature* **402** suppl., pp. C41–C42.

Holland, P. W. H., Garcia-Fernández, J., Williams, N. A., and Sidow, N. (1994). "Gene duplication and the origins of vertebrate development," *Development*, **1994**, pp. 125–133.

Holloway, R. L. (1966). "Cranial capacity, neural reorganization and hominid evolution: A search for more suitable parameters," *American Anthropologist* **68**, pp. 103–121.

(1969). "Culture: A human domain," *Current Anthropology* **10**, pp. 395–407.

(1996). "Evolution of the human brain," in *Handbook of Human Symbolic Evolution*, ed. A. Lock and C. R. Peters (Oxford: Clarendon Press, pp. 74–108).

(2008). "The human brain evolving: A personal retrospective," *Annual Review of Anthropology* **37**, pp. 1–19.

Holy, T. E. and Guo, Z. (2005). "Ultrasonic songs of male mice," *PLOS Biology* **3**, p. e386.

Hopcroft, J. E., Motwani, R., and Ullman, J. D. (2000). *Introduction to Automata Theory, Languages and Computation* (Reading, MA: Addison-Wesley).

Hopfield, J. J. (1982). "Neural networks and physical systems with emergent collective computational abilities," *Proceedings of the National Academy of Sciences, USA* **79**, pp. 2554–2558.

Hopkins, W. D. and Russell, J. L. (2004). "Further evidence of a right hand advantage in motor skill by chimpanzees (*Pan troglodytes*)," *Neuropsychologia* **42**, pp. 990–996.

Hopkins, W. D., Russell, J. L., Freeman, H., Buehler, N., Reynolds, E., and Schapiro, S. J. (2005). "The distribution and development of handedness for manual gestures in captive chimpanzees (*Pan troglodytes*)," *Psychological Science* **16**, pp. 487–493.

Hopkins, W. D., Taglialatela, J. P., and Leavens, D. A. (2007). "Chimpanzees differentially produce novel vocalizations to capture the attention of a human," *Animal Behavior* **73**, pp. 281–286.

Hopson, J. A. (1966). "The origin of the mammalian middle ear," *American Zoologist* **6**, pp. 437–450.

Howie, J. M. (1991). *Automata and Languages* (Oxford: Oxford Univeristy Press).

Hrdy, S. B. (1981). *The Woman Who Never Evolved* (Cambridge, MA: Harvard University Press).

(1999). *Mother Nature* (New York, NY: Pantheon Books).

(2005). "Comes the child before man: How cooperative breeding and prolonged postweaning dependence shaped human potentials," in *Hunter-Gatherer Childhoods*, ed. B. Hewlett and M. Lamb (London: Aldine Transaction, pp. 65–91).

Hu, Y., Meng, J., Wang, Y., and Li, C. (2005). "Large Mesozoic mammals fed on young dinosaurs," *Nature* **433**, pp. 150–152.

Huey, R. B., Hertz, P. E., and Sinervo, B. (2003). "Behavioral drive versus behavioral inertia in evolution: A null model approach," *American Naturalist* **161**, pp. 357–385.

Huffman, M. A. (1997). "Current evidence for self-medication in primates: A multidisciplinary perspective," *Yearbook of Physical Anthropology* **40**, pp. 171–200.

Huffman, M. A. and Seifu, M. (1989). "Observations on the illness and consumption of a possibly medicinal plant Vernonia amygdalina by a wild chimpanzee in the Mahale mountains National Park, Tanzania," *Primates* **30**, pp. 51–63.

Hulse, S. H., Fowler, H., and Honig, W. K. (eds) (1978). *Cognitive Processes in Animal Behavior* (Hillsdale, NJ: Lawrence Erlbaum Associates).

Humboldt, W. von (1836). *Über die Kawi-Sprache auf der Insel Java* (Berlin: Druckerei der Königlichen Akademie der Wissenschaften).

Humphrey, N. K. (1976). "The social function of intellect," in *Growing Points in Ethology*, ed. P. P. G. Bateson and R. A. Hinde (Cambridge: Cambridge University Press, pp. 303–317).

Hunt, G. R. and Gray, R. D. (2003). "Diversification and cumulative evolution in New Caledonian crow tool manufacture," *Proceedings of the Royal Society London, B* **270**, pp. 867–874.

(2004a). "Direct observations of pandanus-tool manufacture and use by a New Caledonian crow (Corvus moneduloides)," *Animal Cognition* **7**, pp. 114–120.

(2004b). "The crafting of hook tools by wild New Caledonian crows," *Proceedings of the Royal Society London, B* **271** Suppl. 3, pp. S88–90.

Hurford, J. (1990). "Nativist and functional explanations in language acquisition," in *Logical issues in Language Acquistion*, ed. I. M. Roca (Dordrecht: Foris Publications, pp. 85–136).

(1994). "Linguistics and evolution: A background briefing for non-linguists," *Discussions in Neuroscience* **10**, pp. 149–157.

(2000). "The emergence of syntax," in *The Evolutionary Emergence of Language: Social function and the origins of linguistic form*, ed. C. Knight, M. Studdert-Kennedy, and J. R. Hurford (Cambridge: Cambridge University Press, pp. 219–230).

(2004). "Language beyond our grasp: What mirror neurons can, and cannot, do for language evolution," in *The Evolution of Communication Systems: A comparative approach*, ed. D. K. Oller and U. Griebel (Cambridge, MA: MIT Press, pp. 297–313).

(2007). *The Origins of Meaning* (Oxford: Oxford University Press).

Huxley, J. S. (1932). *Problems of Relative Growth* (London: Methuen).

Huxley, T. H. (1863). *Evidence as to Man's Place in Nature* (New York, NY: McGraw-Hill).

Huybregts, R. (1985). "The weak inadequacy of CFPSGs," in *Van Periferie naar Kern*, ed. G. de Haan, M. Trommelen, and W. Zonneveld (Dordrecht: Foris Publications, pp. 81–99).

Hyde, J. S. and Linn, M. C. (1988). "Gender differences in verbal ability: A meta-analysis," *Psychological Bulletin* **104**, pp. 53–69.

Iacoboni, M., Molnar-Szakacs, I., Gallese, V., Buccino, G., Mazziotta, J. C., and Rizzolatti, G. (2005). "Grasping the intentions of others with one's own mirror neuron system," *PLOS Biology* **3**, p. e79.

Iacoboni, M., Woods, R. P., Brass, M., Bekkering, H., Mazziotta, J. C., and Rizzolatti, G. (1999). "Cortical mechanisms of human imitation," *Science* **286**, pp. 2526–2528.

Insley, S. J. (2001). "Mother–offspring vocal recognition in northern fur seals is mutual but asymmetrical," *Animal Behavior* **61**, pp. 129–137.

International Chicken Genome Sequencing Consortium, The (2004). "Sequence and comparative analysis of the chicken genome provide unique perspectives on vertebrate evolution," *Nature* **432**, pp. 695–717.

Isaac, G. L. (1978). "Food sharing and human evolution: Archaeological evidence from the Plio-Pleistocene of East Africa," *Journal of Anthropological Research* **34**, pp. 311–325.

Isack, H. A. and Reyer, H.-U. (1989). "Honeyguides and honey gatherers: Interspecific communication in a symbiotic relationship," *Science* **243**, pp. 1343–1346.

Iwatsubo, T., Kuzuhara, S., Kanemitsu, A., Shimada, H., and Toyokura, Y. (1990). "Corticofugal projections to the motor nuclei of the brainstem and spinal cord in humans," *Neurology* **40**, pp. 309–312.

Jablonski, N. G. (1998). "The response of catarrhine primates to Pleistocene environmental fluctuations in East Asia," *Primates* **39**, pp. 29–37.

Jackendoff, R. (1999). "Possible stages in the evolution of the language capacity," *Trends in Cognitive Science* **3**, pp. 272–279.

(2002). *Foundations of Language* (New York, NY: Oxford University Press).

Jackendoff, R. and Lerdahl, F. (1982). "A grammatical parallel between music and language," in *Music, Mind, and Brain: The neuropsychology of music*, ed. M. E. Clynes (New York, NY: Plenum, pp. 83–117).

(2006). "The capacity for music: What is it, and what's special about it?," *Cognition* **100**, pp. 33–72.

Jackson, A. P., Eastwood, H., Bell, S. M., Adu, J., Toomes, C., Carr, I. M., Roberts, E., Hampshire, D. J., Crow, Y. J., Mighell, A. J., Karbani, G., Jafri, H., Rashid, Y., Mueller, R. F., Markham, A. F., and Woods, C. G. (2002). "Identification of microcephalin, a protein implicated in determining the size of the human brain," *American Journal of Human Genetics* **71**, pp. 136–142.

Jacob, F. (1977). "Evolution and tinkering," *Science* **196**, pp. 1161–1166.

Jacobs, G. H. and Rowe, M. P. (2004). "Evolution of vertebrate colour vision," *Clinical and Experimental Optometry* **87**, pp. 206–216.

Jakobson, R. (1941). *Kindersprache, Aphasie, und allgemeine Lautgesetze* (Uppsala: Almqvist and Wiksell).

(1960). "Linguistics and poetics," in *Style in Language*, ed. T. A. Sebeok (Cambridge, MA: MIT Press, pp. 350–377).

(1968). *Child Language, Aphasia, and Phonological Universals* (The Hague: Mouton).

Jakobson, R., Fant, G., and Halle, M. (1957). *Preliminaries to Speech Analysis: The distinctive features and their acoustic correlates* (Cambridge, MA: MIT Press).

James, W. (1890). *The Principles of Psychology* (New York, NY: Henry Holt).

Janik, V. M. and Slater, P. J. B. (1997). "Vocal learning in mammals," *Advances in the Study of Behavior* **26**, pp. 59–99.

(1998). "Context-specific use suggests that bottlenose dolphin signature whistles are cohesion calls," *Animal Behavior* **56**, pp. 829–838.

(2000). "The different roles of social learning in vocal communication," *Animal Behavior* **60**, pp. 1–11.

Jenkins, L. (1999). *Biolinguistics: Exploring the biology of language* (New York, NY: Cambridge University Press).

Jerison, H. J. (1973). *Evolution of the Brain and Intelligence* (New York: Academic Press).

(1975). "Fossil evidence of the evolution of the human brain," *Annual Review of Anthropology* **4**, pp. 27–58.

Jespersen, O. (1922). *Language: Its nature, development and origin* (New York, NY: W. W. Norton & Co.).

Ji, Q., Luo, Z.-X., Yuan, C.-X., Wible, J. R., Zhang, J.-P., and Georgi, J. A. (2002). "The earliest eutherian mammal," *Nature* **416**, pp. 816–822.

Johanson, D. C. and Edgar, B. (1996). *From Lucy to Language* (New York, NY: Simon & Schuster Editions).

Johanson, D. C. and White, T. D. (1979). "A systematic assessment of early African hominids," *Science* **203**, pp. 321–330.

Johnson, M. H. (2005). "Sensitive periods in functional brain development: Problems and prospects," *Developmental Psychobiology* **46**, pp. 287–292.

Johnstone, R. A. (1995). "Sexual selection, honest advertisement and the handicap principle: Reviewing the evidence," *Biological Reviews* **7**, pp. 1–65.

Johnstone, R. A. and Grafen, A. (1992). "The continuous Sir Philip Sidney game: A simple model of biological signalling," *Journal of Theoretical Biology* **156**, pp. 215–234.

Jolly, A. (1966). "Lemur social behavior and primate intelligence," *Science* **153**, pp. 501–506.

Jonas, S. (1981). "The supplementary motor region and speech emission," *Journal of Communication Disorders* **14**, pp. 349–373.

(1982). "The thalamus and aphasia, including transcortical aphasia: A review," *Journal of Communication Disorders* **15**, pp. 31–41.

Jones, G. and Ransome, R. D. (1993). "Echolocation calls of bats are influenced by maternal effects and change over a lifetime," *Proceedings of the Royal Society B* **252B**, pp. 125–128.

Jones, S. W. (1798 [1786]). "On the Hindus: The third anniversary discourse," *Asiatick Researches* **1**, pp. 415–431 (delivered February 2, 1786).

Joshi, A. K. (2002). "Tree-adjoining grammars," in *Handbook of Computational Linguisitcs* (New York, NY: Oxford University Press, pp. 1–31).

Joshi, A. K., Vijay-Shanker, K., and Weir, D. J. (1991). "The convergence of Mildly Context-Sensitive formalisms," in *Processing of Linguistic Structure*, ed. P. Sells, S. M. Shieber, and T. Wasow (Cambridge, MA: The MIT Press, pp. 31–81).

Joyce, G. F. (2002). "The antiquity of RNA-based evolution," *Nature* **382**, pp. 525–528.

Jungers, W. J., Pokempner, A. A., Kay, R. F., and Cartmill, M. (2003). "Hypoglossal canal size in living hominoids and the evolution of human speech," *Human Biology* **75**, pp. 473–484.

Jürgens, U. (1979). "Vocalizations as an emotional indicator: A neuroethological study in the squirrel monkey," *Behaviour* **69**, pp. 88–117.

(1994). "The role of the periaqueductal grey in vocal behaviour," *Behavioural Brain Research* **62**, pp. 107–117.

(1995). "Neuronal control of vocal production in non-human and human primates," in *Current Topics in Primate Vocal Communication*, ed. E. Zimmerman and J. D. Newman (New York, NY: Plenum Press, pp. 199–206).

(1998). "Neuronal control of mammalian vocalization, with special reference to the squirrel monkey," *Naturwissenschaften* **85**, pp. 376–388.

(2002). "Neural pathways underlying vocal control," *Neuroscience & Biobehavioral Reviews* **26**, pp. 235–258.

Jürgens, U., Kirzinger, A., and von Cramon, D. Y. (1982). "The effects of deep-reaching lesions in the cortical face area on phonation: A combined case report and experimental monkey study," *Cortex* **18**, pp. 125–139.

Jürgens, U. and Ploog, D. W. (1976). "Zur Evolution der Stimme?," *Archives of Psychiatrie und Nervenkrankungen* **222**, pp. 117–237.

Jürgens, U. and Pratt, R. (1979). "Cingular vocalization pathway: Squirrel monkey," *Experimental Brain Research* **34**, pp. 499–510.

Jürgens, U. and von Cramon, D. (1982). "On the role of the anterior cingulate cortex in phonation: A case report," *Brain and Language* **15**, pp. 234–248.

Juslin, P. and Sloboda, J. A. (eds) (2001). *Music and Emotion: Theory and research* (Oxford: Oxford University Press).

Kahane, J. (1982). "Growth of the human prepubertal and pubertal larynx," *Journal of Speech and Hearing Research* **25**, pp. 446–455.

Kako, E. (1999). "Elements of syntax in the systems of three language-trained animals," *Animal Learning & Behavior* **27**, pp. 1–14.

Kamil, A. C. and Jones, J. E. (1997). "Clark's nutcrackers learn geometric relationships among landmarks," *Nature* **390**, pp. 276–279.

Kaminski, J., Call, J., and Fischer, J. (2004). "Word learning in a domestic dog: Evidence for 'fast mapping,'" *Science* **304**, pp. 1682–1683.

Kaminski, J., Riedel, J., Call, J., and Tomasello, M. (2005). "Domestic goats, Capra hircus, follow gaze direction and use social cues in an object choice task," *Animal Behavior* **69**, pp. 11–18.

Kandel, E. R. and Schwartz, J. H. (1985). *Principles of Neural Science* (New York, NY: Elsevier).

Kappelman, J. (1996). "The evolution of body mass and relative brain size in fossil hominids," *Journal of Human Evolution* **30**, pp. 243–276.

Karmiloff-Smith, A., Klima, E. S., Bellugi, U., Grant, J., and Baron-Cohen, S. (1995). "Is there a social module? Language, face-processing and theory of mind in individuals with William's Syndrome," *Journal of Cognitive Neuroscience* **7**, pp. 196–208.

Kay, E. D. and Condon, K. (1987). "Skeletal changes in the hindlimbs of bipedal rats," *The Anatomical Record* **218**, pp. 1–4.

Kay, R. F., Cartmill, M., and Balow, M. (1998). "The hypoglossal canal and the origin of human vocal behavior," *Proceedings of the National Academy of Sciences (USA)* **95**, pp. 5417–5419.

Keeley, L. H. (1980). *Experimental Determination of Stone Tool Uses: A microwear analysis* (Chicago, IL: University of Chicago Press).

Kegl, J. (2002). "Language emergence in a language-ready brain: Acquisition issues," in *Language Acquisition in Signed Languages*, ed. G. Morgan and B. Woll (Cambridge: Cambridge University Press, pp. 207–254).

Keith, A. (1948). *A New Theory of the Evolution of Man* (London: Watts).

Kelemen, G. (1963). "Comparative anatomy and performance of the vocal organ in vertebrates," in *Acoustic Behavior of Animals*, ed. R. Busnel (Amsterdam: Elsevier Publishing Company, pp. 489–521).

(1969). "Anatomy of the larynx and the anatomical basis of vocal performance," in *The Chimpanzee*, ed. G. Bourne (Basel: S. Karger, pp. 165–187).

Kelemen, G. and Sade, J. (1960). "The vocal organ of the howling monkey (*Alouatta palliata*)," *Journal of Morphology* **107**, pp. 123–140.

Keller, R. (1995). *On Language Change: The invisible hand in language* (New York, NY: Routledge).

Kellogg, W. N. and Kellogg, L. A. (1933). *The Ape and the Child* (New York, NY: McGraw-Hill).

Kemp, T. S. (2005). *The Origin and Evolution of Mammals* (Oxford: Oxford University Press).

Kendon, A. (1991). "Some considerations for a theory of language origins," *Man* **26**, pp. 199–221.

Kennedy, G. E. (2005). "From the ape's dilemma to the weanling's dilemma: Early weaning and its evolutionary context," *Journal of Human Evolution* **48**, pp. 123–145.

Kenward, B., Weir, A. A., Rutz, C., and Kacelnik, A. (2005). "Tool manufacture by naive juvenile crows," *Nature* **433**, p. 121.

Keysers, C., Kohler, E., Umiltà, M. A., Nannetti, L., Fogassi, L., and Gallese, V. (2003a). "Audiovisual mirror neurons and action recognition," *Experimental Brain Research* **153**, pp. 628–636.

Keysers, C., Wicker, B., Gazzola, V., Anton, J.-L., Fogassi, L., and Gallese, V. (2003b). "A touching sight: SII/PV activation during the observation and experience of touch," *Neuron* **42**, pp. 335–346.

Khaitovich, P., Muetzel, B., She, X., Lachmann, M., Hellmann, I., Dietzsch, J., Steigele, S., Do, H.-H., Weiss, G., Enard, W., Heissig, F., Arendt, T., Nieselt-Struwe, K., Eichler, E. E., and Paabo, S. (2004). "Regional patterns of gene expression in human and chimpanzee brains," *Genome Research* **14**, pp. 1462–1473.

Kier, W. M. and Smith, K. K. (1985). "Tongues, tentacles and trunks: The biomechanics of movement in muscular-hydrostats," *Zoological Journal of the Linneaen Society* **83**, pp. 307–324.

Kimura, D. (1973). "The assymetry of the human brain," *Scientific American* **228**, pp. 70–80.

(1993). *Neuromotor Mechanisms in Human Communication* (Oxford: Oxford University Press).

Kimura, M. (1983). *The Neutral Theory of Molecular Evolution* (New York: Cambridge University Press).

King, J. L. and Jukes, T. H. (1969). "Non-Darwinian evolution," *Science* **164**, pp. 788–798.

Kinzey, W. G. (1987). "Monogamous primates: A primate model for human mating systems," in *The Evolution of Human Behavior: Primate models*, ed. W. G. Kinzey (Albany, NY: State University of New York Press, pp. 105–114).

Kirby, S. (1999). *Function, Selection and Innateness: The emergence of language universals* (Oxford: Oxford University Press).

(2000). "Syntax without natural selection: How compositionality emerges from vocabulary in a population of learners," in *The Evolutionary Emergence of Language: Social function and the origins of linguistic form*, ed. C. Knight, M. Studdert-Kennedy, and J. R. Hurford (Cambridge: Cambridge University Press, pp. 303–323).

(2002). "Natural language from artifical life," *Artificial Life* **8**, pp. 185–215.

Kirby, S., Cornish, H., and Smith, K. (2008). "Cumulative cultural evolution in the laboratory: An experimental approach to the origins of structure in human language," *Proceedings of the National Academy of Sciences* **105**, pp. 10681–10686.

Kirby, S., Dowman, M., and Griffiths, T. L. (2007). "Innateness and culture in the evolution of langauge," *Proceedings of the National Academy of Sciences, USA* **104**, pp. 5241–5245.

Kirby, S., Smith, K., and Brighton, H. (2004). "From UG to universals: Linguistic adaptation through iterated learning," *Studies in Language* **28**, pp. 587–607.

Kirschner, M. W. and Gerhart, J. C. (2005). *The Plausibility of Life: Resolving Darwin's dilemma* (London: Yale University Press).

Kitano, H. (2002). "Computation systems biology," *Nature* **420**, pp. 206–210.

Kittler, R., Kayser, M., and Stoneking, M. (2003). "Molecular evolution of Pediculus humanus and the origin of clothing," *Current Biology* **13**, pp. 1414–1417.

Klatt, D. H. and Stefanski, R. A. (1974). "How does a mynah bird imitate human speech?," *Journal of the Acoustical Society of America* **55**, pp. 822–832.

Kleene, S. C. (1956). "Representation of events in nerve nets and finite automata," in *Automata Studies*, ed. C. E. Shannon and J. J. McCarthy (Princeton, NJ: Princeton University Press, pp. 3–40).

Kleiman, D. G. (1977). "Monogamy in mammals," *Quarterly Review of Biology* **52**, pp. 39–69.

Klein, W. and Perdue, C. (1997). "The basic variety (or: Couldn't natural languages be much simpler?)," *Second Language Research* **13**, pp. 301–347.

Klima, E. S. and Bellugi, U. (1979). *The Signs of Language* (Cambridge, MA: Harvard University Press).

Kluender, K. R., Diehl, R. L., and Killeen, P. R. (1987). "Japanese quail can learn phonetic categories," *Science* **237**, pp. 1195–1197.

Kluender, K. R., Lotto, A. J., Holt, L. L., and Bloedel, S. L. (1998). "Role of experience for language-specific functional mappings of vowel sounds," *Journal of the Acoustical Society of America* **104**, pp. 3568–3582.

Knight, C. (1998). "Ritual/speech coevolution: A solution to the problem of deception," in *Approaches to the Evolution of Language*, ed. J. R. Hurford, M. Studdert-Kennedy, and C. Knight (New York, NY: Cambridge University Press, pp. 68–91).

Knoll, A. H. (2003). *Life on a Young Planet: The first three billion years of evolution on earth* (Princeton, NJ: Princeton University Press).

Koehler, O. (1951). "Der vogelgesang als vorstufe von musik und sprache," *Journal of Ornithology* **93**, pp. 3–20.

(1954). "Vom Erbgut der Sprache," *Homo* **5**, pp. 97–104.

Koelsch, S., Gunter, T. C., Cramon, D. Y. v., Zysset, S., Lohmann, G., and Friederici, A. D. (2002). "Bach Speaks: A cortical 'language-network' serves the processing of music," *NeuroImage* **17**, pp. 956–966.

Koelsch, S., Kasper, E., Sammler, D., Schulze, K., Gunter, T. C., and Friederici, A. D. (2004). "Music, language, and meaning: Brain signatures of semantic processing," *Nature Neuroscience* **7**, pp. 511–514.

Koelsch, S. and Siebel, W. A. (2005). "Towards a neural basis of music perception," *Trends in Cognitive Science* **9**, pp. 578–584.

Kohler, E., Keysers, C., Umiltà, M. A., Fogassi, L., Gallese, V., and Rizzolatti, G. (2002). "Hearing sounds, understanding actions: Action representation in mirror neurons," *Science* **297**, pp. 846–849.

Kohonen, T. (2001). *Self-organizing Maps* (New York, NY: Springer).

Kojima, S. (1990). "Comparison of auditory functions in the chimpanzee and human," *Folia Primatologica* **55**, pp. 62–72.

Kortland, A. (1973). "Commentary on Hewes," *Current Anthropology* **14**, pp. 13–14.

Krakauer, A. H. (2005). "Kin selection and cooperative courtship in wild turkeys," *Nature* **434**, pp. 69–72.

Krantz, G. S. (1980). "Sapienization and speech," *Current Anthropology* **21**, pp. 773–792.

Krause, J., Lalueza-Fox, C., Orlando, L., Enard, W., Green, R. E., Burbano, H. A., Hublin, J.-J., Hänni, C., Fortea, J., de la Rasilla, M., Bertranpetit, J., Rosas, A., and Pääbo, S. (2007). "The derived FOXP2 variant of modern humans was shared with Neandertals," *Current Biology* **17**, pp. 1908–1912.

Krauss, R. M. and Hadar, U. (1999). "The role of speech-related arm/hand gestures in word retrieval," in *Gesture, Speech and Sign*, ed. L. S. Messing and R. Campbell (Oxford: Oxford University Press, pp. 93–116).

Krebs, H. A. (1975). "The August Krogh principle: For many problems there is an animal on which it can be most conveniently studied," *Journal of Experimental Zoology* **194**, pp. 221–226.

Krebs, J. R. and Davies, N. B. (1997). *Behavioural Ecology: An evolutionary approach* (Oxford: Blackwell Scientific Publications).

Krebs, J. R. and Dawkins, R. (1984). "Animal signals: Mind reading and manipulation," in *Behavioural Ecology*, ed. J. R. Krebs and N. B. Davies (Sunderland, MA: Sinauer Associates, pp. 380–402).

Krings, M., Stone, A., Schmitz, R., Krainitzki, H., Stoneking, M., and Pääbo, S. (1997). "Neandertal DNA sequences and the origin of modern humans," *Cell* **90**, pp. 19–30.

Kroodsma, D. and Parker, L. D. (1977). "Vocal virtuosity in the brown thrasher," *Auk* **94**, pp. 783–785.

Kroodsma, D. E. and Byers, B. E. (1991). "The function(s) of bird song," *American Zoologist* **31**, pp. 318–328.

Krubitzer, L. (1995). "The organization of neocortex in mammals: Are species differences really so different?," *Trends in Neurosciences* **18**, pp. 408–417.

Krumhansl, C. L. (1991). "Music psychology: Tonal structures in perception and memory," *Annual Review of Psychology* **42**, pp. 277–303.

Kuczaj, S. A. (1983). *Crib Speech and Language Play* (New York, NY: Springer).

Kuhl, P. K. (1987). "The special-mechanisms debate in speech research: Categorization tests on animals and infants," in *Categorical Perception: The groundwork of cognition*, ed. S. Harnad (New York, NY: Cambridge University Press, pp. 355–387).

  (1991). "Human adults and human infants show a 'perceptual magnet effect' for the prototypes of speech categories, monkeys do not," *Perception and Psychophysics* **50**, pp. 93–107.

Kuhl, P. K. and Miller, J. D. (1975). "Speech perception by the chinchilla: Voiced–voiceless distinction in alveolar plosive consonants," *Science* **190**, pp. 69–72.

Kuhl, P. K. and Miller, J. D. (1978). "Speech perception by the chinchilla: Identification functions for synthetic VOT stimuli," *Journal of the Acoustical Society of America* **63**, pp. 905–917.

Kuhl, P. K., Williams, K. A., Lacerda, F., Stevens, K. N., and Lindblom, B. (1992). "Linguistic experience alters phonetic perception in infants by 6 months of age," *Science* **255**, pp. 606–608.

Kuipers, A. H. (1960). *Phoneme and Morpheme in Kabardian (Eastern Adyghe)* (The Hague: Mouton).

Kunej, D. and Turk, I. (2000). "New perspectives on the beginnings of music: Archaeological and musicological analysis of a middle Paleolithic bone 'flute,'" in *The Origins of Music*, ed. N. L. Wallin, B. Merker, and S. Brown (Cambridge, MA: MIT Press, pp. 235–268).

Kurlansky, M. (1997). *Cod: A biography of the fish that changed the world* (New York, NY: Walker and Co.).

Kurtén, B. (1987). *Dance of the Tiger: A novel of the Ice Age* (New York, NY: J. Curley).

Kuypers, H. G. J. M. (1958). "Corticobulbar connections to the pons and lower brainstem in man: An anatomical study," *Brain* **81**, pp. 364–388.

Lachlan, R. F. (1999). "Cultural evolution of song in theory and in chaffinches Fringilla coelebs," in *Biology* (University of St. Andrews), p. 185.

Lachmann, M., Számadó, S., and Bergstrom, C. T. (2001). "Cost and conflict in animal signals and human language," *Proceedings of the National Academy of Sciences* **98**, pp. 13189–13194.

Ladd, D. R. (1996). *Intonational Phonology* (Cambridge: Cambridge University Press).

Ladefoged, P. (1967). *Three Areas of Experimental Phonetics* (London: Oxford University Press).

(2001). *Vowels and Consonants: An introduction to the sounds of languages* (Oxford: Blackwell).

Ladefoged, P. and Broadbent, D. E. (1957). "Information conveyed by vowels," *Journal of the Acoustical Society of America* **29**, pp. 98–104.

Lahr, M. M. and Foley, R. A. (1998). "Towards a theory of modern human origins: Geography, demography, and diversity in recent human evolution," *American Journal of Physical Anthropology Supplement* **27**, pp. 137–176.

Lai, C. S. L., Fisher, S. E., Hurst, J. A., Vargha-Khadem, F. and Monaco, A. P. (2001). "A forkhead-domain gene is mutated in a severe speech and language disorder," *Nature* **413**, pp. 519–523.

Lai, C. S. L., Gerrelli, D., Monaco, A. P., Fisher, S. E. and Copp, A. J. (2003). "FOXP2 expression during brain development coincides with adult sites of pathology in a severe speech and language disorder," *Brain* **126**, pp. 2455–2462.

Laitman, J. T. (1977). *The ontogenetic and phylogenetic development of the upper respiratory system and basicranium in man* (Yale University, New Haven).

Laitman, J. T. and Heimbuch, R. C. (1982). "The basicranium of Plio-Pleistocene hominids as an indicator of their upper respiratory systems," *American Journal of Physical Anthropology* **59**, pp. 323–343.

Laitman, J. T., Heimbuch, R. C., and Crelin, E. S. (1978). "Developmental change in a basicranial line and its relationship to the upper respiratory system in living primates," *American Journal of Anatomy* **152**, pp. 467–483.

Laitman, J. T. and Reidenberg, J. S. (1988). "Advances in understanding the relationship between the skull base and larynx with comments on the origins of speech," *Journal of Human Evolution* **3**, pp. 99–109.

Laitman, J. T., Reidenberg, J. S., Gannon, P. J., and Johansson, B. (1990). "The Kebara hyoid: What can it tell us about the evolution of the hominid vocal tract?," *American Journal of Physical Anthropology* **81**, p. 254.

Laland, K. N. and Brown, G. R. (2002). *Sense and Nonsense: Evolutionary perspectives on human behaviour* (Oxford: Oxford University Press).

Laland, K. N. and Janik, V. M. (2006). "The animal cultures debate," *Trends in Ecology and Evolution* **21**, pp. 542–547.

Laland, K. N., Odling-Smee, J., and Feldman, M. W. (2001). "Cultural niche construction and human evolution," *Journal of Evolutionary Biology* **14**, pp. 22–33.

Lalueza-Fox, C., Römpler, H., Caramelli, D., Stäubert, C., Catalano, G., Hughes, D., Rohland, N., Pilli, E., Longo, L., Condemi, S., de la Rasilla, M., Fortea, J., Rosas, A., Stoneking, M., Schöneberg, T., Bertranpetit, J., and Hofreiter, M. (2007). "A melanocortin 1 receptor allele suggests varying pigmentation among Neanderthals," *Science* **318**, pp. 1453–1455.

Lamarck, J. B. d. (1809). *Philosophie Zoologique* (Paris: P. Savy).

Lancaster, J. B. (1968). "Primate communication systems and the emergence of human language," in *Primates*, ed. P. C. Jay (New York: Holt, Rinehart & Winston, pp. 439–457).

Lande, R. (1980). "Sexual dimorphism, sexual selection, and adaptation in polygenic characters," *Evolution* **34**, pp. 292–305.

Langer, S. K. (1962). *Philosophical Sketches* (Baltimore, MD: Johns Hopkins Press).
(1972). *Mind: An essay on human feeling (Vol. II)* (Baltimore, MD: Johns Hopkins Press).

Langmore, N. E. (1996). "Female song attracts males in the alpine accentor Prunella collaris," *Proceedings of the Royal Society London, B* **263**, pp. 141–146.
(1998). "Functions of duet and solo songs of female birds," *Trends in Ecology and Evolution* **13**, pp. 136–140.
(2000). "Why female birds sing," in *Signalling and Signal Design in Animal Communication*, ed. Y. Espmark, T. Amundsen, and G. Rosenqvist (Trondhein: Tapir Academic Press, pp. 317–327).

Larson, C. R., Sutton, D., Taylor, E. M., and Lindeman, R. (1973). "Sound spectral properties of conditioned vocalizations in monkeys," *Phonetica* **27**, pp. 100–112.

Lashley, K. (1951). "The problem of serial order in behavior," in *Cerebral mechanisms in behavior: The Hixon symposium*, ed. L. A. Jeffress (New York, NY: Wiley, pp. 112–146).

Lass, R. (1997). *Historical Linguistics and Language Change* (Cambridge: Cambridge University Press).

Laurent, G. (2006). "Shall we even understand the fly's brain?," in *23 Problems in Systems Neuroscience*, ed. J. L. van Hemmen and T. J. Sejnowski (Oxford: Oxford University Press, pp. 3–21).

Leakey, M. D. (1966). "A review of the Oldowan culture from Olduvai Gorge, Tanzania," *Nature* **212**, pp. 579–581.

Leakey, M. D. and Hay, R. L. (1979). "Pliocene footprints in the Laetolil beds at Laetoli, northern Tanzania," *Nature* **278**, pp. 317–323.

Leavens, D. A., Russell, J. L., and Hopkins, W. D. (2005). "Intentionality as measured in the persistence and elaboration of communication by chimpanzees (*Pan troglodytes*)," *Child Development* **76**, pp. 291–376.

Lebedev, O. A. and Coates, M. I. (1995). "The postcranial skeleton of the Devonian tetrapod Tulerpeton curtum Lebedev," *Zoological Journal of the Linnean Society* **114**, pp. 307–348.

Le Douarin, N. M. and Kalcheim, C. (1999). *The Neural Crest* (Cambridge: Cambridge University Press).

LeMay, M. (1975). "The language capability of Neanderthal man," *American Journal of Physical Anthropology* **42**, pp. 9–14.

(1976). "Morphological cerebral asymmetries of modern man, fossil man, and nonhuman priamtes," *Annals of the New York Academy of Science* **280**, pp. 349–366.

(1985). "Asymmetries of the brains and skulls of nonhuman primates," in *Cerebral Lateralization in Nonhuman Species*, ed. S. D. Glick (New York, NY: Academic Press, pp. 233–245).

Lemon, R. E. (1975). "How birds develop song dialects," *Condor* **77**, pp. 385–406.

Lenneberg, E. H. (1967). *Biological Foundations of Language* (New York, NY: Wiley).

Lenski, R. E., Mongold, J. A., Sniegowski, P. D., Travisano, M., Vasi, F., Gerrish, P. J., and Schmidt, T. M. (1998). "Evolution of competitive fitness in experimental populations of Escherischia coli: What makes one genotype a better competitor than another?," *Antonie Van Leeuwenhoek* **73**, pp. 35–47.

Lerdahl, F. and Jackendoff, R. (1983). *A Generative Theory of Tonal Music* (Cambridge, MA: MIT Press).

Levelt, W. J. M. (1989). *Speaking: From intention to articulation* (Cambridge, MA: MIT Press).

Levelt, W. J. M. and Wheeldon, L. R. (1994). "Do speakers have access to a mental syllabary?," *Cognition* **50**, pp. 239–269.

Lewontin, R. C. (1998). "The evolution of cognition: Questions we will never answer," in *An Invitation to Cognitive Science: Methods, models, and conceptual issues*, ed. D. Scarborough and S. Sternberg (Cambridge., MA: MIT Press, pp. 107–131).

Lewontin, R. C. and Hubby, J. L. (1966). "A molecular approach to the study of genic heterozygosity in natural populations II: Amount of variation and degree of heterozygosity in natural populations of *Drosophila pseudoobscura*," *Genetics* **54**, pp. 595–609.

Liberman, A. M. (1957). "Some results of research on speech perception," *Journal of the Acoustical Society of America* **29**, pp. 117–123.

(1996). *Speech: A special code* (Cambridge, MA: MIT Press).

Liberman, A. M., Cooper, F. S., Shankweiler, D. P., and Studdert-Kennedy, M. (1967). "Perception of the speech code," *Psychological Review* **74**, pp. 431–461.

Liberman, A. M., Harris, K. S., Hoffman, H. S., and Griffith, B. C. (1957). "The discrimination of speech sounds within and across phoneme boundaries," *Journal of Experimental Psychology* **53**, pp. 358–368.

Liberman, A. M. and Mattingly, I. G. (1989). "A specialization for speech perception," *Science* **243**, pp. 489–494.

Liebal, K. (2007). "Gestures in organutans (Pongo pygmaeus)," in *The Gestural Communication of Apes and Monkeys*, ed. J. Call and M. Tomasello (London: Lawrence Erlbaum, pp. 69–98).

Lieberman, D. E. and McCarthy, R. C. (1999). "The ontogeny of cranial base angulation in humans and chimpanzees and its implications for reconstructing pharyngeal dimensions," *Journal of Human Evolution* **36**, pp. 487–517.

Lieberman, D. E., McCarthy, R. C., Hiiemae, K., and Palmer, J. B. (2001). "Ontogeny of postnatal hyoid and larynx descent in humans," *Archives of Oral Biology* **46**, pp. 117–128.

Lieberman, E., Michel, J.-B., Jackson, J., Tang, T., and Nowak, M. A. (2007). "Quantifying the evolutionary dynamics of language," *Nature* **449**, pp. 713–716.

Lieberman, P. (1968). "Primate vocalization and human linguistic ability," *Journal of the Acoustical Society of America* **44**, pp. 1574–1584.

(1975). *On the Origins of Language* (New York, NY: Macmillan).

(1984). *The Biology and Evolution of Language* (Cambridge, MA: Harvard University Press).

(1986). "On Bickerton's review of The Biology and Evolution of Language," *American Anthropologist* **88**, pp. 701–703.

(1998). "On the evolution of human syntactic ability: Its pre-adaptive bases, motor control and speech," *Journal of Human Evolution* **14**, pp. 657–668.

(2000). *Human Language and Our Reptilian Brain: The subcortical bases of speech, syntax and thought* (Cambridge, MA: Harvard University Press).

(2006). *Toward an Evolutionary Biology of Language* (Cambridge, MA: Harvard University Press).

(2007a). "Current views on Neanderthal speech capabilities: A reply to Boe *et al.* (2002)," *Journal of Phonetics* **2007**, pp. 552–563.

(2007b). "Human speech: Anatomical and neural bases," *Current Anthropology* **48**, pp. 39–66.

Lieberman, P. and Blumstein, S. E. (1988). *Speech Physiology, Speech Perception, and Acoustic Phonetics* (Cambridge: Cambridge University Press).

Lieberman, P. and Crelin, E. S. (1971). "On the speech of Neanderthal man," *Linguistic Inquiry* **2**, pp. 203–222.

Lieberman, P., Crelin, E. S., and Klatt, D. H. (1972). "Phonetic ability and related anatomy of the newborn and adult human, Neanderthal man, and the chimpanzee," *American Anthropologist* **74**, pp. 287–307.

Lieberman, P., Klatt, D. H., and Wilson, W. H. (1969). "Vocal tract limitations on the vowel repertoires of rhesus monkeys and other nonhuman primates," *Science* **164**, pp. 1185–1187.

Liégeois, F., Baldeweg, T., Connelly, A., Gadian, D. G., Mishkin, M., and Vargha-Khadem, F. (2003). "Language fMRI abnormalities associated with FOXP2 gene mutation," *Nature Neuroscience* **6**, pp. 1230–1237.

Liégeois, F., Connelly, A., Cross, J., Boyd, S. G., Gadian, D. G., Vargha-Khadem, F., and Baldeweg, T. (2004). "Language reorganization in children with early-onset lesions of the left hemisphere: An fMRI study," *Brain* **127**, pp. 1229–1236.

Liem, K. F. (1988). "Form and function of lungs: The evolution of air breathing mechanisms," *American Zoologist* **28**, pp. 739–759.

Lightfoot, D. (1998). *The Development of Language: Acquisition, change and evolution* (Oxford: Blackwell).

Liljencrants, J. and Lindblom, B. (1972). "Numerical simulations of vowel quality systems: The role of perceptual contrast," *Language* **48**, pp. 839–862.

Lindblom, B., MacNeilage, P. F., and Studdert-Kennedy, M. (1983). "Self-organizing processes and the explanation of phonological universals," *Linguistics* **21**, pp. 181–203.

(1984). "Self-organizing processes and the explanation of phonological universals," in *Explanations for Language Universals*, ed. B. Butterworth, B. Comrie, and O. Dahl (Berlin: Mouton, pp. 181–203).

Livingstone, F. B. (1973). "Did the Australopithecines sing?," *Current Anthropology* **14**, pp. 25–29.

Locke, J. L. (1993). *The Child's Path to Spoken Language* (Cambridge, MA: Harvard University Press).

Locke, J. L. and Bogin, B. (2006). "Language and life history: A new perspective on the development and evolution of human language," *Behavioral & Brain Sciences* **29**, pp. 259–280.

Locke, J. L. and Pearson, D. M. (1990). "Linguistic significance of babbling: Evidence from a tracheostomized infant," *Journal of Child Language* **17**, pp. 1–16.

Long, C. H. (1963). *Alpha: The myths of creation* (Chici, CA: Scholars Press).

Long, J. A. (1995). *The Rise of Fishes* (Baltimore, MD: Johns Hopkins University Press).

Longuet-Higgins, H. C. (1978). "The perception of music," *Interdisciplinary Science Review* **3**, pp. 148–156.

Lorenz, E. N. (1963). "Deterministic nonperiodic flow," *Journal of Atmospheric Science* **20**, pp. 130–141.

Lorenz, K. (1965). *Evolution and Modification of Behavior* (Chicago, IL: University of Chicago Press).

Lotto, A. J., Kluender, K. R., and Holt, L. L. (1998). "Depolarizing the perceptual magnet effect," *Journal of the Acoustical Society of America* **103**, pp. 3648–3655.

Lovejoy, C. O. (1981). "The origin of man," *Science* **211**, pp. 341–350.

Lubker, J. and Gay, T. (1982). "Anticipatory labial coarticulation: Experimental, biological and linguistic variables," *Journal of the Acoustical Society of America* **71**, pp. 437–448.

Lyons, J. (1977). *Semantics* (Cambridge: Cambridge University Press).

Mace, R. (2000). "Evolutionary ecology of human life history," *Animal Behavior* **59**, pp. 1–10.

Macedonia, J. M. and Evans, C. S. (1993). "Variation among mammalian alarm call systems and the problem of meaning in animal signals," *Ethology* **93**, pp. 177–197.

MacKay, D. (2003). *Information Theory, Inference, and Learning Algorithms* (Cambridge: Cambridge University Press).

Mackie, G. O. (1990). "The elementary nervous system revisited," *American Zoologist* **30**, pp. 907–920.

MacLarnon, A. M. and Hewitt, G. P. (1999). "The evolution of human speech: The role of enhanced breathing control," *American Journal of Physical Anthropology* **109**, pp. 341–363.

MacLean, P. D. (1990). *The Triune Brain in Evolution: Role in paleocerebral functions* (New York, NY: Plenum Press).

Macnamara, J. (1972). "Cognitive basis of language learning in infants," *Psychological Review* **79**, pp. 1–13.

MacNeilage, P. F. (1991). "The 'postural origins' theory of primate neurobiological asymmetries," in *Biological Foundations of Language Development*, ed. N. Krasnegor, D. Rumbaugh, M. Studdert-Kennedy, and R. Schiefelbusch. (Hillsdale, NJ: Lawrence Erlbaum Associates, pp. 165–188).

  (1998a). "Evolution of the mechanisms of language output: Comparative neurobiology of vocal and manual communication," in *Approaches to the Evolution of Language*, ed. J. R. Hurford, M. Studdert-Kennedy, and C. Knight (New York, NY: Cambridge University Press, pp. 222–241).

  (1998b). "The frame/content theory of evolution of speech production," *Behavioral and Brain Sciences* **21**, pp. 499–546.

  (2008). *The Origin of Speech* (Oxford: Oxford University Press).

MacNeilage, P. F. and Davis, B. L. (1990). "Acquisition of speech production: Frames, then content," in *Attention and Performance 13: Motor representation and control*, ed. M. Jeannerod (Hillsdale, NJ: Lawrence Erlbaum Associates, pp. 453–477).

(2000). "On the origin of internal structure of word forms," *Science* **288**, pp. 527–531.

(2005). "Evolutionary sleight of hand: Then, they saw it; now we don't," *Behavioral and Brain Sciences* **28**, pp. 137–138.

MacNeilage, P. F., Davis, B. L., Kinney, A., and Matyear, C. (1999). "Origen of serial-output complexity in speech," *Psychological Science* **10**, pp. 459–460.

(2000). "The motor core of speech: A comparison of serial organization patterns in infants and languages," *Child Development* **71**, pp. 153–163.

MacNeilage, P. F., Studdert-Kennedy, M., and Lindblom, B. (1987). "Primate handedness reconsidered," *Behavioral and Brain Sciences* **10**, pp. 247–303.

Macphail, E. M. (1982). *Brain and Intelligence in Vertebrates* (Oxford: Clarendon Press).

Maddieson, I. (1984). *Patterns of Sounds* (Cambridge: Cambridge University Press).

Madsen, E. A., Tunney, R. J., Fieldman, G., Plotkin, H. C., Dunbar, R. I. M., Richardson, J.-M., and McFarland, D. (2007). "Kinship and altruism: A cross-cultural experimental study," *British Journal of Psychology* **98**, pp. 339–359.

Malson, L. (1964). *Les Enfants Sauvages: Mythe et réalité* (Paris: Christian Bourgois).

Mandeville, B. (1997 [1723]). *The Fable of the Bees and Other Writings* (Cambridge: Hackett).

Manser, M. B., Seyfarth, R. M., and Cheney, D. L. (2002). "Suricate alarm calls signal predator class and urgency," *Trends in Cognitive Science* **6**, pp. 55–57.

Marcus, G. F. and Fisher, S. E. (2003). "FOXP2 in focus: What can genes tell us about speech and language?," *Trends in Cognitive Science* **7**, pp. 257–262.

Margulis, L. (1992). *Symbiosis In Cell Evolution: Microbial communities in the Archean and Proterozoic eons* (New York, NY: W. H. Freeman and Co.).

Marino, L. (1998). "A comparison of encephalization between Odontocete cetaceans and Anthropoid primates," *Brain, Behavior and Evolution* **51**, pp. 230–238.

Markman, E. M. (1990). "Constraints children place on word meanings," *Cognitive Science* **14**, pp. 57–77.

Markman, E. M. and Hutchinson, J. E. (1984). "Children's sensitivity to constraints on word meaning: Taxonomic versus thematic relations," *Cognitive Psychology* **16**, pp. 1–27.

Markman, E. M. and Wachtel, G. F. (1988). "Children's use of mutual exclusivity to constrain the meaning of words," *Cognitive Psychology* **20**, pp. 121–157.

Markson, L. and Bloom, P. (1997). "Evidence against a dedicated system for word learning in children," *Nature* **385**, pp. 813–815.

Marler, P. (1955). "Characteristics of some animal calls," *Nature* **176**, pp. 6–7.

(1991a). "Song learning behavior: the interface with neuroethology," *Trends in Neurosciences* **14**, pp. 199–206.

(1991b). "The instinct to learn," in *The Epigenesis of Mind: Essays on biology and cognition,* ed. S. Carey and R. Gelman (Hillsdale, NJ: Lawrence Erlbaum Associates, pp. 37–66).

(2000). "Origins of music and speech: Insights from animals," in *The Origins of Music,* ed. N. L. Wallin, B. Merker, and S. Brown (Cambridge, MA: MIT Press, pp. 31–48).

Marler, P. and Evans, C. S. (1996). "Bird calls – just emotional displays or something more," *Ibis* **138**, pp. 26–33.

Marler, P., Evans, C. S., and Hauser, M. D. (1992). "Animal signals: Reference, motivation or both?," in *Nonverbal Vocal Communication: Comparative and developmental approaches,* ed. H. Papousek, U. Jürgens, and M. Papousek (Cambridge: Cambridge University Press, pp. 66–86).

Marler, P., Karakashian, S., and Gyger, M. (1991). "Do animals have the option of withholding signals when communication is inappropriate? The audience effect," in *Cognitive Ethology: The minds of other animals,* ed. C. Ristau (Hillsdale, NJ: Lawrence Erlbaum Associates, pp. 135–186).

Marler, P. and Peters, S. (1982). "Developmental overproduction and selective attrition: New processes in the epigenesis of birdsong," *Developmental Psychobiology* **15**, pp. 369–378.

Marler, P. and Slabbekoorn, H. (2004). *Nature's Music: The science of birdsong* (New York, NY: Academic Press).

Marler, P. and Tamura, M. (1962). "Song 'dialects' in three populations of white-crowned sparrows," *Condor* **64**, pp. 368–377.

Marshall, A. J., Wrangham, R. W., and Arcadi, A. C. (1999). "Does learning affect the structure of vocalizations in chimpanzees?," *Animal Behavior* **58**, pp. 825–830.

Martin, A., Wiggs, C. L., Ungerleider, L. G., and Haxby, J. V. (1996). "Neural correlates of category-specific knowledge," *Nature* **379**, pp. 649–652.

Martin, R. D. (1981). "Relative brain size and basal metabolic rate in terrestrial vertebrates," *Nature* **293**, pp. 57–60.

Martin, R. D. and Harvey, P. H. (1985). "Brain size allometry: Ontogeny and phylogeny," in *Size and Scaling in Primate Biology,* ed. W. J. Jungers (New York, NY: Plenum Press, pp. 147–173).

Martin, R. D., MacLarnon, A. M., Phillips, J. L., and Dobyns, W. B. (2006). "Flores hominid: New species or microcephalic dwarf?," *Anatomical Record* **288A**, pp. 1123–1145.

Martínez, I., Rosa, M., Arsuaga, J.-L., Jarabo, P., Quam, R., Lorenzo, C., Gracia, A., Carretero, J.-M., Bermudez de Castro, J. M., and Carbonell, E. (2004). "Auditory capacities in Middle Pleistocene humans from the Sierra de Atapuerca in Spain," *Proceedings of the National Academy of Sciences* **101**, pp. 9976–9981.

Mather, R. (1992). "A field study of hybrid gibbons in Central Kalimantan Indonesia." Unpublished PhD thesis, University of Cambridge.

Matsuzawa, T. (1985). "Use of numbers by a chimpanzee," *Nature* **315**, pp. 57–59.

Maupertuis, P.-L. M. d. (1768). *Dissertation sur les Différents Moyens dont les Hommes se Sont Servis Pour Exprimer Leurs Idés* (Paris: Husson).

Maynard Smith, J. (1964). "Group selection and kin selection," *Nature* **201**, pp. 1145–1147.

(1976). "Sexual selection and the handicap principle," *Journal of Theoretical Biology* **57**, pp. 239–242.

(1978). "Optimization theory in evolution," *Annual Review of Ecology & Systematics* **9**, pp. 31–56.

(1979). "Game theory and the evolution of behaviour," *Proceedings of the Royal Society, London, B* **205**, pp. 475–488.

(1982). *Evolution and the Theory of Games* (Cambridge: Cambridge University Press).

(1987). "Natural selection: When learning guides evolution," *Nature* **329**, pp. 761–762.

(1991). "Honest signalling: The Philip Sydney game," *Animal Behavior* **42**, pp. 1034–1035.

(1998). "The origin of altruism (Review of Sober & Wilson)," *Nature* **393**, pp. 639–640.

Maynard Smith, J., Burian, R., Kauffman, S., Alberch, P., Campbell, J., Goodwin, B., Lande, R., Raup, D., and Wolpert, L. (1985). "Developmental constraints and evolution," *The Quarterly Review of Biology* **60**, pp. 265–287.

Maynard Smith, J. and Harper, D. (2003). *Animal Signals* (Oxford: Oxford University Press).

Maynard Smith, J. and Holliday, R. (eds) (1979). *The Evolution of Adaptation by Natural Selection* (London: The Royal Society).

Maynard Smith, J. and Price, G. R. (1973). "The logic of animal conflict," *Nature* **246**, pp. 15–18.

Maynard Smith, J. and Szathmáry, E. (1995). *The Major Transitions in Evolution* (New York: Oxford University Press).

Mayr, E. (1951). "Taxonomic categories in fossil hominids," *Cold Spring Harbor Symposia on Quantitative Biology* **15**, p. 109.

(1963). *Animal Species and Evolution* (Cambridge, MA: Harvard University Press).

(1974). "Behavior programs and evolutionary strategies," *American Scientist* **62**, pp. 650–659.

(1982). *The Growth of Biological Thought: Diversity, evolution and inheritance* (Cambridge, MA: Harvard University Press).

Mazak, V. (1981). "Panthera tigris," *Mammalian Species* **152**, pp. 1–8.

McBrearty, S. and Brooks, A. S. (2000). "The revolution that wasn't: A new interpretation of the origin of modern human behavior," *Journal of Human Evolution* **39**, pp. 453–563.

McBride, D. and Williams, S. (2001). "Audiometric notch as a sign of noise induced hearing loss," *Occupational and Environmental Medicine* **58**, pp. 46–51.

McCarthy, J. J. (2002). *A Thematic Guide to Optimality Theory* (New York, NY: Cambridge University Press).

McComb, K., Moss, C., Sayialel, S., and Baker, L. (2000). "Unusually extensive networks of vocal recognition in African elephants," *Animal Behavior* **59**, pp. 1103–1109.

McDaniel, M. A. (2005). "Big-brained people are smarter: A meta-analysis of the relationship between in vivo brain volume and intelligence," *Intelligence* **33**, pp. 337–346.

McDermott, J. and Hauser, M. D. (2005). "The origins of music: Innateness, uniqueness, and evolution," *Music Perception* **23**, pp. 29–59.

McDougal, C. (1987). "The man-eating tiger in geographical and historical perspective," in *Tigers of the World: The biology, biopolitics, management, and conservation of an endangered species*, ed. R. L. Tilson and U. S. Seal (Park Ridge, NJ: Noyes, pp. 435–447).

McGinn, C. (1991). *The Problem of Consciousness* (Oxford: Blackwell).

McGinnis, N., Kuziora, M. A., and McGinnis, W. (1990). "Human Hox-4.2 and Drosophila Deformed encode similar regulatory specificities in Drosophila embryos and larvae," *Cell* **63**, pp. 969–976.

McGonigle, B. and Chalmers, M. (1977). "Are monkeys logical?," *Nature* **267**, pp. 694–696.

McGregor, P. K. (2005). *Animal Communication Networks* (Cambridge: Cambridge University Press).

McGrew, W. C. (1979). "Evolutionary implications of sex differences in chimpanzee predation and tool use," in *The Great Apes*, ed. D. A. Hamburg and E. R. McCown (Menlo Park, CA: Benjamin/Cummings, pp. 441–463).

   (1992). *Chimpanzee Material Culture* (Cambridge: Cambridge University Press).

   (2004). *The Cultured Chimpanzee* (Cambridge: Cambridge University Press).

   (2007). "Savanna chimpanzees dig for food," *Proceedings of the National Academy of Sciences* **104**, pp. 19167–19168.

McGrew, W. C. and Marchant, L. F. (1997). "On the other hand: Current issues in and meta-analysis of the behavioral laterality of hand function in nonhuman primates," *Yearbook of Physical Anthropology* **40**, pp. 201–232.

McGurk, H. and MacDonald, J. (1976). "Hearing lips and seeing voices," *Nature* **264**, pp. 746–748.

McHenry, H. M. (1992). "Body size and proportions in early hominids," *American Journal of Physical Anthropology* **87**, pp. 407–431.

   (1994). "Behavioral ecological implications of early hominid body size," *Journal of Human Evolution* **27**, pp. 77–87.

   (1996). "Sexual dimorphism in fossil hominids and its socioecological implications," in *The Archaeology of Human Ancestry*, ed. J. Steele and S. Shennan (London: Routledge, 91–109).

McNeil, D. (1985). "So you think gestures are nonverbal?," *Psychological Review* **92**, pp. 350–371.

(1992). *Hand and Mind: What gestures reveal about thought* (Chicago, IL: University of Chicago Press).

(ed.) (2000). *Language and Gesture* (New York, NY: Cambridge University Press).

McNeill, D., Bertentahl, B., Cole, J., and Gallagher, S. (2005). "Gesture-first, but no gestures?," *Behavioral and Brain Sciences* **28**, pp. 138–139.

M'Donnel, R. (1860). "Observations on the habits and anatomy of the Lepidosiren annectans," *Natural History Review* **7**, pp. 93–112.

Mehler, J., Bertoncini, J., Barriere, M., and Jassik, D. (1978). "Infant recognition of mother's voice," *Perception* **7**, pp. 491–497.

Mehler, J., Jusczyk, P., Lambertz, G., Halsted, N., Bertoncini, J., and Amiel-Tison, C. (1988). "A precursor of language acquisition in young infants," *Cognition* **29**, pp. 143–178.

Mekel-Bobrov, N., Gilbert, S. L., Evans, P. D., Vallender, E. J., Anderson, J. R., Tishkoff, S. A., Hudson, R. R., and Lahn, B. T. (2005). "Ongoing adaptive evolution of ASPM, a brain size determinant in Homo sapiens," *Science* **309**, pp. 1720–1722.

Mekel-Bobrov, N., Posthuma, D., Gilbert, S. L., Lind, P., Gosso, M. F., Luciano, M. *et al.* (2007). "The ongoing adaptive evolution of ASPM and Microcephalin is not explained by increased intelligence," *Human Molecular Genetics* **16**, pp. 600–608.

Mellars, P. A. (1989). "Major issues in the emergence of modern humans," *Current Anthropology* **30**, pp. 349–385.

(1991). "Cognitive changes and the emergence of modern humans in Europe," *Cambridge Archaeological Journal* **1**, pp. 63–76.

(2005). "The impossible coincidence: A single-species model for the origins of modern human behavior in Europe," *Evolutionary Anthropology* **14**, pp. 12–27.

(2006). "Going east: New genetic and archaeological perspectives on the modern human colonization of Eurasia," *Science* **313**, pp. 796–800.

Mellars, P. A. and Stringer, C. (eds) (1989). *The Human Revolution: Modelling the earlyhuman mind* (Edinburgh: Edinburgh University Press).

Meltzoff, A. N. (1988). "The human infant as *Homo imitans*," in *Social Learning*, ed. T. R. Zentall and J. B. G. Galef (Hillsdale, NJ: Lawrence Erlbaum Associates, pp. 319–341).

Meltzoff, A. N. and Moore, M. K. (1977). "Imitation of facial and manual gestures by human neonates," *Science* **198**, pp. 75–78.

Menn, L. and Stoel-Gammon, C. (2005). "Phonological development: Learning sounds and sound patterns," in *The Development of Language*, ed. J. B. Gleason (Boston, MA: Pearson, Allyn & Bacon, pp. 62–111).

Mercader, J., Panger, M. A., and Boesch, C. (2002). "Excavation of a chimpanzee stone tool site in the African rainforest," *Science* **296**, pp. 1452–1455.

Merker, B. (2000). "Synchronous chorusing and human origins," in *The Origins of Music*, ed. N. L. Wallin, B. Merker, and S. Brown (Cambridge, MA: MIT Press, pp. 315–327).

Merriman, W. E. and Bowman, L. L. (1989). "The mutual exclusivity bias in children's word learning," *Monographs of the Society for Research in Child Development* **54**, pp. 1–129.

Merzenich, M. M., Recanzone, G., Jenkins, W. M., Allard, T. T., and Nudo, R. J. (1989). "Cortical representational plasticity," in *Neurobiology of Neocortex*, ed. P. Rakic and W. Singer (Chichester, NY: John Wiley and Sons, pp. 41–67).

Mesoudi, A., Whiten, A., and Laland, K. N. (2004). "Is human cultural evolution Darwinian? Evidence reviewed from the perspective of 'The Origin of Species,'" *Evolution* **58**, pp. 1–11.

Messing, L. S. and Campbell, R. (eds) (1999). *Gesture, Speech and Sign* (Oxford: Oxford University Press).

Micheau, C., Luboisnki, B., and Lanchi, P. (1978). "Relationship between laryngoceles and laryngeal carcinomas," *Laryngoscope* **88**, pp. 680–688.

Miklosi, A., Kubinyi, E., Topal, J., Gacsi, M., Viranyi, Z., and Csanyi, V. (2003). "A simple reason for a big difference: Wolves do not look back at humans, but dogs do," *Current Biology* **13**, pp. 763–766.

Miles, H. L. (1990). "The cognitive foundations for reference in a signing orangutan," in *"Language" and Intelligence in Monkeys and Apes: Comparative developmental perspectives*, ed. S. T. Parker and K. R. Gibson (New York, NY: Cambridge University Press, pp. 511–539).

Miller, G. A. (1956). "The magical number seven plus or minus two: Some limits on our capacity for processing information," *Psychological Review* **63**, pp. 81–97.

(1967). "Project Grammarama," in *Psychology of Communication*, ed. G. A. Miller (New York, NY: Basic Books).

Miller, G. A., Galanter, E., and Pribram, K. H. (1960). *Plans and the Structure of Behavior* (New York, NY: Henry Holt).

Miller, G. F. (2000). "Evolution of music through sexual selection," in *The Origins of Music*, ed. N. L. Wallin, B. Merker, and S. Brown (Cambridge, MA: MIT Press, pp. 329–360).

(2001). *The Mating Mind: How sexual choice shaped the evolution of human nature* (New York, NY: Doubleday).

Miller, S. L. (1953). "A production of amino acids under possible primitive Earth conditions," *Science* **117**, pp. 527–528.

Milovanov, R., Huotilainen, M., Välimäki, V., Esquef, P. A., and Tervaniemi, M. (2008). "Musical aptitude and second language pronunciation skills in school-aged children: Neural and behavioral evidence," *Brain Research* **1194**, pp. 81–89.

Mitani, J. C. and Brandt, K. L. (1994). "Social factors influence the acoustic variability in the long-distance calls of male chimpanzees," *Ethology* **96**, pp. 233–252.

Mitani, J. C., Hunley, K. L., and Murdoch, M. E. (1999). "Geographic variation in the calls of wild chimpanzees: A reassessment," *American Journal of Primatology* **47**, pp. 133–151.

Mithen, S. (1996). *The Prehistory of the Mind* (London: Thames & Hudson).

(2005). *The Singing Neanderthals: The origins of music, language, mind, and body* (London: Weidenfeld & Nicolson).

Molliver, M. E. (1963). "Operant control of vocal behavior in the cat," *Journal of the Experimental Analysis of Behavior* **6**, pp. 197–202.

Molnar, S. (1972). "Tooth wear and culture: A survey of tooth functions among some prehistoric populations," *Current Anthropology* **13**, pp. 511–526.

Monod, J. (1971). *Chance and Necessity* (New York: NY: Knopf).

Montague, R. (1974a). *Formal Philosophy: Selected papers of Richard Montague* (New Haven, CT: Yale University Press).

(1974b). "Pragmatics," in *Formal Philosophy: Selected papers of Richard Montague*, ed. R. H. Thomason (New Haven, CT: Yale University Press, pp. 95–118).

Moon, S.-J. and Lindblom, B. (2003). "Two experiments on oxygen consumption during speech production: Vocal effort and speaking tempo," *Proceedings of the 15th International Congress of the Phonetic Sciences, Barcelona*, pp. 3129–3132.

Moore, B. C. J. (1988). *An Introduction to the Psychology of Hearing* (New York, NY: Academic Press).

Morgan, C. L. (1903). *An Introduction to Comparative Psychology* (London: Walter Scott Publishing).

Morgan, E. (1997). *The Aquatic Ape Hypothesis* (London: Souvenir Press).

Morse, P. A. and Snowdon, C. T. (1975). "An investigation of categorical speech discrimination by rhesus monkeys," *Perception and Psychophysics* **19**, pp. 137–143.

Morton, E. S. (1977). "On the occurrence and significance of motivation-structural rules in some bird and mammal sounds," *American Naturalist* **111**, pp. 855–869.

Mowrey, R. A. and MacKay, I. R. A. (1990). "Phonological primitives: Electromyographic speech error evidence," *Journal of the Acoustical Society of America* **88**, pp. 1299–1312.

Møller, A. P. (1988). "False alarm calls as a means of resource usurpation in the great tit, *Parus major*," *Ethology* **79**, pp. 25–30.

Mufwene, S. S. (2001). *The Ecology of Language Evolution* (New York, NY: Cambridge University Press).

Mühlhäusler, P. (1997). *Pidgin and Creole Linguistics* (London: University of Westminster Press).

Müller, F. M. (1861). "The theoretical stage, and the origin of language," in *Lectures on the Science of Language* (London: Longman, Green, Longman, and Roberts).

(1873). "Lectures on Mr Darwin's philosophy of language," *Fraser's Magazine* 7–8, pp. 147–233.

Munn, C. A. (1986). "The deceptive use of alarm calls by sentinel species in mixed species flocks of neotropical birds," in *Deception: Perspectives on human and nonhuman deceit*, ed. R. W. Mitchell and N. S. Thompson (Albany, NY: State University of New York Press, pp. 169–175).

Myers, R. E. (1976). "Comparative neurology of vocalization and speech: Proof of a dichotomy," *Annals of the New York Academy of Science* **280**, pp. 745–757.

Myers, S. A., Horel, J. A., and Pennypacker, H. S. (1965). "Operant control of vocal behavior in the monkey Cebus albifrons," *Psychonomic Science* **3**, pp. 389–390.

Myrberg, A. A. and Riggio, R. J. (1985). "Acoustically-mediated individual recognition by a coral reef fish (*Pomacentrus partitus*)," *Animal Behaviour* **33**, pp. 411–416.

Naguib, M. and Kipper, S. (2006). "Effects of different levels of song overlapping and singing behavior in male territorial nightingales (*Luscinia megarhynchos*)," *Behavioral Ecology and Sociobiology* **59**, pp. 419–426.

Naguib, M. and Todt, D. (1997). "Effects of dyadic vocal interactions on other conspecific receivers in nightingales," *Animal Behavior* **54**, pp. 1535–1543.

Nash, J. F. (1996). *Essays on Game Theory* (Cheltenham: Elgar).

Nearey, T. (1978). *Phonetic Features for Vowels* (Bloominton, IN: Indiana University Linguistics Club).

Negus, V. E. (1929). *The Mechanism of the Larynx* (London: Heinemann).

(1949). *The Comparative Anatomy and Physiology of the Larynx* (New York, NY: Hafner Publishing Company).

Neiworth, J. J. and Rilling, M. E. (1987). "A method for studying imagery in animals," *Journal of Experimental Psychology: Animal Behavior Processes* **13**, pp. 203–214.

Nelson, D. A. and Marler, P. (1989). "Categorical perception of a natural stimulus continuum: Birdsong," *Science* **244**, pp. 976–978.

Nelson, K. (1973). "Structure and strategy in learning to talk," *Monographs of the Society for Research in Child Development* **38**, pp. 1–137.

Nettl, B. (2000). "An ethnomusicologist contemplates universals in musical sound and musical culture," in *The Origins of Music*, ed. N. L. Wallin, B. Merker, and S. Brown (Cambridge, MA: MIT Press, pp. 463–472).

Nettle, D. (1999a). "Language variation and the evolution of societies," in *The Evolution of Culture*, ed. R. I. M. Dunbar, C. Knight, and C. Power (Edinburgh: Edinburgh University Press, pp. 214–227).

(1999b). *Linguistic Diversity* (Oxford: Oxford University Press).

Nettle, D. and Dunbar, R. I. M. (1997). "Social markers and the evolution of reciprocal exchange," *Current Anthropology* **38**, pp. 93–99.

Newman, J. D. (1992). "The primate isolation call and the evolution and physiological control of human speech," in *Language Origins: A multidisciplinary approach*, ed. J. Wind, B. A. Chiarelli, B. Bichakjian, and A. Nocentini (Dordrecht: Kluwer Academic, pp. 301–323).

Newmeyer, F. J. (1991). "Functional explanation in linguistics and the origin of language," *Language and Communication* **11**, pp. 3–28.

(1998a). *Language Form and Language Function* (Cambridge, MA: MIT Press).

(1998b). "On the supposed 'counterfunctionality' of Universal Grammar: Some evolutionary implications," in *Approaches to the Evolution of Language*, ed. J. R. Hurford, M. Studdert-Kennedy, and C. Knight (New York, NY: Cambridge University Press, pp. 305–319).

(2003). "What can the field of linguistics tell us about the origins of language?," in *Language Evolution*, ed. M. Christiansen and S. Kirby (Oxford: Oxford University Press, pp. 58–76).

Newport, E. L. (1991). "Contrasting conceptions of the critical period for language," in *Epigenesis of Mind: Essays on biology and cognition*, ed. S. Carey and R. Gelman (Hillsdale, NJ: Lawrence Erlbaum Associates, pp. 113–141).

Niklas, K. J. (1997). *The Evolutionary Biology of Plants* (Chicago, IL: University of Chicago Press).

Nishimura, T., Mikami, A., Suzuki, J., and Matsuzawa, T. (2003). "Descent of the larynx in chimpanzee infants," *Proceedings of the National Academy of Sciences, USA* **100**, pp. 6930–6933.

(2007). "Development of the laryngeal air sac in chimpanzees," *International Journal of Primatology* **28**, pp. 483–492.

Niyogi, P. (2006). *The Computational Nature of Language Learning and Evolution* (Cambridge, MA: MIT Press).

Noad, M. J., Cato, D. H., Bryden, M. M., Jenner, M. N., and Jenner, K. C. S. (2000). "Cultural revolution in whale songs," *Nature* **408**, p. 537.

Noiré, L. (1917). *The Origin and Philosophy of Language* (Chicago, IL, and London: Open Court Publishing).

Northcutt, R. G. and Gans, C. (1983). "The genesis of neural crest and epidermal placodes: A reinterpretation of vertebrate origins," *Quarterly Review of Biology* **58**, pp. 1–28.

Nottebohm, F. (1971). "Neural lateralization of vocal control in a passerine bird. I Song," *Journal of Experimental Zoology* **177**, pp. 229–262.

(1973). "Comment on Hewes," *Current Anthropology* **14**, pp. 5–24.

(1975). "A zoologist's view of some language phenomena, with particular emphasis on vocal learning," in *Foundations of Language Development*, ed. E. H. Lenneberg and E. Lenneberg (New York, NY: Academic Press, pp. 61–103).

(1976a). "Phonation in the orange-winged Amazon parrot, Amazona amazonica," *Journal of Comparative Physiology, A* **108**, pp. 157–170.

(1976b). "Vocal tract and brain: A search for evolutionary bottlenecks," *Annals of the New York Academy of Sci*ence **280**, pp. 643–649.

(1999). "The anatomy and timing of vocal learning in birds," in *The Design of Animal Communication*, ed. M. D. Hauser and M. Konishi (Cambridge, MA: MIT/Bradford, pp. 63–110).

Nowak, M. A., Komarova, N. L., and Niyogi, P. (2001). "Evolution of universal grammar," *Science* **291**, pp. 114–118.

(2002). "Computational and evolutionary aspects of language," *Nature* **417**, pp. 611–617.

Nowak, M. A., Krakauer, D. C., and Dress, A. (1999). "An error limit for the evolution of language," *Proceedings of the Royal Society, London* **266**, pp. 2131–2136.

Nowicki, S., Searcy, W. A., and Peters, S. (2002). "Quality of song learning affects female response to male bird song," *Proceedings of the Royal Society of London, B* **269**, pp. 1949–1954.

Nozick, R. (1974). *Anarchy, State and Utopia* (New York, NY: Basic Books).

O'Connell, J. F., Hawkes, K., and Blurton Jones, N. G. (1999). "Grandmothering and the evolution of Homo erectus," *Journal of Human Evolution* **36**, pp. 461–485.

Odling-Smee, J., Laland, K. N., and Feldman, M. W. (2003). *Niche Construction: The neglected process in evolution* (Princeton, NJ: Princeton University Press).

O'Donnell, T. J., Hauser, M. D., and Fitch, W. T. (2005). "Using mathematical models of language experimentally," *Trends in Cognitive Science* **9**, pp. 284–289.

Ogden, C. K. and Richards, I. A. (1923). *The Meaning of Meaning* (London: Routledge and Keagan Paul).

Ohala, J. J. (1983a). "Cross-language use of pitch: An ethological view," *Phonetica* **40**, pp. 1–18.

  (1983b). "The origin of sound patterns in vocal tract constraints," in *The Production of Speech*, ed. P. F. MacNeilage (New York, NY: Springer, pp. 189–216).

  (1984). "An ethological perspective on common cross-language utilization of F0 of voice," *Phonetica* **41**, pp. 1–16.

  (1993). "The phonetics of sound change," in *Historical Linguistics: Problems and perspectives*, ed. C. Jones (London: Longman, pp. 237–278).

Ohno, S. (1970). *Evolution by Gene Duplication* (Heidelberg: Springer).

Olds, J. and Milner, P. (1954). "Positive reinforcement produced by electrical stimulation of the septal area and other regions of the rat brain," *Journal of Comparative Physiological Psychology* **47**, pp. 419–427.

Orenstein, R. I. (1972). "Tool-use by the New Caledonian Crow (*Corvus moneduloides*)," *Auk* **89**, pp. 674–676.

Orr, W. F. and Cappannari, S. C. (1964). "The emergence of language," *American Anthropologist* **66**, pp. 318–324.

Oudeyer, P.-Y. (2005). "The self-organization of speech sounds," *Journal of Theoretical Biology* **233**, pp. 435–449.

Owen, R. (1835). "On the anatomy of the Cheetah, Felis jubata," *Transactions of the Zoological Society (London)* **1**, pp. 129–136.

Owren, M. J., Dieter, J. A., Seyfarth, R. M., and Cheney, D. L. (1993). "Vocalizations of rhesus (*Macaca mulatta*) and Japanese (*M. fuscata*) macaques cross-fostered between species show evidence of only limited modification," *Developmental Psychobiology* **26**, pp. 389–406.

Owren, M. J. and Rendall, D. (2001). "Sound on the rebound: Bringing form and function back to the forefront in understanding nonhuman primate vocal signaling," *Evolutionary Anthropology* **10**, pp. 58–71.

Packer, C. (1977). "Reciprocal altruism in Papio anubis," *Nature* **265**, pp. 441–443.

Pagel, M. D. (1992). "A method for the analysis of comparative data," *Journal of Theoretical Biology* **156**, pp. 434–442.

Pagel, M. D., Atkinson, Q. D., and Meade, A. (2007). "Frequency of word-use predicts rates of lexical evolution throughout Indo-European history," *Nature* **449**, pp. 717–721.

Pagel, M. D. and Harvey, P. H. (1989). "Taxonomic differences in the scaling of brain on body weight among mammals," *Science* **244**, pp. 1589–1593.

Pagel, M. D., Venditti, C., and Meade, A. (2006). "Large punctuational contribution of speciation to evolutionary divergence at the molecular level," *Science* **314**, pp. 119–121.

Paget, R. A. S. (1923). "The production of artificial vowel sounds," *Proceedings of the Royal Society of London, Series A* **102**, pp. 752–765.

(1930). *Human Speech* (London: Kegan Paul, Trench, Trubner and Co.).

(1944). "The origin of language," *Science* **99**, pp. 14–15.

Palmer, A. R. (2002). "Chimpanzee right-handedness reconsidered: Evaluating the evidence with funnel plots," *American Journal of Physical Anthropology* **118**, pp. 191–199.

Palmer, C. T. (1991). "Kin selection, reciprocal altruism and information sharing among Maine lobstermen," *Ethology and Sociobiology* **12**, pp. 221–235.

Panchanathan, K. and Boyd, R. (2004). "Indirect reciprocity can stabilize cooperation without the second-order free rider problem," *Nature* **432**, pp. 499–502.

Panchen, A. L. (1994). "Richard Owen and the concept of homology," in *Homology: The hierarchical basis of comparative biology*, ed. B. K. Hall (San Diego, CA: Academic Press, pp. 21–62).

Panopoulou, G., Hennig, S., Groth, D., Krause, A., Poustka, A. J., Herwig, R., Vingron, M., and Lehrach, H. (2003). "New evidence for genome-wide duplications at the origin of vertebrates using an amphioxus gene set and completed animal genomes," *Genome Research* **13**, pp. 1056–1066.

Parker, G. A. and Maynard Smith, J. (1990). "Optimality Theory in evolutionary biology," *Nature* **348**, pp. 27–33.

Parkes, A. P. (2002). *Introduction to Languages, Machines and Logic: Computable languages, abstract machines and formal logic* (New York, NY: Springer).

Patel, A. D. (2003). "Language, music, syntax and the brain," *Nature Neuroscience* **6**, pp. 674–681.

(2008). *Music, Language, and the Brain* (New York, NY: Oxford University Press).

Patterson, D. and Pepperberg, I. (1994). "A comparative study of human and parrot phonation: Acoustic and articulatory correlates of vowels," *Journal of the Acoustical Society of America* **96**, pp. 634–648.

(1998). "Acoustic and articulatory correlates of stop consonants in a parrot and a human subject," *Journal of the Acoustical Society of America* **103**, pp. 2197–2215.

Patterson, F. G. (1978). "The gestures of a gorilla: Language acquisition in another pongid," *Brain and Language* **5**, pp. 72–97.

Paulsen, K. (1967). *Das Prinzip der Stimmbildung in der Wirbeltierreihe und beim Menschen* (Frankfurt a. M.: Akademische Verlagsgesellschaft).

Paus, T. (2001). "Primate anterior cingulate cortex: Where motor control, drive and cognition interface," *Nature Reviews Neuroscience* 2, pp. 417–424.

Payne, K. (2000). "The progressively changing songs of humpback whales: A window on the creative process in a wild animal," in *The Origins of Music*, ed. N. L. Wallin, B. Merker, and S. Brown (Cambridge, MA: MIT Press, pp. 135–150).

Payne, R. and McVay, S. (1971). "Songs of humpback whales," *Science* 173, pp. 583–597.

Paz-y-Miño, G., Bond, A. B., Kamil, A. C., and Balda, R. P. (2004). "Pinyon jays use transitive inference to predict social dominance," *Nature* 430, pp. 778–781.

Peccei, J. S. (2006). *Child Language: A resource book for students* (London: Routledge).

Penfield, W. and Welch, K. (1951). "The supplementary motor area of the cerebral cortex: A clinical and experimental study," *AMA Archives of Neurology and Psychiatry* 66, pp. 289–231.

Pepperberg, I. M. (1990). "Conceptual abilities of some nonprimate species, with an emphasis on an African Grey parrot," in *"Language" and Intelligence in Monkeys and Apes: Caomparative developmental perspectives*, ed. S. T. Parker and K. R. Gibson (New York, NY: Cambridge University Press, pp. 469–507).

(1991). "A communicative approach to animal cognition: A study of conceptual abilities of an African grey parrot," in *Cognitive Ethology*, ed. C. A. Ristau. (Hillsdale, NJ: Lawrence Erlbaum Associates, pp. 153–186).

(1994). "Numerical competence in an African Grey Parrot (*Psittacus eithacus*)," *Journal of Comparative Psychology* 108, pp. 36–44.

(1999). *The Alex Studies: Cognitive and communicative abilities of grey parrots* (Cambridge, MA: Harvard University Press).

Pepperberg, I. M. and Brezinsky, M. V. (1991). "Acquisition of a relative class concept by an African Grey parrot (Psittacus erithacus): Discriminations based on relative size," *Journal of Comparative Psychology* 105, pp. 286–294.

Pepperberg, I. M., Garcia, S. E., Jackson, E. C., and Marconi, S. (1995). "Mirror use by African Grey Parrots (Psittacus erithacus)," *Journal of Comparative Psychology* 109, pp. 182–195.

Pepperberg, I. M. and Wilcox, S. E. (2000). "Evidence for a form of mutual exclusivity during label acquisition by grey parrots (Psittacus erithacus)?," *Journal of Comparative Psychology* 114, pp. 219–231.

Peretz, I., Ayotte, J., Zatorre, R. J., Mehler, J., Ahad, P., Penhune, U., and Jutras, B. (2002). "Congenital amusia: A disorder of fine-grained pitch discrimination," *Neuron* 33, pp. 185–191.

Peretz, I. and Zatorre, R. J. (eds) (2003). *The Cognitive Neuroscience of Music* (Oxford: Oxford University Press).

Perkell, J. S. (1969). *Physiology of Speech Production: Results and implications of a quantitative cineradiographic study* (Cambridge, MA: MIT Press).

Perrett, D. I., Smith, P. A. J., Mistlin, A. J., Head, A. S., Potter, D. D., Milner, A. D., Broennimann, R., and Jeeves, M. A. (1985). "Visual analysis of body movements by neurones in the temporal cortex of the macaque monkey: A preliminary report," *Behavioral Brain Research* **16**, pp. 153–170.

Perry, G. H., Verrelli, B. C., and Stone, A. C. (2004). "Comparative analyses reveal a complex history of molecular evolution for human MYH16," *Molecular Biology and Evolution* **22**, pp. 379–382.

Petitto, L. A. and Marentette, P. (1991). "Babbling in the manual mode: Evidence for the ontogeny of language," *Science* **251**, pp. 1493–1496.

Pfungst, O. (1911). *Clever Hans: The horse of Mr. von Osten* (Bristol: Thoemmes).

Piaget, J. (1962). *Play, Dreams and Imitation in Childhood* (New York, NY: Norton Press).

Piattelli-Palmarini, M. (1989). "Evolution, selection, and cognition: From 'learning' to parameter setting in biology and the study of language," *Cognition* **31**, pp. 1–44.

Pinker, S. (1994a). "On language," *Journal of Cognitive Neuroscience* **6**, pp. 92–97.
   (1994b). *The Language Instinct* (New York, NY: William Morrow and Company).
   (1997). *How the Mind Works* (New York, NY: Norton).

Pinker, S. and Bloom, P. (1990). "Natural language and natural selection," *Behavioral and Brain Sciences* **13**, pp. 707–784.

Pinker, S. and Jackendoff, R. (2005). "The faculty of language: What's special about it?," *Cognition* **95**, pp. 201–236.

Plavcan and van Schaik, C. P. (1997). "Interpreting hominid behavior on the basis of sexual dimorphism," *Journal of Human Evolution* **32**, pp. 345–374.

Plooij, F. X. (1984). *The Behavioral Development of Free-living Chimpanzee Babies and Infants* (Norwood, NJ: Ablex Publishing Corporation).

Plotnik, J. M., de Waal, F. B. M., and Reiss, D. (2006). "Self-recognition in an Asian elephant," *Proceedings of the National Academy of Sciences* **103**, pp. 17053–17057.

Plummer, T. (2004). "Flaked stones and old bones: Biological and cultural evolution at the dawn of technology," *American Journal of Physical Anthropology* **39**, pp. 118–164.

Plutynski, A. (2006). "What was Fisher's fundamental theorem of natural selection and what was it for?," *Studies in History and Philosophy of Biological and Biomedical Sciences* **37**, pp. 59–82.

Podos, J. (1997). "A performance constraint on the evolution of trilled vocalizations in a songbird family (Passeriformes: Emberizidae)," *Evolution* **51**, pp. 537–551.

Podos, J., Nowicki, S., and Peters, S. (1999). "Permissiveness in the learning and development of song syntax in swamp sparrows," *Animal Behavior* **58**, pp. 93–103.

Pollard, C. and Sag, I. (1987). *Head-driven Phrase Structure Grammar* (Chicago, IL: University of Chicago Press).

Pomiankowski, A. (1987). "Sexual selection: The handicap principle does work – sometimes," *Proceedings of the Royal Society London, B* **231**, pp. 123–145.

Poole, J. H., Tyack, P. L., Stoeger-Horwath, A. S., and Watwood, S. (2005). "Elephants are capable of vocal learning," *Nature* **434**, pp. 455–456.

Poremba, A., Malloy, M., Saunders, R. C., Carson, R. E., Herscovitch, P., and Mishkin, M. (2004). "Species-specific calls evoke asymmetric activity in the monkey's temporal poles," *Nature* **427**, pp. 448–451.

Portner, P. H. (2005). *What is Meaning: Fundamentals of formal semantics* (Oxford: Blackwell).

Povinelli, D. J., Bierschwale, D. T., and Cech, C. G. (1999). "Comprehension of seeing as a referential act in young children, but not juvenile chimpanzees," *British Journal of Developmental Psychology* **17**, pp. 37–60.

Povinelli, D. J. and Cant, J. G. H. (1995). "Arboreal clambering and the evolution of self-conception," *Quarterly Review of Biology* **70**, pp. 393–421.

Povinelli, D. J., Nelson, K. E., and Boysen, S. T. (1990). "Inferences about guessing and knowing by chimpanzees (*Pan troglodytes*)," *Journal of Comparative Psychology* **104**, pp. 203–210.

Povinelli, D. J., Parks, K. A., and Novak, M. A. (1991). "Do rhesus monkeys (*Macaca mulatta*) attribute knowledge and ignorance to others?" *Journal of Comparative Psychology* **105**, pp. 318–325.

Power, C. (1998). "Old wives' tales: The gossip hypothesis and the reliability of cheap signals," in *Approaches to the Evolution of Language*, ed. J. R. Hurford, M. Studdert-Kennedy, and C. Knight (New York, NY: Cambridge University Press, pp. 111–129).

Premack, D. (1971). "Language in chimpanzee?" *Science* **172**, pp. 808–822.

(1986). *Gavagai! Or the Future History of the Animal Language Controversy* (Cambridge, MA: MIT Press).

Premack, D. and Woodruff, G. (1978). "Does the chimpanzee have a theory of mind?," *Behavioral and Brain Sciences* **4**, pp. 515–526.

Pressing, J. (1983). "Cognitive isomorphisms between pitch and rhythm in world musics: West Africa, the Balkans and Western tonality," *Studies in Music* **17**, pp. 38–61.

Preuschoft, S. (1995). "'Laughter' and 'smiling' in macaques: An evolutionary perspective." Unpublished PhD thesis, Utrecht University.

Prinz, W. (2002). "Experimental approaches to imitation," in *The Imitative Mind: Development, evolution and brain bases*, ed. A. N. Meltzoff and W. Prinz (Cambridge: Cambridge University Press, pp. 143–162).

Prothero, D. R. and Dott, R. H., Jr. (2004). *Evolution of the Earth* (Boston, MA: McGraw Hill).

Pruetz, J. D. and Bertolani, P. (2007). "Savanna chimpanzees, Pan troglodytes verus, hunt with tools," *Current Biology* **17**, pp. 412–417.

Pulleyblank, E. G. (1989). "The meaning of duality of patterning and its importance in language evolution," in *Studies in Language Origins*, ed. J. Wind,

E. G. Pulleyblank, É. d. Grolier, and B. H. Bichakjian (Amsterdam: Benjamins, pp. 53–65).

Pullum, G. K. and Gazdar, G. (1982). "Natural languages and context-free languages," *Linguistics and Philosophy* **4**, pp. 471–504.

Purves, D. (1988). *Body and Brain: A trophic theory of neural connections* (Cambridge, MA: Harvard University Press).

Purves, D. and Lichtman, J. W. (1980). "Elimination of synapses in the developing nervous system," *Science* **210**, pp. 153–157.

Putnam, N., Butts, T., Ferrier, D. E. K., Furlong, R. F., Hellsten, U., Kawashima, T. *et al.* (2008). "The amphioxus genome and the evolution of the chordate karyotype," *Nature* **453**, pp. 1064–1071.

Qiang, J., Currie, P. J., Norell, M. A., and Shu-An, J. (1998). "Two feathered dinosaurs from northeastern China," *Nature* **393**, pp. 753–761.

Quine, W. V. O. (1960). *Word and Object* (Cambridge, MA: MIT Press).

Raff, R. A. and Kaufman, T. C. (1983). *Embryos, Genes and Evolution* (New York, NY: Macmillan).

Rainey, H. J., Zuberbühler, K., and Slater, P. J. B. (2004). "Hornbills can distinguish between primate alarm calls," *Proceedings of the Royal Society, B* **271**, pp. 755–759.

Ralls, K., Fiorelli, P., and Gish, S. (1985). "Vocalizations and vocal mimicry in captive harbor seals, Phoca vitulina," *Canadian Journal of Zoology* **63**, pp. 1050–1056.

Ramachandran, V. S. (2006). "Mirror neurons and imitation learning as the driving force behind 'the great leap forward' in human evolution." Available at www.edge.org/3rd_culture/ramachandran/ramachandran_p1.html

Ramus, F. (2002). "Language discrimination by newborns: Teasing apart phonotactic, rhythmic, and intonational cues," *Annual Review of Language Acquisition* **2**, pp. 85–115.

Ramus, F., Hauser, M. D., Miller, C. T., Morris, D., and Mehler, J. (2000). "Language discrimination by human newborns and cotton-top tamarin monkeys," *Science* **288**, pp. 349–351.

Ramus, F., Nespor, M., and Mehler, J. (1999). "Correlates of linguistic rhythm in the speech signal," *Cognition* **73**, pp. 265–292.

Randolph, M. C. and Brooks, B. B. (1967). "Conditioning of a vocal response in a chimpanzee through social reinforcement," *Folia Primatologica* **5**, pp. 70–79.

Rauschecker, J. P. (2005). "Vocal gestures and auditory objects," *Behavioral and Brain Sciences* **28**, pp. 143–144.

Reader, S. M. and Laland, K. N. (2002). "Social intelligence, innovation, and enhanced brain size in primates," *Proceedings of the National Academy of Sciences, USA* **99**, pp. 4436–4441.

Reby, D. and McComb, K. (2003). "Anatomical constraints generate honesty: Acoustic cues to age and weight in the roars of red deer stags," *Animal Behavior* **65**, pp. 519–530.

Reby, D., McComb, K., Cargnelutti, B., Darwin, C., Fitch, W. T., and Clutton-Brock, T. (2005). "Red deer stags use formants as assessment cues during intrasexual agonistic interactions," *Procedings of the Royal Society London, B* **272**, pp. 941–947.

Reed, D. L., Smith, V. S., Hammond, S. L., Rogers, A. R., and Clayton, D. H. (2004). "Genetic analysis of lice supports direct contact between modern and archaic humans," *PLOS Biology* **2**, p. e340.

Reichard, U. H. and Boesch, C. (eds) (2003). *Monogamy: Mating strategies and partnerships in birds, humans and other mammals* (Cambridge: Cambridge University Press).

Reiss, D. and Marino, L. (2001). "Mirror self-recognition in the bottlenose dolphin: A case of cognitive convergence," *Proceedings of the National Academy of Sciences, USA* **98**, pp. 5937–5942.

Reiss, D. and McCowan, B. (1993). "Spontaneous vocal mimicry and production by bottlenose dolphins (*Tursiops truncatus*): Evidence for vocal learning," *Journal of Comparative Psychology* **107**, pp. 301–312.

Rendall, D., Cheney, D. L., and Seyfarth, R. M. (2000). "Proximate factors mediating 'contact' calls in adult female baboons (Papio cynocephalus ursinus) and their infants," *Journal of Comparative Psychology* **114**, 36–46.

Rendall, D., Owren, M. J., and Rodman, P. S. (1998). "The role of vocal tract filtering in identity cueing in rhesus monkey (Macaca mulatta) vocalizations," *Joural of the Acoustical Society of America* **103**, pp. 602–614.

Rendall, D., Rodman, P. S., and Emond, R. E. (1996). "Vocal recognition of individuals and kin in free-ranging rhesus monkeys," *Animal Behavior* **51**, pp. 1007–1015.

Rendall, D., Vokey, J. R., Nemeth, C., and Ney, C. (2005). "Reliable but weak voice-formant cues to body size in men but not women," *Journal of the Acoustical Society of America* **117**, p. 2372.

Reno, P. L., Meindl, R. S., McCollum, M. A., and Lovejoy, C. O. (2003). "Sexual dimorphism in Australopithecus afarensis was similar to that of modern humans," *Proceedings of the National Academy of Sciences, USA* **100**, pp. 9404–9409.

Rensch, B. (1956). "Increase of learning capability with increase of brain-size," *American Naturalist* **15**, pp. 81–95.

Repp, B. H. (1982). "Phonetic trading relations and context effects: New experimental evidence for a speech mode of perception," *Psychological Bulletin* **92**, pp. 81–110.

Révész, G. (1956). *The Origins and Prehistory of Language* (New York, NY: Philosophical Library).

Reynolds Losin, E. A., Russell, J. L., Freeman, H., Meguerditchian, A., and Hopkins, W. D. (2008). "Left hemisphere specialization for oro-facial movements of learned vocal signals by captive chimpanzees," *PLOS ONE* **3**, p. e2529.

Richerson, P. J. and Boyd, R. (2005). *Not by Genes Alone: How culture transformed human evolution* (Chicago, IL: University of Chicago Press).

Richman, B. (1976). "Some vocal distinctive features used by gelada monkeys," *Journal of the Acoustical Society of America* **60**, pp. 718–724.

(1987). "Rhythm and melody in gelada vocal exchanges," *Primates* **28**, pp. 199–223.

(1993). "On the evolution of speech: Singing as the middle term," *Current Anthropology* **34**, pp. 721–722.

Richmond, B. G., Begun, D. R., and Strait, D. S. (2001). "Origin of human bipedalism: The knuckle-walking hypothesis revisited," *Yearbook of Physical Anthropology* **44**, pp. 70–105.

Ridley, M. (1997). *Evolution* (Oxford: Oxford University Press).

Ridley, M. (2003). *Nature Via Nurture: Genes, experience, and what makes us human* (New York, NY: HarperCollins).

Riebel, K. (2003). "The 'mute' sex revisited: Vocal production and perception learning in female songbirds," *Advances in the Study of Behavior* **33**, pp. 49–86.

Riechert, S. E. (1978). "Games spiders play: Behavioural variability in territorial disputes," *Behavioral Ecology and Sociobiology* **3**, pp. 135–162.

Riede, T. and Fitch, W. T. (1999). "Vocal tract length and acoustics of vocalization in the domestic dog Canis familiaris," *Journal of Experimental Biology* **202**, pp. 2859–2867.

Ritchison, G. (1983). "The function of singing in female black-headed grosbeaks (Pheucticus melanocephalus): Family group maintenance," *Auk* **100**, pp. 105–116.

(1986). "The singing behavior of female northern cardinals," *Condor* **88**, pp. 156–159.

Rizzolatti, G. and Arbib, M. A. (1998). "Language within our grasp," *Trends in Neuroscience* **21**, pp. 188–194.

Rizzolatti, G., Fadiga, L., Gallese, V., and Fogassi, L. (1996). "Premotor cortex and the recognition of motor actions," *Cognitive Brain Research* **3**, pp. 131–141.

Roberts, W. A. (1998). *Principles of Animal Cognition* (New York, NY: McGraw-Hill).

Robinson, J. G. (1984). "Syntactic structures in the vocalizations of wedge-capped capuchin monkeys, *Cebus nigrivittatus*," *Behaviour* **90**, pp. 46–79.

Rodenstein, D. O., Perlmutter, N., and Stanescu, D. C. (1985). "Infants are not obligatory nasal breathers," *American Review of Respiratory Disease* **131**, pp. 343–347.

Roe, A. W., Pallas, S. L., Hahm, J.-O., and Sur, M. (1990). "A map of visual space induced in primary auditory cortex," *Science* **250**, pp. 818–820.

Roede, M., Wind, J., Patrick, J., and Reynolds, V. (1991). *The Aquatic Ape: Fact or fiction?* (London: Souvenir Press).

Rogers, J. and Pullum, G. K. (2009). "Aural pattern recognition experiments and the subregular hierarchy," *UCLA Working Papers in Linguistics* **10**, pp. 1–16.

Rogers, L. J. and Kaplan, G. T. (eds) (2004). *Comparative vertebrate cognition: Are primates superior to non-primates?* (New York, NY: Kluwer Academic).

Roitblat, H. L., Bever, T. G., and Terrace, H. S. (eds) (1984). *Animal Cognition* (Hillsdale, NJ: Erlbaum).

Roland, P. E., Larsen, B., Lassen, N. A., and Skinhoj, E. (1980). "Supplementary motor area and other cortical areas in organization of voluntary movements in man," *Journal of Neurophysiology* **43**, pp. 118–136.

Romer, A. S. (1941). *Man and the Vertbrates* (Chicago, IL: University of Chicago Press).

Rosen, S. and Howell, P. (1981). "Plucks and bows are not categorically perceived," *Perception and Psychophysics* **30**, pp. 156–168.

Ross, E. D. (1981). "The aprosodias: Functional-anatomic organization of the affective components of language in the right hemisphere," *Archives of Neurology* **38**, pp. 561–569.

(1988). "Acoustic analysis of affective prosody during right-sided Wada test: A within-subjects verification of the right hemisphere's role in language," *Brain and Language* **33**, pp. 128–145.

Rothstein, E. (2006). *Emblems of Mind: The inner life of music and mathematics* (Chicago, IL: University of Chicago Press).

Rousseau, J.-J. (1966[1781]). *Essay on the Origin of Languages* (Chicago, IL: University of Chicago Press).

Rubin, D. C. (1995). *Memory in Oral Traditions: The cognitive psychology of epics, ballads, and counting-out rhymes* (New York, NY: Oxford University Press).

Rubin, D. C., Wallace, W. T., and Houston, B. C. (1993). "The beginnings of expertise for ballads," *Cognitive Science* **17**, pp. 435–462.

Ruelle, D. (1991). *Chance and Chaos* (Princeton, NJ: Princeton University Press).

Ruse, M. (1986). *Taking Darwin Seriously* (New York, NY: Basil Blackwell).

Russell, B. and Whitehead, A. N. (1910). *Principia Mathematica* (Cambridge: Cambridge University Press).

Ruvolo, M. E., Zehr, S., and Von Dornum, M. (1993). "Mitochondrial COII sequences and modern human origins," *Molecular Biology and Evolution* **10**, pp. 1115–1135.

Sabater Pi, J., Veà, J. J., and Serrallonga, J. (1997). "Did the first hominids build nests?," *Current Anthropology* **38**, pp. 914–917.

Sacks, O. (1985). *The Man Who Mistook His Wife for a Hat and Other Clinical Tales* (New York, NY: Perennial Library).

Sampson, G. (1980). *Schools of Linguistics* (Stanford, CA: Stanford University Press).

(1997). *Educating Eve: The 'language instinct' debate* (London: Cassell).

Sandberg, R., Yasuda, R., Pankratz, D. G., Carter, T. A., Del Rio, J. A., Wodicka, L., Mayford, M., Lockhart, D. J., and Barlow, C. (2000). "Regional and strain-specific gene expression mapping in the adult mouse brain," *Proceedings of the National Academy of Sciences* **97**, pp. 11038–11043.

Sapir, E. (1921). *Language* (New York, NY: Harcourt, Brace and Co.).

(1929). "A study in phonetic symbolism," *Journal of Experimental Psychology* **12**, pp. 225–239.

Sasaki, C. T., Levine, P. A., Laitman, J. T., and Crelin, E. S. (1977). "Postnatal descent of the epiglottis in man," *Archives of Otolaryngology* **103**, pp. 169–171.

Saussure, F. de (1916). *Course in General Linguistics* (New York, NY: McGraw-Hill).

Savage-Rumbaugh, E. S. (1986). *Ape Language: From conditioned response to symbol* (New York, NY: Columbia University Press).

Savage-Rumbaugh, E. S., Murphy, J., Sevcik, R. A., Brakke, K. E., Williams, S. L., and Rumbaugh, D. M. (1993). "Language comprehension in ape and child," *Monographs of the Society for Research in Child Development* **58**, pp. 1–221.

Savage-Rumbaugh, E. S., Sevcik, R. A., and Hopkins, W. D. (1988). "Symbolic cross-modal transfer in two species of chimpanzees," *Child Development* **59**, pp. 617–625.

Sayigh, L. S., Tyack, P. L., Wells, R. S., and Scott, M. D. (1990). "Signature whistles of free-ranging bottlenose dolphins Tursiops truncatus: Stability and mother–offspring comparisons," *Behavioral Ecology & Sociobiology* **26**, pp. 247–260.

Scharff, C. and Haesler, S. (2005). "An evolutionary perspective on FoxP2: Strictly for the birds?," *Current Opinion in Neurobiology* **15**, pp. 694–703.

Scherer, K. R. (1985). "Vocal affect signaling: A comparative approach," *Advances in the Study of Behavior* **15**, pp. 189–244.

Schlaug, G. (2001). "The musician brain: Evidence for functional and structural adaptation," *Annals of the New York Academy of Science* **930**, pp. 281–299.

Schmidt-Nielsen, K., Bretz, W., and Taylor, C. (1970). "Panting in dogs: Unidirectional air flow over evaporative surfaces," *Science* **169**, pp. 1102–1104.

Schneider, R. (1964). "Der Larynx der Säugetiere," *Handbuch der Zoologie* **5**, pp. 1–128.

Schusterman, R. J. (2008). "Vocal learning in mammals with special emphasis on pinnipeds," in *The Evolution of Communicative Flexibility: Complexity, creativity, and adaptability in human and animal communication*, ed. D. K. Oller and U. Griebel (Cambridge, MA: MIT Press, pp. 41–70).

Schusterman, R. J. and Feinstein, S. H. (1965). "Shaping and discriminative control of underwater click vocalizations in a California sea lion," *Science* **150**, pp. 1743–1744.

Schusterman, R. J. and Gisiner, R. (1988). "Artificial language comprehension in dolphins and sea lions: The essential cognitive skills," *Psychological Record* **38**, pp. 311–348.

Schusterman, R. J. and Krieger, K. (1984). "California sea lions are capable of semantic comprehension," *Psychological Record* **34**, pp. 3–25.

Schwartz, J. and Tallal, P. (1980). "Rate of acoustic change may underlie hemispheric specialization for speech perception," *Science* **207**, pp. 1380–1381.

Scott, S. K. (2005). "The neurobiology of speech perception," in *Twenty-First Century Psycholinguistics: Four cornerstones*, ed. A. Cutler (London: Lawrence Erlbaum, pp. 141–156).

Searle, J. R. (1969). *Speech Acts: An essay in the philosophy of language* (Cambridge: Cambridge University Press).

Seashore, C. (1967). *The Psychology of Music* (New York, NY: Dover).

Sebeok, T. A. (1977). *How Animals Communicate* (Bloomington, IN: Indiana University Press).

Semaw, S., Renne, P., Harris, J. W., Feibel, C. S., Bernor, R. L., Fesseha, N., and Mowbray, K. (1997). "2.5-million-year-old stone tools from Gona, Ethiopia," *Nature* **385**, pp. 333–336.

Senghas, A. and Coppola, M. (2001). "Children creating language: How Nicaraguan Sign Language acquired a spatial grammar," *Psychological Science* **12**, pp. 323–328.

Senghas, A., Kita, S., and Özyürek, A. (2005). "Children creating core properties of language: Evidence from an emerging sign language in Nicaragua," *Science* **305**, pp. 1779–1782.

Seuren, P. (1998). *Western Linguistics: An historical introduction* (Oxford: Blackwell).

Seyfarth, R. M. (2005). "Continuities in vocal communication argue against a gestural origin of language," *Behavioral and Brain Sciences* **28**, pp. 144–145.

Seyfarth, R. M. and Cheney, D. L. (1984). "Grooming, alliances and reciprocal altruism in vervet monkeys," *Nature* **308**, pp. 541–543.

(1997). "Behavioral mechanisms underlying vocal communication in nonhuman primates," *Animal Learning and Behavior* **25**, pp. 249–267.

(2003). "Signalers and receivers in animal communication," *Annual Review of Psychology* **54**, pp. 145–173.

(2005). "Constraints and preadaptations in the earliest stages of language evolution," *Linguistic Review* **22**, pp. 135–159.

(in press). "Primate social cognition as a precursor to language," in *The Oxford Handbook of Language Evolution*, ed. M. Tallerman and K. Gibson (Oxford: Oxford University Press).

Seyfarth, R. M., Cheney, D. L., and Bergman, T. J. (2005). "Primate social cognition and the origins of language," *Trends in Cognitive Science* **9**, pp. 264–266.

Seyfarth, R. M., Cheney, D. L., and Marler, P. (1980a). "Monkey responses to three different alarm calls: Evidence of predator classification and semantic communication," *Science* **210**, pp. 801–803.

(1980b). "Vervet monkey alarm calls: Semantic communication in a free-ranging primate," *Animal Behavior* **28**, pp. 1070–1094.

Shannon, C. E. and Weaver, W. (1949). *The Mathematical Theory of Communication* (Urbana, IL: University of Illinois).

Shattuck-Hufnagel, S. (1979). "Speech errors as evidence for a serial ordering mechanism in sentence production," in *Sentence Processing: Psycholinguistic studies presented to Merrill Garrett*, ed. W. E. Cooper and E. C. T. Walker (Hillsdale, NJ: Erlbaum, pp. 295–342).

Shea, J. J. (2003). "Neandertals, competition, and the origin of modern human behavior in the Levant," *Evolutionary Anthropology* **12**, pp. 173–187.

Sherman, P. W. (1977). "Nepotism and the evolution of alarm calls," *Science* **197**, pp. 1246–1253.

(1985). "Alarm calls of Belding's ground squirrels to aerial predators: Nepotism or self-preservation?," *Behavioral Ecology and Sociobiology* **17**, pp. 313–323.

Shettleworth, S. J. (1998). *Cognition, Evolution, and Behavior* (Oxford: Oxford University Press).

Shieber, S. M. (1985). "Evidence against the context-freeness of natural language," *Linguistics and Philosophy* **8**, pp. 333–343.

Shu, W., Cho, J. Y., Jiang, Y., Zhang, M., Weisz, D., Elder, G. A., Schmeidler, J., De Gasperi, R., Gama Sosa, M. A., Rabidou, D., Santucci, A. C., Perl, D., Morrisey, E., and Buxbaum, J. D. (2005). "Altered ultrasonic vocalization in mice with a disruption in the Foxp2 gene," *Proceedings of the National Academy of Sciences, USA* **102**, pp. 9643–9648.

Shubin, N. (2008). *Your Inner Fish: A journey into the 3.5 billion-year history of the human body* (London: Penguin Books).

Shubin, N., Tabin, C., and Carroll, S. (1997). "Fossils, genes and the evolution of animal limbs," *Nature* **388**, pp. 639–648.

Siegelmann, H. T. and Sontag, E. D. (1991). "Turing computability with neural nets," *Applied Mathematics Letters* **4**, pp. 77–80.

Silk, J. B., Cheney, D. L., and Seyfarth, R. M. (1996). "The form and function of post-conflict interactions between female baboons," *Animal Behavior* **52**, pp. 259–268.

(1999). "The structure of social relationships among female baboons," *Behaviour* **136**, pp. 679–703.

Síma, J. and Orponen, P. (2003). "General-purpose computation with neural networks: A survey of complexity theoretic results," *Neural Computation* **15**, pp. 2727–2778.

Simon, H. A. (1962). "The architecture of complexity," *Proceedings of the American Philosophical Society* **106**, pp. 467–482.

(1972). "Complexity and the representation of patterned sequences of symbols," *Psychological Review* **79**, pp. 369–382.

(1974). "How big is a chunk?," *Science* **183**, pp. 482–488.

Simons, E. L. (1995). "Egyptian oligocene primates: A review," *American Journal of Physical Anthropology* **38**, pp. 199–238.

Singh, I. (2000). *Pidgins and Creoles: An introduction* (London: Arnold).

Sinnott, J. M. and Brown, C. H. (1997). "Perception of the American English liquid /ra-la/ contrast by humans and monkeys," *Journal of the Acoustical Society of America* **102**, pp. 588–602.

Sinnott, J. M. and Saporita, T. A. (2000). "Differences in American English, Spanish, and monkey perception of the say-stay trading relation," *Perception and Psychophysics* **62**, pp. 1312–1319.

Sinnott, J. M. and Williamson, T. L. (1999). "Can macaques perceive place of articulation from formant transition information?," *Journal of the Acoustical Society of America* **106**, pp. 929–937.

Sipser, M. (1997). *Introduction to the Theory of Computation* (Boston, MA: PWS Publishing).

Skinner, B. F. (1957). *Verbal Behavior* (New York, NY: Appleton-Century-Crofts).

Slijper, E. J. (1942). "Biologic-anatomical investigations on the bipedal gait and upright posture in mammals, with special reference to a little goat, born without forelegs," *Proceedings Nederlandse Akademie van Wetenschappen* **45**, pp. 288–295, 407–415.

Sloboda, J. A. (1985). *The Musical Mind: The cognitive psychology of music* (Oxford: Clarendon).

Slobodchikoff, C. N., Kiriazis, J., Fischer, C., and Creef, E. (1991). "Semantic information distinguishing individual predators in the alarm calls of Gunnison's prairie dogs," *Animal Behavior* **42**, pp. 713–719.

Slocombe, K. E. and Zuberbühler, K. (2005). "Functionally referential communication in a chimpanzee," *Current Biology* **15**, pp. 1779–1784.

(2007). "Chimpanzees modify recruitment screams as a function of audience composition," *Proceedings of the National Academy of Sciences* **104**, pp. 17228–17233.

Smith, A. G. (1966). "Speech and other functions after left (dominant) hemispherectomy," *Journal of Neurology, Neurosurgery and Psychiatry* **109**, pp. 95–150.

Smith, D. R. R., Patterson, R. D., Turner, R., Kawahara, H., and Irino, T. (2005). "The processing and perception of size information in speech sounds," *Journal of the Acoustical Society of America* **117**, pp. 305–318.

Smithson, T. R. (1989). "The earliest known reptile," *Nature* **342**, pp. 676–678.

Sober, E. and Wilson, D. S. (1998). *Unto Others: The evolution and psychology of unselfish behavior* (Cambridge, MA: Harvard University Press).

Sommers, M. S., Moody, D. B., Prosen, C. A., and Stebbins, W. C. (1992). "Formant frequency discrimination by Japanese macaques (*Macaca fuscata*)," *Journal of the Acoustical Society of America* **91**, pp. 3499–3510.

Sonntag, C. F. (1921). "The comparative anatomy of the Koala (Phascolarctos cinereus) and Vulpine Phalanger (Trichosurus vulpecula)," *Proceedings of the Zoological Society of London* **39**, pp. 547–577.

Sperber, D. and Wilson, D. (1986). *Relevance: Communication and cognition* (Oxford: Blackwell).

Spoor, F., Leakey, M. G., Gathogo, P. N., Brown, F. H., Antón, S. C., McDougall, I., Kiarie, C., Manthi, F. K., and Leakey, L. N. (2007). "Implications of new early Homo fossils from Ileret, east of Lake Turkana, Kenya," *Nature* **448**, pp. 688–691.

Stabler, E. P. (2004). "Varieties of crossing dependencies: Structure dependence and mild context sensitivity," *Cognitive Science* **28**, pp. 699–720.

Stalnaker, R. C. (1972). "Pragmatics," in *Semantics of Natural Language*, ed. D. Davidson and G. Harman (Dordrecht: Reidel, pp. 380–397).

Stam, J. H. (1976). *Inquiries Into the Origin of Language* (New York, NY: Harper & Row).

Stamenov, M. I. and Gallese, V. (eds) (2002). *Mirror Neurons and the Evolution of Brain and Language* (Amsterdam: John Benjamins).

Stanford, C. B., Wallis, J., Matama, H., and Goodall, J. (1994a). "Patterns of predation by chimpanzees on red colobus monkeys in Gombe National Park, 1982–1991," *American Journal of Physical Anthropology* **94**, pp. 213–228.

Stanford, C. B., Wallis, J., Mpongo, E., and Goodall, J. (1994b). "Hunting decisions in wild chimpanzees," *Behaviour* **131**, pp. 1–18.

Stedman, H. H., Kozyak, B. W., Nelson, A., Thesier, D. M., Su, L. T., and Low, D. W., Bridges, C. R., Shrager, J. B., Minugh-Purvis, N., and Mitchell, M. (2004). "Myosin gene mutation correlates with anatomical changes in the human lineage," *Nature* **428**, pp. 415–418.

Steedman, M. J. (1996). "Categorial grammar," in *Concise Encyclopedia of Syntactic Theories*, ed. E. K. Brown and J. E. Miller (Oxford: Pergamon, pp. 31–44).

Steels, L. (1997). "The synthetic modeling of language origins," *Evolution of Communication* **1**, pp. 1–34.

(2000). "The puzzle of language evolution," *Kognitionswissenschaft* **8**, pp. 143–150.

(2002). "Grounding symbols through evolutionary language games," in *Simulating the Evolution of Language*, ed. A. Cangelosi and D. Parisi (New York, NY: Springer, pp. 211–226).

Steklis, H. D. and Raleigh, M. J. (1973). "Comment on Livingstone," *Current Anthropology* **14**, p. 27.

Stensiö, E. A. (1921). *Triassic Fishes from Spitzbergen* (Vienna: Holzhausen).

Stephan, H., Frahm, H., and Baron, G. (1981). "New and revised data on volumes of brain structures in insectivores and primates," *Folia Primatologica* **35**, pp. 1–29.

Stephenson, P. H. (1974). "On the possible significance of silence for the origin of speech," *Current Anthropology* **15**, pp. 324–325.

Sterelny, K. (2001). *Dawkins vs. Gould: Survival of the fittest* (London: Icon Books).

Stoel-Gammon, C. and Otomo, K. (1986). "Babbling development of hearing-imparied and normally hearing subjects," *Journal of Speech and Hearing Disorders* **51**, pp. 33–41.

Stokoe, W. C. (1960). *Sign Language Structure: An outline of the communicative systems of the American deaf* (Silver Spring, MD: Linstock Press).

(1974). "Motor signs as the first form of language," in *Language Origins*, ed. R. W. Wescott (Silver. Spring, MD: Linstock Press, pp. 35–49).

(2001). *Language in Hand: Why sign came before speech* (Washington, DC: Gallaudet University Press).

Stout, D., Toth, N., Schick, K., and Chaminade, T. (2008). "Neural correlates of Early Stone Age toolmaking: Technology, language and cognition in human evolution," *Philosophical Transactions of the Royal Society of London, Series B* **363**, pp. 1–11.

Street, A., Young, S., Tafuri, J., and Ilari, B. (2003). "Mothers' attitudes towards singing to their infants," *Proceedings of the 5th Triennial ESCOM Conference* **5**, pp. 628–631.

Striedter, G. F. (2004). *Principles of Brain Evolution* (Sunderland, MA: Sinauer).

Stringer, C. and Andrews, P. (2005). *The Complete World of Human Evolution* (London: Thames & Hudson).

Struhsaker, T. T. (1967). "Auditory communication among vervet monkeys (*Cercopithecus aethiops*)," in *Social Communication Among Primates*, ed. S. A. Altmann (Chicago, IL: Chicago University Press, pp. 281–324).

(1970). *The Red Colobus Monkey* (Chicago, IL: Chicago University Press).

Studdert-Kennedy, M. (1998). "The particulate origins of language generativity: From syllable to gesture," in *Approaches to the Evolution of Language*, ed. J. R. Hurford, M. Studdert-Kennedy, and C. Knight (New York, NY: Cambridge University Press, pp. 202–221).

Studdert-Kennedy, M. and Goldstein, L. (2003). "Launching language: The gestural origins of discrete infinity," in *Language Evolution*, ed. M. Christiansen and S. Kirby (Oxford: Oxford Unviersity Press, pp. 235–254).

Suddendorf, T. and Corballis, M. C. (2007). "The evolution of foresight: What is mental time travel, and is it unique to humans?," *Behavioral & Brain Sciences* **30**, pp. 299–351.

Suga, N., Niwa, H., Taniguchi, I., and Margoliash, D. (1987). "The personalized auditory cortex of the mustached bat: Adaptation for echolocation," *Journal of Neurophysiology* **58**, pp. 643–654.

Sugiyama, Y. and Koman, J. (1979). "Tool-using and tool-making behavior in wild chimpanzees at Bossou, Guinea," *Primates* **20**, pp. 513–524.

Sundberg, J. (1987). *The Science of the Singing Voice* (Dekalb, IL: Northern Illinois University Press).

Sundberg, J. and Lindblom, B. (1976). "Generative theories in language and music descriptions," *Cognition* **4**, pp. 99–122.

Sur, M., Garraghty, P. E., and Roe, A. W. (1988). "Experimentally induced visual projections into auditory thalamus and cortex," *Science* **242**, pp. 1437–1441.

Suthers, R. A. and Zollinger, S. A. (2004). "Producing song: Yhe vocal apparatus," *Annals of the New York Academy of Science* **1016**, pp. 109–129.

Sutton, D., Larson, C., Taylor, E. M., and Lindeman, R. C. (1973). "Vocalization in rhesus monkeys: Conditionability," *Brain Research* **52**, pp. 225–231.

Suzuki, R., Buck, J. R., and Tyack, P. L. (2006). "Information entropy of humpback whale songs," *Journal of the Acoustical Society of America* **119**, pp. 1849–1866.

Symington, J. (1885). "On the relations of the larynx and trachea to the vertebral column in the foetus and child," *Journal of Anatomy and Physiology* **19**, pp. 286–291.

Számadó, S. and Szathmary, E. (2006). "Selective scenarios for the emergence of natural language," *Trends in Ecology and Evolution* **21**, pp. 555–561.

Szathmáry, E. (2001). "Origin of the human language faculty: The language amoeba hypothesis," in *New Essays on the Origin of Language*, ed. J. Trabant and S. Ward (Berlin: Mouton de Gruyter, pp. 55–81).

Tallal, P., Miller, S. L., Bedi, G., Byma, G., Wang, X., Nagarajan, S. S., Schreiner, C., Jenkins, W. M., and Merzenich, M. M. (1996). "Language comprehension in language-learning impaired children improved with acoustically modified speech," *Science* **271**, pp. 81–84.

Tallerman, M. (2007). "Did our ancestors speak a holistic protolanguage?," *Lingua* **117**, pp. 579–604.

(2008). "Holophrastic protolanguage: Planning, processing, storage, and retrieval," *Interaction Studies* **9**, pp. 84–99.

Tattersall, I. (1999). *Becoming Human: Evolution and human uniqueness* (New York, NY: Harcourt-Brace).

Tchernichovski, O., Mitra, P. P., Lints, T., and Nottebohm, F. (2001). "Dynamics of the vocal imitation process: How a zebra finch learns its song," *Science* **291**, pp. 2564–2569.

Tebbich, S., Taborsky, M., Fessl, B., and Blomqvist, D. (2001). "Do woodpecker finches acquire tool-use by social learning?," *Proceedings of the Royal Society B* **268**, pp. 2189–2193.

Temeles, E. J. (1994). "The role of neighbours in territorial systems: When are they 'dear enemies'?," *Animal Behavior* **47**, pp. 339–350.

Temperley, D. (2001). *The Cognition of Basic Musical Structures* (Cambridge, MA: MIT Press).

Templeton, C. N., Greene, E., and Davis, K. (2005). "Allometry of alarm calls: Black-capped chickadees encode information about predator size," *Science* **308**, pp. 1934–1937.

Terrace, H. S. (1979). *Nim* (New York, NY: Knopf).

(1987). "Chunking by a pigeon in a serial learning task," *Nature* **325**, pp. 149–151.

(2001). "Chunking and serially organized behavior in pigeons, monkeys and humans," in *Avian Visual Cognition*, ed. R. G. Cook (Cambridge, MA: Comparative Cognition Press; available at: www.pigeon.psy.tufts.edu/avc/terrace/).

Terrace, H. S., Petitto, L. A., Sanders, S. J., and Bever, T. G. (1979). "Can an ape create a sentence?," *Science* **200**, pp. 891–902.

Terrace, H. S., Son, L. K., and Brannon, E. M. (2003). "Serial expertise of rhesus macaques," *Psychological Science* **14**, pp. 66–73.

Thieme, H. (1997). "Lower Palaeolithic hunting spears from Germany," *Nature* **385**, pp. 807–810.

Thomas, J. A. and Golladay, C. L. (1996). "Geographic variation in leopard seal (Hydrurga leptonyx) underwater vocalizations," in *Sensory Systems of Aquatic Mammals*, ed. R. Kastelein, J. A. Thomas, and P. E. Nachtigall (Woerden: DeSpil Publishers, pp. 201–221).

Thomas, J. A. and Stirling, I. (1983). "Geographic variation in the underwater vocalizations of Weddell seals (Leptonychotes weddelli) from Palmer Peninsula and McMurdo Sound, Antarctica," *Canadian Journal of Zoology* **61**, pp. 2203–2212.

Thompson, D. A. W. (1948). *On Growth and Form* (New York, NY: Cambridge University Press).

Thompson, J. A. M. (2002). "The status of bonobos in their southernmost geographic range," in *Developments in Primatology: Progress and Prospects, Vol. 1: African apes*, ed. B. M. F. Galdikas, N. E. Briggs, L. K. Sheeran, G. L. Shapiro, and J. Goodall (New York, NY: Springer, pp 75–81).

Thompson, N. S., Abbey, E., Wapner, J., Logan, C., Merritt, P. G., and Pooth, A. (2000). "Variation in the bout structure of northern mockingbird (Mimus polyglottos) singing," *Bird Behavior* **13**, pp. 93–98.

Thompson-Schill, S. L., D'Esposito, M., Aguirre, G. K., and Farah, M. J. (1997). "Role of left inferior prefrontal cortex in retrieval of semantic knowledge: A reevaluation," *Proceedings of the National Academy of Sciences* **94**, pp. 14792–14797.

Thomson, K. S. (1991). "Where did tetrapods come from?," *American Scientist* **79**, pp. 488–490.

Thorndike, E. L. (1943a). *Man and His Works* (Cambridge, MA: Harvard University Press).

(1943b). "The origin of language," *Science* **98**, pp. 1–6.

Thornton, A. and McAuliffe, K. (2006). "Teaching in wild meerkats," *Science* **313**, pp. 227–229.

Tinbergen, N. (1963). "On aims and methods of ethology," *Zeitschrift für Tierpsychologie* **20**, pp. 410–433.

Tincoff, R., Hauser, M. D., Tsao, F., Spaepen, G., Ramus, F., and Mehler, J. (2005). "Language discrimination based on rhythmic cues: Further experiments on cotton-top tamarins," *Developmental Science* **8**, pp. 26–35.

Tinklepaugh, O. L. (1928). "Multiple delayed reaction with chimpanzees and monkeys," *Journal of Comparative Psychology* **13**, pp. 207–243.

Titze, I. R. (1989). "Physiologic and acoustic differences between male and female voices," *Journal of the Acoustical Society of America* **85**, pp. 1699–1707.

(1994). *Principles of Voice Production* (Englewood Cliffs, NJ: Prentice Hall).

Tobias, P. V. (1965). "The Olduvai Bed I Hominine with special reference to its cranial capacity," *Current Anthropology* **6**, pp. 421–422.

(1987). "The brain of Homo habilis: A new level of organization in cerebral evolution," *Journal of Human Evolution* **16**, pp. 741–761.

Todt, D. (1975). "Social learning of vocal patterns and modes of their application in grey parrots Psittacus erithacus," *Zeitschrift Tierpsychologie* **39**, pp. 178–188.

Tomasello, M. (1990). "Cultural transmission in the tool use and communicatory signaling of chimpanzees?," in *"Language" and Intelligence in Monkeys and Apes: Caomparative developmental perspectives*, ed. S. T. Parker and K. R. Gibson (New York, NY: Cambridge University Press, pp. 274–311).

(1995). "Language is not an instinct," *Cognitive Development* **10**, pp. 131–156.

(ed.) (1998a). *The New Psychology of Language: Cognitive and functional approaches to language structure* (Hillsdale, NJ: Lawrence Erlbaum Associates).

(1998b). "The return of constructions," *Journal of Child Language* **25**, pp. 431–442.

(1999). *The Cultural Origins of Human Cognition* (Cambridge, MA: Harvard University Press).

(2000). "Do young children have adult syntactic competence?," *Cognition* **74**, pp. 209–253.

(2002). "Not waving but speaking: How important were gestures in the evolution of language?," *Nature* **417**, pp. 791–792.

(2003). "On the different origins of symbols and grammar," in *Language Evolution*, ed. M. Christiansen and S. Kirby (Oxford: Oxford University Press, pp. 94–110).

(2005). "Comment on Everrett (2005)," *Current Anthropology* **46**, pp. 640–641.

Tomasello, M. and Call, J. (1997). *Primate Cognition* (Oxford: Oxford University Press).

(2007). "Ape gestures and the origins of language," in *The Gestural Communication of Apes and Monkeys*, ed. J. Call and M. Tomasello (London: Lawrence Erlbaum, pp. 221–239).

Tomasello, M., Call, J., and Hare, B. (1998). "Five primate species follow the visual gaze of conspecifics," *Animal Behavior* **55**, pp. 1063–1069.

(2003). "Chimpanzees understand psychological states – the question is which ones and to what extent," *Trends in Cognitive Science* **7**, pp. 153–156.

Tomasello, M., Carpenter, M., Call, J., Behne, T., and Moll, H. (2005). "Understanding and sharing intentions: The origins of cultural cognition," *Behavioral & Brain Sciences* **28**, pp. 675–735.

Tomasello, M., Hare, B., and Agnetta, B. (1999). "Chimpanzees, Pan troglodytes, follow gaze direction geometrically," *Animal Behavior* **58**, pp. 769–777.

Tomasello, M., Savage-Rumbaugh, E. S., and Kruger, A. (1993). "Imitative learning of actions on objects by children, chimpanzees, and enculturated chimpanzees," *Child Development* **64**, pp. 1688–1706.

Tooby, J. and Cosmides, L. (1990a). "On the universality of human nature and the uniqueness of the individual: The role of genetics and adaptation," *Journal of Personality* **58**, pp. 17–67.

(1990b). "The past explains the present: Emotional adaptations and the structure of ancestral environments," *Ethology & Sociobology* **11**, pp. 375–424.

Toro, J. M., Trobalon, J., and Sebastián-Gallés, N. (2003). "The use of prosodic cues in language discrimination tasks by rats," *Animal Cognition* **6**, pp. 131–136.

Toth, N. (1985). "Archaeological evidence for preferential right-handedness in the lower and middle Pleistocene, and its possible implications," *Journal of Human Evolution* **14**, pp. 607–614.

Toth, N., Schick, K. D., Savage-Rumbaugh, E. S., and Sevcik, R. A. (1993). "Pan the tool-maker: Investigations into the stone tool-making and tool using capabilities of a bonobo (*Pan paniscus*)," *Journal of Archaeological Science* **20**, pp. 81–91.

Townsend, S. W., Deschner, T., and Zuberbühler, K. (2008). "Female chimpanzees use copulation calls flexibly to prevent social competition," *PLOS One* **3**, p. e2431.

Trainor, L. J. (1996). "Infant preferences for infant-directed versus noninfant-directed playsongs and lullabies," *Infant Behaviour and Development* **19**, pp. 83–92.

Trainor, L. J. and Trehub, S. E. (1992). "A comparison of infants' and adults' sensitivity to Western musical structure," *Journal of Experimental Psychology: Human Perception and Performance* **18**, pp. 394–402.

Trehub, S. E. (2000). "Human processing predispositions and musical universals," in *The Origins of Music*, ed. N. L. Wallin, B. Merker, and S. Brown (Cambridge, MA: MIT Press, pp. 427–448).

(2003a). "Musical predispositions in infancy: An update," in *The Cognitive Neuroscience of Music*, ed. I. Peretz and R. J. Zatorre (Oxford: Oxford University Press, pp. 3–20).

(2003b). "The developmental origins of musicality," *Nature Neuroscience* **6**, pp. 669–673.

Trehub, S. E. and Hannon, E. E. (2006). "Infant music perception: Domain-general or domain-specific mechanisms?," *Cognition* **100**, pp. 73–99.

Trevarthen, C. (1999). "Musicality and the intrinsic motor pulse: Evidence from human psychobiology and infant communication," *Musica Scientiae Special Issue 1999–2000*, pp. 155–211.

Trevathan, W. (1987). *Human Birth: An evolutionary perspective* (New York, NY: Aldine De Gruyter).

Trivers, R. L. (1971). "The evolution of reciprocal altruism," *Quarterly Review of Biology* **46**, pp. 35–57.

(1972). "Parental investment and sexual selection," in *Sexual Selection and the Descent of Man*, ed. B. G. Campbell (Chicago, IL: Aldine Press, pp. 136–179).

(1974). "Parent–offspring conflict," *American Zoologist* **14**, pp. 249–264.

Trubetskoy, N. S. (1939/1969). *Grundzüge der Phonologie/Principles of Phonology* (Berkeley, CA: University of California Press).

Tsai, L. S. and Maurer, S. (1930). "'Right-handedness' in white rats," *Science* **72**, pp. 436–438.

Tulving, E. (2002). "Episodic memory: From mind to brain," *Annual Review of Psychology* **53**, pp. 1–25.

Tulving, E. and Thomson, D. M. (1973). "Encoding specificity and retrieval processes in episodic memory," *Psychological Review* **80**, pp. 352–373.

Turing, A. M. (1952). "The chemical basis of morphogenesis," *Philosophical Transactions of the Royal Society of London, Series B* **237**, pp. 37–72.

Tutin, C. E. G. (1979). "Mating patterns and reproductive strategies in a community of wild chimpanzees (Pan troglodytes schweinfurthii)," *Behavioral Ecology and Sociobiology* **6**, pp. 29–38.

Tyack, P. L. and Clark, C. W. (2000). "Communication and acoustic behavior of dolphins and whales," in *Hearing by Whales and Dolphins*, ed. W. W. L. Au, A. N. Popper, and R. R. Fay (New York: Springer, pp. 156–224).

Tyack, P. L. and Miller, E. H. (2002). "Vocal anatomy, acoustic communication, and echolocation," in *Marine Mammal Biology: An evolutionary approach*, ed. A. R. Hoelzel (New York, NY: Blackwell Scientific Publications, pp. 142–184).

Valone, T. J. (2007). "From eavesdropping on performance to copying the behavior of others: A review of public information use," *Behavioral Ecology and Sociobiology* **62**, pp. 1–14.

Van Den Berg, J. (1958). "Myoelastic-aerodynamic theory of voice production," *Journal of Speech and Hearing Research* **1**, pp. 227–244.

van Dommelen, W. A. (1993). "Speaker height and weight identification: A re-evaluation of some old data," *Journal of Phonetics* **21**, pp. 337–341.

van Heyningen, V. and Williamson, K. A. (2002). "PAX6 in sensory development," *Human Molecular Genetics* **11**, pp. 1161–1167.

van Hoof, J. A. R. A. M. (1972). "A comparative approach to the phylogeny of laughter and smiling," in *Nonverbal Communication*, ed. R. A. Hinde (Cambridge: Cambridge University Press, pp. 12–53).

Van Parijs, S. M. (2003). "Aquatic mating in pinnipeds: A review," *Aquatic Mammals* **29**, pp. 214–226.

Van Schaik, C. P., Ancrenaz, M., Borgen, G., Galdikas, B., Knott, C. D., Singleton, I., Suzuki, A., Utami, S. S., and Merrill, M. (2003). "Orangutan cultures and the evolution of material cultures," *Science* **2**, pp. 102–105.

van Schaik, C. P., Fox, E. A., and Sitompul, A. F. (1996). "Manufacture and use of tools in wild Sumatran orangutans: Implications for human evolution," *Naturwissenschaften* **83**, pp. 186–188.

van Valin, R. D. (1996). "Role and reference grammar," in *Concise Encyclopedia of Syntactic Theories*, ed. E. K. Brown and J. E. Miller (Oxford: Pergamon, pp. 281–293).

(2001). *An Introduction to Syntax* (New York, NY: Cambridge University Press).

(2008). "Some remarks on Universal Grammar," in *Crosslinguistic Approaches to the Study of Language*, ed. E. Lieven and J. Guo (Mahwah, NJ: Lawrence Erlbaum Associates, pp. 311–320).

Vandepoele, K., De Vos, W., Taylor, J. S., Meyer, A., and Van de Peer, Y. (2004). "Major events in the genome evolution of vertebrates: Paranome age and size differ considerably between ray-finned fishes and land vertebrates," *Proceedings of the National Academy of Sciences, USA* **101**, pp. 1638–1643.

Vargha-Khadem, F., Carr, L. J., Isaacs, E., Brett, E., Adams, C., and Mishkin, M. (1997). "Onset of speech after left hemispherectomy in a nine-year-old boy," *Brain* **120**, pp. 159–182.

Vargha-Khadem, F., Gadian, D. G., Copp, A., and Mishkin, M. (2005). "FOXP2 and the neuroanatomy of speech and language," *Nature Reviews Neuroscience* **6**, pp. 131–138.

Vargha-Khadem, F., Watkins, K. E., Alcock, K., Fletcher, P., and Passingham, R. (1995). "Praxic and nonverbal cognitive deficits in a large family with a genetically-transmitted speech and language disorder," *Proceedings of the National Academy of Sciences* **92**, pp. 930–933.

Vargha-Khadem, F., Watkins, K., Price, C. J., Ashburner, J., Alcock, K., Connelly, A., Frackowiak, R. S. J., Friston, K. J., Pembrey, M. E., Mishkin, M., Gadian, D. G., and Passingham, R. E. (1998). "Neural basis of an inherited speech and language disorder," *Proceedings of the National Academy of Sciences, USA* **95**, pp. 12695–12700.

Vauclair, J. (1996). *Animal Cognition: An introduction to modern comparative psychology* (London: Harvard University Press).

Vaughan, W. and Greene, S. L. (1984). "Pigeon visual memory capacity," *Journal of Experimental Psychology: Animal Behavior Processes* **10**, pp. 256–271.

Vihman, M. M. (1986). "Individual differences in babbling and early speech: Predicting to age three," in *Precursors of Early Speech*, ed. B. Lindblom and R. Zetterström (New York, NY: Stockton Press, pp. 95–112).

(1991). "Ontogeny of phonetic gestures: Speech production," in *Modularity and the Motor Theory of Speech Perception*, ed. I. G. Mattingly and M. Studdert-Kennedy (London: Lawrence Erlbaum Associates, pp. 69–84).

(1996). *Phonological Development: The origins of language in the child* (Cambridge, MA: Blackwell).

Visalberghi, E. and Fragaszy, D. M. (1990). "Do monkeys ape?," in *"Language" and Intelligence in Monkeys and Apes: Comparative developmental perspectives*, ed. S. T. Parker and K. R. Gibson (New York, NY: Cambridge University Press, pp. 247–273).

Voelkel, B. and Huber, L. (2000). "True imitation in marmosets," *Animal Behavior* **60**, pp. 195–202.

von Frisch, K. (1967). *The Dance Language and Orientation of Bees* (Cambridge, MA: Belknap Press of Harvard University Press).

(1974). *Animal Architecture* (London: Hutchinson).

von Melchner, L., Pallas, S. L., and Sur, M. (2000). "Visual behaviour mediated by retinal projections directed to the auditory pathway," *Nature* **404**, pp. 871–876.

Vorobyev, M. (2004). "Ecology and evolution of primate colour vision," *Clinical and Experimental Optometry* **87**, pp. 230–238.

Vorperian, H. K., Kent, R. D., Lindstrom, M. J., Kalina, C. M., Gentry, L. R., and Yandell, B. S. (2005). "Development of vocal tract length during early childhood: A magnetic resonance imaging study," *Journal of the Acoustical Society of America* **117**, pp. 338–350.

Wada, K., Howard, J. T., McConnell, P., Whitney, O., Lints, T., Rivas, M., Horita, H., Patterson, M. A., White, S. A., Scharff, C., Haesler, S., Zhao, S., Sakaguchi, H., Hagiwara, M., Shiraki, T., Hirozane-Kishikawa, T., Skene, P., Hayashizaki, Y., Caninci, T., and Jarvis, E. D. (2006). "A molecular neuroethological approach for identifying and characterizing a cascade of behaviorally regulated genes," *Proceedings of the National Academy of Sciences, USA* **103**, pp. 15212–15217.

Walker, A. and Leakey, R. E. (eds) (1993). *The Nariokotome Homo Erectus Skeleton* (Cambridge, MA: Harvard University Press).

Walker, S. (1983). *Animal Thought* (London: Routledge & Kegan Paul).

Walkowiak, W. (1988). "Neuroethology of anuran call recognition," in *The Evolution of the Amphibian Auditory System*, ed. B. Fritzsch, M. J. Ryan, W. Wilczynski, T. E. Hetherington, and W. Walkowiak (New York, NY: John Wiley & Sons, pp. 485–510).

Wall, C. E. and Smith, K. K. (2001). "Ingestion in mammals," in *Encyclopedia of Life Sciences*, ed. N. P. Group (London: Macmillan, pp. 1–6).

Wallace, A. R. (1864). "The development of the human races under the law of natural selection," *Journal of the Anthropological Society of London* **2**, pp. clviii–clxxxvii.

(1871). "Limits of natural selection as applied to man," in *Contributions to the Theory of Natural Selection*, ed. A. R. Wallace. (New York, NY: Macmillan).

(1905). *Darwinism: An exposition of the theory of natural selection with some of its applications* (New York, NY: Macmillan).

Wallin, N. L., Merker, B., and Brown, S. (2000). *The Origins of Music* (Cambridge, MA: MIT Press).

Wallman, J. (1992). *Aping Language* (New York, NY: Cambridge University Press).

Walters, J. (1987). "Kin recognition in non-human primates," in *Kin Recognition in Animals*, ed. D. J. C. Fletcher and C. D. Michener (New York, NY: Wiley, pp. 359–394).

Warner, R. R. (1988). "Traditionality of mating-site preferences in a coral reef fish," *Nature* **335**, pp. 719–721.

Watkins, K. E., Dronkers, N. F., and Vargha-Khadem, F. (2002). "Behavioural analysis of an inherited speech and language disorder: Comparison with acquired aphasia," *Brain* **125**, pp. 452–464.

Watkins, W. A., Tyack, P. L., Moore, K. E., and Bird, J. E. (1987). "The 20-Hz signals of finback whales (*Balaenoptera physalus*)," *Journal of the Acoustical Society of America* **82**, pp. 1901–1912.

Webb, D. M. and Zhang, J. (2005). "FoxP2 in song-learning birds and vocal-learning mammals," *Journal of Heredity* **96**, pp. 212–216.

Weber, B. H. and Depew, D. J. (eds) (2003). *Evolution and Learning: The Baldwin Effect reconsidered* (Cambridge, MA: MIT Press).

Webster, D. B., Fay, R. F., and Popper, A. N. (1992). *The Evolutionary Biology of Hearing* (New York, NY: Springer-Verlag).

Weidenreich, F. (1941). "The brain and its rôle in the phylogenetic transformation of the human skull," *Transactions of the American Philosophical Society: New Series* **31**, pp. 321–442.

Weiner, S., Xu, Q., Goldberg, P., Liu, J., and Bar-Yosef, O. (1998). "Evidence for the use of fire at Zhoukoudian, China," *Science* **281**, pp. 251–253.

Weir, A. A. S., Chappell, J., and Kacelnik, A. (2004a). "Shaping of hooks in New Caledonian crows," *Science* **297**, p. 981.

Weir, A. A. S., Kenward, B., Chappell, J., and Kacelnik, A. (2004b). "Lateralization of tool use in New Caledonian crows (Corvus moneduloides)," *Proceedings of the Royal Society London, B* **271** Suppl. 5, pp. S344–346.

Weishampel, D. B. (1981). "Acoustic analysis of potential vocalization in lambeosaurine dinosaurs (Reptilia: Ornithischia)," *Paleobiology* **7**, pp. 252–261.

Weiss, G. (1974). "On Livingstone's "Did the Australopithecines sing?," *Current Anthropology* **15**, pp. 103–104.

Weissengruber, G. E., Forstenpointner, G., Peters, G., Kübber-Heiss, A., and Fitch, W. T. (2002). "Hyoid apparatus and pharynx in the lion (Panthera leo), jaguar (Panthera onca), tiger (Panthera tigris), cheetah (Acinonyx jubatus), and domestic cat (Felis silvestris f. catus)," *Journal of Anatomy (London)* **201**, pp. 195–209.

Wemmer, C. and Mishra, H. (1982). "Observational learning by an Asiatic elephant of an unusual sound production method," *Mammalia* **46**, p. 557.

West-Eberhard, M. J. (1989). "Phenotypic plasticity and the origins of diversity," *Annual Review of Ecology and Systematics* **20**, pp. 249–278.

Westneat, M. W., Long, J. H., Hoese, W., and Nowicki, S. (1993). "Kinematics of birdsong: Functional correlation of cranial movements and acoustic features in sparrows," *Journal of Experimental Biology* **182**, pp. 147–171.

Whalen, D. H. and Liberman, A. M. (1987). "Speech perception takes precedence over nonspeech perception," *Science* **237**, pp. 169–171.

Wheeler, P. E. (1984). "The evolution of bipedality and loss of functional body hair in hominids," *Journal of Human Evolution* **13**, pp. 91–98.

White, S. J., White, R. E. C., and Thorpe, W. H. (1970). "Acoustic basis for individual recognition by voice in the gannet," *Nature* **225**, pp. 1156–1158.

White, S. S. (1968). "Movements of the larynx during crowing in the domestic cock," *Journal of Anatomy* **103**, pp. 390–392.

White, T. D. and Suwa, G. (1987). "Hominid footprints at Laetoli: Facts and interpretations," *American Journal of Physical Anthropology* **72**, pp. 485–514.

Whiten, A. and Byrne, R. W. (eds) (1997). *Machiavellian Intelligence II: Evaluations and Extensions* (Cambridge: Cambridge University Press).

Whiten, A., Goodall, J., McGrew, W. C., Nishida, T., Reynolds, V., Sugiyama, Y., Tutin, C. E. G., Wrangham, R. W., and Boesch, C. (1999). "Cultures in chimpanzees," *Nature* **399**, pp. 682–685.

Whiten, A. and Ham, R. (1992). "On the nature and evolution of imitation in the animal kingdom: Reappraisal of a century of research," in *Advances in the Study of Behavior*, ed. P. J. B. Slater, J. S. Rosnblatt, C. Beer, and M. Milinski (New York, NY: Academic Press, pp. 239–283).

Whiten, A., Horner, V., and de Waal, F. B. (2005). "Conformity to cultural norms of tool use in chimpanzees," *Nature* **437**, pp. 737–740.

Whorf, B. L. (1964). *Language, Thought and Reality: Selected writings* (Cambridge, MA: MIT Press).

Wickler, W. and Seibt, U. (1981). "Monogamy in crustacea and man," *Zeitschrift für Tierpsychologie* **57**, pp. 215–234.

Wild, J. M. (1993). "The avian nucleus retroambigualis: A nucleus for breathing, singing and calling," *Brain Research* **606**, pp. 119–124.

Wildenthal, J. L. (1965). "Structure in primary song of the mockingbird (Mimus polyglottos)," *Auk* **82**, pp. 161–189.

Wildman, D. E., Uddin, M., Liu, G., Grossman, L. I., and Goodman, M. (2003). "Implications of natural selection in shaping 99.4% nonsynonymous DNA identity between humans and chimpanzees: Enlarging genus Homo," *Proceedings of the National Academy of Sciences, USA* **100**, pp. 7181–7188.

Wilkins, A. S. (2002). *The Evolution of Developmental Pathways* (Sunderland, MA: Sinauer).

Wilkinson, G. S. (1984). "Reciprocal food sharing in the vampire bat," *Nature* **308**, pp. 181–184.

(1987). "Altruism and cooperation in bats," in *Recent Advances in the Study of Bats*, ed. M. B. Fenton, P. Racey, and J. M. V. Rayner (Cambridge: Cambridge University Press, pp. 299–323).

Williams, G. C. (1966a). *Adaptation and Natural Selection: A critique of some current evolutionary thought* (Princeton, NJ: Princeton University Press).

(1966b). *Adaptation and Natural Selection.* (Princeton, NJ: Princeton University Press).

Wilson, A. C. and Sarich, V. M. (1969). "A molecular time scale for human evolution," *Proceedings of the National Academy of Sciences, USA* **63**, pp. 1088–1093.

Wilson, E. O. (1975). *Sociobiology* (Cambridge, MA: Harvard University Press).

Wilson, E. O. and Hölldobler, B. (2005). "Eusociality: Origin and consequences," *Proceedings of the National Academy of Sciences* **102**, pp. 13367–13371.

Wilson, M. L., Hauser, M. D., and Wrangham, R. W. (2001). "Does participation in intergroup conflict depend on numerical assessment, range location, or rank for wild chimpanzees?," *Animal Behavior* **61**, pp. 1203–1216.

Wilson, W. A. (1975). "Discriminative conditioning of vocalizations in Lemur catta," *Animal Behavior* **23**, pp. 432–436.

Wimmer, H. and Perner, J. (1983). "Beliefs about beliefs: Representation and constraining function of wrong beliefs in young children's understanding of deception," *Cognition* **13**, pp. 103–128.

Winchester, S. (2001). *The Map that Changed the World: William Smith and the birth of modern geology* (New York, NY: HarperCollins).

Wind, J. (1970). *On the Phylogeny and Ontogeny of the Human Larynx* (Groningen: Wolters-Noordhoff Publishing).

(1976). "Phylogeny of the human vocal tract," *Annals of the New York Academy of Science* **280**, pp. 612–630.

(1983). "Primate evolution and the emergence of speech," in *Glossogenetics: The origin and evolution of language*, ed. É. d. Grolier (New York, NY: Harwood Academic Publishers, pp. 15–35).

Winter, P., Handley, P., Ploog, W., and Schott, D. (1973). "Ontogeny of squirrel monkey calls under normal conditions and under acoustic isolation," *Behaviour* **47**, pp. 230–239.

Wolpoff, M. H., Hawks, J., Frayer, D. W., and Hunley, K. (2001). "Modern human ancestry at the peripheries: A test of the replacement theory," *Science* **291**, pp. 293–297.

Wood, B. and Collard, M. (1999). "The human genus," *Science* **284**, pp. 65–71.

Woods, C. G., Bond, J., and Enard, W. (2005). "Autosomal recessive primary microcephaly (MCPH): A review of clinical, molecular, and evolutionary findings," *American Journal of Human Genetics* **76**, pp. 717–728.

Woods, R. P., Freimer, N. B., De Young, J. A., Fears, S. C., Sicotte, N. L., Service, S. K., Valentino, D. J., Toga, A. W., and Mazziotta, J. C. (2006). "Normal variants of Microcephalin and ASPM do not account for brain size variability," *Human Molecular Genetics* **15**, pp. 2025–2029.

Worden, R. (1998). "The evolution of language from social intelligence," in *Approaches to the Evolution of Language*, ed. J. R. Hurford, M. Studdert-Kennedy, and C. Knight (New York, NY: Cambridge University Press, pp. 148–166).

Wrangham, R. W. (1980). "An ecological model of female-bonded primate groups," *Behaviour* **75**, pp. 262–300.

(1987). "The significance of African apes for reconstructing human social evolution," in *The Evolution of Human Behavior: Primate models*, ed. W. G. Kinzey (Albany, NY: State University of New York Press, pp. 51–71).

Wrangham, R. W., Jones, J. H., Laden, G., Pilbeam, D., and Conklin-Brittain, N. (1999). "The raw and the stolen: Cooking and the ecology of human origins," *Current Anthropology* **40**, pp. 567–594.

Wrangham, R. W., McGrew, W. C., de Waal, F. B., and Heltne, P. (eds) (1994). *Chimpanzee Cultures* (Cambridge, MA: Harvard University Press).

Wrangham, R. W. and Nishida, T. (1983). "Aspilia leaves: A puzzle in the feeding behavior of wild chimpanzees," *Primates* **24**, pp. 276–282.

Wrangham, R. W. and Peterson, D. (1996). *Demonic Males: Apes and the origins of human violence* (Boston, MA: Houghton Mifflin).

Wray, A. (1998). "Protolanguage as a holistic system for social interaction," *Language & Communication* **18**, pp. 47–67.

(2000). "Holistic utterances in protolanguage: The link from primates to humans," in *The Evolutionary Emergence of Language: Social function and the origins of linguistic form*, ed. C. Knight, M. Studdert-Kennedy, and J. R. Hurford (Cambridge: Cambridge University Press, pp. 285–302).

(2002). *Formulaic Language and the Lexicon* (Cambridge: Cambridge University Press).

Wynne, C. D. (2004). *Do Animals Think?* (Princeton, NJ: Princeton University Press).

Yamaguchi, A. (1998). "A sexually dimorphic learned birdsong in the Northern Cardinal," *The Condor* **100**, pp. 504–511.

Yerkes, R. M. and Yerkes, A. W. (1929). *The Great Apes* (New Haven, CT: Yale University Press).

Yip, M. J. (2006). "The search for phonology in other species," *Trends in Cognitive Science* **10**, pp. 442–446.

Zahavi, A. (1975). "Mate selection: A selection for a handicap," *Journal of Theoretical Biology* **53**, pp. 205–214.

(1993). "The fallacy of conventional signalling," *Proceedings of the Royal Society of London, B* **340**, pp. 227–230.

Zahavi, A. and Zahavi, A. (1997). *The Handicap Principle* (New York, NY: Oxford University Press).

Zatorre, R. J., Chen, J. L., and Penhune, V. B. (2007). "When the brain plays music: Auditory-motor interactions in music perception and production," *Nature Reviews Neuroscience* **8**, pp. 547–558.

Zatorre, R. J., Evans, A. C., Meyer, E., and Gjedde, A. (1992). "Lateralization of phonetic and pitch discrimination in speech processing," *Science* **256**, pp. 846–849.

Zatorre, R. J. and Peretz, I. (eds) (2001). *The Biological Foundations of Music* (New York, NY: New York Academy of Sciences).

Zawidzki, T. W. (2006). "Sexual selection for syntax and kin selection for semantics: Problems and prospects," *Biology and Philosophy* **21**, pp. 453–470.

Zemlin, W. R. (1968). *Speech and Hearing Science: Anatomy and physiology* (Englewood Cliffs, NJ: Prentice Hall).

Zimmer, C. (1998). *At the Water's Edge* (New York, NY: Touchstone).

Zimmermann, E. (1981). "First record of ultrasound in two prosimian species," *Naturwissenshaften* **68**, p. 531.

Zipf, G. K. (1949). *Human Behavior and the Principle of Least Effort* (Cambridge, MA: Addison-Wesley Press).

Zoloth, S. R., Petersen, M. R., Beecher, M. D., Green, S., Marler, P., Moody, D. B., and Stebbins, W. C. (1979). "Species-specific perceptual processing of vocal sounds by monkeys," *Science* **204**, pp. 870–872.

Zuberbühler, K. (2000a). "Interspecies semantic communication in two forest primates," *Proceedinsg of the Royal Society of London, B* **267**, pp. 713–718.

(2000b). "Referential labeling in wild Diana monkeys," *Animal Behavior* **59**, pp. 917–927.

(2002). "A syntactic rule in forest monkey communication," *Animal Behavior* **63**, pp. 293–299.

Zuidema, W. H. (2005). "The major transitions in the evolution of language," in *Theoretical and Applied Linguistics* (University of Edinburgh), p. 225.

Author index

Subject index

Acheulean industry, 256, 266f
action syntax, **431**
agents, 51, 381, **382**, 383, 501f
alarm calls, 24, 74, 135, 165, 180, 185, 187ff,
    199, 236, 425, 469, 471, 482
alliteration, **184**, 377
allometry, **282**
amniotes, **224**, 225
analogous, 36, **46**, 57, 65, 99, 229, 262, 306,
    310, 381, 409, 488
animal cognition, 17, 81, 122f, 134, 143ff, **149**,
    159, 171f, 281, 396, 402
anticipatory cognition, **151**, 172
argument from the poverty of the stimulus,
    85
artificial language, **381**, 404, 440
audience effects, **180**
audiogram, **324**, 325
Aurignacian, 275f
automata, **111**, 179f

babbling, 28, 69, 84, 169, 297, **345**, 346, 361,
    372, 375f, 383, 399, 443, 460, 464, 471
basal ganglia, 83, 118, 349, 358ff, 365f, 369f,
    458
base pairs, **49**, 102, 210, 356f
bases, **49**, 50, 66, 208
basicranium, **329**, 330f
basihyoid bone, 300, 312, 323, **331**, 334
beats, **435**, 475, 479
bilaterians, **214**, 215
biological, 74f, 77–81, 87–94, 98, 110, 115f,
    121ff, 136
bipedalism, 251, 255, 257, 259ff, 279, **332**, 373,
    482, 493, 495
bonobo, 236, 240, 264
brainstem chassis, 347, 349
Broca's area, 287f, 350, **351**, 359, 365, 369,
    453f, 458

cache, **151**, 160
call usage learning, **338**
categorical perception, **98**, 99, **146**, 325ff, 475
central nervous system, 62, 215, **218**, 328
cerebral laterality, **449**

chimpanzee, 13ff, 27, 73, 77, 81, 107, 135, 138,
    154, 158, 163f, 166, 173, 188, 207, 233,
    234–244, 258, 260, 262, 265, 272, 275, 279,
    292, 301, 308f, 320, 323, 330, 332ff, 352, 356,
    359, 364, 366, 372, 422, 429f, 443, 458, 493
Chordata, **215**
chunking, **100**, 141
cis-regulatory elements, **357**
clades, **45**, 46, 59, 147, 187, 252, 268, 272, 285,
    363, 426f, 491, 503
co-evolution, **91**, 92
concealed ovulation, **246**, 493
co-speech gestures, **435**, 436
coarticulation, 374, **375**
code model, **131**, 133
codon, 49, **50**, **210**
cognitivist, **86**, 87, 124
color vision, 21, 45f, 206, 228, **229**, 230f
combines, 115, **116**, 138
common ground, **133**
comparative method, 18, **44**, 45f, 70, 149, 206,
    213, 217, 234, 249, 275, 334, 471, 483
complex gill bars, **217**
complex vocal imitation, **338**, 340–362, 382
constraints, 35, 51, 57–68, 79, 86, 88, 95ff, 100,
    106, 110, **116**, 117f, 125–129, 141, 149, 170f,
    174, 185, 195f, 218, 220, 232, 326, 342, 344,
    354, 367, 372–385, 411, 418, 420, 429ff, 467f
context-free grammar, 110, **113**, 114
context-driven inference, **130**, 141
continuity, 47, **149**, 175, 267, 355, 396, 402,
    457, 461f, 497f
control of vocalization, **180**, 302, 348, 360
convergent evolution, **46**, 56, 93, 147, 184, 341,
    470, 495, 503
cooperation, 134, 140, 159, 248, **410**, 414,
    415ff, 489f
cortical control systems, **347**
corvids, 136, **147**, 160, 429
creoles, **379**, 406f, 461
critical periods in early visual development,
    344
cross-modal cognition, **451**, 452f
cue, 96, 114, 143, 178, 193, **195**, 303, 305, 322,
    329, 335

Species index

CPSIA information can be obtained
at www.ICGtesting.com
Printed in the USA
LVHW101721270219
608948LV00006B/149/P

9 780521 677363